Contemporary Terrorism Studies

CONTEMPORARY TERRORISM STUDIES

edited by

DIEGO MURO / TIM WILSON

Diego Muro, Senior Lecturer in International Relations at the Centre for the Study of Terrorism and Political Violence (CSTPV), University of St Andrews, UK.

Tim Wilson, Director of the Centre for the Study of Terrorism and Political Violence (CSTPV), University of St Andrews, UK.

Great Clarendon Street, Oxford, OX2 6DP,
United Kingdom

Oxford University Press is a department of the University of Oxford.
It furthers the University's objective of excellence in research, scholarship,
and education by publishing worldwide. Oxford is a registered trade mark of
Oxford University Press in the UK and in certain other countries

© Oxford University Press 2022

The moral rights of the author[s] have been asserted

First Edition 2022

Impression: 1

All rights reserved. No part of this publication may be reproduced, stored in
a retrieval system, or transmitted, in any form or by any means, without the
prior permission in writing of Oxford University Press, or as expressly permitted
by law, by licence or under terms agreed with the appropriate reprographics
rights organization. Enquiries concerning reproduction outside the scope of the
above should be sent to the Rights Department, Oxford University Press, at the
address above

You must not circulate this work in any other form
and you must impose this same condition on any acquirer

Published in the United States of America by Oxford University Press
198 Madison Avenue, New York, NY 10016, United States of America

British Library Cataloguing in Publication Data

Data available

Library of Congress Control Number: 2021951946

ISBN 978–0–19–882956–0

Printed in Great Britain by
Bell & Bain Ltd., Glasgow

Links to third party websites are provided by Oxford in good faith and
for information only. Oxford disclaims any responsibility for the materials
contained in any third party website referenced in this work.

In memory of our CSTPV colleague, Mark Currie (15 February 1953–30 May 2019). Scholar, teacher, gentleman—and friend.

GUIDED TOUR OF THE LEARNING FEATURES

Contemporary Terrorism Studies provides a range of carefully selected learning tools to help you navigate the text and contextualize your understanding, supporting development of the essential knowledge and skills you need to underpin your comprehension of terrorism studies.

■ CHAPTER SUMMARY

This chapter is designed to offer a ba[sic] begins by looking at attempts to defin[e] traces the evolution of 'mainstream' (o[r]

Each chapter begins with a brief **Chapter Summary** which prepares you for reading, and highlights the key concepts, issues, ideas, and themes which will be covered in the chapter.

KEY CONCEPTS

Terrorism Martha Crenshaw (2011: 23[...]

'Summarizing the basic components [of] following list of essential properties th[...]

Helpful **Key Concepts** boxes throughout the text briefly summarize key ideas, and reinforce your understanding of new terminology.

CASE STUDY 2.2

Terrorism Studies and Western-Ce[ntric]

On the night of the 13 November 2015[...] attack combining suicide bombings, dr[...]

Engaging and relevant **Case Study** boxes in every chapter illustrate how ideas, concepts, and issues are manifested in the real world.

DISCUSSION QUESTIONS

Evaluate the achievements and weaknesses [...]
Has the policy-relevance of terrorism studi[es...]
Why has the field struggled to expand its fo[...]

Useful **Discussion Questions** at the end of each chapter help to encourage critical reflection on what you've learnt, can be discussed and debated in small groups, and provide useful prompts for essay and exam preparation.

GUIDE TO FURTHER REA[DING]

Crenshaw, M. (2011) *Explaining Terrorism*[...] York: Routledge. *A classic collection of articl[es...] terrorism. Explaining Terrorism does a good j[ob...]*

The **Guide to Further Reading** features annotated recommendations for further reading at the end of each chapter to suggest how you can develop your interest in a particular aspect of terrorism studies.

GUIDED TOUR OF THE ONLINE RESOURCES

Contemporary Terrorism Studies is accompanied by a range of online resources, which are available at: www.oup.com/he/Wilson-Muro1e

Student Resources

- Helpful **Question Pointers** help to tackle the end of chapter discussion questions.
- A curated list of **Web Links** for each chapter help students to deepen their understanding of key issues.
- **Guidance on Accessing Databases** help to aid student independent terrorism studies research.

Lecturer Resources

- Customizable **PowerPoint Slides** accompany each chapter and can be used and tailored by lecturers in their teaching.

ACKNOWLEDGEMENTS

Success has many parents. There is therefore a very large number of people whom we need to thank. First, we would like to thank the contributors who gave their time and effort to this textbook. All have given generously of their time. All the contributors are internationally recognized experts: together they greatly enhance the textbook's quality and global relevance.

Second, we owe a huge debt of gratitude to Katie Staal and the whole team at Oxford University Press, who have supported the project from inception to realization: and with great enthusiasm, good humour, and sustained drive.

Third, we also wish to thank our past and present colleagues in the Handa Centre for the Study of Terrorism and Political Violence (CSTPV), at the University of St Andrews. A clifftop in eastern Scotland might not be the most obvious place to study international terrorism: yet it works. Specifically, we are proud to dedicate this book to Mark Currie, our late colleague and resident polymath. We see it as belonging firmly within an unbroken academic tradition of studying terrorism at St Andrews that stretches back to 1994. We have tried to make it worthy of that inheritance.

That CSTPV research tradition is accompanied by a living teaching tradition, of course. We therefore wish to thank all our students at the University of St Andrews. We have benefited enormously from teaching such outstanding cohorts of students; and it is their intellectual curiosity and thirst for learning that has pushed us to deliver this textbook. It has been a common frustration amongst our students that there was no textbook of terrorism studies. *Contemporary Terrorism Studies* is our best attempt at a considered response.

Finally, we would like to thank friends and family who have had to suffer our distraction as we wrestled this textbook into submission. All books steal time from loved ones: this one stole more than most. We hope it has been worth the wait.

CONTENTS

Detailed Contents — xi
List of Case Studies — xx
About the Authors — xxii
About the Editors — xxviii

1. Introduction — 1

PART ONE The State of Terrorism Studies — 15

2. What Are Terrorism Studies? — 17
3. Critical Terrorism Studies — 36
4. Conceptualizations of Terrorism — 56
5. Terrorism in Context — 74
6. The Social Science of Political Violence — 94
7. Terrorism Open Source Databases — 113

PART TWO Issues and Debates in Terrorism Studies — 135

8. The History of Terrorism — 137
9. What Are the Root Causes of Terrorism? — 157
10. When Do Individuals Radicalize? — 178
11. Can Terrorism Be Rational? — 201
12. Target Selection — 218
13. Longevity of Terrorist Groups — 238
14. Can States Be Terrorists? — 260
15. Gendered and Racialized Terrorism — 281
16. Terrorism by Insurgents and Rebels — 302
17. Old and New Terrorism — 325
18. Social Media and Terrorism — 347
19. Is Terrorism Effective? — 368

PART THREE Countering Terrorism — 389

20. Counterterrorism Agencies and Their Work — 391
21. Responding to Terrorism Nonviolently — 413
22. Counterterrorism and Human Rights — 434
23. Foreign Policy and Countering Terrorism — 454
24. International Organizations and Counter-Terrorism — 477
25. Terrorism, Counter-Terrorism, and Technology — 497
26. Preventing and Countering Violent Extremism — 518
27. Disengagement and Deradicalization Programmes — 538
28. Victims of Terrorism and Political Violence — 558
29. The End of Terrorist Campaigns — 575

Index — 595

DETAILED CONTENTS

List of Case Studies	xx
About the Authors	xxii
About the Editors	xxviii

1. Introduction — 1
- 1.1 Introduction — 1
- 1.2 Definition of Terrorism — 1
- 1.3 Design and Learning Features — 4
- 1.4 Structure — 6
  - 1.4.1 Part 1: The state of terrorism studies — 6
  - 1.4.2 Part 2: Issues and debates in terrorism studies — 7
  - 1.4.3 Part 3: Countering terrorism — 11
- 1.5 Conclusion — 14
- References — 14

PART ONE The State of Terrorism Studies — 15

2. What Are Terrorism Studies? — 17
- 2.1 What Is Terrorism? — 18
- 2.2 Terrorism as 'An Essentially Contested Concept' — 19
- 2.3 Evolution of Terrorism Studies — 21
- 2.4 The Nature of Terrorism Studies — 26
- 2.5 Terrorism Studies: Stagnation? — 30
- 2.6 Conclusion — 33
- Guide to Further Reading — 34
- References — 34

3. Critical Terrorism Studies — 36
- 3.1 Introduction — 37
- 3.2 Constructing Terrorism: From the Exceptional to the Everyday — 38
  - 3.2.1 Terrorism — 39
  - 3.2.2 State violence — 40
- 3.3 The Politics of CTS — 48
  - 3.3.1 CTS vs the State: to engage or not? — 49
  - 3.3.2 Broadening CTS' interlocutors — 50
- 3.4 Conclusion: Future Challenges — 51
- Guide to Further Reading — 53
- References — 53

4. Conceptualizations of Terrorism — 56
- 4.1 Introduction — 57
- 4.2 Levels of Analysis — 60
- 4.3 Terrorism as a Method — 61
- 4.4 Components in a Conceptualization of Terrorism — 67
  - 4.4.1 Violence and the threat of violence — 68
  - 4.4.2 Political motive — 69
  - 4.4.3 Civilian targeting? — 69
- 4.5 Conclusion — 71
- Guide to Further Reading — 72
- References — 72

5. Terrorism in Context — 74
- 5.1 Introduction — 75
  - 5.1.1 Normative shift — 75
  - 5.1.2 Victims as innocent bystanders — 78
  - 5.1.3 Current usage — 79
  - 5.1.4 Expanding the concept's scope — 81
  - 5.1.5 In the context of civil wars — 82
  - 5.1.6 The international dimension — 83
  - 5.1.7 Al-Qaeda and ISIS — 87
  - 5.1.8 Lethality and terrorism — 89
  - 5.1.9 Strategy and terrorism — 91
- Guide to Further Reading — 93
- References — 93

6. The Social Science of Political Violence — 94
- 6.1 Introduction — 95
- 6.2 The 'Processual Turn' in Political Violence Research — 96
- 6.3 The Explanatory Logic of Processual Analysis — 100
- 6.4 Mechanisms of Violent Escalation — 102
- 6.5 Micro-Mobilization: Individual Radicalization and Participation in Militant Groups — 107
- 6.6 Conclusion — 109
- Guide to Further Reading — 110
- References — 111

7. Terrorism Open Source Databases — 113
- 7.1 Terrorism Open Source Databases — 114
- 7.2 Terrorism Event Databases — 115
- 7.3 Terrorism Group Databases — 122
- 7.4 Terrorism Perpetrator Databases — 124
- 7.5 The American Terrorism Study — 124

7.6	Profiles of Individual Radicalization in the United States (Pirus)	125
7.7	The Extremist Crime Database	126
7.8	The Western Jihadism Project	126
7.9	Lone Actor Terrorist Data	127
7.10	The Future of Terrorism Event Databases	128
7.11	Conclusions	130
	Guide to Further Reading	131
	References	132

PART TWO Issues and Debates in Terrorism Studies — 135

8. The History of Terrorism — 137

8.1	The Continued Importance of Past Terrorism	138
	8.1.1 Taking long views: terror in the ancient world	140
8.2	The Gunpowder Revolution in Europe	144
8.3	'Terrorism': A New Concept Is Born	145
8.4	Modern Terrorism at Last?	145
	8.4.1 Modern anti-state terrorism: 'The Four Waves of Rebel Terror'	148
	8.4.2 Modern state terror	151
8.5	Conclusion	154
	Guide to Further Reading	155
	References	156

9. What Are the Root Causes of Terrorism? — 157

9.1	Introduction	158
9.2	The Root Causes of Terrorism	158
	9.2.1 Defining the root causes	160
	9.2.2 Types of root cause	161
9.3	Political and Ideological Roots	163
	9.3.1 Nationalism and territorial motivations	163
	9.3.2 Religious extremism	164
	9.3.3 Ideologically-motivated terrorism	165
9.4	Structural Causes of Political Violence	169
	9.4.1 Absence of viable political opportunity	169
	9.4.2 Poverty and economic deprivation	170
	9.4.3 Education	171
	9.4.4 State failure	171
9.5	State (Re-)Action	172
9.6	Conclusion	174
	Guide to Further Reading	175
	References	176

10. When Do Individuals Radicalize? — 178

- 10.1 Introduction — 179
- 10.2 The Early Answers — 179
- 10.3 The Advent of Terrorism Studies — 181
- 10.4 The Road to Radicalization — 187
- 10.5 What Do We Now Know—and What Don't We Know (Yet)? — 193
- 10.6 In the End, What Makes a Terrorist? — 195
- 10.7 Conclusion — 198
- Guide to Further Reading — 199
- References — 199

11. Can Terrorism Be Rational? — 201

- 11.1 Introduction — 202
- 11.2 The Puzzle of Terrorism — 202
- 11.3 Resolving the Puzzle of Terrorism — 208
- 11.4 Counterterrorism Implications — 213
- Guide to Further Reading — 215
- References — 215

12. Target Selection — 218

- 12.1 Introduction — 219
- 12.2 Target Locations for Terrorism — 221
- 12.3 Target Selection, Victims, and Audiences — 224
- 12.4 Democracies as Frequent Targets of Terrorism — 228
- 12.5 Target Selection, Fear, and Public Attention — 230
- 12.6 Conclusion — 234
- Guide to Further Reading — 235
- References — 236

13. Longevity of Terrorist Groups — 238

- 13.1 Introduction — 239
- 13.2 Defining Longevity of Terrorist Groups — 239
- 13.3 Longevity of Terrorist Groups — 241
- 13.4 Factors Influencing Longevity — 244
  - 13.4.1 State characteristics — 244
  - 13.4.2 Group characteristics — 246
  - 13.4.3 Intergroup relations — 250
- 13.5 Motivations to Sustaining Terrorism — 252
- 13.6 Conclusion — 256
- Guide to Further Reading — 257
- References — 258

14. Can States Be Terrorists? — 260
- 14.1 Introduction — 261
- 14.2 Studying Terrorism—What about the State? — 261
- 14.3 What Is State Terrorism? — 262
- 14.4 Objections to the Concept of 'State Terrorism' — 264
- 14.5 Can States Be Terrorists? — 265
- 14.6 How Have States Used Terrorism? — 266
- 14.7 The Effects of State Terrorism — 273
- 14.8 The Limitations of 'State Terrorism' as a Concept — 274
- 14.9 Conclusion — 275
- Guide to Further Reading — 277
- References — 277

15. Gendered and Racialized Terrorism — 281
- 15.1 Introduction — 282
- 15.2 How Gender and Race Work: Essentialization and Idealization — 284
  - 15.2.1 Essentialization — 285
  - 15.2.2 Idealizations — 288
- 15.3 When Gender and Race Are the Driving Forces: The Incel Revolution — 292
- 15.4 Violent Actors Associated with Misogynistic Terrorism — 293
- 15.5 Groups/Online Communities with Misogynistic Idealizations — 294
- 15.6 Conclusion — 297
- Guide to Further Reading — 298
- References — 299

16. Terrorism by Insurgents and Rebels — 302
- 16.1 Introduction — 302
- 16.2 Rebel Relative Strength — 304
- 16.3 Territorial Control, Civilian Compliance and Terrorism — 310
- 16.4 Rebel Social Service Provision — 312
- 16.5 The Strategies of Terrorism — 317
- 16.6 Conclusion — 320
- Guide to Further Reading — 321
- References — 322

17. Old and New Terrorism — 325
- 17.1 Introduction — 326
- 17.2 Origins — 327
- 17.3 Conceptual Issues — 329
- 17.4 Religion — 331
- 17.5 Networks — 335
- 17.6 Lethality — 337
- 17.7 Conclusion — 342

	Guide to Further Reading	344
	References	344
18.	**Social Media and Terrorism**	**347**
	18.1 Introduction	348
	18.2 Concepts and Definitions	349
	18.3 Social Media and the Nature of Terrorism	350
	18.4 Terrorist Use of Social Media	355
	18.5 Social Media as a Double-edged Sword	358
	18.6 Linking Virtual and Physical Worlds	361
	18.7 Conclusion	363
	Guide to Further Reading	365
	References	365
19.	**Is Terrorism Effective?**	**368**
	19.1 Introduction	369
	19.2 Is Terrorism an Effective Tactic?	369
	19.3 Why Can't Scholars Agree?	372
	19.4 When and Where Does Terrorism Work?	377
	19.5 What Do Terrorists Want?	381
	19.5.1 Ways forward for the effectiveness debate?	384
	19.6 Conclusion	384
	Guide to Further Reading	386
	References	387

PART THREE Countering Terrorism 389

20.	**Counterterrorism Agencies and Their Work**	**391**
	20.1 Introduction	392
	20.2 The Demand and Supply Challenge	392
	20.3 Counterterrorism Policy	395
	20.4 Intervention Outcomes	397
	20.5 Implementing Approaches to Counterterrorism	401
	20.5.1 Military	401
	20.5.2 Intelligence	402
	20.5.3 Criminal justice	405
	20.6 Interactions and Collaborations	407
	20.7 Conclusion	408
	Guide to Further Reading	409
	References	410
21.	**Responding to Terrorism Nonviolently**	**413**
	21.1 Introduction	414

	21.2 The Failures of Force-based Counterterrorism	415
	21.2.1 The empirical failure of force-based counterterrorism	416
	21.2.2 The theoretical and ethical failures of force-based counterterrorism	418
	21.3 Alternatives to Force-based Counterterrorism	420
	21.4 Exploring the Potential of Nonviolent Counterterrorism	426
	21.4.1 Counterterrorism and the political	426
	21.4.2 Exploring nonviolent alternatives	427
	21.5 Conclusion	429
	Guide to Further Reading	431
	References	432
22.	**Counterterrorism and Human Rights**	**434**
	22.1 Introduction	435
	22.2 How Counterterrorism Affects Human Rights	436
	22.3 Do Human Rights Standards Shape Counterterrorism?	440
	22.4 Human Rights and the Effectiveness of Counterterrorism	445
	22.5 Conclusion	450
	Guide to Further Reading	451
	References	452
23.	**Foreign Policy and Countering Terrorism**	**454**
	23.1 Introduction	455
	23.2 Concepts and Definitions	455
	23.2.1 Foreign policy	455
	23.2.2 Countering terrorism	457
	23.3 The Overlapping Instruments of Foreign Policy and Countering Terrorism	461
	23.4 Diplomacy and Culture: More Than Dialogue	463
	23.5 The Military Arm—Defence and Deterrence	467
	23.6 Economic Statecraft: Foreign Aid, Sanctions, and the Financing of Terrorism	470
	23.7 Conclusion	473
	Guide to Further Reading	474
	References	475
24.	**International Organizations and Counter-Terrorism**	**477**
	24.1 Introduction	478
	24.2 UN Counter-Terrorism Cooperation	478
	24.2.1 UN Counter-Terrorism Cooperation after 9/11	479
	24.2.2 UN Counter-Terrorism Cooperation after the rise of ISIS	480
	24.2.3 Criticism about the UN Counter-Terrorism Policy	481
	24.3 ASEAN Counter-Terrorism Cooperation	481
	24.4 EU Counter-Terrorism Cooperation	486
	24.4.1 EU Counter-Terrorism Institutions	486
	24.5 Multilateral Counter-Terrorism Cooperation: NATO and the EU	490
	24.6 Conclusion	492

	Guide to Further Reading	493
	References	494
25.	**Terrorism, Counter-Terrorism, and Technology**	**497**
	25.1 Introduction	498
	25.2 Thesis: Our Technology Will Win	498
	25.3 Antithesis: Our Technology Will Not Save Us	507
	25.4 Synthesis: The Nature of the Terrorist Threat	512
	25.5 Conclusion	514
	Guide to Further Reading	515
	References	515
26.	**Preventing and Countering Violent Extremism**	**518**
	26.1 Introduction	519
	26.2 A Short History of P/CVE	520
	26.3 'Western' and 'Eastern' P/CVE Approaches	523
	26.4 Evidence-based Methods and Tools	525
	26.5 Gender Sensitive P/CVE	529
	26.6 Evaluation of P/CVE Programmes	530
	26.7 Conclusion	533
	Guide to Further Reading	535
	References	535
27.	**Disengagement and Deradicalization Programmes**	**538**
	27.1 Introduction	539
	27.2 Conceptualizing and Defining Deradicalization	539
	27.2.1 Theorizing deradicalization	542
	27.3 History and Evolution of Deradicalization Interventions	544
	27.4 Contemporary Deradicalization Policy and Practice	547
	27.4.1 Partnership working in deradicalization initiatives	550
	27.4.2 Deradicalization intervention methods	550
	27.5 Empirical Evidence about Deradicalization	551
	27.5.1 Push and pull factors	552
	27.6 Conclusion	553
	Guide to Further Reading	555
	References	555
28.	**Victims of Terrorism and Political Violence**	**558**
	28.1 Introduction	559
	28.2 The Impact of Terrorism	562
	28.2.1 Terrorism as communication	562

	28.2.2	Terrorism as intent to create harm and fear	563
	28.2.3	The Just World Hypothesis (JWH)	564

28.3 The Ideal Victim — 567
    28.3.1 Hierarchies of victims — 568
28.4 Media and Terrorism Victims — 569
28.5 Conclusion — 571
Guide to Further Reading — 572
References — 573

29. **The End of Terrorist Campaigns** — **575**
    29.1 Introduction — 576
    29.2 Scope and Methods — 578
    29.3 How Terrorism Ends — 579
    29.4 Conclusion — 592
    Guide to Further Reading — 592
    References — 593

Index — 595

LIST OF CASE STUDIES

Case Study 2.1: The Sterling Thesis, 1981   24

Case Study 2.2: Terrorism Studies and Western-Centrism   27

Case Study 3.1: The US Rendition, Detention, and Interrogation Programme   42

Case Study 3.2: Al-Shabaab in Somalia   45

Case Study 4.1: The Israeli/Palestine Conflict   63

Case Study 4.2: Subjective Interpretations of Terrorism   65

Case Study 5.1: The Destruction of Khotso House   77

Case Study 5.2: The 2015 Attack on *Charlie Hebdo*   85

Case Study 6.1: The Red Army Faction (RAF), West Germany   99

Case Study 6.2: The Islamic Group (al-Jamaa al-Islamiyya) in Egypt   106

Case Study 7.1: Defining Terrorism   119

Case Study 7.2: Was the Antifa Attack in Charlottesville, Virginia an Example of Terrorism?   120

Case Study 8.1: David Rapoport's Four Waves of Modern Terrorism   148

Case Study 8.2: The 1970s as the Long Decade of Terrorism   152

Case Study 9.1: RAF   168

Case Study 9.2: GSPC   173

Case Study 10.1: 'I am prepared to die'—Nelson Mandela on Terrorism   182

Case Study 10.2: The European Union at the Cradle of 'Radicalization'   190

Case Study 11.1: Terrorism Failing Politically, Al-Qaeda   203

Case Study 11.2: Terrorism Failing Politically—Islamic State   206

Case Study 12.1: ETA's Mixed Targeting Strategies   226

Case Study 12.2: The IRA Omagh Bombing   232

Case Study 13.1: LTTE in Sri Lanka   248

Case Study 13.2: Revolutionary Organization 17 November in Greece   255

Case Study 14.1: US Torture in the Global War on Terror   270

Case Study 14.2: British Extrajudicial Killings in Northern Ireland   272

Case Study 15.1: Racializations of 'Lone Wolf Terrorism'   287

Case Study 15.2: Ulrike Meinhof and the Assumptions about Women's Political Violence   289

Case Study 16.1: Terrorism by UNITA   308

Case Study 16.2: Explaining the Taliban's Social Service Efforts in the Context of Terrorism   314

Case Study 17.1: How Religious is ISIS?   334

Case Study 17.2: The 2004 Madrid Bombings   340

Case Study 18.1: Christchurch Terror Attacks   353

Case Study 18.2: Lee Rigby   361

Case Study 19.1: The End of ETA   374

Case Study 19.2: Shining Path   379

Case Study 20.1: Countering Terrorism in Russia   399

Case Study 20.2: Co-ordinating Approaches across Agencies   403

Case Study 21.1: Afghanistan: Negotiating with the Enemy   421

Case Study 21.2: The Good Friday Peace Agreement   423

Case Study 22.1: Torture in the US 'War on Terror'   444

Case Study 22.2: British Operations in Northern Ireland in the 1970s   448

Case Study 23.1: US Public Diplomacy in the Post-9/11 Era: Success or Failure?   465

Case Study 23.2: The Use of Sanctions to Combat the Financing of Terrorism   472

Case Study 24.1: UN and EU Financial Sanctions Regime after 9/11   481

Case Study 24.2: The European Court of Justice and the Kadi Case   489

Case Study 25.1: Notting Hill Carnival August 2017   507

Case Study 25.2: Aviation Terrorism—Terrorist Action versus Counter-Terrorist Reaction   509

Case Study 26.1: White Supremacist Online Recruiting in the United States   528

Case Study 26.2: The Prevention Project 'Attention?!' (Achtung?!) in Germany   533

Case Study 27.1: Exit Project   545

Case Study 27.2: The Aarhus Model   548

Case Study 28.1: Paris Terror Attacks, 2015   559

Case Study 28.2: Terrorism at Home and Abroad   566

Case Study 29.1: Aum Shinrikyo   580

Case Study 29.2: Russia's Repression of Chechnya   588

ABOUT THE AUTHORS

MAX ABRAHMS is an Associate Professor of public policy and political science at Northeastern University, where he specializes in international security. Abrahms has published extensively in leading academic and popular outlets such as *International Organization*, *International Security*, *International Studies Quarterly*, *Security Studies*, *Comparative Political Studies*, *Harvard Business Review*, *Foreign Affairs*, *Foreign Policy*, *New York Times*, *Washington Post*, *USA Today*, and *Los Angeles Times*. His book, *Rules for Rebels*, explains why the conventional wisdom about Islamic State was wrong. Abrahms fields questions about the terrorism landscape in the news and for government agencies.

BERNHARD BLUMENAU is a Lecturer at the Centre for the Study of Terrorism and Political Violence at the University of St Andrews. His research focuses on the general history of terrorism, multilateral antiterrorism efforts and the long history of state terror. He is the author, among others, of *The United Nations and Terrorism: Germany, Multilateralism, and Antiterrorism Efforts in the 1970s* (2014) and co-editor of *An International History of Terrorism: Western and Non-Western Experiences* (2013).

LORENZO BOSI is Associate Professor and Director of Graduate Studies at the Faculty of Political and Social Sciences, of the Scuola Normale Superiore, Florence, Italy. He is a political sociologist pursuing comparative analysis into the cross-disciplinary fields of social movements and political violence.

ALEX BRAITHWAITE is Professor and Associate Director in the School of Government & Public Policy at the University of Arizona. His primary research interests centre on the causes and geography of political violence, broadly construed. His recent research has addressed the use of terrorism within democratic and autocratic states, the tendency for terrorism to cluster in time and space, and the targeting of elections by terrorist groups.

NICK BROOKE is an Associate Lecturer at the Handa Centre for the Study of Terrorism and Political Violence at the University of St Andrews. His research has focused on the causes of terrorism and the circumstances under which terrorist movements emerge, and why terrorism has been a feature of some political campaigns but not others. Nick's current research examines the impact of counterterrorist policies on communities rarely directly affected by terrorism.

RIK COOLSAET, PhD, is Professor Emeritus of International Relations at Ghent University (Belgium) and Senior Associate Fellow at Egmont–Royal Institute for

International Relations (Brussels). He was a member of the original European Commission Expert Group on Violent Radicalisation (established 2006) and the subsequent European Network of Experts on Radicalisation (ENER). In the 1980s and 1990s, he served as deputy chief of the Cabinet of the Belgian Minister of Defence and of the Minister of Foreign Affairs.

AUDREY KURTH CRONIN is an academic, practitioner, and award-winning author. She is currently Distinguished Professor at American University in Washington, D.C. Her latest book *Power to the People: How Open Technological Innovation is Arming Tomorrow's Terrorists*, published by Oxford University Press, won the 2020 Airey Neave prize for 'the most significant, original, relevant, and practically valuable contribution to the understanding of terrorism'.

DONATELLA DELLA PORTA is Professor of Political Science, Dean of the Faculty of Political and Social Sciences, and Director of the PhD programme in Political Science and Sociology at the Scuola Normale Superiore in Florence, where she also leads the Center on Social Movement Studies (Cosmos). Among the main topics of her research are social movements, political violence, terrorism, corruption, the police and protest policing.

FRANK FOLEY is Senior Lecturer in International Relations at the Department of War Studies, King's College London. His research focuses on human rights, security, and counterterrorism, and he is the author of *Countering Terrorism in Britain and France: Institutions, Norms and the Shadow of the Past* (Cambridge University Press, 2013). His latest project examines the (de)legitimation of torture and part of this research was published in 2021 in the *European Journal of International Relations*.

CARON E. GENTRY is the Faculty Pro-Vice-Chancellor for Arts, Design, and Social Sciences at the University of Northumbria. Her major research area is gender and terrorism. Her work is published in numerous journals, including *Critical Studies on Terrorism*, *International Feminist Journal of Politics*, *Terrorism and Political Violence*, and *International Relations*. Her books on terrorism include *Disordered Violence* (Edinburgh University Press, 2020) and (with Laura Sjoberg) *Beyond Mothers, Monsters, Whores* (Zed, 2015).

ADRIAN GUELKE is an Emeritus Professor in the School of History, Anthropology, Philosophy and Politics at Queen's University, Belfast and attached to the Centre for the Study of Ethnic Conflict. His publications include *Politics in Deeply Divided Societies* (Polity Press). He is also the author of two works on terrorism: *The New Age of Terrorism and the International Political System* and *Terrorism and Global Disorder*, both published by I. B. Tauris.

DONALD HOLBROOK runs a research consultancy working with law-enforcement and counterterrorism policy bodies in the UK. He is also an Honorary Senior Research

Associate at the Department of Security and Crime Science, University College London and serves as a Senior Research Advisor for the RESOLVE network, part of the United States Institute of Peace. He has published widely on terrorism, online, Islamist and right-wing extremism.

MARTIN INNES is a Professor in the School of Social Sciences and Director of the Crime and Security Research Institute, both at Cardiff University. He is the author of four books and a large number of scholarly articles, spanning a range of topics, including counter-terrorism. He has led several projects for UK government focused upon the Prevent strategy and aspects of counter-terrorism policing, and pioneered the use of social media analytics to understand social reactions to terror attacks.

HELEN INNES is a Research Fellow at Cardiff University's Crime and Security Research Institute. She has degrees in Experimental Psychology (BSc Hons), Social Research Methods (MSc), and Sociology (PhD). During her career at the Institute, Helen's work has significantly contributed to policy and practice on counterterrorism, neighbourhood policing, behavioural change, and digital disinformation.

RICHARD JACKSON is Professor of Peace Studies and Director of the National Centre for Peace and Conflict Studies, University of Otago, New Zealand. He is the editor-in-chief of the journal, *Critical Studies on Terrorism*, and the author and editor of numerous books and papers on critical terrorism studies, political violence, pacifism, and conflict resolution.

CHRISTIAN KAUNERT is Professor of International Security at Dublin City University in Ireland. He is also Professor of Policing and Security, as well as Director of the International Centre for Policing and Security at the University of South Wales, United Kingdom. Prof. Kaunert holds a PhD in International Politics and an MSc in European Politics from the University of Wales Aberystwyth and a BA (Hons) European Business from Dublin City University.

DANIEL KOEHLER works on countering violent extremism, as well as right-wing and jihadist terrorism. He founded the first peer-reviewed open access journal on deradicalization and the German Institute on Radicalization and De-Radicalization Studies (GIRDS). He is a member of the Editorial Board of the International Centre for Counter-Terrorism in The Hague and a Research Fellow at the Polarization and Extremism Research and Innovation Lab of the American University in Washington D.C.

GARY LAFREE is the Founding Director of the National Consortium for the Study of Terrorism and Responses to Terrorism (START) at the University of Maryland. His research is on the causes and consequences of violent crime and terrorism. His most recent books are *Putting Terrorism in Context* (with Laura Dugan and Erin Miller), *The Handbook* *of the Criminology of Terrorism* (with Josh Freilich) and *Countering Terrorism* (with Martha Crenshaw).

PETER LEHR is Senior Lecturer in Terrorism Studies at the CSTPV, School of International Relations, University of St. Andrews whose research revolves around the subject areas of Terrorism/Political Violence in general, and Critical Infrastructure Protection (CIP, with a focus on transportation terrorism) in particular. His first monograph on CIP, *Counter-Terrorism Technologies: A Critical Assessment,* was published by Springer International in 2019 as part of the Springer Advanced Sciences and Technologies for Security Applications series.

SONDRE LINDAHL is Associate Professor in Political Science at Østfold University College, Norway. He holds a PhD from the National Centre for Peace and Conflict Studies, University of Otago, New Zealand. His main research interest is counterterrorism, and he is the author of *A Critical Theory of Counterterrorism: Ontology, Epistemology and Normativity*. He is a regular commentator on issues of security and terrorism in Norway.

ORLA LYNCH is currently a Senior Lecturer in Criminology and Asc. Dean of Graduate Studies at University College Cork, Ireland. Until 2015 she was Director of Teaching and a Lecturer in Terrorism Studies at CSTPV at the University of St Andrews. Orla's background is in International Security Studies and Applied Psychology; her primary training is as a social psychologist. Recent publications include *Applying Psychology: The Case of Terrorism and Political Violence* (Wiley).

LEENA MALKKI is a historian and political scientist specialized in the study of terrorism and political violence. She currently holds a position of University Lecturer at the Centre for European Studies, University of Helsinki. Her fields of interest include political violence in post-war Europe, dynamics of terrorist campaigns, transnational diffusion of extremist narratives, and political and societal resilience to terrorism.

STEFAN MALTHANER is a Research Fellow at the Hamburg Institute for Social Research (HIS) and Visiting Professor at Leuphana University, Lüneburg, Germany. His research interests include terrorism and political violence, processes of radicalization, Islamist movements, and civil wars.

SARAH MARSDEN is Senior Lecturer in the Handa Centre for the Study of Terrorism and Political Violence at the University of St Andrews, prior to which she was a Senior Lecturer at Lancaster University. Her research takes an interdisciplinary approach to questions of terrorism, political violence, and contentious politics. She has published widely on global jihadism, radical social movements, and efforts to counter violent extremism, including in her book, *Reintegrating Extremists: Deradicalisation and Desistance*.

ABOUT THE AUTHORS

KIERAN MCCONAGHY is a Lecturer in International Relations at CSTPV, University of St Andrews. He holds degrees in Law with Politics (LLB) and Irish Politics (MA) from Queen's University Belfast and in International Relations (PhD) from the University of St Andrews. His research interests include conflict in Ireland, state-terrorism, and Irish and British political history more generally.

DIEGO MURO is Senior Lecturer in International Relations at the Handa Centre for the Study of Terrorism and Political Violence at the University of St Andrews and Senior Research Fellow at the Barcelona Centre for International Affairs (CIDOB). His research is centrally concerned with the relationship between identity politics, secession, and political violence, with a comparative-historical focus on Europe. He is the author, among others, of *Ethnicity and Violence: The Case of Radical Basque Nationalism* (2008) and *When Does Terrorism Work?* (2018).

PETER NEUMANN is Professor of Security Studies at the Department of War Studies, King's College London, and served as Director of its International Centre for the Study of Radicalisation (ICSR) from 2008 to 2018. In 2017, he was the OSCE's Special Representative on Countering Violent Radicalisation. Neumann's latest book in English is *Bluster: Donald Trump's War on Terror,* which was published by Hurst and Oxford University Press in early 2020.

IAN ORRINGER is an undergraduate student majoring in German Studies and Political Science with a concentration on International Relations at the University of Arizona. His research interests include terrorist target selection, the effect of border policies on patterns of migration, and foreign policy with regards to global security.

ANTHONY RICHARDS is a Senior Lecturer in the School of Law and Social Sciences at Royal Holloway, University of London and is Co-Director of the MSc in Terrorism and Counter-Terrorism Studies. He has published widely within terrorism studies and is lead editor for *Jihadist Terror: New Threats, New Responses* (Bloomsbury, 2019). He is also the author of *Conceptualizing Terrorism* which was published with OUP in 2015.

RASHMI SINGH is Associate Professor in International Relations at PUC Minas (Brazil), where she has been based since 2016. She is the Co-Founder and Co-Director of The Collaborative Research Network on Terrorism, Radicalization and Organized Crime (TRAC), an Associate Editor of Perspectives on Terrorism and Anniversary Fellow at the Handa Centre for the Study of Terrorism and Political Violence (CSTPV), University of St. Andrews. She was awarded the CnPQ High Research Productivity Grant in 2020.

JAKANA THOMAS is Associate Professor in the School of Global Policy and Strategy at University of California, San Diego. Her research focuses on the behaviour of violent political actors and examines women's participation in rebel, terrorist, and militia organizations, the correlates of terrorist lethality and the determinants of successful peace processes. Her work has appeared in prominent outlets including *American Journal of Political Science*, *American Political Science Review*, *International Organization* and *Journal of Peace Research*.

HARMONIE TOROS is Reader in International Conflict Analysis at the University of Kent (UK). Her research lies at the crossroad between conflict transformation, peace studies, and terrorism studies, developing a critical theory-based approach to terrorism and examining the transformation of conflicts marked by terrorist violence. She has carried out extensive field research in Europe, the Middle East, Southeast Asia, and Africa.

ORI WERTMAN is a Research Fellow at the Institute for National Security Studies (INSS), Israel, and Research Fellow at the University of South Wales, UK.

TIM WILSON is the Director of the Handa Centre for the Study of Terrorism and Political Violence (CSTPV) at the University of St Andrews. He is editor of the CSTPV Monograph Series *Studies in Terrorism and Political Violence* (in conjunction with Lynne Rienner publishers) as well as a member of the editorial board of the *Studies in Conflict and Terrorism* journal. His own research ranges broadly over the history of political violence from state terror to sectarian rioting. His latest book, *Killing Strangers: How Political Violence Became Modern*, appeared with Oxford University Press in September 2020.

ABOUT THE EDITORS

DR DIEGO MURO is Senior Lecturer in International Relations at the University of St Andrews. His main research interests are identity politics, ethnic conflict, and terrorism and counter-terrorism. He has published in *Ethnic and Racial Studies, Ethnicities, Mediterranean Politics, Nationalism and Ethnic Conflict, Nations and Nationalism, South European Society & Politics, Studies in Conflict, and Terrorism and West European Politics*. His latest books on terrorism are *Ethnicity and Violence* (2008), *ETA's Terrorist Campaign* (2017), and *When Does Terrorism Work?* (2018).

DR TIM WILSON is the Director of the Handa Centre for the Study of Terrorism and Political Violence (CSTPV) at St Andrews. His research interests and media appearances range widely over the past, present, and future of terrorism and political violence. He is especially interested in why such horrors take the particular forms that they do. His first book *Frontiers of Violence*—a grassroots comparison of different patterns of ethnic violence in contested borderlands—was published in 2010. His second book *Killing Strangers: How Political Violence Become Modern* appeared in September 2020. Both were published by Oxford University Press.

CHAPTER 1

Introduction

DIEGO MURO AND TIM WILSON

1.1 INTRODUCTION

Welcome to Terrorism Studies: the fastest growing sub-discipline of International Relations in the early 21st century. It was the spectacular conflict unleashed upon the USA by Al-Qaeda suicide hijackers on 11th September 2001 ('9/11') that transformed the study of terrorism from 'an obscure academic field' (Richardson, 2006: 1) into a central arena of debate and research. It has stayed there ever since, and does not appear to be fading in importance any time soon. Terrorism policy continues to remain a major preoccupation of governments and their relations with each other, but it has also increasingly become an important field of interaction between governments and their own citizens. Quite simply: terrorism has become a cutting-edge subject for investigating how power relations are determined in the world today.

1.2 DEFINITION OF TERRORISM

Welcome to a subject area of enormous importance in understanding the contemporary world. Since you are starting out in what may be a new area of investigation, it is natural that you might like to start with a basic definition of terrorism. One place to begin is with the word *terror* itself. In English—as in many other European languages from Spanish to Polish—terror derives directly from the Latin verb *terrere* meaning 'to scare' (Schmid: 41). Terror tends to refer to the end result of this process for its victims: the emotional state of experiencing extreme fear. Such feelings of terror can easily arise from natural disasters (such as earthquakes) or accidents (such as mining explosions). But they can also be a spontaneous reaction to the planned actions of others (such as a bomb attack). The English word 'terror' is closely related to other terms that are relevant here, such as the verb 'to terrify'.

> **KEY CONCEPTS**
>
> **Terror** Terror 'refers to an individual psychological state of mind and has been around for centuries. It received its political connotations only during the French Revolution. It was first signalled in the French language in the 14th century and entered the English language in the sixteenth. Jean Bodin, the French political writer, used the concept "terror" in his *Les six livres de la République* (1577) when referring to fear caused by excessive violence: "Cruelty keeps men in fear, and inactive, inspiring the subject with terror of the prince"' (Schmid: 41).
>
> It is also worth noting that when used as a general label—i.e. 'The Terror'—the term has been used to describe a period when a government uses extreme violence to try to remake society and consolidate its rule. It was first used in this sense during the French Revolution in 1793–4 (Townshend: 36–38). You can read more about this specific usage in Chapter 8, section 8.4.2; and much more about state terror tactics in Chapter 14 ('Can States Be Terrorists?').

In general terms, terrorism studies have tended to see terrorism as this *deliberate* creation of this state of fear in other people; i.e. terrifying by design. Here, the working assumption is that this is being done to advance some *political* goal. In other words, terrorism is not about the deliberate creation of fear for some personal agenda, or as a criminal act (such as threatening a bank cashier with a gun to make them open up the safe). It is always related to some idea of political change.

The good news is that *some* broad degree of convergence does exist around the definitional question of 'what is terrorism'? As a starting point, we can recommend this basic definition from Louise Richardson (2006: 20): 'terrorism, simply put, means deliberately and violently targeting civilians for political purposes'. You can compare this definition with some of the other well-regarded alternatives that have been offered by leading scholars of terrorism, see the Key Concepts box.

> **KEY CONCEPTS**
>
> **Terrorism** Martha Crenshaw (2011: 23):
>
> 'Summarizing the basic components of a definition of the concept of terrorism produces the following list of essential properties that empirical examination of data must reveal:
>
> 1) Terrorism is part of a revolutionary strategy—a method used by insurgents to seize political power from an existing government.
> 2) Terrorism is manifested in acts of socially and politically unacceptable violence.
> 3) There is a consistent pattern of symbolic or representative selection of the victims or objects of acts of terrorism.

> 4) The revolutionary movement deliberately intends these actions to create a psychological effect on specific groups and thereby to change their political behaviour and attitudes.'
>
> Richard English (2009: 24):
>
> 'Terrorism involves heterogeneous violence used or threatened with a political aim; it can involve a variety of acts, of targets, and of actors; it possesses an important psychological dimension, producing terror or fear among a directly threatened group and also a wider implied audience in the hope of maximising political communication and achievement; it embodies the exerting and implementing of power, and the attempted redressing of power relations; it represents a sub-species of warfare, and as such it can form part of a wider campaign of violent and non-violent attempts at political leverage.'
>
> Bruce Hoffman (2017: 44):
>
> 'the deliberate creation and exploitation of fear through violence or the threat of violence in the pursuit of political change'

At this stage, it is worth keeping an open mind about how best to define terrorism. Attempts to achieve a more precise, but widely accepted, definition of terrorism, have generated an impressive amount of academic discussion and disagreement. Alex Schmid (2013: 99–157) once collected a 'short' list of over 250 different definitions of terrorism.

But in itself this variety of interpretation is not unexpected. Terrorism is naturally a controversial subject for two fundamental reasons. First: terrorism is bound up with the use (or, at the very least, threat) of violence in the basic sense of the deliberate infliction of physical injury and, often, death of other human beings. Any discussion of violence is not easily separated from discussion of its morality. Under what conditions is it justified to inflict such harm? And who decides? Secondly: since terrorism is a form of political violence, it is often hard to discuss terrorism without also discussing politics. And politics, by its very nature, is about the clash of rival powers. Deep disagreement over differing values often lies at its core. Or as the political theorist Kenneth Minogue once put it: 'politics is endless public disagreement about what justice requires' (2000: 81).

The important point to note here is that different authors will take different approaches in how they understand terrorism throughout this textbook. As will be explained shortly, they may indeed face in different directions to each other. We recognize that this may seem confusing at first, and that it might be much more convenient for students if all the authors were unified. But that approach would lead to a much less interesting—or useful—textbook. Our design is quite deliberate because it is designed to support you in navigating the field of Terrorism Studies in all its intellectual breadth and variety. Answers to the question 'what is terrorism?' can therefore seem very varied. But it remains a useful starting question in Terrorism Studies for very good reasons. Indeed, attempts to answer it often marks the point at which discussion becomes exciting, because some different assumptions about terrorism begin to surface.

At this stage it may help to note that as far as definitions go, several early chapters have been grouped together to guide your thinking and reading. Chapter 2 therefore looks at 'What Are Terrorism Studies?'—and in doing so, considers briefly why an emerging academic field in the 1970s tended to assume that the study of terrorism should focus upon anti-state violence that was internationally mobile. Chapter 3 takes a rather different stance by considering terrorism as a 'label or category'. Indeed, it deliberately begins with the provocative question of 'whether "terrorism" exists at all'. Chapter 5 considers how the term 'terrorism' has tended to evolve in public discourse. Definitional choices are a recurrent practical challenge in compiling databases of terrorist incidents, as is explored in Chapter 7. Definitional challenges are, however, surveyed at greatest length in Chapter 4 under the general title of 'Conceptualizations of Terrorism'.

It is worthwhile now to take a few moments to explore how best to use *Contemporary Terrorism Studies*, and how its overall structure has been designed to assist your learning.

1.3 DESIGN AND LEARNING FEATURES

How should you read *Contemporary Terrorism Studies*? The short answer is, in whatever way works best for your style of learning. A slightly longer answer is as follows. There *is* a definite logic behind the arrangement of the chapters (as will shortly be explained in Section 1.3). But they certainly do *not* have to be read in strict order. If you like, you can think of this textbook as a sort of giant intellectual 'buffet'. It aims to offer a spread of the chief debates, main actors, and leading issues in a way that encourages you to find your own individual path around them; and, in doing so, to load your 'plate' with ideas to digest later in your own time, and at your own speed.

As has already been mentioned in section 1.2, it is important to note here that the same key concepts and debates may well be discussed across different chapters and from different approaches. Each chapter has been written by a subject expert, and often the same issues and concepts will overlap, but with from perspectives. So, you may find discussion of some themes spread throughout *Contemporary Terrorism Studies*. Here you are encouraged to jump back and forth freely between these related discussions. Cross-references are given as signposts explicitly to help you to do this more effectively.

There are many other learning features to help you as well. These are designed to be eye-catching, and to help you digest key information easily and quickly. You have come across a couple of them already in this chapter in the boxed text sections. *Key Concepts* guide you towards short but contextualized discussions of the foundational ideas that

that chapter explores. Start of chapter summaries introduce you how the author of that particular chapter has understood those concepts. As already indicated, such definitions will vary between chapters, so it is important to be prepared for this.

One other type of boxed text section is worth looking out for. Every chapter (after this one) is supported by two *Case Studies*. As the name suggests, Case Studies are designed to illustrate key themes of the chapter by offering in-depth examples of what they can look like in practice. The Case Studies vary considerably depending on the subject of each chapter. But in general terms they act to bridge the gap between theory and real life. For instance, take the analysis in Chapter 15 ('Gendered and Racialized Terrorism') on how female terrorists have often been presented as more irrational—and hence dangerous—than male terrorists. One of the Case Studies (Case Study 15.2) examines the fascinating career of Ulrike Meinhof (see also Photo 15.2), one of the founding members of the Red Army Faction (RAF) in West Germany in 1970. Controversially, an autopsy of her brain was ordered by the West German government after her death in 1976. Neurosurgeons then tried hard to try to find some clear sign of underlying pathology. They failed. No such autopsy was ever ordered for her male fellow RAF founding member, Andreas Baader.

Case Studies have been selected, therefore, to help establish important concepts with real-life examples. Each one is supported by two questions. In general terms, these are there to aid reflection on the subject at hand. More specifically, they can function as self-test questions to see how well you have absorbed key information contained in the Case Study, and the wider themes it helps you explore.

There are approximately five *Discussion Questions* at the end of each chapter. These are designed to help take your learning beyond the chapter by considering key themes, and act as useful prompts for revision and examination preparation. They can also be discussed in small groups. They are deliberately open-ended. For example, a question from Chapter 28 is: 'Explore how media coverage of terrorism has impacted on your sense of safety. Have you changed your behaviour?' There is no one 'right' answer to such a question: but with luck it should help you reflect on how the information contained in this chapter directly relates to your own personal experience. Another question from Chapter 26 is: 'Can you think of some key challenges for P/CVE [Preventing/Countering Violent Extremism] in the future?' Again, there can be no 'right' answer. By its very nature, the future cannot be known. But it is a line of questioning that is designed to help you build upon what you have already learnt from the chapter.

Contemporary Terrorism Studies is designed to support your continued learning. Every chapter therefore ends with targeted suggestions for your further reading. These suggestions are offered in the form of an annotated *Guide to Further Reading*. Each chapter gives a brief account of *why* this particular book or journal article is useful. This final section of each chapter functions as a springboard from which you can dive into relevant literature to help support your understanding of the chapter, and pursue your own research interests.

1.4 STRUCTURE

We start in Part 1 by introducing the core issues that tend to arise in first studying terrorism. Questions in this section are about the foundations of the subject. How should we study terrorism? What are we looking at? What are we looking for? We then dig deeper throughout Part 2 into debates that are about the nature of terrorism itself. How does it arise? Why does it continue? What forms does it tend to take? Can we see an evolution over time? Part 3 looks at responses to terrorism. What kind of policies and reactions have worked? Which have not? And what do we know about how terrorism ends? Sections 1.4.1 to 1.4.3 provide an outline of each part, and the chapters within.

1.4.1 Part 1: The state of terrorism studies

Part 1 is all about helping to situate yourself in Terrorism Studies. Chapter 2 therefore looks at how terrorism *first* emerged as a subject area for academic study. It concentrates on 'Orthodox Terrorism Studies' (OTS) whose main focus has tended to be upon anti-state international terrorism. Here we note that some intellectual disciplines (i.e. International Relations, Political Science, Psychology, Criminology) have tended to influence the development of Terrorism Studies far more than others that might also appear relevant (such as Anthropology or History). Read more about this aspect in section 2.4 of the chapter. Overall, Chapter 2 notes some basic challenges to researching terrorism, not least, that it can be very dangerous. But it ends on the optimistic note that we know far more about terrorism than we did 50 years ago.

Chapter 3 on 'Critical Terrorism Studies' (CTS) complements Chapter 2, and in some ways they counterbalance each other. CTS emerged in the years after 2001 as a conscious mobilization against OTS priorities. It has been particularly focused upon the actions of states, after all, these are nearly always more powerful than anti-state terrorists—and hence they can do much more damage. In particular, CTS concentrates upon how 'terrorism' is used to label enemies of the state. It asks: what is the place of this label of terrorism in the logics and practices of power? Case Study 3.2 showcases the example of how Al-Shabaab (aS) in East Africa. American policy has been based upon an interpretation of aS as an 'Al-Qaeda-linked terrorist group' that is a direct threat to the USA. But other interpretations are also possible (that stress the emergence of aS from the Islamic Courts Union movement). And these in turn open up the possibility of a more imaginative international policy response to aS than the waging of endless drone strikes.

Chapter 4 is *the* chapter if you wish to explore the debates around definitions of terrorism. However, it is entitled 'Conceptualizations of Terrorism' rather than 'Definitions of Terrorism'. This is quite deliberate. 'Conceptualizing terrorism' can be thought of as a 'less ambitious', but therefore more useful 'approach that acknowledges the social construction of terrorism but at the same time seeks to determine what it is that is analytically distinctive about "terrorism"' (4.2). As Chapter 3 on CTS, you can also find here an uncomfortable discussion of just how often states use terrorism as a label to de-legitimize their opponents (Case Study 4.2).

Context matters greatly. It therefore forms the organizing theme of Chapter 5 on 'Terrorism in Context': 'context remains crucial to the development of an understanding of terrorism in its many manifestations'. Section 5.1.1. explores that up until the mid-20th century there *are* examples of rebel actors who were proud to call themselves 'terrorists'. Since then a 'normative shift' had occurred and 'terrorism has come to mean absolutely illegitimate violence'. In practice, terrorism now applies to a wide range of different types of political violence. Originally, this labelling included assassinations. But popular usage later expanded to emphasize attacks on innocent bystanders (5.1.2). As a general observation, 'the meaning of terrorism in any era inevitably reflects the active campaigns of the time' (5.1.9). Given this shifting pattern, the chapter ends with a sharp question: 'Why is terrorism rarely discussed in the plural as terrorisms?'

Chapter 6 also examines the importance of context: but with a different purpose. It reviews an wide body of sociological literature that analyses political violence as arising through the *process* of 'interactions between multiple actors'. Rather than trying to define upfront what is terrorism and what is not, this approach is far more interested in analysing the emergence of political violence. It sees this as arising through a dynamic *process* of 'interactions between multiple actors'. This is a promising approach. It first emerged out of studying the origins of the Red Army Faction (in West Germany) and the Red Brigades (in Italy): both hard left armed groups at their height in the later 1970s. But there is no reason why this explanatory approach cannot also be adapted to explain the development of other armed anti-state groups motivated by other ideologies. Case Study 6.2, for instance, examines the varying fortunes of The Islamic Group (al-Jamaa al-Islamiyya) in Egypt from the late 1970s to the late 1990s.

Chapter 7 moves away from contextualized approaches. Its subject is the contribution of databases to the study of terrorism. That is, attempts to record systematically information about terrorism that is readily available in the media ('open sources'). Databases take several forms: the most common is the event database that seeks to record terrorist attacks (see section 7.1). There are also invaluable attempts to compile databases of terrorist groups (see section 7.2) and of different types of terrorist perpetrators (see sections 7.3–7.8). All such databases are built upon hard definitional choices. But they also represent the only realistic strategy for charting long-term terrorist trends systematically.

1.4.2 Part 2: Issues and debates in terrorism studies

Part 2 begins by looking back through time. Chapter 8 offers an overview of the long history of terrorism as conducted by both state and non-state actors, but concentrates most upon the period since the French Revolution of the 1790s when the term 'terrorism' was first coined. At its core (see section 8.4.1 and Case Study 8.1) lies a close examination of

David Rapoport's theory that 'rebel terrorism' has occurred in four great 'waves' since 1880. But the chapter also puts terrorism into historical context by noting how it has dramatically changed in form in response to background changes occurring in technology, society, and communication.

Chapter 9 focuses upon 'root causes' of terrorism, i.e. the factors that at a societal level help 'create the conditions in which members of a group or community can feel compelled to actively pursue a terrorist campaign' (9.2: Key Concepts). This is a challenging area for analysis. It involves a consideration of the complex and shifting ways that ideological motivations can interact with background structural factors, including lack of economic development, poor educational opportunities, and so on. Case Study 9.2, for example, examines how the emergence of al-Qaeda in the Islamic Maghreb (AQIM) was facilitated by a combination of such factors. The chapter also contains a wider contextualization of Rapoport's waves of nationalist (see section 9.3.1) and New Left (see section 9.3.3) terrorism, which can be usefully read alongside the discussion of his work in Chapter 8.

Chapter 10 takes the level of explanation down to that of the individual terrorist. What do know about how and why individuals become involved in terrorism? Assuming terrorists are just mentally unwell does not advance explanation very far (see sections 10.2 and 10.3). We need a more systematic approach to analysis of motivation. In this context, Case Study 10.2 explores how the controversial concept of 'radicalization' came to dominate much counterterrorist policy after 2004. Section 10.6 then reviews the existing state of knowledge about 'what makes a terrorist?' It argues that—at least in general terms –a lot is now known about the background conditions behind this process. Just four crucial factors are required: a conducive environment, opportunity, ideology, and local mobilization hubs.

Difficult questions remain about what (anti-state) terrorists are trying to achieve. Schmid and Jongman (1988: 134–135) once drew attention to an 'absurd' quality in terrorism: 'the destruction that terrorists bring about is real; the better world they strive for is an uncertain gamble with history'. Chapter 11 'Can Terrorism Be Rational' tackles this tension head on. Section 11.2 points out that 'political scientists typically view terrorists as rational political actors': as we have already seen (see section 10.3) they are not generally mentally unwell. And yet terrorism often seems to be an unsuccessful political strategy. Even the best-known groups such as al-Qaeda or ISIS can be seen as long-term failures (see Case Studies 11.1 and 11.2). Here lies a great puzzle of Terrorism Studies. But we can get closer to solving it if we understand how terrorists think they may benefit from terrorism. Moreover, this analytical approach supports more effective counterterrorism: 'understanding the thought-process of terrorists is useful for combating them' (see section 11.4).

Chapter 12 on target selection zooms in on a related subject area: the complex relationship between thought and action. It notes that anti-state terrorists try to advance their ideological goals 'only if they are able to convert the fear that their targeted attacks cause within the public into specific demands for changes to policies that would align with the terrorists' goals' (see section 12.5). A key point here is that seemingly 'random' terrorist attacks *are actually* targeted (see section 12.3). A careful study of terrorist target selection can therefore tell us much about *how* terrorists are trying to leverage fear in support of their goals. This discussion is also contextualized with reference to regime type. Democracies are understood here to be particularly vulnerable to attacks by anti-state terrorist groups (see section 12.4).

Yet such anti-state terrorist groups are also often highly vulnerable themselves. Many do not survive for very long (see section 13.3). But others do (see section 13.1). Why? Chapter 13 therefore examines the *longevity* of terrorist groups. Larger groups seem to do better here (see section 13.4.2). So do those that form alliances (see section 13.4.3). Long-running terrorist campaigns generally represent an obvious failure for the security services. But they do not in themselves represent terrorist success because 'mere survival is rarely the only goal' (see section 13.6). Case Study 13.2 presents a fascinating analysis of a group that arose out of the New Left wave of terrorism: The Revolutionary Organization 17 November in Greece. Remarkably, this tiny group stayed active from 1975 to 2002 before coming to an abrupt halt. We can learn much from its career.

Terrorism is often assumed to be *anti*-state political violence. Sometimes this approach has been defended upon grounds of analytical convenience. Terrorism is seen here as the type of clandestine violence that anti-state insurgents commit when they cannot control territory (see section 2.2). But it is hard to overlook the uncomfortable reality that just such an assumption is also highly politically convenient for states themselves (see also Chapter 3 and Case Study 4.2). And in fact, states *do* on occasion also practise such clandestine violence (an example of this is explored in Case Study 5.1). Chapter 14 therefore turns the spotlight on the vital question: Can states be terrorists? It argues forcefully that 'terrorism can be used by a variety of actors, state and non-state, weak and strong, overt and covert' (see section 14.5). State terrorism in practice can take a huge variety of forms that range from acts of unrestrained public intimidation, to more covert forms such as torture and disappearances. All deserve to be analysed within Terrorism Studies (see section 14.6).

Like Chapter 3, Chapter 15 'Gendered and Racialized Terrorism' concentrates upon the *meanings* of terrorism. Chapter 15 adopts a Feminist poststructuralist approach that understands terrorism as 'a subjective term dependent upon the power structures of gender and race'. We have already explored in this chapter how Ulrike Meinhof was understood to be far *more* dangerous and irrational than her male comrades in the Red Army Faction of the 1970s, and this reflects a wider pattern. Case Study 15.1 additionally traces the striking contrasts between how the actions of different violent lone actors of different races have been reported in the media, or investigated by police. The second half of the chapter brings these themes together. It demonstrates how those associated with the Incel ('involuntary celibate') movement 'rely upon the intersecting biases of gender and race to justify their violence' (see section 15.3).

International terrorism often receives far more analytical attention than domestic terrorism. But most terrorism is domestic in the sense that assailants 'reside in the same country they target' (see section 16.1). Much of this terrorism occurs within the context of prolonged insurgency and/or civil war. Chapter 16 examines 'Terrorism by Insurgents and

Rebels', an important, but often neglected, phenomenon. It explores how terrorism may be used by insurgents for very different reasons 'weak groups use terrorism to look strong, while stronger groups use terror to look legitimate'—that is, to help liberate territory and then administer it effectively (see section 16.3). Case Study 16.2 demonstrates just how effectively the Taliban have used such tactics in Afghanistan.

Change lies at the heart of Chapter 17. It examines a significant debate that arose in the 1990s. Researchers argued that a 'New Terrorism' was emerging rapidly. Unlike 'Old Terrorism', this involved 'more networked, religiously motivated terrorists whose attacks are intended to cause mass casualties' (see Key Concepts box in section 17.2). Not all academics were persuaded. Sceptics insisted upon the need to evaluate such claims only against more long-term backgrounds than the immediately preceding few years (see section 17.3). In the chapter's final judgement, 'the debate about the "new terrorism" has made a significant contribution to broadening and deepening our understanding of a constantly evolving phenomenon' (see section 17.7). As such, it is worth noting that this debate on Old versus New Terrorism can be usefully read alongside Chapter 8 on 'The History of Terrorism'. Both dissect the changing nature of terrorism, although over very different time scales.

One very dramatic driver of change in the 21st century has been social media, which is the focus of Chapter 18. The background here has been the communications revolution that has transformed public life across the world. For instance, 'internet bandwidth availability in Africa increased twenty-fold between 2008 and 2012, and mobile phone data-service subscriptions increased sixty-fold in the first decade of the 21st century, making the continent the world's fastest growing mobile phone market' (see section 18.4). Terrorism has not remained unaffected this development. As Case Study 18.1 explores through an analysis of the livestreamed Christchurch Mosque attacks in March 2019, social media has now become central to terrorism. But its adoption also brings downsides and dilemmas for terrorist leaders who may easily lose control over the online debate, and can potentially be more easily tracked down (see section 18.5).

Does terrorism work? It looks like a simple question. But Chapter 19 ('Is Terrorism Effective?') makes clear how difficult it has been for scholars to reach firm agreement in answering it (see section 19.1). Different measures of success may be appropriate at different times. Case Study 19.2 analyses the case of the Shining Path. Between 1980 and 2000, the Shining Path pursued a major insurgency in Peru that 'did not achieve its strategic goal of overthrowing the state by guerrilla warfare and creating the People's Republic of Peru, but [which] did manage to terrorize Peruvian society for decades, especially the impoverished peasantry of rural areas'. Chapter 19 concludes 'that most terrorist groups fail to achieve their strategic goals but often strike some tactical success along the way' (see section 19.6). It is worth noting that this is a chapter that can be very usefully read in conjunction with Chapter 11 ('Can Terrorism Be Rational?'). Both survey political science literatures that interrogate how—and how effectively—(anti-state) terrorists pursue their goals.

We may briefly note here a general tendency for terrorists and counterterrorists to become locked in an 'insecurity spiral' of action and counter-action. Summarizing the content of Part 2, it is clear that both state and anti-state terrorism occur within contexts that are both dynamic and relational. Terrorism cannot be effectively analysed without some reference to these wider dimensions, as Part 2 demonstrates. What brings all these chapters together is an attempt to understand and analyse terrorism from a non-normative perspective, and to avoid being prescriptive with possible solutions.

1.4.3 Part 3: Countering terrorism

By contrast, Part 3 is all about possible solutions. Its organizing theme is counterterrorist responses. It groups together key debates that all, in different ways, relate to the same general question: what should be done about terrorism?

Part 3 begins with the complex apparatus of counterterrorism. Chapter 20 looks at the array of military, intelligence, and criminal justice institutions that liberal democratic states use to try to defeat terrorism, and what we know about their work. Much of this remains hidden normally. But counterterrorism agencies responses to crises—such as successful terrorist attacks—do allow us to gain insight into how they operate (see section 20.1). What is clear is that terrorist threats can evolve and change fast. Social media, for instance, has transformed terrorism, and, by extension, the task of the Intelligence Services as well (see section 20.5). Here it may be worth referring to earlier parallel discussions of how terrorists have struggled to master using social media (see Chapter 18, section 18.5). Terrorists now often generate information about themselves online. But processing all this information also creates its own challenges for those working in counterterrorism. Case Study 20.2 explores just how difficult it can be to coordinate responses effectively across different agencies.

Chapter 21 on 'Responding to Terrorism Nonviolently' takes a more sceptical stance towards standard responses by states to anti-state terrorism, or what it calls 'force-based counterterrorism' (see section 21.2.2). It makes a powerful case for seeing the 'Global War on Terror'—launched by Western powers as a response to al-Qaeda's attacks on the USA in 2001—as both a moral and practical disaster (see section 21.2.1). Against the model of 'force-based counterterrorism' this chapter explores the potential of nonviolent responses such as 'dialogue and direct negotiation with terrorist groups, reconciliation and conflict resolution, concessions and reforms, amnesties and pardons, political settlements, and the like' (see section 21.3). All in all, Chapter 21 forms a companion piece to earlier contributions in *Contemporary Terrorism Studies*: Chapters 3 and 15 (with their sensitivity to the use of delegitimizing labels by states) as well as Chapter 14 (that emphasizes the destructive power of states).

It could also be appropriately read together with the next chapter as well. Chapter 22 concentrates upon the relationship of counterterrorism and human rights (understood in the Key Concepts box in section 22.1 as 'fundamental moral rights, acquired at birth and inherent to all human beings, which are necessary for a life with human dignity'). Counterterrorism has often involved practices that violate such rights, such as detention without trial, torture, and extra-judicial killings. A widespread assumption is that there is a fundamental 'trade off' between security and human rights. In other words, counterterrorist agencies that are obliged to respect human rights will be necessarily less effective. But such thinking can be challenged. Restraint may even be in the state's own long-term interest because repressive measures so quickly alienate key constituencies. And 'while only a small proportion will join terrorist groups, more may become alienated from a draconian state and unwilling to provide it with vital, on-the-ground intelligence on suspected terrorist operatives' (see section 22.5).

In a globalized world where ideas and people circulate, it often makes little sense to draw too clear a line between 'domestic' and 'international' terrorism. Such categories can become blurred and overlapping. So, too, with counterterrorism. Or as Chapter 23 on 'Foreign Policy and Countering Terrorism' puts it: 'to fully understand the formulation of foreign policy and policies countering terrorism, one needs to view the foreign and domestic as two ends of a continuum rather than as separate' (see section 23.1). In practice, the simple label of 'foreign policy' covers a broad array of very different policy responses that can be hard to coordinate effectively. Indeed, 'the instruments of policy discussed here—diplomacy and culture, economic statecraft, and the military—are not sharply delineated' (see section 23.7).

Coordination of foreign policy and counterterrorism at the highest levels of the international community forms the focus for Chapter 24 on 'International Organizations and Counter-terrorism'. This chapter first examines counterterrorism cooperation within the United Nations (UN) (section 24.2). It then moves the discussion to important regional organizations, including the Association of Southeast Nations (ASEAN) (section 24.3), European Union (EU) (section 24.4), as well as multilateral cooperation between the EU and the North-Atlantic Treaty Organization (NATO) (section 24.5). Such efforts can be very different in characters because these organizations are themselves very different. The EU, for instance, has substantial powers in its own right, whereas ASEAN takes the form of a much looser association of different governments. Continued frictions both between, and within, these different international organizations are inevitable. But if the threats from international terrorism continue, so too will attempts to coordinate international counterterrorism better.

Terrorism has always enjoyed an intimate relationship to technology. The invention of dynamite is often seen as introducing the age of modern terrorism (see Chapter 8, section 8.4). But counterterrorism also enjoys a similarly intimate relationship to technology, as is analysed in Chapter 25 'Terrorism, Counter-Terrorism, and Technology'. Section 25.2 explores the diverse ways in which technology has been as way to defeat anti-state terrorism. The focus of the chapter then shifts to consider the downsides to relying upon technology in this way. A key point to consider is 'the onslaught on our privacy, and on our civil liberties, in the name of security is far more severe precisely because our ever-increasing digital footprints render it easy for interested intelligence services to tap into the flow of data and to establish immense data bases' (see section 25.3). In summary, a reliance upon counterterrorist technology is unavoidable. But in helping contain some old problems, it has also created other entirely new ones (see section 25.5).

Chapter 26 puts the spotlight upon 'Preventing or Countering Violent Extremism' (P/CVE). Broadly, this challenging policy field covers efforts 'to support violent actors, or those on the path to violence, to reintegrate into society and leave behind groups which might have recruited and radicalized them' (section 26.2). Cultural context matters here—and distinct 'Western' and 'Eastern' approaches have been a feature of the field (section 26.3). Effective intervention must also pay attention to gender dynamics since 'research has begun to shed light on the potentially different entry and exit pathways of women into, and out of, violent extremism and terrorism' (see section 26.5). Still, research into the effectiveness of such programmes remains challenging: not least because one is often trying to measure a negative outcome—that is, the terrorist attacks that have not happened (see section 26.6). By the end of Chapter 26 you should better equipped to answer its closing question: why is it so difficult to evaluate the impact of P/CVE programmes?

Chapter 27 forms a natural companion chapter to 26, as it looks at disengagement and deradicalization programmes. Disengagement strategies are focused towards changing behaviour. By contrast, deradicalization efforts try to transform underlying attitudes (see section 27.2). Again, this is a young and underdeveloped field for investigation: 'although research has identified some factors relevant to understanding how and when people move away from terrorism, they are less able to explain, through the application or development of theory, why desistance and deradicalization occur' (see section 27.2.1). Nonetheless, a rich body of practical experience has begun to build up. Some 'exit' programmes from the extreme right in Scandinavia date back to the 1990s (see also Case Study 27.1) while the Aarhus model in Denmark is highly regarded for its interagency work encouraging deradicalization from the Islamist scene (explored in Case Study 27.2). But systematic evaluation remains difficult.

In studying terrorism, it is vital not to forget its human cost, the lives lost or instantly transformed. Chapter 28 therefore foregrounds the victims of terrorism. Victimhood is a highly complex phenomenon in part because it is varied. Different people are affected to different degrees, and in different ways by different terrorist attacks (see section 28.1). But it is also important to note that victimhood is itself so often politicized because acts of terrorism are themselves acts of political communication (see section 28.2.1). Different attacks certainly can receive strikingly different international reactions. Some victims seem to 'matter' far more than others. Case Study 28.2 thus examines the different Western reactions to ISIS attacks in Paris and Beirut in November 2015, a contrast that has also been explored from a different perspective in Chapter 2, in Case Study 2.2.

Appropriately, Chapter 29 closes this textbook with what might be seen as an optimistic note: at least from a counterterrorist perspective. What do we know about how terrorist campaigns end? This is a question that has already been touched upon during the discussion of terrorist failure in Chapter 19. But this last chapter systematically traces six pathways by which anti-state terrorism seems to end: Decapitation, Negotiations, Success, Failure, Repression and Reorientation (see section 29.3). Effective counterterrorist analysis seeks to identify some of the policies used by states that can instigate organizational decline. Overall, there is some degree of comfort to the chapter's final conclusions: 'terrorist groups meet their demise in consistent ways. During a terrorist campaign, policymakers should move beyond asking "When will the next attack be?" and arrive at the question "How will it end?"' (see section 29.4).

Reading Part 3 as a whole, you will learn that counterterrorism is an area where there has been considerable organizational learning. But it is also surprising to see how the lessons of the past are often forgotten, hence the need for the systematic study of terrorism.

1.5 CONCLUSION

You are about to be introduced to a fascinating academic field that is concerned with a specific type of political behaviour. What is distinctive about it is that it is focused upon political behaviour in the destructive form of violence. And that is not how we normally think politics 'should' work. So expect Terrorism Studies to be full of puzzles and surprises. This textbook provides a step-by-step analysis, and does not assume you have any previous background in terrorism and/or security studies. It does however, aim to offer a comprehensive overview of the fields of terrorism and counterterrorism, what academics agree and disagree on, and why.

REFERENCES

Crenshaw, M. (2011) *Explaining Terrorism: Causes, Processes and Consequences.* London and New York: Routledge.

English, R. (2009) *Terrorism: How to Respond.* Oxford: Oxford University Press.

Hoffman, B. (2017) *Inside Terrorism.* New York: Columbia University Press.

Minogue, K. (2000) *Politics: A Very Short Introduction.* Oxford: Oxford University Press.

Richardson, L. (2006) *What Terrorists Want: Understanding the Terrorist Threat.* London: John Murray.

Schmid, A. and Jongman, A. J. (1988) *Political Terrorism.* New Brunswick: Transaction Publishers.

Schmid, A. (2013) *The Routledge Handbook of Terrorism Research.* New York: Routledge.

Townshend, C. (2002) *Terrorism: A Very Short Introduction.* Oxford: Oxford University Press.

PART ONE

The State of Terrorism Studies

PART ONE The State of Terrorism Studies — 15

    2 What Are Terrorism Studies? — 17
    3 Critical Terrorism Studies — 36
    4 Conceptualizations of Terrorism — 56
    5 Terrorism in Context — 74
    6 The Social Science of Political Violence — 94
    7 Terrorism Open Source Databases — 113

PART TWO Issues and Debates in Terrorism Studies — 135

PART THREE Countering Terrorism — 389

CHAPTER 2

What Are Terrorism Studies?

TIM WILSON

■ CHAPTER SUMMARY

This chapter is designed to offer a basic overview of the academic study of terrorism. It begins by looking at attempts to define the boundaries of the subject of terrorism. It then traces the evolution of 'mainstream' (or Orthodox) Terrorism Studies since the early 1970s. It pays attention to its basic achievements: but also notes the enduring challenges that have recurred.

2.1 WHAT IS TERRORISM?

'What is terrorism?' looks like an innocent enough question. So, it can come as a bit of a shock to students to learn that it has provoked—and continues to provoke –such intense and endless arguments. As far back as 1977, Walter Laqueur accurately predicted 'endless controversies' about defining terrorism precisely (Schmid, 2013: 42). Brian Jenkins has put it rather memorably: 'definitional debates are the great Bermuda Triangle of terrorism research. I've seen entire conferences go off into definitional debates, never to be heard of again' (Stampnitzky: 5). In short: terrorism is not as straightforward a phenomenon as it may appear.

Why not? Well, there are many reasons. But an important one is that the term 'terrorism' is already in common circulation. Academics do not get to control how it is used; or to fix its meaning in advance. The basic point is that terrorism is a term that is already being heavily used *both* in debates staged in university seminar rooms *and* in the casual conversations that take place in coffee shops and across social media.

In the latter settings, people are understandably not going to be too worried about either the analytical precision or the consistency of their language—however much scholars might wish that they were. And here it is fair to say that the wider contexts that tend to encourage widespread discussion of terrorism often work to undermine attempts to establish conceptual precision.

In popular terms, terrorism conjures up powerful images of sudden, disruptive, and system-shaking political violence. And since such spectacular acts are designed to be iconic, it is tempting for many people to assume that they will know terrorism when they see it: 'the primary characteristic of events of this type seems simply to be that they are, in some sense, the wrong violence in the wrong place' (Ramsay, 2015: 225).

KEY CONCEPTS

Violence Violence is mostly understood by 'Orthodox Terrorism Studies' scholars in straightforward terms: as the deliberate infliction of bodily harm (or the threat of doing so).

Political Violence Political Violence is a term used to refer to a wide range of violence conducted—usually by non-state actors—to increase power. It is a less pejorative term than terrorism. Rioting, for instance, is often not described as terrorism: but could certainly constitute a form of political violence.

Terrorism How terrorism should be defined is debated vigorously. Many 'Orthodox' scholars broadly tend to understand terrorism as a form of violence that is political in motivation and which is intended to have some sort of indirect, or far-reaching, communicative effect. But more precise shared understandings remain hard to achieve.

Such strongly-held assumptions also reach right up to the top of society. As the British Ambassador to the United Nations, Sir Jeremy Greenstock, put it in a keynote speech back in 2001: 'Let us be wise and focused about this: terrorism is terrorism … What looks smells and kills like terrorism is terrorism' (Schmid, 2013: 39). Such thinking can be characterized as 'the common sense' approach to understanding terrorism. But the trouble with 'common sense' is that everyone thinks it is their own property. And what seems so easy to recognize at first glance may still resist more precise definition.

One way of looking at the academic debate around the meaning of terrorism is to see it as a salvage mission. Scholars are like divers scavenging the popular understandings of what terrorism is. They are looking to see whether or not there is something useful that can be brought back to the surface; and then repurposed for value-neutral analysis. But this is no easy task: 'disentangling the word from the world around it has. proved excruciatingly difficult' (Saul, 2019: 34).

Different schools of thought have emerged around this very challenge. One key question is whether to continue with the salvage mission of finding a usable definition of terrorism that can be used across different contexts. Broadly speaking, 'Orthodox Terrorism Studies' (OTS) refers to scholarship that does try to analyse terrorism as a phenomenon in its own right. By contrast, 'Critical Terrorism Studies' (CTS) remains more sceptical: and stresses that the term 'terrorism' tends to be highly politicized. In terms of timing Orthodox Terrorism Studies came first: so, this account starts here.

KEY CONCEPTS

Orthodox Terrorism Studies (OTS) Orthodox Terrorism Studies emerged as a term to distinguish 'mainstream' terrorism studies scholars from the Critical Terrorism Studies (CTS) movement that emerged around 2006. Generally, it is applied to scholars who are more interested in analysing terrorism as a phenomenon 'in its own right' (rather than how the term 'terrorism' is so often used as a stigmatizing label).

2.2 TERRORISM AS 'AN ESSENTIALLY CONTESTED CONCEPT'

We should not see Orthodox Terrorism Studies as monolithic. What has emerged over the past half century is simply a loose tradition of scholars who think there is indeed some sort of recognizable phenomenon called terrorism—even as they continue to disagree amongst themselves about what might make it distinctive. Such disagreement may not matter as much as one might think. The point is that full and final academic agreement on 'what is terrorism' may indeed not be possible: but that does not prevent healthy dialogue and debate between different positions. One cannot expect to please everyone all the time when debating definitions. But the prospect of disagreement is never a good reason to say nothing at all: least of all in the academic world.

Rival definitions of terrorism can also be made workable for different research purposes. So long as our starting assumptions are clearly stated, and differences honestly acknowledged upfront, it is still very possible 'to produce serious scholarship … without ignoring different people's rival understanding of the word' (English, 2016: 136). The great rolling dialogue of scholarship is not silenced just because scholars speak from different corners. Even if inevitably a little hazy around the edges, some general understandings of terrorism can still be developed in that shared space that lies between.

And, finally, we can raise our heads and look around us. When we start to look for 'essentially contested concepts', they begin appearing everywhere, in the world around us. Such unstable concepts are quite common across the Social Sciences. Scholars continue to argue over how we should understand basic concepts such as 'class', 'nation', 'revolution', 'fascism', 'imperialism', and so on. We might therefore conclude along with Richard English that a persistent lack of agreement around the definition of terrorism should cause us 'comparatively little anxiety' (English, 2016: 136).

> ### KEY CONCEPTS
>
> **Terrorist Actors** Who commits terrorism? As so often in the study of terrorism, an apparently simple question has generated very different responses. After all, the term 'terrorism' is frequently applied to the violence of all kinds of very different agents: ranging from lone individuals to the most powerful governments in the world.
>
> It is undeniable that the emergence of Terrorism Studies in the 1970s focused overwhelmingly (and often unthinkingly) upon *non-state* actors: and this—justifiably—attracted criticism. Why should the terror wielded by states be just ignored? In most cases governments have the resources to terrorize far more thoroughly than their challengers. Such criticism notably developed in volume and extent after 2006 with the emergence of the Critical Terrorism Studies movement (Jackson: 2008).
>
> Justifications for an 'actor-based approach' (i.e. that applies the term 'terrorism' exclusively to non-state actors rather than to states) tend to be made on pragmatic rather moral grounds. At heart, the question is whether we need a specific term for the political violence of relatively weak actors that are not able to challenge states directly (Kalyvas and Strauss: 2020).

Debates over '*what* is terrorism' have inevitably been accompanied by parallel debates about *which actors* should be seen as terrorists. Scholars of rioting have long abandoned using the word 'mob' because it is so negative. It risks biasing their analysis. By the same logic, should we also then drop the term 'terrorist'? Or can it still be salvaged as a term of analysis? For those scholars who remain committed to using the term 'terrorist' in this way there are no very easy choices. One approach is to try to apply the term 'terrorist' even-handedly to both state actors *and* their opponents. The challenge here is the 'manageability' of the research design. Such actors often have very different resources at their disposal. Hence their violence often tends to look rather different. Developing an integrated analysis of terrorism when it is conducted by such different types of actors in such different ways can therefore be challenging. Another alternative is simply to reserve the term for 'non-state actors who do not control territory' (Kalyvas and Strauss: 2020). That is both neat and clear. But it is also controversial. Many scholars feel that this approach risks letting state actors off the hook (Jackson: 2008: for a wider discussion, see Chapter 14).

It is easy to get frustrated with how difficult it to disentangle academic dialogue from ever widening debates over 'what is terrorism' in society. Even Facebook and Twitter have been pulled into those whirlpools. But much of the intellectual energy and excitement of Terrorism Studies lies in exactly these cross-currents from the 'real world'. This is an academic field that pursues a subject that is already a hot topic in coffee shops—but also in the halls of power, too. An academic preoccupation is simultaneously a government headache.

And this has always been so. Over 50 years or so, the academic study of terrorism has emerged and taken its shape *primarily* in reaction to sudden and shocking 'real world' events. An instinct of instant curiosity has been an essential force behind its development: and general levels of academic interest have tended to rise and fall on the wider tides of public interest.

2.3 EVOLUTION OF TERRORISM STUDIES

As a concept, terrorism was first used during the French Revolution. As Townshend (2002: 36) notes, '… the first dictionary definition of the word "terrorism", "système, régime de la terreur"—was offered by the Académie française in 1798'. But there was little attempt to refine its usage further. As a consequence, its application remained anything but systematic. It is now standard to see the anarchist assassinations and bombings that erupted in the late 19th century as the first wave of international terrorism. But commentators at the time did not tend to conceptualize this violence as 'terrorism'.

After the term was first coined, as an analytical concept 'terrorism' attracted little sustained academic interest: although it is true that there was something of a 'false dawn' after the international shockwaves caused by the 1934 assassination of King Alexander I of Yugoslavia in France by a Bulgarian assassin (who had trained in both Italy and Hungary). By 1937 legal scholars had come up with a working definition in their Convention for the Prevention and Repression of Terrorism in 1937 (Schmid, 2013: 100). It was submitted to the League of Nations (the predecessor organization to the United Nations). But it was never ratified.

'The advent of what is considered modern, international terrorism' writes Bruce Hoffman 'occurred on July 22, 1968': the day that the Popular Front for the Liberation of Palestine

PHOTO 2.1 The massacre during the 1972 summer Olympics was committed by militant organization Black September. This was the year that the 'systematic study of international terrorism began to develop' (Red quoted in Stampnitzky: 30).

(PFLP) hijacked an airliner bound for Tel Aviv to try to force the release of their members held in Israeli jails. A new era of horror seemed to dawn very abruptly after this event. Aircraft hijackings and bombings were not in themselves unprecedented. But their magnification through TV was. No less than 900 million viewers watched another Palestinian faction, Black September, launch an attack on Israeli Olympic team members at the 1972 Munich Olympics, as shown in Photo 2.1 (Hoffman, 2017: 65, 71).

What particularly attracted academic attention was that the atrocities seemed so free-floating: 'the key factor drawing attention to the problem of terrorism at this time was the transnational character of the events' (Stampnitzky: 26). An early analytical challenge was just making basic sense of this chaos. How could anyone get a handle on these bewildering events? One obvious way was to count them. Some of the most famous terrorist incident databases date back to around this period: ITERATE (1968), RAND (1968), and the Global Terrorism Database or GTD (1970).

 Visit the online resources that accompany this book for guidance on how to access databases: www.oup.com/he/Wilson-Muro1e

Who pioneered the study of terrorism as a serious subject in its early years? The only answer is: a mixture. Some were academics. Some came from think-tanks. Some hailed from military backgrounds. All were self-appointed. As one British ex-officer admitted: 'my becoming a so-called expert on terrorism simply evolved from the fact that I spent such a long time talking about it' (Clutterbuck quoted in Stampnitzky: 45). Historically, most of these new authorities were men. But women were also present from the very start. Indeed, as early as 1972 Martha Crenshaw published her classic essay 'The Concept of Revolutionary Terrorism' in *The Journal of Conflict Resolution*. More than any other theoretical contribution this laid out a powerful case for analysing revolutionary terrorism as a distinctive tradition of political violence in its own right.

Geographically, scholars from the USA (and, to a lesser extent, the UK) were most prominent. So too was the American tradition of close relations between the worlds of government and academia. Conferences organized by the US State Department in both 1972 and 1976 played a major role in consolidating early networks of dialogue (Stampnitzky: 40–41). As one contemporary observer noted: 'while "terror" has hardly had the same impact on the American academic community as Black Studies or Women's Studies, government concern and the media coverage did inspire considerable activity …' even if much of it was little more than speculation on demand (Bowyer-Bell, 1979: 94, 284). Some of the most insightful research was pioneered in both West Germany by scholars such as Friedhelm Neidhardt (whose work is discussed further in Chapter 6): but it took time for these findings to influence English-speaking scholars.

It is important to note that intellectual interest in terrorism continued to remain volatile until the very end of the 20th century. According to one estimate, 1,796 individuals presented at academic conferences on terrorism between 1972 and 2001. Of these, no less than 1,505 (84 per cent) made only one appearance. Such constant 'churn' worked against the emergence of common standards and agreed research agendas. Describing this general picture in sociological language, terrorism studies had emerged as 'a relatively uninstitutionalized field … with highly permeable boundaries' (Stampnitzky: 46). At the core was a small and tight-knit core of scholars who concentrated exclusively on terrorism. Around them lay much larger, and looser, 'cloud' of academics whose interest in terrorism was more transient. To some extent, that basic structure remains recognizable even today.

By the early 1990s, though, the future of terrorism studies as a serious academic subject was in question. As so often, the academic study of terrorism was vulnerable to wider shifts in popular perceptions (see Case Study 2.1). During the 1980s it had been forcefully argued by numerous commentators that international terrorism was primarily sustained and orchestrated by the Soviet Union (Chapman and Chapman, 1980; Sterling, 1981). With the Cold War now over, a common assumption seemed to be that international terrorism would also fade away. As Bruce Hoffman recalled, one of the reasons he left the prestigious policy institute RAND in 1994 was 'that everybody was telling me there was no funding for terrorism research. Everybody was telling me that, with the end of the Cold War and the demise of the Soviet Union, terrorism was going to end' (quoted in Stampnitzky: 140). When a serious attempt was made by an obscure Islamist faction to bomb the World Trade Center in 1993, very few in the American media or government seem to have thought this of much general significance for the future. Eight years later another Islamist plot succeeded to attack the Twin Towers in 2011: now called '9/11' as the attacks took place on 11 September 2001.

> **CASE STUDY 2.1**
>
> *The Sterling Thesis, 1981*
>
> During one of the tensest periods of the Cold War in 1981, journalist Claire Sterling published her book *The Terror Network: The Secret War of International Terrorism*. It was a runaway success. Both Alexander Haig (US Secretary of State from 1981 to 1982) and William Casey (Director of the CIA from 1981 to 1987) both acting under the administration of US President Ronald Reagan (1981–1989) gave it enthusiastic endorsement. Sterling's book received the sort of reception of which most scholars can only dream. The US Senate Subcommittee on Security and Terrorism convened a series of congressional hearings to discuss its findings.
>
> What were its findings? In outline, it seemed to hint that the Soviet Union was conducting a mighty 'orchestra' of international terrorism (Sterling: 286). But it was never quite made clear. One of its academic reviewers pointed out that 'Sterling does not say that the Soviets are cause and master of terrorism. She does say that they have helped the phenomenon along and have benefited from it, and this does not seem such an outrageous or impossible thesis. The problem is that these distinctions are often blurred in the book' (Rubin, 1981: 164). Such key distinctions were glossed over by Sterling's informal writing style.
>
> *The Terror Network* has not aged well. The collapse of the Soviet Union and its satellite regimes allows us to evaluate its claims. The Communist bloc did indeed extend support to the groups that Sterling discusses. But there is little evidence of any master plan at work. Markus Wolf, the former head of the intelligence services of East Germany, describes a more chaotic picture. His regime indeed offered sanctuary to both the Palestine Liberation Organization (PLO) and the Red Army Faction (RAF). It was never entirely clear why to Wolf: but trying to control free-lance terrorism seems to have been a motive, as did contingency planning for a war situation where the RAF could be used as a 'Fifth Column' inside West Germany. Such relationships were anything but straightforward or smooth. In the words of one RAF member who holed up in East Germany, 'By the end we were probably as unbearable for them as they were us' (Wolf, 1998: 279).
>
> What can we still learn from this historical controversy? Arguably, it raises lots of uncomfortable questions. Who is a convincing expert on terrorism? What prevents those in power simply listening to what they want to believe? And how close should terrorism scholars get to the intelligence services anyhow? Some of the Sterling's claims about the links between the Italian Red Brigades and the Soviet Union seem to have had their origin in CIA disinformation campaigns (Stampnitzky, 2013: 121–122). In this case, Sterling simply fed the CIA's creative make-believe back to itself. However, *The Terror Network* still remains 'the most formally influential book on terrorism to date' (Stampnitzky, 2013: 121).

> **QUESTIONS**
>
> 1. Should terrorism studies scholars just keep their distance from the intelligence community?
> 2. Is it natural for intelligence services to exaggerate the threat of international terrorism?

Securing the future of academic research on terrorism was a by-product of the 9/11 terror attacks facilitated by Osama Bin-Laden, leader of terror group al-Qaeda. Never had research into terrorism seemed of greater relevance or urgency than in the immediate aftermath of 11th September 2001. 'Literally overnight with 9/11' writes Magnus Ranstorp (2007: 3) 'the field of terrorism studies catapulted from the relative periphery into the absolute vortex of academic interest and policy concern worldwide'.

9/11 turbo-charged terrorism research. In doing so it also changed it. In effect, the belated realization of al-Qaeda's threat to the US had summoned forth 'an entirely new breed of terrorism expert … whose priority was counter-terrorism policy and American power' (Richardson, 2006: 11). Past terrorism receded in importance (Silke, 2007: 77). Potential future terrorism bulked large. One side effect of 9/11, for instance, was to boost research into Weapons of Mass Destruction: even though the attacks themselves had arisen out of plane hijackings using boxcutters (Silke, 2009: 45). But it is important not to be too dismissive of *all* terrorism research produced in the post-9/11 period. One study of terrorism-related research has found that post-9/11 articles amount for 63 per cent of the 100 most cited articles published between 1952 and 2007 (Chenoweth and Gofas: 3).

How, then, has the academic study of terrorism evolved since 2001? General levels of academic interest have been maintained, even if they are lower than after 9/11. As this textbook demonstrates, the field of terrorism research continues to grow in both breadth and variety, see Chapter 3 (on Critical Terrorism Studies), Chapter 10 (on radicalization), Chapter 18 (on Social Media) and Chapter 26 (on deradicalization/disengagement), which all discuss sub-fields that did not exist in 2001. This 'is a strongly interdisciplinary subject area, and while it has often traditionally been dominated by the political sciences, there have been very significant contributions from other areas, including psychology, criminology, sociology, anthropology, economics, history, religious studies, etc' (Silke and Schmidt-Petersen, 2017: 697).

Such increasing diversification suggests a lively intellectual energy. After all, dying fields do not grow. They simply fade away: graduate programmes are quietly shut down and journals cease publication. So, rolling debates and controversies can be a very good sign: even when they take the form of organized 'breakaway' initiatives such as the Critical Terrorism Studies movement (from 2006 approximately). Other encouraging developments include an increase after 2001 both in collaborative research, such as *The Oxford Handbook of Terrorism* (Chenoweth and Gofas), and in more rigorous statistical analyses (Silke, 2009:

38–43). The latter formed the basis of such heavyweight contributions such as Marc Sageman's *Understanding Terror Networks* (2004) and Robert Pape's *Dying to Win* (2005).

New sub-fields also emerged rapidly after 9/11. In general, these were distinguished by their policy relevance. Suicide terrorism thus quickly emerged the focus of several major studies such as those by Bloom (2005), Gambetta (2005), and Pape (2003). How anti-state terrorist campaigns could be brought to an end also attracted attention (Cronin, 2009). Most strikingly of all, there was a broad upsurge of studies into 'how and why people become involved in terrorism'. Since 2005 this last area has developed its own terminology: as John Horgan (2014: 82) notes 'there are *no* discussions about terrorist psychology today that do not include the word "radicalization"'. Such studies also finally began to pay closer attention to the gendered dynamics of terrorism (Bloom, 2011).

A helpful way to grasp the overall trajectory of terrorism studies is to picture it as a giant rollercoaster course. Three landmark dates mark its sudden gradient shifts. 1972 was the point at which academic research first began to climb sharply: since the attack at the Munich Olympics was 'perceived as launching an era of internationalization of the terrorist threat' (Chenoweth and Gofas, 2019: 2). After 1989 academic research entered its post-Cold War plunge. But 2001 has sent academic interest rocketing back up again. We are all still riding that long post-9/11 crest (Chenoweth and Gofas, 2019: 1–2). With terrorism currently a hot topic in the news, it is surely hard to imagine another sudden downward plunge in interest.

Here the main point to grasp is: the development of academic research into terrorism has been turbulent. Seen in a long-term perspective, there have been some particularly dramatic ups-and-downs. Yet it is still a good idea to have some sense of the early evolution of terrorism studies. As with all academic fields, origins do matter. Basic habits, structures and priorities that were established long ago may still continue to reproduce themselves in the present—and indeed, into the future. Social scientists call this long-term phenomenon 'path dependency'.

Summing this up: through the decades, terrorism studies have evolved and grown exponentially—but not beyond all recognition. Specific areas of research do come and go, sometimes with speed. But general challenges and tendencies tend to recur with some predictability. It is time to examine them more closely in the next section 2.4 on the nature of terrorism studies.

2.4 THE NATURE OF TERRORISM STUDIES

There are patterns in terrorism studies. A good place to start is with the prominence given to *international* terrorism. The origin of the field of terrorism studies was in the early 1970s when there was a preoccupation with the terror tactics of transnational anti-state actors. The tendency has continued: even as the actors have evolved from left-wing militants to Islamist radicals (Crenshaw, 2019: 705–720). Research on terrorism has remained highly reactive in the international system, as Schuurman cites, 'results … indicate that the field remains event-driven and consistently underestimates state terrorism as well as non-jihadist terrorism, such as that perpetrated by right-wing extremists' (Schuurman, 2019: 463).

KEY CONCEPTS

International Terrorism International Terrorism has tended to be used to categorize attacks that are planned in one state but conducted in another: or the targeting of citizens while they are travelling abroad. Conventionally, it was contrasted with Domestic Terrorism that was seen as contained within state borders. The internet has reduced the importance of this analytical distinction, since so many anti-state plots now have a hybrid character with 'home-grown' attackers pledging allegiance to distant leaders and movements.

Why is this? 'Since the late 1960s', observed Martha Crenshaw in 2001, 'the United States has been a preferred target, the victim of approximately one-third of all international terrorist attacks over the past 30 years' (quoted in Crenshaw, 2019: 716). Here we have evidence as to why international terrorism has attracted so much English-language scholarship: because it reflects standard American assumptions. US governments, public, and law all tend to see terrorism as foreign in origin. From this starting point, it makes sense to connect the study of terrorism with International Relations (and related fields such as Political Science). A 2012 survey of American universities found that courses explicitly on terrorism were most frequent in political science (38), international relations (27), and sociology (18), followed by history (14) (Sheehan, 2012: 30).

CASE STUDY 2.2

Terrorism Studies and Western-Centrism

On the night of 13 November 2015, carnage erupted across central Paris. A complex ISIS attack combining suicide bombings, drive-by shootings, and mass hostage-taking killed 130 people, as well wounding over 400. ISIS is an acronym for the terrorist group Islamic State of Iraq and Syria, also known as ISIL (Islamic State of Iraq and the Levant), IS (Islamic State), Daesh or Da'ish (an Arabic-derived acronym).

Following the attack, gestures of international solidarity were shown via Western landmarks from the London Eye to the Brandenburg Gate, and the Sydney Opera House was lit up in the colours of the French tricolour flag.

On 12 November 2015—the day before the horrors in Paris—two ISIS suicide bombers had self-detonated in the Bourj el-Barajneh district of Beirut. It was the most violent attack in Lebanon since the 1975–1990 civil war. 43 people died directly in the attacks: over 200 more were injured. But the Beirut attacks attracted little international attention. No Western landmarks were lit in Lebanese colours.

Such contrasting reactions to atrocities invite us to reflect upon the research priorities of terrorism scholarship as well. At one level, it is unsurprising that English-language scholarship will tend to reflect the priorities of the USA and UK (and their close European partners and allies). But this tendency risks creating a distorted picture of relative risk between different regions of the globe. According to the Global Terrorism Database (GTD), between 2002 and 2017, less than 1 per cent of terrorist attacks occurred in North America and only 2 per cent in Europe. No less than 75 per cent took place in Asia (including the numerous conflicts of the Middle East). 140,000 people died in such attacks in Asia; and another 43,000 people in Africa. At least 587 people were killed in the Mogadishu bombings of 14 October 2017: an atrocity that has been largely forgotten outside Somalia. By comparison, about 5,000 people died in terrorist attacks in Europe in the same period (Python, 2020: 35–36).

There are methodological issues here: disentangling terrorism from the wider contexts of civil wars is challenging. Iraq and Afghanistan were amongst the four countries that saw the highest death tolls (alongside India and Pakistan). Between 2002 and 2017, 124 countries saw lethal attacks. Measured by incidence, the USA ranked 36th (72 attacks), the UK 44th (33), and France 45th (31) (Python, 2020: 3, 38). In other words, the tendency of so much terrorism scholarship to assume that conditions in Western—i.e. American and European—states are somehow the norm is highly problematic.

The study of terrorism should be global. In practice, the structure of its coverage and analysis remains highly uneven. Terrorism studies still lean towards the prioritization of Western concerns and conceptions.

QUESTIONS

1. 'Solidarity gestures such as lighting up famous landmarks after selected terrorist atrocities always conveys the message that other attacks matter less. The practice should be discontinued.' Discuss.

2. How could the study of terrorism studies more accurately reflect, and reflect upon, its actual global occurrence?

Political Science and International Relations do not privilege fine-grained research into specific local contexts. In 2014 the emergence of Islamic State (ISIS) violence across Syria and Iraq (and beyond) posed sharp questions about appropriate research strategies. How should this phenomenon be classified? Was it international anti-state terrorism? Some of it looked that way: such as the November 2015 massacres conducted by ISIS in Paris that killed 130 people (see Case Study 2.2). Or was it state terrorism? There was a clue was in the name of Islamic *State*: and in its heartlands it used terror to consolidate its power. Islamic State also evolved out of simultaneous civil wars in both Iraq and Syria. Against that backdrop, the academic literature on civil wars that emphasizes how often local communities privilege security over ideology might offer more insights into the rise of Islamic State than the terrorism studies tradition (Kalyvas, 2006). In short: there are several different possible research strategies here: but the underlying point is that developing research strategies that try to explain terrorism across quite different levels and contexts is complicated.

The Global Terrorism Database (GTD) is the most extensive database of anti-state terrorist incidents. It consistently demonstrates same basic trend. Most violence that it captures belongs to conflicts *within* states, not to overspill *between* them. In GTD's own framing, it is domestic, not international, terrorism. So most political violence seems local—or at least, national—too. Contexts matter. Several famous scholars of terrorism began by studying specific terror campaigns: Martha Crenshaw (on the *Front Libération Nationale* in Algeria), Bruce Hoffman (on the *Irgun* in Mandate Palestine), Donatella Della Porta (on the Red Brigades) and Richard English (on the Provisional IRA). Later they widened their analytical focus. But such a transition is not always easy to make convincingly. No one can be an expert about everywhere.

Summing this all up, the academic study of terrorism tends to resemble an interdisciplinary sandwich. On top sits a rich layer of traditions that lean towards broad perspectives: International Relations, Political Science and Economics. At the bottom is also a dense layer of scholarship that takes a more micro-focus: typically on individuals or very small groups. Psychology and Criminology are well represented here. What, then, lies in the middle of our sandwich?

The short answer is: less than might be hoped. Our mid-range contextual filling is thin. A recurrent criticism of the academic study of terrorism is that it often lacks detailed contextual data about its subjects. As Schmid and Jongman (1988: 177) put it: 'there are probably few areas in the social science literature on which so much is written on the basis of so little research'. We need such detail to make full sense of violent actors. Anthropology, for instance, is a discipline that closely studies human interaction within bounded situations to make more general claims. In other words, 'Anthropologists don't study villages (tribes, towns, neighbourhoods…): they study *in* villages' (Geertz, 2000: 22). But such approaches are never going to be easily transferred from nonviolent to violent settings (terrorism studies). Observing either anti-state or state terrorism up close in this kind of fashion risks becoming dangerous to one's safety.

If it is difficult to study terrorist actors up close in the act of committing terrorism, it may make more sense to study past examples instead. Yet history does not lie at the core of terrorism studies. One 2009 review of two leading journals, *Terrorism and Political Violence* and *Studies in Conflict and Terrorism,* commented that 'before 9/11, only 1 article in 26 looked at historical conflicts. In the immediate aftermath of 9/11, interest in historical cases effectively collapsed and not even 1 article in 50 was focused away from current events' (Silke, 2009: 46). Or we can look at the 2013 *Routledge Handbook of Terrorism Research*. Its bibliography of 4,600 items are arranged by sub-sections such as 'Aetiology' (the study of causation). No such section exists for 'History' (Schmid, 2013: 475–597, 711). By far the most influential account of the history of modern anti-state terrorism has been provided by a political scientist: David Rapoport. As is discussed in more detail in Case Study 8.1 in this textbook, Rapoport (2003) sees rebel terrorism as arising in giant 40-year waves. His model has sparked lively debate—but largely amongst social scientists. This has remained a history debate without historians. Terrorism studies would certainly benefit from more consideration of past terrorism.

The consideration of future terrorism could be improved. It is hard not to conclude that sometimes there have been some significant downsides to the (relatively close) contacts between terrorism studies and the world of policymaking: Case Study 2.1 explores a concrete example. The aftermath of 9/11 offers another example of the urgency of the orbit of short-term policy concerns exerting a gravitational pull on terrorism research. The US government was concerned that the mass casualty toll of 9/11 foreshadowed a potential turn towards terrorists causing even greater carnage using Chemical, Biological, Radiological, and Nuclear (CBRN) weapons. As Andrew Silke points out in the 20 years between 1989 and 2009, none of the 300 most destructive terrorist attacks had involved CBRN weapons. Yet 'one impact of the 9/11 attacks was that CBRN research—already the most studied terrorist tactic during the 1990s—actually managed to attract even more research attention and funding, doubling the proportion of articles focused on CBRN in the journals' (Silke, 2009: 45).

In short, the academic study of terrorism has hardly been immune to 'latest outrage' effects—the phenomenon by which interpretations of the (supposed) implications of the last big terrorist attack dominates research disproportionately. In general, politicians, policymakers and public officials often seem to want a degree of certainty about terrorism that is simply unattainable. Scholars cannot deliver that. The social sciences cannot predict with the confidence of the natural sciences. Human beings always make choices.

At root here is a question about what the social role of the academic researcher of terrorism should be. Given popular understandings of terrorism, one can assume that the role of the academic should primarily be to study *anti-state* terrorism; and then to help governments fight it more effectively. Some experts (such as Marc Sageman) have indeed seen this as their role. By contrast, other—equally 'orthodox'—scholars (such as Alex Schmid) have not. These latter scholars insist that their duty is simply to pursue knowledge. They see their identity as more like 'students of combustion' than 'fire-fighters' (Schmid and Jongman, 1988, 2008: 40). A public argument brought these issues to the surface in 2014, which is explored in 2.5 Terrorism Studies: Stagnation?

2.5 TERRORISM STUDIES: STAGNATION?

In 2014 the academic journal *Terrorism and Political Violence* published an article where Marc Sageman, a psychologist with 8 years' experience of working in the US intelligence community, accused terrorism studies of intellectual *stagnation*: 'despite over a decade of government funding and thousands of newcomers to the field of terrorism research, we are no closer to answering the simple question of 'What leads a person to turn to political violence?' Such gridlock arose through an intersection of inadequacies between different types of experts. Academics had very little access to the 'necessary source information' they needed. Conversely, intelligence analysts did have that data – but neither the time nor skills to make proper sense of it. Sageman's final verdict was: 'we have a system of terrorism research in which intelligence analysts know everything but understand nothing, while academics understand everything but know nothing' (Sageman, 2014: 565–576).

Academics did not respond well to these sentiments. Some sharp observations were offered in reply. What Sageman had presented as a simple question was not really simple at all. Why speak broadly of 'political violence' rather than the more contentious term 'terrorism' if these matters were ever that simple? Moreover, it is accepted that the social sciences are not able to forecast 'what leads a person to fall in love, to murder another, to choose a particular career path' (Stern, 2014: 607). Why were terrorism studies being held to a different standard? And in fact, some very significant research progress *had* been made in explaining why some people have turned to violent extremism; at least in some specific contexts (Schmid, 2014: 593). Finally, Sageman's assumption that universities and the intelligence services *should* be working closely together was challenged: 'the academic is (or should be) characterized by independence and a striving for knowledge, without fear or favour' (Taylor, 2014: 583).

However, Sageman had certainly highlighted a point that is often overlooked: terrorism is intrinsically *hard* to research. Building explanatory theories and models is a vital long-term goal: but it depends upon a supply of information as its raw material. Sourcing data and then ordering it coherently is the first stage of any such process because 'good description is something that is certainly more useful than bad theory' (Kalyvas, 2020). But reliable detailed information is often hard to find. This issue is significant, as Horgan states: 'to say that terrorism does not easily lend itself to investigation by traditional methods is a considerable understatement' (Horgan, 2014: 41).

However, there are many reasons for optimism. In 1965, Bowyer-Bell discovered 'that the only way you would get to know the IRA is to go and meet them. You couldn't find them in libraries and books' (Breen, 2019). The IRA (Irish Republican Army) were a republican paramilitary organization seeking the establishment of a republic, the end of British rule in Northern Ireland, and the reunification of Ireland, most active from 1969 to a ceasefire in 1997. Developments in technology, including social media has profoundly transformed the possibilities of research from Bowyer-Bell's time. Scholars can now assemble huge amounts of 'open source' (i.e. freely available) information from media sources, trial transcripts, social media, YouTube videos to name but a few.

KEY CONCEPTS

Open Source Information that is widely available in the public domain: such as media reports. By contrast, Closed Source is information held by the security services and only available to those with security clearance.

> **Thick Description** A term coined by anthropologist Clifford Geertz to describe research that places great emphasis upon the importance of close-up in-person observation and contextual awareness to explain human activity.

Detailed and systematic data collation allows researchers to replicate the detailed 'thick description' of terrorist behaviour that previously was hard to achieve (Geertz, 2000). Since social networks have emerged as a new frontier of terrorism, researchers have flocked to investigate them. Such research allows a deeper exploration of the type of extremist sub-cultures that encourage terrorism, and sheds light on patterns of recruitment and their interaction with the offline world. But it also illuminates anti-state terrorist groups' self-image as reflected in their online marketing strategies. As with all areas of human behaviour, the digital sphere has now taken centre stage in the study of terrorism (Scaife, 2017).

New research opportunities also raise new challenges. Morally, there is a risk of harm to the researcher: terrorism is (potentially) a distressing subject indeed. Viewing graphic terrorist material online should only be conducted with appropriate psychological support to hand. Moreover, there is the danger of online harassment from terrorist supporters. As a result, here is that universities have developed elaborate regimes of approval and guidance to reduce the online risks. In the USA these tend to be called Institutional Review Boards (IRBs); in the UK, Ethics Committees.

Legal risks have to be considered as well: not least because showing a sudden online interest in terrorist propaganda can attract the attention of the security services. Here it is also worth being aware that different countries have very different laws on viewing such content. In general, the First Amendment to the American Constitution that guarantees free speech creates a notably permissive environment for such research in the USA. By contrast, the situation in the United Kingdom looks very different. Section 58 of the Terrorism Act 2000 made it an offence to possess an electronic record that contains information 'of a kind likely to be useful to a person committing or preparing an act of terrorism'. Subsequent waves of legislation have been similarly broadly drafted. Effects on terrorism research have been quite profound. On 28 August 2015 the British Library announced with reluctance that, having taken expert legal advice, it would reject a unique archive on Afghanistan that had been offered to it: the Taliban Sources Project. In effect, anti-terrorist legislation had pressured one of the world's great research libraries into an act of self-censorship (Fatima, 2015).

Nonetheless, the big picture remains encouraging. Despite the challenges and complications, the field of terrorism studies has clearly matured as it has grown. Surveys of the discipline have therefore seen the period since 2001 as 'years of bounty': or even a 'Golden Age' of terrorism studies research (Silke and Schmidt-Petersen, 2017: 692–693).

2.6 CONCLUSION

This chapter has traced the evolution of the academic field of terrorism studies: surveying how terrorism came to be seen as a subject worth studying in its own right, as well as some of the main avenues of exploration that have developed since the 1970s. It has emphasized how reactive the field has been to 'real world' events. In that respect, the academic study of terrorism has mirrored the shifting concerns of both governments and publics. And in turn this has raised difficult questions of both perspective and role: most prominently, whether and to what degree, scholars should concentrate upon the study of anti-state violence.

Despite challenges, terrorism studies have survived and thrived. In 1977, Paul Wilkinson published a landmark study *Terrorism and the Liberal State*. He predicted in its introduction that many reviewers would 'shriek and squawk against any project of this kind' (1977: ix). By contrast, it is hard to imagine that any leading scholar on terrorism would feel the need to justify their choice of subject so defensively today. Good research is also needed to help us all understand better one of the most urgent policy—and, indeed, moral—challenges of our age. Cruelty and violence so often seem to lie beyond the reach of all analysis. However, that is an argument for trying to develop better analysis.

And there are far many reasons for hope. The scholarship on terrorism has never been richer and more diverse than it is right now. If curiosity has led you into the study of terrorism, then you are unlikely to find yourself disappointed. Terrorism studies have arrived.

DISCUSSION QUESTIONS

1. Evaluate the achievements and weaknesses of the academic literature on terrorism since 1970.
2. Has the policy-relevance of terrorism studies been a blessing or a curse?
3. Why has the field struggled to expand its focus beyond anti-state international terrorism?
4. Why was the study of counter-terrorism neglected for so long?
5. 'Radicalization is a useful concept for analysing the group process by which key US government officials came to devise a policy of waterboarding torture after 2001.' Discuss.

Visit the online resources for pointers on how to answer the discussion questions, links to useful web sources, and guidance on accessing databases:
www.oup.com/he/Wilson-Muro1e

GUIDE TO FURTHER READING

Crenshaw, M. (2011) *Explaining Terrorism: Causes, Processes and Consequences*. London and New York: Routledge. *A classic collection of articles of great conceptual clarity from the foremost theorist of terrorism.* Explaining Terrorism *does a good job of living up to its title.*

English, R. (2016) 'The Future Study of Terrorism', *European Journal of International Security*, 1 (2): 135–149. *A leading scholar surveys the field. An original piece that manages to hand out both intellectual reassurance and fresh challenge in equal measure.*

Horgan, J. (2014) *The Psychology of Terrorism*. London and New York: Routledge. *A classic introduction to what the psychological study of terrorism can, and cannot, be expected to teach us. It makes a powerful argument for prioritizing accurate description over grand theorizing.*

Schmid, A. (2013) (ed.) *The Routledge Handbook of Terrorism Research*. London and New York: Routledge. *A monumental survey of the state-of-the-field. Highlights include both an extensive bibliography and a monster collection of terrorism definitions.*

Stampnitzky, L. (2013) *Disciplining Terror: How Experts Created 'Terrorism'*. Cambridge: Cambridge University Press. *A sociologist painstakingly recreates who-met-whom on the 1970s conference circuit. In doing so, Stampnitzky sheds light on how the field of terrorism studies first emerged, and why it has continued to remain so volatile.*

REFERENCES

Bloom, M. (2005) *Dying to Kill: The Allure of Suicide Terror*. New York: Colombia University Press.

Bloom, M. (2011) *Bombshell: Women and Terrorism*. London: Hurst.

Breen, S. (2019) 'American behind film of Martin McGuinness with bomb "was suspected CIA agent"', 17 September 2019, *Belfast Telegraph*

Chapman, R. D. and Chapman, M. L. (1980) *The Crimson Web of Terror*. Boulder, Colorado: Paladin Press.

Chenoweth, E. and Gofas, A. (2019) 'The Study of Terrorism' in Chenoweth, E. (et al., eds.), *The Oxford Handbook of Terrorism*. Oxford: Oxford University Press, 1–8.

Crenshaw, M. (2019) 'Constructing the Field of Terrorism', in Chenoweth, E. (et al., eds.), *The Oxford Handbook of Terrorism*. Oxford: Oxford University Press, 705–724.

Cronin, A. K. (2009) *How Terrorism Ends: Understanding the Decline and Demise of Terrorist Campaigns*. Princeton: Princeton University Press.

English, R. (2016) 'The Future Study of Terrorism', *European Journal of International Security*, 1 (2): 135–149.

Fatima, S. (14 September 2015) 'Self-Censorship in Action: The British Library Rejects Taliban Archive', www.justsecurity.org

Gambetta, D. (ed.) (2005, 2012) *Making Sense of Suicide Missions*. Oxford: Oxford University Press.

Geertz, C. (2000) *The Interpretation of Cultures*. New York: Basic Books.

Hoffman, B. (2017) *Inside Terrorism*. New York: Columbia University Press.

Horgan, J. (2014) *The Psychology of Terrorism*. London and New York: Routledge.

Jackson, R. (2008) 'The Ghosts of State Terror: Knowledge, Politics and Terrorism Studies', *Critical Studies on Terrorism*, 1 (3): 377–392.

Kalyvas, S. (2006) *The Logic of Violence in Civil War*. Cambridge: Cambridge University Press.

Kalyvas, S. and Strauss, S. (2020) 'Stathis Kalyvas on 20 Years of Studying Political Violence', *Violence: An International Journal*, 1 (2): 389–407.

Pape, R. (2003) 'The Strategic Logic of Suicide Terrorism', *American Political Science Review*, 97: 343–361.

Python, A. (2020) *Debunking Seven Terrorism Myths Using Statistics*. London: CRC Press.

Ramsay, G. (2015) 'Why Terrorism Can, but Should Not Be Defined', *Critical Studies on Terrorism*, 8 (2): 211–228.

Ranstorp, M. (ed.) (2007) *Mapping Terrorism Research: State of the Art, Gaps and Future Direction*. London and New York: Routledge.

Rapoport, D. (2003) 'The Four Waves of Rebel Terror and September 11', in Kegley, C. W., *The New Global Terrorism: Characteristics, Causes, Controls*. Upper Saddle River, New Jersey: Prentice Hall.

Richardson, L. (2006) *What Terrorists Want: Understanding the Terrorist Threat*. London: John Murray.

Rubin, B. (1981) 'Some Errors on Terror', *The Washington Quarterly*, 4 (3): 164–166.

Sageman, M. (2014) 'The Stagnation in Terrorism Research', *Terrorism and Political Violence*, 26 (4): 565–580.

Saul, B. (2019) 'Defining Terrorism: A Conceptual Minefield' in Chenoweth, E. (et al., eds.), *The Oxford Handbook of Terrorism*. Oxford: Oxford University Press, 34–49.

Scaife, L. (2017) *Social Networks as the New Frontier of Terrorism*. London and New York: Routledge.

Schmid, A. and Jongman, A. (1988, 2008) *Political Terrorism*. New Brunswick: Transaction Publishers.

Schmid, A. (ed.) (2013) *The Routledge Handbook of Terrorism Research*. London and New York: Routledge.

Schmid, A. (2014) 'Comments on Marc Sageman's Polemic "The Stagnation in Terrorism Research"', *Terrorism and Political Violence*, 26 (4): 587–595.

Schuurman, B. (2019) 'Topics in Terrorism Research: Reviewing Trends and Gaps, 2007–2016', *Critical Studies on Terrorism*, 12 (3): 463–480.

Sheehan, I. S. (2012) 'Mapping Contemporary Terrorism Courses at Top-Ranked National Universities and Liberal Arts Colleges in the United States', *Perspectives on Terrorism*, 6 (2): 19–50.

Silke, A. (2007) 'The Impact of 9/11 on Research on Terrorism' in Ranstorp, M. (ed.) (2007), *Mapping Terrorism Research: State of the Art, Gaps and Future Direction*. London and New York: Routledge, 76–93.

Silke, A. (2009) 'Contemporary Terrorism Studies: Issues in Research', in Jackson, R. (et al., eds.), *Critical Terrorism Studies: A New Research Agenda*, 34–48.

Silke, A., and Schmidt-Petersen, J. (2017) 'The Golden Age? What the 100 Most Cited Articles in Terrorism Studies Tell Us', *Terrorism and Political Violence*, 29 (4): 692–712.

Stampnitzky, L. (2013) *Disciplining Terror: How Experts Created 'Terrorism'*. Cambridge: Cambridge University Press.

Sterling, C. (1981) *The Terror Network: The Secret War of International Terrorism*. London: Weidenfeld and Nicolson.

Stern, J. (2014) 'Response to Marc Sageman's "The Stagnation in Terrorism Research"', *Terrorism and Political Violence*, 26 (4): 607–613.

Taylor, M. (2014) 'If I Were You, I Wouldn't Start from Here: Response to Marc Sageman's "The Stagnation in Terrorism Research"', *Terrorism and Political Violence*, 26 (4): 581–586.

Townshend, C. (2002) *Terrorism: A Very Short Introduction*. Oxford: Oxford University Press.

Wilkinson, P. (1977) *Terrorism and the Liberal State*. London: Macmillan Press.

Wolf, M. (1998) *Memoirs of a Spymaster*. London: Pimlico.

CHAPTER 3

Critical Terrorism Studies

HARMONIE TOROS

■ CHAPTER SUMMARY

Critical terrorism studies (CTS) begins its investigation with whether 'terrorism' exists at all, whom the label or category serves, and what is its place in the logics and practices of state power. It then focuses on the violence of states, whether directly involved in terrorism or through prevalent forms of counter-terrorism, and how the state uses terrorism and counter-terrorism language to legitimize its violence. Finally, CTS investigates alternatives to violent counter-terrorism, from nonviolent protests to negotiations with non-state armed groups. The chapter will critically analyse the evolution of CTS and highlight key issues on which it needs to focus on in the future.

3.1 INTRODUCTION

If terrorism studies seek to understand the phenomenon of terrorist violence and how best to respond to it, critical terrorism studies (CTS) begins its investigation with whether 'terrorism' exists at all, whom the label or category serves, and what is its place in the logics and practices of power. Overall it focuses on different actors (state rather than non-state), on different practices (labelling, legislating, and repressing rather than plotting and attacking), and different consequences (discrimination, challenge to the rule of law, and social degradation rather than increased threat and weakening of state security). This chapter will examine the principal contributions of CTS as well as its drawbacks and challenges going forward.

The chapter is divided in two parts. It will first examine the key arguments and contributions of CTS, focusing on how it challenges the very notion of terrorism, first turning the spotlight on the state and then moving the analysis from exceptional acts to the everyday. Here it will outline how the construction of the terrorist threat serves specific political, economic, and social functions, how states have often benefited from such constructions both in exceptional events—waging wars for example to defeat 'terrorist states'—and in the everyday—such as in the provision of health and education services. This section will also highlight the theoretical and methodological innovations put forward by CTS, as well as some of the drawbacks of the choices made by CTS scholars.

The second part of this chapter will examine the politics of CTS. Indeed, CTS scholars have from the very start insisted that the project has to be more than simply an intellectual or academic endeavour. CTS is an intrinsically political project aimed at changing the world—more specifically the policies and practices of security and terrorism (see the key texts of CTS, Jackson, Breen-Smyth, and Gunning, 2009; Jackson, Jarvis, Breen-Smyth, and Gunning, 2011; and Jackson, Toros, Jarvis, and Heath-Kelly, 2018). This explicit engagement in politics is however a road that inevitably leads to contradictions and disagreements that, as this chapter shall argue, continue to keep CTS vibrant and diverse. Indeed, the second part of this chapter will discuss how CTS' political ethos has been challenged by the question of whether scholars should engage in a dialogue with state security officials. In the conclusion, the chapter will examine future challenges facing critical approaches to terrorism, in particular how it can evolve from its principal focus to date on western counter-terrorism to respond to the growing terrorist violence of the far-right.

Before launching into this analysis, a moment of self-reflection is necessary. From a CTS perspective, any research needs to acknowledge, paraphrasing Robert Cox (1986), where it comes from, why it is being written, and for whom. As such, it is essential to set out from the start that my intention is not to neutrally convey to the readers the strengths and weaknesses of CTS scholarship. As will become clear in the chapter, CTS contends that neutrality is neither *possible* nor *desirable*. It is thus important to note that I am a CTS scholar, who has been part of the CTS project since its inception in 2006. I profoundly believe in the contribution the CTS project is making to security and terrorism studies, although I recognize its limitations and contradictions. CTS has neither the monopoly on truth nor on justice, but this chapter is based on the premise that it is one potential path towards good research and better policies.

3.2 CONSTRUCTING TERRORISM: FROM THE EXCEPTIONAL TO THE EVERYDAY

The aim of this first part is to answer two questions: What is critical about CTS and what is it critical of? The simple answer is that it is critical of 'mainstream,' 'orthodox' or 'traditional' terrorism studies—the main precepts of which have been outlined in Chapter 1 (see Silke, 2009 and Raphael, 2009 and Stampinsky, 2013 for a thorough critique of traditional terrorism studies). And it is important to note that numerous traditional scholars have challenged CTS' self-attribution as 'critical' arguing that they have long been critical of power and injustice (see Weinberg and Eubank, 2008 among others and key earlier examples of critical work in Stohl (2006) and Zulaika and Douglass (1996)). Indeed, traditional scholars have accused CTS of building a 'strawman'—i.e. of over-emphasizing negative characteristics of traditional terrorism studies to be able to critique it. CTS did start its intellectual journey as a *critique* of terrorism studies as it existed in the pre- and post-9/11 academic and policy environment. However, this chapter highlights that CTS would not have survived and indeed flourished over the past 15 years if its only motivation were to be in opposition to existing practice, as any field has to be able to propose alternatives and not just simply critique existing practices. As such, this chapter does not examine CTS as opposed to traditional, orthodox, or mainstream terrorism studies but rather as a self-standing approach that takes a different starting point and focuses on different policies and practices. It differs from the approach presented in Chapter 2 but does not exist simply in opposition to it.

The more complex and interesting answer to why 'critical' can be broken down in three areas examined in sections 3.2.1 and 3.2.2. Firstly, it is critical because CTS asks: whether there is such a category as 'terrorism'; what are the repercussions of establishing such a category; and who benefits from it. Second, CTS asks *who* is engaging in terrorism, expanding the range of possible actors beyond non-state groups to include states and other actors. Third, CTS examines terrorism and counter-terrorism beyond the moment of exception—the terrorist attack or the exceptional military counter-terrorism operation—and delves into the everyday violence of terrorism and counter-terrorism policies and practices. The chapter shall now examine each in turn.

3.2.1 Terrorism

Is there a distinct category of violence that can be called terrorism and if so what defines it? More than simply engaging with the definitional question of terrorism studies, CTS questions whether such a category could and should exist. Critical scholars remain divided on this question. Some CTS scholars refuse 'to accept "terrorist" and "terrorism" as objective categories which exist in the world', instead arguing that the only investigation possible is into 'the creation of a discursive reality where the concept of terrorism is used to delegitimise certain actors, achieve policy goals and conceal the ambiguities at the work in the international system' (Heath-Kelly, 2016: 60). It is the discourse of terrorism—the use of the term in political language—and its implications that such authors, who take on post-structuralist and constructivist approaches, focus on (Closs Stephens and Vaughan-Williams, 2008).

> **KEY CONCEPTS**
>
> **Theoretical Foundations of Critical Approaches** CTS draws from two main strands of social and political theory, post-structuralism and constructivism on the one side and Frankfurt School Critical Theory on the other. The first, drawing on early 20th-century linguistic philosophy, is based on the notion that we cannot access an objective 'real world' through research (Finlayson and Valentine, 2002). Instead, we have to investigate how it is constructed by our words and the meanings we ascribe to them, and what these words allow for in terms of systems of power. Frankfurt School Critical Theory, emerging in Germany in the late 1920s (Horkheimer, 1982) instead adopts a 'minimal foundationalist' approach which believes that one can seek out evidence in social science research as well as regularities in human behaviour but must recognize that these can only be understood in their context. Both approaches crucially believe that research cannot be neutral or apolitical: There are important reasons why researchers ask certain questions and it is essential to disclose them.

Others, including many of its founding and leading figures such as Richard Jackson, Marie Breen-Smyth, and Jeroen Gunning (2009), adopted early on a minimal foundational approach largely based on Frankfurt School Critical Theory and the Aberystwyth School of Critical Security Studies (see Toros and Gunning, 2009). This approach agrees with poststructuralists and constructivists that investigating the discourses of terrorism—how it is used, by whom, and with what effect—is an essential part of any investigation into terrorism but still hangs on to the notion that there is a distinct form of violence that can be called 'terrorism.' Jackson (2008: 29–30) thus defines terrorism as 'an intentional and pre-determined strategy of political violence' that 'is intended to cause fear and intimidate' a target audience beyond its victims, who are not necessarily civilians. From a minimal foundationalist perspective, any violence fitting these characteristics can be defined as 'terrorism.' Importantly, however, any investigation into terrorism needs to 'study both the political usages of the discourses of "terrorism" and a historically contextualized form of violence' (Toros and Gunning, 2009: 107).

> **KEY CONCEPTS**
>
> **Terrorism** From a Critical Terrorism Studies perspective, terrorism is understood primarily as a political issue rather than a security issue. What this means is that CTS research is particularly focused on how labelling an individual, group or action as 'terrorist' has political repercussions and who this serves in a political system. CTS scholars disagree on whether there actually exists of discrete form of violence that can be labelled terrorism, with some arguing that it is *only* a label or discourse used to delegitimize anti-state political movements. Others believe it is both a discrete type of political violence *and* a label used to delegitimize anti-state political movements.

This disagreement over what it is we are studying persists in CTS, turning it into a broad church capable of handling different viewpoints that strengthen rather than weaken knowledge. Scholars have also debated on how broadly the notion of political needs to be in discussing political violence. Indeed, feminist scholars have made an important contribution to CTS, introducing the debate on whether domestic violence can be understood and analysed as patriarchal, intimate, or everyday terrorism (see Gentry, 2015 and *Critical Studies on Terrorism* Special Section on Everyday Terrorism 8(3) 2015). The violence is intentional, political (it is aimed at maintaining patriarchal hegemony), and it is aimed at affecting not only the person who is victimized but all 'sub-alterns'—that is, those with less power—of the domestic sphere. 'The use of the term "terrorism" maintains the focus upon the "systematic, intentional nature" of the violence, whereas the use of "patriarchal" draws attention to the ideological, historical and cultural roots of this form of violence' (Gentry, 2015: 365). Others however argue that conflating terrorism and domestic violence actually hinders rather than increases understanding of either form of violence and runs the risk of bringing in violent counter-terrorism approaches into the sphere of domestic violence (see a summary of the debate in Sjoberg and Gentry, 2015). Thus, although disagreements on what terrorism 'is' and if it 'is' anything at all continue, crucially CTS scholars as a whole examine terrorism as part of politics rather than external to it. Importantly, most scholars also agree that the primary source of violence in contexts of the terrorism is actually the state.

3.2.2 State violence

Both of these CTS strands have focused almost exclusively on the state and its violence, whether direct violence (such as torture or extrajudicial killings) or indirect violence (such as repressive legislation, discrimination against ethnic or religious groups). Indeed, a focus on state violence, particularly that of powerful western states, has been one of the central pillars of CTS. From the early work of Ruth Blakeley (2009) on US-backed state terrorism in Latin America and later with Sam Raphael and Blakeley (2016) on the US-directed transnational rendition programme to the work of Charlotte Heath-Kelly (2017) on violent state practices being spread by the British government into social services such as health and education, CTS has as one of its core commitments to '"bring the state back in" to terrorism research. This has been done by exploring the logic and circumstances in which states employ civilian-directed violence to terrorise and intimidate society for political purposes' (Jackson, 2007: 248). Despite important exceptions such as in the work of Michael Stohl, state terrorism and the violence of state counter-terrorism, CTS scholars argue, was largely overlooked by terrorism studies, primarily because many of the key scholars in the field define terrorism as violent acts that can *only* be carried out by non-state actors (among others Hoffman, 1998). CTS is intent on reversing this.

It is challenging to summarize research by dozens of scholars associated with CTS since 2006 (readers can find much of this work in the journal *Critical Studies on Terrorism*), and rather than attempt such a summary, this chapter will highlight the broad lines of enquiry that can be said to characterize CTS' work on state violence. The first examines terrorist acts carried out directly by state actors. The second examines exceptional state violence under the banner of counter-terrorism policies and practices as well as how discourses of terrorism are used to legitimize state violence and delegitimize nonviolent responses. The final line of enquiry is on how states—in particular western liberal democracies—have used such discourses to spread the violence of counter-terrorism into our everyday lives.

CTS research demonstrates that state terrorism not only exists but is a common form of state violence (see for example the early work of Chomsky and Herman, 1979; to Blakeley 2009; Stokes and Raphael, 2010 among others). Blakeley and Raphael (2016: 15) said it best:

'Throughout history a significant portion of state violence has been used to coerce populations into complying with the agendas of political and economic elites by using such violence to instil fear in an audience beyond the direct victim. State violence of this kind is intended to achieve certain political objectives, particularly curtailing political dissent. This is state terrorism.'

As can be noted in this statement, all of the components attributed to terrorism—the non-state kind—can be found in the policies and practices of states. What CTS research has also worked hard to uncover is that state terrorism goes well beyond the 'rogue' states that are often accused of state terrorism or state-sponsored terrorism such as Syria or Iran. From the use of paramilitary units in Latin America, to the systematic use of torture by France in Algeria, to the United States' Rendition programme in the Global War on Terrorism (Blakeley and Raphael, 2016): it is difficult to find a state that *has not* engaged in terrorism at one point or another.

State terrorism, however, has certain specific characteristics that cannot be ascribed to non-state forms of terrorism. Non-state groups often publicly claim responsibility for terrorist attacks to ensure that their political goals are furthered through their actions. States on the other hand often walk a fine line between ensuring that the violence cannot be directly traced back to state officials, while at the same time ensuring that the target audience—those who need to be 'terrorized'—know that the state is behind the violence. Furthermore, such violence takes two forms: the first is limited state terrorism; the second, is generalized, governance, or wholesale state terrorism (Blakeley and Raphael, 2016). Limited state terrorism can be either limited in terms of the number of events or timescale in which this happens or in terms of the target audience, such as certain political or ethnic groups. Generalized, governance or wholesale terrorism refers to using such violence 'for controlling entire populations or for use during war time' (Blakeley and Raphael, 2016: 162). Campaigns of the first limited kind however 'often broaden into more generalized efforts to terrorise entire populations' (Blakeley and Raphael, 2016: 162).

CASE STUDY 3.1

The US Rendition, Detention, and Interrogation Programme

The United States has a long history of covert operations carried out clandestinely, and at times illegally, in the name of counter-terrorism (see Blakeley, 2009). Beginning in the late 1990s but particularly following the September 11, 2001 attacks on New York and Washington, the Central Intelligence Agency's (CIA) attention turned to al-Qaeda, its affiliated organizations, and anyone they deemed potentially linked to violent jihadi groups. What followed was the establishment, according to a decade of research carried out by Blakeley and Raphael in particular, of an elaborate system that involved at least 46 states to varying degree of complicity 'in the kidnap, secret transfer across multiple jurisdictions and arbitrary incommunicado detention, interrogation, and torture of 119 prisoners' (Raphael and Blakeley, 2016: 3, see also www.therenditionproject.org.uk). Following a four-year collaborative project, The Rendition Project and the Bureau of Investigative Journalism found that 'prisoners were held in complete darkness for months on end, chained to bars in the ceiling and forced to soil themselves. Continual loud music, combined with extended sleep deprivation, dietary manipulation and stress positioning were deployed to reduce individuals to a completely dependent state. Interrogations involved being severely beaten, and repeatedly slammed against walls. Some prisoners were placed, for hours at a time, in boxes so small they had to crouch. Others were subjected to water torture which induced vomiting, hypothermia and unconsciousness. Individuals were raped, mutilated, and threatened with guns, drills and being buried alive' (Raphael, Black and Blakeley, 2019: 4). Aside from providing terrible detail on such state violations, research in this secret programme considerably strengthens and changes our understanding of the Global War on Terror (GWOT). For example, Asim Qureshi (2009) states through his research on rendition we must conclude that GWOT did not start with the US-led war in Afghanistan in October 2001, as widely believed, but rather in Bosnia with the detention, rendition and torture of several Bosnian men less than two weeks after the attacks.

Raphael and Blakeley have also demonstrated how the US defence and intelligence officials succeeded in carving out an 'extra-legal space' in which questions of legality did not need to be asked. Finally, Raphael and Blakeley (2016) have revealed the extent of public-private partnerships among the intelligence services and private enterprises—including the collaboration with companies who owned and ran the logistics for the planes used in the intricate flight system—and the extent of the relationship between the US and numerous countries that knowingly supported the US operations. Indeed, from allowing planes to be refuelled on their territory (the UK), to hosting US secret-run prisons (Poland, Romania, and Lithuania), to detaining and interrogating suspects (Jordan, Syria, Egypt, Libya, and Morocco), or to facilitating the capture of suspects (Canada, Sweden, and Italy), states across the world were involved in the rendition programme. Importantly, this includes states with strong anti-US agendas (such as Syria and Libya) which also forces scholars to revisit analyses of US foreign policy, particularly in the Middle East.

QUESTIONS

1. Does the US Rendition, Detention, and Interrogation Programme constitute state terrorism?
2. How does focusing on state violence change our understanding of the Global War on Terror?

The difficulty is that much of this state violence is carried out in the name of counter-terrorism. Apartheid South Africa argued its violence was necessary to defeat the African National Congress (ANC) and other 'terrorist' groups, the violence of state-allied paramilitary units in Colombia was justified to defeat the 'terrorist' Revolutionary Armed Forces of Colombia (FARC), and the US' rendition programme justified its violence as necessary in GWOT. States argued that their violence constituted a legitimate form of counter-terrorism. As such, from a CTS perspective, how does one distinguish between state terrorism and the excesses of state counter-terrorism? To answer this question, CTS challenges the very notion of 'counter-terrorism' and how it has been carried out so far by states.

To begin with, the term *counter*-terrorism needs to be challenged. The assumption in the term is that state violence is *responding* to (non-state) terrorism, i.e. the violence started with actors other than the state. Even in cases in which state counter-terrorism engages in excessive, illegal and/or unjustified violence, the state still maintains the moral high ground of 'not throwing the first punch.' The term also hides the reality that often it is difficult to establish where violence began, and a case can be made that non-state actors are carrying out terrorist violence *in response to* state repression. Secondly, CTS highlights how state counter-terrorism has often been characterized by policies and practices of extreme violence, discrimination, and illegality. This includes: discrimination against entire communities, seen as 'suspect communities' such communities of North African origins in France for example or ethnic Somalis in Kenya; or the killings of thousands in aerial bombings between 2006 and 2009 by the Sri Lankan armed forces to defeat the Tamil Tigers (LTTE) (Chowdhury and Fitzsimmons, 2013).

> **KEY CONCEPTS**
>
> **Counter-terrorism** From a critical terrorism studies perspective, counter-terrorism in the context of this chapter is to be analysed as policies put forward by states to counter the political as well as security effects of terrorism. This means that counter-terrorism is not only investigated to understand whether it is effective or not in ending or reducing terrorist violence, but also to understand whether the measures are actually intended to counter-terrorism (for example whether they are measures that precede the terrorist violence that have been rebranded), and most of all, what are the effects of these measures in terms of legitimizing states and delegitimizing opposition movements (see also Lindahl, 2018).

Thus, CTS exposes the violence of the state but also proposes alternative policies that the state and other actors may use in conflicts marked by terrorist violence grounded in a fundamental concept of Critical Theory: emancipation. In general terms, Critical Security Studies giant Ken Booth (2007: 181) defined emancipation as the 'theory and practice of inventing humanity, with a view of freeing people, as individuals and collectivities, from contingent and structural oppressions.' For CTS, any response to terrorism has to aim for humanity's emancipation from slavery in all its forms (see Horkheimer, 1982). What CTS aims to uncover is what this abstract principle means in practice (MacDonald, 2009; Martini, 2019).

One of the answers that CTS focuses on is the possibility of dialogue and negotiations to end terrorist violence. Directly challenging traditional approaches and policymakers who overall have dismissed the possibility of 'talking to terrorists' (some exceptions include Zartman, 2003; Neumann, 2007) numerous CTS scholars (among others Gunning, 2004; Toros, 2008, 2012; Haspeslagh, 2013) have examined whether negotiations can represent a viable response to terrorist violence (state or non-state) and when and how such negotiations can be undertaken. Indeed, a CTS approach that places terrorist violence within its sociohistorical context and thus sees it as part of a broader social and political conflict. This allows CTS scholars access to the vast array of conflict resolution and transformation tools. Based on interviews and participant observation with non-state armed groups labelled as 'terrorist,' CTS scholars for example have examined how labelling groups and individuals as 'terrorists' has worked to delegitimize nonviolent responses such as negotiations (Haspeslagh, 2013, 2021. Others have analysed how state and non-state actors using terrorist violence can be transformed through dialogue to move away from violence toward nonviolent forms of political struggle (among others Toros, 2012; Toros and Tellidis, 2014; Duhart, 2019).

It must be recognized that despite some headways being made to convince policymakers as well as armed groups to consider negotiations (see in particular the work of the Berghof Foundation and Conciliation Resources), nonviolent responses to terrorism remain marginalized. One of the reasons for this can be found in how state violence and repression are legitimized through the language—or discourses—used by state and other actors that naturalizes this violence as the only solution (Jackson, 2005). Thus, another key pillar of CTS examines how state violence is legitimized and nonviolent responses are delegitimized through discourses on terrorism. In a powerful example of how it can be analysed to uncover power, Jackson (2005: 2) argues that the language of the 'war on terrorism'

> 'is a deliberately and meticulously composed set of words, assumptions, metaphors, grammatical forms, myths and forms of knowledge – it is a carefully constructed *discourse* – that is designed to achieve a number of key political goals: to normalize and legitimize the current counter-terrorist approach; to empower the authorities and shield them from criticism; to discipline domestic society by marginalizing dissent and protest; and to enforce national unity by reifying a narrow conception of national identity. The discourse of the 'war on terrorism' has a clear *political* purpose; it works for someone and for something; it is an exercise in power.'

Such discourses need to be studied precisely because they are an exercise of power, Jackson (2005: 3) continues, and 'unchecked power inevitably becomes abusive.'

CASE STUDY 3.2

Al-Shabaab in Somalia

Al-Shabaab (aS) is one of the largest and most enduring non-state armed groups in East Africa, which despite the efforts of regional states (Ethiopia and Kenya, see Photo 3.1), regional organizations (the African Union), and international actors (in particular the United States) has succeeded in maintaining a presence in large parts of south-central Somalia. Mainstream approaches identify it as an 'al Qaida-linked terrorist group' that poses a threat to the United States both in terms of its interests in the region as well as directly on US soil (Jones, Liepman, and Chandler, 2016: 1). Research published by the US Department of Defense-linked RAND Corporation argued that aS 'possesses a competent external operations capability . . . [has] expressed interest in striking U.S. and other foreign targets in East Africa' (Jones, Liepman, and Chandler, 2016: 2). World powers, particularly the United States, have shared this assessment and have long engaged with the group as part of 'countering the threat of global terrorism' which primarily involves 'targeting terrorists, their training camps, and their safe havens throughout Somalia and the region' (AFRICOM, 2018). From a CTS perspective and drawing on key work by leading East Africa scholars such as Stig Jarle Hansen (2016), Afyare Abdi Elmi (2010), and Roland Marchal (2007), aS is much better understood (and engaged with) as part of a conflict landscape involving clan-based disputes, a history of state violence, and regional and international military interventions. From this perspective, aS emerged from the Islamic Courts Union, a cooperation of armed actors that controlled large parts of Somalia from 1999 until they were ousted by Ethiopian backed-troops in 2006. Some members of the ICU joined the new transitional government, while others formed al-Shabaab that has operated

PHOTO 3.1 The Somalian flag on a map of Somalia, and neighbouring countries Ethiopia and Kenya.

in large sections of south-central Somalia since, although the amount of territory it has under its control has fluctuated substantially in the past decade. Thus, aS is viewed largely as a part of the Somali conflict landscape, although its avowed links with al-Qaeda are recognized and integrated in any analysis of the group. Its primary identity is seen as internal to Somalia rather than the Somali face of an international terrorist network. Aside from leading to a different understanding of the group's purpose, a critical approach brings scholars to focus on how the 'terrorism' label has been used to justify state and international counter-terrorist violence as well as the effects of this violence. Some scholars have examined how drone warfare including in Somalia can be understood as state terrorism, as shown in Photo 3.2 (Calhoun, 2018), while others have looked at how the GWOT in Somalia has turned the country into a rendition site and transit point for suspects detained throughout the region (Qureshi, 2010).

Finally, there has been increasing attention by CTS scholars to the possibility of negotiations with aS, based on research that reveals the group's strong local roots and focus. The research points at how there exists important common ground between the goals of current internationally backed federal government and aS—a 'better Somali-owned governance that is broadly in accordance with local Islamic traditions' (Toros and Harley, 2018: 401)—as well as on the potential role for elders to mediate between the state and aS using traditional conflict resolution processes known as *Xeer*.

PHOTO 3.2 Terrorism scholars including Calhoun have researched drone warfare in Somalia.

QUESTIONS

1. What different aspects of the al-Shabaab and its violence do CTS approaches highlight?
2. What policy responses open up with a CTS approach?

Numerous works carry out similar analyses of official discourses of terrorism, using differing methodologies and techniques, some more quantitative such as content analysis and some more qualitative such as genealogy (for a thorough review of CTS methodologies see Stump and Dixit, 2013; Dixit and Stump, 2016).

Crucially, such policymaking and legislation has effects beyond what could strictly be seen as counter-terrorism operations by the security services. Indeed, research in CTS has demonstrated how dominant CT discourses that in turn enable violent CT practices and legislation have affected how people live their lives even outside the security sphere. Lee Jarvis and Michael Lister (2010, 2013) examined how the notion of citizenship has been affected by US and British counter-terrorism legislation, examining how the latter has conscripted '"ordinary" citizens into the state's security apparatuses' (2010: 174), making it 'a civic obligation to contribute to, and participate in, the monitoring of others' (Jarvis and Lister, 2013: 661). The effect on citizenship is even more detrimental to ethnic minorities, amongst whom many 'believed that their own rights and scope of public participation, as well as their sense of national identity and obligations, had been eroded by anti-terrorism policies; they felt they were becoming, in the words of one individual, "second class citizens"' (Jarvis and Lister, 2013: 672).

Such effects extend even beyond the political sphere. Indeed, in the UK since the establishment of the PREVENT duty in 2015 (also known as The Counter-Terrorism and Security Act 2015) social care, education, and health workers have a statutory duty to prevent the spread of terrorism or counter 'radicalization' (see the work of Francesco Ragazzi, 2017). 'In practice, this has meant that schools, colleges, universities, prisons, social services . . . [and health services] now perform counterterrorism' (Heath-Kelly and Strausz, 2019: 90). Such a diffusion of counter-terrorism duties from the security sector to other public sectors, supported by a discourse of safeguarding of people from extremist ideas, has important implications for the everyday lives of citizens. Indeed, Heath-Kelly and Strausz (2019: 90–91) examine how through the national health service, the British government has extended counter-terrorism screening 'across the entire population,' leading to a 'normalization of counterterrorism within society' and creating a 'tension with the liberal foundations of British political life'. This once again further impacts ethnic minority groups as Heath-Kelly and Strausz (2019:106) found in their survey research that only 'one in three respondents considered themselves confident to tell the difference between radicalization and an interest in Middle Eastern war and politics' leading to a large jump in referrals for potential radicalization from between 500–1000 (prior to the Prevent Duty being established) to more than 7500 in 2015–2016.

CTS thus exposes how states are central actors to be investigated in any research on terrorism, not only or indeed necessarily as the defence that protects us against terrorism, but rather often as the perpetrators of terrorist and counter-terrorist violence and as powerful actors capable of transforming everyday lives in order to justify and legitimate this violence. As this section has explored, CTS is also profoundly political. Aside from being political in its choice of subject matter and approaches, CTS also aims at being political in how research is used and by whom. It is to these questions that the chapter now turns in section 3.3.

3.3 THE POLITICS OF CTS

The politics of CTS and the debates surrounding them are a natural consequence of the research focus of the field outlined in section 3.2: state violence and emancipation. This final section will thus examine how CTS has adopted and struggled with political positions in relation to the state and in relation to supporting scholars, activists, and ordinary people beyond elite academic, policy, and practitioner circles and beyond the Global North.

3.3.1 CTS vs the State: to engage or not?

As outlined in section 3.2, one of CTS' primary goals is to analyse and to *reduce* state violence, particularly its terrorist and counter-terrorist violence. This has been done by investigating covert and illegal state practices including torture and rendition, legal and overt practices that stigmatize certain communities and weaken the democratic fabric of states, and by investigating the potential for nonviolent responses to terrorist violence. In all these areas, changing the behaviour of the state is a crucial aspect of any reduction of direct, structural, and cultural violence. The fundamental question that remains is *how* state violence can be reduced. Here CTS is divided in two very distinct approaches: some scholars, such as Jackson, argue that the state cannot be persuaded or socialized into change; others argue that states are not unitary actors and that all actors are capable of transformation (see Toros, 2016; Fitzgerald, Ali and Armstrong, 2016 for a summary of the debate).

For Jackson (2016: 121), the state-led 'global counterterrorism regime is, in its philosophy, practice, and effects, inherently violent, oppressive, and life-diminishing: it is a set of practices that is deeply anti-emancipatory, anti-human, and regressive'. He goes on to say,

> 'In such conditions, where counterterrorism causes widespread suffering and is an obstacle to progressive change and social justice, it can be argued that working directly with state counterterrorism is akin to medical professionals who collaborate with torturers in an effort to improve prisoner welfare; while there may be some benefit to individual prisoners who perhaps suffer less as a consequence, the broader impact of their participation is the perpetuation and legitimisation of the overall system of torture, and their involvement does nothing to fundamentally change an inherently immoral set of practices' (Jackson, 2016: 122).

Jackson (2016: 122) concludes that 'it is virtually impossible' under such conditions to work toward emancipation while at the same time 'participating in an inherently violence and counter-emancipatory regime of counterterrorism'.

The only path left for CTS scholars is to 'embrace "outsider theorising", "anti-hegemonic" identity', that is 'radical and rebel, dissident and protestor' and 'seek to work with progressive forces outside of the existing structures of power' (Jackson, 2016: 124; as is clear from his chapter in this volume, Jackson believes in nonviolent activism and in no way supports the use of violence). This would mean supporting for example the work and activism of Stellan Vinthagen, the first Endowed Chair in the Study of Nonviolent Direct Action and Civil Resistance at the University of Massachusetts Amherst, who has led numerous campaigns of civil resistance against state violence, whether it be protesting nuclear weapons programmes or Israel's blockade of Gaza and has been arrested numerous times (see https://wagingnonviolence.org/2014/12/meet-stellan-vinthagen-head-first-university-program-civil-resistance/). Such an orientation for CTS would mean supporting—in actions as well as in words—'political nonviolent movements that make claims to contest a dominant and hegemonic power, and act within a society where organized violence and oppression are legitimised, normalized or accepted de facto by a vast population' (Vinthagen, 2015: 2). Some CTS scholars have already brought together activism and research, including Michael Loadenthal (2013a, 2013b, 2019) who has both analysed state vilification of ecological protest movements as 'ecoterrorism' and self-identified as a 'conspirator' and organizer of 'a variety of global direction action movements' (2013b: 15).

Jackson's position does not make unanimity with CTS, and indeed there are scholars who argue that engagement with the state is not only important if one wants to work toward emancipatory social change, but also normatively sound as it is based on the belief that transformation *is* possible, even for the world's most violent actors and institutions. In a published response to Jackson, Toros (2016) has argued that if the greatest violence emerges from the state, then CTS needs to be trying to talk the state out of this violence. Contrary to Jackson's position, Toros argues that this is not a fruitless enterprise as states have 'emancipatory and counter-emancipatory agendas. They are the source of repression and violence but also behind the welfare of millions who are educated, kept healthy, housed and at times fed by state institutions that work for greater social justice' (Toros, 2016: 128). One can thus work to identify the fissures in the state as well as the emancipatory forces that can be strengthened and supported with theoretically solid and empirically grounded research.

KEY CONCEPTS

Impact Academia has been increasingly encouraged to step out of the 'Ivory Tower' of universities to engage with the outside world, be it with state bureaucracies, international organizations, civil society groups, and non-governmental organizations (NGOs). Research is meant to not only further intellectual knowledge but help address salient real-life problems. One can see how this approach is particularly relevant in security and terrorism studies. From a CTS perspective however, impact is particularly thorny. To work with states, often means trying to help them in their *counter-terrorist* policies. This implicitly legitimizes such policies, suggesting that counter-terrorism simply needs improvement not a complete overhaul. It assumes that states are legitimate—another assumption CTS scholars refuse to make. CTS therefore asks scholars to challenge themselves with questions such as: Upon whom do they want to have impact on? And most importantly, for whose benefit?

3.3.2 Broadening CTS' interlocutors

Emerging scholars have questioned whether this debate, in its rather stark positions, is somewhat naïve and fails to take into account the politics of what is labelled 'policy relevant' (Fitzgerald, Ali, and Armstrong, 2016: 2). Indeed, whether it is working with state actors or with resistance movements, one could argue that both approaches tend to focus on elite and/or already highly politicized actors. They tend to overlook less explicitly politicized actors or actors that can bring 'bottom-up perspectives offered by those who operate at the coalface of "radicalisation"' for example (Fitzgerald, Ali, and Armstrong, 2016: 2). Will McGowan (2016) argues that CTS has overlooked the victims and survivors of non-state terrorism, often focusing instead on the victims of state terrorism.

There are good reasons for this: The focus by mainstream media, policymakers, and to a certain extent scholarship on the victims of non-state terrorism has been used to 'champion more aggressive and reactionary policy responses to the war on terror' (McGowan, 2016: 26; see Holland, 2012 for an analysis of media discourses on terrorism). But overlooking these actors silences them, including 'dissenting victims whose vision of civil rights and social justice differs to that of prevailing political, economic, and military hegemony' which deprives CTS of important voices that can challenge dominant representations of the victims of terrorism. Similarly, engaging with authors who have carried out 'everyday' counterterrorism—willingly or reluctantly—is key to understanding and transforming social relations on the ground (Heath-Kelly and Strausz, 2019). Thus, engagement and activism can take a variety of forms, and criticality and policy relevance can be brought together through engagement with a broad range of actors.

In the context of the production of academic knowledge, CTS also sets as its goal to support scholars, activists, and practitioners from the Global South. 'CTS scholars . . . have an additional task of contributing towards the establishment of an alternative "knowledge" and including marginalized views that highlight the asymmetrical relations between Western power and global resistance' (Göl, 2010: 5). This has exposed among innumerable other research areas: how the Global War on Terror has been used to securitize and politicize development aid in Africa (Aning, 2010); the institutionalized role of conspiracy theories in national politics in Pakistan that hinder the development of a terrorism studies field (Feyyaz, 2016: 455); and how the romanticization of resistance to state terrorism in Latin America has been used to 'depoliticise dissent and create obstacles to debate' (Furtado, 2015: 85).

3.4 CONCLUSION: FUTURE CHALLENGES

Critical Terrorism Studies may have begun in opposition to mainstream, orthodox or traditional terrorism studies, but it has since developed into a self-standing subfield with a clear research agenda and the explicit goal of transforming the politics of terrorism and counterterrorism away from its current violent forms. As outlined in this chapter, CTS has made clear contributions by investigating: whether there is a distinct form of violence that can be called 'terrorism' and the effects of using such a label; the violence of the state through state terrorism, violent counter-terrorism, and state discourses on terrorism and counter-terrorism; and a focus on the impact on the everyday of these violent discourses and practices.

Some of its contributions are now widely accepted beyond CTS circles. For example, few would challenge the notion that using the term 'terrorism' has political implications, legitimizing and naturalizing certain policies and practices. Similarly, it has successfully demonstrated that terrorism and counter-terrorism have had an impact far beyond the security and defence spheres, entering our daily lives through laws, health, education, social care, and even affecting our understanding of ourselves as citizens. Finally, it has shown that state terrorist and counter-terrorist violence is not the sole purview of non-Western state terrorism or state-sponsored terrorism (such as Iran and Syria), but a much broader danger affecting the lives of millions across the Western liberal and autocratic world. This latter finding challenges the very distinction between liberal democratic and authoritarian.

Going forward, what is the future of critical approaches to terrorism? State violence—be it terrorist or counter-terrorist, material or discursive—continues, and CTS must continue to shine a light on state abuse and violence. Understanding how such violence is measured out across the world, the role of a variety of actors, including scholars and experts, knowingly and unknowingly sustaining such violence must remain a key focus of CTS. CTS has to also turn toward the study of non-state violence. As argued by McGowan (2016), CTS has largely overlooked the practices and implications of non-state terrorism, arguing that the phenomenon has been overblown by officials, the media, and some scholarship with considerable detrimental effects on communities identified as producing the perpetrators of such violence. CTS has also lamented the selectivity of the latter's focus arguing that it has predominantly focused on so-called 'Islamist terrorism', and overall ignored terrorism from the far-right. However, as state security institutions begin to focus on the far-right using the same illiberal and violent policies and practices as have been used to marginalize ethnic minority communities, CTS faces the challenge of how to engage with state violence being used against communities that support projects directly opposed to CTS' values of emancipation and inclusivity. How does an emancipatory scholarship engage with state violence carried out against violent actors who support a violent politics of supremacy and exclusion? This remains to be seen.

To conclude, CTS offers a wealth of research and innovation for those studying terrorism, that of state and non-state actors. It strengthened the field of terrorism studies more broadly with its pointed critique of mainstream research, and went on to establish a self-standing subfield of its own, which no doubt has deficiencies and faces interesting challenges in the future, but nonetheless offers broad but firm foundations for those interested in combining critical theories and terrorism.

DISCUSSION QUESTIONS

1. Is terrorism a distinct category of violence?
2. Why is there a debate on whether states can engage in terrorist violence?
3. How does research on the Rendition Programme change understandings of the Global War on Terror?

4. Why do some critical terrorism studies scholars argue that counter-terrorism policies and practices have spread into the everyday lives of citizens?
5. Why are critical terrorism scholars divided over whether they can engage with state actors to seek reform of counter-terrorism policies and practices?

 Visit the online resources for pointers on how to answer the discussion questions, links to useful web sources, and guidance on accessing databases: www.oup.com/he/Wilson-Muro1e

GUIDE TO FURTHER READING

Dixit, P. and Stump, J. (2016) *Critical Methods in Terrorism Studies*. London and New York: Routledge. *The book critically engages with the key methodological innovations offered by CTS and how they bring scholars to ask different questions, find different answers, and point toward different futures.*

Heath-Kelly, C. and Strausz, E. (2019) 'The Banality of Counterterrorism "After, After 9/11"? Perspectives on the Prevent Duty from the UK Health Care Sector', *Critical Studies on Terrorism* 12 (1): 89–109. *A key text to understand the concept of 'everyday' counter-terrorism examining how the duty to report signs of radicalization placed on the UK health sector has affected the practices of counter-terrorism and framed it as part of broader safeguarding duties.*

Jackson, R., Breen Smyth, M., and Gunning J. (eds) (2009) *Critical Terrorism Studies: A New Research Agenda*. Abingdon: Routledge. *This edited volume is the seminal text of critical terrorism studies, bringing together most of the first generation of CTS scholars. It offers a pointed critique of mainstream terrorism studies and examines various theoretical foundations for critical theory-based research.*

Stampnitzky, L. (2013) *Disciplining Terror: How Experts Invented 'Terrorism'*. Cambridge: Cambridge University Press. *An in-depth examination of the politics of terrorism studies and its relationship with policymaking, the book investigates how the concept of terrorism has been developed and used over the past decades.*

Toros, H. (2008) '"We Don't Negotiate with Terrorists!": Legitimacy and Complexity in Terrorist Conflicts', *Security Dialogue* 39(4): 407–426. *The article challenges dominant arguments against negotiations with groups using terrorism and looks at how conflict transformation can support in bringing an end to terrorist and counter-terrorist violence.*

REFERENCES

AFRICOM (2018) 'US Statement on Alleged Civilian Casualties in Somalia', 11 May 2018, http://www.africom.mil/media-room/pressrelease/30721/u-s-statement-on-alleged-civilian-casualties-in-somalia (last accessed 5 November 2019).

Aning, K. (2010) 'Security, the War on Terror, and Official Development Assistance', *Critical Studies on Terrorism*, 3 (1): 7–26.

Blakeley, R. (2009) *State Terrorism and Neoliberalism: The North in the South*. Abingdon: Routledge.

Blakeley, R. and Raphael, S. (2016) 'Understanding Western State Terrorism', in Jackson, R. (ed.) *Routledge Handbook of Critical Terrorism Studies*. Abingdon: Routledge, 159–169.

Booth, K. (2007) *Theory of World Security*. Cambridge: Cambridge University Press.

Calhoun, L. (2018) 'Totalitarian Tendencies in Drone Strikes by States', *Critical Studies on Terrorism*, 11 (2): 357–375.

Chomsky, N. and Herman. E. (1979) *After the Cataclysm: Postwar Indochina and the Reconstruction of Imperial Ideology*. The Political Economy of Human Rights, Vol. II, Nottingham: Spokesman.

Chowdhury, A. and Fitzsimmons, S. (2013) 'Effective but Inefficient: Understanding the Costs of Counterterrorism', *Critical Studies on Terrorism*, 6 (3): 447–456.

Closs Stephens, A. and Vaughan-Williams, N. (2008) *Terrorism and the Politics of Response*. London: Routledge.

Cox, R. (1986) 'Social Forces, States and World Orders: Beyond International Relations Theory', in Keohane, R. (ed), *Neorealism and Its Critics*, New York: Columbia University Press, 204–254.

Dixit, P. and Stump, J. (2016) *Critical Methods in Terrorism Studies*. London and New York: Routledge.

Duhart, P. (2019) 'Talking With Terrorists, Talking With Governments: Insurgent Perspectives On Legitimisation And Engagement', *Critical Studies on Terrorism*, 12 (3): 395–415.

Elmi, A. (2010) *Understanding the Somalia Conflagration: Identity, Political Islam and Peacebuilding*. London: Pluto Press.

Feyyaz, M. (2016) 'The Discourse and Study of Terrorism in Decolonised States: The Case of Pakistan', *Critical Studies on Terrorism*, 9 (3): 455–477.

Finlayson. A. and Valentine, J. (eds) (2002) *Politics and Post-Structuralism: An Introduction*. Edinburgh: Edinburgh University Press.

Fitzgerald, J., Ali, N., and Armstrong, M. (2016) 'Editors' Introduction: Critical Terrorism Studies: Reflections on Policy-Relevance and Disciplinarity', *Critical Studies on Terrorism*, 9 (1): 1–11.

Furtado, H. (2015) 'Against State Terror: Lessons on Memory, Counterterrorism and Resistance from the Global South', *Critical Studies on Terrorism*, 8 (1): 72–89.

Gentry, C. (2015) 'Epistemological Failures: Everyday Terrorism in the West', *Critical Studies on Terrorism*, 8 (3): 362–382.

Göl, A. (2010) 'Editor's Introduction: Views from the "Others" of the War on Terror', *Critical Studies on Terrorism*, 3 (1): 1–5.

Gunning, J. (2004) 'Peace with Hamas? The Transforming Potential of Political Participation', *International Affairs*, 80 (2): 233–255.

Hansen, S. (2016) *Al-Shabaab in Somalia: The History and Ideology of a Militant Islamist Group*. New York: Oxford University Press.

Haspeslagh, S. (2013) '"Listing Terrorists": The Impact of Proscription on Third-Party Efforts to Engage Armed Groups in Peace Processes—A Practitioner's Perspective', *Critical Studies on Terrorism*, 6 (1): 189–208.

Haspeslagh, S. (2021) *Proscribing Peace: How Listing Armed Groups as Terrorists Hurts Negotiations*. Manchester: Manchester University Press.

Heath-Kelly, C. (2016) 'Post-structuralism and Constructivism', in Jackson, R. (ed.) *Routledge Handbook of Critical Terrorism Studies*. Abingdon: Routledge, 60–69.

Heath-Kelly, C. (2017) 'The Geography of Pre-Criminal Space: Epidemiological Imaginations of Radicalisation Risk in the UK Prevent Strategy 2007–2017', *Critical Studies on Terrorism*, 10 (2): 297–319.

Heath-Kelly, C. and Strausz, E. (2019) 'The Banality of Counterterrorism "After, After 9/11"? Perspectives on the Prevent Duty from the UK Health Care Sector', *Critical Studies on Terrorism*, 12 (1): 89–109.

Hoffman, B. (1998) *Inside Terrorism*. London: Gollancz.

Holland, J. (2012) *Selling the War on Terror: Foreign Policy Discourses after 9/11*. New York: Routledge.

Horkheimer, M. (1982) 'Traditional and Critical Theory', in Horkheimer, M. *Critical Theory: Selected Essays*. New York: Continuum, 188–252.

Jackson, R. (2005) *Writing the War on Terrorism: Language, Politics and Counter-Terrorism*. Manchester: Manchester University Press.

Jackson, R. (2007) 'The Core Commitments of Critical Terrorism Studies', *European Political Science*, 6 (3): 244–251.

Jackson, R. (2008) 'An Argument for Terrorism', *Perspectives on Terrorism* II, 2 (2): 25–32.

Jackson, R. (2016) 'To Be or Not to Be Policy Relevant? Power, Emancipation and Resistance in CTS Research', *Critical Studies on Terrorism*, 9 (1): 120–125.

Jackson, R., Breen-Smyth, M., and Gunning, J. (eds) (2009) *Critical Terrorism Studies: A New Research Agenda*. Abingdon: Routledge.

Jackson, R., Breen-Smyth, M., Gunning, J., and Jarvis, L. (2011) *Terrorism: A Critical Introduction*. New York: Palgrave Macmillan.

Jackson, R., Toros, H., Jarvis, L., and Heath-Kelly, C. (eds) (2018) *Ten Years of Critical Studies on Terrorism*. Abingdon: Routledge.

Jarvis, L. and Lister, M. (2010) 'Stakeholder Security: The New Western Way of Counter-Terrorism', *Contemporary Politics*, 16 (2): 173–188.

Jarvis, L. and Lister, M. (2013) 'Disconnected Citizenship? The Impacts of Anti-Terrorism Policy on Citizenship in the UK', *Political Studies*, 61: 656–675.

Jones, S., Liepman, A., and Chandler, N. (2016) 'Counterterrorism and Counterinsurgency in Somalia: Assessing the Campaign Against Al

Shabaab', RAND https://www.rand.org/pubs/research_reports/RR1539.html (last accessed 3 November 2019).

Lindahl, S. (2018) *A Critical Theory of Counterterrorism: Ontology, Epistemology and Normativity*. London: Routledge.

Loadenthal, M. (2013a) 'Deconstructing "Eco-Terrorism": Rhetoric, Framing, and Statecraft as Seen through the Insight Approach', *Critical Studies on Terrorism*, 6 (1): 92–117.

Loadenthal, M. (2013b) 'The Earth Liberation Front: A Social Movement Analysis', *Radical Criminology*, 2: 15–36.

Loadenthal, M. (2019) 'Introduction: Studying Political Violence While Indicted – Against Objectivity and Detachment', *Critical Studies on Terrorism*, 12 (3): 481–490.

Marchal, R. (2007) 'Warlordism and Terrorism: How to Obscure an Already Confusing Crisis? The Case of Somalia', *International Affairs*, 83 (6): 1091–1106.

Martini, A. (2019) 'Rethinking Terrorism and Countering Terrorism from a Critical Perspective: CTS and Normativity', *Critical Studies on Terrorism*, 13 (1): 47–55 DOI:10.1080/17539153.2019.1658411.

MacDonald, M. (2009) 'Emancipation and Critical Terrorism Studies', in Jackson, R., Breen-Smyth, M., and Gunning, J. (eds), *Critical Terrorism Studies: A New Research Agenda*. Abingdon: Routledge, 109–123.

McGowan, W. (2016) 'Critical Terrorism Studies, Victimisation, and Policy Relevance: Compromising Politics or Challenging Hegemony?', *Critical Studies on Terrorism*, 9 (1): 12–32.

Neumann, P. (2007) 'Negotiating with Terrorists', *Foreign Affairs*, 86 (1): 128–139.

Qureshi, A. (2009) 'Researching rendition and torture in the War on Terror: lessons from a human rights organization', *Critical Studies on Terrorism*, 2 (2): 376.

Qureshi, A. (2010) '"War on Terror": The African Front', *Critical Studies on Terrorism*, 3 (1): 49–61.

Ragazzi, F. (2017) 'Countering Terrorism and Radicalisation: Securitising Social Policy?', *Contemporary Social Policy*, 37 (2): 163–179.

Raphael, S. (2009) 'In the Service of Power: Terrorism Studies and the US Intervention in the Global South', in Jackson, R., Breen-Smyth, M., and Gunning, J. (eds), *Critical Terrorism Studies: A New Research Agenda*. Abingdon: Routledge, 49–65.

Raphael, S. and Blakeley, R. (2016) 'Rendition in the "War on Terror"', in Jackson, R. (ed.) *Routledge Handbook of Critical Terrorism Studies*. Abingdon: Routledge, 181–189.

Raphael, S. Black, C., and Blakeley, R. (2019) *CIA Torture Unredacted* https://www.therenditionproject.org.uk/documents/RDI/190710-TRP-TBIJ-CIA-Torture-Unredacted-Full.pdf (last accessed 14 October 2021).

Silke, A. (2009) 'Contemporary Terrorism Studies: Issues in Research', in Jackson, R., Breen-Smyth, M., and Gunning, J. (eds), *Critical Terrorism Studies: A New Research Agenda*. Abingdon: Routledge, 34–48.

Sjoberg, L. and Gentry, C. (2015) 'Introduction: Gender and Everyday/Intimate Terrorism', *Critical Studies on Terrorism*, 8 (3): 358–361.

Stampintzky, L. (2013) *Disciplining Terror: How Experts Invented 'Terrorism'*. Cambridge: Cambridge University Press.

Stohl, M. (2006) 'The State as Terrorist: Insights and Implications'. *Democracy and Security*, 2 (1): 1–25.

Stokes, D. and Raphael, S. (2010) *Global Energy Security and American Hegemony*. Baltimore: John Hopkins University Press.

Stump, J. L. and Dixit, P. (2013) *Critical Terrorism Studies. An Introduction to Research Methods*. New York: Routledge.

Toros, H. (2008) '"We Don't Negotiate with Terrorists!": Legitimacy and Complexity in Terrorist Conflicts', *Security Dialogue*, 39 (4): 407–426.

Toros, H. (2012) *Terrorism, Talking and Transformation: A Critical Approach*. Abingdon and New York: Routledge.

Toros, H. (2016) 'Dialogue, Praxis and the State: A Response to Richard Jackson', *Critical Studies on Terrorism*, 9 (1): 126–130.

Toros, H. and Gunning, J. (2009) 'Exploring a Critical Theory Approach to Terrorism Studies', in Jackson, R., Breen-Smyth, M., and Gunning, J. (eds), *Critical Terrorism Studies: A New Research Agenda*. Abingdon: Routledge, 87–108.

Toros, H. and Tellidis, I. (eds) 2014. *Terrorism, Peace and Conflict Studies: Investigating the Crossroad*. London and New York: Routledge.

Toros, H. and Harley, S. (2018) 'Negotiations with al-Shabaab: Lessons Learned and Future Prospects', in Keating, M. and Waldman, M. *War and Peace in Somalia: National Grievances, Local Conflict and Al-Shabaab*. New York: Oxford University Press.

Vinthagen, S. (2015) *A Theory of Nonviolent Action: How Civil Resistance Works*. London: Zed Books.

Weinberg. L. and Eubank, W. (2008) 'Problems with the Critical Studies Approach to the Study of Terrorism', *Critical Studies on Terrorism*, 1 (2): 185–195.

Zartman, I.W. (2003) 'Negotiating with Terrorists', *International Negotiation*, 8 (3): 443–450.

Zulaika, J. and Douglass, W. (1996) *Terror and Taboo: The Follies, Fables, and Faces of Terrorism*. New York: Routledge.

CHAPTER 4

Conceptualizations of Terrorism

ANTHONY RICHARDS

■ CHAPTER SUMMARY

This chapter explores the reasons for seeking a universally agreed conceptualization of terrorism. It will then identify some of the obstacles that have confronted this objective, and why such agreement has been challenging. Key reasons include the subjective application of the term, and the contentious issue as to what components should be featured in any conceptualization of terrorism. One also has to consider that terrorism, like all social science concepts, is ultimately a social construction, and so a concrete definition that speaks 'truth' difficult to attain. Nevertheless, most terrorism scholars view 'terrorism' as a distinctive phenomenon, so what is it that is analytically different about terrorism compared with other forms of political violence, and how can this be captured in an agreed conceptualization of the term?

4.1 INTRODUCTION

> **KEY CONCEPTS**
>
> **Terrorism** For the purpose of this chapter, this is conceptualized as the use of violence or force or the threat of violence or force with the primary purpose of generating a psychological impact beyond the immediate victims or object of attack for a political motive.

Defining terrorism has long been the subject of contentious debates both within policymaking and the terrorism studies literature of the past five decades (see Photo 4.1). It has often been lamented that the international community, and the United Nations in particular, have failed to generate a universally agreed definition of the phenomenon. For example, a UN High-Level Panel in 2004 argued that 'a lack of agreement on a clear and well-known definition undermines the moral and normative stance against terrorism and has stained the United Nations image' (48). The struggle to achieve this has been seen by many policymakers and scholars (though certainly not all) as an important endeavour (for an overview of these perspectives see Richards 2014)—after all, if terrorism has become an increasingly international phenomenon, and if international cooperation is therefore seen

PHOTO 4.1 There is no single definition of terrorism, and this has long been the subject of debate in academic discourse and political decision-making.

as imperative in mounting an effective response, then surely there needs to be agreement as to what it is that is being tackled.

Defining terrorism has long been the subject of contentious debates both within policy-making and the terrorism studies literature of the past five decades.

From an academic research perspective, and if one indeed accepts that it is a distinctive phenomenon within the broad spectrum of political violence, determining what is and what is not terrorism is the starting point that informs many other terrorism theories. It is the foundation upon which all other theories of terrorism rest. How, for example, can we begin to theorize about the causes of terrorism if we haven't agreed what terrorism is? How can we determine why individuals become terrorists or the reasons why groups employ terrorism if we are unclear about what constitutes terrorism? Similarly, the meaning of terrorism is fundamental to theories of disengagement from terrorism, to theories of how terrorism begins and ends, and indeed to counter-terrorism theories. All these theoretical endeavours are dependent on what is meant by terrorism in the first place. So too is any determination as to what is 'terrorist' about a particular Case Study as distinct from insurgency, civil war, guerrilla warfare, and illegal violence in general, for acts of terrorism can take place 'alongside a multitude of other political and criminal acts'. For a list of terrorism related theories and 'approaches' see Schmid, A. (ed.), *The Routledge Handbook of Terrorism Research*, 11–12. It is also integral in attempts to compile chronologies and databases of terrorist incidents in order to determine what acts of violence can and cannot be included in such data-gathering exercises. See, for example, Jenkins, B., 'The Study of Terrorism: Definitional Problems', in Alexander, Y. and Gleason, J., *Behavioural and Quantitative Perspectives on Terrorism*, Pergamon Press, New York and Oxford, 1981, and Schmid, A. (ed.), *The Routledge Handbook of Terrorism Research*, 49. Conceptualizing terrorism, then, importantly and usefully sets the parameters for terrorism research.

One first has to acknowledge, however, that a concrete *definition* that speaks 'truth' is not attainable (Jackson et al., 2011: 119). 'Terrorism', like 'crime', or indeed any other social science concept, is a *social construction* so will forever be a *contested concept*.

KEY CONCEPTS

Social Construction Terrorism, like all social science concepts, is a social construction, meaning that it is something that does on exist in reality, but been created by society and human interaction, and depends on our own interpretation of this idea. This means that there is no concrete truth.

However, this does not mean that there cannot be an agreed conceptualization, even internationally, of terrorism at a given time and context. Yet, even this goal faces challenges. The concept of terrorism has all been employed in common language as a derogatory label, rather than as the outcome of serious analytical scrutiny. As Conor Gearty once remarked, its pejorative connotation has meant that it has become a 'useful insult' (Gearty, 1991: 6).

Terrorism has therefore frequently been associated with particular causes, and, in the context of the Israeli-Palestine conflict in particular, both parties have committed acts of 'terrorism' depending upon which side one sits (see Case Study 4.1: The Israeli/Palestine Conflict). It is often in the context of highly charged and polarized conflict environments that the term continues to be deployed as a rhetorical device to denounce one's enemies.

Rostow remarked that 'the conventional wisdom concludes that the international community will not succeed in this area [of the definition of terrorism] until the conflicts in the Middle East and over Kashmir come to an end' (Rostow, 2002: 489), while Schmid noted that 'the two main issues that obstruct progress are ... "state terrorism" and the "struggle for national liberation"—both of them related to the Palestinian question and to the question of Kashmir' (Schmid, 2004: 389). For context, both India and Pakistan have laid claim to Kashmir since the partition of India in 1947. Tensions have persisted over the region, and it remains a source of conflict, despite the 'line of control' that was agreed in 1972 between Indian administered Kashmir and Pakistan administered Kashmir. It seems therefore, at least in the international policymaking context, that there is little hope of elevating 'terrorism' as an analytical concept for objective analysis above political rhetoric and name-calling.

The subjective use of the term has result in 'little clarity or analytical illumination' (English, 2009: 19). It is in its 'real-world' context, that it is ever more important for the academic community to strive to determine what is *analytically* distinctive about terrorism.

KEY CONCEPTS

Subjectivity Subjectivity is the quality of being based on or influenced by personal feelings, biases, or opinions. In the context of this chapter, it refers to the subjective way that the concept of 'terrorism' has been applied (or not applied).

Beyond the subjective application of 'terrorism', a second fundamental challenge lies in determining the components that should be included in any conceptualization of the phenomenon. Should the motive for terrorism be limited to political goals, or can terrorism be employed for economic or religious objectives too? Should civilian targeting be an integral component (or more broadly 'non-combatant' targeting), or can combatants also be victims of terrorism? Should 'harm' be included as a component rather than 'violence', as harm may be caused or threatened without the use of violence (such as the despatch of anthrax letters) (Shanahan, 2010)? And whatever components one chooses to include, these are themselves socially constructed with their own contested meanings (such as what constitutes 'political' and what counts as a 'civilian target').

KEY CONCEPTS

Components In the context of this chapter, this refers to the challenge of exploring what components should be included in our conceptualization of terrorism.

4.2 LEVELS OF ANALYSIS

The three levels of analysis explored in this section are as follows:

- **Defining terrorism**: the aspiration of achieving a concrete definition of terrorism—the ultimate in analytical endeavour.
- **Conceptualizing terrorism**: rather than being *definitive* this is a less ambitious approach that acknowledges the social construction of terrorism but at the same time seeks to determine what it is that is analytically distinctive about 'terrorism'.
- **Terrorism as merely a pejorative label**: this approach concedes that there is nothing analytically distinctive about terrorism—rather, it has simply been employed as a derogatory label for violence (or causes) that one disagrees with.

As noted in section 4.1, due to its social construction, there can never be the definitive definition of terrorism that speaks truth. Nevertheless, this analytical endeavour has been sought after by generations of scholars and policymakers, dating back to the definitional attempts of the League of Nations (the first global organization who aimed for world peace) in the 1930s. This has primarily been for the purpose of underpinning more effective international counter-terrorism responses against what has been an increasingly international phenomenon. At the national level, legal definitions have been crafted in order to prosecute crimes labelled 'terrorist', but these vary significantly, and are often constructed around the political interests of states (Richards, 2015). There is often a disconnect between academic perspectives (particularly those that seek to draw attention to the social construction of 'terrorism' and that may refrain from being *definitive*) and state perspectives that require definitions for legal precision and certainty (Golder and Williams, 2004: 272).

A second level of analysis steers clear of attempts at being *definitive* about what terrorism means, but rather seeks to *conceptualize* the phenomenon. This softer approach implicitly acknowledges that a concrete definition is not achievable but that there is something analytically distinctive about terrorism that is worth theorizing about. The key question then is to determine where this distinctiveness lies, and then to consider how this can be captured in a conceptualization of terrorism.

> **KEY CONCEPTS**
>
> **Conceptualizing** In the context of this chapter, this refers to the endeavour to form a clear idea of terrorism, as an alternative to *defining* terrorism.

A third level of analysis to consider is that there is nothing distinctive about terrorism as a form of political violence, and that there is therefore little to theorize about. This line of argument is that 'terrorism' is simply a derogatory label for violence that is not qualitatively different to other forms of political violence, with the term's use designed to delegitimize the violence, and the cause one disagrees with or, historically, those who have threatened the status quo. Michael Blain considers that 'the invention of a discourse of terrorism was a strategic response to danger, and could be deployed through basic regulatory practices of subjection' (Blain, 2007: 50–51). This resonates with contemporary critical approaches that argue that 'the accepted knowledge of the field . . . functions ideologically to reinforce and reify existing structures of power within society, particularly that of the state' (Jackson et al., 2009: 67) (see Chapter 3 for coverage of 'Critical Terrorism Studies', or CTS).

It is the second level of analysis, one that deals with conceptualizing terrorism, that this chapter explores. The next section will argue that, notwithstanding its social construction, there is something analytically distinctive about terrorism that is worth theorizing about.

KEY CONCEPTS

Analytical Analytical in general terms means using logical or systematic reasoning and examining things in detail in order to discover more about them. In the context of this chapter, this refers specifically to the endeavour to be analytical about the method of terrorism that we are seeking to conceptualize.

Most terrorism scholars see 'terrorism' as a distinctive phenomenon worthy of study—evidenced by the popularity of university terrorism studies courses. To clarify the conceptualization of terrorism in this chapter is: the use of violence or force or the threat of violence or force, with the primary purpose of generating a psychological impact beyond the immediate victims or object of attack for a political motive.

4.3 TERRORISM AS A METHOD

A key challenge for any such conceptual endeavour has been the inclination, in the public and political spheres, to apply the term 'terrorism' (or refrain from applying it) according to one's perspective on the cause. The more that one is inclined to employ the term 'terrorism' because of opposition to the goal, however, or the more that one prefers *not* to use it because of sympathy with the cause, then the further away we are from viewing terrorism as an analytical concept (that can be dispassionately applied). It is the method of terrorism that we are seeking to analyse here, and this should not be swayed by one's personal perspective on the cause.

Terrorism should, therefore, in keeping with what has been one area of consensus on the definitional issue within the academic literature of the past five decades, be conceptualized as a particular *method* of violence, rather than according to who the perpetrators are, or what the cause is. For example, Schmid, in 1983, suggested that 'terrorism is a method of combat in which random or symbolic victims become targets of violence . . .' and aptly makes no reference as to who carries out this 'method of combat' (Schmid, 1983: 111), and Cooper argues that we 'can no longer afford the fiction that one person's terrorist is another's freedom fighter. Fighting for freedom may well be an individual's purpose, but if the mission is undertaken through the employment of terrorist means, a terrorist they must remain' (Cooper in Griset and Mahan, 2003: 59). Crenshaw also makes the point that 'the identity of the actor does not matter to the specification of the method' (Crenshaw, 2011: 4).

As Richards noted (2014: 225–226), there have been ideologies and causes that are themselves violent (such as those of ISIS and al-Qaeda) but these cannot claim ownership of terrorism, because the latter has been carried out in the name of many causes that are not inherently violent (such as nationalism, animal rights and anti-abortion). In other words, if one aims to capture all forms of terrorism, whether carried out for a violent or a nonviolent ideology, then central to any conceptualization must be an understanding of terrorism as a *method*. This 'method' does not allude to the particular types of violence employed. Rather, it refers to the use of violence (whatever form that violence might take), or the threat of violence, in order to generate a psychological impact beyond the immediate victims. This may then prompt us to consider what the distinction is between terrorism and psychological warfare, or to contemplate terrorism as a form of psychological warfare. For further discussion on this see Richards, 2015, chapter 8.

Understanding terrorism as a method of political violence not only allows us to appreciate that it has been carried out for a variety of different ideologies (both violent and nonviolent), but that it has also been employed by various actors: such as states, guerrilla movements, extreme fringes of social movements, individuals and small groups of collaborators, as well as by terrorist organizations themselves.

Viewing terrorism in this way enhances the prospects for greater analytical illumination. For example, the mantra of 'one person's freedom fighter is another's terrorist', as Leonard Weinberg observed (Weinberg, 2005: 2), confuses the goal with the activity and obscures analytical scrutiny of the activity or method that we are focusing on. So too does the question posed as to whether the late President Nelson Mandela 'was a terrorist or a freedom fighter'. If Mandela, as a member of the Spear of Destiny, carried out acts of violence that satisfy one's criteria for determining them as acts of terrorism, *then acts of terrorism they remain*, notwithstanding the cause and the fact that he went on to become an admired global leader. Using 'terrorism' here would not be a disparaging judgement, but rather the outcome of dispassionate analysis. Again, subject to one's conceptual criteria, any terrorism carried out by the French resistance against Nazi occupation might be viewed by many as terrorism for a good cause (i.e. from an 'allied powers' perspective). In other words, searching for alternative 'positive' labels for the same activity serves to undermine analytical progress on the issue.

CASE STUDY 4.1

The Israeli/Palestine Conflict

In May 1948 Israel declared its independence and this was followed by the Arab-Israeli war. After initial Arab successes, the Israelis achieved military victory and in the process expanded their territory into areas that were beyond what the United Nations had previously envisioned in a partitionist settlement. The war prompted the departure of hundreds of thousands of Palestinians who were to become refugees in the West Bank, the Gaza Strip, Jordan, Lebanon, and Syria. In 1959 Fatah (the Palestinian nationalist social democratic political party) was formed to take up the Palestinian cause, both to pursue a national homeland, and also to represent the plight of the refugees. In 1964 the Palestinian Liberation Organization (PLO) emerged and brought together an amalgamation of Palestinian groups. The Six Day War that

PHOTO 4.2 The Gaza Strip (or simply Gaza) is a self-governing Palestinian territory on the Eastern coast of the Mediterranean Sea.

took place from the 5th to the 10th June 1967 saw the Israeli defeat of Egypt, Syria, and Jordan (and the acquisition of the Sinai peninsula, the Gaza Strip (see Photo 4.2), the West Bank, East Jerusalem, and the Golan Heights), and prompted the departure of many more thousands who found themselves under Israeli control. In 1969 Yasir Arafat, who became the symbolic figurehead of the Palestinian struggle, was elected its chairman. It is in this context that Arafat declared that those fighting for national liberation could not possibly be called terrorists.

In 1972 the most devastating attack ever to have hit the Olympics took place in Munich, where eleven Israeli athletes were killed by a Palestinian organization known as Black September (see also Photo 2.1, Chapter 2). Its impact was magnified by the fact that the event was broadcast live on TV to a watching audience of many millions. Even in the highly charged international environment following the attack, there were difficulties in generating an agreed definition of terrorism in order to mount a unified international response to it. The then Secretary General of the United Nations, Kurt Waldheim, in his efforts to encourage member states to agree to the need for 'measures to prevent terrorist and other forms of violence which endanger or take human lives or jeopardize fundamental freedoms', was confronted by deep concern from some African and Arab states that those engaged in legitimate national liberation struggles would be depicted as terrorists (Wardlaw, 1990: 105). And Syria shortly afterwards argued that 'the international community is under legal and moral obligation to promote the struggle for liberation and to resist any attempt to depict this struggle as synonymous with terrorism and illegitimate violence' (Hoffman, 2002: 16).

There has been a stalemate brought about between those that see certain acts of violence as terrorism, and those that prefer not to use the term to describe the activities of 'independence movements and the legitimate defence of land under foreign occupation' (Dartnell, 1999: 199). This was, for example, the view of the Iranian government (cited in Dartnell). The inclination to associate terrorism or 'freedom fighting' with one cause or another, or with one perpetrator or another, deflects us from our analytical endeavour in focusing on terrorism as a method independent from the cause.

QUESTIONS

1. To what extent is a universally agreed conceptualization of terrorism needed in order to respond effectively to terrorism?
2. Does the Israeli/Palestine conflict demonstrate that an agreed conceptualization of terrorism is likely to remain beyond the grasp of the international community?

As Richards noted (2014: 225), Yasir Arafat was wrong when he declared that:

> 'The difference between the revolutionary and the terrorist lies in the reason for which each fights. For whoever stands by a just cause and fights for the freedom and liberation of his land from the invaders, the settlers and the colonialists, cannot possibly be called a terrorist . . .' (cited in Hoffman, 1998: 26).

The difference between the 'terrorist' and the 'non-terrorist' *does not* lie in the reason for which one fights, as Arafat claimed. National liberation is a cause, and terrorism is a method. Otherwise, we are conceding that terrorism really is 'violence that we don't like' (or whose cause we disagree with) and that there is therefore nothing particularly unique or qualitatively distinctive about the phenomenon compared with other forms of political violence. As Schmid maintains, the mantra of 'one man's terrorist is another man's freedom fighter' is also an 'open invitation to maintain and perpetuate double standards' (Schmid, 2011: 40). Yet, unfortunately, in practice the 'right to self-determination' and terrorism have still not been 'decoupled' and the freedom fighter/terrorist mantra continues to endure (Schmid, 2011: 50). For example (cited on p. 92, footnote 57, in Schmid, 2011), the Organization of the Islamic Conference argued for the 'exclusion of acts done in the pursuance of liberation struggles' and proposed that 'Peoples' struggle including armed struggle against foreign occupation, aggression, colonialism, and hegemony, aimed at liberation and self-determination in accordance with the principles of international law shall not be considered a terrorist crime'.

CASE STUDY 4.2

Subjective Interpretations of Terrorism

A major challenge for students and researchers seeking to generate a universally agreed conceptualization of terrorism is that states tend to interpret 'terrorism' according to their perceived interests. The Policy Working Group on the United Nations and Terrorism, for example, cautioned that:

> 'The rubric of counter-terrorism can be used to justify acts in support of political agendas, such as the consolidation of political power, elimination of political opponents, inhibition of legitimate dissent and/or suppression of resistance to military occupation. Labelling opponents or adversaries as terrorists offers a time-tested technique to de-legitimize and demonize them' (quoted in Schmid, 2011: 56).

Saul also remarked that:

> 'Some States have deployed the international legitimacy conferred by [the UN Security] Council authorization to define terrorism to repress or de-legitimize political opponents, and to conflate them with Al Qaeda . . . Thus China bluntly characterizes Uighur separatists in Xingjiang as terrorists; . . . and India seldom distinguishes militants from terrorists in Kashmir. In Indonesia, insurgencies in Aceh and West Papua have been described and combated as terrorism, as have a Maoist insurgency in Nepal and an Islamist movement in Morocco. Israel has compared Palestinians with Al Qaeda, with Ariel Sharon calling Arafat "our Bin Laden". . . . In the Maldives, an opposition politician was convicted of terrorism offences and sentenced to ten years imprisonment for peacefully protesting against rights violations by the government. . . . Similarly, in Uzbekistan 15 men were convicted of vague terrorism offences for organizing public demonstrations, at which the government indiscriminately fired upon the crowd' (Saul, 2007: 201–202).

Under the Law of Terrorism Crimes and Financing, which came into force in 2014, Saudi Arabia defines terrorism as any act that is 'directly or indirectly intended to disturb the public order of the state, or to destabilize the security of society, or the stability of the state, or to expose its national unity to danger, or to suspend the basic law of governance or some of its articles, or to insult the reputation of the state or its standing, or to inflict damage upon one of its public utilities or its natural resources.'

While interpretations as to what 'destabilizes the state' may be very broad, the most contentious element of this definition is that it includes 'insulting the reputation of the state or its standing'. The UN Human Rights Council's Special Rapporteur on the Promotion and Protection of Human Rights While Countering Terrorism argued that this definition is so broad that 'anyone challenging the authority or policies of the state could qualify as a terrorist' (Emmerson, 2018: 5).

A good example in practice of the selective application of 'terrorism' is the United States' endeavour to support the Northern Alliance in Afghanistan against the Taliban. In the aftermath of 9/11 US Defence Secretary Donald Rumsfeld was quoted as saying that 'there are any number of people in Afghanistan - tribes in the south, the northern alliance in the north—that oppose the Taliban . . . And clearly we need to recognize the value they bring to this anti-terrorist, anti-Taliban effort and, where appropriate, find ways to assist them' (*New York Times*, 1st October 2001). Yet, the Northern Alliance itself had been noted for committing many acts that might themselves be defined as acts of 'terrorism' or 'terror' (depending on one's definitions). According to Human Rights Watch:

> 'Abuses committed by factions belonging to the United Front [formerly the Northern Alliance] have been well documented. . . . including summary executions, burning of houses, and looting, principally targeting ethnic Pashtuns and others suspected of supporting the Taliban . . . Several of the executions were reportedly carried out in front of members of the victims' families. . .' (Human Rights Watch, 2001: 3–4).

The point is that states have often practised double standards when deciding who are terrorists and what constitutes terrorism. The absence of a common understanding as to 'what terrorism is' facilitates this (Schmid, 2004: 379). It may serve strategic interests to sponsor or support terrorism against one's adversaries, and there may indeed be 'terrorisms' that one might sympathize with against certain regimes, providing non-combatants are not targeted. Few policymakers would concede that they are endorsing *terrorism*, such is the stigma attached to the term—as such 'governments characteristically define "terrorism" as something only their opponents can commit' (Held, 2004: 62).

QUESTIONS

1. Given the tendency to define and apply the term terrorism according to one's national interests, is it sensible to abandon attempts to achieve a universally agreed conceptualization of terrorism?
2. Given the obstacles, what prospects does 'terrorism' have as an analytical concept?

4.4 COMPONENTS IN A CONCEPTUALIZATION OF TERRORISM

Alongside the subjective application of 'terrorism', a major challenge is to determine the components that should be included in any conceptualization of the phenomenon. Thus far it has been argued that there are two elements in particular that are fundamental to our understanding of terrorism:

- Firstly, terrorism entails generating a psychological impact beyond the immediate victims, that the target serves as a message generator to a wider audience who are the real target of attention.
- Secondly, terrorism should be viewed as a *method* (rather than conceptualized as a phenomenon that is inherent to any particular cause or perpetrator).

This is not to suggest that there cannot be ideologies where terrorism and violence are intrinsic to them but to reiterate, for conceptual purposes, our understanding of terrorism should not be confined to these—it has also been carried out in pursuit of ideologies that are not inherently violent.

These may not be the most obvious components for many in any conceptualization of terrorism (such as the use or threat of violence or force, or the political motive), but they are integral to differentiate terrorism from other forms of political violence (such as political assassinations, guerrilla warfare, insurgencies or indeed warfare in general). The following subsections briefly consider further components that could be included. The formidable nature of this task is no better exemplified than in Schmid and Jongman's efforts to formulate an 'academic consensus' definition, which ultimately contained no less than sixteen components (Schmid and Jongman, 2008: 28).

Students should also consider that these elements *are themselves disputed concepts* whose parameters are far from clear. What, for example, do we understand by the term 'violence'? Does it include poisoning or the contamination of products, or spraying slogans on a wall? Does it include so-called 'structural violence', a term used to encompass injustices that breed inequality? For a discussion on structural violence see Johan Galtung's landmark work: 'Violence, Peace, and Peace Research', *Journal of Peace Research*, Volume 6, No. 3, 1979. See also Galtung's work on cultural violence: 'Cultural Violence', *Journal of Peace Research*, Volume 27, No. 3, 1990. Also, what are the parameters of 'political', and how do we disentangle the 'political' from the 'religious', the 'economic' or the 'cultural'? While addressing these questions is beyond the remit of this chapter, it is important to note that such components are themselves highly contested.

4.4.1 Violence and the threat of violence

One feature that is commonly associated with terrorism is the use of, or threat of, violence or force. Schmid and Jongman, in their survey of 109 definitions found that the use of the words 'violence' or 'force' appeared in 83.5 per cent of them (Schmid and Jongman, 2008: 5). It is interesting, given the often pejorative use of the term terrorism, that the word 'force' (which is arguably a less emotive term than 'violence') is also included in many definitions. There may be some merit in this—if, for example, we are not to exclude terrorism by the state in any general conceptualization, and if we are to circumvent the inevitably complex debate as to the extent that a state's use of force might constitute terrorism, then the word one could argue that 'force' should indeed be included. There might, for example, be states who have used what they view to be their legal and rightful recourse to employ force that might from others' perspectives be viewed as the *violence* of 'state terrorism' or 'state terror'. As David Claridge remarked 'separating acts that are intended to protect from those that are intended to coerce' can be 'an increasingly challenging task' and that the 'area between legitimate use of force and violent abuse' is a murky one (Claridge, 1996: 49, see also Arendt, 1970).

While 'violence' and the 'the threat of violence' can reasonably be included in any conceptualization of terrorism, there is no universal agreement as to what is meant by violence. *The Oxford English Dictionary* (OED) defines it as 'behaviour involving *physical force* intended to hurt, damage, or kill someone or something' (italics added). Yet, for many, as long as there is the intent or threat to 'hurt, damage or kill' then many acts that do not involve 'physical force' (which is integral to the OED definition of violence) can nevertheless surely be classified as terrorism. It has therefore been proposed that rather than 'violence or the threat of violence' we should instead include, more broadly, 'harm or the threat of harm'. Shannon makes a convincing case for this:

> 'Rather, what matters for 'terrorism' is *harm* or the threat of harm . . . This can be seen by considering cases of terrorism that involve harm but no violence per se. For example, in November 2001, letters containing anthrax spores were mailed to select US news outlets and members of the US Senate. Five people died and seventeen people fell ill from the spores. The news media, following the US government, uniformly described this as a terrorist act, despite the fact that it involved no violence or force' (Shanahan, 2010).

Here, however, one is in danger of labelling any 'direct action' that is intended to cause harm as terrorism, including, for example, vandalism and the daubing of graffiti. Though graffiti can be used as the means to convey a threat of violence which, if credible, could satisfy many definitions of terrorism. This links in to a further discussion as to how *serious* an act of harm or violence has to be to be considered terrorism, and the extent to which, for example, attacks on property should be included in any such conceptualization. However, for the purpose of this chapter we will retain the word 'violence' rather than 'harm'—not least because 'harm' can include a wide range of activity that one wouldn't necessarily refer to as terrorism.

4.4.2 Political motive

Beyond the core element of the 'use of violence or force or the threat of violence or force' terrorism has widely been viewed as being carried out for a *political purpose*. Hoffman has argued that terrorism is ineluctably political (Hoffman, 1998: 43). But does the act of violence or its threat have to be politically motivated to be labelled an act of terrorism? For example, the title of Grant Wardlaw's book *Political Terrorism* implies that there are other forms of (non-political) terrorism (Wardlaw, 1990). Schmid has suggested that 'there are non-political forms of terrorism (such as criminal or psychopathological terrorism) although 'the political motivation of terrorism is one that is often present and stressed by analysts and even more so by terrorists themselves' (Schmid, 2004: 200).

For Schmid, terrorism could be carried out by a psychopath with little or no political motive, or indeed by criminals engaged in organized crime (even if such acts do ultimately have political ramifications). One can suggest, however, that if an act of violence is carried out by a psychopath without a political motive, then this is not an act of terrorism. Nor is an act of violence carried out for private economic gain—for example, in cases of violence or the threat of violence associated with organized crime. Although organized criminals have at times sought to secure political influence through the threat and use of violence in order to protect their illicit interests.

The UK's Terrorism Act 2000 interpreted the motivations for terrorism as including its use for the purpose of advancing a political, religious or *ideological cause*, which is very broad. One might suggest that an act of terrorism could be carried out by an *individual* through purely religious conviction without any political motive, but even here it can be difficult to disentangle political motive from religious, especially if at the 'group level' (on behalf of whom the attack may have taken place) there are clear political goals. The distinction between the motivation of the group and of the individual is an important one to make. See, for example, Gressang, 2001: 93. For a further discussion see Richards, 2015, chapter 9.

4.4.3 Civilian targeting?

For those who define or conceptualize terrorism as entailing attacks on 'civilians' and/or 'non-combatants', there are real challenges in determining what the parameters of these categories are. For example, do civilians include politicians who have key security related decision-making roles in the relevant theatre of conflict? Are those who supply and deliver food, or who manufacture and/or deliver equipment, to armed forces to be considered any less civilian than others? Are there degrees of innocence and should distinctions be made between categories of civilian (for a discussion on this see Tiefenbrun, 2003: 363)—for example between those civilians going about their daily routines in their own homelands (i.e. prior to the 9/11, London 2005 and Madrid 2004 attacks, or, more recently, the November 2015 attacks in Paris and the 2017 attacks in the UK) and those engaged in business contracts in post-conflict zones? Are 'settler' civilians who take up arms within 'disputed' or 'occupied' territory still to be considered civilian?

If terrorism is more broadly conceptualized as targeting 'non-combatants' then who and what constitutes a non-combatant target? Schmid has suggested that military personnel are non-combatants for as long as they are outside a war zone (Schmid, 2011: 46). But does this mean that armed peacekeeping troops in such zones are combatants? Alternatively, were armed military patrols in Northern Ireland during the Troubles non-combatants? For discussions on the Northern Ireland conflict see Case Studies in Chapters 14 and 22. Again, for those who hold to a victim-based approach (that views terrorism as targeting non-combatants) the distinction between combatant and non-combatant is an important one because it determines whether or not an act of violence then constitutes terrorism.

For the purpose of the United States National Counterterrorism Centre World Incidents Tracking System (of terrorist incidents) combatants and non-combatants were defined as the following:

> 'the term "combatant" was interpreted to mean military, paramilitary, militia, and police under military command and control, in specific areas or regions where war zones or war-like settings exist. . . . Non-combatants therefore included civilians and civilian police and military assets outside of war zones and warlike settings. Diplomatic assets, including personnel, embassies, consulates, and other facilities, were also considered non-combatant targets' (NCC, US, 2006).

Thus, 'non-combatant' has been used to refer to both civilians and 'military personnel (whether or not armed or on duty) who are not deployed in a war zone or a war-like setting' (US State Department, quoted in Schmid, 2011: 46) or 'as unarmed or off-duty military personnel or military units stationed in areas where the armed conflict is absent' (US State Department, quoted in European Commission Sixth Framework Programme Project, 2008: 25). Thus, those who define non-combatant in this way and who conceive of terrorism as targeting non-combatants are able to conceptualize acts of violence against military targets in peacetime settings as terrorism, including, for example, the attack on the USS Cole in October 2000 (see discussion and further commentary on the use of the terms 'combatant' and 'non-combatant' in Schmid, 2011: 46–48).

If, however, one takes the view that terrorism can be carried out against *anybody*, including combatants (For a discussion on this see Richards, 2014: 226–229), deliberations as to who or what constitutes a 'civilian' or a 'non-combatant' become less relevant in our conceptual deliberations. Providing the primary intention is to generate a psychological impact beyond the immediate victims, and subject to other conceptual criteria, one can argue that acts of terrorism can be carried out against anybody—whether they be civilians, non-combatants or combatants.

A brief survey of Easson and Schmid's 250 definitions of terrorism endorses the view that terrorism is not just carried out against civilians or non-combatants. In fact, most of the definitions in their compilation do not make explicit reference to civilians or non-combatants as being victims (approximately 70 of the 250 refer to 'civilian,' 'non-combatant,' or 'innocent' victims) (Schmid, 2011, chapter 2).

4.5 CONCLUSION

This chapter demonstrates some of the challenges in determining which elements should be included in any conceptualization of terrorism. Six elements in particular have been identified for inclusion: i) the intent to generate a psychological impact beyond the immediate victims, ii) the use of violence or force or the threat of violence or force, iii) the political motive, iv) that terrorism should be considered as a particular *method* of political violence, v) that (implicitly) anybody can be a victim (including combatants). Hence the following conceptualization: terrorism is the use of violence or force or the threat of violence or force with the primary purpose of generating a psychological impact beyond the immediate victims or object of attack for a political motive. One might plausibly argue from this conceptualization that terrorism is a form of psychological warfare although, rather than being synonymous with the latter, terrorism might be considered as a distinctive subset of this much broader phenomenon, for example, psychological warfare does not necessarily entail the use or threat of force or violence at all. It has, for example, been defined as 'psychological activities in peace or war, directed at the enemy, friendly and neutral audiences in order to influence attitudes and behaviour affecting the achievement of political and military objectives' (Taylor, P., quoted in Schmid, 2005: 141–142).

This chapter has argued that there is something analytically distinctive about terrorism that is worth theorizing about—that it is not simply political violence that one disagrees with. One of the great challenges in trying to infuse some analytical quality into the concept, however, has been the subjective application of the term—the tendency to employ it as a 'useful insult' or to avoid using it at all according to what one's perspective on the cause is—at the expense of a more neutral analytical approach. We have explored how terrorism should be conceptualized as a particular method of violence and if an act of violence or force (or its threat) satisfies one's criteria to be called an act of terrorism, then an act of terrorism it remains regardless of the cause. It is this dispassionate approach that is likely to enhance the prospects for terrorism as an analytical concept.

DISCUSSION QUESTIONS

1. Is there any point in striving for a universally agreed conceptualization of terrorism?
2. What have been the main difficulties in achieving this?
3. To what extent does the failure to craft a universally agreed conceptualization of terrorism hinder counter-terrorism responses?
4. Is terrorism really a distinctive form of political violence?
5. How would you conceptualize terrorism?

Visit the online resources for pointers on how to answer the discussion questions, links to useful web sources, and guidance on accessing databases:
www.oup.com/he/Wilson-Muro1e

GUIDE TO FURTHER READING

Carlile, A. (2007) *The Definition of Terrorism*, available at: https://www.gov.uk/government/publications/the-definition-of-terrorism-a-report-by-lord-carlile-of-berriew (last accessed 14 June 2021).

Jackson, R. (2011) 'In defence of "terrorism": finding a way through a forest of misconceptions', *Behavioural Sciences of Terrorism and Political Aggression*, 3: 2. *This article argues that, while there are grounds for dispensing with 'terrorism' (not least due to its social construction), there are a number of reasons for retaining it as a research concept.*

Richards, A. (2015) *Conceptualizing Terrorism*. Oxford:Oxford University Press. *This is a monograph published by the author of this chapter that explores the prospect for 'terrorism' as an analytical concept (this is also discussed in an article version of the book in Richards, A. (2014), 'Conceptualizing Terrorism', Studies in Conflict and Terrorism, 37: 3).*

Schmid, A. (2004) 'Terrorism – The Definitional Problem', *Case Western Reserve Journal of International Law*, 36: 2-3. *Schmid has made a major contribution to the definitional literature and this piece is an excellent starting point on the subject.*

Schmid, A., (2011) (ed.) *The Routledge Handbook of Terrorism Research*. London and New York: Routlege. *This is a valuable source that provides comprehensive coverage of many of the conceptual debates around terrorism.*

Weinberg, L., Pedahzur, A., and Hirsch-Hoefler, S. (2004) 'The Challenges of Conceptualising Terrorism', *Terrorism and Political Violence*, 16: 4. *This article explores the reasons as to why a widely agreed definition has proved elusive before contemplating a potential consensus definition of terrorism.*

REFERENCES

Arendt, H. (1970) *On Violence*. Houghton Miffin: Harcourt Publishing.

Blain, M., (2007) 'On the Genealogy of Terrorism', in Staines, D. (ed.), *Interrogating the War on Terror: Interdisciplinary Perspectives*. Newcastle (UK): Cambridge Scholars Publishing.

Claridge, D. (1996) 'State Terrorism? Applying a Definitional Model', *Terrorism and Political Violence*, 8 (3).

Crenshaw, M. (2011) *Explaining Terrorism, Causes, Processes and Consequences*. Routledge.

Dartnell, M. (1999) 'A legal inter-network for terrorism: Issues of globalization, fragmentation and legitimacy', *Terrorism and Political Violence*, 11 (4).

Emmerson, B. (2018) 'Report of the Special Rapporteur on the promotion and protection of human rights and fundamental freedoms while countering terrorism—Mission to Saudi Arabia' (A/HRC/40/52/Add.2).

English, R. (2009) *Terrorism, How to Respond*. Oxford: Oxford University Press.

European Commission Sixth Framework Programme Project (2008) 'Defining Terrorism' (WP3 Deliverable 4).

Gearty, C. (1991) *Terror*. London: Faber and Faber.

Golder, B. and Williams, G. (2004) 'What is Terrorism – Problems of Legal Definition', *University of New South Wales Law Journal*, 27: 2.

Gressang IV, D. (2001) 'Audience and Message: Assessing Terrorist WMD Potential', *Terrorism and Political Violence*, 13 (3).

Griset, P. and Mahan, S. (2003) *Terrorism in Perspective*. Thousand Oaks (California) and London: Sage.

Held, V. (2004) 'Terrorism and War', *The Journal of Ethics*, 8.

Hoffman, B. (1998) *Inside Terrorism*. Columbia: Columbia University Press.

Hoffman, B. (2002) 'Defining Terrorism', in Howard, R. and Sawyer, R. (eds.), *Terrorism and Counterterrorism, Understanding the New Security Environment, Readings and Interpretations*. London: McGraw-Hill.

Human Rights Watch (2001) 'Military Assistance to the Afghan Opposition', 3–4, available at: http://www.hrw.org/legacy/backgrounder/asia/afghan-bck1005.pdf (last accessed 14 June 2021).

Jackson, R. (2009) 'Knowledge, power and politics in the study of political terrorism', in Jackson, R.,

Breen Smyth, M., and Gunning, J. (eds.), *Critical Terrorism Studies*. London: Routledge.

Jackson, R., Jarvis, L., Gunning, J., and Breen Smyth, M. (2011) *Terrorism, A Critical Introduction*. London: Palgrave Macmillan.

Levitt, G. (1986) 'Is Terrorism Worth Defining?', *Ohio Northern University Law Review*, 13: 1.

Richards, A. (2015) *Conceptualizing Terrorism*. Oxford: Oxford University Press.

Richards, A. (2014) 'Conceptualizing Terrorism', *Studies in Conflict and Terrorism*, 37 (3).

Rostow, N. (2002) 'Before and After: The Changed UN Response to Terrorism since September 11, *Cornell International Law Journal*, 35: 3.

Saul, B. (2006) *Defining Terrorism in International Law*. Oxford: Oxford University Press.

Saul, B. (2007) 'Defining Terrorism to Protect Human Rights', in Staines, D. (ed.), *Interrogating the War on Terror: Interdisciplinary Perspectives*. Newcastle (UK): Cambridge Scholars Publishing.

Schmid, A. (1983) *Political Terrorism: A Research Guide to Concepts, Theories, Data Bases and Literature*. New Brunswick: Transaction.

Schmid, A. (1992) 'The Response Problem as a Definition Problem', *Terrorism and Political Violence*, 4 (4).

Schmid, A. (2004) 'Terrorism – The Definitional Problem', *Case Western Reserve Journal of International Law*, 36: 2–3.

Schmid, A. (2005) 'Terrorism as Psychological Warfare', *Democracy and Security*, no. 1.

Schmid, A. (2011) (ed.) *The Routledge Handbook of Terrorism Research*. London and New York: Routledge.

Schmid, A. and Jongman, A. (2008) *Political Terrorism*. Transaction Books.

Shanahan, T. (2010) 'Betraying a Certain Corruption of Mind: How (and how not) to Define "Terrorism"', *Critical Studies on Terrorism*, 3 (2).

Tiefenbrun, S. (2003) 'A Semiotic Approach to a Legal Definition of Terrorism', *ILSA Journal of International and Comparative Law*, 9: 2.

Wardlaw, G. (1990) *Political Terrorism*. Cambridge: Cambridge University Press.

Weinberg, L. (2005) *Global Terrorism, A Beginner's Guide*. Oneworld.

CHAPTER 5

Terrorism in Context

ADRIAN GUELKE

■ CHAPTER SUMMARY

Generalization about terrorism is difficult. An agreed definition of the concept remains an elusive quest (see Chapters 2 and 4 for more). Terrorism has been most commonly used to describe violence from below directed at the power of the state. That has been the dominant usage during the last century and a half through successive waves of terrorism. But the form that such violence takes has varied widely so that terrorism has had multiple meanings across time and in different contexts. Context remains crucial to the development of an understanding of terrorism in its many manifestations, as this chapter seeks to demonstrate.

5.1 INTRODUCTION

The purpose of this chapter is to explain why establishing generalizations about terrorism is difficult, despite the efforts of scholars to pin down the concept. Lack of clarity on what terrorism encompasses limits what quantitative analysis on the occurrence of terrorist incidents at a global level can achieve, and explains in part the prevalence of qualitative case studies in this field. As we have established in Chapter 2, the study of terrorism cuts across a number of disciplines, including law, history, and the social sciences. But the focus of this chapter is on the study of the subject largely from the perspective of Comparative Politics and International Relations. Due regard will be paid to historical circumstance as that remains of profound importance to an understanding of a concept that has undergone a number of changes of meaning. Indeed, a significant theme of this chapter will be explaining the circumstances in which these changes have occurred. The chapter will underline the difficulty of attaching a fixed meaning to a concept that has been employed in a variety of contrasting political contexts.

Terror, terrorist, terrorism, and their variants in other languages are commonly used terms in public discourse. Read news coverage anywhere in the world, and it is likely that one or other of these words will be found in the text. That has not always been the case. The employment of these terms in virtually daily usage dates back to the late 1960s during the onset of the 'age of terrorism', as it was widely referred to, until that description was superseded by the Global War on Terror following the September 11th attacks on the US in 2001. But if the regular use of these terms in a variety of forms and combinations is a product of a little more than the last half a century, the terms themselves were far from novel at the beginning of this period. Indeed, coinage of the terms can be traced as far back as the French revolution at the end of the 18th century. Admittedly, its meaning then used to refer to the most repressive actions of the state, and bore little relationship to the types of violence to which the term terrorism has primarily come to be applied to, that is, political violence from below directed at existing power structures, (particularly the state).

5.1.1 Normative shift

The most significant change that has taken place in the use of the term terrorism is a normative one. Terrorism has come to mean absolutely illegitimate violence. That is reflected in the disappearance of the use of the term terrorist as a self-identification. Put simply, individuals engaged in a campaign of violence against political authority do not describe themselves as terrorists.

> **KEY CONCEPTS**
>
> **Normative** Normative refers to the established social 'norms' which designate some actions or outcomes as good. It is commonly used in the context of behaviour.

What may surprise students is that people **did** self-identify as terrorists in previous centuries. Boris Savinkov was a member of the combat organization of the Socialist Revolutionary Party in Russia at the start of the 20th century. In 1906 he was sentenced to death for his involvement in the assassinations of the Russian Minister of Interior and of Grand Duke Alexandrovich. He escaped from custody and went on to serve in the Kerensky government following the February 1917 revolution. In the same year an account of his exploits as a terrorist were published in Russia. An English edition of the book was published in 1931, with the title, *Memoirs of a Terrorist* (Savinkov, 1931). Geulah Cohen joined the militant group, Lehi, which was better known as the Stern Gang, in mandatory Palestine in 1943. Among the actions carried out by the group were high-level assassinations. They included the killing of Lord Moyne, the British minister of state for the Middle East, in November 1944 and that of Count Folke Bernadotte, the UN's mediator in the Arab-Israeli war, in September 1948. Cohen's account of her experiences in Lehi was first published in Hebrew. A translation was published in English in 1966 as *Woman of Violence: Memoirs of a Young Terrorist, 1943–1948* (Cohen, 1966).

At the time of the English publication of Cohen's memoirs, it was still possible to view terrorism as a tactic that might be compared for its utility to others that those seeking revolutionary change might pursue, such as rural guerrilla warfare or urban insurrection. Within a few years, terrorism came to be viewed very differently. As a consequence, the difference between guerrilla warfare and terrorism was no longer seen simply as the pursuit of different tactics, but as distinct normatively. Guerrilla was perceived as a relatively neutral description, as were terms such as insurgent or rebel. By the time that Doris Lessing's novel, *The Good Terrorist*, was published in 1985, the association of terrorism with morally completely unacceptable violence was well established (Lessing, 1985). The title was an oxymoron and widely recognized as such in reviews of the book. While terrorism continued to be seen as involving at the least the threat of lethal violence, what had fundamentally changed were the perceived targets of terrorists. These were no longer high-level members of political or security establishments or symbolic figures such as royalty, but ordinary members of the public. The event that provided the inspiration for Lessing's novel illustrates the change. This was the bombing of Harrods, a department store in London, in December 1983. Six people were killed and 90 injured in the attack.

So well established was the connection between terrorism and threats to the lives of the general public that by this stage such attacks had come to typify terrorism. The association had been forged much earlier by the episodes that had marked the onset of the age of terrorism in the late 1960s. These were the hijackings of commercial airliners by Palestinian groups. In the course of the hijackings, the passengers were taken hostage and their safety used as a bargaining chip to secure the release of Palestinian prisoners in Israel. The hijacking of aircraft was by no means a novel tactic. A spate of hijackings of commercial jets had taken place to and from Cuba in the early 1960s. But they had been condemned as air piracy rather than terrorism, in part because the perpetrators were intent on forcing a change to the plane's destination and did not directly threaten the lives of the passengers. The subsequent use of commercial airliners as aerial bombs causing the deaths of all aboard the flight, as well as others on the ground, represented a different, even more extreme use of hijacking as a method of violence. The scale of the September 11th attacks on the US in 2001 were to provide the basis of further modification of what the term terrorism encompassed.

CASE STUDY 5.1

The Destruction of Khotso House

On 31st August–1st September 1988, Khotso House in the centre of Johannesburg, South Africa, was destroyed by a massive explosive blast. The bomb injured 19 people in the vicinity of the building, but no one was killed. Khotso House was the headquarters of the South African Council of Churches (SACC). The building had also contained the national offices of the United Democratic Front (UDF), an umbrella organization for a number of civil society groups opposed to apartheid, before the government restricted its activities in February 1988. Prior to its banning, the UDF had been aligned ideologically to the outlawed African National Congress (ANC). As recounted in the report of the Truth and Reconciliation Commission (TRC), this attack, along with a number of others, such as the bombing of the offices of the Congress of South African Trade Unions (COSATU) in May 1987, was carried out by members of the security police acting on explicit instructions from the State Security Council at the apex of government under President P.W. Botha (Truth and Reconciliation Commission of South Africa Report: Volume 2, 291–3).

The then Minister of Law and Order, Adriaan Vlok, the former Commissioner of Police, General Johan van der Merwe, and various members of the security police applied for, and, in 1999, were granted amnesty in relation to the attack on Khotso House, as well as for their attempts to defeat the ends of justice in the subsequent investigation of the bombing. As explained by Vlok in his application to the TRC, the principal motivation for the attack was President Botha's animus against the SACC and its campaigning against apartheid.

At the time of the attack on Khotso House, the police attributed its destruction to use of the building by the ANC underground for the storage of explosives. Extra detail was added to this narrative in the course of the police investigation. In particular, the police identified a member of the ANC underground, Shirley Gunn, as their prime suspect. She had previously been detained by the security police for a period of three months in 1985, but had been acquitted on the criminal charges the police brought against her. The police told the media that a taxi driver had spotted Gunn in the environs of Khotso House on the day of the attack. In addition, they speculated that the explosion at Khotso House had happened when a bomb that Gunn had been preparing to use elsewhere had been accidentally triggered and this was what had set off the entire arsenal. A nation-wide hunt for Gunn, identified in the media as a 'white woman terrorist', ensued. Subsequently, Gunn stated that she had feared that the intent of the police would be to shoot her on sight when they found her, as she knew the allegations against her were false and would not stand up in court, as at the time of the destruction of Khotso

House, she had been a thousand miles away in Cape Town. She eluded the police for a year and a half. When they eventually found her with her infant son in June 1990, she was arrested. The fact that by this point the ANC was no longer an illegal organization did not protect Gunn. She was held for over two months during the course of which she was subjected to torture that formed the subject of evidence she later presented at a public hearing of the TRC in 1996. She also sued the police over her ill-treatment and received substantial compensation in an out of court settlement.

QUESTIONS

1. How would you categorize the attack on Khotso House? And how would you justify your choice, bearing in mind both the covert nature of the attack and the absence of fatalities?
2. What considerations affect the use of terms such as terrorism or state terror in societies beset by widespread civil conflict?

5.1.2 Victims as innocent bystanders

The conclusion that terrorism primarily threatened the lives of innocent bystanders, not as an end in itself, but as a means to other ends, was widely accepted by the time of the publication of Alex Schmid's monumental study of the scholarship on terrorism in 1988 (Schmid, 1988). What flowed from this assumption, and was reflected in numerous laws adopted by states to tackle terrorism was a belief that putting the general public in fear formed the primary method of terrorism. The objection that even at the height of most terrorist campaigns, tiny numbers of the public fell victim to such terrorist outrages was met by the argument that the purposively indiscriminate nature of terrorism meant that anyone, anywhere **might** become a victim of an act of terrorism and that possibility in itself was capable of sustaining a climate of fear, or so, it was contended, the terrorists hoped. While other forms of violence by state and non-state actors commonly resulted in many more deaths of innocent bystanders as collateral damage, they could be distinguished from terrorism in their not seeking to achieve their aims through such deaths. At the same time, it was also argued that terrorists were indifferent to the identity of their victims. On this issue, Schmid contrasted terrorism and assassination: 'while assassination aims at having the victim dead, terrorism does not care about the victim itself' (Schmid, 1988: 8).

The shift that Schmid's view represented in the understanding of the essence of terrorism was striking. Prior to the age of terrorism in the late 1960s, the assassination of high-level figures had been seen as typical of terrorism. For example, following the assassination by Croatian nationalists of the King of Yugoslavia and the French foreign minister in Marseilles in 1934, the League of Nations established a committee of experts to study the problem of terrorism. The outcome was an international conference in 1937 to approve two international conventions. One was on the prevention and punishment of terrorism and the other on the creation of an international criminal court. Thanks largely to the outbreak of war, neither came into force. The main focus of the first of the conventions was on attacks on heads of state, as well as 'their hereditary or designated successors' and on holders of public offices 'when the act is directed against them in their public capacity', though it also included within its broad definition of terrorism 'any wilful act calculated to endanger the lives of members of the public' (Article 1).

Schmid's insistence on excluding political assassinations from his definition of terrorism was the logical outcome of his emphasis on terrorism as a way of communicating a larger political message through the medium of shockingly transgressive violence. A widely quoted precept that encapsulated this view before 9/11 was that what terrorists wanted was few dead but millions watching. With the advent of mass casualty terrorism, that proposition no longer holds. However, the notion that the deliberate killing of civilians or non-combatants distinguishes terrorism from other forms of political violence remains largely unchallenged. Thus, Jeff McMahan has described 'intentional attacks on non-combatants as a means of achieving political or other ideological goals' as 'the orthodox definition' (McMahan, 2004: 729). This approach underpins much of the discussion of terrorism in philosophical journals. In particular, debate on whether there might be any circumstances in which terrorism might be justified commonly takes a definition along these lines as its point of departure. This could be seen as tilting the outcome in favour of the unconditional and universal condemnation of terrorism.

5.1.3 Current usage

The larger problem of this approach, for all its clarity and logical rigour, is that it does not entirely accord with how the words, terror, terrorist and terrorism, are used in current public discourse, let alone how they were used in the past. The point can be illustrated by drawing on some examples of the use of the term, terrorism and terrorist, in the course of 2020. In June, a number of stabbings attracted the attention of the media in the UK. By far the most serious of these took place in Reading. Three people died in this attack and three were seriously wounded. A suspect was arrested on the spot. The episode was not labelled an act of terrorism at the very outset. The description of it as 'a terror incident' followed the determination that the suspect, a Libyan refugee, was considered a person of interest by counter-terrorist police. This interpretation was further underlined by reporting from the committal hearing that he had shouted out 'Allahu Akbar' ('God is the greatest', a common Arabic expression used by Muslims) during the attack (*The Independent*, 29 June 2020). At the same time, the suspect's criminal record and questions over his mental health, as well as the fact that he appears to have acted alone, casts doubt on whether his conduct should be considered part of any terrorist campaign, except in a very loose sense of that concept. But in this, it was entirely typical of the many attacks by single individuals that Europol, the European Union law enforcement agency, has classified as cases of jihadist (militant Islamic movements perceived as rooted in political Islam) terrorism.

Three men in their 20s were stabbed in brawls in Bournemouth in what was described in reports as a day of chaos across Britain's beaches (*Sky News,* 26 June 2020). There was never any suggestion of any terrorist aspect to any of these incidents. In Glasgow, six people were seriously injured in a stabbing rampage at a hotel providing temporary accommodation for asylum seekers. The perpetrator, an asylum seeker from Sudan, was shot dead at the scene by a police officer. On the same day as the attack, a police statement was issued that the stabbings were not being treated as a terrorist incident. But it was also subsequently reported that detectives were investigating whether the perpetrator had been inspired by the stabbings in Reading (*The Telegraph,* 27 June 2020).

In circumstances in which the perpetrator dies in an attack or its immediate aftermath, whether as a result of police actions or suicide, it is often difficult to determine the perpetrator's motivation. In the absence of perpetrator's leaving behind a clear indication, the nationality and/or religion of the perpetrator may influence media coverage as to whether an incident is likely to be one of terrorism or not. The dominant role played by jihadist groups in terrorism around the world in this century makes this bias explicable. It underscores the view that has prevailed through the course of all of the terrorist waves identified by Rapoport that the source of terrorism lies outside society, particularly where the society in question is a long-standing democracy (Rapoport, 2013: 282). The assumption that terrorism presents an externally generated threat also accounts for the nature of the political measures, such as immigration controls, that have tended to be adopted in response to the onset of terrorism. An example is the Anarchist Exclusion Act of 1903 introduced by President Theodore Roosevelt after he had denounced anarchism as a threat to mankind in language remarkably similar to that used by President George W. Bush in the aftermath of 9/11 about terrorism with a global reach.

Episodic jihadist attacks that have targeted ordinary members of the public, such as the van attack in Barcelona in August 2017 that killed 14 people, to use an example involving multiple perpetrators and where their adherence to Islamic State in Iraq and Syria (ISIS) was unambiguous, have provided the primary context for the current application of this concept. At the same time, the association of the terms, terror, terrorism and terrorist, with absolutely illegitimate violence has facilitated their use in other, very different contexts. Thus, the Chinese government characterized those protesting against the security crackdown in Hong Kong in 2020 as terrorists. The Chinese case is far from being unusual. There have been numerous instances of the characterization of anti-government protestors as terrorists by authoritarian leaders, including those in Turkey, Egypt, Russia, Thailand, the Philippines, Venezuela, and Zimbabwe. Violent clashes between demonstrators and the police typically form the justification for the invoking of this language. Further, rhetoric of this kind is by no means confined to autocracies. After the eruption of widespread protests by the Black Lives Matter movement following the killing of George Floyd in May 2020, US President Donald Trump announced his intention to add Antifa (shortened from 'Anti-fascist', a left-wing political movement in the US) to the country's list of designated terrorist organizations, as he sought to blame Antifa for violence that had accompanied some of the protests (Shatz, 2020: 5). Trump was frustrated in doing so because the designation of terrorist organizations under existing legislation was limited to foreign groups and individuals. While each of these cases might be dismissed as overblown polemic, with little relevance for the study of terrorism, the aggressive characterization of one's adversaries as terrorists carries with it, given the absolutism of current usage, a readiness to justify extreme measures up to and including killing anyone so labelled.

5.1.4 Expanding the concept's scope

This needs to be a consideration when examining more serious proposals for expanding the scope of the language of terrorism to situations other than political violence. For example, in a piece in the *New York Review of Books*, the American author, Caroline Fraser, suggested that a more apt term for the increase in domestic violence against women that had resulted globally in approximately 50,000 deaths in 2017 might be 'intimate partner terrorism' (Fraser, 2020: 14). Such a development could affect how the actions of women in abusive relationships might themselves be judged. But while male violence towards partners might satisfy the criterion of being absolutely illegitimate, it lacks two other common characteristics of terrorism, as the term is currently used in public discourse. While such violence is global in its extent, it generally lacks the transnational dimension associated with most terrorism, and most particularly with the terrorism with a global reach that has preoccupied much of the world since 9/11. It is also difficult to argue that instances of the murder of female partners form part of a campaign. Such killers rarely articulate justifications for their actions on the basis of a defence of patriarchy. While forums such as Incel (short for Involuntarily Celibate) could be seen as providing a rationale for male violence, Incel's influence is far too limited to sustain a claim that a global network exists to abuse women. While male violence may cause fear among people in general, it is rarely an explicit aim of the individual perpetrator.

A more cogent case can be made for including criminal gangs, especially drug cartels, within the remit of the efforts to suppress terrorism. The violence of gangs takes place on an ongoing basis and the intent to intimidate members of the public so as to facilitate the gang's control in particular communities is a common feature of their violence, when not directed at rival gangs in turf wars. Drug cartels have even been willing to use violence to press for changes in the state's stance on political matters such as extradition. Also significant in advancing the case for the treatment of drug cartels under the rubric of terrorism are their transnational character and the types of violence they engage in, including bombings and attacks on security personnel. Towards the end of 2019 the Mexican authorities arrested a major figure in the Sinaloa drug cartel, the son of its imprisoned leader, Joaquin Guzmán. In response heavily armed members of the cartel launched a wave of violence. This included taking soldiers hostage, attacking the homes of their family members, setting up roadblocks, and instigating a riot in a prison. Eight people died in these events which resulted in the government's release of Oxidio Guzmán Lopez. In the same period, another cartel murdered the family of an American Mormon, including six children. These outrages prompted the US Administration under President Trump to consider designating the Mexican drug cartels as foreign terrorist organizations.

5.1.5 In the context of civil wars

In this chapter terrorism has been examined against the backdrop of relatively stable and effective governance of a society. In situations in which the authority of government has broken down, it becomes much more difficult to draw clear distinctions between terrorism and other forms of collective violence. While it may seem perfectly reasonable to describe, say, a clandestine bomb attack that leads to a large number of casualties among the general public as an act of terrorism, identifying the groups from whom such perpetrators may have come as terrorists remains open to question, particularly where the group has a share of power in the overall governance of the society. In civil wars, the killing of civilians takes a number of forms and in some cases is carried out openly by soldiers in uniform. Other terms than terrorism are available to describe such violations of fundamental human rights, including crimes against humanity and war crimes. Further, since the founding of the International Criminal Court in 2002, a mechanism exists for the prosecution and punishment of perpetrators, though the jurisdiction of the court remains far from universal.

The remit of the court does not include among its high crimes, terrorism, but it does apply to genocide. In the past this term referred to the purposeful attempt to eliminate entire peoples, but it has been extended to include virtually any mass killings, particularly when directed at a particular racial, religious or ethnic group. The perpetrators of genocide are known as *génocidaires*, a French term that is gradually making its way into English. An example of the use of this term in 2020 was a description of Julius Caesar as 'the first *génocidaire* in European history' (Kulikowski, 2020: 15).

This example does not fit with other established aspects of current usage of the term, terrorism, in particular, that it applies to violence from below. A case might be made for the application of the derivative term, state terrorism (or terror). While terrorism generally refers to political violence with a transnational dimension, use of the term, domestic terrorism provides a basis for the condemnation of the killing of civilians that takes place within national boundaries in pursuit of purely internal political objectives. In this context, a distinction can be drawn between the indiscriminate and random killing of members of the public and the targeting of particular communities, as is more typical in cases of internal conflict, though the latter may also be called terrorism. In a number of jurisdictions, the judgement as to whether an act is one of terrorism hinges simply on the weaponry employed, with **means** that are considered likely to put the lives of members of the public at risk being included within the scope of anti-terrorist measures. Powerful explosive devices provide an obvious example of what tends to be treated as terrorism, without regard to motive or perpetrator or, indeed, whether the group or individual planting the bomb issued any kind of warning beforehand.

5.1.6 The international dimension

> **KEY CONCEPTS**
>
> **Transnational Terrorism and International Terrorism** Like piracy, terrorism naturally transcends national boundaries. The terms, **transnational terrorism** and **international terrorism**, are used but they mean more than simply that the terrorism in question has external connections. All terrorism, unless explicitly characterized as **domestic terrorism**, is assumed to arise from foreign influences. **Transnational terrorism** refers specifically to networks of non-state groups that cross state boundaries.
>
> **International terrorism** as widely used in the 1980s highlighted the support of foreign states for non-state terrorist groups. After 9/11 President George W. Bush coined the term, **terrorism with a global reach**. He did so to avoid the impression that the Global War on Terror could rid the world of all political violence and to dispel the notion that the United States would aid any government that called its internal opposition terrorists.

Part of the illegitimacy of terrorism stems from its international or transnational nature. This may seem counter-intuitive in respect of the numerous nationalist groups that states designate as terrorist organizations, but international support often plays as important a role for nationalists that adopt violent strategies, as it does in the case of groups with objectives that transcend the nation-state. Common to many of the nationalist groups that have resorted to violence is the use of the rubric, national liberation, to justify their violence. It appears in the names of numerous groups around the world, translated into the appropriate language for the territory in question. The fusion of nationalism with social revolution formed a potent combination in the second half of the 20th century. While groups on the far left and far right of the political spectrum in West Germany, Italy and Japan achieved a measure of notoriety at the start of the age of terrorism in the late 1960s and early 1970s, nationalist groups in the Middle East, Sri Lanka, Spain, and Ireland proved more durable and their actions came to be seen as typifying terrorism. This was until they were superseded by jihadist groups employing novel methods of violence, including simultaneous attacks aimed at maximizing casualties and often carried out by perpetrators on a suicide mission.

After 9/11 it was widely assumed by political leaders and by commentators that al-Qaeda (see section 5.1.7) had established a new norm, and that attacks of this nature would be what terrorist groups in future might seek to accomplish. But these fears seem to have been overdone. There have been no further terrorist attacks to date on the scale of 9/11. It might be argued that the counter-terrorist measures states have put in place are primarily responsible for this outcome. But part of the answer is also that very few of the groups that the United States or countries in Europe have officially designated as terrorist organizations possess the capacity or will to carry out another 9/11. The assumption that it is the aim of every terrorist organization to kill as many members of the general public as possible is mistaken. It does not correspond to how many terrorist organizations behave in practice or how they have behaved in the past.

What is more accurate is that terrorist groups remain shockingly indifferent to the deaths among the general public that their operations might cause. However, even this judgement requires modification when applied to some of the self-described terrorist organizations of the past. Thus, the International Relations scholar, Louise Richardson notes:

> 'Credited with creating the notion of propaganda by the deed, the Russian anarchists in fact produced more propaganda than deeds. This was true even of more extreme groups like the Russian Socialist Revolutionary Party, whose members carefully sought to avoid the deaths of innocents and constrained themselves within clearly defined limits' (Richardson, 2006: 53).

Furthermore, restraint can be found among groups that are currently listed by states as terrorist organizations or which have appeared on such lists in recent decades. Most, if not all, of these are also treated as terrorist organizations in the scholarly literature on terrorism. The clearest example of restraint is the African National Congress (ANC) that prior to South Africa's transition in the 1990s employed violence in its struggle against apartheid. It sought to do so in a way that would not jeopardize the support it enjoyed internationally. Thus, the ANC publicly undertook to adhere to the Geneva Convention's additional protocol on guerrilla warfare, though it was later criticized by the South African Truth and Reconciliation Commission for engaging in some activities that ran counter to its commitment to the avoidance of civilian casualties, such as the use of land mines against army patrols in border areas (*Truth and Reconciliation Commission of South Africa Report*, Volume 5, 1999: 241). The Provisional Irish Republican Army (IRA) justified its operations on the basis that its violence was directed against legitimate targets, a concept that encompassed a far larger group of people than simply those in the security forces. Even so, many ordinary civilians that did not fit even into the widest possible interpretation of this concept were killed by the organization, sometimes deliberately, but also due to mistakes. The Harrods bombing of December 1983 in the UK, also provides an example.

Few terrorist groups have any compunction about killing members of a state's security forces or those of any other state, should there be foreign intervention in the conflict. Within any state, such attacks are likely to be viewed as acts of terrorism and described as such in the media within the country. This also applies to states intervening in the conflict. This explains why countries such as Iraq, Syria, Afghanistan, and Libya, which have been subject to long-running foreign military interventions, loom so large in the global statistics on terrorism, while by no means accounting for most of the civilians that have been killed in armed conflicts around the world. The rubric of terrorism is also often applied to another tactic that many revolutionary groups adopt, that of the assassination of leading figures in the regime they are seeking to overthrow. External judgements and hence the language used will depend on perceptions of the legitimacy of the regime under attack. The language used by the World Service of the British Broadcasting Corporation (BBC) has been the source of a long-running controversy stemming from its policy of avoiding the unattributed use of the term terrorism in its reporting of foreign conflicts. It has encountered strong criticism when that reluctance has even extended to jihadist outrages, including the attack on the offices of *Charlie Hebdo* in Paris in January 2015 (see Case Study 5.1) (Shariatmadari, 2015).

CASE STUDY 5.2

The 2015 Attack on *Charlie Hebdo*

On 7 January 2015, two brothers, Säid and Chérif Kouachi, who identified themselves as members of the jihadist group al-Qaeda on the Arabian Peninsula, forced their way into the Paris offices of the satirical weekly, *Charlie Hebdo*. They opened fire on the occupants, killing 12 people and injuring another 11 before fleeing. Two days later the brothers died in a confrontation with the police after a long siege at an industrial estate outside Paris. During the siege, an associate of the brothers, Amedy Coulibady, took hostages at a kosher supermarket. He killed four of his hostages before he was killed himself. The previous day he had killed a policewoman near a Jewish centre and school. All three of the jihadists were born in France.

These events prompted protests by millions of people in France and around the world. The phrase, *Je suis Charlie* ('I am Charlie', see Photo 5.1), was widely adopted by demonstrators to express their solidarity with the victims of the attacks who included well-known cartoonists. And it was their murders, as much as those of innocent bystanders who were caught

PHOTO 5.1 'Je suis Charlie' graffitied on a wall on 11 January 2015 during a march after the brutal Paris attacks.

up in the events of 7–9 June, that prompted the strength of the public's outrage. If it was plain who the perpetrators primarily wished to kill; there was also clarity on their reasons for targeting the satirical weekly. This was because the magazine had reproduced cartoons portraying the Prophet Muhammad that had first appeared in the Danish paper, *Jyllands-Posten*, in September 2005. The weekly had also published cartoons of its own in much the same vein as the Danish ones. This was in keeping with the non-conformist and secular outlook of the weekly. Religion was often a target of its cartoons.

The editors of the Danish paper were well aware that much of the Muslim world considered the pictorial representation of the Prophet Muhammad to be blasphemous. Their motivation was to challenge what they saw as growing self-censorship among non-Muslims in this area and they solicited contributions from Danish cartoonists for this purpose. The nature of the cartoons, particularly the linking of the religion of Islam to terrorism, was bound to cause controversy. This theme was exemplified by a cartoon that portrayed Muhammad with a bomb tucked into his turban. Representatives of Danish Muslims objected to the publication of the cartoons both on religious grounds and as inciting hatred towards Muslims through the inflammatory coupling of the religion with terrorism. The Danish government refused to engage with these arguments on the grounds that they did not provide a justification for official interference with the freedom of the press.

A consequence of the impasse was that Danish Muslims sought support for their stance from outside Denmark. Information as well as misinformation about the cartoons spread rapidly. There were large demonstrations protesting against their publication in a number of countries such as where Muslims constituted a majority of the population. In some instances, the demonstrations were violent, and lives were lost. The internationalization of the issue of the cartoons presented the news media in other countries with a dilemma, as to whether their coverage of the controversy necessitated reproduction of the cartoons. The option generally followed by American and British papers was to describe the cartoons in words, though some critics argued that this was tantamount to self-censorship. The internet gave anyone in the world access to the images. Another argument advanced for reproducing the cartoons was to express solidarity with the Danish cartoonists whose lives were being threatened by jihadists.

This was the spirit that underlay *Charlie Hebdo*'s reproduction of the cartoons in an issue in February 2006. The issue published the full set of Danish cartoons, with the addition of cartoons of its own portraying Muhammad. Its front cover portrayed a weeping Muhammad, with a text bubble that proclaimed that he found being loved by idiots trying. A court case followed in which the weekly was cleared of inciting hatred through the publication of the cartoons. In 2011 the offices of the weekly were fire-bombed. This was on the eve of the publication of a special issue that the editors had dubbed *Charia Hebdo*, with Mohammad as its supposed guest editor. Further threats by jihadists against the weekly culminated in the attack of 7 June 2015.

Conflict over the issue of Danish cartoons has continued to give rise to acts of terrorism. In October 2020 a schoolteacher, Samuel Paty, was beheaded by a jihadist, Abdullah Anzorov, after the teacher showed his pupils the cartoons in the context of a class on freedom of expression. Criticism of Paty on social media drew this to the attention of Anzorov who had no connection with the school where Paty taught. In an echo of the *Je suis Charlie* demonstrations, there were rallies across France protesting against Paty's murder as a challenge to free speech. There was particularly forthright condemnation of the attack by the President of France, Emmanuel Macron. He strongly defended Paty's conduct. His stance on this case and the measures he initiated to address what he described as the threat of Islamic separatism to French republican values contributed to a diplomatic row between France and Turkey. Controversy over Macron's actions also led to calls for a boycott of French goods in a number of Muslim countries.

QUESTIONS

1. How typical of jihadist terrorism was the attack on the offices of *Charlie Hebdo* in 2015?
2. How useful is the notion of a conflict of civilizations as an explanation for the violence arising out of publication of the Danish cartoons?

The inclusion of the targeting of particular groups or individuals under the rubric of terrorism does not affect the general impression that what terrorists typically do is to kill or threaten to kill civilians at random or indiscriminately for some political purpose. Further, the converse holds that it is considered legitimate to attach the label terrorist to any agency that carries out such attacks, including states. The commonest way for states to deflect such charges is to claim that their operations are directed against terrorists. Frequent incidents in which large numbers of civilians are killed, as collateral damage or due to mistakes and misinformation tend to undermine such claims and explain the efforts of states to suppress reporting of such episodes. Contemporary impressions of the nature of terrorism reflect the overriding influence of two jihadist groups, al-Qaeda and ISIS, which are covered in section 5.1.7.

5.1.7 Al-Qaeda and ISIS

From its creation in 1988, al-Qaeda adopted a strategy of attacking the far enemy, by which it meant countries outside the Muslim world that lent support to regimes in majority Muslim countries that pursued policies al-Qaeda considered un-Islamic. Al-Qaeda's assumption was that this would create a crisis in relations between these regimes and their external backers that would provide opportunities for the advancement of the cause of rule according to Islamic principles. This provided the rationale for its 9/11 attacks on Americans and on the United States of America itself. While ISIS has provided the inspiration for most of the jihadist attacks in the last decade or so, its initial strategy had been to create a caliphate or Islamist state within the Middle East and to recruit foreign fighters to aid in its defence. So different was this approach that some scholars questioned whether ISIS could be characterized as a terrorist organization at all (Cronin 2015). Alternatively, it was proposed that ISIS represented a new, fifth wave of terrorism (Honig and Yahel 2019).

ISIS attacks outside of the Middle East were initially just an adjunct to its main objective. After 2017 they came to represent the organization's response to foreign intervention and the defeat of its efforts to establish a territorial base for its new caliphate anywhere. A feature of many of the attacks in Europe and in the United States has been that they were carried out by 'lone wolves' with seemingly little or no contact with ISIS as an organization. Few of these perpetrators have sought to justify their actions on the basis of any strategy. More frequently, they have given revenge for bombings carried out by American and European forces in Muslim countries as a justification for their own killings.

> ### KEY CONCEPTS
>
> **Lone Wolf Terrorism** The idea of **lone wolf terrorism** seems a contradiction in terms, since terrorism is a form of **collective violence**, while a lone wolf refers to someone who acts on their own without the assistance of others. The solution to this conundrum is that the internet and social media have created the possibility for the socially isolated individual to be part of a network that exists only in cyberspace and to act as if part of a larger **terrorist campaign** while forging few, if any, other links to any **terrorist group**. Terrorist attacks quite often end in the death of the perpetrator and that has led to increased reliance on the browsing history of the individual and activity on social media to draw conclusions about motivation.

Similar questions arose over the role that revenge for past jihadist attacks had played in the motivation of Brenton Tarrant, the single perpetrator of the Christchurch New Zealand attacks in March 2019. Prior to the attacks, Tarrant had put a lengthy manifesto online that included praise for the Norwegian mass killer, Anders Breivik (who committed attacks in 2011) and expressed white supremacist and anti-immigrant opinions. Material Tarrant left at the scene of the attacks referenced recent jihadist outrages, as well as allusions to historical conflicts between Christians and Muslims in Europe. But missing was any connection to an ongoing terrorist campaign, or that Tarrant conceived the attacks as a means to some other end.

In conflicts in ethnically divided societies, cycles of 'tit for tat' violence are common. In these cases, the victims are not simply random members of the general public whose identity is incidental to the pursuit of much larger political aims. While the attacks are indiscriminate in the sense that particular individuals are not singled out to be killed, but simply people belonging to a large category of people without distinction as to age, gender or other basic characteristic, the killing or injuring of people within this wide range is the primary objective of the perpetrators. In this they closely resemble hate crimes and indeed may be categorized as such in periods of peace. In this context, two other attacks, both in the United States, are worth examining. They were also the two most lethal attacks in the United States since 9/11 and deserve attention for that reason as well.

5.1.8 Lethality and terrorism

The attacks in question were examples of what has come to be called 'lone wolf terrorism' (Simon, 2016). Both were carried out by American-born perpetrators. The first of these was on 12 June 2016. Before being killed himself by police, Omar Mateen, the son of immigrants who had come to the United States from Afghanistan, killed 49 people and wounded 53 others at Pulse, a gay nightclub in Orlando, Florida (see Photo 5.2). At the time, it was the deadliest shooting by a single gunman in American history. That figure was surpassed the following year. Stephen Paddock, a Nevada retiree, opened fire on a large crowd attending a country music festival in Las Vegas. On 1 October 2017 he killed 58 people and injured hundreds more before committing suicide.

Before the shooting, Mateen had phoned the police and declared his adherence to ISIS. He also proclaimed in the phone call and in posts online that the killing of an ISIS leader, Abu Waheeb, in an American airstrike in Iraq the previous month had spurred him to act. However, Mateen's explanation of his motivation was not universally accepted, especially in the absence of any earlier signs of his commitment to the jihadist cause. His choice of Pulse as his target prompted speculation that his actions had been driven by homophobia and should therefore be characterized as a hate crime, rather than, or as well as, an act of terrorism. But once it came out that Mateen had considered attacking other targets without any connection to the LGBTQIA+ community, the interpretation

PHOTO 5.2 Orlando, FL— 12 June 2021: Mourners pay their respects to those killed at the Pulse Nightclub memorial on the fifth anniversary of the Pulse mass shooting.

of the attack as driven by homophobia became questionable. The investigation also uncovered evidence that there had been concerns about his mental health and the effect of drug abuse on his behaviour.

In the Las Vegas, Nevada case involving Steven Paddock, too, the significance of the target he had chosen diminished when it emerged that he had researched events at other venues. They had little or nothing in common beyond the fact that they also attracted large crowds of people. His ultimate choice seems simply to have been determined by the fact that the country music festival offered the best opportunity for a shooter to kill a very large numbers of people in a short space of time. No evidence emerged as to any political or ideological motive for Paddock's actions. In the immediate aftermath of the killings rumours circulated on the internet about possible motives but none stood up to any scrutiny. In the absence of any other pointers, the assumption tended to be made that he was 'very sick', to use former President Donald Trump's words (*Washington Post,* 4 October 2017). Paddock's life as a businessman, heavy drinker, and gambler contained no clues to his future notoriety. One consequence was that the response to the shootings focused less on the perpetrator himself than on the means he had employed. A federal ban was enacted on bump stocks, the mechanism that had enabled Paddock to fire a thousand rounds in a short space of time.

The scale, gravity, and lethality of Paddock's attack demanded that it should be treated as an act of terrorism (Dolliver and Kearns, 2019). A concept that is widely used by governments and counter-terrorist agencies to explain why individuals would carry out such lethal attacks on civilians is radicalization. Radicalization may take a variety of forms, including self-radicalization to cover instances where the individual becomes indoctrinated through the internet without any social interaction with other people. However, Paddock's case fits neither version.

> ### KEY CONCEPTS
>
> **Self-Radicalization** The term **self-radicalization** is commonly used in this context to describe the individual's evolution into a killer. Some scholars have raised objections to the term, lone wolf, on the grounds of its potential to romanticize perpetrators (Borum, Fein, and Vossekuil, 2012: 390), but the term, like that of terrorism itself, is freely and widely used in public discourse, which justifies its use here.

A note explaining why, nevertheless, the Las Vegas attack had been included in a database of global terrorism observed: 'Lack of evidence of radicalization—a cognitive process—is not evidence of the lack of radicalization' (Miller, 2018). Scale matters in relation to the public's reaction to violent events. Whereas in cases where there are relatively small numbers of victims, the conclusion by the police that the attack was not a terrorist one relieves public anxiety, mass casualty attacks with multiple fatalities prompt the demand that the episode is categorized in a way that accords with the seriousness of its consequences.

5.1.9 Strategy and terrorism

These cases covered in section 5.1.8 prompt a question. Is it possible to have terrorism without terrorists? The converse of that is also worth considering. Is it possible to have terrorists without terrorism? Governments of many kinds have answered this question in the affirmative by seeking to use the whole array of counter-terrorist laws against individuals and groups in situations where no terrorism has taken place, where no-one has died and where any violence that has taken place has posed no threat to life. A case in point was a fight in a bar in Navarre, Spain in 2016 in which a group of Basque nationalists attacked two members of the civil guard. The Spanish authorities used counter-terrorist legislation to prosecute the nationalist individuals involved in the encounter (Sagardoy-Leuza, 2020). The public's fear of terrorism is a potent weapon in the hands of any government to quell any form of disorder, including stigmatizing peaceful protests that give rise to incidental violence. The era of mass casualty attacks since 9/11 has intensified the public's fear and that has opened the way to political exploitation of the issue of terrorism in a variety of contexts. An example is the mobilization of opposition to immigration and, more particularly, the settlement of refugees and asylum seekers on the grounds that those fleeing conflicts may contain terrorists within their ranks. One of the findings of a survey of why the UK voted to leave the EU (Brexit) in 2016 was that there was a belief among leave voters that EU membership fuelled increasing terrorist threats (Clarke, Goodwin, and Whiteley, 2017: 461).

Focus on the consequences of terrorism tends to deflect attention away from the concept's main value in comparative analysis. This is to gain an understanding of the strategies behind terrorism on the assumption that in terrorist campaigns killing is not an end in itself but a means to a political goal. It begs the following questions. What is the group's theory of change? What works and what doesn't? For example, the adoption of the method of mass casualty attacks may in part be traced back to the success achieved by suicide bombs in driving American forces out of Lebanon in 1983. But, in the long run, few campaigns are sustainable in the absence of continuing validation of their assumptions about the relationship between means and ends. At the same time, as Kalyvas points out in his path-breaking work on the subject, violence takes place in civil wars for all manner of motives unrelated to the strategic objectives of the contending forces (Kalyvas, 2006). The same is true of terrorist campaigns. Their existence may also provide a rationale for violence, for motives that have nothing to do with the strategic calculations of any campaign.

The sheer variety of groups that might be compared under the rubric of terrorism is a reason why the existence of many different terrorisms might be posited. And it is quite common in public discourse to refer to domestic terrorism and to distinguish rebel or revolutionary terrorism from terrorism in support of the status quo. But, overwhelmingly, the term terrorism is employed in the singular, while the increasingly used shortened form, terror, is even more resistant to pluralization. Further, unless the contrary is stated, use of the term is assumed to apply to active, ongoing campaigns that are transnational in scope. The point can be illustrated by the very different reactions to two highly lethal mass shootings in the United States in 2015.

In the first shooting, on 1 October 2015, a lone wolf perpetrator killed nine people in a community college in Oregon before he killed himself. His motivation remained obscure and led to a focus on his history of mental illness. Another theme in the coverage was his hostility to religion, leading to the characterization of the shootings as a hate crime. Very little significance was attached to the perpetrator's admiration for the IRA and that was not seen as a reason to classify the shootings as an act of terrorism (Hensch, 2 October 2015). On 2 December, 14 people were killed in a shooting at a training session and party for health officials in San Bernardino, California, USA. The two perpetrators, a married couple, subsequently died in an exchange of fire with police. The FBI investigation concluded that the couple had no links with any foreign terrorist group but had been inspired by ideas of jihad and martyrdom they had acquired from the internet. That was sufficient to ensure coverage of the attack as a major terrorist assault on the United States and prompted Donald Trump, who had started his presidential campaign at the time, to demand a total and complete ban on Muslim immigration into the United States.

What the contrast in reactions to the two cases underscores is the importance in the public mind as to whether violence forms part of an ongoing terrorist campaign, however tenuously. While terrorist campaigns wax and wane, as long as there is an active campaign, it is likely to be a cause of intense public concern. Past terrorist campaigns leave their marks on survivors and the bereaved but have little influence on the public discourse on terrorism. The meaning of terrorism in any era inevitably reflects the **active** campaigns of the time. Though location matters in perceptions of what constitutes terrorism, it has less significance because of terrorism's transnational dimension and the connections that governments and others seek to make among the wide variety of ongoing campaigns. The role that imitation plays in the means employed by different groups and individuals also tends to reduce the significance attached to the specific political context.

DISCUSSION QUESTIONS

1. What accounts for the shifts in the meaning of terrorism over the course of the last century and a half?
2. How important is the domestic political context to the nature and perceptions of terrorism?
3. What role does the killing of innocent bystanders play in terrorism?
4. What has been the place of the assassination of political leaders in the history of terrorism?
5. Why is terrorism rarely discussed in the plural as terrorisms, given its different manifestations and meanings?

 Visit the online resources for pointers on how to answer the discussion questions, links to useful web sources, and guidance on accessing databases: www.oup.com/he/Wilson-Muro1e

GUIDE TO FURTHER READING

Richard English in his short book, *Terrorism: How to Respond* (Oxford: Oxford University Press, 2009) considers the subject from both an analytical and practical perspective and is fully alert to changing contexts and their significance. Marc Sageman's *Understanding Terror Networks* (Philadelphia: University of Pennsylvania Press, 2004) remains a valuable guide to innovative aspects of most recent wave of terrorism.

Chaliand, G. and Arnaud, Blin. (2016) *A History of Terrorism: From Antiquity to ISIS*. Oakland, Calif.: University of California Press.

Crenshaw, M. (2011) *Explaining Terrorism: Causes, Processes and Consequences*. Abingdon: Routledge.

Mueller, J. (2006) *Overblown: How Politicians and the Terrorism Industry Inflate National Security Threats and Why We Believe Them*. New York: Free Press.

Richardson, L. (2006) *What Terrorists Want: Understanding the Terrorist Threat*. London: John Murray.

Townshend, C. (2002) *Terrorism*. Oxford: Oxford University Press.

REFERENCES

Borum, R., Fein, R., and Vossekuil, B. (2012) 'A Dimensional Approach to Analyzing Lone Offender Terrorism', *Aggression and Violent Behaviour*, 17 (5): 389–396.

Clarke, H. D., Goodwin, M., and Whiteley, P. (2017) 'Why Britain Voted for Brexit: An Individual-Level Analysis of the 2016 Referendum Vote', *Parliamentary Affairs*, 70 (3): 439–464.

Cohen, G. (1966) *Woman of Violence: Memoirs of a Young Terrorist, 1943–1948*. New York: Holt, Rinehart and Winston.

Cronin, A. K. (2015) 'ISIS Is Not a Terrorist Group: Why Counterterrorism Won't Stop the Latest Jihadist Threat'. *Foreign Affairs*, 94 (2): 87–98.

Dolliver, M. J. and Erin M. K. (2019) 'Is It Terrorism?: Public Perceptions, Media, and Labelling the Las Vegas Shooting', *Studies in Conflict and Terrorism*, 12 (3).

Fraser, C. (2020) 'When Will We Care About Domestic Violence?', *New York Review of Books*, 67 (9): 14–16.

Hensch, M. (2015) 'Report: Oregon shooter hated religion, liked the IRA', *The Hill*. 2 October.

Honig, O. and Ido Y. (2019) 'A Fifth Wave of Terrorism? The Emergence of Terrorist Semi-States', *Terrorism and Political Violence*, 31 (6): 1210–1228.

Kalyvas, S. N. (2006) *The Logic of Violence in Civil War*. Cambridge: Cambridge University Press.

Kulikowski, M. (2020) 'A Very Bad Man', *London Review of Books*, 42 (12): 15–16.

Lessing, D. (1985) *The Good Terrorist*. London: Jonathan Cape.

McMahan, J. (2004) 'The Ethics of Killing in War', *Ethics*, 114 (4): 693–733.

Miller, E. (2018). 'Global Terrorism Database Coding Notes: Las Vegas 2017'. *START*. 7 December.

Rapoport, D. (2013) 'The Four Waves of Modern Terror: International Dimensions and Consequences' in Jussi Hanhimäki and Bernhard Blumenau (eds), *An International History of Terrorism: Western and Non-Western Experiences*. London: Routledge. 282–310.

Richardson, L. (2006) *What Terrorist Want: Understanding the Terrorist Threat*. London: John Murray.

Sagardoy-Leuza, I. (2020) 'The Altsasu Case: Terrorism Without Terrorists', *Critical Studies on Terrorism*, 13 (2): 296–311.

Savinkov, B. (1931) *Memoirs of a Terrorist*. New York: Albert and Charles Boni.

Schmid, A. P. and Jongman, A. J. (1988) *Political Terrorism: A New Guide to Actors, Authors, Concepts, Data Bases, Theories and Literature*, Amsterdam: North-Holland Publishing Company.

Shariatmadari, D. (2015) 'Is It Time to Stop Using the Word 'Terrorist'?', *The Guardian*. 27 January.

Shatz, A. (2020) 'America Explodes'. *London Review of Books*, 42 (12): 4–8.

Truth and Reconciliation Commission of South Africa Report: Volume 2. 1999. London: Macmillan.

Simon, J. D. (2016) *Lone Wolf Terrorism: Understanding the Growing Threat*. Amherst, NY: Prometheus Books.

Truth and Reconciliation Commission of South Africa Report: Volume 5. 1999. London: Macmillan.

CHAPTER 6

The Social Science of Political Violence

STEFAN MALTHANER, DONATELLA DELLA PORTA, LORENZO BOSI

■ CHAPTER SUMMARY

Research on political violence has been re-shaped by what can be described as a 'processual turn'. Instead of focusing on socio-structural conditions ('root causes') or individual predispositions, political violence has increasingly been analysed as emerging from—and being shaped by—processes of radicalization, escalation, transformation, and disengagement that result from interactions between multiple actors. This chapter will present and critically discuss some of the main processual approaches in the study of political violence, focusing, in particular, on their conceptual and theoretical foundations and their explanatory logic, but also discussing exemplary empirical works that have adopted a processual perspective in their research.

6.1 INTRODUCTION

The 'German Autumn' of 1977 marked the peak of a violent campaign by the so-called 'Red Army Faction' (RAF), a radical left-wing armed group, aimed at forcing the government of the Federal Republic of Germany to release the group's founders from prison (see Case Study 6.1). The kidnapping of a leading representative of German industry, Hans Martin Schleyer, combined with the hijacking of a Lufthansa plane by a Palestinian group in support of the RAF, turned into one of the most severe political crises of post-war West Germany. It ended with the rescue of all hostages by an elite counterterrorism unit, the killing of Hans Martin Schleyer, and the suicide of the RAF founders in prison.

These dramatic events prompted the Ministry of the Interior to initiate a comprehensive research programme into the 'root-causes of terrorism', involving some of the country's leading social scientists. As one of them, Friedhelm Neidhardt, later explained, this did not go as planned. In fact, their final conclusions did not correspond to the original search for 'root causes' of political violence at all:

> 'Psychological research, which was looking for personality traits as predisposing or triggering factors, as well as social science research that was looking for socio-structural factors, only yielded very limited results. Terrorism emerges from quite ordinary samples of people under very different societal conditions' (translated from Neidhardt 1981: 244).

What Neidhardt and his colleagues had realized was that political violence emerges over time—and here the very *process* of escalation is crucial to outcomes. Various parties—radical fringes of a protest movement, militant groups, the police, the news media—interact and influence each other, contributing to a 'circular dynamic' of increasing political violence:

> 'It seems that the crucial factors/dynamics are found not in individual or societal predispositions, but in process trajectories in which various conditions shape a system of action, and which, in circular interaction, affect each other and themselves. They are cause and effect at the same time, shaped by and depending on the changing constellations in which interactions take place. The search for "root causes" ends up becoming circular. The system becomes its own, best explanation – and our main task is to understand it' (translated from Neidhardt 1981: 244).

Neidhardt's 1981 paper is one of the earliest—and clearest—expressions of an approach to studying political violence that takes inter-action between different actors seriously. We call such an analysis 'processual' simply because it focuses on these key *processes* of inter-action.

> **KEY CONCEPTS**
>
> **Processual Approaches** Processual approaches offer a dynamic way of trying to understand phenomena that are themselves dynamic and continuously changing. Arguing that outcomes are not determined by preceding conditions alone, they focus on the causal effects of sequences of events over time, often drawing on a notion of 'mechanisms' to capture recurring patterns in the effectuation of change.

Examining political violence within a processual perspective means taking into account that it emerges *gradually*, in sequences of encounters between protest movements, militant groups, and government authorities, and as result of the gradual transformation of political contexts, organizational structures, and frameworks of interpretation. In other words, it means conceiving of political violence as fundamentally emerging from interactions (Della Porta 2013: 18–21; Bosi/Demetriou/Malthaner 2014; Alimi/Demetriou/Bosi 2015).

Such an approach has serious implications for how we explain political violence, including the phenomena usually called 'terrorism'. When (and how) do such processes start? Or end? What is the relationship between 'initial conditions' (Goldstone 1998) and the dynamics of these processes? And how can we understand recurring patterns of causal relationships within processes of political violence?

There is a lot to think about here. But the basic point about processual approaches is that they offer a dynamic way of trying to understand phenomena that are themselves dynamic and always changing. In this chapter, we present core-elements of a processual perspective and outline how it can help us to explain why violence occurs, escalates, and declines. To that end, it is helpful to distinguish between recurrent mechanisms that contribute to the radicalization of militant groups and those dynamics that shape individual pathways of participating in political violence (Malthaner 2017).

6.2 THE 'PROCESSUAL TURN' IN POLITICAL VIOLENCE RESEARCH

It is worth asking a very basic question initially: why try to look at things this way at all? How does it help us to see more clearly? To understand the benefits of concentrating our analysis, we need to understand a little about the limitations of previous approaches to studying political violence in the social sciences.

Before the 1960s, the study of political violence tended to focus on unconscious psychological forces. At the macro-level, the key causes were thought to be some sort of 'strain' in the social system or breakdown of societal order. Violence was the reaction to those changes (i.e. frustration-aggression theory; relative deprivation). At the micro-level, those who participated in that violence were often seen in sociopathic terms—putting it simply, there was something wrong with them as people (Victoroff 2005).

> **KEY CONCEPTS**
>
> **Political Violence** Political violence involves a heterogeneous repertoire of actions oriented at inflicting physical, psychological, and symbolic damage to individuals and/or property with the intention of influencing various audiences for affecting or resisting political, social, and/or cultural change (Bosi and Malthaner 2015).

Such answers became more and more inadequate in the light of the turbulent events of the late 1960s. Over the next decade attempts at analysis became more sophisticated. A key advance was to take the phenomenon of protest, or contentious politics, more broadly speaking, seriously: those who were seeking to achieve change—whether violently or nonviolently—were now seen as self-organizing in complex ways. Such 'social movements' were now recognized as developing their own 'repertoires' of action: that is, loosely standardized ways of exerting pressure. Social movements, in short, had now arrived as a serious subject for academic investigation. Different traditions of scholarship developed to try to understand them better (Della Porta and Diani 2020).

One group of scholars concentrated on how (some) social movement organizations (SMOs) got going—or 'mobilized'—in the first place. They looked at how they needed both to find resources—time, energy, money, etc.—but also to build networks of solidarity if they were to stand any chance of converting discontent into potential for activism (McCarthy and Zald 1973, 1977; Obershall 1978; Tilly 1978). Without these steps, even deeply oppressive situations might never see collective mobilization. Such work can be grouped together under the heading of Resource Mobilization Theory (RMT).

From the early 1980s, another approach, which shared with RMT the vision of social movement organizations as strategic actors, focused more on the wider contextual conditions that needed to exist for SMOs to be able to exploit opportunities for change (McAdam 1982; Tarrow 1998; Kriesi et al. 1995). When do such opportunities emerge? Or disappear? What happens when governing elites break down into different factions? Or when a regime's capacity for repression suddenly weakens? We can call this body of work the Political Opportunity Structure (POS) approach.

A third approach that shaped the study of social movements focused more upon the area of meanings and communication. This approach begins with the notion of 'frames'. Frames are 'schema of interpretation'—that is: simplified ways of organizing experience and making sense of a very complex world. A key notion here is that of 'frame alignment'. For instance, someone or some organization may try to frame an event in public life a certain way (for instance, as a gross injustice that belongs in a longer prior catalogue of similar injustices). If enough people find the frame convincing—and feel deeply enough about the issues—then a social movement may be either be born or else dramatically rejuvenated (Snow and Benford 1998). An example of frame alignment in action are the protests against police brutality that erupted across the USA (see Photo 6.1) after the murder of George Floyd, an African American man, at the hands of the police (25 May 2020).

A couple of comments about the study of social movements are worth making here. First, those who studied social movements tend to see their members as rational political actors. Activists might make all kinds of misjudgements and commit all kinds of moral lapses of course: like any other group of human beings. But they should not be assumed to be inherently irrational: even if the nature of their passions may seem very puzzling at first glance. Secondly, scholars of social movements tend to be interested in both violence and nonviolence: and in particular the switch between nonviolence to violence; that is: in processes of radicalization. They are sensitive to just how differently political violence could develop in different settings; and what very different forms it could take. As a result, they tend to be sceptical about using the concept of 'terrorism', given that it has 'strong normative and political connotations, is much more contested, has doubtful heuristic value, and has often been used to stigmatize rather than to explain the social phenomena under examination' (Bosi, Della Porta, and Malthaner 2018: 133). But the problems go even

PHOTO 6.1 An image of George Floyd being held up at a protest in front of the White House, Washington DC on 6 June 2020.

deeper than this. A concept of terrorism treats some violence as utterly exceptional. It thus cuts off the violence that has been designated 'terrorism' from the study of broader movements and their repertoires of both violent (and nonviolent) action (Della Porta 2008).

Overall, the rise of social movement theory enriched the study of political violence massively. Both resource mobilization theory and political opportunity structure approaches had established the basic idea that political violence emerges, under particular circumstances, and from the strategic interactions between protest movements and state actors or political elites, and counter-movements.

CASE STUDY 6.1

The Red Army Faction (RAF), West Germany

The 1968 student revolt in West Germany spawned several small left-wing militant groups. Names mattered here: the 'Movement 2nd of June', for instance, highlighted the background of lethal state repression that its members saw as justifying their own armed struggle—it had been on 2 June 1967 that an unarmed protestor had been shot dead by a police officer. Greatest impact was achieved by the Red Army Faction, or Baader-Meinhof Gang (after two of its leaders, Ulrike Meinhof and Andreas Baader). Between 1970 and 1972 the group killed five people and injured over 50 in a series of bomb attacks. After the arrest of most of the group's first-generation members, the RAF demonstrated a striking capacity for self-regeneration: a second and a third generation of RAF militants were to follow, driven in part by the desire to free their imprisoned comrades.

The RAF never enjoyed mass support: but to the West German government (and, indeed, wider public opinion) they loomed very large as a security threat. As a result, the state security apparatus at both federal and state levels grew dramatically. Extensive police measures multiplied. (Malthaner and Waldmann 2003). Still, there was some political pushback: the radical left mobilized energetically around the questions of whether the incarcerated RAF members should be recognized as political prisoners. This was also an issue that drew in intense criticism from liberal intellectuals.

1977 represented a sort of high noon for the RAF campaign. The spectacular kidnapping (and subsequent killing) of Hans Martin Schleyer triggered crisis. Arrests and drop-outs followed. Yet the RAF attempted to kickstart their campaign in the next decade with a renewed offensive of assassinations and bombings. Internal controversy followed: particularly driven by doubts around the murder of a US solider for his ID card (to facilitate entry into US military facilities in Frankfurt). Debate and factionalism accelerated among the RAF's members, prisoners, and sympathizers: leading, in the end, to the end of its violent campaign.

This did not happen quickly: until 1991 the RAF carried on assassinating economic and political leaders. Dissolution followed in 1998. Over nearly 30 years, this small group had killed over 40 individuals—and injured a further 100 more.

> **QUESTIONS**
> 1. How did policies aimed at controlling the protest movement and the RAF contribute to escalating and sustaining political violence?
> 2. In what way were the broader protest movement and sympathizing milieus relevant to the RAF's decisions to escalate or end their violent campaign?

6.3 THE EXPLANATORY LOGIC OF PROCESSUAL ANALYSIS

Before presenting processual analytical approaches in more detail, it is important to outline the basic explanatory logic that they share. The common starting point for most works adopting a processual perspective is a critique of explanations of political violence as an effect of socio-economic structural conditions, individual predispositions, or particular ideologies. Instead, they focus on the way sequences of events, involving a variety of actors, produce changes in strategies, frameworks of interpretation, and organization. In turn, these contribute to the gradual emergence of political violence: and its increase (or decline).

At the core of a processual perspective on political violence lies the notion that processes matter in their own right. To put it in more formal language: they *have autonomous causal efficacy* (Bosi, Demetrious, and Malthaner 2014: 3). They are autonomous because—at least to some extent—they develop their own momentum. They are causal because they have direct consequences: they cause things to happen. And they are efficacious because of these other qualities. In other words, such processes themselves put further changes into effect.

Nothing comes from nowhere: and conditions at the outset do influence what happens afterwards. But the key point about process trajectories leading into political violence is that they are driven and shaped by dynamics that they themselves generate. They therefore transform initial conditions and generate new goals and motives for political violence (Della Porta 2013; Neidhardt 1981; Kalyvas 2006; Wood 2003).

So, processual analyses do not see causation as a one-way process. They instead try to capture a dynamic pattern of developments, guided by the notion of *emergence*. To reconstruct the unfolding of a process, from this perspective, is to explain it (Bosi, Demetriou, and Malthaner 2014: 4).

This is an important difference from other approaches to terrorism introduced in this textbook (Chapter 8 that focuses upon examining 'root causes', for instance). Such a perspective does not prioritize factors and conditions that are conceived of as being somehow located 'at the root' of the phenomenon, either as 'underlying' structural conditions or as the all-important initial factors that 'kickstarted' subsequent events. Even if social and political orders are inherently prone to conflict, these conflicts do not always—and not necessarily—lead to confrontational protest or violence. This means that processual factors, mechanisms, or even contingent trigger events have the same causal impact in producing the outcome—violence—as presumed 'root causes'. Consequently, political violence is seen as emergent to the process, arising in a gradual manner, often in the context of broader collective mobilizations. This understanding has several important implications that are now reviewed in turn.

Continuity. First, when examining a particular form of political violence from a processual perspective, the focus of attention turns to continuities with other forms of political violence as well as with nonviolent forms of action (Della Porta 2013: 20–21; Bosi, Demetriou, and Malthaner 2014: 2–3; see also Crenshaw 2001: 3, 5). For example, you cannot understand the emergence of the Provisional IRA (PIRA) armed campaign in the early 1970s if you do not trace how the broad Irish republican movement changed in the aftermath of the failed Border Campaign (1956–1962) and in the interaction with the emergent civil right movement in the region (Bosi 2006). And you have to recognize that the PIRA, to stay with this example, used violence in combination with other, nonviolent strategies, with shifting priorities.

Interaction. Sequences of events produce changes that lead to the adoption and increase of political violence because the individuals and groups involved react and adapt to each other, thereby transforming relationships, perceptions, and frameworks of interpretation. One pattern of interactive escalation are revenge cycles, in which events perceived as unprovoked atrocities by an 'enemy' call for a violent response on par or exceeding the original attack. In some cases, as the Red Army Faction (see Case Study 6.1), avenging 'comrades' killed by the police can become a powerful driver of a violent campaign. But the different parties involved in a process of political violence mutually adapt their practices and perspectives also in other ways.

Context. This leads to a third, important point: the relationship between process and *context* (or *structure*). This can be a difficult area to understand on first encounter. On the one hand, processes are seen as having 'autonomous causal efficacy'—in other words, they act more or less as forces in their own right. On the other hand, they are not seen as independent from the political and organizational context in which they emerge. How can we reconcile these apparently contradictory viewpoints? Once again it is helpful to return to the early insights of Friedhelm Neidhardt here. Neidhardt pointed out that dynamics of interaction depended on and were shaped by particular *relational configurations*, or patterns of relationships and power-balances between actors involved (Neidhardt 1981: 244). Let us take the example of the RAF as an armed group that operates 'underground': that is in secrecy. Operating clandestinely, thereby, significantly affected how the RAF interacted not only with their 'enemies', but also with supportive milieus or broader movements, and with the audience, it sought to influence. Instead of persuading others of their cause in face-to-face encounters, the militants could reach their audience only in mediated ways, via pamphlets or media-reporting. Organizational structures thus shape what kind of interactions can take place. At the same time, processes of violent escalation re-shape these contextual conditions as well as the constellation of parties involved in the conflict. For example, escalating violence may lead to increasing repression, forcing militants to adopt more clandestine forms of operation, which, in the end, produces a spiral of isolation and radicalization. 'Boundary activation' kicks in: interactions are reorganized around a single us-versus-them boundary, and exclusionary conceptions of identity are reinforced.

Political violence, in other words, is not merely a 'product' of a process of escalation. It is part of it, and reacts with patterns of interaction as well as environmental conditions. This in turn can give processes of violent escalation a circular, self-reinforcing dynamic. Or if the process develops differently it can lead to a final disengagement from political violence.

Contingency. Processes of escalation and radicalization can reproduce themselves, particularly when they trigger self-reinforcing dynamics, such as cycles of revenge. But this tendency is neither linear nor deterministic—in other words, this does not happen inevitably or in ways that are easily forecast (Bosi, O'Dochartaigh, and Pisoiu 2015). And while some violent processes do indeed display more distinct, 'wave-like' patterns of escalation and decline (Crenshaw 2001: 14), others evolve in discontinuous or even erratic patterns. Why? Here it is crucial to acknowledge contingency in sequences of events that turn violent (Bosi, Demetriou, and Malthaner 2014: 4). Contingency simply refers to the role of the unexpected in rearranging patterns. Unexpected events can become turning points in a process (McAdam and Sewell 2001; Sewell 2005), depending on their timing and how they coincide and become enchained with other events, but also on how they are perceived and interpreted by the groups and individuals involved.

6.4 MECHANISMS OF VIOLENT ESCALATION

A key challenge in developing processual perspectives on political violence has been to identify the mechanisms of political violent escalation. Can we understand more systematically when protest movements turn violence? Can we map more systematically how initial spontaneous violence turns into more sustained and systematic campaigns of political violence?

Fortunately, processual perspectives have begun to broaden out with an increasing number of comparative studies covering more diverse sets of cases (including militant Islamist groups). A further development has been the growing influence of the *contentious politics* paradigm pioneered by McAdam, Tarrow, and Tilly (2001) and Tilly and Tarrow (2007). At heart, the basic idea behind much of this recent research has been to identify recurring causal mechanisms which, in varying combinations and with context-specific outcomes, have shaped processes of radicalization and escalation.

> **KEY CONCEPTS**
>
> **Contentious Politics** Contentious Politics includes repertoires of non-routine and often disruptive, nonviolent and violent collective action used to make political claims and achieve political goals, involving the state as direct or indirect target of claims. Repertoires of action include civil disobedience, protest, strikes, and different forms of political violence.

Alimi, Bosi, and Demetriou, for example, developed an analytical framework specifying a set of causal mechanisms—including 'upward spirals of political opportunities', 'competition for power', and 'outbidding'—as well as three corresponding *arenas of interaction* out of which these mechanisms emerge (2012/2015). In addition, Bosi, Demetriou, and Malthaner (2014) have proposed a framework of four types of dynamics that shape processes of radicalization and escalation (dynamics of interaction between oppositional movements and the state, dynamics of intra-movement competition, dynamics of meaning formation and transformation, and dynamics of diffusion).

> **KEY CONCEPTS**
>
> **Radicalization** Radicalization here denotes a collective or individual shift from nonviolence to violent forms of actions. It can involve cognitive transformations ('radicalization of ideas'), as well as shifts in patterns of relations, but the connection between ideas and actions is complex.
>
> **Disengagement** Disengagement denotes a collective or individual shift from political violence to nonviolent forms of actions.

In this section, we focus on a set of four interconnected mechanisms developed by Della Porta on clandestine political violence. The first is termed: *Escalating Policing*. It refers to the reciprocal adaptation of forms of policing and repertoires of protest. By contrast, *Competitive Escalation* is a mechanism that emerges from a dynamic of competition between different groups within the same overall movement. *Organizational Compartmentalization* refers to patterns of increasing social isolation and detachment. Finally, *Ideological Encapsulation* relates to a shift in ways of thinking. In other words, it refers to the cognitive dynamic that triggers a shift towards more exclusive ideological frameworks (Della Porta 2013: 67–69, 74–76, 146–152, 176–178, 206–209).

Escalating Policing. As protests challenge public order, they often trigger interactions between the protestors and the police. Police strategies can and do vary broadly in terms of their respect for the right to demonstrate, their toleration of minor violations, and whether tactics of intervention are 'harder' or 'softer'. The key point here is that escalating policing happens when, the radicalization of the forms of protest interacts with repressive policing styles. These are typically not only brutal, but also often diffuse. Put simply, in these types of situation, the police just tend to hit a lot of people—both the violent and the nonviolent. The result is a process of 'double diffusion'—that is a spread of (increasingly violent) tactics amongst both police and protestors (Della Porta and Tarrow 2012).

What each side does influences the other. So tactical interactions then move through reciprocal adaptation to innovative turns by the adversary (McAdam 1983). Violence spreads especially fast when the state is perceived as overreacting to the emergence of protest and taking the sides of its opponents. Everyday experiences of physical confrontation with police tend to spread the image of an unfair state, ready to use brutal force against its citizens. A perception of indiscriminate repression brings about increased solidarity amongst protestors: the dynamics we call solidarization. This in turn helps to delegitimize both the police, and the state which they claim to serve.

Repression then spreads to countercultural milieus sympathetic to violence. These resuscitate old myths; and create new ones. Brutal charges against demonstrators, or the killing of comrades represent particularly transformative events (Beissinger 2002; Sewell 1996). They trigger intense emotions of identification with those prepared to fight. And the state becomes designated unambiguously as an enemy. Elaborated within a broader narrative of oppression and resistance, escalating policing is then read by protestors as a sign that there is no other way out. They become convinced, that peaceful protest is insufficient to reach their goals, or simply suicidal in the face of violent repression.

Competitive escalation. During waves of protests different actors cooperate with each other. But they also are rivals, such as different activist groups who compete for public attention and the same pool of recruits. While large part of these interactions are peaceful, radicalization also happens at times. Generally, more occasional and defensive at the beginning of a cycle of protests, violent repertoires may then become increasingly organized and ritualized as protests spread. Towards the end of the cycle, as the number and size of protest events decline, some forms of protest may become 'institutionalized'. In other words, street protests as energy is channelled into setting up new campaigning organizations on a more long lasting basis. But clandestine forms of violence may also survive.

Indeed, the use of violence may become a resource in the organizational competition within dense milieus of specific social movements. Such social movement are often related to other social movements. We can call these 'social movement families'—that is, different, but related, social movements that share general orientations and at times join together for broader campaigns.

Large networks of old and new social movement organizations tend to cooperate with each other as protest is building to a peak. But the opposite occurs after that peak. Fissions and tensions typically increase during the decline of mobilization. Conflicts emerge over the best strategies and tactics that could help in order to overcome the perceived crises.

Moreover, counter-movements tend to emerge during cycles of protests, to resists claims for reform, with often physical conflicts between militants of different fronts.

Experimentation with violent tactics emerge therefore from attempts to outbid the other groups and adaptations to the tactics of adversaries. Radicalization develops then in connection with organizational competition over tactics (McCarthy and Zald 1973: 6).

Especially during these declining phases of mobilization, violence can therefore become a trademark that attracts radicalized activists. Through these adaptations of practices, activists are socialized into violence. Organizations also adapt their structures to its use. A typical example is the creation of martial bodies, devoted at first to self-defence. But they can easily instead be reoriented towards attack. All in all, structures that specialize in violent repertoires are created during fights with political adversaries and the police. Eventually, some occasion of violence or repression pushes these members into the underground.

Organizational compartmentalization. Once underground, clandestine organizations tend to change profoundly. They depart from the organizational repertoires (Clemens 1996) that had characterized their social movement families. In a nutshell, they have to adapt fast to a hostile context.

With a very different balance between hierarchical and horizontal formats and different internal divisions of function, new compartmentalized structures develop in clandestinity. Faced with increasing repression and reduced external support, the clandestine organizations tend to become more hierarchical. The sheer difficulty of holding meetings open to both militants and wider sympathizers tends to increase the power of a small core of leaders.

But there are counter-pressures as well. Attempts to implement hierarchical control are often jeopardized by centrifugal trends. When members are forced to go underground, small cells are formed with looser and looser contacts not only with each other but also with the leaders. In addition, the difficulty in participating in visible forms of protests tends to give more and more relevance to the military skills and the military organizational bodies over the political ones. As isolation increases, factions are formed and often physically attack each other. They frequently split into smaller and smaller units. Internal purges may occur.

During this process, then, action becomes increasingly violent. There are frequent shifts from actions against property to actions against people, and from wounding to killing. Actions for propaganda can give way to actions intended merely to help the organization to survive. A logic of war emerges as the organizational isolation intensifies. Defining themselves as soldiers and heroes, militants tend to target the so-called repressive apparatuses (police, army, judges, and so on).

Ideological encapsulation. Radical ideologies are preconditions for the turn to political violence. But they can also be effects of the use of violent repertoires of action: and sometimes overwhelmingly so. Narrative about one's own identity constructs a path going from a glorious past, to a long decadence, and then to a rebirth. A sense of moral superiority develops. Moving away from the political visions shared by the broader social movements that they were initially rooted in and that they had wanted to influence, and adapting their discourse to organizational transformations, the clandestine groups tend to present themselves as heroic soldiers and/or martyrs.

More and more brutal forms of action are then justified through the building of an image of an absolute evil and the 'de-humanization' of the enemy. Giving up attempts at coordinating their views with those of activists in the social movement environments, their discourse becomes self-contained and self-referential. In effect, militants are left only to talk among themselves: and that talk becomes more extreme. Violence, which might have been initially justified simply as a means of opposing a powerful and unjust adversary, then becomes framed as an existential response. Increasingly, they see their choice as to kill or be killed.

This analysis leads to some startling conclusions. According to this approach, political ideologies may well not be the direct causes of clandestine violence. Rather they are the twisted products of process: belief systems that have, in part, been transformed by the militants themselves (Bosi 2012).

CASE STUDY 6.2

The Islamic Group (al-Jamaa al-Islamiyya) in Egypt

Al-Jamaa al-Islamiyya ('The Islamic Group') emerged in the late 1970s at the radical fringe of a (non-militant) Islamist student movement in Egypt, mainly at Upper-Egyptian universities, which had become a potent challenger to president Anwar al-Sadat, his pro-Western policies, and peace treaty with Israel. The government's attempts to curb the movement's growing influence with repression triggered further protests as well as, eventually, the assassination of Sadat in 1981, as an act of revenge by a small group called al-Jihad in collaboration with some members of al-Jamaa al-Islamiyya.

The assassination was followed by a major crackdown on the Islamist movement, which was effectively eliminated from the political stage in the mid-1980s. After a number of middle-ranking leaders were released from prison, al-Jamaa re-appeared across universities in Upper Egypt, but also in poor neighbourhoods in the suburbs of Cairo. By the late 1980s, al-Jamaa's followers among university students and around local mosques again counted in the thousands. Police tried to uproot the militants from local neighbourhoods, which resulted in a series of violent clashes, such as in the Ayn Shams area of Cairo in August 1988. There, police met with fierce resistance that turned into prolonged street battles, in which not only militants, but also local residents, who perceived the police as attacking their neighbourhood, took part.

After the group's spokesman was allegedly killed by the secret police in August 1990, the group started a campaign of violent attacks against policemen, foreign tourists, and members of the Christian minority, mainly in Upper Egypt and Cairo, which lasted until 1998 and claimed about one and a half thousand lives (see Photo 6.2).

Notably, over the course of this campaign, initial support among the local population gradually eroded as a result of increasing pressure from government forces which arrested

PHOTO 6.2 The Temple of Luxor, Egypt, was the site of a massacre in 1997 by the terrorist organization al-Jamaa al-Islamiyya.

hundreds of alleged militants and cordoned off whole villages. But the militants' increasing isolation was also the result of their attempts to impose an Islamic order and their brutal punishment—including public executions—of alleged collaborators.

QUESTIONS

1. How would you explain the escalation of the Islamic Group's tactics using a processual approach?
2. In what way might interactions with supportive milieus have affected the group's violent campaign?

6.5 MICRO-MOBILIZATION: INDIVIDUAL RADICALIZATION AND PARTICIPATION IN MILITANT GROUPS

How do individuals become involved in militant activism? Exploring such individual pathways has become a major concern of processual scholarship (Viterna 2006, 2013; Bosi 2012, 2016; Bosi and Della Porta 2012; Blee 2016). An emphasis upon social ties and interpersonal processes tends to lead away from seeing individual participation in protest and political violence as stemming from psychological or social 'pathologies' (McAdam 1986: 65; Snow, Zurcher, and Ekland-Olson 1980: 789; Della Porta 1992: 6/7).

At this level of analysis, it is the relational dimension of radicalization that is stressed. Cognitive processes are shaped by this dimension in complex ways within specific social contexts. Radical networks and milieus operate as 'micromobilization-settings'. But it is important as well not to overlook how broader processes of escalation impact on individual pathways. Analysis of individual pathways is most persuasive when it is integrated with other levels of analysis: including the research on collective radicalization (Della Porta 1995/2013; Bosi and Della Porta 2012; Weinstein 2007).

A key notion here is that of *mobilization via pre-existing social ties*. Consistently, research has found that personal relationships (friendship or kinship) come first: they can then pave the way into participation in movements (i.a. Snow et al. 1980; McAdam 1986; Della Porta 1992: 8; McAdam and Paulsen 1993; Passy 2003). Other experienced observers have also come to similar conclusions: Marc Sageman once described al-Qaeda cells as typically evolving from just a 'bunch of guys' (Sageman 2004).

Interpersonal networks are not just the entry gate into radicalization. They continue to matter later on as well—but with different dynamics. Once involved in armed groups, the networks formed through action frequently come to matter most (Bosi 2012; Della Porta 2013; Viterna 2006/2013). Such subcultural milieus and radical networks can forge close personal bonds which in turn become a powerful inducement to continued participation. Commitment under pressure can indeed only be sustained through such intense bonds of trust and loyalty (Snow, Zurcher, and Eckland-Olson 1980; McAdam 1986; Della Porta 1992).

Such bonds are often forged gradually. The sympathizer who distributes propaganda materials successfully may then be called upon for more ambitious duties as well. 'High-risk' forms of activism are often preceded by more 'low-risk' activism in broader social movements: these early forays provide the opportunity for trying out new roles while facilitating connections to other activists. With them comes a process of socialization that facilitates the adoption of perceptions, attitudes, values, and identities (McAdam 1986: 69/70). Seen this way, cognitive radicalization is bound up with social processes of dense interaction. Ideological affinity is not irrelevant. But the attitudes and motivations for participation are themselves formed through the process itself. As Snow, Zurcher, and Eckland-Olson put it strikingly: *'the "whys" or "reasons" for joining arise out of the recruitment itself'* (1980: 799).

From left-wing through to ethno-nationalist and religious movements, comparative analysis has thus stressed social ties and personal networks as crucial. Still, radical networks and milieus vary greatly—and thus shape individual pathways in very different ways (Bosi and Della Porta 2012; Della Porta 2013; Malthaner and Waldmann 2012/2014). Several authors have identified varieties of individual motivations (i.e. ideological, instrumental, and solidaristic) as well as varieties of pathways among the members of particular groups (Bosi and Della Porta 2012; see also Dorronsoro and Grojean 2004). The particular motivations and trajectories of female activists has also attracted attention (i.e. Passerini 1992; Viterna 2013; Blee 2008).

Yet a balanced perspective is needed here. An emphasis on personal networks alone does not explain radicalization: *'Focusing on affective ties provides only a partial explanation of individual motivations, since they cannot account for the specific form that social networks take'* (Della Porta 1992: 10/11). Della Porta emphasizes the importance of examining *'the environmental conditions that make an individual receptive to the use of political violence'* (Della Porta 1992: 11). Effects of repression and confrontations with counter-movements on individuals need to be factored in here (Della Porta 1995 161/2; Bosi and Della Porta 2012). Solidarity among activists is reinforced by confrontation with the police (as well as by persecution and arrest). Such episodes also create powerful 'frames'—ways of presenting experience—that stress injustice and legitimize violence as necessary revenge.

In summary, it is important not to reduce radicalization to abstract ideological processes. Arguably, it is more illuminating to see it as unfolding via the lived experience of activism. A specific type of activism will be connected to wider processes of escalation. Episodes of collective action entail powerful experiences. And these, in their turn, re-shape perceptions and frames of interpretation.

6.6 CONCLUSION

Arising out of the study of social movements, processual perspectives have made a distinctive and valuable contribution to the study of political violence. First, their emphasis on relational dynamics in explaining violence has been a major step forward. It has introduced the idea of political violence not as something that just springs into life fully formed, but which emerges only gradually.

Secondly, this approach calls for us to embed our analysis of radical movements and militant groups within a broader relational field of actors involved in political conflict, including broader protest movements, militant groups, and state actors. Rather than try to mark out a separate category labelled 'terrorists' this approach seeks to understand how violent militants relate to other political actors: and if they become highly isolated, to explain how and why.

Finally, this perspective helps us to understand the actors' motives and beliefs more adequately, as a dynamic product of processes of escalation and radicalization. Intentions and goals are neither pre-given nor stable. Militant groups as well as individual activists form and adapt their perceptions and frameworks of interpretation in interactions with opponents and rivals. At the same time—by shaping their actions—these beliefs and perceptions reinforce or drive the escalation of violence. Beliefs and actions are locked in a feedback-circle.

In summary, the study of processes remains an exciting and fresh area of investigation into political violence even as it has matured and become more 'mainstream'. The reasons for this are obvious enough. At the most basic level, a dynamic phenomenon needs to be analysed using a dynamic theory.

Over the past 50 years the study of social movements has offered many invaluable suggestions for how we might better study violent groups. And here, processual approaches have proven their worth many times over. They have been able to explain changes in the nature and levels of violent campaigns, including their endings. Even if those working on processual approaches have tended to remain reluctant to see themselves as 'terrorism studies' scholars, there is no doubt that the study of terrorism is far richer for their efforts.

DISCUSSION QUESTIONS

1. How does a concentration on processes help us to understand the development of political violence?
2. Processual approaches emerged out of the study of social movements in liberal democracies from the late 1960s. What might the challenges be in transferring this analytical approach to very different contexts?
3. Which of the factors considered in processual approaches seems more relevant and why?
4. Does terrorism always emerge as gradually as processual approaches seem to assume?
5. 'Rather than reducing radicalization to abstract ideological processes, it is arguably much more helpful to see it as unfolding via the lived experience of activism.' Discuss.

 Visit the online resources for pointers on how to answer the discussion questions, links to useful web sources, and guidance on accessing databases:
www.oup.com/he/Wilson-Muro1e

GUIDE TO FURTHER READING

Bosi, L., Demetriou C., and Malthaner, S. (eds., 2014) *Dynamics of Political Violence: A Process-Oriented Perspective on Radicalization and the Escalation of Political Conflict*. Farnham/London: Ashgate. *This book brings together a broad array of authors from social movement studies, civil war research, and research on political violence, who analyse different types of dynamics in processes of radicalization and the escalation of violence.*

Della Porta, D. (2013) *Clandestine Political Violence*. Cambridge: Cambridge University Press. *Della Porta's monograph comparatively examines the processes by which clandestine groups emerge in the context of broader movements.*

McCauley, C. and Moskalenko, S. (2009) *How Radicalization Happens to Them and Us*. Oxford: Oxford University Press. *Clark McCauley and Sophia Moskalenko, both social psychologists, offer an alternative, though similar perspective on mechanisms in processes of radicalization.*

Tilly, C. (2003) *The Politics of Collective Violence*. Cambridge: Cambridge University Press. **Charles Tilly suggests to go beyond conventional typologies and examine common dynamics in very different forms of collective violence.**

Viterna, J. (2013) *Women in War: The Micro-processes of Mobilization in El Salvador*. New York: Oxford University Press. **Focusing on individual pathways towards joining armed groups, Jocelyn Viterna brings together social movement theory and civil war studies.**

REFERENCES

Alimi, E. Y., Demetriou, C., and Bosi, L. (2015) *The Dynamics of Radicalization: A Relational and Comparative Approach*. Oxford: Oxford University Press.

Beissinger, M. R. (2002) *Nationalist Mobilization and the Collapse of the Soviet State*. Cambridge: Cambridge University Press.

Blee, K. (2008) 'The Hidden Weight of the Past: Paths and Micro-History in the Study of Social Movements,' in J. Walton, C. DeCorse, and J. Brooks (eds.), *Small Worlds: Method, Meaning, and Narrative in Microhistory*. Sante Fe: School of Americas Research (SAR) Press.

Blee, K. (2016) 'Personal Effects from Far-Right Activism', in L. Bosi, M. Giugni, and K. Uba (eds.), *The Consequences of Social Movements: People, Policies, and Institutions*. New York: Oxford University Press, 66–84.

Bosi, L. (2006) 'The Dynamic of Social Movement Development: Northern Ireland's Civil Rights Movement in the 1960s', *Mobilization*, 11 (1): 81–100.

Bosi, L. (2012) 'Etat des savoirs et pistes de recherche sur la violence politique' *Criticque Internationale*, 54: 171–189.

Bosi, L., and Della Porta, D. (2012), 'Micro-mobilization into Armed Groups: Ideological, Instrumental and Solidaristic Paths', *Qualitative Sociology*, 35: 361–383.

Bosi, L., Della Porta, D. and Malthaner, S. (2018) 'Organizational and Institutional Approaches: Social Movement Studies Perspectives on Political Violence', in Erica Chenoweth, Richard English, Andreas Gofas, and Stathis Kalyvas (eds.) *The Oxford Handbook of Terrorism*. Oxford: Oxford University Press. 133–147.

Bosi, L., Demetriou, C., and Malthaner, S. (2014) (eds.), *Dynamics of Political Violence. A Process-Oriented Perspective on Radicalization and the Escalation of Political Conflict*. Farnham: Ashgate.

Bosi, L., and Malthaner, S. (2015), 'Political Violence,' in D. Della Porta and M. Diani (eds) *Oxford Handbook of Social Movements*. Oxford: Oxford University Press. 439–451.

Bosi, L., O'Dochartaigh, N. and Pisoiu, D. (2015), 'Contextualizing Political Violence', in L. Bosi, N. O'Dochartaigh, and D. Pisoiu (eds.), *Political Violence in Context: Time, Space, and Milieu*. Colchester: ECPR Press. 1–14.

Clemens, E. (1996) 'Organizational form as frame: collective identity and political strategy in Amercian labour movement, 1880–1920', in McAadam, McCarthy and Zald (eds.) *Comparative Perspectives on Social Movements*. Cambridge: Cambridge University Press. 205–226.

Crenshaw, M. (2001) 'Theories of Terrorism: Instrumental and Organizational Approaches', in D. Rappoport (ed.), *Inside Terrorist Organizations*, 2nd edition. London: Frank Cass. 13–31.

Della Porta, D. (1992) 'Introduction: On Individual Motivations in Underground Political Organizations', in D. della Porta (ed.), *Social Movements and Violence: Participation in Underground Organizations*. Greenwich/London: Jai Press Inc. 3–28.

Della Porta, D. (1995) *Political Violence and the State*. Cambridge: Cambridge University Press.

Della Porta, D. (2008) 'Research on Social Movements and Political Violence', *Qualitative Sociology*, 31: 221–230.

Della Porta, D. (2013) *Clandestine Political Violence*. Cambridge: Cambridge University Press.

Della Porta, D. and Diani, M. (2000) *Social Movements: An Introduction*. Oxford: Blackwell Publishers.

Della Porta, D. and Tarrow, S. (2012), 'Double Diffusion: Police and Protestors in Transnational Contention', *Comparative Political Studies*, 20: 1–34.

Dorronsoro, G. and Grojean, O. (2004), 'Engagement militant et phénomènes de radicalisation chez les Kurdes de Turquie', *European Journal of Turkish Studies* (http://www.ejts.org/document198.html).

Goldstone, J. (1998) 'Initial Conditions, General Laws, Path Dependence, and Explanation in Historical Sociology', *American Journal of Sociology*, 104 (3): 829–845.

Kalyvas, S. N. (2006) *The Logic of Violence in Civil War*. Cambridge: Cambridge University Press.

Kriesi, H., R. Koopmans, Dyvendak, J. W., and Giugni, M. G. (1995) *New Social Movements in Western Europe: A Comparative Perspective*. Minneapolis: University of Minnesota Press.

Malthaner, S. (2014) 'Contextualizing Radicalization: The Emergence of the "Sauerland-Group" from Radical Networks and the Salafist Movement', *Studies in Conflict and Terrorism*, 37 (8): 638–653.

Malthaner, S. (2017) 'Radicalization: The Evolution of an Analytical Paradigm', European Journal of Sociology, 58 (3): 369–401.

Malthaner, S. and Waldmann, P. (2003) 'Terrorism in Germany: Old and New Problems', in M. van Leeuwen (ed.), *Confronting Terrorism. European Experiences, Threat Perceptions and Policies*. The Hague, London, New York: Kluwer Law International. 111–128.

Malthaner, S. and Waldmann, P. (2012) (eds.), *Radikale Milieus: Das soziale Umfeld terroristischer Gruppen*. Frankfurt/New York: Campus.

Malthaner, S. and Waldmann, P. (2014) 'The Radical Milieu: Conceptualizing the Supportive Social Environment of Terrorist Groups', *Studies in Conflict and Terrorism*, 37 (12): 979–998.

McAdam, D. (1982) *Political Process and the Development of Black Insurgency, 1930—1970*. Chicago and London: University of Chicago Press.

McAdam, D. (1983) 'Tactical Innovation and the Pace of Insurgency', *American Sociological Review*, 48: 735–754.

McAdam, D. (1986) 'Recruitment to High-Risk Activism: The Case of Freedom Summer', *American Journal of Sociology* 92/1, 64–90.

McAdam, D. and R. Paulsen (1993) 'Specifying the Relationship between Social Ties and Activism', *American Journal of Sociology* 99, 640–667.

McAdam, D., Tarrow, S., and Tilly, C. (2001) *Dynamics of Contention*. New York: Cambridge University Press.

McAdam, D. and Sewell, W. H. (2001) 'It's about Time: Temporality in the Study of Social Movements and Revolutions', in R. R. Aminzade, J. G. Goldstone, D. McAdam, E. J. Perry, W. H. Sewell, S. Tarrow, and C. Tilly (eds.), *Silence and Voice in the Study of Contentious Politics*. Cambridge: Cambridge University Press. 89–125.

McCarthy, J. and Zald, M. (1973) The trend of social movements in America: Professionalization and resource mobilization. Morristown, NJ: General Learning Press.

McCarthy, J. D. and Zald, M. N. (1977) 'Resource Mobilization and Social Movements: A Partial Theory', *American Journal of Sociology*, 82 (6): 1212–1241.

Neidhardt, F. (1981) 'Über Zufall, Eigendynamik und Institutionalisierbakeit absurder Prozesse: Notizen am Beispiel einer terroristischen Gruppe', in H. v. Alemann and H. P. Thurn (eds.), *Soziologie in weltbürgerlicher Absicht. Festschrift für René König zum 75. Geburtstag*. Opladen: Westdeutscher Verlag. 243–257.

Passy, F. (2003) 'Social networks matter. But how?', in M. Diani and D. McAdam (eds), *Social Movements and Networks. Relational Approaches to Collective Action*. Oxford: Oxford University Press. 21–48.

Sageman, M. (2004) Understanding Terror Networks. University of Pennsylvania Press.

Sewell, W. H. (1996) 'Three Temporalities: Toward an Eventful Sociology', in T. J. McDonald (ed.), *The Historic Turn in the Human Sciences*. Ann Arbor: University of Michigan Press. 245–280.

Sewell, W. H. (2005) *Logics of History. Social Theory and Social Transformation*. Chicago and London: University of Chicago Press.

Snow, D. A., Zurcher, L. A., Ekland-Olson, S. (1980) 'Social Networks and Social Movements: A Microstructural Approach to Differential Recruitment', *American Sociological Review*, 45 (5): 787–801.

Snow, D. A. and Benford, R. D. (1998) 'Ideology, Frame Resonance, and Participant Mobilization', in Bert Klandermans, Hanspeter Kriesi, and Sidney Tarrow (eds.), *From Structure to Action: Social Movement Participation Across Cultures*. Greenwich, Conn.: JAI Press.

Tarrow, S. (1989) *Democracy and Disorder*. Oxford: Clarendon Press.

Tarrow, S. (1998) *Power in Movement. Social Movements and Contentious Politics*. Cambridge: Cambridge University Press.

Tilly, C. (1978) *From Mobilization to Revolution*. Reading, MA: Addison-Wesley.

Tilly, C. and Tarrow, S. (2007) *Contentious Politics*. Boulder, CO: Paradigm Publishers.

Victoroff, J. (2005) 'The mind of terrorists: A review and critique of psychological approaches', *Journal of Conflict Resolution*, 49 (1): 3–42.

Viterna, J. (2006) 'Pulled, Pushed, and Persuaded: Explaining Women's Mobilization into Salvadoran Guerrilla Army', *American Journal of Sociology* 112, 1–45.

Viterna, J. (2013) *Women in War. The Micro-Processes of Mobilization in El Salvador*. Oxford: Oxford University Press.

Weinstein, J. (2007) *Inside Rebellion. The Politics of Insurgent Violence*. Cambridge: Cambridge University Press.

Wood, E. J. (2003) *Insurgent Collective Action and Civil War in El Salvador*. Cambridge: Cambridge University Press.

CHAPTER 7

Terrorism Open Source Databases

GARY LAFREE

■ CHAPTER SUMMARY

Open source databases on terrorism are created from unclassified, publicly available information retrieved from print (e.g. newspapers) and digital (e.g. online news reports) media. Over the past two decades the number and scope of open source databases on terrorism has greatly increased. The unit of analysis for these databases have either been events, organizations or individuals. Of the three types, event databases have been the most common. Terrorism event databases provide systematized descriptive information about terrorist attacks where the attack is the unit of analysis. Databases on terrorist organizations gather group-level characteristics including dominant ideology, attacks claimed, and estimated number of followers. Individual level databases generally focus on demographic, group affiliation, and contextual information about perpetrators of terrorism.

Most commonly, event and group-level databases have been worldwide in scope while most individual level databases have focused on perpetrators in a single country. Because terrorism is a type of behaviour that is difficult to study by more traditional means (e.g. police reports or victim or perpetrator surveys), open source databases have come to fill an essential niche. However, they have important weaknesses, most notably media inaccuracies; conflicting information or false, multiple, or no claims of responsibility; government censorship and disinformation; and a lack of systematic empirical validation. Nevertheless, open-source databases on terrorism can be justified in part because many terrorist perpetrators seek publicity. Likely future improvements include better coverage of domestic terrorism, more extensive automated coding, enhanced geo-spatial information, better links to related databases, and more detailed data on the effectiveness of countermeasures.

7.1 TERRORISM OPEN SOURCE DATABASES

Let's say you are interested in knowing how many terrorist attacks happen in the world or whether the number of attacks is increasing or decreasing. Where do you go for information? Compared to collecting data on more commonly studied crime like homicide and robbery, collecting data on terrorism raises unique challenges. First, (as this textbook has already explored) there is no universally accepted definition of terrorism. A survey of terrorism studies by Schmid and Jongman (1988: 5) famously concluded that there were more than 100 different definitions of terrorism. The definition we adapt in this chapter is 'the threatened or actual use of illegal force and violence by non-state actors to attain a political, economic, religious, or social goal through fear, coercion or intimidation' (LaFree, Dugan, and Miller 2015: 13). But while this definition includes some of the most obvious characteristics of terrorism (e.g. use of violence, political goals), it by no means reflects a universally agreed upon definition. This means that the designers of open source terrorism databases must make some difficult decisions about how to conceptualize and count terrorism.

Second, because definitions of terrorism vary, and because terrorism has a strong political dimension, not all individuals or governments agree on exactly what constitutes terrorism. Researchers face a difficult challenge in terms of defining and counting terrorist incidents.

And finally, most of the data collection methods used by social scientists to study ordinary crime are difficult or impossible to use in the case of terrorism. For example, victimization surveys are useful for studying common types of crime but are of little value in the case of terrorism, where victims are often randomly selected, have little information about the perpetrators, and often do not survive the attack. So-called 'self-report' surveys, where researchers interview informants about their prior criminal behaviour have been valuable in criminology, but are difficult in the case of terrorism where most perpetrators actively avoid researchers. And while governments collect a great deal of information about ordinary crimes, government data collection on terrorism has been hampered by the fact that most terrorist perpetrators are arrested and convicted not on terrorism charges but for common crimes based on terrorist activity, such as murder, arson, and money laundering. Moreover, even when governments (for example, the US State Department and the Israeli Ministry of Foreign Affairs) collect data on terrorism, the political nature of the phenomenon generally produces a good deal of scepticism about the validity of the data reported. Open source databases are a response to these challenges.

Open source terrorism databases concentrate on three units of analysis: events, organizations, and individuals. Of the three types, event databases have been the most common. Terrorism event databases provide systematized descriptive information about terrorist attacks. Databases on terrorist organizations gather group-level characteristics including dominant ideology, attacks claimed, and basic features like estimated number of followers. Individual level databases most often focus on demographic, group affiliation, and contextual information related to perpetrators. There have been a dozen or more systematic efforts to build terrorism event databases while databases on groups and individuals have been less common. Event and group-level databases have usually been worldwide in scope while most individual level databases have focused on perpetrators in a single country. In fact, a disproportionate amount of research attention in this area has focused on highly industrialized Western countries. All three types of terrorism databases are similar in that they rely on information from unclassified, open sources, like newspaper articles and court documents.

> **KEY CONCEPTS**
>
> **Open Source Databases and OSINT** Open source data are gathered from public sources, including scientific articles, newspapers, and digital media. Open source intelligence (OSINT) involves the collection and analysis of these unclassified open sources for intelligence purposes (Best and Cumming 2008). During the early part of the post-World War II period intelligence professionals were sceptical of open source information and valued secret information above all else. However, this began to change in the United States after the collapse of the Soviet Union, and especially as the intelligence community came under intense scrutiny after the 9/11 attacks and the perceived intelligence failures surrounding the 2003 war in Iraq. More generally, intelligence experts increasingly recognized that the explosive growth of the internet and online media were providing an ever increasing amount of potentially useful information. In recognition of these changes in 2005 the US Congress created the National Open Source Center whose mission is to perform specialized OSINT acquisition in support of all US intelligence agencies. An emerging consensus now exists that OSINT must be systematically collected and should constitute an essential component of analytical products for intelligence purposes.

While open source databases fill an important niche for an area of great policy interest that is generally lacking in data that are more traditional, they also have several weaknesses. In this chapter, we will review event, group, and individual-level terrorism databases. This chapter considers how each type of database is organized, what it tells us about terrorism, and considers some of its main strengths and weaknesses. The chapter is concluded with a discussion of how open source terrorism databases are likely to evolve in the future.

7.2 TERRORISM EVENT DATABASES

Starting in the late 1960s, the availability of satellite technology and portable video equipment made it much easier for researchers and policymakers to gather information on events like war, political violence, and conflict. Terrorism databases were a natural outgrowth of these developments. These are summarized in Table 7.1.

TABLE 7.1 World Wide Open Source Event Databases on Terrorist Attacks

	SCOPE	PERIOD	NUMBER
TWEED	Domestic (Europe only)	1950–2004	11,245
ITERATE	International	1968–2020	15,534
RAND	International	1968–1997	8,509
PGIS	Domestic & International	1970–1997	67,179
US Dept. of State	International	1980–2003	10,026
RAND-MIPT/RDWTI [a]	Domestic & International	1968–2009	40,129
GTD (Stage 1)	Domestic & International	1970–2011	104,658
WITS	Domestic & International	2004–2011 [b]	79,795
GTD (Stage 2)	Domestic & International	1970–2019	201,183

[a] Funding for MIPT data collection ended in 2008 and after a brief pause, RAND continued the series as the RAND Database of Worldwide Terrorism.
[b] Data reported through March 31, 2011.

All of the event databases listed in Table 7.1 draw upon 'open source' or unclassified digital and print media and use terrorist attacks as the unit of analysis. Their intention is to provide descriptive information about terrorist attacks on a systematic basis that follow basic journalistic conventions: *who* is responsible for an attack, *what* happened, *where* and *when* did it happen, and *how* did it happen.

The Global Terrorism Database (GTD), located at the University of Maryland (LaFree, Dugan, and Miller 2015) is the most extensive. Current data collection for the GTD is wide-ranging. Two million articles published daily worldwide are reviewed; the aim is to isolate the small subset of articles that refer to terrorist attacks. The GTD team of 15–20 initially uses customized search strings; natural language processing methods then 'weed out' duplicate source articles.

Feedback from trained staff guides a machine-learning model to classify digital and print media. Manual reviews of the source documents identify both false-positives (source documents that appear to describe terrorist attacks but do not) and false-negatives (source documents that appear to not describe terrorist attacks but actually do).

All source documents that have been classified as relevant by the machine-learning model are reviewed by the GTD team; generating database entries for individual attacks that satisfy the GTD inclusion criteria. An event definition process is then conducted using automated tools (including natural language processing, named entity recognition, and machine learning models). At present, the GTD team reviews 10,000–30,000 articles each month.

PHOTO 7.1 Gary LaFree and the team that collects the Global Terrorism Database (GTD).

The GTD's impact has been huge across both terrorism research and policy. Every year it receives over 1,000 citations on Google Scholar and its website attracts over two million page visits. Every US agency concerned with defence or intelligence consults it. So, too, do governments and businesses around the world.

Another influential worldwide terrorism event database is the International Terrorism: Attributes of Terrorist Events (ITERATE) database (Mickolus et al. 2010). ITERATE contains two different types of files: quantitatively coded data on international terrorist incidents and a qualitative description of each incident included in the quantitative files. The quantitative data are arranged into four files, containing: (1) information on the type of terrorist attack, including location, name of group taking responsibility, and number of deaths and injuries; (2) information on the fate of the terrorists or terrorist group claiming responsibility; and (3) information on terrorist attacks involving hostages and skyjackings. The ITERATE data are limited to transnational terrorist attacks, which are a small subset of all terrorist attacks. ITERATE data began in 1968 and has been updated through 2021. Use of ITERATE data requires a substantial fee.

Several other event databases are worth mentioning, although each has limitations. With the support of the US Department of State and the Defense Advanced Research Projects Agency (DARPA), in 1972, Brian Jenkins at the RAND Corporation began to develop a 'Chronology of International Terrorism' dating back to 1968. Like ITERATE, the original RAND data were generally limited to international attacks. However, RAND began collecting data on domestic attacks in 1998. Funding for the RAND data collection ended in 2008. According to the RAND website, data on terrorism are available free from 1968 through 2009.

> ### KEY CONCEPTS
>
> **Domestic Versus International Attacks** Both policymakers and the public frequently draw sharp distinctions between domestic and international terrorist attacks. Particularly in the wake of the coordinated attacks of 9/11, it has become common to hear the argument that international terrorism poses a more serious threat than domestic terrorism (Johnson 2012). At the same time, Chermak and Gruenewald (2006) argue that terrorism motivated by domestic ideologies can be every bit as deadly as international terrorism. How do we tell the two apart? In general, every terrorist attack has three main nationalities associated with it: that (1) of the country in which the attack took place, (2) of the perpetrators, and (3) of the targets. The simplest and most common distinction between domestic and international terrorism is to assume that attacks where one or more of these nationalities differs from the others is international, while attacks where all three are the same are domestic (LaFree, Dugan, and Miller 2015). However, a major challenge of distinguishing domestic from international attacks is that in most open source terrorism databases, the nationality of the perpetrators is only known about half the time.

The National Counterterrorism Center (NCTC) collected the Worldwide Incidents Tracking System data (WITS) from 2004 to 2011. Collection depended upon a manual search of open sources: commercial subscription news services, the US Government's Open Source Center, local news websites in both English and foreign languages (Wigle 2010). Both international and domestic data were gathered, generating extremely inclusive coverage. Between 2004 to 2011, WITS reported nearly 80,000 terrorist attacks—far more than any other events database.

Event databases have profound weaknesses. Inaccuracies and lies turn up in media reports. Conflicting information as well as false, multiple or no claims of responsibility present challenges. So, too, does government censorship and disinformation. Dictatorships like North Korea report extremely low numbers of terrorist attacks. Is this because of actual low numbers? Or merely the ability of these regimes to minimize coverage by the print or digital media? It is impossible to say for certain. Overall, then, the key weaknesses of event databases include: (1) lack of a generally accepted definition of terrorism, (2) biases and inaccuracy in open source data, and (3) lack of consistency over time.

First, because there is no universally accepted definition of terrorism, individual event databases generally rely on different operational definitions. In some cases, definitions are similar, but important differences remain. Different definitions will result in different data outcomes. It is challenging to distinguish terrorist attacks from other violent behaviour that shares certain terrorism characteristics, notably insurrection, guerrilla warfare, hate crime, ethnic cleansing, and organized crime (for a review, see LaFree, 2018a). Terrorism definitions for the major open source event databases are compared in Case Study 7.1.

CASE STUDY 7.1

Defining Terrorism

Sheehan (2012) identified 12 of the most common elements in definitions of terrorism and checked for their application in five open source databases: GTD, ITERATE, RAND, TWEED (Department and Terrorism in Western Europe: Events Data) and WITS (The Worldwide Incidents Tracking System). RAND includes nine of these elements in their definition of terrorism, ITERATE and GTD include seven, WITS includes six, and TWEED includes five. Only two elements are included in terrorism definitions for all five databases (perpetrators are sub-state groups or clandestine agents and the act is outside the context of legitimate warfare or a coup d'état). Two additional elements are included in the terrorism definitions of four of the five databases (use of violence and intended to influence or coerce an audience). The remaining eight elements are divided between different combinations of three or fewer of the five databases. While differences in definitions of terrorism across databases make it more difficult to directly compare them, open source databases that are transparent in terms of what their definitions are, and consistent in terms of how they apply them, may nonetheless provide extremely valuable information about terrorism and its characteristics.

QUESTIONS

1. How does the problem of defining terrorism differ from the problem of defining more ordinary crimes like robbery or burglary?
2. Does the fact that there are no universally accepted definitions of terrorism have any advantages for researchers?

Second, some general biases are unavoidable (Dugan and Distler 2016). Event databases draw upon news sources which are themselves affected by the degree of freedom of the local press. Unsurprisingly (but crucially) in strongly undemocratic states, the press is not free (such as China, Iran, or Cuba). Conversely, in strongly democratic states, the press is generally free (Norway, Finland, and Sweden are the top three according to the world press freedom index in 2021) (Drakos and Gofas 2006). The potential implications are profound. Research has often linked the incidence of terrorist attacks to democratization levels. But here under reporting of terrorist attacks in countries with low press freedom (which are often more undemocratic or authoritarian) may be distorting results. Even in countries with high levels of press freedom the more serious attacks are more likely to be reported.

International press coverage varies considerably. Let us take the percentage of terrorist attacks in the GTD where responsibility for attacks cannot be attributed to a specific group.

In over 60 per cent of the attacks in South America and Western Europe, perpetrators could be identified. By contrast, the equivalent figure for Russia and the states of the former Soviet Union, Eastern Europe, and Central Asia was less than 20 per cent (Crenshaw and LaFree 2017). Human rights coverage has also fluctuated over time (Fariss 2014). So, a possibility remains: apparent increases in terrorism that show up in the open sources may simply be picking up media change (rather than more attacks).

Another possibility is that open source databases underreport terrorism for some countries or regions of the world because their data collection has leaned toward coverage of English language sources. Resource constraints have limited the monitoring of non-English sources for the GTD, RAND and WITS, fluctuating over time.

And the media itself has its own biases. Fishman (1980) noted the tendency for new sources to be fitted into news 'frames'. Such preselected themes (e.g. 'suicide attacks') are more likely to be covered. Even conscientious media sources remain vulnerable to unintentional inaccuracy and intentional misinformation.

Given the desirability of developing time series longitudinal analyses of terrorist attacks, the complexities of maintaining event databases become even more challenging. The more time elapsed between real events and data collection the greater the chances that some data are no longer available. Thus, GTD data from 1998 to 2006 were collected after 2006 while GTD from 2006 on have been collected in close to real time (LaFree et al. 2015). If newspaper and digital media are unarchived, availability of original sources erodes over time. Missing data increase: especially for small, regional, and local newspapers.

Moreover, as event databases evolve, the size of the media 'fire hose' supplied by news aggregators increases. Media sources that the GTD relies on have moved from one million per day to nearly two million per day. These increases raise the possibility that trends in terrorist attacks over time are affected by increasing access to information rather than a real escalation in the total number of attacks. It becomes difficult to identify and resolve duplicate cases (King and Lowe 2003; Schrodt and Van Brackle 2013). Case Study 6.2 illustrates how difficult it is to classify an attack as terrorism by considering a recent attack attributed to a group called Antifa (an anti-fascist network of groups) in Charlottesville, Virginia.

CASE STUDY 7.2

Was the Antifa Attack in Charlottesville, Virginia an Example of Terrorism?

During clashes between right-wing extremists and left-wing supporters in Charlottesville, Virginia in August 2017, one person was killed, and 35 others were injured when James Fields, a man with links to white-supremacist groups, drove his car into a crowd of left-wing protesters (Hawes and Perez-Penadec 2017). The GTD team included the attack by Fields, but did not include as terrorism the violence committed by the left-wing Antifa supporters.

PHOTO 7.2 The Antifa flag. Antifa are an anti-fascist left-wing network of groups who were deemed to have not committed terrorism in Charlottesville, Virginia by the GTD. This was counter to the views of the US President at the time, Donald Trump.

The GTD team looked at six major issues to decide whether an attack should be counted as terrorism (START 2019). Five of these characteristics appear to be met in this case (LaFree 2018b). First, the incident involved the immediate threat of violence (Astor et al. 2017; Penny 2017). Second, the incident was committed by an individual rather than a government. Third, there is evidence that the act was aimed at attaining a political goal (counter protesters in Charlottesville saw themselves as taking a political stand by countering racism and hate crime; Astor et al. 2017; Beinart 2017). Fourth, there was evidence of an intention to coerce, intimidate, or convey some other message to a larger audience than the immediate victims. Fifth, the action took place outside the context of legitimate warfare activities. Yet the Antifa actions in the Charlottesville case lack a final necessary element: that the attack be intentional. The GTD requires that the attack be a conscious calculation on the part of the perpetrators. The GTD team did not count the attack as terrorism because they could not find any evidence that Antifa supporters came to the demonstration with the intention of engaging in violence or doing harm. This is counter to the perspective put forward by former President Donald Trump, who at the time Tweeted that Antifa could be to blame.

> **QUESTIONS**
> 1. How do we determine the intent of someone's actions in everyday life?
> 2. Based on this description of the case in Charlottesville, would you classify the actions leading to the storming of the US Capitol on 6 January 2021 as terrorism?

Event databases also have key strengths. Media attention is key to terrorist groups: unlike most common criminals, they *want* to be noticed. 'Terrorism is theatre' as Brian Jenkins (1975) declared: terrorist attacks are often designed to win the attention of digital media and the international press. Open source information can be uniquely illuminating here; because terrorists seek the attention of the media, the coverage of terrorism is likely to be more comprehensive than coverage of more common crimes. Tracking burglary or fraud rates by studying digital and print media would present profound methodological problems, but it makes more sense for tracking terrorist attacks. Global media are unlikely to miss an aerial hijacking or politically motivated assassination, even in remote areas.

And there is another advantage to such event databases on terrorism. Cross-national crime research has been severely weakened by its focus on highly industrialized Western-style democracies: in practice, fewer than 40 of the world's countries which spotlight Europe and North America, neglect Africa, the Middle East, and Asia (Nivette 2011; LaFree, Carrillo, and McDowall 2015). By contrast, open source terrorism databases do cover all countries (albeit imperfectly).

In summary, open source event databases have their limitations—like all crime databases. The US's FBI's Uniform Crime Reports, for instance, have long been criticized for many of the same issues as event databases (Lynch and Addington 2007; O'Brien 1985). However, in the final analysis, for those interested in tracking terrorism, at present there is no obvious alternative to using event databases.

7.3 TERRORISM GROUP DATABASES

Of the serious efforts to construct databases on terrorist organizations, the most extensive to date is the Big, Allied, and Dangerous Dataset (BAAD) collected by Asal and colleagues (Asal and Rethemeyer 2008; Asal, Rethemeyer, and Anderson 2011). BAAD data collection began in 2005 and relied especially on group-level data originally collected by the Memorial Institute for the Prevention of Terrorism's (MIPT) Terrorism Knowledge

Base (Houghton 2008). The original BAAD contained a snapshot of 395 terrorist organizations that committed at least one attack between 1998 to 2005 (START 2015). BAAD includes information on incidents, injuries, and fatalities for each terrorist organization. Organizations that were either aliases, covers, or temporary fronts for other members are excluded. Information collected includes size, date of founding, ideology, state sponsors, connection to other terrorist groups, and territory the group controls (Asal, Pate, and Wilkenfeld 2008).

BAAD was first used to understand why some terrorist organizations were more lethal than others and the variables that contribute to the lethality of these organizations (Asal, Pate, and Wilkenfeld 2008). In later iterations, researchers added data to BAAD to allow analyses of relationships between terrorist organizations and between countries and terrorist organizations. BAAD has continued to expand over time, gradually including a longer time frame and additional variables. BAAD now includes group names, whether the organization is supported by the state, the organization's home-base country, the total number of deaths associated with the group, the age of the organization, size, whether the organization controls territory, the number of alliance connections, and the ideology of the group. These relationships are coded for suspected allies, factions, splinter groups, rivals, enemies, targets and state sponsors. These data now allow researchers to examine the evolution of terrorism networks over time.

In a 2015 update of BAAD, researchers included more than 2,800 primary terrorist and insurgent groups and more than 3,400 associated aliases. The expanded BAAD allows scholars to examine the organizational behaviour of terrorist organizations and to compare terrorist attacks to war, insurgency, and nonlethal forms of political violence. BAAD is the most extensive open source database on group-level terrorism yet assembled.

BAAD suffers from the same weaknesses as open source event databases, such as missing or biased information. The early BAAD data did not allow longitudinal analysis and even the most recent versions include only a limited time series capability. This restricts researchers' ability to analyse the relationships between terrorist behaviours and terrorist network formation. Because information in BAAD relies heavily on the internet it was not practical to gather data earlier than 1998; a date at which the internet had reached enough maturity to be a viable source of information about terrorist groups. Still, the difference in internet penetration over time may affect the quality and availability of information. Another limitation is that most of the coding and sources are either in English or are machine translated into English. At times, the project had coders who spoke other languages (e.g. Arabic, Spanish) but generally data collection has relied on automated translation. To the extent that English language sources are treated differently than sources in other languages bias in outcomes may be introduced.

7.4 TERRORISM PERPETRATOR DATABASES

Collecting information on all individuals involved in terrorism around the world is a more complicated endeavour than collecting data on terrorist attacks or groups; in large part because a single attack may involve multiple perpetrators (who may never all be identified). Conversely, individuals may be charged with terrorism-related offences before they have actually committed a planned attack. For these reasons, the few open source databases on individuals that now exist focus on specific countries rather than on the world as a whole. Three of the most extensive of these are from the United States: (1) the American Terrorism Study (ATS; Smith and Damphousse 2007); (2) the Profiles of Individual Radicalization in the United States (PIRUS; Jensen, James, and Tinsley 2015; LaFree et al. 2018); and (3) the Extremist Crime Database (ECDB; Freilich et al. 2014). Two additional individual-level studies focus on Islamist cases in Europe and the United States (the Western Jihadism Project, Klausen et al. 2016) and on lone actor perpetrators in the United Kingdom and the United States (the Lone Actor Terrorist Database, Gill, Horgan, and Deckert 2014). In sections 7.4–7.7 we will review these databases.

7.5 THE AMERICAN TERRORISM STUDY

In 1989, Professor Brent Smith began the American Terrorism Study (ATS) with a list of perpetrators from the FBI who had been indicted on criminal charges for domestic terrorism. For each indicted suspect, Smith and his colleagues obtained individual information from US District Court case records (Smith and Damphousse 2007). The initial list included more than 200 perpetrators from over 20 terrorist groups that were active in the United States from 1980 to 1989. Subsequent FBI lists were collected through the 2000s. With Department of Justice funding, the ATS was expanded beyond the sources supplied by the FBI (Fitzpatrick et al. 2017). For all those indicted, the ATS includes criminal counts, background information, conviction and sentencing outcomes. The data also include information on the terrorist organizations with which the indicted are associated. As of 2018, the ATS had data for the years 1980 to 2017 (Freilich et al. 2018).

One limitation of the ATS is that it is collected primarily from administrative sources, which may contain errors because of processing differences between federal courts. Another drawback is that information is limited to individuals who were indicted in federal courts, excluding state courts. Despite these limitations, the ATS is one of the longest running and most extensive sources of open source terrorism data in the United States. ATS is especially useful for examining the characteristics and actions of individual perpetrators operating in the United States, the groups in which they operate and how these individuals and groups respond to prosecutorial and sanctioning strategies. The dataset provides important insights into the impact of federal guidelines on the sentencing outcomes for terrorists and similarly situated non-terrorists (Smith and Damphousse 2007). It includes information on nearly all individuals indicted in federal courts for terrorism-related charges, and it allows geospatial and temporal analysis of terrorist attacks and the individuals and groups that perpetrated them.

7.6 PROFILES OF INDIVIDUAL RADICALIZATION IN THE UNITED STATES (PIRUS)

PIRUS is a cross-sectional, quantitative dataset of individuals in the United States who radicalized to the point of violent or nonviolent ideologically motivated criminal activity, or had an ideologically motivated association with a foreign or domestic extremist organization from 1948 until 2017 (Jensen et al. 2016). The PIRUS team defines radicalization as the psychological, emotional, and behavioural processes by which an individual adopts an ideology that promotes criminal behaviour for the attainment of political, economic, religious, or social goals (LaFree et al. 2018). Indicators of radicalization within the PIRUS dataset are set broadly and do not have to involve violence. They span arrests, indictments, as well as convictions for engaging in (or simply planning to engage in) ideologically motivated unlawful behaviour. Membership in a designated terrorist organization or extremist group is also included. Under PIRUS criteria, then, an individual who runs a website for a violent extremist group can be included in the database. PIRUS only includes cases of 'domestic radicalization:' where most or all of the individuals' radicalization occurred while they were residing in the United States. PIRUS is based entirely on publicly available sources, including court documents, online news articles, newspaper archives, open-source non-government reports (e.g. the Southern Poverty Law Center), unclassified government reports (e.g. annual FBI terrorist reports), and existing terrorism-related datasets (e.g. the Global Terrorism Database).

The PIRUS data collection team uses random sampling methods to maximize the representativeness of the data. Yet problems remain. First, a reliance on open sources may reflect news reporting trends. As groups come under intense media scrutiny, it becomes easier to identify those who are involved. Conversely, individuals affiliated with ideologies or movements that are not being spotlighted may find it easier to keep a low profile. In concrete terms the post-9/11 period likely over-represents Islamist extremists (in comparison to those associated with other extremist ideologies). Second, there is a potential 'foreshortening effect' caused by limited access to digital historical sources before the 1990s. More recent cases are likely, therefore, to be over-represented in the PIRUS database. If not corrected for, this will distort the results of any longitudinal trend analysis.

At the same time, PIRUS has provided a rich set of empirical studies on political extremism in the United States. Researchers using PIRUS have tested and compared a wide range of theoretical explanations of domestic terrorism (Holt et al. 2018; Becker 2020; LaFree et al. 2017; Jasko, LaFree, and Kruglanski 2017; Jensen, Atwell Seate, and James 2020; Carson, James, and O'Neal 2019). PIRUS has also been used to examine the strengths and weaknesses of open source data on terrorism (Safer-Lichtenstein, LaFree, and Loughran 2017). And PIRUS data have been used to further our understanding of how political violence is linked to criminal gangs (Pyrooz et al. 2017), the perpetrator's prior criminal record (LaFree et al. 2017; Jensen et al. 2020), the leadership structures of terrorist organizations (Jasko and LaFree 2020), and imprisonment (LaFree, Jiang, and Porter 2020).

7.7 THE EXTREMIST CRIME DATABASE

The Extremist Crime Database (ECDB) includes individual level open source data that fulfils two requirements. First, the illegal violent incident or financial scheme must have been committed within the United States. Second, at least one of the suspects who perpetrated the illegal act must adhere to a far-right, Islamist-inspired, or extremist animal/environmental rights belief system. The ECDB includes incidents in which extremists commit homicide, suicide, bombing, arson, or are killed by law enforcement. The ECDB also collects information on ideologically motivated financial crimes. To create the ECDB researchers first reviewed existing databases and unclassified official sources, such as FBI reports (Freilich et al. 2014). They then examined journal articles, books and case studies, material published by private watch groups, and media publications. The ECDB includes over 370 homicides committed by far-right extremists and close to 700 financial schemes perpetrated by al-Qaeda inspired Islamist extremists or far-right extremists (Freilich et al. 2014: 376).

7.8 THE WESTERN JIHADISM PROJECT

Professor Jytte Klausen started the Western Jihadism Project (WJP) in 2006 to understand Islamist extremism and Western homegrown terrorist movements. The project is a multimedia archive that contains quantitative and qualitative data on the growth of jihadism (militant and politically rooted Islamic movements) in Western democracies across Europe, North America, and Australia. It contains data on terrorist offenders from 20 countries. The data are collected from government press releases, court records, and autobiographical statements made by perpetrators on social media or in jihadist forums. The data currently include about 6,200 individuals, 850 plots, local and international terrorist organizations that are linked to western jihadist extremists, and 27,000 links between either persons or persons and organizations (Brandeis University n.d.). The data contains demographic information and records of criminal acts, charges and convictions.

The WJP provides a comprehensive dataset on Jihadist-inspired terrorist offenders that allows social network analyses of the recruitment processes of terrorist organizations and the radicalization patterns for individuals (Brandeis University n.d.). The project can provide insight on cross-national and personal networks of the organization and recruitment of Jihadist terrorists in western nations (Brandeis University n.d.). It can also shed light on radicalization patterns and behaviours of homegrown Jihadist offenders to inform law enforcement and policymakers. Much of the information about the terrorist offenders in the data are from court or prosecution documents. This potentially limits what is included in the data. For example, information unrelated to the adjudication of criminal offences is often lacking (Klausen 2016).

7.9 LONE ACTOR TERRORIST DATA

Gill and colleagues (2014) collected data on behavioural aspects of 119 lone actor offenders who engaged in or planned to engage in lone actor terrorism within the United States and Europe after 1990 and were convicted for their actions or died during the offence. These include perpetrators who planned and executed violent attacks as well as those who engaged in nonviolent behaviours that encouraged violence or actions that only intended to cause property damage. Data were collected by building a list of individuals from academic sources, LexisNexis search archives (including open source news reports, sworn affidavits, openly available firsthand accounts, biographies), the Global Terrorism Database, and lists of those who were convicted of terrorism-related offences in the United States and the United Kingdom (Gill et al. 2014).

Lone actor terrorists in the database include both individual terrorists and isolated dyads. Individual terrorists include those with and without command and control links who operate autonomously and independently of organizations. Some individuals are completely independent of groups in terms of training, preparation, and target selection, while others radicalized within a group, but later left to engage in terrorist activities on their own. There are also perpetrators that received training from organizations, but carried out attacks on their own (Gill et al. 2014). The lone actor dataset includes information on sociodemographic characteristics, behaviour antecedent to the event, event specific behaviour (e.g. attack methods, targets), and post-event behaviour (e.g. claims of responsibility, arrest details; Corner and Gill 2015; Gill et al. 2014).

As with other open source data, the lone actor data only includes individuals whose stories are reported in the media. If the incidents led to convictions but they were not covered in national media or if they were only reported in local media sources not covered by LexisNexis, then the individuals involved are excluded. Another limitation is that the amount of information provided by different media sources varies. In addition, newspaper reporting does not cover the information of each variable or behaviour that the offender did not do (e.g. the offender did not have a substance abuse history). This makes it hard for coders to distinguish between actual missing data and 'no' answers (Gill et al. 2014).

7.10 THE FUTURE OF TERRORISM EVENT DATABASES

Given continued interest in tracking terrorism around the world, event databases are likely to be with us for the foreseeable future. There are five considerations about the future of these databases. First, terrorism event databases will routinely include both domestic and international data. Many of the early event databases were limited to international data. However, prior research that has compared domestic and international terrorist attacks (Enders et al. 2011; LaFree, Dugan, and Miller 2015) concludes that the former outnumbers the latter by as much as seven to one. Moreover, as Falkenrath (2001: 164) points out, dividing bureaucratic responsibility and legal authority according to a domestic-international distinction is 'an artifact of a simpler, less globally interconnected era.'

Second, we can expect increasingly automated data collection in the future. Schrodt and Van Brakle (2013: 26) make the argument simply: '… human-machine comparisons are of little practical consequence, since human coding is not an option.' This is well illustrated by the current data collection of GTD which now digests two million articles each day: in the face of an ever-growing 'fire hose' of media information, a fully human coding protocol is no longer a serious option.

But at the same time, there are still important limitations to automation. A recent study by Wingenroth et al. (2016) tested the accuracy of the semi-automated data collection procedures used by the GTD against three fully automated data systems: the

Global Database of Events, Language and Tone (GDELT); the Integrated Conflict Early Warning System (ICEWS) and Phoenix. To compare the databases the researchers chose as a test bed world-wide suicide bombing in January and February 2015. The authors found that the GTD was able to pick up 97 per cent of the incidents identified in a 'ground truth' exercise where a research team combed through sources and carefully verified actual events. By contrast, GDELT picked up 70 per cent of the events, ICEWS 57 per cent and Phoenix only 10 per cent. A major challenge for the fully automated databases was the presence of duplicates. Eighty-three per cent of ICEWS cases, 79 per cent of GDELT cases, and 65 per cent of Phoenix cases were duplicate interpretations of the same event. While automation is likely to improve our ability to detect and record terrorist attacks, human validation is likely to remain as a critically important part of the process.

Third, event databases will increasingly provide geographic information system (GIS) enhancements. All GTD data are now geo-referenced. Such GIS data are critical for supporting the growing amount of research on geo-spatial patterns of terrorism (Berrebi and Lakdawalla 2007; Behlendorf, LaFree, and Legault 2012).

Fourth, future databases will increasingly be linked to other related databases, including those on countermeasures and other types of political and non-political violence and crime. For example, Eck (2012) provides the framework for integrating two of the preeminent armed conflict event datasets (the Uppsala Conflict Data Program's Georeferenced Event Data [UDCP-GED] and the Armed Conflict Location and Event Data Project [ACLED]). Donnay et al. (2019) have developed a dashboard that integrates the Global Terrorism Database with UCDP-GED, ACLED, and the Social Conflict Analysis Database (SCAD). There has also been research on integrating terrorism data across different units of analysis. The Terrorism and Extremist Violence in the United States (TEVUS) Database and Portal is based on four related open source databases (START 2020). The portal compiles behavioural, geographic, and temporal characteristics of extremist violence in the United States dating back to 1970.

Finally, future open source data bases are likely to more fully examine how specific anti-terrorism and counter-terrorism efforts impact the likelihood of terrorist attacks. At present, we have relatively little systematic information on the impact of government programmes on trajectories of terrorist activities. Such research could help us better understand what separates successful and unsuccessful countermeasures, which variables predict the countermeasures implemented by governments, and whether the same countermeasures may have different impacts when implemented in response to different groups. An illustration is provided by Dugan and Chenoweth (2012) who collected extensive counter terrorism data for Israel and used the data to compare terrorism data from the GTD to countermeasures adopted by the Israeli government. See Table 7.2 for a list of websites for the databases reviewed in this chapter.

TABLE 7.2 Websites for Major Open Database Sources

ATS	https://doi.org/10.3886/icpsr04639.v1
BAAD	https://www.start.umd.edu/data-tools/big-allied-and-dangerous-baad-database-1-lethality-data-1998-2005
DVN/GPEUFH	
ECDB	https://www.start.umd.edu/publication/introducing-united-states-extremist-crime-database-ecdb
GTD	https://www.start.umd.edu/gtd/
ITERATE	https://library.duke.edu/data/sources/iterate
10.7910/DVN/TH4ADJ	
PIRUS	https://www.start.umd.edu/data-and-tools/start-datasets
RAND	https://www.rand.org/nsrd/projects/terrorism-incidents.html
TEVUS	https://www.start.umd.edu/tevus-portal
TWEED	https://dss.princeton.edu/catalog/resource380
WJP	https://www.brandeis.edu/klausen-jihadism/staff.html

7.11 CONCLUSIONS

The nature of terrorism makes it difficult to track through traditional criminological sources such as victimization or self-report surveys or police data. Contemporary terrorism event databases have become more feasible over time, first with the availability of satellite technology and portable cameras and later with the explosive growth of the internet. The number and scope of open source databases on terrorist attacks has greatly expanded since the early 1970s. Open source databases are generated from print and digital media and face associated limitations. In particular, the media may report misinformation, there may be conflicting information or false, multiple or no claims of responsibility and despite improvements, coverage still relies more on Western than non-Western news organizations.

It is worth pointing out that all of these problems are also frequently mentioned as drawbacks of official crime data. Certainly, government censorship and disinformation affects not only media sources but official government sources. It is especially challenging to disentangle terrorism from acts of war, insurrection or massive civil unrest: as have predominated in countries such as Iraq, Afghanistan, and Syria. Even though the media now reach every corner of the world, media coverage still varies across time and geographic space. On the other hand, event databases have the great strength of tracking a type of behaviour whose success is in large part a function of its ability to be publicized. At present there is likely no other type of crime that has data as universally available for all countries of the world as terrorism.

Efforts to compare event databases have been slow to develop, hampered especially by major differences between definitions, scope and years of coverage. However, in recent years there have been an increasing number of comparative studies of the available databases and this is likely to accelerate in the future.

Because event databases provide data on terrorism that are not available from any other source, they are likely to continue. Some of the major developments we can expect from event databases in the future include routine collection of domestic as well as international events, increased use of automated data collection and verification, geo-referencing of events, more comprehensive linkage to other data sources, and more sophisticated efforts to measure and evaluate the impact of government countermeasures on terrorism.

DISCUSSION QUESTIONS

1. In what ways is collecting data on terrorism more difficult than collecting data on other types of illegal behaviour?
2. In the interconnected world in which we live is it possible to meaningfully distinguish domestic from international terrorism?
3. Why do you suppose most of the existing databases on terrorist attacks began after the late 1960s?
4. Which type of open source data—event, group or individual—is most difficult to collect and why?
5. Why not collect data on terrorism the same way that we collect data on other more typical types of crime?

Visit the online resources for pointers on how to answer the discussion questions, links to useful web sources, and guidance on accessing databases:
www.oup.com/he/Wilson-Muro1e

GUIDE TO FURTHER READING

Crenshaw, M. and LaFree, G. (2017). *Countering Terrorism: No Simple Solutions*. Washington, DC: Brookings. *For an overview of major challenges to doing counterterrorism and how these challenges are made apparent by data on terrorism.*

Freilich, J. D., Chermak, S. M., Belli, R., Gruenewald, J., and Parkin, W. S. (2014) 'Introducing the United States Extremist Crime Database (ECDB).' *Terrorism and Political Violence* 26(2): 372–384. *Another major individual-level database on terrorism.*

Klausen, J., Campion, S., Needle, N., Nguyen, G., and Libretti, R. (2016) 'A Behavioural Model of "Homegrown" Radicalization Trajectories'. *Studies in Conflict & Terrorism.* 39(1): 67–83. *A close look at a large data set on individual terrorist perpetrators and what the data tell us about terrorist careers.*

LaFree, G., Dugan, L., and Miller, E. (2015). *Putting Terrorism in Context: Lessons from the Global Terrorism Database*. London: Routledge. *The most extensive current data base on terrorist attacks is introduced in detail.*

Schmid, A. and Jongman, A. (1988) *Political Terrorism: A New Guide to Actors, Authors, Concepts, Data Bases, Theories, and Literature*. New Brunswick and London: Transaction Publishers. *This critical review of terrorism research, data, and methods is useful to consult.*

REFERENCES

Asal, V. and Rethemeyer, R. K. (2008) 'The Nature of the Beast: Organizational Structures and the Lethality of Terrorist Attacks', *The Journal of Politics*, 70 (2): 437–49.

Asal, V., Pate, A., and Wilkenfeld, J. (2008) Minorities at Risk Organizational Behaviour Data and Codebook Version 9/2008. Available at http://www.cidcm.umd.edu/mar/data.asp#marob

Asal, V., Rethemeyer, R. K. and Anderson, I. (2011) 'Big Allied and Dangerous (BAAD) Database 1 - Lethality Data, 1998–2005 [Dataset].' (https://dataverse.harvard.edu/dataset.xhtml?persistentId=doi:10.7910/DVN/GPEUFH).

Astor, M., Caron, C., and Victor, D. (2017) 'A guide to the Charlottesville aftermath', *The New York Times*. August 13. https://www.nytimes.com/2017/08/13/us/charlottesville-virginia-overview.html.

Beinart, P. (2017) 'The rise of the violent left: antifa's activists say they're battling burgeoning authoritarianism on the American right. Are they fuelling it instead?' *The Atlantic's Politics and Policy*, 9, September. https://www.theatlantic.com/magazine/archive/2017/09/the-rise-of-the-violent-left/534192/

Becker, M. (2020) 'When Extremists become Violent: Examining the Association between Social Control, Social Learning, and Engagement in Violent Extremism', *Studies in Conflict & Terrorism*, October 28: 1–21.

Behlendorf, B., LaFree, G., and Legault, R. L. (2012) 'Predicting Microcycles of Terrorist Violence: Evidence from FMLN and ETA', *Journal of Quantitative Criminology*, 28: 49–75.

Berrebi, C. and Lakdawalla D. (2007) 'How Does Terrorism Risk Vary Across Space and Time? An Analysis Based on the Israeli Experience', *Defence and Peace Economics*, 18: 113–131.

Best, R. and Cumming, A. (2008) *Open Source Intelligence (OSINT): Issues for Congress*. Washington, DC: Congressional Research Service.

Brandeis University. n.d. 'About the Project | Jytte Klausen's Western Jihadism Project.' Retrieved July 10, 2019 (https://www.brandeis.edu/klausen-jihadism/about.html).

Brandeis University. n.d. 'Data Collection | Jytte Klausen's Western Jihadism Project.' Retrieved July 10, 2019 (https://www.brandeis.edu/klausen-jihadism/data-collection.html).

Carson, J. V., James, P. A., and O'Neal, T. A. (2019) The radicalization of the Kanes: family as a primary group influence? *Dynamics of Asymmetric Conflict*, 12 (1): 67–89.

Chermak, S. M. and Gruenewald, J. (2006) 'The Media's Coverage of Domestic Terrorism', *Justice Quarterly*, 23: 428–461.

Corner, E. and Gill, P. (2015) 'A False Dichotomy? Mental Illness and Lone-Actor Terrorism', *Law and Human Behaviour*, 39 (1): 23–34.

Crenshaw, M. and LaFree, G. (2017) *Countering Terrorism: No Simple Solutions*. Washington, DC: Brookings.

Donnay, K., Dunford, E. T., McGrath, E. C., Backer, D., and Cunningham, D. E. (2019) 'Integrating conflict event data', *Journal of Conflict Resolution*, 63 (5): 1337–1364.

Drakos, K. and Gofas, A. (2006) 'The Devil You Know but Are Afraid to Face Underreporting Bias and its Distorting Effects on the Study of Terrorism', *Journal of Conflict Resolution*, 50: 714–735.

Dugan, L. and Chenoweth, E. (2012) 'Moving Beyond Deterrence: The Effectiveness of Raising the Expected Utility of Abstaining from Terrorism in Israel', *American Sociological Review*, 77: 597–624.

Dugan, L. and Distler, M. (2016) 'Measuring Terrorism', in G. LaFree and J. Freilich, eds. *The Handbook of the Criminology of Terrorism*. New York: Wiley.

Eck, K. (2012) 'In Data We Trust? A Comparison of UCDP, GED and ACLED Conflict Events Datasets', *Cooperation and Conflict*, 47: 124–141.

Enders, W., Sandler, T., and Gaibulloev, K. (2011) 'Domestic Versus Transnational Terrorism: Data, Decomposition and Dynamics', *Journal of Peace Research*, 48: 319–337.

Falkenrath, R. (2001) 'Analytic Models and Policy Prescription: Understanding Recent Innovation in US Counterterrorism', *Journal of Conflict and Terrorism*, 24: 159–181.

Fariss, C.J. (2014) 'Respect for Human Rights Has Improved Over Time: Modelling the Changing Standard of Accountability', *American Political Science Review*, 108: 297–318.

Fishman, M. (1980) *Manufacturing the News*. Austin, TX: University of Texas Press.

Fitzpatrick, K. M., Gruenewald, J., Smith, B. L. and Roberts, P. (2017) 'A Community-Level Comparison of Terrorism Movements in the United States', *Studies in Conflict & Terrorism*, 40 (5): 399–418.

Freilich, Joshua D., Steven M. Chermak, Roberta Belli, Jeff Gruenewald, and William S. Parkin (2014) 'Introducing the United States Extremist Crime Database (ECDB)', *Terrorism and Political Violence*, 26 (2): 372–384.

Freilich, J. D., Chermak, S. M., Gruenewald, J., Parkin, W.S. and Klein, B. R. (2018) 'Patterns of Fatal Extreme-Right Crime in the United States.' *Perspectives on Terrorism*, 12 (6): 38–51.

Gill, P., Horgan, J., and Deckert, P. (2014). 'Bombing Alone: Tracing the Motivations and Antecedent Behaviours of Lone-Actor Terrorists', *Journal of Forensic Sciences*, 59 (2): 425–35.

Hawes, S. and Perez-Penadec, R. (2017) 'Murder charge increases in Charlottesville protest death', *The New York Times*, December 14. https://www.nytimes.com/2017/12/14/us/charlottesville-fieldswhite-supremists.html.

Holt, T., Freilich, J., Chermak, S., and LaFree, G. (2018) 'Examining the utility of social control and social learning in the radicalization of violent and non-violent extremists', *Dynamics of Asymmetric Conflict*, 11 (3): 125–48.

Houghton, B. K. (2008) 'Terrorism Knowledge Base: A Eulogy (2004-2008)', *Perspectives on Terrorism*, 2 (7). Retrieved from http://www.terrorismanalysts.com/pt/index.php/pot/article/view/43/html.

Jaśko, K., LaFree, G., and Kruglanski, A. (2017) 'Quest for Significance and Violent Extremism: The Case of Domestic Radicalization', *Political Psychology*, 38 (5): 815–831.

Jaśko, K. and LaFree, G. (2020) 'Who is more violent in extremist groups? A comparison of leaders and followers.' *Aggressive Behaviors*, 46 (2): 141–150.

Jenkins, B. M. (1975) *Will Terrorists Go Nuclear?* Santa Monica, CA: RAND Corporation.

Jensen, M., LaFree, G., James, P. A., Atwell-Seate, A., Pisoiu, D., Stevenson, J., and Tinsley, H. (2016) 'Empirical Assessment of Domestic Radicalization (EADR)'. Final Report to the National Institute of Justice, Office of Justice Programs, U.S. Department of Justice. College Park, MD: START. (https://www.start.umd.edu/pubs/START_NIJ_EmpiricalAssessmentofDomesticRadicalizationFinalReport_Dec2016_0.pdf)

Jensen, M., James, P. A., and Tinsley, H. (2015) 'Profiles of Individual Radicalization in the United States: Preliminary Findings'. January. https://www.start.umd.edu/pubs/PIRUS%20Research%20Brief_Jan%202015.pdf.

Jensen, M., Safer-Lichtenstein, A., James, P. A., and LaFree, G. (2020) 'The link between prior criminal record and violent political extremism in the United States', 121–146 in *Understanding Recruitment to Organized Crime and Terrorism*. Springer.

Jensen, M., Atwell-Seate, A., and James, P. A. (2020) 'Radicalization to Violence: A Pathway Approach to Studying Extremism', *Terrorism and Political Violence*, 32 (5): 1067–1090.

Johnson, D. (2012) Interview with a former counter-terrorism expert at the US Department of Homeland Security, CNN.

King, G. and Lowe, W. (2003) 'An Automated Information Extraction Tool for International Conflict Data with Performance as Good as Human Coders: A Rare Events Evaluation Design', *International Organization*, 57: 617–642.

Klausen, J. (2016) 'A Behavioural Study of the Radicalization Trajectories of American "Homegrown" Al Qaeda-Inspired Terrorist Offenders'. Report to the U.S. Department of Justice. 62.

Klausen, J, Campion, S., Needle, N., Nguyen, G. and Libretti, R. (2016) 'A Behavioural Model of "Homegrown" Radicalization Trajectories', *Studies in Conflict & Terrorism*, 39 (1): 67–83.

LaFree, G. (2018a) 'Conceptualizing and Measuring Terrorism: Evidence from the Global Terrorism Database', 22–33 in A. Silke (ed.). *The Handbook on Terrorism and Counter-terrorism*. London: Routledge.

LaFree, G. (2018b) 'Is Antifa a terrorist group?', *Society*, 55 (3): 248–253.

LaFree, G., Jiang, B., and Porter, L. (2020) 'Prison and Violent Political Extremism in the United States', *Journal of Quantitative Criminology*, 36 (3): 473–498.

LaFree, G., Dugan, L., and Miller, E. (2015) *Putting Terrorism in Context: Lessons from the Global Terrorism*. London: Routledge.

LaFree, G., Carrillo, K., and McDowall, D. (2015) 'How effective are our "Better Angels?" Evidence for a world-wide decline in violent crime since the 1990s', *European Journal of Criminology*, 12: 482–504.

Lynch, J. P. and Addington, L. (2007) *Understanding Crime Statistics: Revisiting the Divergence of the NCVS and UCR*. Cambridge studies in criminology. Cambridge University Press.

Mickolus, E. F., Sandler, T., Murdock, J. M., and Flemming, P. (2010) *International Terrorism:*

Attributes of Terrorist Events (ITERATE). Dunn Loring, VA: Vinyard Software.

Nivette, A. E. (2011) 'Cross-national Predictors of Homicide: A Meta-analysis', *Homicide Studies*, 15 (2): 103–131.

O'Brien, R. (1985) *Crime and Victimization*. Beverly Hills, CA: Sage.

Penny, D. (2017). An intimate history of antifa. *The New Yorker*. August 22. https://www.newyorker.com/books/page-turner/an-intimate-history-of-antifa.

Pyrooz, D., LaFree, G., Decker, S., and James, P. (2017) 'Cut from the Same Cloth? Comparing Gangs and Violent Political Extremists', *Justice Quarterly*, 35 (1): 1–32.

Safer-Lichtenstein, A., LaFree, G., and Loughran, T. (2017) 'Studying Terrorism Empirically: What We Know about What We Don't Know', *Journal of Contemporary Criminal Justice*, 33: 273–291.

Schmid, A. and Jongman, A. (1988) *Political Terrorism: A New Guide to Actors, Authors, Concepts, Data Bases, Theories, and Literature*. New Brunswick and London: Transaction Publishers.

Schrodt, P. A. and Van Brakle, D. (2013) 23–48 in V. S. Subrahmanian (ed.), *Handbook of Computational Approaches to Counterterrorism*. New York: Springer.

Sheehan, I. S. (2012) 'Assessing and Comparing Data Sources for Terrorism Research', 13–40, in C. Lum and L. Kennedy (eds.), *Evidence-Based Counterterrorism Policy*. New York: Springer.

Smith, B. L. and Damphousse, K. R. (2007) 'American Terrorism Study, 1980-2002: Version 1 [Data set].' (https://doi.org/10.3886/icpsr04639.v1).

START Center. (2015) Big, Allied and Dangerous (BAAD) Fact Sheet. https://www.start.umd.edu/publication/big-allied-and-dangerous-baad-fact-sheet.

START Center. (2019) Global Terrorism Database Codebook. http://www.start.umd.edu/gtd/downloads/Codebook.pdf.

START Center. (2020) The Terrorism and Extremist Violence in the United States (TEVUS) Database and Portal. https://www.start.umd.edu/tevus-portal.

Wigle, J. (2010) 'Introducing the Worldwide Incidents Tracking System (WITS)', *Perspectives on Terrorism*, 4: 3–23.

Wingenroth, B., Miller, E., Jensen, M., Hodwitz, O, and Quinlan, K. (2016) 'Event Data and the Construction of Reality'. Poster presented at the June, 2016 International Conference on Social Computing, Behavioural-Cultural Modelling, and Prediction and Behaviour Representation in Modelling and Simulation, Washington, DC.

PART TWO

Issues and Debates in Terrorism Studies

PART ONE The State of Terrorism Studies	15

PART TWO Issues and Debates in Terrorism Studies	135
8 The History of Terrorism	137
9 What Are the Root Causes of Terrorism?	157
10 When Do Individuals Radicalize?	178
11 Can Terrorism Be Rational?	201
12 Target Selection	218
13 Longevity of Terrorist Groups	238
14 Can States Be Terrorists?	260
15 Gendered and Racialized Terrorism	281
16 Terrorism by Insurgents and Rebels	302
17 Old and New Terrorism	325
18 Social Media and Terrorism	347
19 Is Terrorism Effective?	368

PART THREE Countering Terrorism	389

CHAPTER 8

The History of Terrorism

BERNHARD BLUMENAU AND TIM WILSON

■ **CHAPTER SUMMARY**

Every human phenomenon has a backstory. If we want to understand terrorism *now* it also make sense to think about terrorism's *past*. This chapter considers how we can best do so. First, it looks at what we might gain by looking to the past. Secondly, it offers an overview of the history of pre-modern terrorism. Thirdly, it looks closely at the dominant survey account of the historical evolution of modern anti-state terrorism since 1880: David Rapoport's 'Four Waves' model. Lastly, it briefly traces the evolution of modern state terrorism.

> **KEY CONCEPTS**
>
> **Terrorism** This chapter follows standard popular usage in distinguishing between *terrorism* (for non-state actors) and *terror* (for state oppression). It is important to recognize that both concepts are closely related by origin and association in the French Revolution of the 1790s: when this terminology first emerged.
>
> *Terrorism*, as it is understood in this chapter, is the deliberate use or threat of violence by non-state actors in order to achieve power and implement political goals. Its intended reach goes beyond those immediately attacked and terrorism is meant to create psychological effects (such as fear and anxiety) in a broader target audience. In that sense it is often a strategy of (extreme) communication.
>
> **Terror** If committed by a state, *terror* in the context of this chapter is understood to consolidate the power of a leader or elite through a campaign of deliberate and orchestrated violence carried out by agents of the authority.

8.1 THE CONTINUED IMPORTANCE OF PAST TERRORISM

Why study past terrorism at all? It is a fair question; and the answers are not obvious, so they are worth exploring early on. A first good reason to study past terrorism is practical. We might learn something useful. By its very nature, human experience lies in the past. Recorded history thus represents examples that we can freely explore. A lack of primary source research has often been identified as a key area of weakness of Terrorism Studies. There are good reasons for that. In general, it is not a good idea to try to study contemporary terrorists at close quarters. You might get arrested (or harmed). By contrast, data about past terrorism is available. And it is usually safe to access.

Some of this old information can prove very illuminating: especially if we believe that human nature does not change that much over time. If we can study more or less the same experiment repeated again and again, we can learn a lot about how violence is actually conducted. Let us take assassination as an example. Historical study shows that the close-quarter killing of leaders without warning is often surprisingly difficult. Would-be killers are typically highly nervous. As a result, they often fail. Assassination is not a practice that lends itself to realistic rehearsal.

Another strong argument for historical study is that it helps us understand the sheer complexity of past terrorism better. Very often, supposed 'lessons of history' are presented by either terrorists or governments as justifications for what they wanted to do anyway. Some knowledge of history allows us to interrogate these claims. In other words: it helps make us better sceptics. To give just one example: the American government's policy of 'enhanced interrogation' of al-Qaeda suspects was always likely to turn into a propaganda disaster. Historians of torture could have warned about that from past examples.

A further, and closely related, reason to study past terrorism is to support a sense of proportion about the *present*. Is the current terrorist threat that we happen to face now the worst ever? We are often told it is: by media commentators, by governments, and opposition politicians. Are they right? How can we know? We need comparative measurements to help us judge. And it is here that past records can give us the tools we need to measure the present. Knowledge of past terrorism, in short, can help protect us against accepting overexaggerated claims about contemporary terrorism.

Historical knowledge also helps to put current events into perspective: and to understand the deep roots of present crises. Some troubled regions, such as countries in the Middle East, provide case studies on terrorism. We cannot hope to understand these unless we have some sense of their historical background. Local actors themselves will often reference that past: and make contemporary claims based on their understanding of what happened long ago.

Let us take an example in more detail to make the point more fully. In Great Britain and France the diplomats Mark Sykes and Francois Georges-Picot are almost entirely forgotten figures. But they remain infamous names in the Middle East. Some brief background is needed here to explain why. At the time of the First World War, the Middle East was under the control of the Ottoman Empire. By tradition, its Sultan Abdulmejid II took the title of 'Caliph': that is, the ruler of the Islamic world (and guardian of the Islamic Holy Places) who stands in direct descent from the Prophet Muhammed himself. This ancient tradition was to be a casualty of the wider global conflict in which the Middle East became a direct battleground between the Ottoman Empire as an ally of Imperial Germany (on the one side); and of Great Britain and France (on the other).

The secret Sykes-Picot deal of 3 January 1916 was the French-British blueprint for carving up the territory of the Ottoman Empire between themselves and according to their own interests. In 1917–18, military victory allowed them to put this plan into action—with consequences (and borders) that still remain relevant to this day. In the aftermath of the Ottoman Empire's collapse, the Caliphate was formally abolished. But its memory lingered. Thus, when Islamic State declared *their* Caliphate and demolished border posts between Syria and Iraq in 2014, they celebrated it as 'The End of Sykes Picot'. They knew that framing would resonate deeply across the Middle East: because it could be presented as the righting of a great historic injustice to the Muslim *umma*, or global community.

A final good reason to study the past record of terrorism is that it might help us see the *future* shape of terrorism more clearly. All forecasts of the future involve some attempt to estimate the likely projected direction of current trends on the basis of past experience. All change is itself conditioned by the past. We need to know something of that past to evaluate the significance of any change.

Claims of total change always deserve to be carefully evaluated. The basic analytical point remains: we cannot hope to recognize what is genuinely 'new' terrorism if do not also study 'old' terrorism (see also Chapter 17). Historians can be sceptical of claims of total 'newness': because they recognize that even the processes that drive future changes themselves emerge out of the past, although often in ways that seem startling. It is precisely here that the study of some very old terrorism can prove illuminating.

8.1.1 Taking long views: terror in the ancient world

Historians face the same challenge as all other scholars of terrorism: to decide first how to define their subject area. If power means getting other people to do things that they do not want to do, then terrifying them is a method to get results. So, if we understand both terror and terrorism along these broad lines—the communicative use of violence to achieve wider political effects—we can trace its development back a very long way.

Starting from this viewpoint, we can see terror as 'old as human civilization' (Law, 2011: 1). A systematic use of intimidation has been a tool of state-building since the dawn of recorded time. The Assyrian Empire that ruled much of the Middle East between the ninth and seventh centuries *before* the so-called 'Common Era' (BCE) ago is often identified as a pioneer of such tactics. Across what is now Iraq, it consolidated its power through injustice and cruelty. Rebels met awful fates: public skinning, impaling, burning, and starvation.

If the Assyrian rulers were the first to apply such tactics systematically, they were not the last. Rulers in the ancient world generally used terror to broadcast their power. It is important to understand the wider context here: in an age of difficult communications and relatively undeveloped bureaucracies, terror was useful. It represented a short cut for rulers to establish their authority. As an ancient Chinese saying put it: 'Kill one, frighten ten thousand' (in Wilkinson, 1977: 49).

Such terror tactics were also not just a feature of consolidating authority, but of expanding it as well. Terror was instrumental to the practice of ancient warfare. Capturing fortified cities one after another was nearly always a very slow and difficult process. How might it be sped up? One tactic was to use a captured city as an example of what others might expect if they did not surrender quickly. Again and again, the same pattern emerges: an combination of arson, looting, murder, and rape was used by conquering forces to intimidate neighbouring cities into submission.

In short, ancient states were brutal. But they were also often potentially unstable. The death of an emperor or king might instantly create wider chaos. Attempts at violent change therefore targeted rulers directly because power was concentrated in leaders. Even the Roman Empire at its height remained highly vulnerable in this regard. In 69 of the Common Era (CE) power thus passed from Galba (who was assassinated) to Otho (who committed suicide after defeat in battle) to Vitellius (who was also assassinated) and, finally, to Vespasian (who consolidated his authority) in what was called 'the Year of the Four Emperors'.

> **KEY CONCEPTS**
>
> **Assassination** The relationship between assassination and terrorism is widely debated (Schmid, 2013: 62). Assassination implies the killing of an elite figure, but the term tends to imply little about the motivation behind the attack. Not all assassinations are political: some would-be killers just want to achieve publicity such as John Hinckley Jr who shot the American President, Ronald Reagan, on 30 March 1981 in an attempt to impress the actress Jodie Foster. Even if they are motivated by political calculation, that aim may be narrowly focused on the removal of a particular leader—rather than calculated to broadcast a message more widely (which is often considered a core element of terrorism). That said, assassinations *may* be reasonably understood as acts of terrorism if at least part of their motivation is to achieve some wider destabilization (as killings of truly powerful leaders will almost certainly do).
>
> **Before Common Era (BCE)/Common Era (CE)** This derives from the standard 'Western' or Christian calendar that takes the (assumed) date of the birth of Jesus Christ as the Year Zero. CE refers to dates after this starting point: BCE to dates before.

Assassination is as old as human hierarchy itself. But the key question is how *assassination* relates to the history of *terrorism*. And here there is no one general answer that fits all cases. Put simply: the motivations behind individual assassinations vary greatly. Sometimes a leader is targeted. Any wider effect is secondary: the main point of the killing is the removal of a unique personality (Schmid, 2013: 62). As early as the 4th century BCE ancient theorists of 'tyrannicide' across the ancient world emphasized this point: the Indian philosopher Kautilya made this assumption, as did Aristotle and Plato in ancient Greece (Law: 13). In exceptional cases they assumed it might indeed become necessary to kill a tyrant. Yet these thinkers understood this in limited terms: as an act of corrective surgery. Or as the medieval churchman John of Salisbury described it much later (in 1160 CE): 'it has been honourable to kill [tyrants] if they could not be otherwise restrained' (in Law, 2011: 35).

By contrast, on other occasions leaders have indeed been killed as symbols: and with the more ambitious goal of broadcasting some message to wider society. Such killings fit more neatly within standard understandings of what terrorism is: especially so when they are repeated in a serial pattern. Can we find any examples of such assassination campaigns from the deep past?

We can. But they are rare. It is hard to say why with any confidence. This absence may simply reflect a lack of surviving evidence. Or it may more accurately reflect ancient realities. After all, news travelled very slowly for most people before the transport revolutions of the past 200 years. Most people lived in a state of poverty. People remained preoccupied with the daily struggle of survival. Most politics were court politics—played out by a small number of elites in a distant and hidden arena. Yet despite these structural differences to our own age, two case studies stand out as similar to modern terrorism. The first are the Jewish 'dagger-men'—or Sicarii—of the 1st century Common Era (CE). The second are the hitmen of the Nizaris, an off-shoot of the Shia tradition of Islam: better known in English as 'the Assassins'. Each is worth exploring briefly.

By the mid-1st century CE Judea had emerged as a major trouble spot for the Roman Empire. At the heart of the instability lay the question of politico-religious legitimacy: and the claim of the Roman Empire (which officially recognized many Gods) to rule a distinct people (who believed in the existence of only one God). Here the Jewish priesthood had emerged as crucial, but compromised, agents of Roman control. Their cooperation with the Roman authorities was essentially pragmatic only. But it remained opposed by those Jews who believed *any* such cooperation was heretical. Against this unstable backdrop, the Jewish writer Josephus tells us of the sudden emergence of the Sicarii whose:

> … favourite trick was to mingle with festival crowds, concealing under their garments small daggers with which they stabbed their opponents. When their victims fell the assassins melted into the indignant crowd, and through their plausibility entirely defied detection. First to have his throat cut by them was Jonathan the High Priest, and after him many were murdered every day (Josephus, translated by Williamson, 1981: 147).

What are we to make of this account? First, the Sicarii were something new. Josephus seems to have struggled to find an appropriate vocabulary for them, introducing them as simply 'bandits in different form'. Secondly, they were sophisticated political killers who did not target *Romans* directly. Instead, they deliberately attacked high-profile *Jewish* 'collaborators': an indirect strategy to advance the long-term goal of overthrowing Roman rule. Tactics were also finely calculated. They operated in broad daylight; amidst urban crowds; and in a pattern that all could recognize. As such, the Sicarii became efficient agents of fear: 'the panic created was more alarming than the calamity itself' (Josephus, quoted in Taylor and Gautron, 30).

We do not know much more about the Sicarii. Josephus is our only source: and he was not a disinterested witness. He was also unreliable and considered a traitor as a Jewish ex-rebel leader who defected to the Roman side. But his account of the Assassins has echoed through the ages. Elements on the Israeli far-right who remain opposed to any negotiated peace with Palestinians have found inspiration here. During the late 1980s, for instance, the Kach movement sought to advance an Orthodox Jewish and ultranationalist agenda to expand settlements throughout the occupied territory. One sub-group of its activists even adopted the name 'Sikarikin' (from the Sicarii): although they achieved little beyond 'setting fire to property and sending threatening letters to media figures, judges, and political leaders from the ultra-Orthodox, moderate right, and left-wing parties' (Pedahzur and Perliger: 93).

A thousand years after the Sicarii, the Nizari movement revived broadly similar tactics— but over the much longer period of two centuries (roughly, from c. 1081 to 1271 CE). The Nizaris (or Nizari Isma'ilis) are an offshoot of the Shia tradition of Islam that still survive

PHOTO 8.1 Hassan-i Sabbah, founder of the Nizari state and its military group known as the Order of Assassins.

to this day. In Hassan-i Sabbah (1050s to 1124, see Photo 8.1) the Nizaris found a political leader of great ability. He first established secure defensive bases in mountain-top castles; and then launched a campaign of long-range assassination against key regional opponents both Muslim and Christian. Such tactics allowed the Nizari movement to consolidate their movement south of the Caspian Sea; and in Syria (at the time a frontier region with the Crusader kingdoms).

As Christians, the Crusader chroniclers had no interest in the Nizaris' political aims. But they were deeply impressed by their attention-grabbing tactics. They noted that the Nizari leadership was using assassination as a *systematic* policy of power-projection; and that its manner amplified its message. Such killings were typically very public: and assassins did not prioritize their own escape. Effectively, these were often suicide missions. As one 12th-century chronicler explained such assassins were 'feared everywhere because they kill kings with disregard for their own life' (quoted in Taylor and Gautron, 39).

Often the assassins had also lived with their targets for years and had become loyal confidants before finally committing their murder. This only increased the perception of terror that they created. Such new tactics caused enormous confusion. Christian explanations therefore tended to fall back on fictional accounts of narcotic-fuelled control to explain the assassins' behaviour. In most European languages today, the word 'assassin' derives directly from hashish: a faint, but enduring, linguistic trace of the cultural shock that the Nizaris' prolonged campaign had once caused.

8.2 THE GUNPOWDER REVOLUTION IN EUROPE

Between about 1450 and 1800 CE European societies underwent 'a military revolution'. Gunpowder lay at the heart of this military transformation. It was actually old technology: having been invented in China over 500 years earlier. But the systematic ways in which Europeans now learnt to harness this borrowed technology allowed them to transcend new thresholds of destructive power. All this was happening against a social backdrop in which military and civilian life had not yet separated out into distinct spheres. Hence it was inevitable that the impact of this military revolution would not stay confined to the battlefield. Gunpowder suggested brand new possibilities for political violence also.

Assassins, for instance, now had more options as firearms spread. Guns allowed attackers to strike at a distance. In January 1570 James Stewart, Earl of Moray was the first head of state in the world to be shot dead—blasted from an upstairs window as he rode through Linlithgow, Scotland. In 1584 the Dutch leader William the Silent was similarly killed. Attempts were also made to shoot Elector Christian II of Saxony (1603); King Gustavus Adolphus of Sweden (during the 1630s); and Oliver Cromwell, Lord Protector of the English Republic (1657). As a tool of individual assassination, the gun had become commonplace.

Gunpowder also encouraged more ambitious plots. The Earl of Darnley's house outside Edinburgh was detonated in 1567: although the Earl survived this (and was strangled instead). An attempt to blow up William the Silent by packing his cellars with gunpowder barrels also was unsuccessful. Also unsuccessful was The Gunpowder Plot of 1605 where a group of English Catholics planned to blow up both their King and Parliament (now celebrated as Guy Fawkes Night on 5 November each year in the UK). Where gunpowder could be transported and concealed more reliably, the results could be truly destructive. At the siege of Antwerp in 1585, the Dutch defenders floated 'hellburners' (explosive-packed ships) into a pontoon bridge; and killed a thousand Spanish soldiers. Over 400 years later—in October 2000—al-Qaeda attacked the American warship USS Cole in Aden harbour in the same fashion: although with more limited results.

Such technologies remained highly experimental throughout this early modern period from the 15th to 18th centuries. And it is also important to note the dynamics that had *not* changed fundamentally. Defences had evolved to cope with artillery; so, siege warfare remained both difficult and slow. Conquerors in a hurry therefore still turned to terror as a quick fix—just as the Assyrians had done 2,000 years earlier. Some cities met such devastation that they are still remembered locally to this day. Examples include Drogheda in Ireland, brutally sacked by Oliver Cromwell's English army in 1649.

In summary: such atrocities remained a central feature of *warfare* in the 17th century. Random attacks on civilians in *peacetime*, however, still belonged to the future. Revolutionary changes—and a new conceptual vocabulary to describe them—had to appear first. By the end of the 18th century that new world was finally beginning to emerge.

8.3 'TERRORISM': A NEW CONCEPT IS BORN

Historians see the later 18th century as the key watershed between the modern world and earlier ages (Hobsbawm: 17). Two background revolutions coincided here. The intellectual revolution called 'the Enlightenment' advanced bold new claims that human rationality, not tradition and religion, could form the foundations of a better society. Around the same time, it also became clear that an industrial revolution was emerging in north Western Europe. Over the next two hundred and fifty years the multiple impacts of these twin shifts in society would impact the entire world. Unending change, and not long-held traditions, would now influence humanity. In many ways: the twin concepts of terror and terrorism *belong* to this modern world. They have shaped its politics profoundly.

To explore a specific example, as a concept, terrorism belongs to the French Revolution. Charles Townshend notes that the first dictionary definition of the word 'terrorism' appeared in 1798: 'in the light, plainly, of recent French experience' (2002: 36). The key point here is that this new *term* of 'terrorism' reflected a new *phenomenon*: the 'Reign of Terror' from 1793 to 1794. If we follow this language trail, the first 'terrorists' in history were the state actors of a highly insecure French revolutionary government.

As we have explored in section 8.1.1, rulers using terror is not new. Tyrants have always done that. What seemed new to contemporaries about the state terror of the 1790s in France was its ambition. It aimed to create a new world. It aimed to make society better: indeed, perfect. Or as the revolutionary leader Jacques Nicolas Billaud-Varenne put it: 'we must re-create the people that we wish to make free, for we need to destroy old prejudices, change outdated customs, restore jaded feelings, restrain excessive wants and annihilate deep rooted vices' (quoted in Wilson, 2013: 17). At heart, this experiment 'was informed by the Enlightenment assumption that the social order can be changed by human agency' (Townshend, 2002: 37). It thus aimed to intimidate the 'forces of reaction': those ultra-conservatives who were trying to return society to the times before the Revolution.

It is very striking that for about 200 years the term 'terrorism' tended to remain popularly associated in this way with revolutionary violence from the Left—whether in government or opposed to it. Within these parameters, though, the usage of the term continued to evolve. By the 1990s, the label of terrorism had long come to be applied more and more frequently to small anti-state groups: and not to governments. How did this shift happen?

8.4 MODERN TERRORISM AT LAST?

General histories of modern anti-state terrorism often begin in the late 19th century. On 13 March 1881, the People's Will activist Ignaty Grinevitsky killed Tsar Alexander II of Russia (and himself): the first suicide bombing. On 30 October 1883, 72 people were injured when

Irish Republicans bombed underground trains in London at Praed Street (near Paddington Station) and at Charing Cross: the first mass casualty attacks on a public transport system. On 26 August 1896 Armenian nationalists occupied the Ottoman Bank in Constantinople (today, Istanbul, Turkey) and took 150 prisoners: the first barricade hostage crisis. If we are searching for examples of (anti-state) terrorism that just *look* familiar, this seems to be the key period. Why?

Like our own age, the last quarter of the 19th century was a period of massive and accelerating change: a first age of globalization. Then (as now) many things were changing simultaneously: but two revolutionary developments stand out as key drivers of innovation. To be clear: these did not *cause* modern terrorism as such. But they did help create the background conditions in which it could then flourish. Neither were directly linked to violence—at least initially. Both arose out of the emerging world economy: and not on any battlefield.

> **KEY CONCEPTS**
>
> **Globalization** Globalization refers to an overarching process where communication between distant locations increases dramatically. It is often associated with accelerated mobility: of people, ideas, information, and money. It is important to grasp that for much of the past our ancestors lived lives that were much more static than our own, and which were conducted within much more limited locations. Broadly speaking, these were not conditions to encourage the emergence of modern terrorism. Conversely, the sudden emergence of terrorism towards the end of the 19th century can plausibly be understood as one of the 'dark sides' of globalization. Likewise, the spread of terrorism in the late 20th and early 21st centuries is linked in complex ways to processes of globalization.

The first revolution lay in information circulation. Electric telegraph now instantly flashed news around the world: creating a global stage for drama. Newspapers with mass readerships began to emerge: the assembling of a global audience. Here for the first time in human history was an opportunity for simultaneously influencing different people in different places. Publicity promised power potential. Out of an awareness of these emerging possibilities arose the anarchist theory of 'propaganda by the deed': the dream that a few exemplary acts of violence might inspire a more general revolt.

Such thinking was new. As practical assassins, the militant anarchists were often unimaginative. Often, they relied upon highly traditional tools: the knife and the gun. But in terms of international terrorism, they broke new ground entirely. On 10 September 1898, for instance, Empress Elisabeth of Austria was stabbed to death in Switzerland by an Italian anarchist, Luigi Lucheni. His weapon was a homemade knife. Yet his intentions were truly global. Under interrogation he justified his act 'as part of the war on the rich and great'. Lucheni further declared that he had simply intended to kill 'a high personage, no matter which one' (quoted in Pernicone and Ottanelli: 119–120). As a logic of assassination, such impersonal thinking bore no resemblance to the assumption of highly individualized targeting that lay behind medieval theories of tyrannicide.

> **KEY CONCEPTS**
>
> **Propaganda of the Deed (also rendered as 'Propaganda by Deed')** 'Propaganda of the Deed' is a 19th-century political soundbite. It seems to have been first used by the Italian Federation of the Anarchist International in 1876. As a strategy, it rested upon twin assumptions: that violent actions could advertice a revolutionary cause far more effectively than any other more conventional means; and that the oppressed masses were just waiting to be aroused to rebellion by such attacks because they exposed the governing system to be far weaker than it looked. Such calculation is often seen as the foundation of modern terrorism as a strategy (Townshend: 55–56). In that sense, 21st-century terrorist groups such as al-Qaeda and ISIS follow a 19th-century template.

The second revolution was in civil engineering. In 1866 Alfred Nobel combined the high explosive nitroglycerine with kieselguhr clay (as a stabilizing agent). He called his new commercial product dynamite. Engineering triumphs followed all over the world because this transportable and affordable new explosive allowed brand new possibilities. Above all, its energy density was unprecedented: the blast waves travelled twelve times faster than gunpowder. Dynamite thus forced the railroad tunnels through the Alps and Rockies; and opened up the Panama Canal.

This could effectively demolish mountains, but also societies and governments. Dynamite instantly appealed to rebels and was adopted (amongst others) by: Anarchists, Russian revolutionaries, Irish Republicans, Armenian nationalists and American labour militants. By 1880, 17 dynamite bombings had already taken place. By early March 1881, a dynamite bomb had killed one of the most powerful men in the world: Tsar Alexander II of Russia. By 1934 at least 1,291 dynamite bombings had occurred globally. According to one careful study 'the global wave of terrorism that dynamite unleashed involved bombing incidents in 52 countries' (Cronin, 2020: 69–125). By late 20th or early 21st-century standards, such globalized terrorism remained a highly limited phenomenon. But its emergence pointed the way towards that future.

Summing all this up: anti-state terrorism appeared in fully recognizable form near the end of the 19th century. But explaining its historical development since then has still been challenging. That evolution has not been linear. Anti-state terrorism at times has become a major preoccupation of international politics. However, at other times it seems to have all but disappeared; only to increase in scrutiny again without warning. Can we find any deeper patterns that might help us make sense of this randomness?

Amongst theoretical attempts to do so, one approach holds the field. David Rapoport's Four Waves of Rebel Terror is considered a classic contribution to the historical study of anti-state terrorism. We turn to consider it now in section 8.4.1.

8.4.1 Modern anti-state terrorism: 'The Four Waves of Rebel Terror'

Reviewing the entire period from 1880, the political scientist David Rapoport (2003) suggested that what he called 'rebel terrorism' had tended to collect in major 'waves'. Rapoport's focus was on what he saw as broad, swelling patterns of terrorism: and not on individual terrorist groups. He argued that there had been just four giant waves of terrorism:

1. An Anarchist wave had arisen around 1880: and lasted until about 1920.
2. Anti-colonial terrorism then dominated for the next 40 years up until c. 1960.
3. A New Left wave arose in that decade; but had broken well before the dawn of the 21st century.
4. Finally, a global wave of Religious terrorism had gathered force after 1979: and was—at the time Rapoport was writing, in 2001—ongoing.

CASE STUDY 8.1

David Rapoport's Four Waves of Modern Terrorism

David Rapoport's (2003) model highlights that the history of modern terrorism over the past 150 years can be divided into four periods, or waves, with distinct features: The Anarchist, Anti-colonial, New Left, and Religious waves. The waves are marked by a high international dimension, so that similar events happen in different regions of the globe, and the terrorist organizations share certain traits. What is common across the waves is that groups strive for revolution, a complete overhaul of exiting social, political, or economic conditions. However, each organization's goals might differ. While some want to achieve independence and self-determination (especially in the second wave), others might aim for radical alteration of the social and political fabrics (in waves 1, 2, and 4). Important to the concept of waves is that they build up, climax, and fade out. They can also overlap, which can be seen for instance in the 1970s (defined in a Key Concepts box) where anticolonial and New Left terrorists co-existed and collaborated.

The first, or Anarchist wave, started in Russia and benefitted from the advances in transport and communication, making it easier for people, ideas, and news to travel. It also built on the radical writings of figures such as Peter Kropotkin which provided the philosophical foundation for first wave terrorists. Terror was deemed the only feasible method to achieve timely and radical change to the society and 'propaganda by the deed'—acts that would get attention—was supposed to ensure that the terrorists' demands would be heard and acted upon. Dynamite was their weapon of choice. The ideas and tactics spread from Russia to Europe but also towards the Americas and Asia.

The second, Anti-colonial wave, occurred after the upheavals of the First World War. It is intimately linked to the phase of decolonization, where the colonial empires retreated from their colonies. However, when states did not want to cease control over a territory, groups resorted to terrorism, for instance in Israel (when it was a British mandate and Jewish groups used terrorism to drive the British out, just like a few decades later Palestinian groups would use terrorism to try to get rid of Israeli control), Algeria, or Cyprus. They followed an approach, which did not rely so much on assassinations (unlike in the first wave) but had a staggered strategy of provoking the police and military into overreactions that would drive more people into the arms of the anticolonial groups. This would often include guerrilla-like tactics of hit and run.

The third, or New Left wave, was an offspring of the protests against the US war in Vietnam. It was social-revolutionary in nature, aiming at the overthrow of states and societies. Groups existed in many Western countries and used hijackings and hostage-takings as tactics of choice. They were also highly international in nature with collaborations occurring between groups. Some states such as Libya also supported groups.

The last, Religious, wave started in the late 1970s and early 1980s as a new Islamic century began, the Iranian revolution unrolled, and the Soviets invaded Afghanistan. While Christian groups also existed, this wave is predominantly Islamic (or indeed Islamist) in nature. Suicide bombings became a cheap and oft-used tactic, and while fewer groups existed than in previous waves, those which were active turned out to be bigger and to last longer. The US was seen as the chief enemy and many groups aimed at forming a single Islamic state under Sharia law.

QUESTIONS

1. What is the advantage of Rapoport's model to the study of terrorism?
2. How convincing is Rapoport's account of how external and internal factors combine to produce waves of terrorism?

Rapoport's work has become *the* dominant account of the evolution of modern terrorism. Although slightly different versions exist, Rapoport drafted the original text in late 2001. As Western societies struggled to come to terms with the shock of the September 11th 2001 attacks in the US, Rapoport offered some much-needed historical background. Even more importantly, he offered a model that suggested the possible outline of *future* terrorism. Here was a history lesson for non-historians. Moreover, that lesson was both short and accessible. Rapoport's 'Four Waves of Rebel Terrorism' became by far the most influential 15 pages ever written on the history of terrorism.

However, it is also important to note what Rapoport's 'Four Waves' model does not do. Several important phenomena are not addressed. His coverage of 'rebel terrorism' deliberately does not include single-issue movements (such as the Suffragettes in the UK or anti-abortionists). Nor does he consider extreme right-wing actors and groups (who have re-emerged as a major threat in the early 21st century). Defining global conflicts of the period—the First World War (1914–18), Second World Wars (1939–45) and the Cold War (c. 1945–89)—are also hardly mentioned.

This last point draws attention to Rapoport's account of causation. Rapoport combines both background factors and 'agency'—that is, actors' own choices—in his overview account. Background factors are briefly acknowledged with reference to world events and emerging new technologies. But the driving motor of his explanation remains agency: the terrorists' own beliefs and actions.

Rapoport's priorities are reflected here in the naming of his Four Waves. He spotlights single ideologies as key drivers of terrorist energy. As a short-hand formula, this may be a convenient simplification—but it does tidy up some messy realities. Much of the most important anti-state terrorism between 1880 and 1920 was *not* conducted by anarchists. By far the most significant attack here was the shooting of Archduke Franz Ferdinand on 28 June 1914. The First World War thus arose out of an act of nationalist terrorism that had been state-sponsored by Serbia. There was nothing anarchist about it. Rapoport is aware of such realities—but assigns anarchism a leading inspirational role in his account. It is not always clear why.

Generalizations are only ever meant to be generally true, of course: there can be value in deliberately sketching in broad strokes. Some exceptions can be tolerated if a model is still useful in outline. The question is: how many? Rapoport writes that the IRA 'began the anti-colonial wave in the 1920s and is still here'. But armed campaigns by Irish Republicans are far older than that: we have already encountered their 1883 bombing of the London Underground (in the explosions at Praed Street and Charing Cross). And anti-colonial bomb attacks and assassinations were also well established in India long before 1920. Rapoport's Four Waves is designed to offer a *generalized* theory: not to account for every terrorist incident in modern history. It takes a 'big picture' approach to its subject.

Rapoport's model resembles earlier wave theories. Nikolai Kondratieff (1935) proposed that capitalism was prone to 50-year waves of expansion and depression. Samuel Huntington (1991) suggested that democratization occurred in great, although irregularly spaced, waves. Both Kondratieff and Huntington were trying to chart human behaviour at a mass level. A highly original feature of Rapoport's work was that he applied a wave model to anti-state terrorism: a phenomenon, typically, of clandestine groups with limited memberships. Here he stressed that the fortunes of individual groups would indeed rise and fall within waves: yet the wave itself remained the key unit of the model.

Rapoport here seemed to anticipate the insights of radicalization theory: that the violent actions of the extreme few are committed on behalf of much larger ideological constituencies. In other words: more people will think about radical ideas than will ever commit terrorism. Moreover, active support for radical agendas is likely to fluctuate wildly over time. Like most things in public life radical politics have their own cycles which change over time.

Still, 40 years is a long period. In a key passage Rapoport reflects upon his chosen time frame:

> The first three waves lasted approximately 40 to 45 years, but the new left wave was somewhat abbreviated. The pattern suggests a human life-cycle pattern, where dreams that inspire fathers lose their attractiveness for the son.

Does a 40-year pattern actually suggest this? After all, human generations are shorter: perhaps 20 to 30 years. But Rapoport's more fundamental assumption here seems to be that it is the *inner momentum* of the wave that will determine how long it lasts. Yet how such *inner* momentum is affected by *external* developments is not explored in depth. Rapoport, for instance, was writing before the rise of the social media. By accelerating shifts of mass attention, it is clear that the emergence of mass communication has profoundly altered patterns of terrorism. What such trends will look like over the longer term is still unclear.

In the final analysis, Rapoport's model does leaves room for acknowledging some variation between waves, even if it also contains a strong suggestion of predictable regularity as well. As he himself acknowledges, the New Left wave clearly did not last anything like 40 years: here the 'Long 1970s' was the peak period. Conversely, the Religious Wave of the late 20th century should by now be fast running out of momentum: *if* it is like the earlier Anarchist and Anti-colonial waves. But time will tell.

Within the field of Terrorism Studies, Rapoport's reputation as *the* leading historical authority on the development of modern terrorism is certainly secure. His Four Waves model looks set to survive as the most popular general account for the time being. No other account has come close to being adopted so widely. Any academic work that forces scholars to rethink their own positions is always valuable. In summary: Rapoport's ground-breaking work repays close study.

> **KEY CONCEPTS**
>
> **Long 1970s** We tend to think in terms of tidy decades or centuries. However, significant turning points do not come at regular intervals. Historians often find it helpful therefore to think in terms of slightly stretched or compressed time periods. A 'Long 1970s of Terrorism' therefore emerges around 1968 and lasts to the early 1980s.

8.4.2 Modern state terror

Modern states may be just as brutal as their ancient predecessors. But they tend to be more resilient. Only in a few corners of the globe today is there an effective absence of *any* state authority: yet in previous centuries this was a very common reality. Such an expansion of governmental control over its citizens' daily lives makes modern states very different in reach from their more distant ancestors. The Nazi genocide of 6 million Jews from 1939 to 1941, for instance, depended upon their direct control of the sophisticated bureaucracies and transport networks of modern Europe. By contrast, even the Roman Empire lacked any police force at all.

Governments, in short, could now kill millions at speed. Back in the mid-1790s France 'The Terror' pioneered such ambitious social engineering and the concept of 'terrorism' was its by-product. This experiment was short (9 months) but devastating (16,000 guillotined). Later applications of this leftist revolutionary template were even more ambitious. Stalin's Great Terror of (1936–38) consumed 700,000 lives across the Soviet Union. Chairmen Mao Zedong's Cultural Revolution (1966–76) likely killed far more in China.

> **KEY CONCEPTS**
>
> **The Terror** This term has occasionally been applied to periods of spectacularly intense state terrorism. The most infamous examples are: the French Terror (1793–94) and Stalin's Great Terror (1936–38).

Such periods represent the truly 'excessive excesses' of state terror (Mayer: 101). More common has been less spectacular, but relentless, oppression. Out of the chaos of the French Revolution emerged Napoleon's France (1804–14): the world's first police state. This Napoleonic model has formed the basic template for a wide array of modern dictatorships ever since: the centralized state that obsessively monitors society for dissent.

By the end of the 20th century, such dictatorships had become very hard to overthrow directly through armed challenge. Where revolutionary struggles degenerated into auctions of violence, state terror won convincingly. Argentina's 'Dirty War' (1976–83) is a good example of such an unequal contest: the left-wing guerrillas had no effective answer to the systematic oppression unleased by a military junta. Rodolfo Walsh recognized this early on: '… in practice our theory has galloped kilometres ahead of reality. When that occurs, the vanguard runs the risk of becoming a lost patrol' (in Moyano, 1995: 1). Walsh's image of the vulnerable 'lost patrol' was to prove all too far-sighted: both nationally and personally. Caught alone on a Buenos Aires street, he was gunned down by the army on 25 March 1977.

> **CASE STUDY 8.2**
>
> *The 1970s as the Long Decade of Terrorism*
>
> The years around the 1970s marked an important, long, decade of terrorism. For one, different forms of terrorism (or 'waves') coincided: nationalists used terrorism to try to free their countries from Israeli (in Palestine), South African (in Namibia), or English (Northern Ireland) occupation whilst the Spear of the Nation committed terrorism to overthrow apartheid in South Africa. At the same time, social revolutionary terrorist groups were growing. Left-wing groups such as the Red Brigades (Italy), Red Army Faction (West Germany. See also Chapter 6, Case Study 6.1), Weather Underground (USA), Action Directe (France), or the Japanese Red Army (Japan) used assassinations, hijackings, or hostage-takings to challenge their governments in an attempt at overthrowing societies and states.
>
> Meanwhile, right-wing terrorist groups were also active (for instance in West Germany or Italy). They often escaped the radar screens of the police as left-wing groups were considered more serious threats to the state and committed more attacks. And the latter also targeted prominent politicians or civil servants, which explains the alarm they caused in government

circles. However, some of the most fatal attacks of the Long 1970s were committed by right-wing terrorists: in 1969, members of the group Ordine Nuovo exploded a bomb in Milan's Piazza Fontana and killed 17 people while wounding 88 others. In August 1980, the Nuclei Armati Rivoluzionari bombed Bologna's central railway station and killed 85 people while more than 200 were wounded. Just a month later, right-wing terrorist Gundolf Köhler planted a bomb at Munich's Oktoberfest and killed 12 people with more than 200 other people wounded.

As social-revolutionary and nationalist groups thrived, state terror was also globally represented: Chairman Mao Zedong re-established power in China with the Cultural Revolution (1966–76, see Photo 8.2), as various Latin American, Asian, and African countries were also terrorized by their governments.

Other states, such as Uganda, and later Libya, directly supported terrorists whereas most Eastern European states allowed Western terrorists to hide inside their borders; or granted training and support to Third World groups. The Americans would replicate this in the 1980s with support for the Mujahideen in Afghanistan or the Contras (right-wing rebel groups) in Nicaragua. And the late 1970s laid the groundwork for religious terrorism also, with the Soviet invasion of Afghanistan, and the Iranian revolution in 1979.

PHOTO 8.2 1960s propaganda poster for the Cultural Revolution led by Chairman Mao Zedong in the People's Republic of China.

> The 1970s saw an amalgamation of different forms of terrorism. Importantly, this long decade of terrorism was marked by a boom in globalization: air travel became faster and more affordable for the masses, making it a more attractive target for terrorists. Meanwhile, live broadcasts on TV and the radio brought terror attacks from across the globe into the living rooms of the global public. This was ideal as terrorism feeds off attention. Technological progress, thus, helped terrorists to spread their message and to commit attacks. At the same time, groups of various backgrounds also cooperated: Palestinian groups trained European left- and right-wing terrorists in their camps (though, wisely, not at the same time), members of the Japanese Red Army permanently relocated to the Middle East to help their Palestinian comrades in their struggle, and joint hijacking operations by Palestinian and German terrorists in Entebbe (Central Uganda) and Mogadishu (Somalia) were meant to blackmail states into making political concessions.
>
> The 1970s thus mark a unique juncture in the history of terrorism. It was also the decade when many states established antiterrorism laws, or counterterrorism units, and agreed to cooperate bilaterally, multilaterally, and globally to fight terrorism. It is in the 1970s, for instance, that the United Nations became involved in the efforts to fend off terrorism.
>
> **QUESTIONS**
> 1. Was the threat of terrorism worse in the 1970s than now?
> 2. Why would nationalist terrorists cooperate with social-revolutionary terrorists?

Accelerating global communications during the later 20th century also affected patterns of state terror: 'disappearances emerged as a core tactic of the Dirty War in Argentina in part because the regime wished to avoid the international isolation of post-1973 Chile' (Wilson, 2013: 26). With the end of the Cold War in the early 1990s it was tempting to see such developments—especially when followed by the rise of the internet—as constraining state terror by putting human rights abuses firmly under the spotlight. Such illumination did succeed in embarrassing Western democratic governments for their mistreatment of prisoners during the US Global War on Terror after 2001. However, it has also become increasingly clear that repressive governments can also learn how to utilize social media skilfully: not least by sowing widespread confusion, propaganda, misinformation, and 'fake news'. State terror looks here to stay, and the rise of the Islamic State's Caliphate in 2014 has offered an additional template of how quickly tactics of anti-state terrorism can be converted into those of state-building terror.

8.5 CONCLUSION

Terrorism Studies remains an academic field that is largely focused upon present and future threats. This chapter has demonstrated that there is also much to be gained from looking into the past. In that spirit it has reviewed some ancient examples: both the atrocities committed by the Assyrian Empire and the assassination campaigns of both the Sicarii and Nizaris. An explicit concept of state terror was only to emerge much later: during the 1790s. Anti-state terrorism in the form of mass casualty bombings appeared later still: in the 1880s. Much about this past terrorism looks unfamiliar to us now. But human nature does not appear to change much down the ages, and we ignore past experiences at our peril.

Searching the past for lessons is never going to be an *exact* science. What happened in the past is no automatic guide to what will happen in the future. No historical situation ever repeats itself exactly. Circumstances always differ. And historians will always debate over *why* what happened, happened. But we should not despair. Even some suggestive half-parallels between past and present situations are more effective than no guidance at all. As Walter Laqueur asked (1978: 8): 'Historical experience, it is said, cannot teach us much about terrorism: but what else can?'

DISCUSSION QUESTIONS

1. Is there an end to terrorism, or is it here to stay?
2. Do social scientists and historians need one another to properly research terrorism?
3. How can the knowledge of the joint histories of terror and terrorism help with dealing with such phenomena today?
4. Why have forms of terrorism changed so radically over time?
5. What alternatives to Rapoport's model could you think of to categorize the history of terrorism?

 Visit the online resources for pointers on how to answer the discussion questions, links to useful web sources, and guidance on accessing databases:
www.oup.com/he/Wilson-Muro1e

GUIDE TO FURTHER READING

Survey accounts remain a good place to start introductory reading. Walter Laqueur's *A History of Terrorism: Expanded Edition* (1977, 2016) is a revised version of one of the first general histories of anti-state terrorism. It remains a standard monograph in the field. Gérard Chaliand and Arnaud Blin offer a long overview in *The History of Terrorism: From Antiquity to ISIS* (2016): Martin Miller's *The Foundations of Modern Terrorism: State, Society and the Dynamics of Political Violence* focuses upon more recent centuries (2012).

Tim Wilson's *Killing Strangers: How Political Violence Became Modern* (2020) deliberately avoids a Four Waves approach to trace the evolution of political violence through a close study of its changing patterns of action. Growing state control over societies limited rebel violence: but changing technology allowed new experimentation with new and more impersonal forms.

Edited volumes of essays are also valuable: thus, Jussi M. Hänhimaki and Bernhard Blumenau's *An International History of Terrorism: Western and Non-Western Experiences* (2013) brings together experiences with terrorism and counterterrorism in different parts of the world over the past 150 years and contains an updated version of Rapoport's Four waves model. *The Cambridge History of Terrorism* (2021), edited by Richard English, gathers together an impressive panorama of perspectives on studying past terrorism.

REFERENCES

Chaliand, G. and Blin, A. (2016) *The History of Terrorism: From Antiquity to ISIS* (Updated edition. Oakland, CA: University of California Press.

Cronin, A. (2020) *Power to the People: How Open Technological Innovation is Arming Tomorrow's Terrorists*. Oxford: Oxford University Press.

English, R. (ed.), (2021) *The Cambridge History of Terrorism*. Cambridge: Cambridge University Press.

Hänhimaki, J. M. and Blumenau, B. (2013) *An International History of Terrorism: Western and Non-Western Experiences* Routledge.

Huntington, S. P. (1991) 'Democracy's Third Wave', *Journal of Democracy*, 2 (2): 12–34.

Kondratieff, N. (1935) 'The Long Waves in Economic Life', *The Review of Economic Statistics*, 17 (6): 105–115.

Laqueur, W. (1977, 1978) *Terrorism*. London: Abacus.

Laqueur, W. (1977, 2016) *A History of Terrorism Expanded* Routledge.

Law, R. D. (2009, 2011) *Terrorism: A History*. Cambridge: Polity.

Mayer, A. (2000) *The Furies: Violence and Terror in the French and Russian Revolutions*. Princeton: Princeton University Press.

Miller, M. A. (2012) *The Foundations of Modern Terrorism: State, Society and the Dynamics of Political Violence*. Cambridge: Cambridge University Press.

Moyano, M. J. (1995) *Argentina's Lost Patrol: Armed Struggle, 1969-1979*. London: Yale University Press.

Pedahzur, A. and Perliger, A. (2009) *Jewish Terrorism in Israel*. New York: Columbia University Press.

Pernicone, N. and Ottanelli, F. M. (2018) *Assassins Against the Older Order: Italian Anarchist Violence in Fin de Siècle Europe*. Urbana: University of Illinois Press.

Rapoport, D. (2003) 'The Four Waves of Rebel Terror and September 11', in Kegley, C. W., *The New Global Terrorism: Characteristics, Causes, Controls*. Upper Saddle River, New Jersey: Prentice Hall.

Schmid, A. (2013) *The Routledge Handbook of Terrorism Research*. Abingdon: Routledge.

Taylor, D. and Gautron, Y. (2015) 'Pre-modern Terrorism: The Cases of the Sicarii and the Assassins', in Law, R. D. (2015) *The Routledge History of Terrorism*. Abingdon: Routledge.

Townshend, C. (2002) *Terrorism: A Very Short Introduction*. Oxford: Oxford University Press.

Wilkinson, P. (1977, 1979) *Terrorism and the Liberal State*. London: Macmillan Press.

Williamson, G. A. (ed.) (1959, 1981) *The Jewish War*. London: Penguin.

Wilson, T. (2013) 'State Terrorism: An Historical Overview', in Duncan, G. (et al., eds.), *State Terrorism and Human Rights: International Responses Since the End of the Cold War*. London: Routledge.

Wilson, T. (2020) *Killing Strangers: How Political Violence Became Modern*. Oxford: Oxford University Press.

CHAPTER 9

What Are the Root Causes of Terrorism?

NICK BROOKE

■ CHAPTER SUMMARY

At the heart of the study of terrorism is a question often posed but rarely answered satisfactorily: why? Why do people use violence for political means, especially when their victims are unconnected civilians? Whilst this is so often a cry of desperation, for scholars of terrorism this question seeks to get to the root of why terrorist actors behave in the manner that they do, and explain the relationship between societal factors and political violence. This chapter considers the accuracy and validity of the term 'root causes', outlines the varied attempts to identify the root causes of terrorism, and engages with those who would question the purpose of this endeavour.

9.1 INTRODUCTION

A strong part of terrorism's emotional and political resonance is that it can be perceived as a sign of desperation or depravity, an act outside the realms of normality. As a result, in the wake of terrorist acts and campaigns, the public, the media and policymakers inevitably look to understand why this happened. Journalists attempt to track down details of the attackers' childhood by speaking with school friends and teachers. Family members and loved ones are interviewed—if not by the media, by the police—to ascertain what they knew and when they knew it. In an increasingly digital age, social media posts and online profiles are scoured for indications of ideological leanings. Finally, in the event that the attacker has made any public utterances on their acts, each word is carefully weighed and measured to strip out every detail of meaning.

One of the most profound challenges associated with the study of terrorism is understanding why terrorism happens. The use of terrorism by a wide variety of groups from different time periods and cultural contexts immediately suggests that there is not a simple answer to the question: 'why does terrorism emerge?'. In the study of terrorism and political violence, the search for an explanation has often led policymakers and scholars to look for the 'root causes' of terrorism. This chapter examines how scholars have attempted to conduct this search, why this question is important, and the key motivating and precipitating factors commonly provided in the literature on the causes of terrorism.

9.2 THE ROOT CAUSES OF TERRORISM

> **KEY CONCEPTS**
>
> **Root Causes** 'Root causes' are societal factors that create the conditions in which members of a group or community can feel compelled to actively pursue a terrorist campaign.

Effectively identifying the causal factor behind human decision-making is challenging. Studies to date have identified many factors that may lead to terrorist violence, such as relative deprivation and religious extremism. Before examining the root causes themselves, it is useful to clarify the terminology, and the limits of this study. It is also useful to set out the purpose of studying the causes of terrorism.

Beyond simple comprehension, understanding the root causes of terrorism is good practice in formulating a response to terrorism. Within the literature on terrorism and political violence, there is a consensus that—where possible—addressing the root causes of a conflict is an important step in ending terrorist campaigns. Paul Wilkinson suggests that 'experience of past terrorist struggles indicates that the government cannot win unless it energetically produces reforms to meet the major grievances or demands of the citizens' (1974: 138). Richard English also notes that resolving the 'underlying problems' can 'lessen or even – in some cases – remove the likelihood of that violence continuing' (2009: 123). Louise Richardson (2006: 245) highlights that efforts to:

> 'look behind the violence and to understand the factors that fuel it and . . . introduce social, political and religious reforms to alleviate the conditions that breed support for violence represent a model of what can be done in the face of terrorism'.

Each comes to the same conclusion: that an effective response to an act of terrorism requires an understanding of the causes of the terrorist act.

This conclusion has also been reached by practitioners and high-level policymakers. Jonathan Evans (2007), then head of the British Security Service (MI5) stated:

> 'The work of the intelligence and security agencies will not be enough. We will do our utmost to hold back the physical threat of attacks, but alone, this is merely containment. Long-term resolution requires identifying and addressing the root causes of the problem.'

Likewise, a UN High-Level Panel (2003) convened by former Secretary-General Kofi Annan (who held this position from 1997–2006) on the topic of 'Threats, Challenges and Change' made the case that it was 'imperative to develop a global strategy of fighting terrorism that addresses root causes and strengthens responsible states and the rule of law and fundamental human rights'. A key reason to study the root causes of terrorism more closely is to enable state actors to respond more effectively.

Scholars have a key role to play in this endeavour, and the study of the causes of terrorism has inspired much academic engagement broadly (Bjørgo 2006; Crenshaw 1981; Richardson 2006) and on specific alleged causes of terrorism such as national liberation, often highlighting specific movements (English 2008; Laitin 1995 and Muro 2013); on religion (Gunning and Jackson 2011; Juergensmeyer 2000 and Stern 2003); on economic causes of political violence (Berrebi 2007; Gurr 1970 and Krueger and Malečková 2003) and on state failure or the absence or weakness of democracy (Abadie 2006; Newman 2007; Piazza 2007 and Eubank and Weinberg 1994).

However, the search for the root causes of terrorism has not been without controversy. Lisa Stampnitzky (2013: 191) makes the case that, in the wake of the US September 11th attacks in 2001, those who tried to explain the actions of the attackers were met with accusations that they were almost defending the attacks: 'Attempts to seek reasons for the attacks were heard as justifications. The slippage between reason, reasons and justifiable reasons led to a situation in which explanation itself became suspect.' Whilst terrorism, as a subject, is emotive and contentious, it is important to continue to develop our understanding of terrorism occurs.

The search for the root causes of terrorist violence throws up many challenges and many inconsistencies. Whilst various terrorist organizations might have a stated political, religious, or ideological motivating aim, the root causes of their campaign are often far deeper, as the 'root' analogy suggests. Furthermore, the factors that inspire one individual to become involved within a political movement may differ from the reasons why another member, pursuing the same goals, chooses to become involved (see Alonso 2006). Another key question is understanding why patterns of terrorist violence are uneven: why violence occurs in one location, but a neighbouring location with similar socio-political conditions is spared. Research to understand this uneven pattern can shed further light on the causes of terrorism (see Brooke 2018; de la Calle 2015 and Conversi 1997).

Scholars should also be wary about treating motivations as fixed temporally: over time different members might join the same movement or cause for wildly different reasons. Equally, the primary motivating factors of terrorist movements engaged in long-lasting campaigns might change over time, as they adapt to a change in circumstances or respond to new developments. It is important to understand the motivations to commit violence can be simultaneously deeply rooted and entirely contemporary. This chapter proceeds by laying out the definitional debate on the term 'root causes'.

9.2.1 Defining the root causes

The next step is to clearly set out what is meant by the term root causes, and identify the parameters of this study. The term 'root causes' is often applied by scholars within the literature as if it does not require explanation, but it is vital that we have clarity and specificity if we are to understand what this entails. Precisely why the prefix 'root' has been added by some scholars of the topic is unclear. What the addition of the term 'root' adds is questionable, but it has nonetheless become standard terminology. It is likely the conflation of suggestions that a held belief or behaviour is 'deep rooted', drawing on an understanding of tree roots being deep, powerful, and historical. However, as we will move on to discuss, the root causes of a conflict can also be jarringly recent.

As an example of this: the conflict in Northern Ireland in the second half of the 20th century (also called 'the Troubles') was partly motivated by a deep historical sense of injustice felt by the Catholic community of Northern Ireland about the role of the United Kingdom in Irish affairs. It was also an active time for the PIRA (Provisional Irish Republican Army, see Photo 9.1) who sought to end British rule in Northern Ireland. The conflict was simultaneously the result of entirely modern socio-economic conditions in which members of the Catholic community felt an intense (and arguably, justified) sense of discrimination. Thus, root causes can be simultaneously deeply historical and entirely contemporary. Both are structural factors: the result of the political system, and impacting the community broadly, rather than individuals specifically.

In terms of a definition, we can take the concept of 'root causes of terrorism' to mean: structural factors that create the conditions in which members of a group or society can feel compelled to actively pursue a terrorist campaign.

PHOTO 9.1 West Belfast, Northern Ireland, Beechmont Estate neighbourhood children next to a street mural depicting armed members of the Provisional Irish Republican Army (PIRA).

9.2.2 Types of root cause

Within the study of the causes of terrorism, scholars have sought to clarify this term further—most notably Martha Crenshaw (1981), who does not invoke the prefix 'root' and Tore Bjørgo (2006). In her influential work on the causes of terrorism, Crenshaw (1981: 381) argues that they can be broken down into:

- *Preconditions*: 'factors that set the stage for terrorism over the long run'
- *Precipitants*: 'specific events that immediately precede the occurrence of terrorism'

This classification further breaks preconditions down into 'enabling' or 'permissive' causes. The former 'provide opportunities for terrorism to happen', and the latter are 'situations that directly inspire and motivate terrorist campaigns' (Crenshaw 1981: 381). Tore Bjørgo, in an influential edited collection on the root causes of terrorism, identifies what he describes as 'various levels of causes of terrorism' (2006: 3). Utilizing Crenshaw's *preconditions* and *precipitants,* Bjørgo goes further and categorizes:

- *Structural causes*: 'causes which affect people's lives in ways that they may or may not comprehend'

- *Facilitator/accelerator causes:* 'make terrorism possible or attractive without being prime movers'
- *Motivational causes:* 'the actual grievances that people experience at a personal level'
- *Triggering causes:* 'the direct precipitators of terrorist acts. They may be momentous or provocative events'

From these two approaches, we can see that the term 'root causes' includes a wide variety of elements: long-standing political and societal arrangements that affect governance, equality and liberty, as well as modern events, declarations or developments that create an immediate 'need' for a response. The former can create and energize identity groups and political movements, or shape common views on desired political outcomes among a community or subset of society. The latter highlight the immediacy of the need for change and shape the form action should take. Taken together the historical conditions, and the disruptive development can bring about terrorist violence. It is important to note that the 'root causes' of one conflict may not spark violence when present elsewhere. The study of root causes cannot predict where violence *will* occur but can help to explain why violence *has* occurred in a particular pattern.

A key part of understanding what we mean by the 'root causes' of terrorism is identifying what we are *not* referring to. Most crucially, we are not focusing on 'radicalization', although the two concepts both provide ways to try to understand terrorists' actions. 'Radicalization' typically refers to the process by which **an individual or small group** becomes involved in political violence, and this will be the focus of Chapter 10. 'Root causes' as a concept is focused on **structural** or **societal level**, reasons that may inspire the emergence of terrorism. This is not to diminish the importance of psychological research on terrorism and why people become involved in this phenomenon, however it is important to reflect that these two debates, whilst overlapping, are seeking to understand this phenomenon in different ways.

KEY CONCEPTS

Root Causes v Radicalization Although similar, these two studies differ in important ways:

'Root causes' as a concept is focused on **structural** or **societal level**, reasons that may inspire the emergence of terrorism.

'Radicalization' typically refers to the process by which **an individual** or **small group** becomes involved in political violence

This chapter now examines some of the most frequently cited root causes of terrorist violence highlighted in the existing literature and by terrorist actors themselves. It starts with a focus on the political and ideological motivations behind some of the most impactful and violent terrorist campaigns, before focusing on what we referred to as 'preconditions' or 'structural causes'. It will conclude with a discussion of how state action can motivate violence, considered a 'precipitant' or 'triggering' factor.

9.3 POLITICAL AND IDEOLOGICAL ROOTS

The first aspect to consider is the specific political causes at the heart of terrorist campaigns. Terrorist violence has been utilized by activists with a wide variety of political goals in a myriad of social contexts. Yet, by grouping similar organizations in a historical overview of the development of terrorism, we can see that a certain set of particular motivations have been responsible for a substantial amount of terrorism violence.

9.3.1 Nationalism and territorial motivations

Violent outcomes to territorial disputes have occurred throughout history. As empires have risen and fallen territory has changed hands throughout the development of the modern political system. As the authority and military resolve of the state as a political actor increased, non-state territorial challenges had to adapt and take on a form that negates the comparative martial weakness. Thus, terrorism and other forms of political violence have been used in a variety of campaigns for national liberation, or to achieve other territorial aims in contexts such as Palestine, Cyprus, and Sri Lanka.

Nationalism as a political phenomenon is—in the words of nationalism scholar Ernest Gellner (1983: 1)—the belief that 'the political unit and the national unit should be congruent'. Nationalist political movements (whether violent or nonviolent) argue that each national community should govern itself, regardless of how this community is defined (whether that be as an ethnic group, a language community or by other attributes). Due to the often-haphazard erection of national borders (especially when this process was carried out by colonial authorities), there are many national or ethnic groups around the world who do not have their own state, and lack decision-making authority. The common motivating goal for a number of these groups has been the creation of new self-governing nation-states, the expulsion of foreign ruling authorities, or the integration of their territory with existing kin states. Prominent examples include Kurdish groups operating in Turkey, Syria, Iran, and Iraq, Basque separatists principally operating in Spain but also claiming territory in France, Palestinian groups engaged in a campaign against Israel, and Tamil groups operating in Sri Lanka (including LTTE—Liberation Tigers of Tamil Eelam).

In David Rapoport's (2004) influential framework of terrorist history, he refers to these movements as part of the 'anti-colonial' wave, which arguably have been motivated by the same nationalist energies as those described above, occurring in (among other cases) Algeria and Cyprus. Terrorist campaigns aimed at bringing about national independence or re-unification have often been among the longest campaigns of terrorist violence: conflict in Sri Lanka over the future of Tamil Eelam persisted between 1983 and 2009, and ETA's (Basque Homeland and Freedom) campaign against the Spanish state officially ended in 2018, after 50 years.

In any territorial dispute, there is a section of society at odds with the nationalist pursuit of an independent homeland—often because they feel a greater emotional attachment to the state against which the group is fighting. This can, on occasions lead to **responsive** or **oppositional** terrorist campaigns that seek to protect the status quo, also carried out in the name of a national movement. An example of this would be the violent campaigns carried out by Loyalist paramilitary groups in Northern Ireland, such as the Ulster Defence Association and the Ulster Volunteer Force in defence of the continued status of Northern Ireland as part of the United Kingdom. In these circumstances, the violence is often intended to convince state authorities that capitulation to a nationalist challenger for a given territory would bring about an equally bloody campaign in response.

Nationalism was arguably the principal motivating cause of terrorist groups operating in the 20th century. Whether because of changes to the international system, military stalemate or strategic success, nationalist movements are less prominent in the 21st century as religiously-motivated groups have increasingly come to the fore.

9.3.2 Religious extremism

Religiously-motivated extremists have been responsible for some of the most infamous terrorist acts since the start of the 21st century. Religion was not a new phenomenon, but its prominence as a justification for violence has increased since the 1980s and certainly since the US attacks of September 11th 2001. From that point onwards, the actions of terrorist organizations such as al-Qaeda and the Islamic State (also known as ISIS) have re-shaped the popular understanding of the archetypal terrorist actor, as one with a distinctly religious character.

To highlight their religious character, these groups draw heavily from scripture and invoke religious language. This can be observed in public statements released by Osama bin Laden (founding member of al-Qaeda and credited for 9/11 attacks) who described members of the anti-coalition insurgency in Iraq as 'the soldiers of God, the spears of Islam . . . on the front line in the defence of the Muslim community' (Kepel and Milelli 2008: 69), and described attacks in Europe and Russia as the actions of 'the zealous sons of Islam in defence of their faith and in response to the order of their Lord and Prophet' (Ibrahim 2007: 231). The exploitation of religion can also be seen in the appropriation of religious symbols and language by these organizations: militant jihadist groups have used black banners bearing scripture as their flag. These claims of divine support are based on a specific interpretation of holy texts, and many interpretations of the same sources dismiss any justification for committing violence in the name of a higher power.

Religiously-inspired terrorists often portray their violence as part of a broader religious struggle between those who follow the true path and those who do not. For many religiously-inspired terrorist movements the long-term ambition for their campaign is to bring about a theocratically-governed and ordered society, without the excesses of secular capitalist systems. However, they also regularly cite motivating factors associated with political goals: al-Qaeda regularly framed their violence in reference to the presence of American military personnel in Saudi Arabia, and later, Iraq. This combination is not uncommon in discourse from supposedly religiously-motivated groups in a variety of different contexts, and it emphasizes the extent to which terrorism is rarely motivated by a single factor. Millenarian groups believe that their violent acts will bring about a prophesized event such as the 'end of days' or similar. Members of the Japanese group Aum Shinrikyo, responsible for the 1995 Tokyo Sarin attacks, were inspired by a belief that an apocalyptic third world war was imminent.

In modern popular discourse, religious terrorism is overwhelmingly associated with attacks carried out by Islamists. Yet terrorist violence has been carried out 'in the name' of all major religions. Anti-abortion political violence in the United States is justified through Christian scripture; prior to the formation of the state of Israel, Jewish terrorist organizations such as the Irgun fought for a Jewish homeland (see Hoffman 2015), and sporadic attacks by Jewish extremists have continued since; and militant forms of Buddhism have brought about violent clashes in Southeast Asia (see Lehr 2019). There will always be conditions in which religious adherents (of any faith) feel sufficiently threatened that they will turn to violence to protect their community.

Despite the attention paid to religiously-motivated violence in popular discourse and academic scholarship, it must be remembered that the vast majority of religious adherents do not engage in violent campaigns. Moreover, throughout human history religion has inspired many more acts of love, devotion, and charity as acts of destruction. Nonetheless, the rise to prominence of al-Qaeda and their successors ISIS have created (in the public's mind at least) a notion that religion is the primary cause of terrorism. Through highly-publicized attacks in locations such as New York, Bali, London, Nairobi, Dar es Salaam, Madrid, and Paris, as well as long-running campaigns in Iraq, Pakistan, and Somalia, religiously-motivated terrorism has dominated the news cycle and the policy sphere. Yet it is important to remember at all times that religiously extremism does not hold a monopoly on the use of terrorist violence and that other motivating factors need equal attention.

9.3.3 Ideologically-motivated terrorism

> **KEY CONCEPTS**
>
> **Ideology** A belief system about how to understand, order, and structure social life.

Linked to, and arguably overlapping with, religiously-motivated terrorism are terrorist acts that are conducted by violent actors in the name of a specific ideology. An ideology is a belief system about how to understand, order and structure social life. They are differentiated from political theories in that they set out a course of action to be followed. Ideological devotion can inspire the same emotional feelings as religious and national attachments and can form an important part of an individual's identity. This is a broad and somewhat artificial categorization that brings together a number of political ideologies, explored further in sections 9.3.3.1–9.3.3.4.

9.3.3.1 Far-right terrorism

A prominent example of ideological forms of terrorist violence are terrorist actions carried out by extreme far-right attackers (see Bjørgo 1995, Taylor, Currie, and Holbrook 2013). Often associated with neo-Nazi political views—and often drawing from the symbolism of Nazism—extreme right-wing attacks have been carried out in the United Kingdom, Norway, New Zealand, Germany, and the United States in recent years. In many cases their targets are minority groups: David Copeland targeted immigrants and LGBT+ people throughout London in 1999, and the 2019 Christchurch attack was directed against mosques in the city, indicating a clear targeting of the Muslim community. Islamophobic, anti-Semitic, and anti-immigrant political narratives are often cited by those involved in these types of acts.

One notable characteristic of recent extreme right-wing terrorist acts is that they have often been carried out by a single actor rather than a broader terrorist movement, as attacks in Norway (2011) and New Zealand (2019) demonstrated. This partly reflects a de-centralization of terrorist violence in the wake of increasing state surveillance, enabled by communication and expertise-sharing opportunities that the internet provides. This, however, has not made right-wing violence any less potent: the Oslo and Utøya attacks in Norway in July 2011 killed 77 people, and the Christchurch mosque attacks in New Zealand in March 2019 resulted in 51 deaths.

9.3.3.2 Anarchist terrorism

> **KEY CONCEPTS**
>
> **Anarchism** A political philosophy that rejects the need for central political authority.

The main terrorist threat in the late 19th century and at the start of the 20th century was posed by insurrectionary anarchism. Drawing on the works of (among others) Russian and French social philosophers, these campaigns were directed at bringing about a revolution within the host society to end the inequalities of the existing hierarchical system of government and provide for a more equitable distribution of resources (see Jensen 2004). As such violence was often directed at political leaders and monarchs, and assassinations were one of the principal tactics utilized by these groups. In fact, anarchists were responsible for a series of high-profile assassinations in that period: Spanish Prime Minister Antonio Cánovas del Castillo was assassinated by an Italian anarchist in August 1897, King Umberto I of Italy died at the hands of an anarchist terrorist in

July 1900, and US President William McKinley died after being shot by an anarchist attacker in September 1901.

Anarchist groups were also responsible for attacks against the general public: The US Wall Street Bombing in September 1920 was arguably a precursor to the vehicle-borne terrorism more prevalent in later terrorist 'waves'. Anarchist terrorism faded as a societal threat after the First World War. When a socialist-inspired terrorism did re-emerge, it was typically referred to as 'new left' or 'far left' terrorism.

9.3.3.3 New left/far left terrorism

In Rapoport's framework he labels his 'third wave' of terrorism as 'new left' terrorism (see also Chapter 8, Case Study 8.1). Inspired by the increasing attraction of revolutionary ideas and socialism to the post-war generation disillusioned by the Cold War and the inequalities perpetuated by a capitalist system that was facing international competition from communism. This form of terrorism was particularly prevalent between the 1960s and late 1980s. It was also broadly geographically distributed: groups such as the Weather Underground in the United States, the Communist Party of Nepal, the French *Action Directe*, and the Peruvian Shining Path (see Chapter 19, Photo 19.2) all had their roots in socialist ideologies.

Across these different contexts, tactics differed with some groups relying more on rural guerrilla struggles and others focusing on 'urban guerrilla' activities including the kidnapping or assassinations of prominent politicians and businessmen or bombings against military infrastructure. Many existing groups fighting for entirely different reasons also incorporated left-wing ideologies into their vision for the future. Nationalist movements in Northern Ireland and the Basque Country were split by those who advocated for a greater emphasis on class struggle. These new left movements declined in potency and visibility following the collapse of the Soviet Union and the subsequent diminishing power of communism as an international political ideology.

9.3.3.4 Single issue terrorism—anti-abortion, animal rights, and environmental groups

A number of terrorist campaigns are carried out by actors who are focused on a single emotive political issue. Among these types of campaigns include those who carry out violence against abortion clinics in the United States; those targeting testing labs in the name of animal rights, and in the name of environmental protection. These are often grouped together and referred to as 'single-issue' campaigns. Many of the acts of political violence carried out by groups such as the Animal Liberation Front are often directed against property rather than human life—but within the anti-abortion movement in the United States especially, a number of doctors who performed abortions have been killed by militant members of the movement. Whilst there is a religious element to the actions of these groups, their campaigns have largely focused on the single issue of abortion. Single-issue campaigns rarely pose the same level of threat to society at large as other terrorist movements, as they are often intensely focused on the specific motivating issue and the targets with which it is associated.

CASE STUDY 9.1

RAF

The *Rote Armee Fraktion* (Red Army Faction—RAF) was a left-wing revolutionary terrorist movement that operated in West Germany between 1970 and the group's dissolution in April 1998 (see also Chapter 6, Case Study 6.1). The movement was also referred to by the press as the Baader-Meinhof Gang, based on the name of two key figures in the group Andreas Baader and Ulrike Meinhof. The group itself went through a number of 'iterations' as new generations took over the mantle of leadership when the previous generation was imprisoned or passed away. Baader and Meinhof committed suicide whilst imprisoned along with other members of the group. During their nearly 30-year campaign, the group was involved in a number of assassinations, kidnappings, bombings, and bank robberies.

The ideological roots of the Red Army Faction were in socialist ideals put forward about the need to overthrow capitalism through mass activism, to bring about a more equal and just distribution of resources within society. The RAF, as well as a plethora of left-wing groups operating in Europe drew ideological inspiration from the student protest movements of the 1960s. This broad movement took on causes such as racial and gender equality, and protested against what they perceived as American imperialism in the invasion of Vietnam. These movements also concerned themselves with other (in their view) colonial struggles: the liberation of Palestine and support for guerrilla movements in Latin America. In Germany, another key cause played into the motivations of those involved in the Red Army Faction: concerns that German society had not heeded the lessons of the Second World War, and that key figures from the Nazi regime were still empowered in West Germany, providing the possibility of a return to Nazism.

The root causes, therefore, of the Red Army Faction (and groups like them) were a desire to overthrow a capitalist political system (far-left political ideology), to respond to American imperialist actions (state action) and to support liberation movements across the world (territorial motivations). One specific incident: the shooting of a student protester by the West German police in June 1967, has been cited as a precipitating factor in the group's emergence (Aust 2009: 27).

These root causes manifested in the targets the group chose: The West Berlin British Yacht Club was bombed in 1972, as were American military and diplomatic targets in Frankfurt. Industrial and political leaders were also targeted through assassination and kidnapping. Like-minded movements across Europe—such as the *Brigate Rosse* (Red Brigades) in Italy and the 17 November Revolutionary Organization (often known as 17N) in Greece—engaged in similar campaigns with equally limited success. These actions were intended to inspire a popular uprising, but the Red Army Faction failed to build a popular movement to support them. In 1998, the third generation of the movement released a statement in which they admitted that the group had not succeeded in their campaign.

QUESTIONS

1. What were the root causes of the Red Army Faction's campaign?
2. Can you think of a contemporary equivalent to the RAF? Have the root causes changed at all for these modern groups?

9.4 STRUCTURAL CAUSES OF POLITICAL VIOLENCE

So far, this chapter has looked at a variety of the key political root causes that have inspired terrorism. Whilst they can enlighten us as to why people would become politically active, they do not always help us to shed light on why they choose to express their political demands through violence. Therefore, it is important to consider reasons why those engaged in terrorist movements feel that violent action was their only way forward.

9.4.1 Absence of viable political opportunity

In a modern democratic system, citizenry has a great deal of power in shaping the future of society. Trade unions, political parties, advocacy groups and other forms of political movements have been shown to have the power to make immense political change, and regular elections allow for a smooth and orderly transfer of power. However, in some societies the ability of society to change their government through political means is weak or absent.

It is when individuals feel that they lack political agency through democratic means or mass peaceful action that terrorist violence may be utilized. The lack of viable mechanisms for change can cause certain elements within a political movement to turn to alternative available methods until there is little option left but to consider violence. Scholars such as Jeff Goodwin (2001) and John Schwarzmantel (2011) have highlighted how democratic deficits within society can make some political activists feel they have no viable alternative for political change other than armed rebellion. Some militant leaders have cited the lack of alternative as a key reason for their choice of violent methods: Richardson (2006: 35) records claims from Osama bin Laden, LTTE (LTTE Liberation Tigers of Tamil Eelam) leader Velupillai Prabhakaran, and key Red Army Faction figure Ulrike Meinhof, that no other strategy was available to their groups.

There can be little doubt that the weakness or absence of political institutions through which redress can be achieved peacefully can contribute to the emergence of terrorist organizations. Yet we should be cautious of terrorist claims that violence was the last resort in their political struggle: many terrorist movements subvert this very claim by aligning themselves with electoral and mass-membership movements that pursue similar goals through nonviolent means. Equally, there are many groups operating in democratic countries who justify their violence with the claim that the system is unjust or inherently flawed, and that engaging in this process only grants legitimacy to an illegitimate authority.

9.4.2 Poverty and economic deprivation

One cause identified by policymakers as key to understanding the conditions that give rise to terrorism is poverty. In December 2001, World Bank President James Wolfensohn remarked that 'The war [on terror] will not be won until we have come to grips with the problem of poverty and thus the sources of discontent'. The following year, in a speech to the United Nations, then President of the United States George W. Bush (2002) claimed that the fight against poverty was connected to the fight against terrorism because 'hope is an answer to terror'. Other international leaders including French President Jacques Chirac and Pakistani President Pervez Musharraf echoed this sentiment. During the post-9/11 period, it has been argued that international development funding was increasingly tied to security objectives, with defeating poverty perceived as a key strand of the response to international terrorism (Abrahamsen 2004; Brown and Grävingholt 2016).

Advocates of this connection suggest that poverty can contribute to feelings of hopelessness and futility, and that in these circumstances potential terrorists view violence as the only way to make an impact. The offers of salaries and loot are also highlighted as likely to influence those with limited means towards terrorist organizations. The notion of a connection between deprivation and political violence is not particularly new: influential scholars of civil conflict such as Ted Robert Gurr (1970) have made the case that it is not absolute deprivation per se, but *relative* deprivation that inspires individuals to adopt militant behaviour.

Yet this explanation has not been universally accepted. Alan Krueger and Jitka Malečková (2003) present research drawing on the cases of Lebanon and Palestine that shows that poverty was not an effective explanation of why people turned to terrorism in these contexts. They showed that members of Hezbollah (a Lebanese Shia Islamist political party and militant group) and Palestine groups were equally likely to come from 'economically-advantaged' families as they were from 'the ranks of the economically disadvantaged' (2003: 141). James Piazza (2007: 170) also found 'no empirical evidence to support the crux of the "rooted-in-poverty" thesis'. Thus, whilst poverty and relative deprivation may contribute to feelings of helplessness and futility, and could contribute to a sense of suffering that others seek to relieve with violent action, it is not clear that they are *directly* correlated with involvement in terrorism.

9.4.3 Education

Another policy measure cited by politicians and policymakers as key to reducing terrorism is education. The UN Global Counter-Terrorism Strategy, agreed in September 2006, argued that 'more educational initiatives are needed to weaken support and sympathy for terrorist activities and groups'. The explanation commonly given for this focus is that without formal education the populace lacks the opportunity to improve their own personal circumstances and lacks the critical faculties to challenge terrorist narratives. In many forms of domestic modern counterterrorism, education is held up as the key to success. The evidence between the lack of education and terrorism is contestable. Referring again to the work of Krueger and Malečková (2003: 119), they suggest that 'any connection between . . . education and terrorism is indirect, complicated and probably quite weak', instead linking violence to political conditions.

Other scholars, such as Diego Gambetta and Steffen Hertog (2016) have also challenged this connection, in their work on the correlation between individuals with engineering backgrounds and terrorist violence. When these aspects are considered, a lack of education would seem to be a poor indicator of potential involvement in terrorism, and certainly cannot be considered (by itself) a root cause. However, we can accept that it may contribute to the absence of opportunity that can convince an individual that they have limited prospects.

9.4.4 State failure

State failure or state weakness—the collapse of the state's infrastructure and ability to secure its own territory—is another systemic explanation often proclaimed by policymakers as a causal factor in the emergence, growth and 'incubation' of terrorist groups. The logic behind this claim is that ungoverned spaces allow terrorists opportunities to build an infrastructure that allows the group to train, recruit and earn money through taxation. In the absence of state welfare assistance, terrorist movements have been known to provide basic necessities such as food and medication, as well as to implement a specific form of local justice. The rise of ISIS, controlling parts of Syria and Iraq at the height of their strength in mid- to late 2014, does give this theory some weight, as the weakness of the Syrian state (involved in a bloody and destructive civil war at that time) and the Iraqi state allowed the organization to take control of major cities in both countries.

Scholars such as Karin von Hippel (2002: 31) have challenged some of the assumptions about the role of weak and failed states, highlighting instead that 'these attractions may be countered by the difficulties facing terrorists when operating in an insecure and foreign environment, where security is itself highly fragmented and infrastructure unreliable'. Moreover, this assumption rests on Western premises of state behaviour which may be at odds with expectations in other parts of the world. Finally, if this claim is true, it does not explain why terrorist actors haven't sought to base their operations in a wide variety of other states that perform poorly in indicators of stability.

Taken together this series of factors are important in understanding why actors choose *violent* means to pursue political goals. The absence of political opportunity has been highlighted by a variety of terrorist movements in different contexts. Other explanations focus on how economic deprivation, the lack of education and state failure may contribute to the emergence of terrorist movements. The final set of factors to engage with in this chapter relate not to the ideas behind terrorist movements, or the socio-political circumstances that can provide a permission structure for violent behaviour, but the actions of state actors in sparking and sustaining terrorist conflict.

9.5 STATE (RE-)ACTION

Another approach to take when studying the root causes of terrorism is to consider terrorism as a response to state behaviour. Repressive acts—from the imposition of emergency measures curtailing civil liberties, the implementation of curfews, and imprisonment of protesters to the use of violence against citizens—have been held up as directly inciting a violent, in-kind, response. In many of the longest-lasting terrorist campaigns, the state's response to violent and nonviolent political protest has often set the tone for what is permissible in the ongoing conflict. One of the principal reasons for this is that repressive state action—especially deadly violent repression—often creates martyrs out of those killed in this response. In her work on terrorism and what terrorists hope to achieve, Louise Richardson (2006) cites 'revenge' as one of the principal motivating factors. Seeking vengeance against a state actor can inspire many to join terrorist organizations when they had no notions of engaging in violent struggle prior to their loss. For some, a particular grievance may be more of a perception of injustice, but it is no less influential in shaping their behaviour.

This type of root cause would fit under the label of a 'precipitant' or 'triggering' cause that was explained in Section 9.2, as it immediately precedes the terrorist action. An inflammatory political measure, repressive state response to a political protest or an overreaction to an individual act of terrorism escalate the situation if tensions run high. McConaghy (2017) highlights that this results from the fact that state organizations consist of individuals whose decision-making is not flawless, and who are prone to responding emotionally.

It has been argued that some terrorist actors deliberately try to provoke the state and state officials into a heavy-handed response in the belief that a public demonstration of the state's illegitimacy can sway a wavering constituency towards the group. Louise Richardson argues that 'very often the goal of a particular action is to provoke the government to retaliate forcibly' (2006: 103). Although they refer to it as 'jujitsu politics', Clark McCauley and Sophia Moskalenko also identify this approach in terrorist decision-making, claiming that the 'state response, to the extent that it hurts or outrages those less committed than the terrorists, does for the terrorists what they cannot do themselves' (2017: 178).

Thus, a key root cause of terrorist violence is state behaviour: whether provoked or otherwise. Repressive government measures create a perception that normal politics is unable to bring about the change, and can swell the ranks of their adversaries with new members seeking revenge.

CASE STUDY 9.2

GSPC

The *Groupe Salafiste pour la Prédication et le Combat* (Salafist Group for Preaching and Combat—GSPC) was a North African militant organization that operated mostly in Algeria, but also in several countries in North Africa and the wider Sahel region, such as Chad, Mauritania, and Niger. The group was formed in 1998 by former members of the *Groupe Islamique Armé* (Armed Islamic Group—GIA), an Algerian militant organization. The group gained international attention in 2003 following the kidnapping of 32 European tourists in Algeria. The group later pledged allegiance to al-Qaeda and in early 2007 the group was renamed al-Qaeda in the Islamic Maghreb (AQIM).

The motivating causes of the GSPC's campaign are varied, and there is evidence that they shifted as their local struggle was overtaken by global events. The initial set of causes were inherited from their predecessors in the GIA: a desire to bring about a theocratic revolution in Algeria. The GIA came into existence as a result of the Algerian Civil War, which itself was brought about by the cancellation of the 1991 election following a military coup, to prevent the theocratic *Front Islamique du Salut* (Islamic Salvation Front—FIS) from winning. From the outset, there were related and overlapping root causes from the GIA's violent campaign: a desire for a political revolution through the overthrow of the Algerian government, Algerian state brutality and the absence of democratic means of political redress. The name of its successor organization, the GSPC—including the term 'Salafist'—illustrated the strong religious motivations of the group.

The alliance sought by the leaders of the GSPC with al-Qaeda illustrates also the group's desire to contribute to an international struggle in support of co-religionists in conflicts in other parts of the world: principally Iraq and Afghanistan at that point in time. In particular, key figures in the GSPC hoped to aid the al-Qaeda affiliate in Iraq in the aftermath of the 2003 coalition invasion. When the GSPC united under the al-Qaeda banner, the deputy leader of al-Qaeda highlighted the antipathy towards France shared by both parties. This development illustrates the extent to which local actors can be simultaneously motivated to contribute to a local and a global struggle.

Through the kidnapping of European tourists another motivation can be determined that speaks not to terrorist motivations, but potentially criminal: the extraction of ransom payments from Western governments. Whereas kidnapping by other religiously motivated groups in this period often ended in the deaths of the hostages, the GSPC sought a ransom payment in exchange for their release.

PHOTO 9.2 Soldiers secure the area in front of Splendid Hotel in Ouagadougou, Burkina Faso, 17 January 2016, a day after security forces retook the hotel from AQIM fighters who seized it in an assault that killed two dozen people from at least 18 countries and marked a major escalation of Islamist militancy in West Africa.

In early 2007, the GSPC dropped their own name and became AQIM (al-Qaeda in the Islamic Maghreb). This development diminished the highly local roots of their origins in the politics of Algerian governance, in an attempt to contribute to the force projection of the global al-Qaeda brand. Since that point, AQIM has been responsible for a number of deadly attacks, most notably targeting hotels in Bamako, Mali (November 2015) and Ouagadougou, Burkina Faso as shown in Photo 9.2 (January 2016). The changing nomenclature and regional spread of the GSPC/AQIM help illustrate the extent to which the motivations of terrorist groups can fluctuate over time.

QUESTIONS

1. Why did the GSPC have to evolve?
2. How do the root causes of terrorism differ *within* organizations that you have studied?

9.6 CONCLUSION

In this chapter, a variety of explanations for terrorist violence have been laid out. For as long as terrorism has impacted society, different factors have been held up as the 'root cause' of militant activity: from poverty and state failure to religious and separatist extremism.

The vast array of studies on these topics have significantly aided our comprehension of this phenomenon, but there remains scope to study the root causes of terrorism further. Understanding why terrorism occurs is important not only to scholars and students, but to policymakers in guiding the response to terrorism. Without a clear understanding of the root causes of terrorism, state actors have shown a tendency to respond inappropriately and insensitively, often exacerbating an issue that a more nuanced approach might have been able to resolve. Thus, it is important to continue to ask the question why does terrorism occur?

This chapter has demonstrated that there are a variety of *types* of root causes—whether deeply historical or pressing and immediate. This variety reflects the myriad forms terrorism has taken around the world, and is not only between terrorist groups, but also within terrorist groups: both between different members and throughout the timeframe in which the groups operate. Any study of the causes of terrorism would be wise to look not for one root cause but an array of root cause*s*.

DISCUSSION QUESTIONS

1. Are there some root causes that are common to all (or most) forms of terrorism?
2. Can we identify a single 'root cause' of a specific terrorist movement?
3. Do specific types of terrorist violence, such as suicide terrorism, have unique causes?
4. What impact might our understanding of root causes have on counterterrorism?
5. How has technological innovation impacted upon the root causes of terrorism?

Visit the online resources for pointers on how to answer the discussion questions, links to useful web sources, and guidance on accessing databases:
www.oup.com/he/Wilson-Muro1e

GUIDE TO FURTHER READING

Bjørgo, T. (ed.) (2006) *Root Causes of Terrorism. Myths, Reality and Ways Forward*. London and New York: Routledge. *Bjørgo's edited collection examines the idea behind 'root causes' as a phenomenon and assesses the validity of a number of supposed 'root causes' of terrorism.*

Crenshaw, M. (1981) 'The Causes of Terrorism,' *Comparative Politics*, 13/4: 379–399 *Crenshaw's 1981 article on the causes of terrorism remains influential for those examining why terrorism occurs, breaking the causes down into different 'types' such as preconditions and precipitants.*

Pedahzur, A. (ed.) (2006) *Root Causes of Suicide Terrorism: The Globalisation of Martyrdom*. London: Routledge. *Pedahzur's collection brings together a series of essays on the different factors at play in suicide terrorism. An important text for understanding whether different types of terrorism have different causes*

Richardson, L. (ed.) (2006) *The Roots of Terrorism*. London: Routledge. *The authors of this edited collection were brought together in the wake of the 2004 Madrid bombings to address the causes of terrorism further—this wide-ranging book covers their findings very effectively.*

REFERENCES

Abadie, A. (2006) 'Poverty, Political Freedom, and the Roots of Terrorism', *American Economic Review*, 96 (2): 50–56.

Abrahamsen, R. (2004) 'A Breeding Ground for Terrorists? Africa & Britain's "War on Terrorism"', *Review of African Political Economy*, 31 (102): 677–684.

Alonso, R. (2006) 'Individual Motivations for Joining Terrorist Organisations: A Comparative Qualitative Study on Members of ETA and IRA', in J. Victoroff (ed.), *Tangled Roots: Social and Psychological Factors in the Genesis of Terrorism*. Amsterdam: IOS Press, 187–202.

Aust, S. (2009) *Baader-Meinhof: The Inside Story of the RAF*. Oxford: Oxford University Press.

Berrebi, C. (2007) 'Evidence About the Link Between Education, Poverty and Terrorism Among Palestinians', *Peace Economics, Peace Science and Public Policy*, 13 (1).

Bjørgo, T. (1995) *Terror from the Extreme Right*. London: Routledge.

Bjørgo, T. (ed.) (2006) *Root Causes of Terrorism. Myths, Reality and Ways Forward* (London and New York: Routledge).

Brooke, N. (2018) *Terrorism and Nationalism in the United Kingdom: The Absence of Noise*. Basingstoke: Palgrave Macmillan.

Brown, S. and Grävingholt, J. (2016) *The Securitization of Foreign Aid*. Basingstoke: Palgrave Macmillan.

Bush, G. (2002) 'Remarks by Mr. George W. Bush, President, at the International Conference on Financing for Development', Available at: https://www.un.org/ffd/statements/usaE.htm

Conversi, D. (1997) *The Basques, the Catalans and Spain: Alternative Routes to Nationalist Mobilization*. Reno, NV: University of Nevada Press.

Crenshaw, M. (1981) 'The Causes of Terrorism', *Comparative Politics*, 13 (4): 379–399.

De la Calle, L. (2015) *Nationalist Violence in Postwar Europe*. Cambridge: Cambridge University Press.

English, R. (2008) *Irish Freedom: A History of Nationalism in Ireland*. London: Pan Macmillan.

English, R. (2009) *Terrorism: How to Respond*. Oxford: Oxford University Press.

Eubank, W. and Weinberg, L. (1994) 'Does Democracy Encourage Terrorism?', *Terrorism and Political Violence*, 6 (4): 417–435.

Evans, Jonathan (2007) 'Intelligence, Counter-terrorism and Trust'. Available at: https://www.mi5.gov.uk/fa/node/404

Gambetta, D. and Hertog, S. (2016) *Engineers of Jihad: The Curious Connection between Violent Extremism and Education*. Princeton, NJ: Princeton University Press.

Gellner, E. (1983) *Nations and Nationalism*. Oxford: Blackwell.

Goodwin, J. (2001) *No Other Way Out: States and Revolutionary Movements, 1945–1991*. Cambridge: Cambridge University Press.

Gunning, J. and Jackson, R. (2011) 'What's so "Religious" About "Religious Terrorism"?', *Critical Studies on Terrorism*, 4 (3): 369–388.

Gurr, T. (1970) *Why Men Rebel*. Princeton, NJ: Princeton University Press.

Hoffman, B. (2015) *Anonymous Soldiers: The Struggle for Israel, 1917–1947*. New York: Vintage.

Ibrahim, R. (2007) *The Al Qaeda Reader*. New York: Broadway Books.

Jensen, R. (2004) 'Daggers, Rifles and Dynamite: Anarchist Terrorism in Nineteenth Century Europe', *Terrorism and Political Violence*, 16 (1): 116–153.

Juergensmeyer, M. (2000) *Terror in the Mind of God*. Oakland, California: University of California Press.

Kepel, G. and Milelli J. P. (2008) *Al Qaeda in its Own Words* [Translated by Pascale Ghazaleh]. London: Harvard University Press.

Krueger, A. and Malečková, J. (2003) 'Education, Poverty and Terrorism: Is There a Causal Connection?', *Journal of Economic Perspectives*, 17 (4): 119–144.

Laitin, D. (1995) 'National Revivals and Violence', *European Journal of Sociology*, 36 (1): 3–43.

Lehr: (2019) *Militant Buddhism: The Rise of Religious Violence in Sri Lanka, Myanmar and Thailand*. Basingstoke: Palgrave Macmillan.

McCauley, C. and Moskalenko, S. (2017) *Friction: How Radicalization Happens to Them and Us*. Oxford: Oxford University Press.

McConaghy, K. (2017) *Terrorism and the State: Intra-state Dynamics and the Response to Non-State Political Violence*. Basingstoke: Palgrave Macmillan.

Muro, D. (2013) *Ethnicity and Violence: The Case of Radical Basque Nationalism*. London: Routledge.

Newman, E. (2007) 'Weak States, State Failure, and Terrorism', *Terrorism and political violence*, 19 (4): 463–488.

Pedahzur, A. (2006) *Root Causes of Suicide Terrorism: The Globalisation of Martyrdom*. London: Routledge.

Piazza, J. (2007) 'Draining the Swamp: Democracy Promotion, State Failure, and Terrorism in 19 Middle Eastern countries', *Studies in Conflict & Terrorism*, 30 (6): 521–539.

Rapoport, D. (2004) 'The Four Waves of Modern Terrorism', in A. Cronin and J. Ludes (eds.), *Attacking Terrorism: Elements of a Grand Strategy*. Washington, D: Georgetown University Press. 46–73.

Richardson, L. (ed.) (2006) *The Roots of Terrorism*. London: Routledge.

Richardson, L. (2006) *What Terrorists Want: Understanding the Terrorist Threat*. London: John Murray.

Schwarzmantel, J. (2011) *Democracy and Political Violence*. Edinburgh: University of Edinburgh Press.

Stampnitzky, L. (2013) *Disciplining Terror: How Experts Invented 'Terrorism'*. Cambridge: Cambridge University Press.

Stern, J. (2003) *Terror in the Name of God*. New York: Ecco.

Taylor, M., Currie: M., and Holbrook, D. (2013) *Extreme Right Wing Political Violence and Terrorism*. London: Bloomsbury.

UN (2003) 'Transmittal letter dated 1 December 2004 from the Chair of the High-level Panel on Threats, Challenges and Change addressed to the Secretary-General', Available at: https://www.un.org/ruleoflaw/blog/document/the-secretary-generals-high-level-panel-report-on-threats-challenges-and-change-a-more-secure-world-our-shared-responsibility/

Von Hippel, K. (2002) 'The Roots of Terrorism: Probing the Myths'. *The Political Quarterly*, 73 (1): 25–39.

Wilkinson (1974) *Political Terrorism*. London: Macmillan.

CHAPTER 10

When Do Individuals Radicalize?

RIK COOLSAET

■ CHAPTER SUMMARY

For more than a century now, observers have been trying to understand why and how individuals become terrorists. Every time the international community was confronted with a significant wave of terrorist attacks, a sense of urgency boosted this quest for answers. Each time, fierce academic and public debates on the causes of terrorism ensued and answers varied widely, ranging from mental health problems to social injustice. Beyond scholarly differences and competing paradigms, however, broad areas of consensus have over time matured into solid research-based findings on some of the key variables that play a crucial role in the making of a terrorist. There is now a broad academic consensus that involvement in terrorism results from an interaction of personal trajectories with group dynamics and contextual factors. Acknowledging the progress made in the field of terrorism studies over the past hundred years and establishing its current state of play is useful for putting the ongoing scholarly and public debates into perspective.

10.1 INTRODUCTION

Writing to President Nixon in March 1969, US National Security Advisor Henry A. Kissinger summarized the main findings of a secret CIA survey of the global student unrest of the late 1960s. With its 'behavioural, social-psychological emphasis', it represented an attempt to understand 'what makes Johnny riot'. Radicalization, Kissinger pointed out, is the process 'whereby more and more participants are drawn into protest (not unlike a lynch mob)'. However, there is 'no agreement as to the dynamics involved', but 'adolescent rebellion, existential "Angst", systemic alienation' may be purged through participating in the protest movement. 'Nihilism' was the actual programme of this 'New' Left: 'There is very little prescription and no discussion of the apocalyptic future. The system must be destroyed; then the future will be dealt with.' As to the future of the protest movement, he was less certain: 'It is not possible to assess whether the crest has been reached' (Kissinger 1969).

Kissinger referred to the work of sociologists who had been studying how individuals joined mass protest movements. Nowadays, 'radicalization' is commonly understood as the process through which an individual gets involved in terrorism. Ideally, the concept of radicalization should provide answers to questions such as: why do individuals join terrorist groups or commit terrorist acts? What goes on in their mind? What is the trigger that makes an individual cross the threshold to actually using violence? In short: What makes a terrorist?

While the concept of radicalization is recent, such questions are not. Walter Laqueur (1977a), one of the pioneers of modern terrorism studies, opined in the 1970s: 'Questions about what motivates the terrorist have been asked for a long time and the answers have varied enormously.' Over time, however, our knowledge about the dynamics that lead individuals towards violence has advanced significantly.

This chapter will first identify how scholars and observers reacted to the first truly global wave of terrorism at the end of the 19th century. The worldwide wave of political violence of the 1960s then allowed for the early sporadic observations on political violence to develop into a thriving research field that offered more insightful answers to the old questions. The post 9/11 environment saw the emergence of new models, concepts and mechanisms, that tried to systematize the knowledge on political violence. The chapter will conclude with a state of play concerning the 'making of a terrorist', that identifies the degree of broad consensus on the old question of what makes a terrorist.

10.2 THE EARLY ANSWERS

When the world faced the first truly global terrorist campaign in the 1880s, the most common view of the perpetrators was that they had to be senseless. The culprits were anarchists. Most anarchists were not terrorists. But a minority strongly believed that violence was the only way to achieve the anarchists' goal of upending bourgeois society. To the well-off public, violent anarchism was an enigma at odds with the unparalleled material wealth, the scientific progress, and the ensuing optimism that marked the epoch of the late 1800s. Physicians considered them 'insane' 'irresponsible persons affected by a desire for martyr glory and irresistibly drawn towards the scaffold' (New York Times 1909). Some viewed anarchists as vulnerable youngsters, 'weak minds without education and without defence against the harmful ideas of agitators', as an observer noted in 1882, during the trial of a 19-year-old weaver who had attempted to kill a French industrialist (Bataille 1882).

Not everybody subscribed to the weak-minded or vulnerable youth theses, however. The late 19th-century psychiatrist Edward C. Spitzka was persuaded that violent anarchism represented a 'conspiracy among sane men'. While not excluding that some of them were 'unquestionably insane', they were nevertheless part of 'an international army organized to war upon society, directed by skilful generals (. . .)' (New York Times 1909).

Ernst Viktor Zenker, an Austrian journalist and MP, was more nuanced as to motivations. He strongly emphasized that context had to be taken into account (Zenker 1897). Anarchism could not be explained sufficiently—perhaps not at all—by mere poverty, he pointed out. It is not an economic but a political question. It results from 'a confused mass of injustice and wrongdoing, of which the bourgeois State is daily and hourly guilty towards the weak':

> The average man does not much mind his rich fellow-man riding in his carriage while he himself cannot even pay his tram fare; but that he should be abandoned by society to every chance official of justice, as a prey that has no rights (. . .) that makes his blood boil, and causes him to seek the origin of this injustice in the institution itself instead of in the way it works. How many Anarchists have become so merely because they were treated as common criminals when they happened to have the misfortune to be suspected of Anarchism? How many became Anarchists because they were outlawed by society on account of free and liberal views? (Zenker 1897: 322).

Zenker thus concluded with an outline of a whole-of-government disengagement strategy before the term was invented:

> A movement like Anarchism cannot be conquered by force and injustice, but only by justice and freedom (Zenker 1897: 323).

Notwithstanding all the efforts at identifying the terrorist mindset, no single profile of the anarchist terrorist existed. Some were *solitaires* (as lone wolves were then called by the French police), others were part of small cells, where it was 'often hard to distinguish the devoted anarchist militant, moved by a deep passion for justice, from the psychopath whose shadowy voices prompt him to take his private revenge on society by means of actions of which the anarchists had given him the example' (Joll 1964: 128). Anarchist violence was not necessarily the work of the destitute and the desperate. Depending on national contexts, violent anarchism could attract artisans threatened by rising industrialization, landless peasants or industry workers and miners, convinced the 'Social Revolution' was near. Some were middle class. 'Long live the Social Revolution' was often their battle cry when they went into action—or their last words before the blade of the guillotine fell. They believed that their act—or their death—would set an example and inflame the masses. The masses were not particularly moved, but revenge for their death became a powerful motive for fellow anarchists to act in turn.

When put on trial, terrorists always blamed their violence on society, which left them no choice but violence. At his trial in 1892, a notorious French terrorist who went by the name of Ravachol, half anarchist, half criminal, explained his motivations as follows: 'I was forced to do so by necessity. [. . .] I was the one who had the right to expect everything from society. But society didn't give me anything' (Bataille 1892).

The early attempts to understand why individuals chose to perpetrate acts of political violence resulted in widely diverging diagnoses. But interest in the topic was largely sporadic. It took a new wave of terrorism, half a century later, to transform these observations into more systematic insights.

10.3 THE ADVENT OF TERRORISM STUDIES

By the 1960s, the interest in the old questions received a significant boost by the simultaneous advent of national liberation movements in the 'Third World' (as it was then called, generally considered paternalistic and derogatory terminology today), urban guerrilla movements in Latin America, the Basque and Irish republican turns to violence, student protests, and violent left-wing groups.

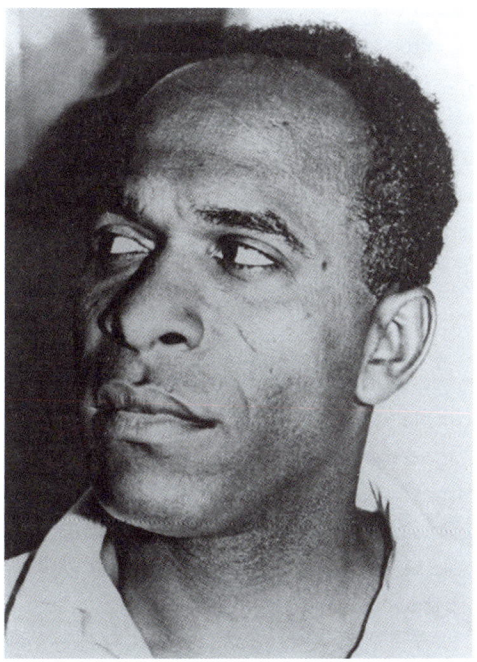

PHOTO 10.1 Frantz Fanon (1025-196) psychoanalysist and social philosopher.

Outside the West, the focus was mostly on the structural drivers of political violence. This was typically justified as a response to the intrinsic injustice and violence of colonialism. Frantz Fanon (1925-1961) was among the most influential voices claiming the need and the right for colonized people to resort to political violence in order to shed the burden of colonialism, both politically and culturally. Born in 1925 in Martinique, he left for Algeria in 1953, where he started to work as a psychiatrist and soon joined the National Liberation Front. Speaking on behalf of the have-nots of the world, Fanon considered violence not so much as the only means left, but as the only way for the colonized to reclaim both their own identity and a sense of national identity. Introducing Fanon's *The Wretched of the Earth* (1961), the French philosopher Jean-Paul Sartre explicitly rejects psychological considerations to explain Fanon's call to arms: '... you need not think that hot-headedness or an unhappy childhood have given him [Fanon] some uncommon taste for violence'. Violence, according to Sartre, is a necessary evil to combat entrenched violence, when nonviolence 'serves only to position you in the ranks of the oppressors' (Sartre 1961).

CASE STUDY 10.1

'I am prepared to die'—Nelson Mandela on Terrorism

At the time apartheid ruled in South Africa, Nelson Mandela (1918–2013, see Photo 10.2) was its most prominent opponent. He was labelled a 'terrorist' by the authorities, as well as by many Western states. On 20 April 1964, he was brought to justice for acts of violence in a court trial. He used this opportunity to explain his point of view on the use of violence. In 1993, he received the Nobel Peace Prize. A year later, he became president of South Africa. As late as 2008, he was still on the US terrorism watch list. The extracts from his speech below were given at the Rivonia Trial, and are considered one of the great speeches of the 20th century:

'Some of the things so far told to the Court are true and some are untrue. I do not, however, deny that I planned sabotage. I did not plan it in a spirit of recklessness, nor because I have any love of violence. I planned it as a result of a calm and sober assessment of the political situation that had arisen after many years of tyranny, exploitation, and oppression of my people by the whites.

[...]

I have already mentioned that I was one of the persons who helped to form Umkhonto [armed wing of the African National Congress, the main resistance movement to apartheid]. I, and the others who started the organization, did so for two reasons. Firstly, we believed that as a result of Government policy, violence by the African people had become inevitable, and that unless responsible leadership was given to canalize and control the feelings of our people, there would be outbreaks of terrorism which would produce an intensity of bitterness and hostility between the various races of this country which is not produced even by war. Secondly, we felt that without violence there would be no way open to the

PHOTO 10.2 Nelson Mandela in 1993. Mandela was labelled a terrorist, and was on terrorist watch lists until 2008.

African people to succeed in their struggle against the principle of white supremacy. All lawful modes of expressing opposition to this principle had been closed by legislation, and we were placed in a position in which we had either to accept a permanent state of inferiority, or to defy the Government. We chose to defy the law. We first broke the law in a way which avoided any recourse to violence; when this form was legislated against, and then the Government resorted to a show of force to crush opposition to its policies, only then did we decide to answer violence with violence.

[...]

Four forms of violence were possible. There is sabotage, there is guerrilla warfare, there is terrorism, and there is open revolution. We chose to adopt the first method and to exhaust it before taking any other decision.

[...]

But we in Umkhonto weighed up the whites' response with anxiety. The lines were being drawn. The whites and blacks were moving into separate camps, and the prospects of avoiding a civil war were diminishing. The white newspapers carried reports that sabotage would be punished by death. If this was so, how could we continue to keep Africans away from terrorism?'

Mandela's stance on terrorism illustrates Franz Fanon's argument that a highly oppressive state ('a land ruled by the gun' as Mandela described South Africa under the apartheid regime), renders the use of armed struggle inevitable, since all peaceful means to eradicate the entrenched oppression have proven futile. Through this armed struggle a nation acquires its self-determination and identity. Since 1960, United Nations resolutions have legitimized this specific use of violence by recognized liberation movements.

QUESTIONS

1. How do Mandela's words relate to the 1960s maxim that 'one man's terrorist is another man's freedom fighter'?
2. Is this description of the different forms of political violence still valid in today's world?

In Europe and the United States, too, the worldwide wave of political violence enhanced the relevance of the study of political violence. Combining two existing notions—the relationship between frustration and aggression and relative deprivation—the American political scientist Ted Gurr argued that men become discontented when they do not get that to which they think they are entitled. Actual material deprivation is thus not the cause of their discontent (Zenker suggested the same in 1897), but rather it is the gap between what they expected and what they actually get: 'Men who are frustrated have an innate disposition to do violence to its source in proportion to the intensity of their frustration' (Gurr 1970: 37).

Gurr offered a powerful argument, but not everyone was convinced about its utility in explaining terrorism or, in particular, individual motivations. While sharing Gurr's observation that 'it is ultimately the perception of grievance that matters, not the grievance itself', Walter Laqueur (1976: 103, 1977b) warned against grand schemes to explain such a complex phenomenon as terrorism.

The British scholar of terrorism Paul Wilkinson was also of the opinion that Gurr's relative deprivation propositions were 'pitched at such a high level of generality that it is hard to see how they could be invalidated' (Wilkinson 1974: 126). Nevertheless, he was adamant that 'context was all in the study of political violence' (Wilkinson 1986). But he insisted that the study of terrorism should also take into account the ideologies, beliefs and lifestyles of the terrorists: '. . . every international terrorist movement or group requires an extremist ideology or belief-system of some kind to nourish, motivate, justify and mobilize the use of terror violence' (Wilkinson 1988: 95). Personal characteristics such as 'passionate idealism and conviction' should not be discarded. He warned, however, against the tendency to stereotype terrorists as 'psychopaths' based on intelligence measurement scales (Wilkinson 1974: 132–133).

The American scholar Martha Crenshaw offered the most elaborate model put forward by the pioneers of terrorism studies. In her landmark 1981 contribution on the causes of terrorism (Crenshaw 1981), she too insisted that context was of the essence in understanding terrorism. Its causes lie in a conducive environment that permits its emergence *and* in direct motivating factors that propel people to violence. Crenshaw was the first scholar to propose an integrated approach to the study of terrorism by looking into the interplay between the societal context, psychological considerations and group dynamics. Terrorism, Crenshaw insisted, is never an automatic reaction to conditions. But answering the question of why specific individuals engaged in political violence was a tough question (Crenshaw 1981: 390).

The insights of these early scholars of terrorism laid the foundation of what was to become a thriving research field, with a rapidly growing scholarly output in the first half of the 1980s. It was essentially the work of political scientists, but some psychologists too entered the field. The difficulties scholars were facing at the time included the small number of individuals to study, the near impossibility of interviewing them, the confusion and lack of consensus as to what exactly constituted terrorism, and the need for interdisciplinary research.

Nevertheless, the research led to a broad consensus on some findings and offered promising insights on trajectories, role models and beliefs that were flagged for further research. By the mid-1980s, most scholars in the field would agree that terrorism was the result of a complex interplay of factors. There was also broad consensus that no single terrorist profile existed, that terrorists were not necessarily the most destitute, and that psychiatric diagnoses were not particularly relevant (Corrado, 1981: 304).

But still, Martha Crenshaw (1986) argued in a review of the state of play concerning the psychology and motivations of terrorists and terrorist groups, the decision to join a terrorist group can be 'influenced or, in some cases, even determined by subconscious or later psychological motives'. The decision to become a terrorist often corresponds to personal needs, different from case to case. Some terrorists see it as an 'act of personal futility ... when there is nowhere else to go' (Crenshaw 1986: 386). Others are seeking adventure or grandeur or see it as compensating for feelings of inferiority. Some are looking for recognition, acceptance, warmth, and solidarity.

For a majority of terrorists who are followers, Crenshaw makes clear, a dominant motive is to become a member of the group. Personal connections and relatives were of the essence in the process of joining a group, with the group becoming 'a family substitute' (Crenshaw 1986: 389–390). Becoming a terrorist was rarely a mere individual decision but was instead closely linked to group interactions. It was often the result of a gradual process and not a sudden conversion. But once a member of a group, the individual found that peer pressure within the group started to exert an inexorable influence, socializing them into its subculture, regulating all aspects of life, including the sexual relations of members. Embracing violence resulted from group pressure:

> The decision to use violence came only after association with the group, the choice was then between participating in violence or leaving the group. The individual who was already in need of the things a group could supply and who had over time become dependent on the group found it costly, in psychological terms, to go back (Crenshaw 1986: 389, 395).

A final broad consensus among terrorism scholars of the 1970s and 1980s concerned the role of ideology. Ideology was an important component of terrorism, but less than the general public or policymakers imagined: '. . . it is certainly not true that scratching a terrorist will necessarily reveal an ideologue,' Laqueur pointed out (1977b: 4). Sometimes it was mere 'camouflage', as was the case with almost all West-German RAF leaders (see Case Studies 6.1 and 9.1 for more), who never attempted to detail the future society they envisaged (Pridham 1981: 25).

Their 'ideology' was not so much a fixed set of axioms as a 'belief system': 'a set of lenses through which information concerning the physical and social environment is received. It orients the individual to his environment, defining it for him and identifying for him its salient characteristics ... In addition (...), the belief system has the function of the establishment of goals and the ordering of preferences.' (Holsti 1969: 544).

This brings the context back in. Many scholars subscribed to the view that terrorism cannot be studied in isolation from its political and social context (Crenshaw 1986: 384). 'Terrorism always assumes the protective colouring of certain features of the *Zeitgeist* (the defining mood of an epoch), which was fascist in the 1920s and 1930s but took a different direction in the 1960s and 1970s', Laqueur asserted (1977a). Though political terrorism was considered a transnational phenomenon, in individual countries it necessarily reflected 'local conditions, cultural and political no less than economic and social' (Furlong 1981: 60).

By the mid-1980s, the study of terrorism had thus received a real scholarly boost compared to previous decades. But this hadn't resulted in a straightforward answer to the question of what makes a terrorist. Results were disparate and non-cumulative. Important questions remained unanswered. Why did only some individuals become terrorists, while others with the same background did not? Mental illness was largely discredited as a satisfactory explanation, but it nevertheless 'continued to survive as a resilient source of inspiration on which to base theories' (Silke 1998: 53).

At this point terrorism research began to decline. A small group of terrorism scholars nevertheless pursued their research. Their contributions would bridge the 1970–1980s wave of terrorism studies with a new wave that emerged after the 9/11 attacks.

The Italian political sociologist Donatella Della Porta is one of them. Her comparative study of radical-left movements in Italy and West-Germany refined the integrated model Martha Crenshaw had sketched in 1981 (see also Chapter 6). She viewed terrorist groups as part of social movements and applied the earlier research on mass movements to the much smaller and more violent militant groups. In order to grasp their dynamics, all three levels of analysis should be explored simultaneously. External conditions are crucial in the emergence of political violence, the group level in its development and the individual level in gauging motivations and perceptions of the militants (Della Porta 1995: 187). Among the external conditions, her work concentrated on the state's policies. She viewed terrorism as a relational dynamics, determined by the interaction between state and protest movement. At the group and the individual levels, she explored how group dynamics shapes the minds of its members and forges militant identities, whereby the environment is framed as unfair, the state as the enemy and themselves as an heroic elite.

Terrorism as a complex phenomenon might be the best description of the state of play in the field of terrorism studies on the eve of the 20th century. While diverging on the relative importance of the different dimensions of the phenomenon, scholars broadly shared the overall assessment that it resulted from a complex interaction between personal characteristics, group dynamics, belief systems, and contextual factors.

10.4 THE ROAD TO RADICALIZATION

The attacks in New York of September 11, 2001 gave terrorism studies a renewed boost, surpassing the 1970s-1980s era in academic frenzy and scholarly output. 'Why do they hate us?' President George W. Bush rhetorically asked in his address to the joint session of Congress less than a week after the attacks. 'Root causes', the European Union asserted, have to be identified if we are to understand why 9/11 happened and prevent it from repeating itself (see Chapter 9 for more on Root Causes).

The terrorist organization al-Qaeda was perceived by authorities and security agencies in the West as a worldwide recruitment ring. The West was a target for al-Qaeda, as well as a 'place for recruitment and logistical support for jihad in Afghanistan, Iraq and Chechnya' (Europol 2004). Jihad literally means 'a struggle', and 'jihadism' is newly coined term in Western-languages to describe Islamic movements perceived as 'existentially threatening'. Al-Qaeda's foreign recruiters were targeting angry, vulnerable young people, especially in Europe's diasporic communities, who 'are often in search of their identity', the Dutch intelligence service AIVD alleged (AIVD 2002b: 10–11). By implanting 'extreme religious convictions' in young people's minds, recruiters sought to persuade them to participate in terrorist attacks (AIVD 2002a: 10, 18). In the United States, too, the 'key assumption . . . was that there was some mysterious process of indoctrination or brainwashing that transformed "vulnerable" or "at risk" *naïve* young people into fanatic killers' (Sageman 2014: 567).

The American forensic psychologist Randy Borum (2003) was the first to present a simplified model of the process that leads to the emergence of a terrorist mind-set. His model was intended to enable investigators to 'better identify persons who represent desirable candidates or recruitment [. . .], possible sites of indoctrination [. . .], and extremists or groups that may use violent tactics' (2003, 8) (see Figure 10.1). Echoing similar warnings from the pioneers of terrorism studies, he argued that: '[. . .] ideology may be *a* factor, but not necessarily *the* factor in determining motive' (2003, 9).

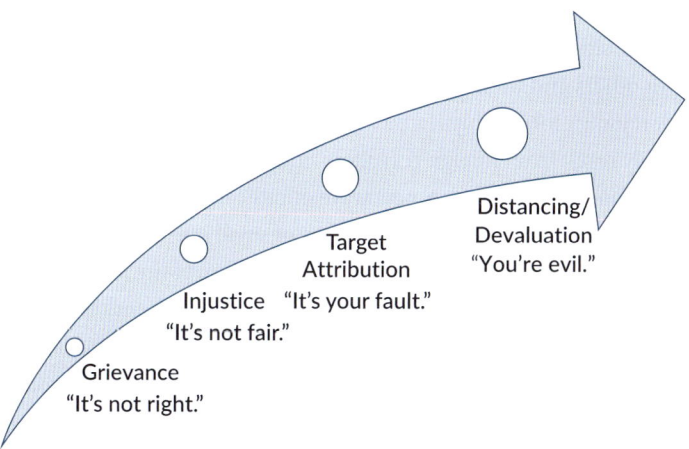

FIGURE 10.1 Borum's four-stage model of the terrorist mind-set. Source: Borum (2011).

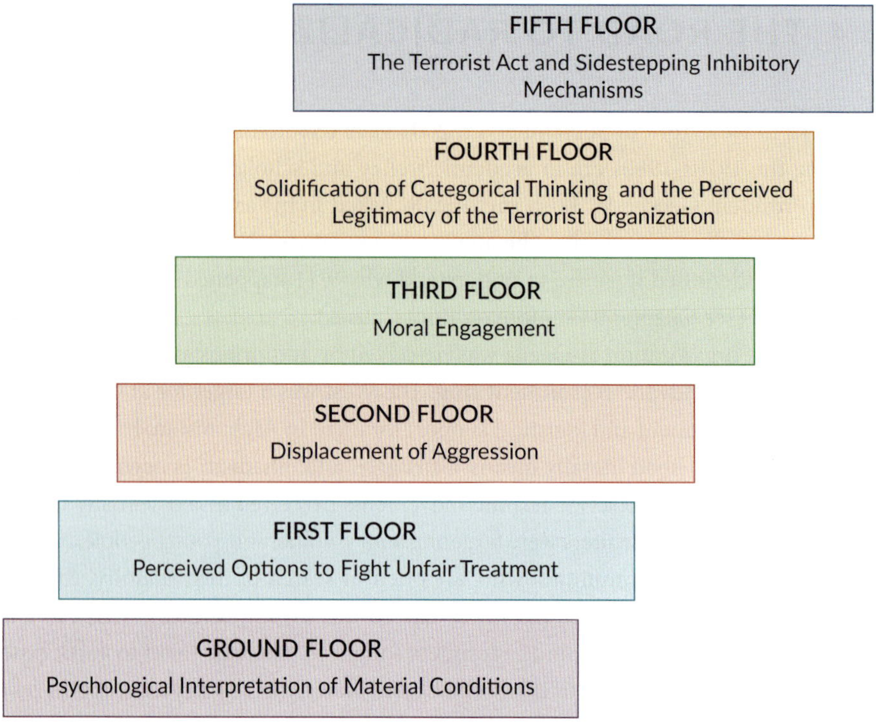

FIFTH FLOOR
The Terrorist Act and Sidestepping Inhibitory Mechanisms

FOURTH FLOOR
Solidification of Categorical Thinking and the Perceived Legitimacy of the Terrorist Organization

THIRD FLOOR
Moral Engagement

SECOND FLOOR
Displacement of Aggression

FIRST FLOOR
Perceived Options to Fight Unfair Treatment

GROUND FLOOR
Psychological Interpretation of Material Conditions

FIGURE 10.2 **Moghaddam's staircase to terrorism.** Source: Moghaddam, F. A. (2005).

A more elaborated model was offered by the American psychologist Fathali M. Moghaddam (2005). It became one of the most popular and influential representations of a staged process of 'radicalization'—even if this word was not yet widely used. Moghaddam offered a metaphor of an ever-narrowing staircase leading to the top of a building—terrorism (see Figure 10.2). On the ground floor, perceptions of fairness and feelings of relative deprivation dominate. Step-by-step, an individual, 'influenced by leaders', eventually gets recruited to terrorist organizations and might reach the top floor, where they are 'trained to sidestep inhibitory mechanisms that could prevent them from injuring and killing both others and themselves'.

Models grew rapidly more sophisticated when it became clear that engagement in terrorism did not necessarily result from foreign recruiters' efforts. The US invasion of Iraq in 2003 had reinvigorated a waning jihadi scene. A new wave of radicals emerged. This wave was labelled 'home-grown'. It represented a bottom-up dynamic of small self-radicalizing groups and individuals not directed by al-Qaeda, but mobilized by outrage over the invasion. They essentially got involved through kinship and friendship bonds—a crucial dimension of terrorism that the pioneers of terrorism studies had identified decades earlier (see section 10.2).

In *Understanding Terror Networks*, the American scholar and former CIA case officer Marc Sageman offered a biographical study of 172 al-Qaeda members. His research not only confirmed the earlier findings that terrorists were not 'poor, desperate, naïve single young men from third world countries, vulnerable to brainwashing and recruitment into terror' (Sageman 2004: 69), but also described how they typically joined the global jihad through pre-existing social bonds (family and friends), that often preceded ideological commitment to the cause of jihadism.

In Europe, the Madrid train bombings of March 2004, the assassination of the Dutch film director Theo van Gogh in November 2004, and the London bombings of July 2005 redirected the focus from foreign recruitment to home-grown self-mobilization.

The murder of van Gogh was the action of a young second-generation Moroccan-Dutchman of Berber origin, who was part of a loose grouping of mostly Moroccan descent who had been born or raised in the Netherlands. The perpetrators of the Madrid bombings with their mixture of Spanish and foreign backgrounds did not conform to the standard terrorist profile of a fundamentalist Muslim extremist coming from abroad either. The four perpetrators of the 2005 London bombings were all British citizens, three of whom were born in Britain from parents who immigrated to the UK.

How did all these individuals come to resort to terrorism and turn against their own countrymen? To what degree religion played a role, or feelings of discrimination? Something, it was argued, must turn a person from a 'normal' individual into a terrorist. Unpacking this became of paramount importance, lest European societies be undermined by a growing polarization between Muslims and non-Muslims and between natives and migrant communities, European officials feared (Coolsaet 2019: 36).

KEY CONCEPTS

Radicalization There is no agreed definition of radicalization. It can simply refer to an idea or a behaviour that is not mainstream. Historically, it referred to efforts to broaden the realm of democracy. Since 2004, it often is often associated with the process by which an individual becomes a terrorist, starting with embracing radical (extremist) ideas that inexorably pushes them down the road toward terrorist violence. Originally, it was thought that this pathway needed some time to develop (hence the idea of a 'process'), but now it appears that the decision to act is not necessarily preceded by a preliminary phase of acquiring radical ideas. When studying radicalization, sometimes all three levels of analysis (individual, group, conducive environment) are taken into account, but often the micro-level of the individual is privileged. It can be limited to ideas ('cognitive radicalization') or to action ('behavioural radicalization'), with the relationship between the two being subject to (scholarly and public) debate.

KEY CONCEPTS

Extremism Often conflated with radicalism. Extremism too has no universally agreed definition. While radicalism can function within the realm of democratic action, extremism projects itself outside this realm, by refusing diversity in opinion and the rule of law, as well as not rejecting the use of violence as a legitimate policy tool.

These attacks propelled a novel concept to centre stage in EU counterterrorism thinking and policies—radicalization. Until then, it had been loosely used to describe growing expressions of anger and frustration among young people. In October 2004, the European Commission, for the very first time released a public paper that introduced the concept of 'radicalization' (European Commission 2004). Convinced of the need to address the root causes of this resurgence of terrorism, Commission officials nevertheless preferred to use the concept of 'radicalization', judging it to be more neutral (see Case Study 10.2).

CASE STUDY 10.2

The European Union at the Cradle of 'Radicalization'

Before 2004, the concept of radicalization wasn't part of the counterterrorism terminology. Within academia, the concept was hardly used. In the wake of the 9/11 attacks, it started to be loosely utilized by European police and intelligence officials as a synonym of 'anger' among young people in immigrant communities. What exactly was the source of this anger? Finding an answer to this question became all the more urgent after the terrorist attacks of March 2004 in Madrid which killed 193 people. European Commission officials were acutely aware that without tackling the 'root causes' of this anger, European societies risked being undermined by a growing polarization between Muslims and non-Muslims, between natives and migrant communities.

In May 2004, a confidential assessment of the 'underlying factors in the recruitment to terrorism' was elaborated. It was the very first time an EU document mentioned 'radicalization' in relation to terrorism. Radicalization was essentially understood as 'anger among Muslims or Islamists'. Its potential causes were considered wide-ranging: regional conflicts and failed or failing states (and the perception of Western double standards), globalization and socioeconomic factors, alienation, propagation of an extremist worldview, and of systems of education (madrasas).

A second confidential report, in November 2004, zoomed in on the personal trajectories of individuals. Doing so, it privileged an essentially ideological understanding of the process of radicalization, disconnected from the potential political, social, and economic causes of radicalization, identified in the first report as causes of anger.

In between these reports, in October 2004, the European Commission (EC) released *Prevention, Preparedness and Response to Terrorist Attacks*. This document contained the first public reference to 'radicalization', accompanied by the qualification 'violent'. EC officials were convinced that the root causes behind the current wave of 'Islamic terrorism' had to be addressed upstream, but they hesitated to use the words 'root causes', since they could be interpreted as condoning certain terrorist acts. They thus seized the opportunity offered by the novel concept of 'radicalization', judging it to be more neutral than 'root causes'.

They were evidently aware of the intricate, interlinked and complex nature of the label 'radicalization', by which individuals turn into terrorists. In 2006, the European Commission set up its 'Expert Group on Violent Radicalization' to establish the state of play of academic knowledge about radicalization. In its report, the group emphasized that the concept of 'radicalization' had originated in EU policy circles, and that it had not been widely used in social science.

Cautioning against its ambiguity, they suggested an alternative: 'socialization to extremism which manifests itself in terrorism'—although this was not widely adopted.

Among its main conclusions, the expert group confirmed that:

- Radicalization always takes place at the intersection of that enabling social environment and individual trajectories towards greater militancy;
- Individuals involved in terrorist activities exhibit a diversity of social backgrounds, undergo fairly diverse processes of violent radicalization and are influenced by various combinations of motivations;
- There is no single root cause for radicalization processes leading to terrorism, but a convergence of several contributing variables can usually be found at the origin of the radicalization process;
- Precipitant ('trigger') factors vary according to individual experience and personal pathways to radicalization;
- Personal experiences, kinship and bonds of friendship, as well as group dynamics, are critical in triggering the actual process of radicalization escalating to engagement in acts of terrorism against civilians (EC Expert Group 2008).

By the time the report was released in May 2008, the new concept of radicalization had gained traction, notwithstanding its ambiguity. Born as a Eurocentric concept, it has pervaded official and scholarly discourses beyond the West.

QUESTIONS

1. How to explain Europe's pioneering role in the emergence of 'radicalization' as a globally used concept?
2. Assess the possible overlap between 'radicalism' as a political and historical movement, and the premise that terrorism is the result of radicalization.

The notion of radicalization was contested from its very inception. Critics called it ill-defined, complex, and controversial. It nevertheless became the central terminology of counterterrorism, first in Europe and then worldwide. It became the dominant paradigm for addressing the old question of why and how individuals chose to join a terrorist group or to opt for terrorist violence.

In 2011–2012, a civil war in Syria muted into the largest jihadi mobilization ever, drawing tens of thousands of foreign fighters from all over the world to the Middle East. By then, explanatory models had become more multifaceted to catch up with the growing realization that the earlier staged process models (see Figures 10.1 and 10.2) were no longer adequate. Scholars began to opt for multi-factor dynamics which involved a considerable amount of variables and mechanisms.

The American social psychologists Clark McCauley and Sophia Moskalenko presented a set of mechanisms of radicalization at the individual, group, and mass levels that could generate a wide variety of combinations pushing individuals into a radicalization pathway (McCauley and Moskalenko 2011, 2017). But, they insisted that there are two kinds of radicalization—radicalization of opinion and radicalization of action. The relationship between these two is weak, since radical ideology is not a 'conveyor belt' that mechanically moves an individual on to violent action, contrary to the popular image. McCauley and Moskalenko thus confirmed an earlier observation of the 1970s and 1980s: not all individuals carrying radical ideas are willing to act upon these ideas and use violence to impose them.

In *Leaderless Jihad* (2008) Marc Sageman (Sageman 2008) pursued his investigation into the bottom-up mobilization into terror networks through kinship and friendship bonds—a 'bunch of guys', as he labelled it (2008: 66-69). He viewed radicalization as a dynamics including four 'prongs', that interact in a non-linear way: moral outrage about the way Muslims worldwide are being treated; interpretation that this is part of a war on Islam, constituting a mobilizing narrative; resonance of this perception with one's personal experience of discrimination; and, finally, mobilization of a small number of those who share this perception through networks of kin and friends.

Explicitly rejecting models based upon an orderly sequence of steps that produce an output, the American scholars Mohammed Hafez and Creighton Mullins proposed an alternative metaphor of a 'puzzle', consisting of four pieces or factors that come together to produce violent radicalization: personal and collective grievances; networks and interpersonal ties; political and religious ideologies, and enabling environments and support structures (Hafez and Mullins 2015).

KEY CONCEPTS

CVE 'Countering Violent Extremism' was adopted by the US State Department at the start of the Obama Presidential administration (2009) as an acronym for the US global counter-terrorism approach, with 'violent extremism' as an alternative for 'terrorism'. It was based on the recognition that even the best 'intelligence operations and law enforcement efforts alone' would not be sufficient in countering the 'long-term challenge'. The aim of CVE was to 'make environments non-permissive for terrorists seeking to exploit them'. This required a broad range of 'non-coercive' instruments, such as messaging, capacity-building, outreach to civil society and educational campaigns. In August 2011, it was broadened to designate also the domestic counter-radicalization programme of the US government. The domestic CVE strategy of the Obama administration explicitly stated: 'Violent extremists prey on the disenchantment and alienation that discrimination creates, and they have a vested interest in anti-Muslim sentiment.' (2011, available at https://www.dhs.gov/sites/default/files/publications/empowering_local_partners.pdf)

PVE Stands for Preventing Violent Extremism. Launched in December 2015 by the United Nations, it essentially covers the same wide-ranging agenda as CVE under the Obama administration. By adopting the acronym 'PVE', the United Nations wanted to distinguish itself from the American programme.

In short, the post 9/11 research on terrorism developed new concepts and tools that systematized the early observations and insights since the late 19th century. But did these allow for a definitive answer to the question of why someone becomes a terrorist?

10.5 WHAT DO WE NOW KNOW—AND WHAT DON'T WE KNOW (YET)?

With hindsight, the concept of radicalization has been less helpful at explaining individual motivations than its European advocates envisaged in 2004. A wide gap looms between scholarly understanding and its everyday public and political use. Contrary to early expectations, we're no closer to a one-size-fits-all model which explains why and how individuals become terrorists. Identifying them as 'radicalized' is not very helpful, since many others sharing the same ideas never go beyond this point. At a more general level, no metrics have ever been developed to measure radicalization.

But the huge increase in funding, the massive output of scholarly studies, and the availability of more hard data and primary sources than ever before (through interviews, intercepted communication and social media analyses, testimonies of (former) terrorists, courtroom documents, journalistic accounts and statistical evidence) have made it possible to test the exploratory insights originating in the early days of terrorism research. More solid research methodologies have been developed and the involvement of a wider pool of scholars with different academic backgrounds has resulted in fewer impressionistic frameworks.

There is now a broad research-supported consensus that involvement in terrorism results from an interaction of personal trajectories with group dynamics and contextual factors. As far as the latter is concerned, empirical studies have led to robust findings that:

> 'Group-based feelings of injustice reliably predict collective action. However, two specifications must be highlighted here. First, it is the emotions elicited by the injustice—not only the cognitive awareness of the injustice—that predict collective action. Second, it is group-based relative deprivation, as opposed to personal deprivation, that predicts collective action' (King and Taylor 2011: 610).

That an individual isn't part of a group that experiences the injustice is therefore less important in explaining their turn to terrorism than the fact that they identify with another group's grievances.

It will always remain a thorny issue to relate context to individual motivations and behaviour. Moreover, it is not easy to compare granular analyses of local and regional contexts in widely different parts of the world. As a result, many radicalization studies have zoomed in on the micro-level of individual processes (Sedgwick 2010: 480–481). This de-contextualization of individual behaviour was a step backwards, compared to the broad consensus among the pioneers of terrorism studies that joining and bonding in a terrorist group did not happen in a vacuum.

One has to bear in mind, however, that terrorism is not an automatic response to a given context (Crenshaw 1981: 389). Other factors need to come into play for terrorism to emerge. As scholars such as Martha Crenshaw have been suggesting since the 1970s and 1980s, it is now well established that group processes and social bonds are a crucial ingredient. Involvement in terrorism is as much an individual choice as the result of exposure to a specific social environment and peer influence.

Radicalization studies have deepened our understanding of what happens to individuals once they get involved in a group. In most cases, the process of socialization into extremism and eventually, into terrorism, happens gradually. Jihadi plots by small hubs and so-called 'lone actors' alike, in particular from 2015 onwards, have challenged earlier assumptions that the socialization process always needed time to mature into action. A number of terrorist plotters literally jumped from drug trafficking and petty crime or living a 'normal' life into a jihadi plot without any protracted process. This has also been noted with left-wing and right-wing terrorists. In fact, before these individuals decided to act, there was not much of a 'radicalization process' going on.

This observation is connected to another broad consensus, which also confirms an insight from the 1970s and 1980s: there is no single profile and no uniform trajectory into terrorism. No specific 'terrorist mindset' has ever been found. And contrary to what some early radicalization studies assumed, personal trajectories or pathways are murky processes that are neither fixed nor predetermined, but highly individualized and nonlinear (Emmerson 2016). It is thus problematic to try to generalize personal trajectories and capture them in one-size-fits-all radicalization models. This observation also implies that the risk assessment tools which have been developed since the 2000s to evaluate the risks and vulnerabilities an individual represents for sliding into terrorism, are to be taken with great caution.

> ### KEY CONCEPTS
>
> **Deradicalization and Disengagement** Deradicalization generally refers to efforts at changing the way an individual thinks, i.e. bringing one to abandon extremist ideas. This is considered to be a challenging endeavour, in particular when pursued by authorities. **Disengagement** in turn refers to efforts to alter an individual's attitude towards the use of violence in pursuit of their ideas.

Mental illness is now largely discarded as an explanation. This observation too rests on a broad scholarly consensus. But the debate is still ongoing on how personal characteristics enter into the equation. There is broad consensus, based upon empirical studies, that among 'lone actors' the number of individuals with mental disorders of different kinds tends to be significantly higher than among members of structured terrorist groups and than people on average. From his detailed study of the data in the Dutch police files on individuals who left for Syria and Iraq after 2012, Anton Weenink concluded that individuals who experienced adversity and distress, or had mental health issues or with criminal pasts, seem to have been relatively more susceptible to radicalization (and other forms of delinquency) than their age-matched peers (Weenink 2019). But exactly how these characteristics relate to their decision to travel to Syria and engage in jihadi groups, remains an open question.

There is also strong evidence that terrorists who perpetrate attacks in their own country and (at least some of the) foreign fighters are not to be lumped together in one and the same category. The Norwegian scholar Thomas Hegghammer found that 'a majority of Western jihadis choose foreign fighting over domestic fighting, most likely because they have come to view the former as more legitimate' (Hegghammer 2013: 8). It echoes an observation Walter Laqueur had already offered in the 1970s: 'terror is always far more popular against foreigners than against one's own countrymen' (1976: 104). This is supported by the fact that the vast majority of returnees from Syria and Iraq have not been involved in terrorist plots upon their return to their home countries.

Finally, a last area of broad consensus among scholars concerns the weak relationship between ideas and action, or between cognitive and behavioural radicalization—even if policymakers often continue to simplify terrorism into a question of ideology and still view radicalization as embracing extremist ideas that then pushes an individual inexorably into terrorism. In academia the 'conveyor belt' theory is now largely discredited. But at the same time, most scholars acknowledge that ideology (alternatively called 'narrative' or 'discourse') plays a role in terrorism. How exactly it relates to terrorism remains matter of febrile discussion. To some, ideology is merely camouflage and a justification of violence in search of a cause (which, in some cases, it undoubtedly is). To others, it chiefly serves as a means of cementing group cohesiveness and identity. Still others will consider ideology as the last straw that helps individuals overcome their inhibitions about killing innocent people. Finally, some do consider ideology as a key driver of terrorism, albeit with some variance. Some judge it to be an indispensable transit station before the commitment of terrorist acts, while others emphasize that it is not by itself a root cause, but only when it meets specific outside conditions.

10.6 IN THE END, WHAT MAKES A TERRORIST?

For more than a century now, scholars and observers have been trying to understand what makes a terrorist. Why, how and when do individuals become terrorists (see Figure 10.3)? The study of terrorism has developed in successive waves. It is common to highlight scholarly differences and competing paradigms among students of terrorism. Taking a bird's-eye

FIGURE 10.3 What makes a terrorist?

view, however, it appears—a bit surprisingly perhaps—that over the decades the study of terrorism has reached broad but real scholarly consensus on some of the key variables that play a crucial role in the making of a terrorist. For sure, discussions and debates are ongoing and gaps in our knowledge exist. But what we do know, is that an individual does not embrace political violence in a void. And, most crucially, that there are as many trajectories into terrorism as there are individuals.

Reviewing the literature on radicalization, Alex Schmid (2013), former Officer-in-Charge of the Terrorism Prevention Branch of the UN and editor of the journal *Perspectives on Terrorism*, noted that 'the popularity of the concept of "radicalization" stands in no direct relationship to its actual explanatory power regarding the root causes of terrorism'. The propensity to focus on 'vulnerable' young people and on the individual level has produced inconclusive results. He therefore suggested re-conceptualizing radicalization as a socialization and mobilization process, usually in a situation of political polarization, whereby one or both sides show 'a growing commitment to engage in confrontational tactics of conflict-waging'. He also pleaded for the integration of the individual micro-level into an overall approach including the group level of the radical milieu as well as the macro-level of structural factors in and between societies and states.

Starting from this observation and fusing the insights offered by the founders of the study of terrorism with the contemporary research on radicalization, terrorism can be conceptualized as the interplay between a conducive environment, an opportunity, an ideology and group dynamics. Take away any of these dimensions and no terrorism campaign will be able to emerge and certainly not to sustain itself. It is in this dynamic interplay that people radicalize, with some going to the extreme choice of considering violence at the only adequate way to act.

Conducive environment—The specifics of contextual factors (also called 'push' factors or preconditions) may differ from one form of terrorism to another and vary according to time and place. But the cocktail of social malaise, perceived injustice and existential threat to a segment of society appears to be a, if not the, crucial push factor behind the successive waves of transnational terrorism since the 1880s. Group-based dissatisfaction with the existing order certainly has been an important dimension of the conducive environment that allowed jihadism to prosper. It is not about the material aspect of it per se (poverty, discrimination), but about the emotions elicited by such an environment—frustration, anger, perceived threat to a group's identity, and, crucially, a polarized Us vs. Them social context, whereby a specific group within society is 'othered' and so portrayed as a suspect community. Who the Other is, depends upon the local and national contexts, but the Manichean mechanism itself is the same on all continents and in all countries.

Opportunity—A conducive environment does not automatically lead to terrorism. But it potentially creates the space for competing offers promising to deal with the source of the dissatisfaction. These can range from modestly reformist to very radical. They can be nonviolent or violent. In this arena of political competition, the most credible offer is stand to win the largest following. In case the violent offer gains momentum, it acts as a 'pull factor' that not only encompasses a (self-proclaimed) vanguard that believes it can arouse the masses by its actions; it also requires promising signs that history is on its side and the proclaimed goal within reach. This offer has to be perceived as credible, as riding the tailwind of history, with real-world events seemingly confirming that revolutionary change is imminent.

Ideology—A narrative is needed to mobilize a large group of individuals. Ideology is here understood as a belief system—a set of lenses through which the environment is framed, the dissatisfaction articulated and violence identified as the only adequate response. The ideological factor is all about the credibility of the narrative, not about doctrinal fine print. Its capacity to mobilize is contingent on outside conditions. It must also be able to tap into the aforementioned emotions. When an overarching narrative can wrap a range of individual motivations into a collective storyline and a shared perception of injustice and group-based anger, its mobilization and socialization power can be consequential—at least for a certain amount of time.

Local mobilization hubs—For terrorism to take root, a physical link has to be established between a conducive environment, the offer and the narrative. Kinship and friendship ties are key components of the socialization process that leads individuals into terrorism.

Mobilization via pre-existing social bonds is a solid finding of decades of research. Such 'bunches of guys' make the difference between street gangs and terrorist groups. An individual joining a given group evolves with the group of which they are part. Such hubs form cohesive counterculture in-groups that enhance the emotional dimension of getting involved in the cause. Groupthink and peer pressure can gradually socialize the members of the group into extremism and, eventually, terrorism. Personal characteristics will influence the roles and functions individuals assume in these group interactions. Without such terrorism-oriented hubs, individuals seldom link up with terrorism in large numbers. Lone actors exist, but in most cases they see themselves as acting on behalf of a community at risk.

10.7 CONCLUSION

Terrorism is a complex phenomenon. How individuals get involved in it, is even more complex. This observation is neither new nor original. We have to resist simple answers, models and diagnoses. No one chooses to become a terrorist by simply viewing an extremist video. What we do know is that one does not become a terrorist in a void. The decision to perpetrate a terrorist attack or to join a terrorist group is as much an individual decision as the result of the interplay of contextual factors, kinship and friendship dynamics, belief systems, and personal trajectories. These factors do not play in the same way for all individuals. Routes into terrorism are as varied as there are individuals—but all these factors need to be present for terrorism to emerge.

DISCUSSION QUESTIONS

1. Is there any practical difference between political and religious narratives in the process of radicalization of individuals?
2. How would you assess the conducive environment that allowed for the emergence of left-wing terrorism in the United States and in Europe in the 1970s-1980s?
3. How can you elucidate that ISIS (Daesh, Islamic State) has been able to attract more than 40,000 volunteers with widely different backgrounds and from very different locations in the world to join its ranks?
4. What might make extremists change their mind with regard to the ideas they hold? And what might make them change their attitude towards the use of violence?
5. How can you explain that so few people end up becoming terrorists, while so many grow up in the same circumstance as those who decide to become terrorists? Does the same observation also apply to national liberation movements?

Visit the online resources for pointers on how to answer the discussion questions, links to useful web sources, and guidance on accessing databases:
www.oup.com/he/Wilson-Muro1e

GUIDE TO FURTHER READING

Bjørgo, T. and Horgan, J. (2009) *Leaving Terrorism behind. Individual and Collective Disengagement.* New York: Routledge. *A collection of essays on how disengagement from terrorism works (of fails) in many parts of the world.*

Crenshaw, M. (1981) 'The causes of terrorism', *Comparative Politics*, 13/4: 379–399. *A pioneering grand theory on the emergence of terrorism.*

McCauley, C. and Moskalenko, S. (2011) *Friction: How Radicalization Happens to Them and Us.* Oxford: University Press. *Historical analysis of the mechanisms of radicalization by two leading social psychologists.*

Neumann, P. (2016) *Radicalized. New Jihadists and the Threat to the West.* London/New York: I.B. Tauris. *Explaining the dynamics behind the ISIS mobilization of thousands of Western youngsters.*

Schmid, A. (2013) *Radicalization, De-Radicalization, Counter-Radicalization: A Conceptual Discussion and Literature Review.* The Hague: ICCT Research Paper, March (https://www.icct.nl/download/file/ICCT-Schmid-Radicalization-De-Radicalization-Counter-Radicalization-March-2013.pdf). *A state of play on 'radicalization' and its re-conceptualization as a socialization and mobilization process.*

REFERENCES

AIVD (2002a) *Annual Report 2001.* The Hague, National Security Service (precursor agency to the AIVD) (https://english.aivd.nl/publications/annual-report/2002/09/06/annual-report-2001).

AIVD (2002b) *Recruitment for the Jihad in the Netherlands.* The Hague, General Intelligence and Security Service, December.

Bataille, A. (1882) 'Affaire Fournier. Tentative d'assassinat par un ouvrier sur un patron', *Le Figaro*, 28, 20 June (https://gallica.bnf.fr/ark:/12148/bpt6k278238z/f3.image.texteImage)

Bataille, A. (1892) 'Procès Ravachol', *Le Figaro*, 38, 22 June (https://gallica.bnf.fr/ark:/12148/bpt6k282205c/f2.item.r=soci%C3%A9t%C3%A9).

Borum, R. (2003) 'Understanding the Terrorist Mind-set', *FBI Law Enforcement Bulletin*, 72 (7): 7–10.

Borum, R. (2011) 'Radicalization into Violent Extremism II. A Review of Conceptual Models and Empirical Research', *Journal of Strategic Security*, 4 (4): 37–62.

Coolsaet, R. (2019) 'Radicalization – The origins and Limits of a Contested Concept', in Fadil, N., de Koning, M., and Ragazzi, F., *Radicalization in Belgium and the Netherlands: Critical Perspectives on Violence and Security* (London: I.B. Tauris).

Corrado, R. R. (1981) 'A Critique of the Mental Disorder Perspective of Political Terrorism', *International Journal of Law and Psychiatry*, 4 (3–4): 293–309.

Crenshaw, M. (1981) 'The Causes of Terrorism', *Comparative Politics*, 13 (4): 379–399.

Crenshaw, M. (1986) 'The Psychology of Political Terrorism', in Hermann, M. G. (ed.), *Political psychology* (San Francisco: Jossey-Bass).

Della Porta, D. (1995) *Social Movements, Political Violence and the State. A Comparative Study of Italy and Germany.* Cambridge: Cambridge University Press.

Emmerson, B. (2016) *Report of the Special Rapporteur on the promotion and protection of human rights and fundamental freedoms while countering terrorism*, A/HRC/31/95, 22 February. Geneva: Human Rights Council.

European Commission (2004) *Prevention, Preparedness and Response to Terrorist Attacks. Communication from the Commission to the Council and the European Parliament.* COM(2004) 698, 20 October.

European Commission Expert Group on Violent Radicalization (2008) *Radicalization Processes Leading to Acts of Terrorism*. Reprinted in Coolsaet, R. (2011) (ed.), *Jihadi Terrorism and the Radicalization Challenge: European and American Experiences*. Farnham: Ashgate.

Europol (2004) *Terrorist Activity in the European Union: Situation and Trends Report* (TE-SAT). The Hague, 2 December.

Furlong, P. (1981) 'Political Terrorism in Italy', in Lodge, J. (ed.), *Terrorism: A Challenge to the State*. Oxford: Martin Robertson.

Gurr, T. R. (1970, 2016) *Why Men Rebel*. Oxon/New York: Routledge.

Hafez, M. and Mullins, C. (2015) 'The Radicalization Puzzle: A Theoretical Synthesis of Empirical Approaches to Homegrown Extremism', *Studies in Conflict & Terrorism*, 38 (11): 958–975.

Hegghammer, T. (2013) 'Should I Stay or Should I go? Explaining Variation in Western jihadists' Choice Between Domestic and Foreign Fighting', *American Political Science Review*, 107 (1): 1–15.

Holsti, O. R. (1969) 'The Belief System and National Images: A Case Study', in Rosenau, J., *International Politics and Foreign Policy* (New York: Free Press).

Joll, J. (1964) *The Anarchists* (London: Methuen & Co)

King, M., Taylor, D. (2011) 'The Radicalization of Homegrown Jihadists: A Review of Theoretical Models and Social Psychological Evidence', *Terrorism and Political Violence*, 23 (4): 602–622.

Kissinger, H. A. (1969) *Memorandum to the President. Summary of CIA Survey 'Restless Youth'*. White House, 7 March (https://www.cia.gov/library/readingroom/document/loc-hak-1-2-21-4).

Laqueur, W. (1976) 'The Futility of Terrorism', *Harper's Magazine*, March, 99–105.

Laqueur, W. (1977a) 'Interpretations of Terrorism: Fact, Fiction and Political Science'. *Journal of Contemporary History*, 12: 1–42.

Laqueur, W. (1977b) *Terrorism. A Study of National and International Political Violence*. Boston/Toronto: Little, Brown and Company.

McCauley, C. and Moskalenko, S. (2011) *Friction: How Radicalization Happens to Them and Us*. New York: Oxford University Press.

McCauley, C. and Moskalenko, S. (2017) 'Understanding Political Radicalization: The Two-pyramids Model', *American Psychologist*, 72 (3): 205–216.

Moghaddam, F. A. (2005) 'The Staircase to Terrorism. A Psychological Explanation', *American Psychologist*, 60 (2): 161–169.

Pridham, G. (1981) 'Terrorism and the State in West Germany During the 1970s', in Lodge (1981: 11–56).

Sageman, M. (2004) *Understanding Terror Networks*. Philadelphia: University of Pennsylvania Press.

Sageman, M. (2008) *Leaderless Jihad. Terror Networks in the Twenty-First Century*. Philadelphia: University of Pennsylvania Press.

Sageman, M. (2014) 'The Stagnation in Terrorism Research', *Terrorism and Political Violence*, 26 (4): 565–580.

Sartre, J.-P. (1961), Preface to Frantz Fanon, *Les damnées de la terre*. Paris: Maspero, Cahiers Libres 27–28.

Schmid, A. (2013) *Radicalization, De-Radicalization, Counter-Radicalization: A Conceptual Discussion and Literature Review* (The Hague: ICCT Research Paper), March (https://www.icct.nl/download/file/ICCT-Schmid-Radicalization-De-Radicalization-Counter-Radicalization-March-2013.pdf).

Sedgwick, M. (2010) 'The Concept of Radicalization as a Source of Confusion', *Terrorism and Political Violence*, 22 (4): 479–494.

Silke, A. (1998) 'Cheshire-Cat Logic: The Recurring Theme of Terrorist Abnormality in Psychological Research', *Psychology, Crime, and Law*, 4 (1): 51–69.

Weenink, A (2019) 'Adversity, Criminality, and Mental Health Problems in Jihadis in Dutch Police Files', *Perspectives on Terrorism*, 13 (5): 130–142.

Wilkinson, P. (1974) *Political Terrorism*. London: Macmillan.

Wilkinson, P. (1986) 'Fighting the Hydra: International Terrorism and the Rule of Law', in Noel O'Sullivan (Ed), *Terrorism, ideology and revolution*. Boulder: Westview Press.

Wilkinson, P. (1988) 'Support Mechanisms in International Terrorism', in Robert O. Slater and Michael Stohl, *Current Perspectives on International Terrorism*. New York: St. Martin's Press.

X (1909) 'The Workings of Anarchists', *New York Times*, 6 June (https://timesmachine.nytimes.com/timesmachine/1909/06/06/issue.html).

Zenker, E. V. (1897) *Anarchism. A Criticism and History of the Anarchist Theory*. New York/London: G.P. Putnam's Sons.

CHAPTER 11

Can Terrorism Be Rational?

MAX ABRAHMS

■ CHAPTER SUMMARY

This chapter explores how, on one hand, terrorists are presumed to be rational political actors and on the other, terrorism is an ineffective method for achieving political demands. This chapter demonstrates how terrorists can still be rational, even though their attacks on civilians seldom advance the stated political agenda. The conclusion explores the counterterrorism implications, depending on the presumed thought process of the terrorists.

11.1 INTRODUCTION

Terrorism is puzzling behaviour to scholars. On one hand, social scientists generally regard terrorists as rational political actors. On the other hand, empirical research on terrorism suggests that it is a losing political tactic. Not only do terrorists seldom achieve their political platform with terrorism, but their attacks on civilians dissuade governments from granting concessions. If terrorism is ineffective, even counterproductive for achieving their political goals, then can the perpetrators still be understood as rational? For the purposes of this chapter, this will be called 'the puzzle of terrorism'. This chapter lays out the puzzle, and then resolves it by showing how terrorists can still be rational, regardless of whether their violence pays off politically. The conclusion explores the counterterrorism implications depending on the presumed goals of the terrorists.

11.2 THE PUZZLE OF TERRORISM

Political scientists typically view terrorists as rational political actors (e.g. Gaibulloev and Sandler 2019; Kydd and Walter 2006; Lake 2002; Pape 2003; Perry and Hasisi 2015). Demographic research on terrorists confirms that they do not appear to disproportionately suffer from mental health problems. In his studies of failed suicide bombers, Ariel Merari (2004) finds that they are not prone to psychopathology or any other known personality disorders. Anat Berko (2007: 9), a criminologist in the Israel Defence Forces who interviewed dozens of failed Palestinian suicide terrorists, likewise finds that they seldom have 'an emotional disturbance that prevents them from differentiating between reality and imagination.' In his analysis of Salafi terrorists, Scott Atran (2004) also concludes that they do not tend to exhibit any conspicuous cognitive infirmities. Similarly, Marc Sageman (2006) reports a lack of mental illness in his sample of al-Qaeda affiliated terrorists. Martha Crenshaw (1981: 383) was an early proponent of this view, maintaining that 'The outstanding common characteristic of terrorists is their normality' (see also Chapter 10). Louise Richardson (2007: 41) agrees that 'The one shared characteristic of terrorists is their normalcy.' In sum, psychological assessments of terrorists suggest that their brains operate much like those of non-terrorists.

The puzzle of terrorism is its practitioners are presumed rational political actors, and yet this mode of violence is ineffective, even counterproductive for their political cause (Abrahms and Lula 2012). For decades, terrorism specialists have noted that terrorists are political 'losers'. In the 1970s, Walter Laqueur (1976) published an article entitled 'The Futility of Terrorism' in which he claimed that terrorist groups do not attain their political platforms. In the 1980s, Crenshaw (1980: 15) likewise observed that terrorists do not obtain their given political ends, and 'Therefore one must conclude that terrorism is objectively a failure.' Similarly, a RAND study (Cordes at al. 1984: 49) noted that 'Terrorists have been unable to translate the consequences of terrorism into concrete political gains ... [I]n that sense terrorism has failed. It is a fundamental failure.' In the 1990s, Thomas Schelling (1991: 20) proclaimed that 'Terrorism almost never appears to accomplish anything politically significant.' Virginia Held (1991: 70) went even further, claiming that the 'net effect' of terrorism may actually be counterproductive. Case studies 11.1 and 12.1 further explore the puzzle of terrorism by illustrating how this tactic has backfired politically on perpetrators.

CASE STUDY 11.1

Terrorism Failing Politically, Al-Qaeda

According to Osama Bin Laden (founder and former leader of al-Qaeda), al-Qaeda attacked the United States on September 11th 2001 to redress four grievances. First, the leader's most salient ultimatum was for the US to withdraw its military forces from the Persian Gulf. Bin Laden was particularly critical of the US presence in Saudi Arabia because of this status as the 'Land of the Two Holy Mosques' and Iraq because its bases facilitated military operations throughout the region. Bin Laden therefore threatened to continue attacking the United States until it withdrew from the entire Persian Gulf. Second, the al-Qaeda leader said the purpose of the September 11th attacks were to deter America from participating in military interventions that harm Muslims. Bin Laden was deeply critical of what he called 'Crusader wars,' for example, the bloodshed against Muslims in Bosnia, Chechnya, East Timor, Iraq, and Israel. Third, al-Qaeda said the purpose of 9/11 was also to dissuade the US from supporting so-called 'apostate regimes,' that is, pro-West Muslim leaders that suppress the will of their population. In particular, Bin Laden objected to US support for the House of Saud (the ruling royal family of Saudi Arabia) and Pervez Musharraf's Pakistan (a former general who was President of Pakistan from 2001 to 2008). Bin Laden said the final objective of 9/11 was to destroy the US–Israel relationship, which he derided as the 'Zionist-Crusader alliance'.

Sceptics may question whether Bin Laden truly cared about these stated grievances. In theory, he could have mentioned them simply to help recruit aggrieved Muslims. But Bin Laden appears to have obsessed about these grievances even in private. In October 2001, for example, Scotland Yard seized letters allegedly written by the al-Qaeda leader in which he railed against the same four grievances that he complained about publicly. The convergence of his public and private statements suggests that Bin laden truly hoped for 9/11 to eject American forces from the Persian Gulf; to dissuade the US from backing conflicts that harm Muslims; to stop Americans from interfering in regional politics, especially in Pakistan and Saudi Arabia; and to halt US support for Israel.

PHOTO 11.1 The north and south towers of the World Trade Center behind the Statue of Liberty before 9/11. In 2001 both towers were destroyed by two planes hijacked by terrorists.

The September 11th attacks (see Photo 11.1) were not only ineffective at redressing these grievances, but also exacerbated each of them. The 9/11 attacks did not diminish American inference in the Gulf. On the contrary, responding to al-Qaeda helped to sell to the American public on the 2003 invasion of Iraq (Operation Iraqi Freedom or OIF). The main motivation for assassinating Saddam Hussein from the US perspective was that he would supply terrorists after 9/11 with weapons of mass destruction to strike the American homeland again. Polls confirm that most Americans did not favour invading Iraq until the summer of 2002, when the Bush administration began to connect Bin Laden with the international terrorism threat (Kaufman 2004). Without 9/11, it is inconceivable that the American public would have consented to increase the US troop presence by a factor of fifteen in the Gulf from 11,000 9/11 to 177,000 in the course of the Iraq War and its aftermath.

September 11th also failed in destroying US relations with Pakistan and Saudi Arabia. Before the attack, US relations with Pakistan were at a low point: Pakistan had questionable strategic value with the end of both the Cold War and Soviet occupation of Afghanistan; the Pakistani federal government in Islamabad posed a challenge to America's non-proliferation policy and was the main sponsor of the Taliban (a jihadist military organization); and

General Musharraf, who had staged a coup against his country's democratically elected leader in 1999, successfully became President in 2001. September 11th helped Musharraf to depict Pakistan as a critical counterterrorism American ally. He broke off diplomatic relations with the Taliban, and offered support for the Global War on Terrorism in Afghanistan. Following the 9/11 attack, the Pakistani military killed hundreds of terrorists in South Waziristan, and Musharraf froze financial assets of terrorist entities connected to al-Qaeda. The US and Washington reciprocated by ignoring Musharraf's crackdowns on political dissidents, as well as repealing sanctions over the Pakistani government's unauthorized 1998 nuclear weapons tests. To bolster Musharraf further, Bush worked with Congress to alleviate Pakistan's $400 million debt to the United States. The September 11th attack thus strengthened US-Pakistani relations militarily and economically, while bolstering Musharraf.

In several respects, the Saudi government led by King Fahd of Saudi Arabia (in power from 1982 to 2005) was in a similar position as Pervez Musharraf before the 9/11 attack. Both Fahd and Musharraf had friendly relations with the military group the Taliban, both were unelected, and both presided over Muslim populations sceptical of engaging with the United States. Fifteen of the nineteen plane hijackers who attacked the World Trade Center towers, Pentagon building, and United Airlines Flight 93 were from Saudi Arabia. Many foreign policy analysts assumed that the 'special relationship' forged between Franklin Roosevelt and Abdulaziz bin Abdulrahman Al Saud (King Fahd's father) was over. But the basic terms of the relationship remain unchanged. The US continued to be dependent on oil from Saudi Arabia, and the Saudis remained dependent on the American market, and security guarantees in the Persian Gulf. As with Musharraf, the Saudi government ingratiated itself with Washington in the area of counterterrorism by severing diplomatic relations with the Taliban, and mounting military operations against local al-Qaeda operatives. Contrary to Bin Laden's stated goal, the United States strengthened relations with Saudi Arabia, especially in counterterrorism cooperation.

Rather than deterring military interventions that harm Muslims, 9/11 galvanized Washington to wage an unprecedented counterterrorism campaign predominantly in the Muslim world, killing countless civilians, mostly in Afghanistan and Iraq. Lastly, US–Israeli relations actually strengthened after the September 11th attacks, particularly in the area of counterterrorism. The Bush administration did not intervene when the Israel Defense Forces detained Political Leader Yasser Arafat in his headquarters and reoccupied swathes of the Palestinian West Bank in Spring 2002. An April 2004 'Letter of Understanding' between Bush and Israeli Prime Minister Ariel Sharon formally recognized Israel's right to retain indefinitely 'major population centres' (i.e. settlements) in the West Bank of Palestine. Public opinion surveys confirmed that the American public shared Bush's pro-Israel response to 9/11 ('The US and the Middle East After 11 September', 2002). Prior to the attack, 41 per cent of Americans expressed support for Israel and 13 per cent for Palestinians. Following the attack, 55 per cent supported Israel while support for Palestinians fell almost in half, to 7 per cent. Such high levels of American support for Israel were unseen since the 1991 Iraq war, when Saddam Hussain (5th President of Iraq) authorized rocket attacks on Israel. The American public also expressed less support for trying to resolve the Israeli-Palestinian conflict with a peace process. In sum, 9/11 was not only ineffective in redressing Bin Laden's grievances, but appears to have rendered them even more urgent (Abrahms 2006a).

QUESTIONS

1. Why did Osama Bin Laden authorize the al-Qaeda attacks against the United States on September 11, 2001?
2. Were those terrorist attacks politically successful?

CASE STUDY 11.2

Terrorism Failing Politically—Islamic State

The so-called Islamic State (ISIS) group's leader, Abu Bakr al-Baghdadi, spoke at the Great al-Nuri Mosque in the Iraqi city of Mosul on 5 July 2014 proclaiming his determination to create a new caliphate (a spiritual leader of Islam who claims succession from Muhammad). In his sermon, the self- proclaimed caliph (chief Muslim civil and religious ruler) announced to the Muslim community that his foot-soldiers were building an Islamic State in Iraq and Syria. Initially, the ISIS may have appeared successful. By year's end, ISIS would control one-third of Iraq and one-third of Syria—land mass roughly equal to the size of Britain—where the terrorists ruled over 9 million people. ISIS was bolstered by the largest influx of international jihadis in history. Over 40,000 foreign fighters from 110 countries headed to Syria and Iraq, more than four times the number of mujahidin (guerrilla fighters against non-Muslim forces) who travelled to Afghanistan to battle the Soviet Armed Forces in the 1980s. By 2016, Abu Bakr al-Baghdadi had accepted the allegiance of 43 terrorist group affiliates from Boko Haram in Nigeria to Abu Sayyaf in the Philippines. Not only did ISIS have territory and fighters, but money. Billed as the world's richest terrorist group, ISIS obtained over a billion dollars a year from oil sales, taxes, looting, antiquity smuggling, and hostage-taking.

But the ISIS caliphate died as quickly as it had appeared. In 2015, ISIS territory shrank by 40 per cent in Iraq and 20 per cent in Syria. ISIS lost another quarter of its territory the following year. By early 2017, ISIS had ceded two-thirds of its land. By springtime, the group controlled less than 7 per cent of Iraq, and was getting attacked in Syria by the Syrian Arab Army, its Shia militia partners, American and Russia airpower, Kurdish warriors, and a smattering of other militants.

In his May 2017 Pentagon press conference, Defence Secretary James Mattis noted that ISIS had lost 55,000 square kilometres and regained none of it. That June ISIS blew up the al-Nuri mosque—the very site where the caliphate had been declared. As the group lost land, its revenues also shrank until it could no longer pay fighters, which spurred defections and dissuaded recruits from joining the losing team. The political scientist James DeNardo (2014: 63) remarks that we cannot ever be sure whether terrorists get what they want; at best, we

PHOTO 11.2 Aleppo, Syria in November 2017: Logos written by ISIS fighters on the walls.

can evaluate whether they got what they claimed to want. The Islamic State project imploded by this standard (Abrahms 2018). To retain old fighters and attract new ones, terrorist leaders are reluctant to admit political failure (Lichbach 1998). To this end, terrorist leaders frequently invent new political motivations when their previous agenda failed (Abrahms 2008; Stern 2003). Perhaps the Islamic State will try to claim that its latest territorial gains outside of Iraq and Syria such as in Mozambique constitute a major success notwithstanding the death of the Caliphate (Mroszczyk and Abrahms 2021; Mwakideu 2021).

QUESTIONS

1. What was the main goal of the Islamic State
2. To what extent was the group politically successful?

The al-Qaeda and Islamic State cases are not unique. With few exceptions, the history of terrorism is a story of political failure. In the 1960s and 1970s, the Baader-Meinhof gang failed to coerce West Germany into adopting communism as its national ideology. In the 1980s, the Libya-based Aby Nidal Organization failed to destroy the state of Israel, while the Shining Path of Peru failed to spur a communist revolution. In the 1990s, the Japanese doomsday cult known as Aum Shinrikyo failed to spark a global Armageddon. In the early 21st century, the Sunni fundamentalist terrorist group, Asbat an-Ansar, failed to overthrow the more secular Lebanese government, or to coerce it into adopting a Salafi form of Islam.

These examples of political failure are anecdotal, but in 2006 Abrahms (2006b) published in *International Security* the first major study to assess whether terrorism works politically. To make this assessment, Abrahms analysed the political plights of 28 Foreign Terrorist Organizations (FTOs), as designated by the US State Department. The analysis yields two main findings. First, the FTO success rate is low, as only ten per cent of the groups managed to achieve their political demands. And second, all the successful FTOs used terrorism only as a secondary tactic. Although non-state actors are known to employ a hybrid of asymmetric tactics, the politically successful FTOs directed their violence against military targets, not civilian ones. By disaggregating the FTOs by target selection, Abrahms therefore revealed the full extent to which terrorism—defined as non-state attacks on civilian targets—has historically been a losing political tactic. Seth Jones and Martin Libicki (2008) subsequently examined a larger sample, the universe of known terrorist groups between 1968 and 2006. Of the 648 groups identified in the RAND-MIPT Terrorism Incident database, only 4 per cent obtained their strategic demands. Audrey Cronin (2009) has reexamined the success rate of these groups, confirming that less than 5 per cent prevailed.Statistical studies find that terrorism is not only correlated with political failure, but actually lowers the odds of government concessions even after taking into account the capability of the perpetrators and the nature of their demands (Abrahms 2012, 2013; Abrahms and Gottfried 2016; Fortna 2015; see also Stanton 2016). Terrorism often backfires politically by raising popular support for right-wing leaders opposed to appeasing the perpetrators. For example, terrorist fatalities within Israel significantly boost local support for right-bloc parties opposed to accommodation, such as the Likud (Berrebi and Klor 2006). The most lethal terrorist incidents in Israel are also the most likely to induce this rightward electoral shift. The authors conclude that heightening the pain to civilians tends to 'backfire on the goals of terrorist factions by hardening the stance of the targeted population' (Gould and Klor 2010: 1507). Christophe Chowanietz (2010) likewise finds in France, Germany, Spain, the United Kingdom, and the United States that terrorist attacks have shifted the electorate to the political right in proportion to their lethality. A RAND study (Berrebi 2009) summarizes this literature: 'terrorist fatalities, with few exceptions, increase support for the bloc of parties associated with a more intransigent position. Scholars may interpret this as further evidence that terrorist attacks against civilians do not help terrorist organizations achieve their stated goals.' In sum, terrorism is puzzling for social scientists because its practitioners are presumably rational, but the violence against civilians seldom result in political concessions, and may even impede them. In the remainder of this chapter, we explore how terrorism may still be understood as rational behaviour, even if its perpetrators seldom benefit from the tactic politically.

11.3 **RESOLVING THE PUZZLE OF TERRORISM**

As with 'terrorism,' the word 'rational' is difficult to define. But few social scientists would conclude that someone acted irrationally simply because they did not achieve the intended outcome (Lupia et al. 2000). When it comes to assessing the rationality of behaviour, its outcome is generally seen as less important than the thought process behind it. At the most basic level, rational behaviour requires only that a person has a goal in mind and acts to achieve it (Jones 1999). As Herbert Simon (1976) noted, even rational people have limited human cognition, and are never omniscient. Because we cannot always know the outcome of our behaviour, or even which actions of are most likely to further our goals, terrorism's low political success rate does not necessarily mean that its perpetrators are irrational.

> **KEY CONCEPTS**
>
> **Rational Behaviour** At the most basic level, rational behaviour requires only that a person has a goal in mind and acts in a reasonable manner to achieve it based on his or her understanding of the world.

Furthermore, the history of terrorism is not entirely bereft of political triumphs. Terrorism is generally an ineffective political tactic, but its perpetrators have been known to occasionally achieve their strategic demands (Asal et al. 2019; Chenoweth et al. 2009; Muro 2018; Thomas 2014). And in some cases, terrorist attacks have arguably been critical to political achievement, such as when Spain hastily withdrew from Iraq after the 2004 Madrid train attacks in accordance with al-Qaeda's demands. Although 'quite rare' (Rose et al. 2007: 188), such victories may convince reasonable people that they, too, stand a chance of prevailing politically by attacking civilians. That is, rational individuals may conclude that the odds of political success are apparently not zero, so decide to use terrorism, particularly if alternative courses of action have previously not worked.

> **KEY CONCEPTS**
>
> **Rationality** Rationality has less to do with the outcome of a decision than the thought-process behind it. Regardless of whether terrorism tends to pay politically, it is still a rational decision if perpetrators believe they will benefit more than from alternative tactical approaches.

Indeed, terrorism is often selected as a tactic only after alternative options have failed. In the parlance of political science, the decision to use terrorism is a 'last resort', a 'constrained choice' imposed by the absence of political alternatives (McCormick 2003: 483; Crenshaw 1992: 72). Although some research casts doubt on the external validity of this presumed sequencing (Abrahms 2008), there are many historical cases in which aggrieved individuals escalated to violence after determining that nonviolence would remain politically ineffectual (see Abrahms 2018). In the late 19th century, the leader of the Irish National Invincibles (a group of assassins) declared: 'There comes an hour when protest no longer suffices. After philosophy, there must be action.' Michael Collins, an Irish revolutionary, soldier, and politician in 1920s was convinced that 'Irish Independence would never be attained by constitutional means' and that 'when you're up against a bully you've got to kick him in the guts' (Boot 2013: 250). In his memoir, the leader of the paramilitary organization The Irgun, Menachem Begin (1978: 43), described the Zionist group's predicament after nonviolence failed to protect the Jews: 'What use was there in writing memoranda? What value in speeches? No, there was no other way. If we did not fight we should be destroyed.' When asked why they adopted violence in the 1950s during the Algerian War, Algerian nationalists striving to gain independence from France cited that the French colonizers had ignored their strikes and boycotts. In her autobiography from the American Weather Underground, Susan Stern (2007: 130–131) explained why her radical left-wing group escalated: 'As the years have passed, I've seen my efforts fail with thousands of others in the Civil Rights and anti-war movements. The time has come not merely to protest but to fight for what we believe in.' Accounts of the Syrian rebels who fought against President Bashar Assad after the Arab Spring suggest that many 'picked up weapons as a last resort.' According to the Palestinian academic and politician Ziad Abu-Amr: 'as it became evident that the peace negotiations were not yielding any tangible results …[the Islamist Palestinian group] Hamas was emboldened and became more aggressive in its opposition to the PLO and its tactics against Israel.' For this reason, some scholars, such as McCormick, expect terrorism and other forms of violence whenever mass-based nonviolent movements fail (McCormick 2003).

Yet terrorism is not cost-free for perpetrators. Terrorism may seem like a reasonable decision for the politically desperate, but only for those willing to bear the costs. Compared to nonviolence, terrorism is a far riskier enterprise for the participants. Whereas protesters generally risk getting arrested, terrorists risk getting killed (Chenoweth and Lawrence 2010; DeNardo 1985). The rational course of action is therefore arguably to 'free-ride' by allowing others to assume the risk for the 'public good' because any political concessions gained by the perpetrators will also be enjoyed by those who remain on the sidelines. Social scientists refer to this dynamic as a 'collective action' problem (Lichbach 1994; Tullock 1971); even if terrorism were to succeed politically, which is unlikely, rational individuals may reason that they are better off reaping the public good of whatever concessions are granted without risking their own lives by partaking in the dangerous violence. Terrorism may thus seem irrational because it is unlikely to work politically, and even if it does, free-riders who refrain from violence will enjoy the same political benefits without assuming the personal risks of participating in the violence. Leaders try to overcome this collective action problem by offering what are known as selective incentives. Unlike public goods which are shared equally with free-riders, selective incentives are benefits that accrue only to participants (Weinstein 2006).

KEY CONCEPTS

Public Good An outcome that benefits everyone including those who do not help to earn it. In the case of terrorism, political concessions may be regarded as a public good from the vantage of the terrorists and those who support their cause.

Free-Riders Those who benefit from the public good even though they did not help to earn it. In the case of terrorism, free-riders may be understood as those who share the terrorists' political goals but refrain from violence and thus assume less personal risk.

Collective Action Problem The challenge of motivating rational individuals not to free-ride. Terrorism poses a collective action because the rational course of action for terrorist sympathizers may be to refrain from violence, free-ride to minimize personal risks, and reap the public good of whatever political gains result from the terrorism.

Selective Incentive Benefits that accrue only to those who participate in trying to achieve public good. Selective incentives from terrorism are benefits enjoyed only by those who partake in the violence.

A major selective incentive is financial compensation. The former President of Iraq Saddam Hussein, for example, bribed the families of Palestinian suicide bombers up to $25,000 to martyr themselves (Esterbrook 2002). Turkish president Recep Tayyip Erdoğan paid the medical bills for Syrian rebels who agreed to fight on Turkey's side in Libya (McKernan and Akoush 2020). Such terrorists are not necessarily irrational to pursue those financial rewards if they value them above other considerations.

Selective incentives need not take the form of a material or even tangible benefits. They may be anything that benefits participants for assuming the risk of acting violently. Social solidarity, for example, can be an alluring benefit of joining a terrorist group. Terrorist groups foster unusually close friendship precisely because they are so dangerous. The prospect of getting caught engenders trust and shared, memorable experiences conducive to bonding. For this reason, terrorists have been described as social utility—rather than political utility—maximizers. Terrorist groups disproportionately draw members from the socially alienated, such as unassimilated second-generation immigrants struggling in society (Abrahms 2008). Suicide attackers may seem like an irrational anomaly because they do not reap such social benefits, at least for long. But suicide attackers are not irrational if they attach supreme importance to the posthumous celebrations of their bravery, media attention, or simply want to end their state of depression as the criminologist Adam Lankford (2013) believes. Lankford (2011) highlights evidence that suicide bombers may disproportionally suffer from depression, making the decision to martyr themselves more understandable, if no less tragic.

KEY CONCEPTS

Expected Utility An action may be deemed rational whenever chosen for its presumed value or what economists refer to as expected utility.

A common misperception is that rational decision-making is emotionless. But an action may be deemed rational whenever chosen for its presumed value or what economists refer to as utility. Vengeance is thus another common selective incentive of terrorism. Attacking civilians is almost always counterproductive for the political success of groups, but can offer emotional value to perpetrators in settling the score. Success for them may be achieved from inflicting costs on the target regardless of whether it grants political concessions. Historical accounts confirm that revenge is often a powerful motive in militant groups especially among the rank-and-file. Assaf Moghadam (2003) finds that Palestinian terrorists are often motivated by the vengeance impulse. In her El Salvador fieldwork, the political scientist Elisabeth Wood (2003) discovered that insurgents fought for the feeling of vengeance, not political reform, against those who had wronged their family and friends. A Polish underground fighter during World War II acknowledged that 'life had ceased to mean anything to him after he had lost his sister and his brothers, his parents, his wife and his three daughters in a [Ukrainian] raid [and so he] continued to exist only for the purpose of killing and torturing Ukrainians' (Lotnik 1999: 70). A Lebanese woman in the civil war captures the desire for vengeance in conflict zones: 'It concerns me when three hundred and sixty-five Lebanese Muslims are murdered. I feel the seeds of hatred and the desire for revenge taking root in my very depths. At this moment I want the [militia] or anybody else to give the Phalangists back twice as good as we got. I would like them to go into offices and kill the first seven hundred and thirty defenceless Christians they can lay their hands on' (Tabbara 1979: 54).

Although terrorism is frequently understood as random violence against civilians, the targeting choices are seldom entirely arbitrary. Charles Drake (1998) and Michael Becker (2014) find that the stated grievances of terrorists are generally a reliable predictor of which targets they will attack. Some general examples include: anti-abortion terrorists targeting abortion clinics; anti-Semites targeting Jews; islamophobes targeting Muslims; anarchists targeting the government; ecoterrorists targeting factories. Robert Pape (2003) finds that suicide terrorists tend to strike countries occupying their nation. Similarly, Claude Berrebi and Darius Lakdawalla (2007) find that Palestinian terrorists are more likely to direct their attacks against Israeli regions with higher concentrations of military and other government targets. In sum, terrorism may seem irrational with its high risks and poor political return, but offers perpetrators the selective incentive of making their enemies suffer. Success for these perpetrators may be achieved from inflicting costs on the target country regardless of whether it grants political concessions. In addition to slaying their foes, terrorist attacks can help perpetrators to gain respect among their peers and ascend into leadership positions within the group. Attacks can boost a member's organizational standing even if the violence backfires politically. Based on his interviews with Irish Republican Army members, the terrorism researcher Gary Ackerman (2017) found that 'the goal of attacks was more often than not about personal glorification and the desire to be seen as a hero amongst one's peers'. Ahmed Chaabani climbed the ranks of the Algerian Armed Islamic Group because he was 'so aggressive' and acted as 'a daredevil' in attacking civilians (Gacemi et al. 2006: 48). Mohammed Emwazi ascended the ranks of Islamic State foreign fighters in Syria for his recorded beheadings of James Foley, Kenji Goto, Steven Sotloff, David Haines, Alan Henning, and Abdul-Rahman Kassig. These gruesome acts only encouraged the United States to increase energies on countering ISIS. From a personal perspective, however, they propelled him up the latter of ISIS foreign fighters until he died in a drone strike in November 2015.

Not only is it arguably rational to use terrorism for its selective incentives, but terrorist groups are known to adjust their tactics when confronted with operational impediments, that is, barriers to carrying out attacks. When metal detectors were first introduced in airports in the 1970s, for example, terrorists increased their attacks against non-aviation targets (Enders et al. 1990). As Martha Crenshaw (1981: 390) noted in the 1980s, terrorist 'decisions are based on logical processes' in the sense that the perpetrators scheme to commit attacks that will not be foiled. Such behaviour may be 'substantively irrational' as the violence almost never helps the perpetrators to redress their political grievances. But the violent act is often 'procedurally rational' in terms of exhibiting logistical calculations that enable the perpetrator to perpetrate the violence despite government countermeasures (Abrahms 2004).

> **KEY CONCEPTS**
>
> **Substantively Irrational and Procedurally Rational** In the context of this chapter, terrorism is substantively irrational when it stands no chance of helping the perpetrators to resolve their political grievances. Terrorism is procedurally rational when perpetrators adjust their operational approach to elude authorities. Some terrorist attacks are both substantively irrational but procedurally rational.

11.4 COUNTERTERRORISM IMPLICATIONS

This chapter has revealed that terrorism is seemingly puzzling behaviour. It is puzzling because terrorists are presumed to be rational political actors, but this tactic has an abysmal political record. The two Case Studies (11.1 and 11.2) of al-Qaeda and Islamic State are representative of a broader pattern; terrorism is not only highly correlated with political failure, but the attacks on civilians appear to bolster government resolve by empowering hardliners most opposed to concessions. Yet this paradox of terrorism does not mean its practitioners are necessarily irrational. Many people who become terrorists initially tried other strategies that proved no more effective, sometimes terrorists beat the odds and win, and rationality does not require individuals to be either omniscient or successful.

Still, terrorism cannot be easily explained from the rational actor model unless the perpetrators believe that they can benefit from participating in some way that they would not by remaining on the sidelines. Otherwise, there would be no point to assume the risks particularly when the political spoils will be enjoyed equally among those who picked up arms and those who did not. To overcome this collection action problem and minimize free-riders, militant leaders reward members financially and with other selective incentives. Accounts of terrorists and studies of their behaviour suggest that many people participate in terrorism not only for the material benefits, but also for the social solidarity, notoriety, respect among their peers, and out of vengeance to harm their enemy irrespective of the political consequences. The important take-away is that terrorists can derive all sorts of benefits, or what economists call utility, from their actions regardless of whether the violence results in political concessions. For this reason, terrorism can still be rational even if terrorism is a losing political strategy.

Knowing the priorities of terrorists is essential to combating them. If the conventional wisdom is correct that terrorists are rational political actors, then they may be deterred upon learning the unlikelihood that their violence will resolve their stated grievances. Indeed, many militant leaders have eschewed civilian attacks, and even punished operatives for perpetrating them upon learning about the negative political effects of terrorism. David Ben-Gurion, the leader of the Zionist militant group called Haganah, punished Jews in the 1940s for attacking civilians because he believed that the terrorism only discouraged Britain's withdrawal from Palestine. When caught terrorizing civilians, members of Uganda's National Resistance Army have faced public trials before elders who administered punishment brutally. Leaders of the Kurdish militant group called the PKK (Kurdistan Workers' Party) have handed out prison sentences when their members attacked civilians because doing so undermines the goal of an independent Kurdish state. Even al-Qaeda affiliates, such as in Syria, came to avoid terrorism upon discovering its political ineffectiveness and then punished members for attacking civilians (Abrahms 2018). When militant leaders are politically motivated, they often turn against terrorism and even help to fight it to help achieve their cause. For this reason, teaching militants especially the leaders about the political costs of terrorism can deter them from using it.

For prospective terrorists motivated by money, counterterrorism should focus on improving their financial prospects. For terrorist members driven by social solidarity, governments should plant spies to erode trust, while assimilating alienated young people to reduce the incentive of like-minded recruits to join terrorist organizations (Abrahms 2008). Depriving terrorists of media attention may disincentivize terrorists motivated by the attention. And governments must not mistreat or isolate populations and communities, for doing so risks increasing the supply of terrorists motived by revenge. Because terrorists tend to be procedurally rational, governments can reduce terrorist attempts by hardening targets, and thereby convincing would-be attackers that there is no point trying to strike them in the first place.

In sum, terrorists are generally presumed to be rational political actors. The history of terrorism indicates that it seldom helps the perpetrators to achieve their political goals. Yet this poor political success rate is not necessarily evidence of irrationality. Rationality depends more on the thought-process of the individual than the outcome. Understanding the thought-process of terrorists is useful for combating them.

DISCUSSION QUESTIONS

1. What is the puzzle of terrorism?
2. How does terrorism pose a collective action problem?
3. What are three selective incentives from the chapter that may motivate terrorists?
4. How can terrorism be substantively irrational but procedurally rational?
5. What are some counterterrorism implications of this chapter?

 Visit the online resources for pointers on how to answer the discussion questions, links to useful web sources, and guidance on accessing databases: www.oup.com/he/Wilson-Muro1e

GUIDE TO FURTHER READING

Abrahms, M. (2018) *Rules for Rebels: The Science of Victory in Militant History*. Oxford University Press.

Forest, J. (2012) *The Terrorism Lectures: A Comprehensive Collection for Students of Terrorism, Counterterrorism, and National Security*. Nortia Press. **There is widespread agreement among scholars that understanding the thought-process of terrorists is essential to combating them, Forest explores this in The Terrorism Lectures.**

Lake, D.A. (2002) 'Rational extremism: Understanding terrorism in the twenty-first century'. Dialogue IO 1, no. 1: 15–28. **Despite its political limitations, terrorism is usually seen by social scientists as rational behaviour. These two studies treat terrorism as a rational tactic.**

Muro, D., ed. (2018) *When Does Terrorism Work?* London: Routledge. **A growing body of research indicates that terrorism is not politically effective behaviour. These two books include relevant research.**

Pape, R. A.. (2006) *Dying to Win: The Strategic Logic of Suicide Terrorism*. Random House Incorporated.

REFERENCES

Abrahms, M. (2004) 'Are Terrorists Really Rational? The Palestinian Example'. *Orbis*, 48, 3: 533–549.

Abrahms, M. (2006a.) 'Al Qaeda's Scorecard: A Progress Report on Al Qaeda's Objectives'. *Studies in Conflict & Terrorism*, 29 (5), 509–529.

Abrahms, M. (2006b.) 'Why Terrorism Does Not Work'. *International Security*, 31, 2: 42–78.

Abrahms, M. (2008) 'What Terrorists Really Want: Terrorist Motives and Counterterrorism Strategy'. *International Security*, 32 (4): 78–105.

Abrahms, M. (2012) 'The Political Effectiveness of Terrorism Revisited'. *Comparative Political Studies*, 45 (3): 366–393.

Abrahms, M. (2013) 'The Credibility Paradox: Violence as a Double-edged Sword in International Politics'. *International Studies Quarterly*, 57 (4), 660–671.

Abrahms, M. (2018) *Rules for Rebels: The Science of Victory in Militant History*. Oxford: Oxford University Press.

Abrahms, M. and Gottfried, M. S. (2016) 'Does Terrorism pay? An empirical analysis'. *Terrorism and Political Violence*, 28 (1): 72–89.

Abrahms, M. and Lula, K. (2012) Why Terrorists Overestimate the Odds of Victory. *Perspectives on Terrorism*, 6 (4–5).

Asal, V., Gustafson, D., and Krause, P. (2019) 'It Comes with the Territory: Why States Negotiate with Ethno-Political Organizations'. *Studies in Conflict & Terrorism*, 42 (4): 363–382.

Atran, S. (2004) 'Mishandling Suicide Terrorism'. *The Washington Quarterly*, 27 (3): 65–90.

Becker, M. (2014) 'Explaining Lone Wolf Target selection in The United States'. *Studies in Conflict & Terrorism*, 37 (11): 959–978.

Begin, M. (1978) *The Revolt*. New York: Dell Publishing.

Berko, A. (2007) *The Path to Paradise: The Inner World of Suicide Bombers and their Dispatchers*. Greenwood Publishing Group.

Berrebi, C. (2009) 'The Economics of Terrorism and Counterterrorism: What Matters and Is Rational-Choice Theory Helpful?' In *Social science for counterterrorism: Putting the pieces together*, eds., Davis, P. K., and Cragin, K. Santa Monica: Calif.: Rand. 189–190.

Berrebi, C. and Klor, E. F. (2006) 'On Terrorism and Electoral Outcomes: Theory and Evidence from The Israeli-Palestinian Conflict'. *Journal of conflict resolution*, 50 (6): 899–925.

Berrebi, C. and Lakdawalla, D. (2007) 'How does Terrorism Risk Vary Across Space and Time? An Analysis Based on The Israeli Experience'. *Defence and Peace Economics*, 18 (2), 113–131.

Boot, M. (2013) *Invisible Armies: An Epic History of Guerrilla Warfare from Ancient Times to the Present*. 1. ed. New York, NY: Norton.

Chenoweth, E. and Lawrence, A. (2010) *Rethinking Violence: States and Non-State Actors in Conflict*. MIT Press.

Chenoweth, E., Miller, N., McClellan, E., Frisch, H., Staniland, P., and Abrahms, M. (2009) 'What Makes Terrorists Tick'. *International Security*, 33 (4): 180–202.

Chowanietz, C. (2010) 'Rallying Around the Flag or Railing Against the Government? Political Parties' Reactions to Terrorist Acts'. *Party Politics*, 17 (5): 673–698.

Cordes, B., Hoffman, B., Jenkins, B.M., Kellen, K., Moran, S., and Sater, W. (1984) 'Trends in International Terrorism, 1982 and 1983' (No. RAND/R-3183-SL). RAND: Santa Monica, CA.

Crenshaw, M. (1980) 'The Logic of Terrorism: Terrorist Behaviour as a Product of Strategic Choice' in *Origins of Terrorism: Psychologies, Ideologies, Theologies, States of Mind*. Walter Reich, ed., Washington, DC: Woodrow Wilson.

Crenshaw, M. (1981) 'The Causes of Terrorism'. *Comparative politics*, 13 (4): 379–399.

Crenshaw, M. (1992) *How Terrorists Think: What Psychology Can Contribute to Undersatnding Terrorism*.

Cronin, A. K. (2009) *How Terrorism Ends*. Princeton University Press.

DeNardo, J. 1985. *Power in Numbers: The Political Strategy of Protest and Rebellion* (Vol. 41). Princeton University Press.

Drake, C. J. (1998) 'The Role of Ideology in Terrorists' target selection'. *Terrorism and Political Violence*, 10 (2): 53–85.

Enders, W., Sandler, T., and Cauley, J. (1990) 'Assessing the Impact of Terrorist-thwarting Policies: An Intervention Time Series Approach'. *Defence and Peace Economics*, 2 (1): 1–18.

Esterbrook, J. (2002) Salaries for Suicide Bombers. CBS, April, 3.

Fortna, V.P. (2015) 'Do Terrorists Win? Rebels' Use of Terrorism and Civil War Outcomes'. *International Organization*, 69 (3): 519–556.

Gacemi, B., Colonna, F., and Burke, E. (2006) 'I, Nadia, Wife of a Terrorist' (xvii 157). University of Nebraska Press.

Gaibulloev, K. and Sandler, T. (2019) 'What we Have Learned About Terrorism Since 9/11', *Journal of Economic Literature*, 57 (2): 275–328.

Gould, E. D. and Klor, E. F. (2010) 'Does terrorism work?' *The Quarterly Journal of Economics*, 125 (4): 1459–1510.

Held, V. (1991) 'Terrorism, Rights, and Political Goals', in *Violence, Terrorism, and Justice*, eds., R. G. Frey and Christopher W. Morris. Cambridge: Cambridge Press.

Jones, B. D. (1999) 'Bounded Rationality'. *Annual Review of Political Science* 2, 1: 297–321.

Jones, S. and Libicki, M. C. (2008) 'How Terrorist Groups End: Lessons for Countering Al Qaeda', RAND Corporation, Washington, DC.

Kaufman, C. (2004) 'Threat Inflation and the Failure of the Marketplace of Ideas: The Selling of the Iraq War', *International Security*, 29 (1) (Summer 2004).

Kydd, A. H. and Walter, B. F. (2006) 'The Strategies of Terrorism'. *International security*, 31 (1): 49–80.

Lake, D. A. (2002) 'Rational Extremism: Understanding Terrorism in the Twenty-first Century'. *Dialogue IO*, 1 (1): 15–28.

Laqueur, W. (1976) 'The Futility of Terrorism'. *Harper's*, 252 (1510): 99–105.

Lankford, A. (2013) *The Myth of Martyrdom: What Really Drives Suicide Bombers, Rampage Shooters, and Other Self-destructive Killers*. St. Martin's Press.

Lankford, A. (2011) 'Could Suicide Terrorists Actually be Suicidal?', *Studies in Conflict & Terrorism*, 34 (4): 337–366.

Lichbach, M. I. (1994) 'What Makes Rational Peasants Revolutionary? Dilemma, Paradox, and Irony in Peasant Collective Action'. *World Politics*, 46 (3): 383–418.

Lichbach, M. I. (1998) *The Rebel's Dilemma*. University of Michigan Press.

Lotnik, W. (1999) *Nine Lives: Ethnic Conflict in the Polish-Ukrainian Borderlands*. London: Serif.

Lupia, A., McCubbins, M.D., and Popkin, S. L. (2000) 'Beyond Rationality: Reason and the Study of Politics'. *Elements of Reason: Cognition, Choice, and the Bounds of Rationality*: 1–20. Cambridge, UK: Cambridge University Press.

McCormick, G. H., (2003). 'Terrorist Decision Making'. *Annual Review of Political Science*, 6 (1): 473–507.

McKernan, B. and Akoush, H. (2020) '2,000 Syria fighters deployed to Libya to support government', *The Guardian*. Accessed at: https://www.theguardian.com/world/2020/jan/15/exclusive-2000-syrian-troops-deployed-to-libya-to-support-regime

Merari, A. (2004) 'Suicide Terrorism in the Context of the Israeli-Palestinian Conflict', presented at the National Institute of Justice Suicide Terrorism Conference, Washington, DC, October 25–26.

Moghadam, A. (2003) 'Palestinian Suicide Terrorism in the Second Intifada: Motivations and Organizational Aspects'. *Studies in Conflict and Terrorism*, 26 (2): 65–92.

Mroszczyk, J. and Abrahms, M. 'Terrorism in Africa: Explaining the Rise of Extremist Violence Against Civilians'. E-IR (April 2021). Available at https://www.e-ir.info/2021/04/09/terrorism-in-africa-explaining-the-rise-of-extremist-violence-against-civilians/.

Muro, D. ed. (2018) *When Does Terrorism Work?* London: Routledge.

Mwakideu, C. (2021) 'Mozambique's Extremist Violence Poses Threat for Neighbors'. Deutsche Welle, 29 March. Available at: https://www.dw.com/en/mozambiques-extremist-violence-poses-threat-for-neighbors/a-57043563

Pape, R. A. (2003) The Strategic Logic of Suicide Terrorism. *American Political Science Review*, 97 (3): 343–361.

Perry, S. and Hasisi, B. (2015) 'Rational Choice Rewards and the Jihadist Suicide Bomber'. *Terrorism and Political Violence*, 27 (1): 53–80.

Richardson, L. (2007) *What Terrorists Want: Understanding the Enemy, Containing the Threat.* Random House Incorporated.

Rose, W., Murphy, R., and Abrahms, M. (2007) 'Does Terrorism Ever Work? The 2004 Madrid Train bombings'. *International Security*, 32 (1): 185–192.

Sageman, M. (2006) 'Global Network Terrorism: Comparative Anatomy and Evolution', NSC briefing. Washington, DC: White House, April 28.

Schelling, T. C. (1991) 'What Purposes Can International Terrorism Serve?', in Raymond Gillespie Frey and Christopher W. Morris eds., *Violence, Terrorism, and Justice*, New York: Cambridge Press.

Simon, H. A. (1976) 'From Substantive to Procedural Rationality', in *25 Years of Economic Theory*, 65–86. Boston, MA: Springer.

Stanton, J. A. (2016) *Violence and Restraint in Civil War: Civilian Targeting in the Shadow of International Law*. Cambridge: Cambridge University Press.

Stern, J. (2003) 'The Protean Enemy'. *Foreign Affairs*: 27–40.

Stern, J. (2007) *With the Weathermen: The Personal Journal of a Revolutionary Woman*. New Brunswick, N.J: Rutgers University Press.

Tabbara, L. M. (1979) *Survival in Beirut: Diary of Civil War*. London: Onyx Books.

'The US and the Middle East After 11 September', *Strategic Survey*, 102(1) (May 2002), 182.

Thomas, J. (2014) 'Rewarding Bad Behaviour: How Governments Respond to Terrorism in Civil War'. *American Journal of Political Science*, 58 (4): 804–818.

Tullock, G. (1971) 'The Paradox of Revolution'. *Public Choice*, 89–99.

Waldemar, L. (1999) *Nine Lives: Ethnic Conflict in the Polish-Ukrainian Borderlands*. 1st edition. London: Serif Publishing.

Weinstein, J. M. (2006) *Inside Rebellion: The Politics of Insurgent Violence*. Cambridge: Cambridge University Press.

Wood, E. J. (2003) *Insurgent Collective Action and Civil War in El Salvador*. Cambridge: Cambridge University Press.

CHAPTER 12

Target Selection

ALEX BRAITHWAITE AND IAN ORRINGER

■ CHAPTER SUMMARY

This chapter provides an overview of theoretical and empirical models of terrorist target selection. This overview begins with a discussion of the distinction between targets of violence and targets of attention (audiences) in definitions of terrorism. This is followed by a description of the empirical record, with data on different target types and regions affected. The main body of the chapter is then divided between discussions of hard versus soft targets, the perceived vulnerability of democratic institutions to terrorist violence, and the use of target selection in terrorist strategies, including to provoke a fearful response from targets and audiences. We draw upon brief illustrations of white nationalism in the USA, ETA in Spain, and the IRA in the United Kingdom to demonstrate these concepts in real world cases.

12.1 INTRODUCTION

At approximately 10:40am on Saturday 3rd August 2019, a young white male carried out a mass shooting at a Walmart Supercenter in the Cielo Vista Mall in El Paso, Texas. Patrick Wood Crucius, aged 21, used a semi-automatic civilian analog to an AK-47 rifle to kill 22 individuals and injure 24 more. This attack is best thought of as an act of domestic terrorism and a hate crime, because the 'manifesto' that the perpetrator issued was replete with the language and imagery of white nationalism and anti-immigrant rhetoric.

Crucius's choice of target speaks volumes about his probable motivations. As with the vast majority of cases of terrorist violence, this attack was not a random occurrence but, rather, a purposive and intentional act. Selecting a target is a fundamental decision taken in the early stages of the terrorist event cycle (Horgan 2004). In this instance, the decision to target a shopping centre suggests that Crucius recognized that he was not sufficiently capable to be able to target government forces or a secured facility, such as a border crossing. Accordingly, he needed to select a popular public gathering space that is a prime example of a soft target in a democratic society that is commonly not secured or fortified in any way. A soft target is one that is only minimally secured, whereas a hard target would be one that features a police or armed presence to provide security, such as an embassy. A soft target such as a shopping centre was likely selected because of the relative ease with which an attack can be planned and executed. Shopping centres are lightly secured spaces through which individual access and free movement is protected. Therefore, attacks against members of the public in shopping centres can have the effect of generating fear more broadly within a population of individuals who might themselves commonly frequent such spaces.

KEY CONCEPTS

Hard vs. Soft Targets When terrorist groups or individuals select a target, their decision is likely affected by the level of security or protection at specific locations. A 'soft' target is generally a minimally secured public place frequented by civilians. A 'hard' target, by contrast, usually includes greater levels of security, and may house government and/or military personnel. The choice of a soft or hard target will be influenced by what goal(s) the terrorists are trying to achieve.

Crucius travelled for 10 hours and 600 miles from his home in Dallas, Texas, to carry out the attack. This is presumably because of the symbolic value of this target, and the likely characteristics of its victims. The shopping centre is located in El Paso, a city on the US border with Mexico that is next to the Mexican city of Ciudad Juárez. The shopping centre is known locally to be a popular shopping location for Mexicans making the short journey across the border, as well as local immigrant communities. As such, we might conclude that Crucius selected the location, rather than one in his hometown of Dallas, because of the greater probability of attacking Mexican people, and because the closer proximity to the border would provide an elevated stage for the attack, generating more media attention given the significance of the border in political debate during the Trump Administration's time in office. Donald Trump was the US President from 2017–2021, and the signature promise of his 2016 election campaign was to build a barrier wall between the US and Mexico.

The target choice in this case can reflect a clear ideological motivation on the part of the perpetrator. The attack occurred at the heart of a debate about border security and immigration which was central to the Trump Administration's time in office. This debate involved members of the President's Administration and their supporters on the far right of the political spectrum in the USA drawing upon xenophobic, racist, and anti-immigrant tropes. The attack in Texas (see Photo 12.1) can be viewed, therefore, as an attempt to elicit excitement and support from those that espouse white supremacist and replacement theory logics. Replacement theory—the fear that white people will be replaced by ethnic minority people—was directly referenced in the so-called manifesto of the killer. Crucially, the words used to justify this attack from Crucius were reflected at the highest levels of government in the US, with Representative Steve King of Iowa and President Trump both espousing key talking points from replacement theory, identifying 'invasions' of migrants, and claiming the need for a border wall with Mexico to limit the threat. The so-called

PHOTO 12.1 El Paso, Texas, USA, August 2019. Memorabilia left by citizens in support of the victims of the Walmart shooting on 3 August.

'extinction' of the white people appears central to the motivation of many of the deadliest terrorist violence in recent US history, including attacks in Oklahoma City (1995), Pittsburgh (2018), and Charleston (2015). As such, rather than an isolated incident, it is important to view the El Paso terror attack in 2019 as one of a long series of similar terrorist targets. Viewing Crucius's individual attack as being part of a sequence is important for terrorism research, as this helps researchers understand how societal trends affect the likelihood of violence and the types of targets that may be attacked.

This chapter provides an overview of theoretical and empirical models of terrorist target selection. In the process of doing so, we discuss scholarly debates and empirical trends that highlight important aspects of the El Paso terrorist attack. We explore violence against soft targets as compared to the targeting of hardened locations. We examine the role of public fear in generating more media attention and publicity for the group and, thus, accelerating their perceived gains toward achieving policy change. We then consider the possibility that this same public fear, if reaching too great a level, could prove to be counterproductive for terrorist organizations if it provides governments with support for coercive counterterrorism tactics. We then finally discuss the claim that democracies are especially vulnerable to terrorist targeting. Before proceeding to each of these discussions, however, we first place this attack in a broader empirical context by assessing trends in terrorism targeting over the past five decades.

12.2 TARGET LOCATIONS FOR TERRORISM

The attack in El Paso fits within the empirical literature's common definition of terrorism as a tactic involving the threat or use of violence by non-state actors against public interests with a view towards affecting some policy change (Hoffman 2006; Enders and Sandler 2011). Using this standard definition, the Global Terrorism Database (GTD) (see Chapter 7) records more than 190,000 qualifying violent attacks globally between 1970 and 2018 (National Consortium for the Study of Terrorism and Responses to Terrorism 2018). Each attack involves a perpetrator that carried out the attack, a method through which an attack is executed, a goal behind the attack, and a target for the attack.

KEY CONCEPTS

Target Selection Target Selection refers to the purposeful way terrorist organizations choose the location of an attack. It is important to note that the where these groups choose to target reflects some strategic goal, including recruiting members, striking fear into the public, or causing maximum damage (Heymann 2003: 52). Each of these goals is then a means to achieve the organizations' ultimate political objective that they desire from targeted governments.

In a simple, stylized sense, countries can be thought of as the targets of terrorist attacks. What this really means is that given their sovereign authority, governments get to define what is and what is not terrorism, as well as who is to be considered a terrorist or terrorist group. Accordingly, they will typically identify violent attacks against their interests and those of their constituents as being terrorist in nature. We will not directly address the debate surrounding whether governments' actions can be considered 'terrorism' (see, e.g., Tilly 2004 and Chapter 14 in this volume). Instead, we are going to build our discussion upon the premise that terrorism is carried out by non-state actors (Hoffman 2006). From this perspective, we pay initial attention to the countries and regions that are most frequently targeted by terrorism.

In 2018, the greatest density of attacks was observed in Syria, Iraq, Afghanistan, Nigeria, and Yemen. These countries have in recent years have experienced large-scale civil wars, and the density of attacks highlights that terrorism is likely to be employed as a tactic within these ongoing wars (Findley and Young 2012; Stanton 2013; Fortna 2015). The observation of most terrorist attacks in conflict zones and non-democratic environments is a relatively recent phenomenon (as will be noted below in the discussion of Figure 12.1). This trend reflects an empirical record that shows that while groups employing terror rarely achieve their goals, their marginal successes are achieved when they target military, rather than civilian targets (Abrahms 2006).

The targeting of military assets by non-state actors has increased notably in the last four decades. Pape (2006) contends that this is likely because of the demonstration in the early 1980s of the effectiveness of suicide terrorism, primarily through attacks in Lebanon, which prompted the withdrawal of French and American troops. At the same time, empirical trends support the idea—as we will see later in this chapter in Case Study 12.2—that excessive uses of force against public (rather than government or military) targets can often undermine any level of public support or sympathy for the movement of the perpetrators of the violence (Fortna 2015; Gould and Klor 2010).

We can also look at the distribution more broadly across the regions of the world. This perhaps provides a more stable perspective on where terrorists tend to target their violent attacks. To this end, Figure 12.1 displays the total numbers of attacks across twelve regions of the world. These numbers are total counts of attacks observed across the period between 1970 and 2017. The numbers do not take account of variation between countries in terms of the size of their land area or population. In other words, we are not accounting here for the possibility that some countries and regions are simply larger or have larger populations, which would mean that they also potentially are home to more soft and hard targets for terrorist violence. Nonetheless, they reflect an interesting spatial distribution. First, the Middle East/North Africa and South Asia regions top the charts for volume of attacks. This is likely because both regions have experienced a combination of long running terrorist campaigns and a growth in use of terrorist tactics within civil wars. In the Middle East this is reflected in the combination of traditional campaigns in occupied Palestinian territories and Kurdish claimed territories, as well as the more recent wars in Syria and Iraq. In South Asia, these

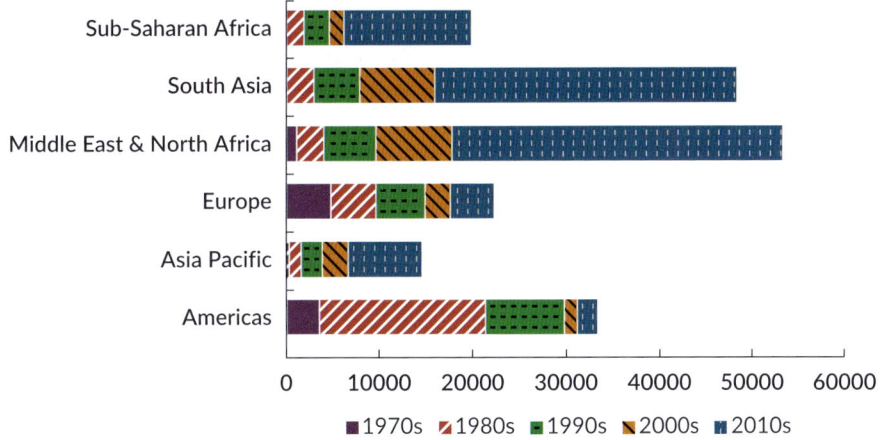

FIGURE 12.1 Total number of terrorist attacks by region, 1970–2017. Source: Global Terrorism Database (GTD).

numbers are bolstered by traditional campaigns in disputed Kashmir territories and India's so-called 'red corridor' of states disturbed by left-wing insurgencies, as well as ongoing war in Afghanistan and insurgency in the Afghan-Pakistan border region, as shown in Figure 12.1.

Also reflected in this exploration of regional trends are changes over time. Two dominant shifts are worth commenting upon. Firstly, the Americas were the primary target of terrorist violence in the 1980s, but have experienced much less violence each decade since. This reflects how this is the hemisphere in which democracy and capitalism were being strengthened by government policy, but also challenged by leftist opponents. In the 1980s, therefore, leftist terrorists, like the Shining Path, a group of communist extremists in Peru, were responsible for attacks targeting right-wing governments and economic actors and interests.

Secondly, into the 1990s and up to the present day, we see violence shifting across other regions, with a rapid escalation of the use of terrorism across the Middle East, South Asia, and Sub-Saharan Africa in response to the continued military presence of Western states, and escalation of anti-government civil wars (Enders and Sandler 2006). There is little evidence of a slowdown in this second trend.

From a practical perspective, terrorist organizations rarely target a country as a whole. Even the deadliest attacks that we have observed are concentrated at specific locations within a country. For instance, the 9/11 attacks targeted the USA's economic and political hubs of New York City and Washington, DC. Thus, whilst their effects may have been felt nationwide (if not even further afield globally), the direct targets of the violence were isolated. Two recent empirical studies in political science provide an opportunity to grapple with the precise locations of terrorist violence and to identify the local correlates of terrorism (Nemeth et al. 2014; Marineau et al. 2020). These studies explore, respectively, the local correlates of domestic and transnational terrorist violence, where domestic attacks involve perpetrators, targets, and victims all from the same country, and transnational attacks affect at least two countries' citizens or targets.

With respect to domestic terrorism, Nemeth et al. (2014) contend that the risk of violence is uneven across the territories of any individual state. Their empirical analyses highlight that attacks are most likely in areas with higher levels of population density, which would fit with the notion that terrorists commonly target non-combatants. They also demonstrate that within democratic countries, attacks are most likely in areas with relatively mountainous terrain and where there exist greater levels of ethnic diversity (see, also, Fearon and Laitin 2003). Furthermore, they demonstrate that terrorist attacks are likely in both rich and poor regions of a given country, but not in areas of medium wealth. In each case, these findings parallel those of the broader civil war literature, identifying spaces in which governmental control is increasingly subject to contestation.

A number of these relationships also appear to hold in the case of transnational terrorism. Arguing that terrorists select locations with respect to their intrinsic value and practical vulnerability to attack, Findley et al. (2019) uncover the local correlates of transnational terrorism. They demonstrate that groups are most likely to target attacks in areas with ongoing civil conflict, in areas closer to international borders and the capital city, elsewhere in urban areas, and where there is economic productivity. In other words, as with domestic terrorism, transnational terrorist attacks are locally targeted in potentially predictable patterns.

12.3 TARGET SELECTION, VICTIMS, AND AUDIENCES

The locations of terrorist attacks highlight that target selection is best thought of as being purposive, intentional, and strategic, with valuable locations often prioritized. Targets are selected on purpose to cause greatest damage or to generate the most fear or to attract recruits and supporters (Heymann 2003: 52) and to communicate a specific message to a target audience that is likely broader than the target victims (Hoffman 2006: 229). As such, targets are not selected at random but may occasionally appear that way because they will be chosen to be representative of a broader set of possible targets. This perception of randomness is something that fuels anxiety within the audience population (Enders and Sandler 2006; Braithwaite 2013). Violence can be thought of, therefore, as being targeted in such a manner that a broader audience observing an attack could believe that they will be the next victims.

The target audience is identified by the perpetrating group as being pivotal to achievement of their strategic goals. If ideologies define goals, then strategies can be thought of as central to identifying suitable targets. For example, left-wing groups are notorious for targeting actors that are deemed responsible for perpetuating economic inequalities and injustices as a means of appealing to their broad constituencies interested in achieving some systemic revolution. This means that left-wing groups commonly target government and business actors as representatives of the capitalist and neoliberal markets. For example, the Red Army Faction in Germany, a leftist militant organization, set off several bombs at the Axel-Springer (a German conservative media group) headquarters in Hamburg in 1972. Two years later, they would follow this up with the murder of the president of the Berlin district court, and in 1975 with the kidnapping of a mayoral candidate in West Berlin (see also Case Study 6.1 and Case Study 9.1). Given their focus on justice, though, Leftists are more likely to be constrained with respect to the level of harm they will generate.

By contrast, right-wing groups, such as white supremacists in the USA, and ethnic-nationalist groups, such as the Palestinian Liberation Organization (PLO), are more likely to inflict harm when targeting leftist governments and ethnic out-groups (a social group with which an individual does not identify), respectively. This is because their violence will be designed to demonstrate the fundamental weakness of the government and its inability to provide security to all members of society. Finally, religiously-motivated groups are identified as being consistently most deadly in their application of force, as they face fewer constraints on their use of indiscriminate violence against a broader set of out-groups.

The GTD distinguishes between 22 categories of direct target (victim) types. This includes business, government, police, public citizens, and military targets as the primary groups. Each of these 22 target categories can be further disaggregated. For instance, government targets could be from legislative, judicial, or executive branches, or indeed from a royal family, or the intelligence services. Figure 12.2 focuses upon the first level of aggregation, with a few uncommon categories collapsed for ease of presentation. This means that we are highlighting the total numbers of attacks against each of 15 categories of targets for the period 1970 to 2017.

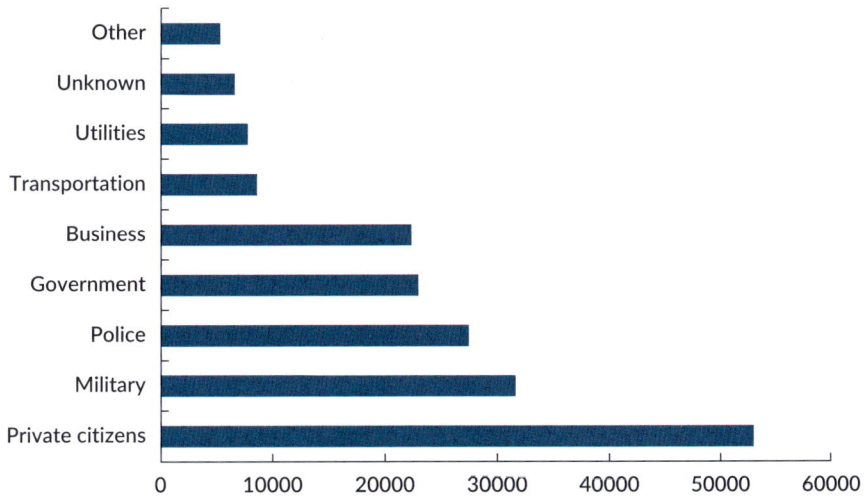

FIGURE 12.2 Total number of terrorist attacks by target category, 1970–2017. Source: Global Terrorism Database (GTD).

The graph demonstrates that attacks have been most commonly carried out against private citizens. This fits with the traditional perspective of terrorism as violence against non-combatant citizens. Fifth on the list are business targets. This reflects the common practice of targeting private, (non-governmental) economic interests as a means of attempting to coerce strategic and self-interested actors to alter their support for state policies. For example, rebels in Colombia and Nigeria have long targeted pipelines owned and controlled by Western multi-national corporations (see, e.g., Bibes 2001; Onuoha 2008, respectively). The goal of these attacks is to undermine these private interests' confidence in the ability of the local government to protect their property rights and economic viability.

In between these two categories of non-governmental target types are three categories of government targets: the military, the police, and other elements of the structure of government. Collectively, these attacks are likely motivated as part of campaigns of attrition designed to target the policymakers directly that stand in the way of change to convince them that they are vulnerable to direct violence. Outside of the top five primary target types, there is a precipitous drop-off in total numbers of attacks per category. Nonetheless, what is perhaps most noteworthy is that terrorists rather commonly attack elements of public infrastructure, such as utilities and transportation networks (such as the bombing of the St Petersburg metro train in 2017, or the bombing of the Brussels airport and subway station in 2016). These are essentially public targets and attacks against them are highly likely to generate fear within a broader public audience. Many groups identify a strategic advantage in targeting both governmental and non-governmental targets in concert, as shown in our description of the case of ETA in Spain (see Case Study 12.1).

The location and timing of violent terrorist attacks are often highly symbolic. Buildings and property (e.g. the World Trade Center towers, oil pipelines, political institutions) may often be targeted because they are viewed as being symbolic of the sources of problems inherent in political or economic systems. Such targets may also be selected to undermine confidence in economic institutions by targeting specific industries (Lutz and Lutz 2006), deter tourists (Enders et al. 1992), or force governments to divert scarce resources into counterterrorism (Gaibulloev and Sandler 2008). However, attacks against property alone are highly unlikely to move governments to affect policy change. Thus, groups will become increasingly likely to target civilians and military personnel to induce fear or demonstrate strength, both of which are likely pre-requisite for moving governments to change policies.

CASE STUDY 12.1

ETA's Mixed Targeting Strategies

The Basque separatist group, ETA ('Euskadi Ta Askatasuna' or Basque homeland and freedom) killed at least 850 people in the 50 years during which it operated leading up to being disbanded in 2018. Over the course of its lifetime, ETA has opposed a series of Spain's governments, beginning with that controlled by General Francisco Franco in the 1950s. Throughout, ETA maintained a steadfast desire to increase the autonomy of the Basque populations and, ultimately, create an independent Basque state.

To achieve this goal, it designed numerous violent attacks against a variety of public and government targets. As such, ETA stands as a prime example of a group identifying various targets with distinct objectives at the same time (Horgan 2004). Take, for instance, their violent campaigns in the Summer of 1996, during which ETA deployed a series of bombs in tourist locations across Spain. This included at the ticket counter of the Alhambra in Granada that came with a forewarning and thus, inflicted no loss of life, and a bombing at the Reus airport that injured 35 holiday-makers. This was followed by two more explosions at some nearby hotel airport. These attacks were intended to place pressure on the increasingly right-leaning Spanish government whose economy was heavily reliant upon the tourist industry.

In that same year, ETA engaged in more direct attacks against the government. The organization kidnapped José Antonio Ortega Lara, a prison officer who aligned with Spain's right-wing People's Party, in an attempt to exchange him for the release of ETA prisoners. Then, in 1997, they abducted People's Party politician Miguel Ángel Blanco, with the same goal to exchange him in a swap for Basque prisoners. After their demands were not met, the group murdered Blanco, which led to mass demonstrations against ETA and the formation of some anti-terrorist groups, including Foro Ermua, which formed to as a direct response to Blanco's assassination and sought to personally counteract Basque Nationalists. Later, in 2000, ETA was deemed responsible for targeting and murdering several Spanish politicians as a direct show of force to the Spanish authorities. Therefore, ETA also directly attacked individuals who stood in the way of the specific economic and political interests of the group. While they only achieved mixed results in their direct goals, their attacks still demonstrated a combination targeting strategy aimed at both creating fear with attacks on the public, and displaying power with attacks on the government.

Therefore, the targeting of both public and government actors and interests can be thought of as strategically motivated. On the one hand, public targets are selected to elicit a fearful response from the broader population with a view towards compelling members of the public to demand policy changes from their government. On the other hand, the targeting of government interests directly can be viewed as a means of demonstrating the strength of the group and their ability to directly challenge their enemy through a campaign of sustained attack (Kydd and Walter 2006).

QUESTIONS

1. What do ETA's target selections tell us about their strategic motivations?
2. Why would ETA target foreign tourists if those tourists are not able to vote in local elections to affect policy change?

Evidence suggests that while terrorist violence rarely proves effective in achieving strategic or outcome goals, such as coercing regime change, it can be effective in bringing about tactical or process goals, such as troop withdrawal (e.g. Pape 2006). It is for this reason, perhaps, that groups which focus on military targets appear to be more effective than those that focus on civilian targets. While this may appear counter-intuitive on face value, it is likely that this stems from civilian targeting being treated by victims and their government as maximalist in nature. That is to say that attacks against civilian soft targets will be viewed more directly as an existential threat targeting the state. By contrast, attacks against hardened military targets may be viewed in a more piecemeal fashion as a tactic aimed at achieving a more incremental outcome (Abrahms 2006; Abrahms et al. 2018). Therefore, relatively deadly attacks against the military, such as the attacks against US and French troops in Lebanon in the early 1980s (see section 12.2 Target Locations for Terrorism) precipitated the withdrawal of those countries' troops from the area. To some analysts, these cases reinforce the long-held contention that democracies are especially vulnerable to violence targeted against their interests (Pape 2005).

12.4 DEMOCRACIES AS FREQUENT TARGETS OF TERRORISM

Recent trends in terrorism have centred upon the use of the tactic in the context of ongoing civil wars in a series of undemocratic countries. This trend emerges with the end of the Cold War, when the loss of bipolarity globally exposes a series of long-simmering civil conflicts involving non-state actors (see, e.g., Kaldor 2013). This new trend reverses the record of earlier decades in which the tactic appeared most commonly in more democratic environments. Countries with democratic institutions, rules, and norms have long been deemed to be especially vulnerable to being targeted by terrorist violence (Posen 2001/2). There is reasonably strong empirical evidence that this is the case (Li 2005), and there are several theoretical explanations for why this might be the case. First, the protection of civil liberties by democratic states facilitates attacks occurring in these contexts, with the freedom of movement and association enabling potential terrorists to plan and execute their attacks.

Secondly, and in addition, a desire to protect rights of privacy and due process represent a notable burden on the state's deployment of more coercive counterterrorism operations (Piazza 2008). Democratic governments are subject to greater levels of executive constraints that require them to strike a balance between demonstrating an active response to violence without overstepping the mark and violating civil liberties. This is often referred to in discourse as the proactive response dilemma (Kydd and Walter 2006). In a democratic setting, this dilemma or pressure stems from electoral constraints. Recent studies suggest that a similar constraint may also exist in autocracies, where other elites may limit the executive authority of the leader (Wilson and Piazza 2013; Conrad et al. 2014). In single party systems, the party can limit a leader's autonomy. In a military dictatorship, the generals may serve in this constraining role.

> **KEY CONCEPTS**
>
> **Proactive Response Dilemma** The proactive response dilemma (Kydd and Walter 2006) refers to the likelihood that democratic governments will be held to high standards both domestically and internationally, forcing them to respect concerns about proportionality in the ways that they respond to terrorism (Wilkinson 2015). A second important facet of this dilemma is the potential with which democracies may be expected to offer partial concessions to their opponents in the interest of preserving or restoring security and stability.

Thirdly, the freedom of the press that is protected within democracies provides an opportunity for individuals and groups to disseminate their message to a broad audience (Rid and Hecker 2009: 10). This is central to enabling relatively weak actors to compensate for their inferior strategic position. Crucially, given their need to generate profits for corporate bosses and shareholders, the media in democracies also have an incentive to report prolifically on dramatic and compelling violent attacks that capture the public's imagination. In other words, groups employing violence and the media enjoy a kind of symbiotic relationship, helping to sustain one another's relevance (Nacos 2016).

> **KEY CONCEPTS**
>
> **Democracies in Target Selection** It is a well recorded observation that democracies tend to be more likely to be targeted by terrorist violence. This can be explained in a number of ways, including the protection of rights and liberties in democracies that give terrorists more freedom to operate, rights of privacy and due process that constrain counterterrorist measures, freedom of the press that allows messages from organizations to be shared more widely, foreign policies that are often easy to criticize, and questions of legitimacy that plague recently forged democracies.

Fourthly, democracies are viewed as being especially vulnerable to coercive force from non-state actors because of the foreign policies that they maintain (Pape 2005). As part of this, democracies (perhaps most notably, the USA) engage in aggressive foreign policies that often generate grievances in areas in which they remain a military presence (Savun and Phillips 2009; Braithwaite 2015). They also are accused of exhibiting double standards by supporting illiberal regimes in the Middle East, Latin America, and elsewhere. Democracies are also typically unwilling to pay the costs of casualties incurred overseas (Pape 2005).

Finally, scholars hold that democracies may be especially vulnerable in their early years post-transition (Wilkinson 2015; Eyerman 1998; Chenoweth 2013; Piazza 2013). The logic holds that recently transitioned democracies will face stronger challenges against their legitimacy, including from non-state actors with a tradition of relying upon violence. Moreover, these fledgling democracies will face a great pressure to manage the threat of terrorism without resorting to excessive uses of force. As such, it might be that new democracies are the most vulnerable to terrorist violence.

In combination, these characteristics exacerbate democratic vulnerability to terrorist targeting. In the next section, we explore the main point of this vulnerability: public fear and desire for security. Before doing so, however, we detail a notable case in which public resolve in the face of casualties actually led to the strengthening of anti-terrorism practices and the demise of a terrorist group (see Case Study 12.2 below).

12.5 TARGET SELECTION, FEAR, AND PUBLIC ATTENTION

Terrorism is commonly described as a tool of the weak (Crenshaw 1981), and as a tactic employed to help its perpetrators overcome an asymmetry of power in its relationship with a wealthier or militarily capable government (Merari 1993). According to rationalist logics of terrorism, violence is believed by its perpetrators to be a means of overcoming this asymmetry (Pape 2005; Kydd and Walter 2006). Specifically, violence is employed in order to attract attention and garner popular support by spreading information about a cause, grievance, and/or set of demands (Crenshaw 1981; Nacos 2016).

At its crux, this instrumental logic of terrorism turns on the suggestion that violence against public interests will elicit and spread fear among a broad public audience and, by doing so, may manipulate public sentiment to demand that the government change its policy or stance towards the violent group (Braithwaite 2013). According to this logic, it is suggested that public sentiments and perceptions—rather than transportation, military, government, or private property, per se—ought to be thought of as the primary targets of terrorist attacks. By focusing upon public perceptions, terrorists employ dramatic violent attacks to communicate an exaggerated sense of their ability to do harm and to undermine the perception of the government's ability to protect its citizens.

Terrorists will prove successful in achieving their goals through this strategy of intimidation (Kydd and Walter 2006) only if they are able to convert the fear that their targeted attacks cause within the public into specific demands for changes to policies that would align with the terrorists' goals (Crenshaw, 1981). This is what Crenshaw (1998) refers to as the agenda-setting quality of terrorism. By attracting attention, terrorism '… makes the claims of the resistance a salient issue in the public mind' (Crenshaw 1998: 17).

If their violence receives enough media coverage, terrorists may prove able to communicate to the public that the violence to which they are victims is likely to remain a consistent feature of the status quo political order (Braithwaite 2013). Consequently, their political terror campaign, if successful, will have the effect of encouraging citizens to pressure their government to give into the demands of the terrorists to be able to restore public safety

(Hoffman 2006). In other words, terrorists, 'use the unreasonable fear and the resulting political disaffection it has generated among the public to intimidate governments into making political concessions in line with its political goals' (Long 1990: 5). This theoretical logic is shown to have some marginal empirical support. Hewitt (1993), for example, shows incumbent governments in Germany and Italy in the 1970s and 1980s tended to be blamed by their publics for general threats to the state's security.

This logic of intimidation through public fear appears plausible, and receives some minor empirical support. However, there remain at least two problems that warrant some additional consideration. First, as time passes, publics surely grow familiar with the occurrence of terrorism and, thus, more easily able to cope with the violence that terrorists target against them. Consequently, media attention is less likely to be drawn to each new violent event. Accordingly, to be able to grab attention, elicit fear, and intimidate their audiences, terrorists must continually innovate and escalate their violence, including by identifying new targets that will be noticed. Hoffman (1993) makes this claim and supports it with evidence that while tactics remained consistent, terrorist group lethality increased markedly between the 1970s and 1980s. Hoffman concludes that the most plausible explanation for this trend was that terrorist groups were escalating their violence and lethality to grab attention.

Secondly, we have already noted that under certain conditions, violence against public, and especially military targets, can have a limited effectiveness in changing policy and helping groups achieve their goals (Abrahms 2006). However, there are also clearly cases in which violence perpetrated by terrorist groups has the opposite effect and actually generates a backlash, instead. Indeed, it appears to be the case that some attacks that purposefully target civilians and produce (whether intentionally or otherwise) higher civilian casualties prove counterproductive. Such attacks, rather than undermining trust in government, can have the effect of firming up popular opposition to the groups espousing and using violence. This latter dynamic was observed, for example, in Turkey, Russia, and Northern Ireland in the late 1990s (see Case Study 12.2 below for a discussion of this last example).

The Kurdistan Worker's Party (PKK) is still a very active terrorist group that employs violence against Turkish government, civilians, and global interests with a view toward trying to coerce concessions to enhance the rights and territorial autonomy of the Kurdish peoples. However, a series of their attacks against Turkish civilians through the mid-1990s severely undermined their cause in the minds of the Turkish population. Perhaps the pinnacle of this period was their bombing of Istanbul's covered bazaar in April 1994. The attack killed two and injured another dozen but also caused serious damage to the support of the PKK. The attack followed a series of incidents in which the PKK targeted members of its own community that it deemed treacherous. The attacks prompted dissent against and opposition to the group throughout the country, which forced them to stray away from employing attacks against civilian targets and instead towards military and government targets.

> **KEY CONCEPTS**
>
> **The Role of Fear in Target Selection** When choosing soft targets for attacks, terrorists likely consider how their violence will elicit a fearful response from the public. The presence of the general population at soft targets increases the likelihood of a fearful response. This fearful response could then be used by the violent organization to help bring about a desired policy concession from the government representing the population. However, generating the right amount of public attention can be a difficult balance for the terrorist organization to achieve. Too much violence can cause a country's people to lash out at the organization, which could lead to support for stronger counterterrorist measures.

A final example from the end of the 1990s rests upon similar dynamics on the face of it but may reveal a more strategic interest on the part of the state. Following the First Chechen war from 1994–5, many Russian citizens believed that the war was unnecessary and that granting more autonomy to Chechnya (the Chechen Republic, a constituent republic of Russia situated in the North Caucasus) was a preferred alternative. In light of this, Boris Yeltsin (President of Russia from 1991 to 1999) publicly proposed granting Chechnya rights as an independent state. In September 1999, however, several bombs were detonated in Russian apartment buildings, killing hundreds. The Russian government quickly blamed Chechen terrorists for these attacks, which likely contributed to a rapid decline in public support for an independent Chechnya (Bruce Ware 2005). Critics of the Russian government have long argued, however, that the attacks were actually carried out by Russian agents of the Federal Security Service (FSB) with the goal of framing Chechens and undermining public sympathies for the Chechen cause (Sattar 2003). Whether the result of Chechen aggression or, more likely, Russian government agents, the excessive attacks had the effect of dramatically changing public perceptions.

> **CASE STUDY 12.2**
>
> *The IRA Omagh Bombing*
>
> The Irish Republican Army (IRA) was an organization made up of mostly Catholics that sought to unite Catholic Ireland with the more Protestant, UK-governed Northern Ireland. On 15 August 1998, the IRA carried out one of its deadliest attacks in the market town of Omagh, in Northern Ireland. The attacks, which killed 29 people and injured more than 200 others, were the first large-scale attacks during the period of ceasefire ushered in by the Good Friday agreement of 1997.

A renegade element of the IRA, who disagreed with the terms of the peace with the British government, split off and formed the Real IRA. This was their first signature attack. Several members of the group drove an explosive-laden car to the town's symbolic courthouse, but they became distressed when they saw a police officer near the building and instead parked it in the crowded market. Unfortunately, not all of the Real IRA affiliates were aware of the change of location and issued several warnings, 30 minutes and 15 minutes before the bomb was to be set off, to the town about an explosive near the originally targeted courthouse. The police then decided to move civilians near the courthouse towards the market, the actual location of the bomb, where it eventually detonated. This attack killed many civilians, including both Catholics and Protestants, and was condemned internationally.

Gerry Adams, the leader of Sinn Féin, an Irish political party that previously aligned with the IRA in many of its views and members, also condemned the attack stating, 'I am totally horrified by this action. I condemn it without any equivocation whatsoever.' Meanwhile even Martin McGuinness, a former IRA leader and at the time a Sinn Féin member called the act of violence 'appalling'. This widespread condemnation and attention to the bombing led to serious and quick action from the UK's and Ireland's governments with strict anti-terrorism laws. This included the UK's Criminal Justice (Terrorism and Conspiracy) Act of 1998, which allowed the government to try conspiracies that would lead to offences abroad, and Ireland's counterterrorist amendment to the Offences against the State Act, demonstrating the consequences of excessive civilian targeting in democratic settings. Public interest in the Omagh bombing (see Photo 12.2) was reignited in July 2021 when a judge ruled that the attack could have been prevented by the security services, and called for new investigations on both sides of the Irish border.

PHOTO 12.2 The Omagh Bomb Memorial Gardens in County Tyrone, Northern Ireland.

Similar dynamics have prevailed in other cases in which terrorist targeting has resulted in levels of casualties deemed excessive by local populations. In the wake of the attacks on 9/11 in the US (see also Case Study 11.1) and 7/7 in the UK in 2005, both governments escalated restrictions on civil liberties and expanded the reach of their surveillance practices. Likewise, Chechen attacks against Russian apartment buildings and PKK attacks against soft targets in Turkey proved counterproductive for the groups' goals.

Rather than displaying power and compelling concessions from governments, these attacks enhanced public resolve and tolerance for strengthened anti-terrorism practices. Thus, these attacks and reactions to them show that terrorist organizations must be cautious with their attacks on civilians. They must be able to balance the level of attack in order to avoid a hard push-back from the government and the public, while still striking enough fear into these parties to gain the organization's desired concessions.

QUESTIONS

1. Why effect did the Omagh attack have on public sentiments?
2. When will civilian targeting and casualties help terrorists to achieve their goals and when will they undermine those goals?

12.6 CONCLUSION

This chapter has provided an overview of theoretical and empirical models of terrorist target selection. In the process of doing so, we discussed scholarly debates and empirical trends that highlight important aspects of the August 2019 El Paso terrorist attack, as well as the campaigns of groups such as ETA and the IRA. As part of this discussion, we have explored the targeting of soft targets, the role of public fear both in terms of accelerating terrorists' gains and undermining their mission, and the claim that democracies are especially vulnerable to terrorist targeting.

The most important take away points are as follows: Terrorist violence is rarely random. Targets are selected as part of a decision-making process that is purposive and intentional, however dreadful its loss of life may be. This decision-making process appears to centre upon organizations selecting targets with a view toward eliciting a fearful response from the broader public. This is intended to be one means of trying to force a government into offering some policy concessions. Finally, the growing familiarity of violence in many societies means that violent organizations appear now to have to escalate the deadliness of their attacks to elicit sufficient responses from the public. At the same time, however, evidence supports that attacks against the public are rarely useful in helping groups to achieve their goals. Rather, historical records suggest that terrorist targeting of military interests overseas might be most likely to prove effective.

DISCUSSION QUESTIONS

1. What are the most common targets of terrorist violence?
2. Why do you think that terrorists typically select these targets?
3. Why are democracies often considered vulnerable targets to terrorist violence?
4. What is the difference between soft and hard targets?
5. What is the role of fear in the terrorism process?

 Visit the online resources for pointers on how to answer the discussion questions, links to useful web sources, and guidance on accessing databases:
www.oup.com/he/Wilson-Muro1e

GUIDE TO FURTHER READING

The following five recommended further readings provide a solid overview of the theoretical and empirical trends and puzzles discussed in this chapter. They also serve the purpose of providing a connection between our discussion of the targeting decisions taken by violent groups and the broader causes and consequences of their campaigns. Each reading builds fundamentally upon the rationalist or instrumental logic that underlies our discussion in this chapter.

Enders, W. and Sandler, T. *The Political Economy of Terrorism*. Cambridge University Press. **Enders and Sandler provide a series of econometric and political analyses of trends in terrorism over time and space. Their study weaves together a series of prior studies addressing the impact of new policies and watershed events upon the frequency of terrorist violence and the efficacy of government antiterrorism policies.**

Findley, M. G. and Young, J. K. (2012) 'Terrorism and civil war: A spatial and temporal approach to a conceptual problem'. *Perspectives on Politics*, 10(2), 285–305. **Findley and Young provide an empirical investigation of the overlap between violence observed in civil wars and terrorist campaigns. They show that a high proportion of so-called terrorist attacks are carried out by actors engaged in broader campaigns of violence against their governments.**

Hoffman, B. (1993) 'Terrorist targeting: Tactics, trends, and potentialities'. *Terrorism and Political Violence* 5(2): 12–29. **Hoffman provides an assessment of the effect of tactical and technological innovations. The study shows that while many terrorist organizations are radical in their politics, they prove to be consistently quite conservative in their operations.**

Kydd, A. H. and Walter, B. F. (2006) 'The strategies of terrorism'. *International Security*, 31(1), 49–80. **Kydd and Walter conceptualize and contextualize five common strategies of terrorism in the modern era: attrition, intimidation, provocation, spoiling, and outbidding. Their study demonstrates the conditions under which each strategy is employed by terrorist groups, as well as the variety of methods governments employ to try to counter each strategic use of violence.**

Nemeth, S. C., Mauslein, J. A., and Stapley, C. (2014) 'The Primacy of the Local: Identifying Terrorist Hot Spots Using Geographic Information Systems'. *The Journal of Politics*, 76(2), 304–317. **Nemeth et al. provide an analysis of the local-level correlates of violent terrorist events globally. Their analysis demonstrates that there are significant differences in the causes of violent events in democratic and autocratic states. For example, terrorism occurs in closer proximity to capital cities in democracies, as compared to international borders in autocracies.**

REFERENCES

Abrahms, Max (2006) 'Why Terrorism Does Not Work'. *International Security*, 31: 42–78.

Abrahms, M., Ward, M., and Kennedy, R. (2018) 'Explaining Civilian Attacks: Terrorist Networks, Principal-Agent Problems and Target Selection'. *Perspectives On Terrorism*, 12(1).

Bibes, P. (2001) 'Transnational Organized Crime and Terrorism: Colombia, a Case Study'. *Journal of Contemporary Criminal Justice*, 17 (3): 243–258.

Braithwaite, A. (2013) 'The Logic of Public Fear in Terrorism and Counter-terrorism'. *Journal of Police and Criminal Psychology*, 28 (2): 95–101.

Braithwaite, A. (2015) 'Transnational Terrorism as an Unintended Consequence of a Military Footprint'. *Security Studies*, 24 (2): 349–375.

Bruce Ware, R. (2005) 'Revisiting Russia's Apartment Block Blasts'. *Journal of Slavic Military Studies*, 18 (4): 599–606.

Chenoweth, E. (2013) 'Terrorism and Democracy'. *Annual Review of Political Science*, 16: 355–378.

Conrad, C. R., Conrad, J. and Young, J. K. (2014) 'Tyrants and Terrorism: Why some Autocrats are Terrorized While Others are not'. *International Studies Quarterly*, 58 (3): 539–549.

Crenshaw, M. (1981) 'The Causes of Terrorism'. *Comparative Politics*, 13 (4): 379–399.

Crenshaw, M. (1998) 'The Logic of Terrorism: Terrorist Behaviour as a Product of Strategic Choice', in W. Reich (Ed.), *Origins of Terrorism: Psychologies, Ideologies, Theologies, States of Mind*, Washington, DC: Woodrow Wilson Center Press, 7–24.

Enders, W. and Sandler, T. (2006) 'Distribution of Transnational Terrorism Among Countries by Income Class and Geography After 9/11'. *International Studies Quarterly*, 50 (2): 367–393.

Enders, W. and Sandler, T. (2011) *The Political Economy of Terrorism*. Cambridge University Press.

Enders, W., Sandler, T. and Parise, G. F. (1992) 'An Econometric Analysis of the Impact of Terrorism on Tourism'. *Kyklos*, 45 (4): 531–554.

Eyerman, J. (1998) 'Terrorism and Democratic States: Soft Targets or Accessible Systems'. *International Interactions*, 24 (2): 151–170.

Fearon, J. D. and Laitin, D. D. (2003) 'Ethnicity, Insurgency, and Civil War'. *American Political Science Review*, 97 (1): 75–90.

Findley, M. G. and Young, J. K. (2012) 'Terrorism and Civil War: A Spatial and Temporal Approach to a Conceptual Problem'. *Perspectives on Politics*, 10 (2): 285–305.

Fortna, Virginia Page. (2015) 'Do Terrorists Win? Rebels' Use of Terrorism and Civil War Outcomes'. *International Organization*, 69 (3) 519–556.

Gaibulloev, K. and Sandler, T. (2008) 'Growth Consequences of Terrorism in Western Europe'. *Kyklos*, 61 (3): 411–424.

Gould, E. D. and Klor, E. F. (2010) 'Does Terrorism Work?' *Quarterly Journal of Economics*, 125 (4): 1459–1510

Hewitt, Christopher (1993) *The Consequences of Political Violence*. Aldershot: Dartmouth.

Heymann, P. B. (2003). *Terrorism, Freedom, and Security: Winning Without War*. MIT press.

Hoffman, B. (1993) 'Terrorist Targeting: Tactics, Trends, and Potentialities'. *Terrorism and Political Violence*, 5 (2): 12–29.

Hoffman, Bruce (2006) *Inside Terrorism*. New York: Columbia University Press.

Horgan, J. G. (2004) *The Psychology of Terrorism*. Routledge.

Kaldor, M. (2013) *New and Old Wars: Organized Violence in a Global Era*. John Wiley & Sons.

Kydd, A. H. and Walter, B. F. (2006) 'The Strategies of Terrorism'. *International Security*, 31 (1): 49–80.

Li, Q. (2005) 'Does Democracy Promote or Reduce Transnational Terrorist Incidents?' *Journal of Conflict Resolution*, 49 (2): 278–297.

Long, D. E. (1990) *The Anatomy of Terrorism* (5). New York: Free Press.

Lutz, J. M. and Lutz, B. J. (2006) 'Terrorism as Economic warfare'. *Global Economy Journal*, 6 (2): 1850086.

Marineau, J., Pascoe, H., Braithwaite, A., Findley, M. and Young, J. (2020) 'The Local Geography of Transnational Terrorism'. *Conflict Management and Peace Science*, 37 (3): 350–381.

Merari, A. (1993) 'Terrorism as a Strategy of Insurgency'. *Terrorism and Political Violence*, 5 (4): 213–251.

Nacos, B. (2016) *Mass-mediated Terrorism: Mainstream and Digital Media in Terrorism and Counterterrorism*. Rowman & Littlefield.

National Consortium for the Study of Terrorism and Responses to Terrorism (START) (2018) Global Terrorism Database [Data file]. Retrieved from https://www.start.umd.edu/gtd

Nemeth, S. C., Mauslein, J. A. and Stapley, C. (2014) 'The Primacy of the Local: Identifying Terrorist Hot Spots Using Geographic Information Systems'. *The Journal of Politics*, 76 (2): 304–317.

Onuoha, F. C. (2008) 'Oil Pipeline Sabotage in Nigeria: Dimensions, Actors and Implications for National Security'. *African Security Studies*, 17 (3): 99–115.

Pape, R. A. (2006) *Dying to Win: The Strategic Logic of Suicide Terrorism*. Random House Incorporated.

Piazza, J. A. (2008) 'Incubators of Terror: Do Failed and Failing States Promote Transnational Terrorism?' *International Studies Quarterly*, 52 (3): 469–488.

Piazza, J. A. (2013) 'Regime Age and Terrorism: Are New Democracies Prone to Terrorism?' *International Interactions*, 39 (2): 246–263.

Posen, B. R. (2001/2) 'The Struggle Against Terrorism: Grand Strategy, Strategy, and Tactics'. *International Security*, 26 (3): 39–55.

Rid, T. and Hecker, M. (2009) 'The Terror Fringe'. *Policy Review*, (158): 3.

Sattar, D. (2003) *Darkness and Dawn: The Rise of the Russian Criminal State*. New Haven: Yale University Press.

Savun, B. and Phillips, B. J. (2009) 'Democracy, Foreign Policy, and Terrorism'. *Journal of Conflict Resolution*, 53 (6): 878–904.

Stanton, J. A. (2013) 'Terrorism in the Context of Civil War'. *The Journal of Politics*, 75 (4): 1009–1022.

Tilly, C. (2004) 'Terror, Terrorism, Terrorists'. *Sociological Theory*, 22 (1): 5–13.

Wilkinson, P. (2015) *Terrorism & the Liberal State*. Macmillan International Higher Education.

Wilson, M. C. and Piazza, J. A. (2013) 'Autocracies and Terrorism: Conditioning Effects of Authoritarian Regime Type on Terrorist Attacks'. *American Journal of Political Science*, 57 (4): 941–955.

CHAPTER 13

Longevity of Terrorist Groups

LEENA MALKKI

■ CHAPTER SUMMARY

Why do some terrorist groups endure longer than others? This chapter summarizes the findings of academic research on the average lifespan of terrorist groups, as well as on the characteristics typical of those groups, and their operational environment, that remain involved in terrorism for a longer period of time. A large number of groups do not survive their first year, while the average lifespan of terrorist organizations is around 8–9 years. The characteristics of the state in which terrorist groups operate—regime type, for example—appear largely insignificant. Larger groups have a longer lifespan, as do those that form alliances. The chapter also looks at what kind of considerations are at play when groups decide on whether to continue with terrorist attacks. It ends with a reflection on whether the longevity of a terrorist group is a sign of success.

13.1 INTRODUCTION

Many of those terrorist groups that have regularly appeared in the headlines have existed for years or decades. Al-Qaeda, for example, traces its origins to the late 1980s. The IRA and ETA engaged in such violence for decades before agreeing to lay down their weapons. Not all terrorist groups, however, endure this long. Even a brief look at the Global Terrorism Database (GTD, see also Chapter 7) reveals a plethora of terrorist groups that one has likely never heard of, and which only existed for a few months or years.

Why do some terrorist groups endure longer than others? What is the average lifespan of a terrorist group? What motivates groups to sustain their involvement in terrorism? There is a growing body of literature that addresses these questions. Many of these studies are quantitative in nature, and use statistical methods to analyse the longevity of terrorist groups and the factors that influence such longevity.

This chapter begins by looking at what these studies tell us about the average longevity of terrorist groups, as well as what kind of characteristics are typical of those groups, and their operational environment, that stay involved in terrorism for longer periods of time.

After that, the chapter turns to studies on terrorist decision-making in order to discern those factors that motivate groups to carry on with their violent attacks. While the processes and factors that lead to terrorism have been extensively studied, and how terrorism ends has similarly received an increasing amount of scholarly focus, less attention has been explicitly directed towards studying why terrorism continues. Even so, research on terrorist decision-making and the internal dynamics of terrorist groups provide insight into what kind of motivations, needs and considerations may be relevant. The chapter ends with a reflection on whether the longevity of a terrorist group is a sign of success.

13.2 DEFINING LONGEVITY OF TERRORIST GROUPS

First, it is necessary to look more closely at how the 'longevity of terrorist groups' is understood by research. Even though this expression leads to thinking about organizational survival, it is not the duration of terrorist groups but instead the longevity of terrorist activity that forms the main topic of interest here.

This becomes clear when looking at how a 'terrorist group' is usually defined when its longevity is measured by research. Most statistical studies employ what Brian Phillips (2015a) calls an inclusive definition. By this definition, 'terrorist groups are subnational political organizations that use terrorism' (231). There are also studies that use a more exclusive definition or, in other words, place additional limitations to what groups are included in the analysis. This is done by, for example, excluding groups that control territory or use terrorism only sporadically. What unites both inclusive and exclusive definitions is that the terrorist group is only understood to be terrorist in nature during the time it uses terrorism. It becomes a terrorist group with the first terrorist attack and ceases to be one when such attacks are definitively ceased.

This means that what is usually analysed as the 'longevity of a terrorist group' is, in fact, the *longevity of involvement in terrorism under the name of a particular group*, not the longevity of the group's existence as such. There are numerous examples of groups that have continued to exist after their terrorist campaigns ended. This is demonstrated by studies on how terrorism ends (e.g. Cronin 2009). Groups that transform from politically motivated actors to criminal organizations are one example of the phenomenon.

> ### KEY CONCEPTS
>
> **Longevity** Longevity of a terrorist group is usually understood by research as longevity of involvement in terrorism under the name of a particular group, beginning from its first attack and ending with the last. The group may well exist before and after the use of terrorism, but is regarded as a terrorist group only for the period of time during which it conducts terrorist attacks.

Likewise, many groups have existed for years before deciding to resort to terrorism. The ETA (Euskadi Ta Askatasuna or Basque homeland and freedom, see also Case Study 12.1), for example, was founded already in 1959 but committed its first terrorist attack nearly a decade later, in 1968. Certain long-lived organizations have only perpetrated one or two attacks, thereby qualifying for a very short lifespan as a 'terrorist group'.

The relationship between a group and a terrorist campaign is, furthermore, not altogether clear-cut in the sense that a group might take a different name when claiming attacks, yet these attacks would nevertheless form a part of one and the same terrorist campaign. Indeed, is not uncommon for groups to temporarily use other names to claim attacks. It is also not uncommon that a group might cease to exist but the terrorist campaign be continued by a successor organization (Miller 2016: 7; Malkki 2010: 19–20). Splintering is very common in terrorist groups (Jones and Libicki 2008). It is also worth noting that ceasing to use terrorism is rarely a sudden event but rather a long process. It is, indeed, quite possible that the decision to stop using terrorism comes well after an attack that, in fact, turns out to have been the last one. For example, The Red Army Faction (see also Case Studies 6.1 and 9.1), a German far-left group which started its terrorist campaign in the early 1970s, officially disbanded in 1998. It had, however, conducted its last terrorist attack already in the early 1990s (Moghadam 2012).

> **KEY CONCEPTS**
>
> Are all groups that commit terrorist acts automatically considered as such by research? Below is a summary of three common ways to define the criteria of a 'terrorist group':
>
> **Inclusive definition** Any subnational political organization that uses terrorism
>
> **Action-based exclusive definition** Any subnational political organization that engages primarily or regularly in terrorism
>
> **Actor-based exclusive definition** Any subnational political organization that uses terrorism and does not hold territory
>
> Source: Phillips 2015a

13.3 LONGEVITY OF TERRORIST GROUPS

How long do terrorist groups endure, or to be more precise, how long do groups continue to use terrorism? The possibilities for analysing this question have improved during the 2000s with the development of new and more extensive databases on terrorism.

Researchers had concluded, already before the publication of recent studies drawing on large datasets, that the use of terrorism did not last very long on average. The most famous 'guestimate' was brought forth by David C. Rapoport in the early 1990s: 'modern terrorist organizations, in contrast to their ancient counterparts, do not survive long. Perhaps as many as 90 per cent last less than a year. Nearly half of those which persist beyond the first year are out of existence by the tenth.' (Rapoport 1992: 1067).

Rapoport provided no source for this claim. It was most likely not meant to be taken literally, but rather as a suggestion of just how short-lived most terrorist groups might be.

During the recent decade, new studies have been conducted that allow us to evaluate this claim against empirical evidence. These studies show that terrorist groups do indeed face a common phenomenon called the *liability of newness*. This means that the failure rates of new groups are higher than those of groups that have existed for a longer period of time (Young and Dugan 2014). A significant number of terrorist groups—like most businesses—cease their operations during the first year. The per centage, however, is not as high as 90 per cent. Different studies have produced varying figures that range from 25 to 74 per cent of the groups discontinuing their involvement in terrorism within the first year. The results depend partly on the inclusiveness of the dataset used. Some researchers have excluded the most sporadic uses of terrorism from their study. The average per centage of dropouts during the first year across different studies is 52 per cent (Phillips 2019).

Among the studies that have produced the highest figures are those that draw upon data from the Global Terrorism Database (GTD), as shown in Figures 13.1 and 13.2. Erin Miller (2016), for example, studied 2437 groups included in the database. These groups

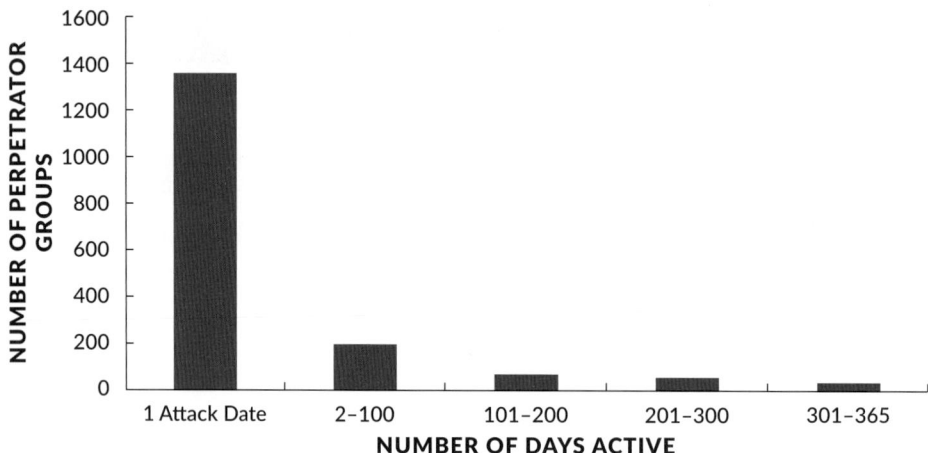

FIGURE 13.1 Time span of terrorist violence, perpetrator groups active < 365 days. Source: Miller 2016: 11.

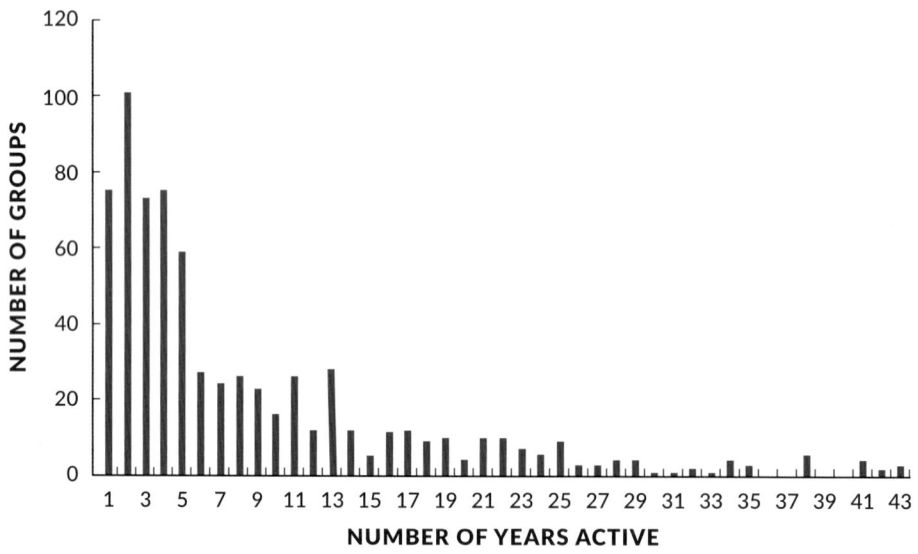

FIGURE 13.2 Time span of terrorist violence, perpetrator groups active > 365 days. Source: Miller 2016: 13.

were active between the years 1970 and 2013. Her analysis reveals that 71 per cent of these groups (1726) engaged in terrorism for less than a year. A large majority of such short-lived groups (1198 groups) have only one recorded attack in the Global Terrorism Database. Those studies that report lower percentages of groups with less than a one-year lifespan use datasets from which the most sporadic uses of terrorism have been excluded.

With respect to those cases where terrorism was used for less than a year, many concern groups of which little more is known than the (typically small-scale) attack(s) that they have committed. It would appear, in short, that starting terrorism in any sustained fashion is relatively difficult.

Whether modern terrorist groups have a shorter lifespan than their 'ancient counterparts', as Rapoport also claims, remains unverified. Since virtually all larger datasets begin from circa 1968–1970, it is currently not possible to evaluate this claim by means of systematic empirical data.

What about the lifespan of those groups that carry out terrorist attacks for more than a year? Rapoport also suggests that over half of these groups do not endure for ten years. While per centages vary from one dataset to the other, figures generally do support Rapoport's claim. According to Erin Miller's study (2016), for example, 55 per cent of those groups that use terrorism for more than one year do not engage in such activity for a time period that exceeds 5 years. The average life span stands at 8.7 years.

While groups on average do not engage in terrorism for long periods of time, a number have perpetrated acts of terror for decades. Among the most long-lived terrorist groups (during the period covered by the databases) are the Provisional Irish Republican Army (PIRA) in Northern Ireland, Euskadi Ta Askatasuna (ETA) in Spain, the Popular Front for the Liberation of Palestine (PFLP) in Israel/Palestine, the Ku Klux Klan in the United States (see Photo 13.1),

PHOTO 13.1 The Ku Klux Klan (KKK) are a long-lasting terrorist group, pictured here receiving new members in the 1920s.

and the LTTE (aka Tamil Tigers) in Sri Lanka (Blomberg et al. 2011: 445). The overall number of terrorist attacks perpetrated, as well as the distribution of such attacks over time, vary significantly between these groups. While the IRA and ETA, for example, have carried out a high number of attacks, others such as the PFLP have perpetrated considerably fewer recorded attacks under their own name (Miller 2016: 14–15).

Al-Qaeda usually does not make it on the list of the most durable terrorist groups as it is a relative newcomer compared to those organizations that have existed since the late 1960s or early 1970s—the period of time from where the most widely-used and extensive databases begin. It is, however, without question among the most durable terrorist groups of recent decades. The first recorded terrorist incident for Hamas in the Global Terrorism Database is from 1989 while terrorist attacks by Hezbollah date back to the early 1980s. Islamic State of Iraq and the Levant (ISIL) has similarly shown significant persistence. It operated under different names (Monotheism and Jihad, al-Qaeda in Iraq, and Mujahideen Shura Council) before adopting the title ISIL in 2013. The group is also called Islamic State in Iraq and Syria (ISIS).

13.4 FACTORS INFLUENCING LONGEVITY

How can we explain why some groups use terrorism for longer periods of time than others? Conducting statistical analyses on the relationship between the lifespan of a terrorist group and various other factors has been the most common way of approaching this question. This has meant, in effect, investigating what kind of group characteristics, and those of the operating environment, seem to go together with the longevity of terrorist groups. In this way, researchers have sought to uncover the factors explaining the longevity of some terrorist groups over others.

13.4.1 State characteristics

It seems logical to expect that a terrorist group's longevity depends on the kind of state in which it functions, for example whether the state is a democracy or autocracy. However, the research results so far have been mixed. Studies have generally demonstrated that the relationship between the longevity of a terrorist group and various indicators of state characteristics is not very strong. Moreover, different studies have produced somewhat conflicting results with regard to specific state characteristics.

The most typical state characteristics included in the statistical analyses are those related to regime type, state capabilities, repression, population and geographical location.

Regime type does not appear to correlate with the duration of a group's use of terrorism. In other words, there does not appear to be any significant and systematic difference between democracies, authoritarian regimes and other regime types with respect to how long groups in their territory persist in the use of terrorism (e.g. Phillips 2015b; Young and

Dugan 2014). This may come as a surprise, as countering terrorism has often been considered a particularly complicated challenge to democracies.

State capabilities refers to how well resourced and effective at governing the state is. State capabilities are included in the analysis of longevity, as they are assumed to influence the effectiveness of counterterrorism measures which, in turn, have an effect on the ability of groups to perpetrate terrorist attacks. The more capable the state is in monitoring and intervening in the activities of a terrorist group, such thinking holds, the more difficult it is expected that the continued use of terrorist attacks will be.

So far, there is no clear empirical evidence for the relevance of state capabilities. However, the results should be treated with caution due to methodological challenges. There are no ready indicators for measuring counterterrorism capabilities, so researchers have had to rely on indirect ways of measurement. Such measures have included Gross Domestic Product (GDP), measures of the state's ability to extract tax revenue from its citizens, and measures concerning the severity of civil conflicts (e.g. Piazza and Piazza 2020). It is not clear how suitable these measures are.

Analyses have thus far consistently demonstrated that GDP does not appear to be of relevance (e.g. Blomberg et al. 2011; Phillips 2015b). There is some evidence, though, that—somewhat surprisingly—the state's weak ability to extract tax revenues, which is used as a measure of state weakness, reduces the longevity of terrorist groups (Piazza and Piazza 2020). Weak and failed states therefore do not necessarily provide a favourable environment for maintaining terrorist groups. Since these factors are not particularly good indicators of counterterrorism capabilities, the results should be treated as preliminary observations.

Repression has typically been studied by using the Political Terror Scale which measures the use of violence by the state. Again, the results have been somewhat mixed. Particularly interesting are the findings of a study conducted by Ursula E. Daxecker and Michael L. Hess (2013). According to their study, the effects of repression on the longevity of the use of terrorism depend on the regime type so that repression shortens the duration of a group's involvement in terrorism in authoritarian regimes, but not in democratic regimes.

Daxecker and Hess suggest that this correlation derives from how repression affects a government's legitimacy. Democracies are more dependent on public legitimacy, which repression is likely to hurt. This backlash effect may in turn increase support for the terrorist group subjected to repression. Daxecker and Hess also suggest that repression may decrease the willingness of local communities to cooperate with the authorities, as they fear that the potential suspects would not be treated fairly. More authoritarian regimes, however, do not rely on public support to the same degree, and the backlash effect of repression is therefore less significant. Daxecker and Hess furthermore point out that compliance with the authorities is more likely to be based on the fear of punishment than the perception of legitimacy, and repression is therefore unlikely to weaken it.

What is good to keep in mind in this context is that the new surveillance technology may be significantly changing the counterterrorism landscape. Especially new technologies that utilize artificial intelligence, such as face recognition, provide new powerful ways for governments to monitor citizens. Extensive surveillance systems are easier to introduce for autocracies than for democracies which are constrained by privacy laws and the need to maintain government's legitimacy. In fact, there is evidence that autocracies have already become more resilient against protest movements (Kendall-Taylor et al. 2020).

Population is the indicator that has perhaps produced the most consistent results. Most studies demonstrate a correlation between a large population and the longer duration of the use of terrorism (e.g. Phillips 2015b; Blomberg et al. 2011). Why this is so has not received an explanation thus far. The composition of the population may also matter. Blomberg et al. (2011) find that the use of terrorism tends to continue for a longer period of time in those countries with an intermediate level of ethnic diversity than in those that are ethnically very homogeneous or heterogeneous.

Geographic location also seems to correlate with the longevity of terrorism's use, although this correlation is most likely explained by other factors. Groups which operate in the Middle East and North Africa survive longer than groups in Europe, Latin America and North America (Blomberg et al. 2011).

In sum, exploring the relationship between the longevity of terrorist groups and state characteristics has thus far failed to provide strong and systematic evidence about the conditions under which terrorist groups endure. While regime type as such does not appear to matter, repression does, and in ways that are conditioned by regime type. The average lifespan of a terrorist group tends to be longer in those countries which have larger population and more ethnic diversity. The lack of systematic research results does not necessarily mean that the state characteristics do not matter, but rather that their effect is not systematic in a way that would allow for global generalization.

13.4.2 Group characteristics

Besides state characteristics, the analyses on longevity have often looked at group characteristics. Among these are ideology, capabilities, group size and involvement in crime.

Ideology is the group characteristic that has been subject to the greatest amount of analyses and hypotheses. It has been commonly argued that nationalist-separatist (and later religious) groups have more staying power than left-wing or right-wing groups. So common is this claim, in fact, that it is treated as more or less conventional wisdom by terrorism studies. The argument has been furthered, among others, by Bruce Hoffman in his widely read book *Inside Terrorism* (first edition 1998, third edition 2017). According to Hoffman, nationalist-separatist and religious terrorist groups tend to survive longer because 'they are able to draw sustenance and support from an existing constituency, namely, the fellow members of their national or ethnic group or religious persuasion' (Hoffman 2017: 255). It is believed that recruiting successive generations of members and supporters is easier for such groups. Secondly, Hoffman connects the longevity of nationalist-separatist groups with their goals and vision for the future. While the nationalist-separatist groups' visions of the desired state of affairs are easily understood and communicated, this has not generally been the case with left-wing groups in particular.

How well does the above claim withstand empirical scrutiny? Thus far, the results have been mixed. Some studies (such as Vittori 2009) find no support for the relevance of ideological orientation, while others (Phillips 2015b; Acosta 2014) have established that groups with an ethnic motivation are likely to endure for longer periods of time than those groups without such a motivation. Still others (Blomberg et al. 2011) have found that religious groups survive longer than nationalist, left-wing or right-wing groups. Among the body of research that has produced this result is a study by Hou et al. (2020), which uses a dataset that covers the time period closest to the present day (1970–2016). There is also some evidence that those terrorist groups which have a clear ideological identity survive longer than those which are more hybrid in their ideology and identity (Olzak 2016).

It is important to keep in mind that an overwhelming majority of current religious terrorist groups are of a relatively recent origin. This means that they are unavoidably underrepresented among those groups with the longest lifespan that are included in the period of time covered by most quantitative analyses.

Group capabilities are also often assumed to influence staying power. It is believed that groups with greater capabilities will be able to continue perpetrating terrorist attacks for a longer period of time than those with less capabilities. Such a belief derives from the perception that if a group has more expertise and resources at its disposal, it will be more resilient in the face of countermeasures. Empirical tests of this claim have usually measured group capabilities through such factors as the ability to conduct complicated or multiple attacks, use various methods of action (bombings, kidnappings, etc.) or operate in multiple countries. The results demonstrate, indeed, that those groups which have been capable of engaging in these more demanding forms of operation have also been likely to survive for a longer period of time (e.g. Young and Dugan 2014; Blomberg et al. 2011; Vittori 2009; Hou et al. 2020).

Group (peak) size shows similar results. The overwhelming majority of studies demonstrate that groups with more members are likely to continue terrorist attacks for a longer period of time.

How these results should be interpreted is another question. Based on these studies alone, it is not clear why group capabilities and size seem to enhance longevity, or even whether the dynamics at play are of an inverse nature. In other words, whether it is actually the group's longevity that tends to increase its size and capabilities. What is clear, in any case, is that larger and more capable groups survive for a longer period of time.

Finally, *involvement in crime* is also among those group characteristics assumed to influence the staying power of terrorist groups. A study by James A. Piazza and Scott Piazza (2020) points to the direction that 'engagement in criminal activities seems to enhance rather than degrade terrorist group lifespan' (18). Here too, it is unclear what kind of causal relationship exists between these two issues. This means that it is not clear whether involvement in crime makes involvement in terrorism last longer—or the other way around. As Piazza and Piazza themselves point out, it may also be that involvement in crime is simply more typical of terrorist groups that have operated for a longer period of time.

CASE STUDY 13.1

LTTE in Sri Lanka

Liberation Tigers of Tamil Eelam (LTTE), as shown in Photo 13.2, was formed in 1976 and continued until 2009 when it was unexpectedly defeated by the Sri Lankan army. It was one of the most durable groups that have used terrorism in recent decades.

PHOTO 13.2 Tamil Eelam Flag from the LTTE era.

The LTTE emerged as part of a larger Tamil political mobilization for an independent homeland in the 1970s. This mobilization was sparked by policies that favoured the Sinhalese majority over the Tamil minority, and were introduced after Sri Lanka gained independence in 1948. The ethnic and linguistic tensions eventually led to a series of violent conflicts known as the Eelam wars (1983–2009).

When the LTTE was founded, it was one of many Tamil militant groups that were all in the margins of Tamil politics. This started to change quickly after the conflict escalated in 1983 and new recruits flooded to Tamil militant organizations. In the latter half of the 1980s, the LTTE managed to outplay almost all other militant groups and become a major Tamil political and military force.

The LTTE used guerrilla tactics combined with terrorist attacks and even waged conventional war against the Sri Lankan armed forces. It is particularly well known for being one of the first modern organizations to conduct suicide missions. The LTTE's 'Black Tigers' committed their first suicide attack in 1987. The most famous victims of its suicide operations were the president of Sri Lanka, Ranasinghe Premasada, in 1993, and the prime minister of India, Rajiv Gandhi, in 1991.

The LTTE had considerable resources at its disposal. At its height, it was estimated to have 10,000 armed combatants. The Tamil diaspora played a significant part in financing and facilitating its operations. The LTTE also received support and training from India in the 1980s. During the 1990s, the LTTE managed to build an impressive infrastructure in its sanctuary areas, including schools, health care, taxation and military training.

The LTTE's resilience derives in large part from a skilful leadership that allowed it to tap into the Tamil mobilization and build a coherent and disciplined organization. Establishing such an organization was initially facilitated by the fact that it was built on a small and close-knit social base. The LTTE leadership came from the same subset of the same small caste, so it was built strongly on pre-existing social networks. After 1983, when the Tamil militant organizations were flooded with new potential recruits and received Indian help, these foundations helped it to manage growth. At the same time, other militant organizations suffered from internal disputes and fragmentation. These internal disputes made it easier for the LTTE to wipe out virtually all of its competitors during the late 1980s.

The LTTE's staying power and cohesion also derived from its internal culture and socialization of new recruits. The LTTE developed its own distinctive culture during the 1980s including symbols, various kinds of rituals, and narratives praising individual discipline, and the mythologization of its leaders.

Finally, the LTTE has widely been credited as one of the most innovative terrorist and insurgent organizations in recent decades. The use of suicide operations is one sign of its capacity to innovate. Its tactical and strategic choices also show that it was able to navigate its political, social, and security context much more skilfully than other Tamil militant organizations (Staniland 2014).

QUESTIONS

1. Compare the LTTE and the research results presented in the section 'Factors Influencing Longevity'. How does the longevity of the LTTE support these findings?
2. Compare the LTTE and the research results presented in the section 'Factors Influencing Longevity'. How does the longevity of the LTTE contradict these findings?

There are also grounds to think that involvement in crime prolongs the lifespan of terrorist organizations. Support for this thinking comes from literature on the 'crime-terror nexus', in other words the literature that examines the overlap and interrelationship between terrorism and organized crime (see e.g. Felhab-Brown 2019). It is not uncommon for terrorist groups to finance their activities through bank robberies, extortion, trafficking or drug trade, for example, but the extent of their involvement in such activities varies. In some cases, the groups that commit terrorist attacks have also become extensively involved in illicit economies. In such cases, involvement in crime can help the group to build more political support and freedom of action. Especially in the areas that are poor and where the state is weak, the actors involved in illicit economies can provide the local population with employment opportunities and services that would otherwise not exist. This includes, for example, social services and the provision of security. This can strengthen the group's legitimacy and resources, and thereby its chances of survival.

To sum up, groups that are larger and have better resources in their disposal tend to continue terrorism for a longer time, as do those that are involved in crime. It is not clear, however, whether longevity results from large size, good resources, and involvement in crime, or vice versa. There is also some evidence to suggest that nationalist-separatist and religious terrorist groups operate for a longer period of time.

13.4.3 Intergroup relations

Terrorist groups do not exist in a vacuum. Instead, they often operate in an environment shared with other terrorist groups. These groups may be political enemies that fight each other. On the other hand, they can also represent the same cause or movement, in which case they may cooperate or compete for supporters and resources. All this can have an effect on their decision to continue with the use of terrorist tactics, and the resources that they are able to allocate for such a purpose.

With respect to competition between different terrorist groups, empirical research has thus far produced somewhat mixed results. According to a study by Joseph K. Young and Laura Dugan (2014), the higher the number of terrorist groups is in the country, the less likely these groups are to survive. However, the group that can be considered 'top dog' in its national context has a much higher likelihood of survival—competition, in fact, makes its failure less likely. A good example of this is the Liberation Tigers of Tamil Eelam (LTTE) in Sri Lanka, which defeated all its competitor organizations over time (see also Case Study 13.1). What needs to be remembered, however, is that the above study does not seem to pay attention to the nature of the relationship between groups that operate in the same context—in other words, whether they compete against each other, or whether their relationship is rather one of collaboration (see Miller 2016: 8).

Brian Phillips (2015b), for his part, has analysed the impact that terrorist groups may have on each other by focusing specifically on the violent rivalry between them. His study indicates that violent rivalry between opposing groups (inter-field violent rivalry) increases the longevity of terrorist groups. Intra-field violent rivalry between groups that are part of the same social movement does not have this effect. In other words, if a terrorist group has a rival that represents an opposing political standpoint, this increases its longevity. If the group, on the other hand, has a rival that represents the same cause, this is not the case.

The studies by Young and Dugan, as well as by Phillips, are purely quantitative and do not produce more detailed evidence on the causal mechanisms behind their observations. Phillips does, however, provide a good discussion of what may lie behind his findings.

According to Phillips, one possible explanation is that if the group has rivals, it may encourage hitherto unaffiliated supporters to become active. The competition with other groups can also function as an impetus and accelerator for learning and innovation. This pattern is also detectable in the relationship between terrorist groups and security authorities, with both parties trying to circumvent and counter new innovations by the other. As Phillips points out, this is also in line with what we known about firms and social movements among which competition is also known to drive innovation.

Furthermore, violent rivalries produce new incentives for existing and potential participants in terrorist groups. Rivalries between groups can act as an additional purpose and motivation for participation (purposive incentives). Violent confrontations with a rival can also increase the sense of togetherness between participants (solidary incentives). Finally, there are so-called spoiler situations in which the opposition to a peace treaty by one terrorist group may lead another one to continue its involvement in terrorism for a longer time than would have otherwise been the case. While there is quite a lot of evidence of such patterns in individual cases, there is a need for comparative research that would analyse their prevalence—and identify other potential causal mechanisms that concern violent rivalries between terrorist groups.

Another type of a relationship that terrorist groups may have with other actors is an *alliance*. Large groups are more likely to form alliances than small ones. Alliances are most likely to be formed with other groups of a similar ideological orientation (e.g. Asal et al. 2016).

Increasing the chances of survival has long been perceived as a major reason for terrorist groups to cooperate with each other (see e.g. Karmon 2005). Groups with allies do indeed tend to use terrorism for a longer period of time (Pearson et al. 2017; Phillips 2014). This effect, however, seems to be limited only to those groups that operate in more capable and more autocratic states which, assumingly, are the most difficult setting for such groups to operate in. One explanation for this is that having allies helps terrorist groups as it increases the resources at their disposal. This is not only because the groups thereby share their resources, but also because being able to commit attacks more frequently can help in acquiring more resources. Committing more attacks, that is, usually means more visibility, and increased attention can help in recruiting new members and donors.

In sum, having allies helps terrorist groups to survive, and having rival opposing groups may also be of assistance. Competition from other terrorist groups that seek to advance similar goals is, on the other hand, less likely to be good news in this respect—unless the group is able to come out as top contender.

13.5 MOTIVATIONS TO SUSTAINING TERRORISM

So far, we have focused on quantitative studies on the longevity of terrorist groups. Studies of this kind are helpful in many ways, but they do not provide answers to all relevant questions. One of the questions left unanswered is *why* groups continue using terrorism and what kind of considerations affect their decision-making.

While the sustained use of terrorism obviously requires that the group has the necessary resources to mount attacks, groups do not commit terrorist attacks just because they can. In fact, terrorist groups do not always put their resources to full use and continue their use of terrorism for as long as they can (neither do they commit as many attacks as possible, see Busher et al. 2019). Therefore, understanding why groups continue their involvement in terrorism also requires some understanding of decision-making and priority-setting in terrorist groups. What kind of considerations play a role when such groups decide on whether or not to continue terrorist attacks?

Studies that look at terrorism as a group activity typically envision a terrorist group as outlined by the exclusive definition, even though individual studies rarely offer any explicit definition. They quite typically focus on those groups that use terrorism primarily or regularly (action-based definition) and do not hold territory (actor-based definition). As we shall see, not all studies are based on the premise of such an organization, and can therefore also be applied to the sporadic use of terrorism by a wide range of different actors.

Studying anything that concerns the internal dynamics of terrorist groups is difficult due to limited access to data. What is clear by now, however, is that many of those theories that are used to explain decision-making and collective action by other types of organizations can also be applied to terrorism. Terrorist groups, too, weigh the costs and benefits of different courses of action even if the preferred outcomes and methods may be different. They also need to think about how to acquire the necessary resources, recruit new members, and keep existing members motivated.

At the same time, it is necessary to recognize that those groups which commit terrorist attacks often have certain special (but not unique) features that derive from the need to act clandestinely in particular.

There are two models that terrorism studies widely apply to explaining terrorist decision-making: the instrumental and organizational models (Crenshaw 1987; McCormick 2003). Both are to a large degree adaptations of more general theories and models used to explain strategic calculation and organizational dynamics. These models are introduced.

The instrumental model maintains that a group will continue to commit terrorist attacks for as long as it deems them a good means to advancing political objectives. This model is sometimes also referred to as the strategic model.

The main premise here is that the decision to commit a terrorist attack results from strategic calculation where the available courses of action are compared with each other and the one deemed to be the most optimal chosen. Such calculations are conditioned by the possibilities and constraints that the prevailing situation places. Different versions of the instrumental model hold different assumptions of the constraints to rational decision-making. The strong variants assume that terrorist groups have all the necessary information and ability to fully predict the consequences of their actions. Weak variants, by contrast, assume that terrorist groups act rationally, but also acknowledge that such groups view reality through the prism of their beliefs and are likely to operate with incomplete information (McCormick 2003).

Terrorist groups are particularly likely to face significant challenges in maintaining good situational awareness, as their need to operate clandestinely is also likely to limit their information flow. The same need to operate clandestinely has a tendency to make the group turn inward and increase the likelihood that its reasoning becomes increasingly biased by ideological beliefs and expectations (Crenshaw 1992).

Following the logic of the instrumental model, a group is assumed to continue perpetrating terrorist attacks for as long as it is considered as the preferable course of action. The instrumental benefits that the group expects to gain from the attacks can be several. The use of terrorism is not always directly related to the group's long-term political objectives, but it often serves goals of a more short-term nature. Terrorist attacks may aim to gain publicity for the group and its objectives, provoke an overreaction from the state and thereby turn the public against it, spoil negotiations, polarize society, or intimidate or wear out the enemy in order to force concessions from it (e.g. Kydd and Walter 2006; Merari 1993; Richardson 2006).

The instrumental model is too simple to capture the complex dynamics of terrorism in their entirety. The decision to commit or refrain from committing acts of terrorism is influenced by a host of other considerations, not just mere instrumental or strategic calculation of how to reach long-term or short-term political objectives most efficiently.

An important point to recognize here is that terrorist groups do not persist in their use of terrorism only for those reasons that initially led to the start of the campaign (Bjørgo 2005). It is quite well documented by now that once a group begins its involvement in terrorism, other motivations and considerations come into play.

The most often mentioned motivation that comes into play when the group becomes involved in terrorism is revenge. While revenge is undeniably one of the motivators for engaging in terrorism in the first place (both on the individual and collective level), it is also well known that conflict situations tend to produce a cycle of revenge that sustains the conflict itself. Attacks that target a terrorist group create the pressure to retaliate against those believed to be responsible for such attacks, which in turn gives the adversaries a motivation and a need to retaliate.

Shifting objectives are by no means typical to terrorism alone, but to collective human behaviour in general. In the most extreme cases, terrorist attacks continue even after the grievances that initially led to the start of the campaign have disappeared. It is also entirely possible for a terrorist group to change its objectives over time.

> **KEY CONCEPTS**
>
> **Instrumental Model** The instrumental model claims that the decision to commit a terrorist attack results from strategic calculation where the available courses of action to further a group's political objectives are compared with each other, and the one deemed as most optimal chosen.
>
> **Organization Model** The organizational model posits that decision-making within the group is influenced by its need to survive and organizational dynamics such as the need to provide incentives for members and the struggle for power within the group.

The second, organizational model provides further insight into what other kind of considerations may affect terrorist decision-making apart from the struggle to achieve political objectives (see e.g. Crenshaw 1985). This approach draws from a wide body of organizational research. The organizational model, too, starts from the assumption that those who make the decisions over terrorist attacks act rationally, but it proposes another set of objectives and incentives. Like any organization, terrorist groups are also affected by various kinds of organizational considerations and dynamics.

Individuals do not join terrorist groups or remain involved merely because of their political objectives, but also because of the incentives that being a member of the group presents. Among these incentives are the belonging to a group and the sense of solidarity it entails, acquiring a new kind of social status, respect among the wider community, and sometimes also material incentives and a source of income. Occasionally the decision to continue can be motivated by an unwillingness to abandon profitable criminal activities.

These incentives mean that terrorist groups are more than just a means towards political objectives. The survival and operational capabilities of terrorist groups are dependent upon their continued ability to provide crucial incentives for participants and to keep up morale among their ranks. Such organizational demands may sometimes create the need to commit attacks even when they are not deemed necessary for political reasons. Conspiratorial organizations like terrorist groups have shown a tendency to substitute political objectives with group solidarity as their dominant incentive over time. Securing the survival of the organization thereby becomes its primary logic of action. This happened, for example, to the Red Army Faction in West Germany. The campaign of its second generation strongly focused on pressuring the state to release the imprisoned leaders of the first generation (e.g. Della Porta 1995).

There is also evidence of how committing attacks can become the tool of an intra-organizational competition for power. Case studies document various instances where leadership competition within the organization has led to the escalation of attacks. Intra-organizational disputes can also mean that the leadership is not always entirely in control of decision-making (e.g. Shapiro 2013).

Furthermore, the fate of imprisoned or dead comrades may elevate the threshold to giving up the fight. The sacrifices made by these comrades may create an obligation for the others to continue fighting in order to ensure that those sacrifices were not made in vain. This has been documented, for example, by Alison Jamieson (1990) in the case of the Red Brigades, a left-wing organization that operated in Italy during the 1970s and 1980s. Sometimes the use of terrorism may continue for longer than would have otherwise been necessary, as those involved do not see a way out.

CASE STUDY 13.2

Revolutionary Organization 17 November in Greece

Revolutionary Organization 17 November (17N, *Epanastatiki Organosi Dekaefta Noemvri*) was a Greek Marxist-Leninist group that operated in Greece during 1975–2002. It got its name from the day in 1973 when the military junta violently ended a large uprising against it. This group outlived all other violent leftist groups that were part of the New Left wave of terrorism. This wave began in the late 1960s and early 1970s, and largely declined by the early 1990s (Rapoport 2004). What is particularly striking and unusual about 17N is that through all these years, the authorities never managed to infiltrate it or arrest any of its members. This is why it was often called the 'phantom organization,' and the Greek National Intelligence Agency suspected it might not even exist as a proper organization (Kassimeris 2005; Karyotis 2007).

17N started its violent campaign in 1975 by murdering the CIA station chief in Athens. During the following decades, it conducted over 100 attacks which resulted in over 20 deaths. These included bombings, assassinations and rocket attacks. 17N targeted the representatives of those institutions and powers that it considered imperialist or corrupt enemies of the Greek people. Among them were US diplomats, Greek politicians, police officers, public prosecutors, businessmen and international companies, and representatives of the Turkish state.

17N finally ran out of luck in June 2002 when a bomb exploded prematurely and injured the 17N member carrying it. This man shared information with the police, helping the authorities to get on 17N's trail. Several other key members were soon arrested and the safehouses of the 17N found. The group practically ceased to exist within a month.

Why did 17N manage to continue its operations for so long? Researchers have offered two main reasons for this. First, 17N indisputably benefited from an inefficient and under-resourced counterterrorism apparatus and the indecisiveness of the Greek state. The key political parties were unable to reach consensus on how to define terrorism and what kind of legislation should be introduced. Terrorism was generally not considered a major security threat or a political priority. Small leftist groups such as 17N were seen as marginal phenomena eventually likely to destroy themselves. It took until the late 1990s before significant progress was made in developing counterterrorism capabilities (Karyotis 2007; Kassimeris 2007).

What further strengthened 17N's vitality was its composition. The 17N members were very committed to the cause and the group. That several of those involved were close relatives further strengthened mutual bonds and loyalty (Kassimeris 2005; Kassimeris 2013). The group remained small throughout its existence.

While the apparent group cohesion had its benefits, it also had its downsides. The testimonies of former members give the impression that most 17N members 'lived in a closed, self-referential world where terrorism became a way of life from which they found it impossible to walk away' (Kassimeris 2007: 142). The group's political achievements were marginal at best.

The end of 17N did not mean the end of left-wing terrorism. Even if 17N had been relatively closed and self-referential, Greece has a long-standing tradition of revolutionary politics. The demise of 17N was immediately followed by the emergence of other violent groups continuing this tradition. Unlike 17N, most of these groups have been more loosely organized and much less security-minded. The authorities have nevertheless struggled to suppress their activities as new activists seem to constantly appear to replace those arrested (Kassimeris 2016; Xenakis 2012).

QUESTIONS

1. Would you consider 17N a successful terrorist group?
2. Studies show that larger groups are more likely to have more staying power. 17N, in contrast, was a small group. Can you think of any benefits that being a small group can have for survival?

13.6 CONCLUSION

The longevity of terrorist groups, as we have seen, varies greatly. A significant number of groups do not continue with terrorism for more than one year. Others carry on with terrorist attacks for decades. We also know that the intensity of terrorist campaigns varies over time and between groups.

Continued terrorist attacks, despite all the countermeasures employed against the group, do indeed come across as a success to the terrorist groups and a failure for the security authorities and an achievement for the terrorists.

It is, however, problematic to equate the longevity of a terrorist group with success. Being able to sustain a campaign in the face of countermeasures is admittedly an achievement itself (Phillips 2018). But mere survival is rarely the only goal. Instead, involvement in terrorism can be expected to last only for a short period of time. It is not uncommon for groups that commit terrorist attacks to expect a quick victory. These expectations are rarely met, and what follows instead is a prolonged conflict with many more terrorist attacks. Few groups expect terrorist attacks to take them all the way to their ultimate goal.

Sometimes terrorism is seen as the first phase, or one part, of a larger conflict. This means that the group expects terrorist attacks to help it expand its membership and resources, and to switch to more demanding forms of operations or instigate a popular insurrection. Such ideas are embedded in many classic theories of revolutionary warfare (Malkki 2019). The conditions ripe for escalation may never materialize. Therefore, a prolonged reliance on terrorist attacks can sometimes be seen as symptomatic of a failure to escalate.

Finally, there are no studies providing such comparative data that would allow one to contrast the longevity of involvement in terrorism with that of involvement in other forms of political or violent activity. While the average duration of involvement in terrorism may seem rather short and the share of groups that abandon it quickly very large. What is less clear, however, is whether terrorist groups any different from other violent or nonviolent political groups in terms of longevity.

DISCUSSION QUESTIONS

1. Regime type does not appear to have any systematic effect on terrorist group survival. Still, democratic and authoritarian states are very different types of operating environments for terrorist groups. What kind of possibilities and constraints does each of these regime types pose for continuing terrorist attacks?
2. Is there any relationship between the longevity of terrorist groups and population size? How would you explain it?
3. Why do you think so many groups stop using terrorism within one year after the first attack?
4. Can you think of other factors that might affect the longevity of terrorist groups than those discussed in this chapter?
5. What kind of learnings can be drawn from this chapter for developing counterterrorism policies?

Visit the online resources for pointers on how to answer the discussion questions, links to useful web sources, and guidance on accessing databases: www.oup.com/he/Wilson-Muro1e

GUIDE TO FURTHER READING

Blomberg, S. B., Gaibulloev, K., and Sandler, T. (2011) 'Terrorist Group Survival: Ideology, Tactics and Base of Operations', *Public choice* 149: 441–463. **The article presents a large study on the determinants of terrorist group survival.**

Crenshaw, M. (2011) *Explaining Terrorism: Causes, Processes, and Consequences.* London and New York: Routledge. **Martha Crenshaw is one of the pioneers of the academic study of terrorism. This volume includes her most important contributions, including her seminal articles on instrumental and organizational approaches to terrorism.**

Dugan, L. (2012) 'The Making of the Global Terrorism Database and its Applicability to Studying the Life Cycles of Terrorist Organizations', in D. Gadd et al. (eds.), *Sage Handbook of Criminological Research Methods*. Newbury Park, CA: Sage Publications. *This article by one of the key researchers behind the Global Terrorism Database shows how it can be used for studying longevity of terrorist groups.*

Miller, E. (2012) 'Patterns of Onset and Decline Among Terrorist Organizations', *Journal of Quantitative Criminology* 28: 77–101. *Erin Miller has conducted one of the most extensive studies on terrorist group longevity and this article summarizes part of her work. It draws attention to the fact that the frequency of attacks varies widely between different groups and uses trajectory models to analyse organizations' frequency of attacks.*

Phillips, B. J. (2019) 'Do 90 Per cent of Terrorist Groups Last Less Than a Year? Updating the Conventional Wisdom', *Terrorism and Political Violence* 31/6: 1255–1265. *This article gives an excellent overview of existing literature on the longevity of terrorist groups, as well as debunks some common myths.*

Young, J. K. and Dugan, L. (2014) 'Survival of the Fittest: Why Terrorist Groups Endure', *Perspectives on Terrorism* 8/2: 2–23. *The article analyses how competition between terrorist groups which operate in the same environment affect their duration of activity.*

REFERENCES

Acosta, B. (2014) 'Live to Win Another Day: Why Many Militant Organizations Survive Yet Few Succeed', *Studies in Conflict and Terrorism*, 37 (2): 135–161.

Asal, V. H., Partk, H. H., Rethemeyer R. K., and Ackerman, G. (2016) 'With Friends Like These … Why Terrorist Organizations Ally', *International Public Management Journal*, 19 (1): 1–30.

Bjørgo, T. (2005) 'Conclusions', in T. Bjørgo (ed.), *Root Causes of Terrorism: Myths, Realities, and Ways Forward*. London: Routledge, 256–264.

Blomberg, S. B., Gaibulloev, K., and Sandler, T. (2011) 'Terrorist Group Survival: Ideology, Tactics and Base of Operations', *Public choice*, 149: 441–463.

Busher, J., Holbrook, D., and Macklin, G. (2019) 'The Internal Brakes on Violent Escalation: A Typology', *Behavioural Sciences of Terrorism and Political Aggression*, 11 (1): 3–25.

Crenshaw, M. (1985) 'An Organizational Approach to the Analysis of Political Terrorism', *Orbis*, 29 (3).

Crenshaw, M. (1987) 'Theories of Terrorism: Instrumental and organizational approaches', *Journal of Strategic Studies*, 10 (4): 13–31.

Crenshaw, M. (1992) 'Decisions to Use Terrorism: Psychological Constraints on Instrumental Reasoning', in D. della Porta (ed.), *Social Movements and Violence: Participation in Underground Organizations*. International Social Movement Research, 4. Greenwich: JAI Press.

Cronin, A. K. (2009) *How Terrorism Ends: Understanding the Decline and Demise of Terrorist Campaigns*. Princeton and Oxford: Princeton University Press.

Daxecker, U. E. and Hess, M. L. (2013) 'Repression Hurts: Coercive Government Responses and the Demise of Terrorist Campaigns', *British Journal of Political Science*, 43 (3): 559–577.

Della Porta, D. (1995) *Social Movements, Political Violence and the State: A Comparative Analysis of Italy and Germany*. Cambridge: Cambridge University Press.

Felhab-Brown, V. (2019) 'The Crime-Terrorism-Nexus and its Fallacies', in E. Chenoweth et al. (eds.), *The Oxford Handbook of Terrorism*. Oxford: Oxford University Press.

Hoffman, B. (2017) *Inside Terrorism*. Third Edition. New York: Columbia University Press.

Hou, D., Gaibulloev, K., and Sandler, T. (2020) 'Introducing Extended Data on Terrorist Groups (EDTG), 1970 to 2016', *Journal of Conflict Resolution*, 64 (1): 199–225.

Jamieson, A. (1990) 'Entry, Discipline and Exit in the Italian Red Brigades', *Terrorism and Political Violence*, 2 (1): 1–20.

Jones, S. G. and Libicki, M. C. (2008) *How Terrorist Groups End: Lessons for Countering Al Qaeda*. Santa Monica: RAND Corporation. Available at https://www.rand.org/content/dam/rand/pubs/monographs/2008/RAND_MG741-1.pdf.

Karmon, E. (2005) *Coalitions Between Terrorist Organizations: Revolutionaries, Nationalists and Islamists*. Leiden/Boston: Martinus Nijhoff Publishers.

Karyotis, G. (2007) 'Securitization of Greek Terrorism and Arrest of the "Revolutionary Organization November 17"', *Cooperation and Conflict, 42* (3): 271–293.

Kassimeris, G. (2005) 'What Not to Do When Dealing with Terrorism: The Greek Experience', *Democracy and Security, 1* (1): 105–117.

Kassimeris, G. (2007) 'For a Place in History: Explaining Greece's Revolutionary Organization 17 November', *Journal of Conflict Studies, 27* (2): 129–145.

Kassimeris, G. (2013) 'Greece: The Persistence of Political Terrorism', *International Affairs, 89* (1): 131–142.

Kassimeris, G. (2016) 'Greece's Terrorism Problem: A Reassessment', *Studies in Conflict and Terrorism, 39* (9): 862–870.

Kendall-Taylor, A., Frantz, E., and Wright, J. (2020) 'The Digital Dictators: How Technology Strengthens Autocracy', *Foreign Affairs* March-April: 103–115.

Kydd, A. H. and Walter, B. F. (2006) 'The Strategies of Terrorism', *International Security, 31* (1): 49–80.

Malkki, L. (2010) *How Terrorist Campaigns End: The Campaigns of the Rode Jeugd in the Netherlands and the Symbionese Liberation Army in the United States*. PhD Dissertation, University of Helsinki. Available at https://blogs.helsinki.fi/leenamalkki/files/2012/07/Malkki-PhD.pdf.

Malkki, L. (2019) 'Left-wing Terrorism', in Andrew Silke (ed.), *Routledge Handbook of Terrorism and Counterterrorism*. Abingdon and New York: Routledge: 87–97.

McCormick, G. H. (2003) 'Terrorist Decision Making', *Annual Review of Political Science, 6*: 473–507.

Merari, A. (1993) 'Terrorism as a Strategy of Insurgency', *Terrorism and Political Violence, 5* (4): 213–251.

Miller, E. (2016) 'Patterns of Collective Desistance from Terrorism: Fundamental Measurement Challenges', *Perspectives on Terrorism, 10* (5): 5–21.

Moghadam, A. (2012) 'Failure and Disengagement in the Red Army Faction', *Studies in Conflict and Terrorism, 35* (2): 156–181.

Olzak, S. (2016) 'The Effect of Category Spanning on the Lethality and Longevity of Terrorist Organizations', *Social Forces, 95* (2): 559–584.

Pearson, F. S., Akbulut, I., and Olson Lounsbery, M. (2017) 'Group Structure and Intergroup Relations in Global Terror Networks: Further Explorations', *Terrorism and Political Violence, 29* (3): 550–572.

Phillips, B. J. (2014) 'Terrorist Group Cooperation and Longevity', *International Studies Quarterly, 58*: 336–347.

Phillips, B. J. (2015a) 'What Is a Terrorist Group? Conceptual Issues and Empirical Implications', *Terrorism and Political Violence, 27* (2): 225–242.

Phillips, B. J. (2015b) 'Enemies with Benefits? Violent Rivalry and Terrorist Group Longevity', *Journal of Peace Research, 52* (1): 62–75.

Phillips, B. J. (2018) 'Terrorist Group Survival as a Measure of Effectiveness', in D. Muro (ed.), *When Does Terrorism Work*. London and New York: Routledge, 52–70.

Phillips, B. J. (2019) 'Do 90 Per cent of Terrorist Groups Last Less Than a Year? Updating the Conventional Wisdom', *Terrorism and Political Violence, 31* (6): 1255–1265.

Piazza, J. A. and Piazza, S. (2020) 'Crime Pays: Terrorist Group Engagement in Crime and Survival', *Terrorism and Political Violence, 32* (4): 701–723.

Rapoport, D. C. (1992) 'Terrorism', in M. Hawkesworth and Maurice Kogan (eds.), *Encyclopedia of Government and Politics*, 2. London: Routledge.

Rapoport, D. C. (2004) 'The Four Waves of Modern Terrorism', in A. K. Cronin and J. M. Ludes (eds.), *Attacking Terrorism: Elements of a Grand Strategy*. Washington, DC: Georgetown University Press: 46–73.

Richardson, L. (2006) *What Terrorists Want: Understanding the Terrorist Threat*. London: John Murray.

Shapiro, J. N. (2013) *The Terrorist's Dilemma: Managing Violent Covert Organizations*. Princeton and Oxford: Princeton University Press.

Staniland, P. (2014) *Networks of Rebellion: Explaining Insurgent Cohesion and Collapse*. Ithaca and London: Cornell University Press.

Vittori, Jodi (2009) 'All Struggles Must End: The Longevity of Terrorist Groups', *Contemporary Security Policy, 30* (3): 444–466.

Xenakis, S. (2012) 'A New Dawn? Change and Continuity in Political Violence in Greece', *Terrorism and Political Violence, 24* (3): 437–464.

Young, J. K. and Dugan, L. (2014) 'Survival of the Fittest: Why Terrorist Groups Endure', *Perspectives on Terrorism, 8* (2): 2–23.

CHAPTER 14

Can States Be Terrorists?

KIERAN MCCONAGHY

■ CHAPTER SUMMARY

This chapter looks at the use of political violence by states and asks whether it can (or ought to) be considered terrorism. It explores terminology common in the literature and its rhetorical impact, and asks questions regarding the legitimacy of state violence.

It concludes that states can and do use terrorism, but that the terms 'state terrorism' and non-state terrorism' are simplistic, overlooking the range of ways that states commit, facilitate and contribute to political violence. It suggests that we need more studies which explore state involvement in political violence in nuanced ways and which do not naïvely accept the legitimacy of state violence while rendering all violence by non-state actors as morally repugnant.

14.1 INTRODUCTION

State terrorism is among the most divisive subjects in an already contentious field. To answer the question, 'can states be terrorists?' this chapter traces the emergence of 'terrorism studies' as a discrete field of enquiry, and the meaning of terrorism that developed which excluded state actors. It then explores the cases for and against the inclusion of states in definitions of terrorism. Finally, it points to the limitations of state terrorism as a concept, and the need to look beyond it to understand political violence.

14.2 STUDYING TERRORISM—WHAT ABOUT THE STATE?

The emergence of the term 'terrorism' can be traced to the Jacobin regime in revolutionary France (Primoratz 2004: 113). *La Terreur*, or the 'Reign of Terror', was violence perpetrated by elements of the French Revolutionary state in efforts to consolidate their fledgling government, and is sometimes cited as one of the first modern examples of terrorism (see also Chapter 8) (Hoffman 2006: 3). While the term terrorism may have been born at this time, terroristic violence by repressive regimes can be found from antiquity onwards. The First Mesopotamian Empire under Sargon of Akkad (2334–2284 BCE) was founded on despotic violence (Chaliand and Blin 2007: vii). Roman rule of 1st-century CE Judea under Emperor Nero, relied on theatrical public executions such as crucifixions in order to quash Jewish resistance (Bloom 2010: 169). The expansion of the Mongol Empire under Genghis Khan (1162–1227) and his heirs similarly depended on subjugating peoples through fear of tyrannical violence (Giessauf 2008: 88–90).

Despite ancient roots, the language of terrorism took some time to gain currency. The term 'terrorism' had been used in the 19th century sporadically to describe a range of violence. With very few exceptions however, it was a term that was applied to violence used against the state. It was the 1970s before the language of 'international terrorism' became commonplace, after events like the 'skyjackings' by Palestinian revolutionary organizations, and the Black September assault at the Munich Olympics in 1972 captured the attention of governments and the media. These acts were 'violence from below'. For people in the West, terrorism came to refer only to the actions of non-state actors using these and similar methods (Claridge 1996: 48) to alter the political status quo. This ignored the vast array of political violence perpetrated against non-Western interests and violence against ethnic minority people, which nonetheless relied on fear to achieve their ends. By the early 1990s in the public discourse there had been a virtual appropriation of the term 'terrorism' to signify 'atrocities targeting the West' (George 1991: 1; Blakeley 2007: 229).

The rising political importance of terrorism led to increased scholarly attention (Stampnitzky 2013: 27). Since states were closely linked to the emergence of the field of terrorism studies, the questions pursued and concepts developed reflected states' agendas (Jackson 2007: 225). Academics who chose not to orient their research towards informing counterterrorism policy found it more difficult to publish in mainstream journals on terrorism, and to attract funding for their research (Wight 2009: 99). Thus, the main focus of the field became non-state violence that challenged the existing political order. Intentional or not, studies of state violence, violence against ethnic minority people, and 'pro-state' violence were marginalized—a trend that was exacerbated after 11 September 2001 when non-state terrorism became seen as the predominant threat to freedom and security (Koch 2016: 1).

Despite this, some academics remained committed to the study of state violence (Herman 1985; Stohl and Lopez 1986; George 1991; Sluka 2000). Much work exists which examines 'state sponsorship of terrorism' (see Key Concepts box in section 14.3) but this literature has tended to be selective and addresses different dynamics of state involvement in terrorism. Since 2006, the focus on state terrorism has been boosted by the emergence of Critical Terrorism Studies (see also Chapter 3) (Blakeley 2007; Blakeley 2009; Jackson et al. 2010). 'State terrorism' has not been the only framework through which state violence has been addressed. There have been many studies across a range of disciplinary backgrounds that have sought to explain and understand the use of state violence that might well be considered terrorism (Jamieson and McEvoy 2005; Sluka 2000; Gunneflo 2016; Baum 2008; Hajjar 2013; Ott 2011; Blakeley 2009). Literatures on civil wars, revolutions, counter-insurgency, policing, and social and military history have all contributed much to our understanding of violence that might be classified as state terrorism. Students hoping for a wide-angled understanding of state terrorism must pay heed to the formal literature on 'state terrorism' but also be prepared to look beyond to other disciplines.

14.3 WHAT IS STATE TERRORISM?

Defining state terrorism is difficult, since it relies first on a definition of terrorism and then seeks to identify state responsibility. Rather than provide a holistic definition, this section looks at some of the core components that any definition of state terrorism ought to include. The first four points pertain to *all* terrorism, the latter two to state terrorism specifically:

The first necessary component is actual or threatened violence. This ought to be physical rather than 'structural' violence (where structures in society cause harm to people, rather than that harm being the direct result of physical violence). While structural violence potentially serves similar political objectives, it manifests differently, and ought to be dealt with separately. Sometimes states are keen to distinguish between practices that cause psychological harm or 'mental pressure' and those that cause physical harm. The distinction between the two is however not clear cut. Frequently mental pressure rests on the threat of physical harm. In many cases, extreme mental pressure can cause real and severe physiological harm because of the stress it puts on the body.

Most academics would agree that to be considered terrorism, violence must be in pursuit of a political objective. The objective need not be political 'change' since terrorism is often concerned with *preventing* political change and with state terrorism, the objective is frequently to preserve the political status quo.

For political violence to be considered terrorism, there must be intent to affect a wider audience than just the direct targets. This is true of both state and non-state terrorism. Terrorism is about communication of a political message—there must be someone to communicate with. That audience can vary in scale from one person to the entirety of society.

The psychological dimension is also an important aspect of both state and non-state terrorism. It is, after all, what gives terrorism its name. Different to other forms of political violence that might cause fear as a by-product of other strategic aims, triggering a psychological response among a category of people *is* a calculated effect of terrorism. Through this, those who use terrorism aim to coerce the secondary audience in the hope of achieving a political objective.

Blakeley (2009: 30) building on Walter (1969) argues that in order for terrorism to be state terrorism, it must be perpetrated by the state or on behalf of the state with its approval. This could be by permitting or contracting violence to third parties such as militias, private companies, or gangs. Discerning when something has been perpetrated by the state or on its behalf is not always straightforward. States are usually keen to obscure their involvement, to avoid reputational damage. Domestically, the knowledge that the state has relied on terroristic violence to achieve its policy goals can damage its legitimacy in the eyes of the citizens. Internationally, knowledge that a state engages in terrorism might see it isolated by former allies unwilling to be associated with such practices.

There are other difficulties—at what point do the illegal acts of members of state forces pass from individual culpability to state culpability? There are also related phenomena like 'pro-state' or 'conservative' terrorism, where non-state actors seek to achieve by political violence what the state struggles to achieve legally (Bruce 1992; Drake 1996) and 'state-sponsored terrorism'. States frequently sponsor or assist violent groups internationally because it serves their foreign policy objectives (see Key Concepts box in this section).

KEY CONCEPTS

State Terrorism versus State-Sponsored Terrorism A separate sub-field of 'state-sponsored terrorism' has emerged, the complexity of relationships and the dynamics involved necessitating a different kind of focus (Wilson 2019: 331). Byman (2005: 10) defines state sponsorship of terrorism as a 'government's intentional assistance to a terrorist group to help it use violence, bolster its political activities, or sustain the organization'. Thus, the work on state sponsorship distinguishes between state terrorism which has tended to refer to direct involvement in terrorism by states and their personnel and state sponsorship which refers to

> instances where states fund or assist pre-existing or separate non-state groups using terrorism which have command structures and objectives separate from those of the state itself. This distinction is not always clear and it can be difficult to decide whether some examples should be deemed 'state terrorism' or state-sponsored terrorism. This dilemma is also dealt with in the conclusion to this chapter.
>
> During the Cold War, the study of state sponsorship focused on alleged Soviet patronage of insurgent groups globally, including some pseudo-academic work that attempted to pin all world terrorism on the USSR in what was later acknowledged to be thinly veiled CIA propaganda (see Sterling 1981). While work on state sponsorship of terrorism has become more nuanced, much of this work has remained skewed towards a focus on states which are seen as enemies by Western state elites such as Iran, Libya, North Korea, Cuba, Nicaragua, Syria, Pakistan, and Afghanistan (O'Sullivan 2003; Byman 2005; Roberts 1987: 255) and has largely ignored Western state sponsorship of organizations in Latin America, the Middle East, and Southeast Asia.

State terrorism must exclude legitimate state action. Every state is underpinned by recourse to the legitimate means of coercion (Weber 1919). They exist because they retain the right to coerce the population to comply with laws and social conventions. If you do not pay your taxes, you might go to prison. If you threaten to punch someone, you may be arrested. The use or threat of such force is designed to coerce the public into behaving a certain way so that the state maintains its power. Where that violence is legitimate, it ought not to be considered as 'state terrorism'. To consider it such would mean that much of the function of the coercive apparatus of the state would be included within the definition. Deciding what is and what is not legitimate is riven with difficulties, both conceptual and political. Legitimacy is not co-determinate with legality, since states are sometimes in a position to make their violence legal or to exploit grey areas in international law, while still perpetrating acts of violence that extend beyond what might be considered legitimate.

14.4 OBJECTIONS TO THE CONCEPT OF 'STATE TERRORISM'

We have seen how state terrorism became marginalized with the focus of the field remaining squarely on certain types of non-state political violence. States have a clear interest in avoiding the application of a term that is so heavily laden with censure of their own actions (Schmid 2011: 39–98). As Wilkinson (2011: 10) put it, 'the tendency of modern governments to apply the terms terror and terrorism exclusively to sub-state groups is blatantly dishonest and self-serving'.

Some academics object to the term 'state terrorism'. In some cases, the decision to rule out the existence of 'state terrorism' comes down to fundamental differences of definitions.

Some adopt an actor centric view of terrorism (Kalyvas 2019: 23; Hoffman 2006: 40). For them, 'terrorists' are a type of non-state actor, and 'terrorism' is the name for their violence, thus terrorism cannot possibly be used to describe violence from the state. This can create jarring and intellectually uncomfortable scenarios. On 6 September 1938, a lorryload of British soldiers from the Royal Ulster Rifles struck an improvised bomb outside the village of al-Bassa near Acre in what was then British Mandate Palestine (the British mandate was from 1918, ending in 1948 when it became the State of Israel). The blast mortally wounded four riflemen. The following day, soldiers from that same regiment loaded 20 villagers onto a bus and directed the bus over a similar explosive device planted by the British Army's Royal Engineers. Many of the passengers on that bus were killed instantly in this brutal reprisal attack (Allport 2020: 48–50). Here, state and non-state actors used identical means with the same intent to kill. An actor-centric understanding of terrorism would mean that despite their similarity, the attack by the non-state actor is considered to be terrorism, while the attack by the state actor is not.

Others point to the Weberian (attributed to German sociologist Max Weber) monopoly that states have over legitimate violence as excluding the possibility that they can perpetrate terrorism (Sproat 1991, 1997, cited in Jarvis and Lister 2014: 74). However, just because states have the legitimacy to use violence in limited circumstances does not mean that state violence is always legitimate (Stohl 2006: 5). There are instances where state violence would be illegimate; shooting unarmed peaceful protestors for example.

Others still have argued that a concept of 'terrorism' that would include both state and non-state terrorism is overstretched since there is no analytical benefit from their comparison (Richardson 2006: 21; Gearty 1991: 1; Crenshaw 2011: 4). This argument hinges on the idea that state and non-state violence serve fundamentally different motives and have different effects (Laqueur 1986: 89). However, both state and non-state rely on violence to excite a psychological response in order to coerce, and while the two can look very different, there are times when they are virtually indistinguishable.

Finally, it might be argued that state terrorism is redundant, since such violence is already covered by concepts like ethnic cleansing, assassination, war crimes, and human rights abuses (Jackson, Murphy and Poynting 2010: 5). Yet many concepts overlap and are still analytically useful. One can find characterizations of non-state terrorism under titles such as murder, assault, treason, and subversion. The concept of state terrorism might allow us to study these issues in new ways and to examine aspects that might otherwise remain unexplored.

14.5 CAN STATES BE TERRORISTS?

How useful is the term 'terrorist', as a descriptor for those who perpetrate terrorism? Unlike the term 'terrorism' which can tell us something about the nature of violence, 'terrorist' does not tell us anything. Terrorism can be used by a variety of actors, state and non-state, weak and strong, overt and covert. All that the term 'terrorist' does, is convey moral censure. By adopting a view of an actor simply as a 'terrorist', we might ignore other actions they carry out, such as protests, providing social goods, or engaging in organized crime, for example. The term 'terrorist' thus contributes to simplistic understandings of violent actors and their contexts.

The literature on terrorism sometimes speaks of 'terrorist states'. Objective criteria for what constitutes a terrorist state is difficult to find. It is not applied uniformly, but rather is usually reserved to describe totalitarian regimes and has also been used to discuss states that sponsor acts of terrorism that have targeted the West, such as North Korea, Libya under Muammar Gaddafi (1969–2011), and Iran after the Islamic Revolution (7 January 1978–11 February 1979). Yet there are many states that have resorted to terroristic violence against their own populations, but which are seldom talked about as 'terrorist states'. The term is rarely applied to Western states or their allies internationally. This generates the misunderstanding that state-terrorism is the preserve of a small number of despots at odds with the international order. So, while the important job of studying and understanding state violence remains, there is little analytical utility in the term 'terrorist state' or in referring to states simply as 'terrorists'.

14.6 HOW HAVE STATES USED TERRORISM?

State terrorism has appeared in many forms. It has varied in terms of its intensity, scale and duration, from generation-long programmes of systematic violence against entire populations to quell dissent, to individual acts designed to coerce a small number of individuals. At times, state terrorism has been overt, with the publicity and panic generated designed to terrify the public into compliance. At others, it has been covert, where plausible deniability (which allows the state to deny involvement in such acts and thus retain its legitimacy and authority) is calculated to isolate the target audience and make them conform to the state's wishes.

Totalitarian regimes (regimes which aim for total social and political control, expect total subservience, and refuse citizens a private life in principle) have often institutionalized and systematized policies of state terrorism. Regimes like Hitler's Third Reich, Cambodia's Khmer Rouge, and Iraq under Saddam Hussein's Ba'ath Party instituted terrorism as a policy to maintain power and reshape society, purging political opponents or eradicating ethnic groups. The absence of accountability meant that violence could be unrestrained. Perpetual fear of secret police or paramilitary forces served to insulate the regime from popular uprisings and challenges to the established order. Victims were often denigrated and characterized as enemies of the state or traitors to the nation. Where acknowledged, state terrorism was rationalized as a necessary measure in order to build the utopia envisaged by regime elites. The sense that anyone could be a victim of state violence added to the terrorizing effect and demonstrated the need for compliance and total submission to the state.

Authoritarian regimes lack the all-encompassing grip on society of totalitarian states, but have nonetheless engaged in some widespread programmes of state terrorism. After the US backed coup d'etat in 1973 that deposed the democratically elected President of Chile Salvador Allende, torture was used heavily to repress leftists and consolidate the coup. Chile's secret police, intelligence agencies and armed forces established detention centres where up to 50,000 people were tortured (Crenzel 2011: 2). The objective was not simply to secure intelligence from supporters of Allende's government, but to 'extirpate communism'. Thus, torture and murder by the regime meant that voicing political dissent, and even public mourning of the victims was rendered impossible (Wright 2007: 67).

'Enforced disappearances' is a term which was first used with regards to the victims of authoritarian regimes in Latin American countries such as Colombia and Mexico, beginning in the 1970s (Lippman 1988: 121; Berman and Clark 1981: 531). This refers to the practice of:

> '(. . .) the arrest, detention, abduction or any other form of deprivation of liberty by agents of the State or by persons or groups of persons acting with authorization, support or acquiescence of the State, followed by a refusal to acknowledge the deprivation of liberty or by the concealment of the fate or whereabouts of the disappeared person, which place such a person outside the protection of the law' (International Convention for the Protection of all Persons from Enforced Disappearance 2006).

Such tactics were utilized widely in Guatemala under Efrain Rios Montt, de facto President from 1982 to 1983, as part of a wider campaign of ethnic cleansing of indigenous peoples under the guise of 'counter-insurgency' (Brett 2016: 47). Disappearing has in some circumstances replaced the rule of law and formal arrest and detention, enabling the state to circumvent legal process and accountability (Berman and Clark 1981: 531). The United Nations Working Group on Enforced or Involuntary Disappearances (WGEID) reported in 2012 that there were 42,889 cases under active consideration in 84 states across all continents (Bargu 2014: 39). Requests for information by families or humanitarian groups are typically met with complete denial by the state. It is only the pain caused by disappearance but having no recognition and no explanation, and being unable to process the loss that serves to terrorize. Opposition to the state in these circumstances becomes almost impossible. Disappearances and presumed killings by the state become 'ungrievable' (Butler 2004: 34–35).

Colonial powers in the 20th and 21st centuries have relied heavily on state terrorism as a means to dominate populations and retain control of territory. Aerial bombardment was developed to provide superior capacity against conventional military targets and was central to efforts by Western states to develop a more scientific and 'sanitized' form of warfare (Gregory 2010: 159–161). This language masked the often-indiscriminate ways that air power has been deployed. From the 1920s onwards, colonial powers such as Britain, Italy and France used aerial bombardment not only to counter armed insurrection, but to ensure acquiescence of native populations to colonial rule through the destruction of civilian settlements, agriculture, and food supplies (Neocleous 2013: 581–585).

Torture was used extensively by colonial powers during the wars of national liberation in the 20th century. France systematically tortured suspects during the Algerian War of Independence from 1954 to 1962. They subjected those believed to be Front de Liberation Nationale (FLN or National Liberation Front Algeria) guerrillas to beatings, stress positions, electrocutions, and sexual violence including rape (Branche 2007: 552). The British state deployed tactics developed during the Second World War against guerrilla forces in Malaya (1948–1960; now Malaysia), Kenya (1952–1960), Cyprus (1955–1959), and Nigeria and Cameroon (1960–1961), varying the scale and intensity of violence depending on the perceived level of impunity (Cobain 2013).

The wars of decolonization often saw the use of extrajudicial killings to terrorize enemy combatants and those perceived to be sympathetic towards them. At times these were performed by uniformed units of the state apparatus. In Ireland in the 1920s, British army officers created a procedure for sanctioning attacks against civilian settlements as 'reprisal' for Irish Republican Army attacks on the British military (see also Case Study 14.2) (Townshend 1975: 149) described by one historian as a 'counter-murder campaign' (Jeffrey 1984: 85 cited in Bennett 2013: 100). The incorporation of 'counter-gangs' into British counterinsurgency practice in Malaya and Kenya demonstrated a commitment to the use of extra-judicial killings (Sluka 2000: 134). These unofficial groups organized by the state provided deniability while attacking suspected guerrilla and their presumed support base. Similar units were deployed by France in Algeria during the War of Independence. They targeted strongholds of European colonists in attacks that were intended as both revenge for opposition to the state and to terrorize them into acquiescing to government policy (McConaghy 2017: 59).

Despite the separation of powers and purported respect for the rule of law, **liberal democracies**, have used state terrorism as a tool of statecraft. Democratic elections are supposed to act as a safety valve, where governments can be ousted for such wrongdoings. However sometimes the electorate does not know of these transgressions and at other times they may actually approve of it. Even in cases where the electorate vote out particular governments, the coercive apparatus of the state (intelligence agencies, military and police), which are usually most directly involved in perpetrating state-terrorism, typically remain intact and cultures which permit the use of state terrorism remain.

Israel claims liberal democratic status, seeing itself as the beacon of Western-style democracy in the Middle East, surrounded by autocracies and failing states. Oren Yiftachel characterizes Israel more accurately as an 'ethnocracy' (1999: 369), having some of the outward characteristics of a democracy, but with an ethnocentric basis to society that renders it otherwise. Supported by the USA and reliant on a narrative of existential threat from Palestinians and neighbouring states, Israel has adopted a plethora of measures which are 'designed to instil fear, humiliate, injure or otherwise cause harm' to the civilian population of the Occupied Territories (including the West Bank, East Jerusalem, and the Gaza Strip) for political gain (Nasr 2010: 68). Indiscriminate cluster-bombings during the 2006 invasion of Lebanon led to the death of around 1,000 civilians during the bombardment and hundreds more since (Finkelstein 2013: 197; Human Rights Watch 2008). In 2000, Israel admitted that they operated a policy of targeted killing which saw the Israeli Defence Forces assassinate suspected enemies of the state in Israel and the Occupied Territories rather than try to bring them to justice (Kretzmer 2005: 172; Alston 2010: 6). The bombing of civilian areas in Gaza during Operation Cast Lead in 2008–2009, see Photo 14.1, led to the deaths of somewhere in the region of 1,300 or 1,400 civilians in retribution for Hamas (The Islamic resistance movement) attacks on Israel (Slater 2012: 55; Amnesty International 2009: 6). Thus, Israel is among the most prolific perpetrators of state terrorism. Combined with other instruments of statecraft, including embargoes on Gaza, and the creeping expansion of Israeli settlements into the Occupied Territories, state terrorism is used to make Israel's domination of Palestine unassailable.

Other states claiming the status of liberal democracy have tended to be less brazen in perpetrating terrorism, opting for more covert methods. One year after the transition to democracy in Spain, elements of the state founded the GAL (*Grupos Antiterrorista de Liberación*), an illegal clandestine group partially comprised of members of the state's security forces, funded by the Ministry of the Interior. Between 1983 and 1987, the GAL

PHOTO 14.1   The Gaza Strip in November 2009. An Israeli tank crew prepares for a land incursion into the Gaza Strip during Operation Cast Lead.

killed 27 people, nine of whom had no link at all to the radical Basque group ETA (see Case Study 12.1) who were allegedly the targets of these attacks (Woodworth 2001: 7). The attacks were designed to demoralize Basque nationalists and damage the support for ETA. However, Basque nationalists identified that GAL was the work of the state undermining their trust in the still fledgling democracy (Aretxaga 2000: 50; Woodworth 2001: 408; McConaghy 2017: 36). Elsewhere, evidence suggests that *stragismo* or false flag attacks in Italy, which were designed to look like the work of radical leftists, were in fact orchestrated by neofascists in concert with elements of the Italian security apparatus. The ultimate aim was to justify a crackdown on the radical left in the 1960s and 1970s (See Hajek 2010: 205; Bull 2005: 264–265). In the Italian case, as with the Spanish, plausible deniability was central to the effectiveness of the tool.

CASE STUDY 14.1

US Torture in the Global War on Terror

The 'Global War on Terror' has brought state terrorism back into the spotlight as the US and its allies have resorted to tactics seen by many to fit that description. Since the invasion of Afghanistan in 2001, the USA has exploited legal grey areas to defend its actions from criticism and shield against legal challenges. The use of Guantanamo Bay facilities in Cuba for detention and interrogation evades the application of US domestic law and allows the treatment of prisoners to derogate widely from the acceptable standards on US territory. Detainees at Guantanamo have no recourse to rights of freedom from unlawful detention or the right to fair trial. Suspects have been brought before military tribunals as enemy combatants, where they have no access to writs of *habeas corpus*, their legal counsel is appointed by the US military, and trials are held in secret (Steyn 2004: 9).

Despite centuries old legal and moral norms prohibiting torture, public and academic debate on its permissibility re-emerged after September 11th (Dershowitz: 2004). Much of the discussion centred on arguments around the novelty and scale of the threat faced from terrorism; arguments which had been used in defence of such tactics during the Algerian War of Independence (1954–1962) where terrorism had been used extensively (MacMaster 2004: 5). President George W. Bush authorized the use of psychological torture in Afghanistan and Iraq against captured suspects, euphemistically referred to as 'enhanced interrogation' (McCoy 2012: 4). While the language used by the US government was sanitized and scientific sounding, the methods used often resulted in brutal suffering and long-term damage (McCoy 2012: 6). The methods had been based on fifty secret experiementation and research by the CIA over 50 years. However, scientific evidence suggests that 'interrogational torture', designed to elicit confessions and intelligence does not work (O'Mara 2015). Waterboarding (as one example), is not a safe and modern interrogation technique, but a severe form of torture with precedents in medieval Europe, having been used during the Spanish Inquisition (Cox 2018).

PHOTO 14.2 Washington DC, USA, January 2019: Witness Against Torture activists demonstrating at the White House calling for the closing of the Guantanamo Bay detention camp on the 17th anniversary of its opening.

The list of officially sanctioned techniques designed to assist US service personnel in interrogations has included an array of methods from stress positions, sensory deprivation, forced nudity, and intimidation using dogs, to more grave ones such as the use of scenarios designed to convince the detainee that death or harm for them or their loved ones was imminent, as well as waterboarding (Danchev 2009: 181–182). It has become clear that the treatment of prisoners in detention has gone far beyond even these proscribed techniques.

The now infamous photographs of the torture and abuse of detainees held in Abu Ghraib prison in Iraq emerged in 2004 (Cohen 2005: 27). These photographs, taken by US security force personnel depicted naked prisoners being sexually and physically assaulted, humiliated, electrocuted, raped, and in some cases murdered. Abu Ghraib was not an isolated case. In 2005, evidence of an incident was leaked to *The New York Times* which said that two prisoners had been beaten to death by American soldiers during interrogation at Bagram Internment Facility in Afghanistan (Golden 2005). Other evidence emerged in 2004 of torture in Guantanamo Bay in Cuba by US personnel, including beatings, strangulation and burning with cigarettes (Luban 2005: 60). A Report by The Centre for Constitutional Rights collated evidence of torture in Guantanamo, detailing sexual humiliation, extreme sleep deprivation, beatings, stress positions, and rape, as well as desecration of holy books, exposure to sustained loud music, and sensory deprivation (Centre for Constitutional Rights 2006). A statement in 2017 from the UN

Special Rapporteur on Torture, Nils Melzer, indicated that measures amounting to torture were still in use at Guantanamo Bay and other CIA 'Black Site' facilities (Melzer 2017). The extent of the abuse of prisoners demonstrates that in some cases, torture was used for reasons other than intelligence gathering. As Heath Kelly has argued, the unconcealed existence and use of detention facilities to imprison and torture detainees was an act of terror, designed to intimidate and to communicate the USA's defiance of international norms (2019: 233).

QUESTIONS

1. Consider the impact that US use of torture in the Global War on Terror has had on global security
2. What other contemporary practices in the 'Global War on Terror' might be seen as state-terrorism?

CASE STUDY 14.2

British Extrajudicial Killings in Northern Ireland

Throughout the Northern Ireland conflict that began in the mid-1960s, the British state was engaged in practices that amounted to state terrorism. In 1969, as civil unrest worsened, the British Army were deployed to Northern Ireland where they used colonial style counterinsurgency practices developed during engagements fighting national liberation movements in Malaya, Aden (temporary capital of Yemen), Cyprus, and Kenya (McConaghy 2017: 80).

In the early 1970s, the British Army's Parachute Regiment gained a reputation for atrocities. They killed 11 unarmed civilians over a three day period in Belfast in August 1971 during civil unrest (which became known as the Ballymurphy Massacre) and a further 13 civilians at a Civil Rights protest in Derry in January 1972, with another civilian dying later of his injuries (which became known as the Bloody Sunday Massacre) (Mulholland 2002: 97). Both areas were zones where the population opposed the presence of the British Army and where state control was waning. The deployment of such violent military units into nationalist areas at times of high tension had a disastrous effect, contributing to a surge in violence. It was seen by the local community as a move designed to stamp out political dissent through exemplary force.

Between the 1970s and 1990s in Northern Ireland, British security forces conducted a number of 'shoot to kill' attacks against suspected members of republican paramilitaries, rather than attempting to arrest and seek prosecutions (Hearty 2014: 50, 63). These targeted killings were conducted by specialist army and police units (Stalker 1988: 253; Ellison and Smyth 2000: 116–133; White et al. 2021: 267) and became more common in the 1980s, coinciding with a surge in support for Sinn Féin, the political party linked to the IRA (White et al. 2020: 4). The attacks aimed to demoralize republicans at a time when they had unprecedented strength. Loyalist paramilitaries were rarely targeted in such attacks (Ní Aoláin 2000: 62); the British government's objective in this period became destroying the IRA rather than resolving the conflict (MoD 2006: 242; McGovern 2019: 66–69). 'Shoot to kill' incidents had a profoundly negative human and moral cost and served the exacerbate violence in the long run. They undermined the UK state's efforts to position itself as a neutral arbiter in the conflict. While British Prime Minister during this period, Margaret Thatcher, applauded the use of such tactics, (Hearty 2014: 64–65) these were criticized by human rights experts and damaged the reputation of the UK internationally (Amnesty International 1994, McCann and Others v United Kingdom 21 ECHR 97 GC, Re McCaughley and Anor [2011] UKSC 20).

Northern Ireland also saw a substantial number of cases of 'collusion' where elements of the state worked with illegal paramilitaries. Some British soldiers and police officers were also members of loyalist paramilitary groups, carrying out attacks on civilians and suspected IRA members. A report commissioned by the British government in 1974 found that a substantial portion of the British Army's Ulster Defence Regiment were members of loyalist paramilitary organizations (Cadwallader 2013: 35). The loyalist Ulster Volunteer Force's (UVF) 'Glennane Gang' contained substantial numbers of serving and former security force personnel and is believed to be responsible for around 120 murders. In other instances, British intelligence agents working within illegal paramilitary groups like the IRA and UVF were permitted to continue killing people to maintain their cover, and at times were given intelligence in order to allow them to target specific individuals more effectively (Mulcahy 2006: 73–74). The use of such force by the British state aimed not simply to defeat the IRA, but also to terrify the wider nationalist community and to diminish the IRA's support base.

QUESTIONS

1. Consider the impact of states using targeted killings against their own citizens on domestic legitimacy.
2. Why do you think the UK resorted to state-terrorism in the Northern Ireland conflict?

14.7 THE EFFECTS OF STATE TERRORISM

There are many studies which seek to discern whether non-state terrorism 'works' (English 2016; Muro 2018; Abrahms 2006, 2011, 2012). No such studies exist for state terrorism. While the literature on the effectiveness of non-state terrorism has tended focus on whether armed groups have achieved strategic victory, states seldom have a preconceived endgame in sight, theirs is the perpetual task of survival. Similarly, illicit state violence often runs in tandem with licit state policies, making it harder to discern the effect that state terrorism has. The desire for silence and secrecy that cloaks most state terrorism makes it difficult to even quantify its human cost. We can never know with any certainty. What we can say of terrorism, be it state or non-state is that it 'works' in so far as it serves to generate fear in society. Its consistent ability to amplify the political message that far outweighs the initial violence is one of the most durable features of terrorism. This is why terrorism is likely to remain a tool wielded by state and non-state actors for centuries to come.

When the state is prepared to use wholesale terroristic violence, the re-modelling of society is often achieved with devastating effectiveness and speed, though the human and moral cost associated is an exorbitant price to pay for such control. Terrorism might have assisted totalitarian and authoritarian regimes control their societies in the short to medium term, but ultimately may have sharpened the resolve of their opponents to foment revolution or launch a coup d'etat.

As for terrorism perpetrated by liberal democracies and retreating colonial powers, the result has been damage to reputation and legitimacy both domestically and internationally. It is difficult to argue that the terroristic violence perpetrated by nominal liberal democracies against their citizens and colonial subjects in the course of decolonization campaigns achieved anything but the alienation of the populace and the acceleration of independence. Post 9/11, the evidence regarding the torture and abuse of prisoners in Bagram Airbase, Guantanamo Bay, and Abu Ghraib (see Case Study 14.1) punctured narratives of 'civility' versus 'barbarism'. Images of smiling US soldiers torturing prisoners in Abu Ghraib, and of manacled detainees in orange boiler suits in Guantanamo Bay became the definitive images of the Global War on Terror (see Photo 14.2), deposing those of the crumbling World Trade Centre in the public imagination.

Yemeni Youth Activist and Writer Farea Al-Muslimi, told the US Senate Judiciary Subcommittee on the Constitution (2013) that the US drone strike on his village targeting al-Qaeda in the Arabian Peninsula, which killed multiple civilians, served the opposite of the intended effect:

> 'What radicals had previously failed to achieve in my village, one drone strike accomplished in an instant: there is now an intense anger and growing hatred of America' (Al-Muslimi 2013).

State terrorism has served as the justification for acts of non-state terrorism. Mohammad Sidique Khan, one of the principal planners of the 7 July 2005 bombings in London, stated in his pre-recorded 'martyrdom' video that 'Until we [Muslims] feel security, you [British citizens] will be our targets. And until you stop the bombing, gassing, imprisonment and torture of my people we will not stop this fight' (2005).

14.8 THE LIMITATIONS OF 'STATE TERRORISM' AS A CONCEPT

As this chapter has demonstrated, states do perpetrate terrorism and while it might be overlooked, 'state-terrorism' remains an analytically useful term. But what are the limitations of this concept? Terrorism continues to be a pejorative term that states are unlikely to accept as a descriptor of their actions. There may be limits to what academics can do about this as states seek to distance themselves from a term that has such negative connotations. Nonetheless, for as long as terrorism remains a concept in use, academics ought to commit to ensuring that they apply the term to the acts of both state and non-state actors. This will help challenge the polarizing view that has developed of 'good' states and 'evil' (non-state) 'terrorists'. There ought to be scholarly clarity and honesty, even if policymakers will seek to pursue their own agendas.

Definitions of terrorism often depend on intent, which is notoriously difficult to prove with any certainty, both for state and non-state actors. Where terrorizing intent exists, it can often be masked by assertions of a strategic utility, leaving the fear induced and coercive impact look like unintended side effects. Establishing state responsibility for terrorism is also difficult. States seeking deniability will rarely produce official documentation that associates the state elites with acts of state terrorism. In instances where state personnel have engaged in terroristic violence, there have been efforts by elites to distance themselves from the actions, explaining them away as the actions of 'bad apples' who have abused their positions rather than acting in line with orders. Academics are left with difficult questions, which may have no easy answer. When is it a case of bad apples and when is it a case of rotten barrels?

States have sometimes relied on omission rather than acts–*not* penalizing subversion, looking the other way when state personnel perpetrate acts of terrorism, or by allowing a culture that makes terrorism by individual state personnel permissible. Proving state responsibility in these circumstances is difficult. In recent times, 'outsourcing' of state action, (where the state makes arrangements for another entity to perform tasks on its behalf) either to third party states through 'extraordinary rendition' (where individuals are covertly transported to another country to circumvent laws on the treatment of prisoners), or to corporate entities such as mercenaries, private military contractors, private security companies, and for-profit prisons have complicated matters. It is even more difficult in such instances to follow the thread of responsibility back to the state, which is precisely what has made such practices attractive.

14.9 CONCLUSION

This chapter has highlighted that states can, and do, perpetrate terrorism. The scale of this terrorism is much greater than that of non-state actors. If state terrorism has fallen from the public consciousness, it is not for want of examples, but rather because policymakers, media, and academics in the west have been more focused on 'revolutionary' or 'insurgent' violence than the excesses of states. There are many obstacles which make studying state terrorism difficult, not least the lack of funding incentives, the lack of conceptual clarity, the secrecy surrounding state violence, and a repudiation of the terminology of terrorism for state violence. Yet, despite these barriers, some academics have produced excellent work and demonstrated the necessity of further work in this area.

State terrorism does not exist in a vacuum. In order to understand why it manifests, how it is used, and what effect it has, it is essential to study the wider political and social context. It would be counterproductive to adopt a narrow focus on 'state terrorism' to the exclusion of other categories of violence (some abutting and some overlapping with state terrorism) such as forced population transfers, detention without trial, or ethnic cleansing. Similarly, states frequently rely on oppressive legal frameworks which curtail rights and fundamental freedoms in order to induce fear and create subservient compliance. To call this 'state terrorism' might be to over-stretch that concept, but to ignore it would limit our understanding of state power and repression. Our efforts to understand state terrorism will be more fruitful if they pay attention to other strategies of state repression too.

We live in a world where the concepts we use are too simplistic for the complicated conflicts they are applied to. How useful are distinctions of state and non-state terrorism in instances where conflicts involve proto-states, pseudo-states, and counter-states? How should one characterize the so-called Islamic State of Iraq and Syria (ISIS) when it controlled a territory during the years when it held vast swathes of territory, employed public servants, and discharged public duties? How can we describe the various gradations of state involvement in terrorism? Some violence is patently designed and directed by elites in the highest offices. Other violence is ordered by chiefs of state organizations who break the law to pursue their own objectives. Other violence still is the work of small groups of low-level public servants perhaps working with illegal organizations. In such cases the level of ignorance or complicity of their superiors is hard to establish. The binary terms of 'state terrorism' and 'non-state terrorism' do a great disservice to our understanding of these complex relationships. To deny that states partake in terrorism is to skew our understanding of one of the most prevalent and contentious forms of political violence in modernity. To achieve a fine-grained understanding of complex conflicts and modern states, we will need a wider-angled view, and more nuanced concepts than those we currently possess.

DISCUSSION QUESTIONS

1. Why might actor-centric definitions of terrorism be problematic?
2. Why has there been such little research on state terrorism compared to non-state terrorism?
3. How is 'state terrorism' different to 'non-state terrorism? How clear is the distinction between the two phenomena?
4. Why have some scholars chosen to reject 'state terrorism' as a concept?
5. What are the main obstacles to research on state terrorism?

Visit the online resources for pointers on how to answer the discussion questions, links to useful web sources, and guidance on accessing databases:
www.oup.com/he/Wilson-Muro1e

GUIDE TO FURTHER READING

Blakeley, R. (2009) *State Terrorism and Neoliberalism: The North in The South*. London and New York: Routledge. *A theoretically and empirically rich study that examines the range of ways that states in the global north have contributed to terroristic violence in the global south.*

Jarvis, L. and Lister, M. (2014) 'State Terrorism Research and Critical Terrorism Studies: An Assessment', *Critical Studies on Terrorism*, 7/1: 43–61. *This article reviews much of the literature on state terrorism and highlights its successes and failures.*

Pisoiu, D. and Hain, S. (2018) *Theories of Terrorism: An Introduction*, in Pisoiu, D. and Jackson, R. (2018), (eds.) *Contemporary Debates on Terrorism*. London: Routledge. 152–165. *Another excellent chapter taking a theoretical angle and asking why states resort to state terrorism.*

Wilson, T. (2019) 'State Terrorism', in *The Oxford Handbook of Terrorism*. Oxford: Oxford University Press, 331–348. *A historically informed study that reviews efforts to study state-terrorism and suggests a series of interesting questions for students and scholars of political violence to pursue.*

REFERENCES

Abrahms, M. (2006) 'Why Terrorism Does Not Work', *International Security*, 31 (2): 42–78.

Abrahms, M. (2011) 'Does Terrorism Really Work? Evolution in the Conventional Wisdom Since 9/11', *Defence and Peace Economics*, 22 (6): 583–594.

Abrahms, M. (2012) 'The Political Effectiveness of Terrorism Revisited', *Comparative Political Studies*, 45 (3): 366–393.

Allport, A. (2020) *Britain At Bay: The Epic Story of the Second World War: 1938–1941*. London: Profile Books.

Al-Muslimi, F. (2013) United States Senate Judiciary Committee Subcommittee on the Constitution, Civil Rights and Human Rights Drone Wars: The Constitutional and Counterterrorism Implications of Targeted Killing. 23 April 2013. Accessible at https://www.judiciary.senate.gov/imo/media/doc/04-23-13Al-MuslimiTestimony.pdf

Alston, P (2010) Report of the Special Rapporteur on Extrajudicial, Summary or Arbitrary Executions, Addendum—Study on Targeted Killings, United Nations General Assembly, United Nations Human Rights Council (A/HRC/14/24/Add.6).

Amnesty International (1994) *Political Killings in Northern Ireland EUR 45/001/94*. London: Amnesty International.

Amnesty International (2009) *Israel/Gaza—Operation 'Cast Lead': 22 Days of Death and Destruction*. London: Amnesty International.

Aretxaga, B. (2000 'Playing Terrorist: Ghastly Plots and the Ghostly State', *Journal of Spanish Cultural Studies*, 1 (1): 43–58.

Bargu, B. (2014 'Sovereignty as Erasure: Rethinking Enforced Disappearances', *Qui Parle: Critical Humanities and Social Sciences*, 23 (1): 35–75.

Baum, S.K., (2008) *The Psychology of Genocide: Perpetrators, Bystanders, and Rescuers*. Cambridge: Cambridge University Press.

Bennett, H. (2013) *Fighting the Mau Mau: The British Army and Counter-insurgency in the Kenya Emergency*. Cambridge: Cambridge University Press.

Berman, M. R. and Clark, R. S. (1981) 'State Terrorism: Disappearances', *Rutgers Law Journal*, 13: 531–577.

Blakeley, R. (2007) 'Bringing the State Back into Terrorism Studies', *European Political Science*, 6 (3): 228–235.

Blakeley, R. (2009) *State Terrorism and Neoliberalism: The North in The South*. London and New York: Routledge.

Bloom, J. J. (2010) *The Jewish Revolt Against Rome, AD 66–135. A Military Analysis*. London: Jefferson.

Branche, R. (2007) 'Torture of terrorists? Use of Torture in a "War Against Terrorism": Justifications, Methods and Effects: The Case of France in Algeria, 1954–1962', *International Review of the Red Cross*, 89 (867): 543–560.

Brett, R. (2016) *The Origins and Dynamics of Genocide: Political Violence in Guatemala*. London: Palgrave Macmillan.

Bruce, S. (1992), 'The Problems of "Pro-state" Terrorism: Loyalist Paramilitaries in Northern Ireland', *Terrorism and Political Violence*, 4 (1): 67–88.

Butler, J. (2004). *Precarious Life: The Powers of Violence and Mourning*. London and New York: Verso.

Bull, A.C. (2005). 'Casting a Long Shadow: The Legacy of Stragismo for the Italian Extreme Right', *The Italianist*, 25 (2): 260–279.

Byman, D. (2005) *Deadly Connections: States That Sponsor Terrorism*. Cambridge: Cambridge University Press.

Cadwallader, A. (2013). *Lethal Allies: British Collusion in Ireland*. Cork: Mercier Press.

Centre for Constitutional Rights (2006) Report on Torture and Cruel, Inhuman and Degrading Treatment of Prisoners at Guantánamo Bay, Cuba. Accessible at https://ccrjustice.org/sites/default/files/assets/Report_ReportOnTorture.pdf.

Claridge, D. (1996) 'State Terrorism? Applying a Definitional Model', *Terrorism and Political Violence*, 8 (3): 47–63.

Chaliand, G. and Blin, A. eds., (2007) *The History of Terrorism: From Antiquity to ISIS*. Los Angeles: University of California Press.

Cobain, I. (2013) *Cruel Britannia: A Secret History of Torture*. London: Portobello.

Cohen, S. (2005) 'Post-moral Torture: From Guantanamo to Abu Ghraib', *Index on Censorship*, 34 (1): 24–30.

Crenshaw, M. (2011) *Explaining Terrorism: Causes, Consequences and Processes*. New York and London: Routledge.

Crenzel, E. (2011) 'Present Pasts: Memory (ies), of State Terrorism in the Southern Cone of Latin America'. *The Memory of State Terrorism in the Southern Cone: Argentina, Chile, and Uruguay*: 1–13.

Cox, R. (2018) 'Historicizing Waterboarding as a Severe Torture Norm', *International Relations*, 32 (4): 488–512.

Danchev, A. (2009) *On Art and War and Terror*. Edinburgh: Edinburgh University Press.

Dershowitz, A. (2004) 'Tortured Reasoning', in Levinson, S. (2004) (ed.) *Torture: A Collection*. New York: Oxford University Press, 257–280.

Drake, C. J. M. (1996) 'The Phenomenon of Conservative Terrorism', *Terrorism and Political Violence*, 8 (3): 29–46.

Ellison, G. and Smyth, J. (2000) *The Crowned Harp: Policing Northern Ireland*. London: Pluto Press.

English, R. (2016) *Does Terrorism Work?: A History*. Oxford: Oxford University Press.

Finkelstein, N. G. (2013) 'US Support for Israeli State Terror', in Bailes, J. and Aksan, C. (2013) (eds.), *Weapon of the Strong: Conversations on US State Terrorism*. London: Pluto Press.

Gearty, C. (1991) *Terror*. London: Faber and Faber.

Giessauf, J., (2008) 'A Programme of Terror and Cruelty: Aspects of Mongol Strategy in the Light of Western Sources', *Chronica*, 7: 85–96.

Golden, T. (2005) 'In U.S. Report, Brutal Details of 2 Afghan Inmates Deaths', *New York Times*, 20 May 2005. Accessible at https://www.nytimes.com/2005/05/20/world/asia/in-us-report-brutal-details-of-2-afghan-inmates-deaths.html

George, A. ed. (1991) *Western State Terrorism*. Cambridge: Polity Press.

Gregory, D. (2010) 'War and Peace', *Transactions of the Institute of British Geographers*, 35 (2): 154–186.

Gunneflo, M. (2016) *Targeted Killing: A Legal and Political History*. Cambridge: Cambridge University Press.

Hajek, A. (2010) 'Teaching the History of Terrorism in Italy: The Political Strategies of Memory Obstruction', *Behavioural Sciences of Terrorism and Political Aggression*, 2 (3): 198–216.

Hajjar, L. (2013) *Torture: A Sociology of Violence and Human Rights*. London: Routledge.

Hearty, K. (2014) 'The Political and Military Value of the "Set Piece" Killing Tactic in East Tyrone 1983-1992', *State Crime Journal*, 31 (1): 50–72.

Heath Kelly, C. (2019) 'Critical Approaches to the Study of Terrorism', in Chenoweth, E, English, R., Gofas, A, and Kalyvas, S. (2019), *The Oxford Handbook of Terrorism*. Oxford: Oxford University Press, 224–250.

Herman, E. S. (1985) *The Real Terror Network: Terrorism in Fact and Propaganda*. Montreal: Black Rose Books.

Hoffman, B. (2006) *Inside Terrorism*. New York: Columbia University Press.

Human Rights Watch (2008) *Flooding South Lebanon: Israel's Use of Cluster Munitions in Lebanon in July and August 2006*. New York: Human Rights Watch https://www.hrw.org/report/2008/02/16/flooding-south-lebanon/israels-use-cluster-munitions-lebanon-july-and-august-2006 (last accessed 24 October 2019).

International Convention for the Protection of all Persons from Enforced Disappearance (ICPPED), Opened for signature (2006), Entered into force (2010) No. 48088.

Jackson, R. (2007) 'The Core Commitments of Critical Terrorism Studies', *European Political Science*, 6 (3): 244–251.

Jackson, R. Murphy, E., and Poynting, S. (2010) (eds.), *Contemporary State Terrorism: Theory and Practice*. London: Routledge.

Jamieson, R. and McEvoy, K. (2005) 'State Crime by Proxy and Juridical Othering', *British Journal of Criminology*, 45 (4): 504–527.

Jarvis, L. and Lister, M. (2014) 'State Terrorism Research and Critical Terrorism Studies: An Assessment', *Critical Studies on Terrorism*, 7 (1): 43–61.

Jeffrey, K. (1984) *The British Army and the Crisis of Empire, 1918–1922*. Manchester: Manchester University Press.

Kalyvas, S.N. (2019) 'The Landscape of Political Violence', in *The Oxford Handbook of Terrorism*. Oxford: Oxford University Press, 11–33.

Koch, B. (2016) 'Terror, Violence, Coercion: States and the Use of (Il)legitimate Force', in Koch, B. 2016 (ed.), *State Terror, State Violence: Global Perspectives*. Gottingen: Springer.

Kretzmer, D. (2005) 'Targeted Killing of Suspected Terrorists: Extra-judicial Executions or Legitimate Means of Defence?', *European Journal of International Law*, 16 (2): 171–212.

Laqueur, W. (1986) 'Reflections on Terrorism', *Foreign Affairs*, 65: 86–100.

Lippman, M. (1988) 'Disappearances: Towards a Declaration on the Prevention and Punishment of the Crime of Enforced or Involuntary Disappearances', *Connecticut Journal of International Law*, 4: 121–143.

Luban, D. 'Liberalism, Torture, and the Ticking Bomb', in Greenberg, K. J. (2005) (ed.) *The Torture Debate in America*. Cambridge: Cambridge University Press, 35–83.

MacMaster, N. (2004) 'Torture: From Algiers to Abu Ghraib', *Race and Class*, 46 (2): 1–21.

McConaghy, K. (2017) *Terrorism and the State: Intrastate Dynamics and the Response to Non-State Political Violence*. Basingstoke: Palgrave Macmillan.

McCoy, A. W. (2012) *Torture and Impunity: The US Doctrine of Coercive Interrogation*. Madison: University of Wisconsin Press.

McGovern, M. (2019) *Counterinsurgency and Collusion in Northern Ireland*. London: Pluto Books.

Melzer (2017) 'US must stop policy of impunity for the crime of torture', UN rights expert. Accessible at ://www.ohchr.org/EN/NewsEvents/Pages/DisplayNews.aspx?NewsID=22532andLangID=E

Ministry of Defence (UK) (2006) *Operation Banner: An Analysis of Military Operations in Northern Ireland: Army Code 71842*. London: MoD. McCann and Others v United Kingdom 21 ECHR 97 GC.

Mulcahy, A. (2006) *Policing Northern Ireland: Conflict, Legitimacy and Reform*. Cullompton: Willan.

Mulholland, M. (2002) *The Longest War: Northern Ireland's Troubled History*. Oxford: Oxford University Press.

Muro, D. (2018) (ed.), *When Does Terrorism Work?* London: Routledge.

Nasr, SM. (2010) 'Israel's Other Terrorist Challenge', in Jackson, R., Murphy, E., and Poynting, S. (2010) (eds.), *Contemporary State Terrorism: Theory and Practice*. London: Routledge. 68–85.

Neocleous, M. (2013) 'Air Power as Police Power', *Society and Space*, 31 (4): 578–593.

Ní Aoláin, F. (2000) *The Politics of Force: Conflict Management and State Violence in Northern Ireland*. Belfast: Blackstaff Press.

O'Sullivan, M.L. (2003) *Shrewd Sanctions: Statecraft and State Sponsors of Terrorism*. Washington DC: Brookings Institution Press.

O'Mara, S. (2015) *Why Torture Doesn't Work: The Neuroscience of Interrogation*. Cambridge MA and London: Harvard University Press.

Ott, L. (2011) *Enforced Disappearance in International Law*. Cambridge-Antwerp-Portland: Intersentia.

Pisoiu, D. and Jackson, R. (2018) (eds.) *Contemporary Debates on Terrorism*. London: Routledge.

Primoratz, I. (2004) 'State Terrorism and Counter-terrorism', in Primoratz, I. *Terrorism: The Philosophical Issues*. London: Palgrave Macmillan, 113–127.

Richardson, L. (2006) *What Terrorists Want: Understanding the Terrorist Threat*. London: Random House. Re McCaughley and Anor [2011] UKSC 20.

Roberts, G. B. (1987) 'Self-Help in Combatting State-Sponsored Terrorism: Self Defence and Peacetime Reprisals', *Case Western. Reserve. Journal of International Law*, 19: 243–294.

Schmid, A. P. (2011) *The Routledge Handbook of Terrorism Research*. London: Routledge.

Sidique Khan, M. (2005) Accessible at http://news.bbc.co.uk/1/hi/uk/4206800.stm

Slater, J. (2012) 'Just War Moral Philosophy and the 2008–09 Israeli Campaign in Gaza', *International Security*, 37 (2): 44–80.

Sluka, J. A. (2000) Death Squad: The Anthropology of State Terror.

Sproat, P. (1991) 'Can the State Be Terrorist?', *Terrorism*, 14 (1): 19–29.

Sproat, P. (1997) 'Can the State Commit Acts of Terrorism?: An Opinion and Some Qualitative Replies to a Questionnaire', *Terrorism and Political Violence*, 9 (4): 117–150.

Stalker, J. (1988) *Stalker: Ireland 'Shoot to Kill' and the 'Affair'*. London: Penguin Books.

Stampnitzky, L. (2013) *Disciplining Terror: How Experts Invented 'Terrorism'*. Cambridge: Cambridge University Press.

Sterling, C. (1981) *The Terror Network: The Secret War of International Terrorism*. New York: Weidenfeld and Nicolson.

Steyn, J. (2004) 'Guantanamo Bay: The Legal Black Hole', *International and Comparative Law Quarterly*, 53 (1): 1–15.

Stohl, M. (2006) 'The State as Terrorist: Insights and Implications', *Democracy and Security*, 2 (1): 1–25.

Stohl, M. and Lopez, G. A. (eds.) (1986) *Government Violence and Repression: An Agenda for Research* (No. 148). New York: Greenwood Press.

Townshend, C. (1975) *The British Campaign in Ireland, 1919-1921: The Development of Political and Military Policies*. Oxford: Oxford University Press.

Walter, E. V. (1969) *Terror and Resistance: a Study of Political Violence, with Case Studies of Some Primitive African Communities* (Vol. 1). New York: Oxford University Press.

Weber, M. (1919) *Politics as a Vocation*. Munich: Duncker and Humboldt.

White, R. W., Demirel-Pegg, T., and Lulla, V. (2021) 'Terrorism, Counter-terrorism and "The Rule of Law": State Repression and "Shoot to Kill" In Northern Ireland', *Irish Political Studies*, 36 (2): 263–290.

Wight, C. (2009) 'Theorising Terrorism: The State, Structure and History', *International Relations*, 23 (1): 99–106.

Wilkinson, P. (2011) *Terrorism Versus Democracy: The Liberal State Response*. London: Routledge.

Wilson, T. (2019) 'State Terrorism' in *The Oxford Handbook of Terrorism*. Oxford: Oxford University Press, 331–348.

Woodworth, P. (2001) *Dirty War Clean Hands: ETA The GAL and Spanish Democracy*, Cork: Cork University Press.

Wright, T. C. (2007) *State Terrorism in Latin America: Chile, Argentina, and International Human Rights*. Plymouth: Rowman and Littlefield.

Yiftachel, O. (1999) '"Ethnocracy": The Politics of Judaizing Israel/Palestine', *Constellations*, 6 (3): 364–390.

CHAPTER 15

Gendered and Racialized Terrorism

CARON E. GENTRY

■ CHAPTER SUMMARY

This chapter relies upon poststructuralism to understand how terrorism is a subjective term dependent upon the power structures of gender and race. In simple terms, poststructuralism looks at how meaning and power are constructed through discourse—text, speech, and/or images (Devetak 2013). It recognizes that all knowledge is manufactured and often aligned with power. The first part of the chapter draws out that the very understanding of what terrorism *is* is dependent upon gendered and racialized assumptions. It uses the Feminist theory of intersectionality, which looks at how oppressions, such as race and gender, intersect to cause harm. Therefore, 'terrorism' immediately imparts certain meanings to an audience, meanings that all individuals respond to differently, or subjectively. Therefore, an objective idea of terrorist does not exist, and this chapter aims to demonstrate that this is owed to gender and race. The second part of the chapter shifts focus and looks at the rise of Incel violence, and who those associated with the Incel 'revolution' rely upon the intersecting biases of gender and race to justify their violence.

15.1 INTRODUCTION

When Shamima Begum, a 15-year-old from Bethnal Green, London, took her passport, flew to Turkey with two friends, and crossed the border into Syria to join ISIS in February 2015, she was portrayed in the media as a manipulated schoolgirl, one who had been groomed by ISIS fighters to join them. Little attention was paid to her own motivations or commitment to the ideology ISIS articulated. Begum was simply a confused British girl who the general public and media wanted home. This all changed when Shamima Begum materialized in a refugee camp in February 2019. Eight months pregnant with her third child, she was widowed, and her first two children were both dead from suspected malnutrition. She expressed a desire to return to UK to give her child a chance at survival. Instead of sparking further sympathy, her unrepentant belief in ISIS' cause was met with outrage from a once supportive audience. Instead of an innocent 'schoolgirl', the British public (and beyond) were confronted by a young woman who, after everything, still saw validity in ISIS' fight. They then regarded her as monstrous and a traitor to British values. Within days, she was stripped of British citizenship and not allowed to return to the UK. Her third child died within weeks of birth. Currently, Begum's appeal to restore her citizenship is ongoing.

A year after Begum left for Syria, an armed right-wing militia of white men, Citizens for Constitutional Freedom, took over the Malheur National Wildlife Refuge in Harney County, Oregon, USA, in January 2016. Ammon Bundy, a middle-class Mormon man whose father is a rancher in Harney County, led the militia. Bundy was driven by the belief that God had directed him to end the federal government's ownership of land in the County. During the siege, other militias protected the headquarters by setting up a parameter. Law enforcement allowed militia members to come and go as they liked until the fourth week. At this time, police tried to intercept a few of the leaders. This led to a car chase, shootings, and arrest, yet it did not end the siege which went on for another two weeks. Even though these men used violence against law enforcement, physically challenged the US federal government's authority in Harney County, and resisted arrest, none of the militia members were charged with terrorism. Later, all of were acquitted of the criminal charges brought against them.

> **KEY CONCEPTS**
>
> **Gender** Understood as a social construction of the expectations placed on to sexed bodies, varying from one social context to the next; additionally, understood as social structure that orders the relationships between objects gendered as masculine and objects gendered as feminine.

> **KEY CONCEPTS**
>
> **Intersectionality** The belief that oppressive structures, such as gender and race, often intersect harming some individuals more than others; it is also a form of analysing both the lived experiences of people and a method of inquiry.

> **KEY CONCEPTS**
>
> **Race** A socially constructed division of humanity based upon biological characteristics not shared by all humans.

These examples illustrate the subjectivity of who is seen, or not, as a terrorist actor and how such 'seeing' does not follow an objective definition of what terrorism is. Those now recognized internationally as 'heroes', such as Nelson Mandela who was found guilty of terrorist offences and imprisoned only to become the first black president of South Africa, or José 'Pepe' Mujica, a former Tupamaro (a left-wing urban guerrilla group) who from 2010 to 2015 served as President of Uruguay, have been through similar shifts in perception. The subjective nature of terrorists and terrorism has often been noted by Terrorism Studies scholars (Hoffman 2006: 21–23; Jenkins 1980: 10). Yet, this chapter goes beyond these studies to examine the subjectivity to gender and race. This chapter, alongside other work by Gentry (2020, 2018), argues that the subjectivity of terrorism is dependent upon gendered and racialized (amongst other) notions of who a terrorist is and what a terrorist looks like.

This chapter analyses the relationship between terrorism and intersectional structures, such as gender and race, and does so in two different ways. First, how terrorism is *understood* by those who describe it, such as academics, government officials, and media sources, is dependent upon gendered and racialized assumptions. To demonstrate this, the chapter relies upon a post structural Feminist theoretical perspective. In simple terms, poststructuralism looks at how meaning and power are constructed through discourse—text, speech, and/or images (Devetak 2013). It recognizes that all knowledge is manufactured, and closely aligned with power. Poststructuralism deconstructs texts by looking at the hidden (and not hidden) meaning in chosen words or imagery. Thus, terror, terrorist and terrorism are all words that immediately impart certain meanings to an audience, meanings that all individuals respond to differently (subjectively). When 'terrorism' or 'terrorist' are spoken, different social meanings of who a terrorist is, what forms of violence they use, and why they use violence accompany these words, meaning that objectivity is lost. Therefore, an objective idea of terrorist does not exist, and this chapter aims to highlight how this is owed to gender and race.

> **KEY CONCEPTS**
>
> **Discourse and Post-structuralism: Logocentric Binaries and Deconstruction** Logocentrism is a complex idea within poststructuralism (and structuralism before it) that looks at the privileging of spoken words to convey deeper, hidden meanings. As this chapter is not solely focused on poststructuralism (for more information and background, see E-International Relations resources on poststructuralism at www.e-ir.info/resources/poststructuralism), it introduces one piece of the discussion: the logocentric binary. The logocentric binary looks at the relationship between contrasting terms such as masculine/feminine, white/Black, reason/emotion, or rationality/irrationality. Before poststructuralism, it was held that the first terms from this list, such as masculine, white, reason, rationality, were dominant and preferred. Thus, the use of these terms, or ones that indicated such biases, revealed the author's own preferences and highlighted the 'correct' way of being or knowing for an audience. The second term (feminine, Black, emotion, irrationality) therefore were presented as inferior, illustrating a lack or a negation. Poststructuralism nuances the relationship between the two terms, seeing them as co-constitutive and complications of each other instead of clear-cut binaries. It has been argued that terrorist/counterterrorist or state/non-state exist in similar tensions, where one term is significantly superior to the other.

The second objective of this chapter is to examine how gendered and racialized beliefs play a part in justifying and shaping terrorists' agendas. Thus, the chapter explores the ideological discourse and violence perpetrated by groups and actors united by misogyny and toxic masculinity (a set of attitudes and ways of behaving stereotypically associated with or expected of men, which has a negative impact on men and society as a whole). These actors include Marc Lépine, Eliott Rodger, and Alek Minassian, but also Dylann Roof and Anders Breivik, who are widely recognized for their white supremacy rather than their misogyny (see Boxes 15.3 and 15.4). The purpose of section 15.3: When Gender and Race Are the Driving Focus is to amplify how misogynistic and white supremacist attitudes are political and ideological beliefs. This helps to clarify how this violence is the *politically driven* violence commonly labelled terrorism.

15.2 HOW GENDER AND RACE WORK: ESSENTIALIZATION AND IDEALIZATION

Structures order, often hierarchically, the relationship between actors, organizations, and individuals. These relationships are power-filled and, as Feminism is driven by the need to uncover the operation of power, this chapter will uncover how the various structures determine Western understandings of terrorism, reproducing and reconfiguring pre-existing power relationships. Gender or race are often attributed to biological characteristics; yet these 'biological' and therefore immutable traits derive their meaning from what individuals and society make of them (they are social constructions). Additionally, gender and race are not just applied to people, but to institutions, concepts, actors, and objects. Therefore, this part of the chapter will tease out how gender and race structures utilize *essentialization* and *idealization* to create and maintain hierarchical relationships between people and objects such as states and terrorist groups, and the perception of state violence versus terrorist violence.

15.2.1 Essentialization

The study of gender and terrorism began with the classic Feminist question, 'where are the women?' At first, Feminist terrorism studies academics (Sjoberg and Gentry 2007 and 2011; Gentry 2004; Parashar 2011 and 2009; McEvoy 2009; Cunningham 2003; Alison 2003; Hamilton 2013) explored various groups active in the recent past, dating from the 1960s onward, such as the West German Red Army Faction, the Italian Red Brigades, the Liberation Tigers of Tamil Elam, ETA, and the Popular Front for the Liberation of Palestine. They also studied places, such as Chechnya, Kashmir, and Northern Ireland, where women participated in terrorist violence and planning. Thus, it is well known amongst these scholars that women have been engaged in the planning and enacting of terrorist violence ever since the term terrorism came into existence. It is largely agreed that 'terrorism' was first used to describe the state violence of Robespierre's Reign of Terror during the French Revolution (Hoffman 2006). It later morphed, describing the pro-nationalist violence of the mid-19th-century Europe, later coming to be identified with the anarchist violence that marked the end of the 19th century in Europe (see Crenshaw 1995). Women were immersed in these groups: actively writing ideology, planning attacks, and even carrying them out (Gentry 2019). And, yet, surprise over women's participation in terrorism persists (see Gentry 2020; Gentry 2019; Loken and Zelenz 2018).

The notion that women are often not involved in terrorist violence is a gendered notion: one that relies too heavily on the gendered ideal that women are not violent, but passive, and men inherently violent. Gender *essentialization* proposes that men and masculinity are *naturally* tied to superior intelligence, rationality, logic, and the ability to be violent and aggressive, whereas women and femininity are the opposite and *naturally* tied to inferior intelligence, emotion, nurturing, and peaceability (Elshtain 1981 and 1987). The assumption that these attributes or characteristics are innate is something that is now seen as fundamentally flawed, if not completely false. Yet, it persists: if a woman is violent she is seen as 'flawed' or a corrupted (Gentry and Sjoberg 2015). This does all people a disservice, as it essentializes violence, and does consider socio-political motives. Additionally, it relies too heavily on the idea that women only operate in the private sphere (home) and men naturally fit best into the public sphere (politics, government, war, commerce) (Elshtain 1981; Pateman 1980). Such notions are limiting, failing to see the engagement of all people in political violence as complicated, and stemming from personal as well as political reasons.

Since women's participation in terrorism has been studied (starting in the 1970s), women's involvement has tended to be described or explained in terms of gendered idealizations or essentializations (see Sjoberg and Gentry 2007 and 2011; Gentry and Sjoberg 2015). On the one hand, it was assumed that women affiliated with terrorism were simply not capable of violence, because all women were presented as nurturing and peaceable. In the 1980s, women's participation in terrorism was described in terms of keeping house or 'mothering' the men (Weinberg and Eubank 1987) or as simply the partners supporting their men (Morgan 1989). On the other hand, women involved with terrorism were presented as corrupt, they had an erotic malfunction that drove their violence (Anonymous 1976) or mentally unwell, and far more ruthless and violent than male terrorists (MacDonald 1991; see also Cooper 1979).

Additionally, feminists studying gender and terrorism go beyond how individuals are characterized by gender by looking at how gender constructs society, and the relationship of actors and organizations within society. Masculinity has long been affiliated with the legitimate operations of the state in the international system. Because masculinity and femininity exist in a logocentric dynamic, where masculinity marks the superior term and femininity the inferior term, the masculinity of states demarcates the feminization of non-state actors and activities. Within a state-centric system, Terrorism Studies prioritizes the state over non-state actors, and legitimizes the violence of the state, while delegitimizing non-state violence. The values that are seen as important to a state—rationality, sovereignty, power—are also traditionally masculine traits. Thus, the state system is a masculine structure (see Tickner 1992; Sjoberg 2013). Terrorism, often defined as a non-state activity (see Richardson 2006; Wight 2015; Blakeley 2009), is 'feminized' or 'de-valourized' and therefore seen as illegitimate (Sjoberg 2009; Gentry 2020, 2018, 2014).

Equally, Terrorism Studies as a predominantly Western academic subject, operates within a 'white supremacist' system as it values European ways of doing and being, as prioritized in colonialism, over other ways (see Muppidi 2006; Barkawi and Laffey 2006). Thus, intersectional oppressions are seen in the social relationships between states, the violence of states, actors affiliated with states versus non-state actors, and in particular the violence of non-state actors. Racialized essentializations related to skin colour and ethnicity also play a role in how a person's use of violence is perceived. Colonial imperialism assumes that white Europeans (and their descendants) were superior in intellect, rationality, and judgement to ethnic minority people (Smith 2012). Thus, the activities of colonized people are presented as inferior—this ranged from cleanliness (McClintock 2013), the treatment of women (Chakrabarty 1992), to the ability to suppress violent impulses (Smith 2012). Instead of seeing the anti-colonial violent rebellions that rose up after World War II as legitimate and linked to self-determination, the violence was often understood and described by Western states as terrorism and illegitimate (Barkawi and Laffey 2006; Smith 2012).

CASE STUDY 15.1

Racializations of 'Lone Wolf Terrorism'

Lone Wolf terrorism is defined as 'terrorist activities carried out by lone individuals from those carried out on the part of terrorist organizations or state bodies' (Spaaij 2010: 856; Berntzen and Sandberg 2014). These individuals may be politicized in a larger community, or an online one, yet they tend to plan and carry out their attacks alone (Kirby 2007). Prominent lone wolf terrorists include Theodore Kaczynski, 'the Unibomber' (years active 1978–1995), and Timothy McVeigh, who bombed the federal building in Oklahoma City, USA in 1995. Yet, attention in the post-9/11 era is often given to ethnic minority people, and violence by white men is often dismissed due to poor mental health.

Anders Breivik's two-part attack in Norway started with a car bomb in Oslo and massacre on the island summer camp of Utøya on 22 July 2011. His attack was the largest violent act in Norway since World War II. The car bomb in Oslo killed 8 people. The island massacre killed 69 people, many of them young people under the age of 20. In total, he wounded another 319 people. As the attack unfolded, the media first assumed it was being committed by a radical Islamist. It soon became clear that it was a Norwegian citizen who had shared his 1,500-page ideological statement with multiple people before the attack. He used Islamophobia and misogynistic white supremacy to justify his attacks. Yet, as his case went through the judicial system, Breivik's political motivations were met with suspicion as his mental health came into question.

This is in stark contrast with the assumptions around Major Nidal Hassan's mass shooting on Fort Hood, Texas, the largest Army base in the United States. On 5 November 2009, Major Hasan entered Fort Hood's Soldier Readiness Processing Centre, shouted 'Allahu Akbar' ('God is greatest' in Arabic) and shot 200 bullets from his handgun. He harmed 45 and killed 13 people. He was sentenced to death in 2013 (Kenber 2013). Before the attack, his superiors were concerned about his well-being, including one instructor who worried Hasan risked developing a psychosis, and others who sent him for counselling and extra supervision (BBC 2010). Even though he was not charged with terrorist offences, Hassan's attack is often conceived of by the media as a terrorist attack.

An additional example of racialized assumptions of guilt happened during the March 2018 mail-bombing campaign by Mark Anthony Conditt in Austin, Texas, USA. The first victim of the bomber was Anthony Stephan House, a 39-year-old Black man and graduate from Texas State University (Wallace-Wells 2018). Initially, the police refused to treat his death as murder because 'we can't rule out that Mr. House didn't construct this himself and accidentally detonate it . . .' (Wallace-Wells 2018). When it was discovered that Conditt was a 23-year-old white man from a Christian family, the response from the police was telling in their contrast as his actions were seen as the 'outcry of a very challenged young man' (Hanna, Karimi, Morris, and Almasy 2018). This was after he died effectively as a suicide-bomber by setting off his own bomb, in his car, while driving it along I-35, the interstate that runs through the middle of Austin (Almasy 2018). In looking at these examples, a person's race and identity has implications for how their violence and motivations are understood. Therefore, thinking intersectionally helps one to critically evaluate common depictions of individuals and different acts of violence.

QUESTIONS

1. How do the racial assumptions about lone wolf terrorism correspond to racial assumptions about people of colour more generally?
2. How do those who study or counter terrorism begin to challenge these assumptions?

Within this racialization of anti-colonial violence is the construction of rationality/irrationality as a logocentric binary. White Europeans were historically assumed to be more rational, and therefore more in control of their impulses. In this complex hierarchy, as noted by the Austin, Texas example, ethnic minority people are constructed as irrational and less in control of impulses, such as violence. In more recent years, when looking at terrorism, this has become particularly problematic with the prominence of neo-Orientalism, which racializes Islam, assuming that all people who live in the Middle East and other parts of the world, such as Afghanistan, Pakistan, and Indonesia, are Muslims and that, somehow, all Muslim men are violent. Neo-Orientalist bias believes that Muslim men are prone to hyperviolence (unthinking violence), hyper-aggression, and hypersexuality, whereas Muslim women are overly submissive, passive, and victimized by Muslim men (Martini 2018). This is particularly clear in the literature that surrounds the US Global War on Terror and the justifications for it (see Gentry 2018; Nayak 2006; Shepherd 2006).

15.2.2 Idealizations

Structures that create assumptions about how things operate, as gender and race do, also make assumptions about an ideal-type, or an exaggerated expectation, of what a certain object should look or act like. *Idealizations* perform the structuring—first, that the state is the 'normal' preferred actor in International Relations; second, that (Western/white) men are the preferred agent of the state, as they are most able to control their violent impulses (see Case Study 14.1); and thirdly, that most women and all colonized people are inferior in multiple respects. Even though these are clear exaggerations, idealizations work through these assumptions and the acceptance of them. In the current state-centric international system, the state has the monopoly on legitimate violence. The state becomes the elected and accepted way of fighting terrorism: terrorist violence after all often attacks the state. Thus, the counter-terrorist agent, as an agent of the state, is imbued with the legitimacy of the state. On the other side of this logocentrism, in more recent events, terrorists exist as an illegitimate and (frequently) non-state actor from the Global South. As non-state actors, the use of violence is conceived of as illegitimate. Yet, there are other ways of signifying illegitimacy.

Poststructuralism helps us to analyse language, looking to see what words are connotated with other words; it examines how the use of one word immediately brings to mind another one, leading to a conflation of meaning. For instance, how has terrorism become associated with 'Arab,' 'Islam,' and 'Muslim' to create a prejudiced fear of *all* Muslims without recognizing how biased and unproblematized these associations are (see Ahmed 2004)? For instance, Lisa Stampnitzky (2013) traces out the historical development of the field of Terrorism Studies. Stampnitzky (2013: 70–75) highlights how the definition of terrorism went from violence associated with post- and anti-colonial violence to violence associated with irrationality, immorality, and illegitimacy. As highlighted by the Austin male-bombing case, gender and race can both determine whether or not an individual is viewed as 'rational' or 'irrational'. When terrorist violence becomes tied with an estimation of 'rationality' gender and race are not absent from these estimations.

Idealizations of gender and race become the way an actor's violence is evaluated, like Shamima Begum's support for ISIS outlined the introduction to this chapter, or the discussion of lone wolf actors and race in Case Study 15.1. Men and other masculine actors are idealized as rational, just as white people (mainly white men) are seen as more rational than ethnic minority people (thus why the takeover of Malheur Nature Reserve was perhaps not seen as terrorism—see section 15.1). 'Female terrorists' are not rational because women are not meant to be violent, see Case Study 15.2. Anti-colonial violence is 'terrorist' because it is a threat to a white Western (rational) order. Therefore, even though states are the ideal actor and terrorists are not, there still exists an idealization of a terrorist, or the 'normal' terrorist. The structures of gender and race impact who is seen as terrorists. If terrorism is known to be political, strategic, and ideologically motivated, then the 'ideal' (assumed normal) terrorist is driven by these. If women are never violent (supposedly), then they are never (typically) deemed terrorists. If illegitimate non-state violence becomes associated with ethnic minority people and the Global South, then terrorism belongs to those from the Global South.

CASE STUDY 15.2

Ulrike Meinhof and the Assumptions about Women's Political Violence

Ulrike Meinhof (see Photo 15.1) was one of three leaders of the first generation of the Red Army Faction (RAF), a Marxist-Leninist terrorist group, that formed in West Germany in the late 1960s. Born in 1934, Meinhof grew up in Nazi Germany although her parents and later her foster mother were all dissenters. As a teenager she was politically active as an anti-atom bomb Christian pacifist, although moving to communism as a university student. She became a well-known left-wing journalist. She married and had twin daughters. During her pregnancy, she was diagnosed with a possible brain tumour. She refused surgery to protect her pregnancy. After an early caesarean, Meinhof had an emergency surgery that revealed a large brain aneurysm, which required a permanent clamp (Aust 2008).

PHOTO 15.1   Ulrike Meinhof, German journalist and member of the RAF (Red Army Faction).

In 1968, as a journalist, she reported on the fire-bombing of a department store carried out by Gudrun Ensslin and Andreas Baader. Later, Meinhof joined Ensslin in breaking Baader out of prison. Together the three of them formed and led the Red Army Faction. While investigating the RAF, Alfred Klaus, head of the West German Special Commission on Terrorism, labelled Meinhof the 'head' as she articulated the beliefs of the group; Baader the 'engine' because he was committed to violent actions; and Enslinn the 'soul' for her ability to captivate an audience (Aust 1987, 267). The first generation of RAF militants operated from 1970 until the time of their arrest in 1972. They were found guilty and, unable to find political asylum in sympathetic countries, the imprisoned leadership committed suicide in 1977 (except for Meinhof, who committed suicide in 1976), which they staged to look like they were murdered by agents of the West German state. Meinhof was the first one to commit suicide, hanging herself in her prison cell.

Meinhof's violence poses a problem for those who believe women are not violent. Her successful career as a journalist and personal 'success' being married to konkret's Editor-in-Chief suggested to some that Meinhof had mental health problems when she joined Ensslin and Baader. Some suggested that the brain surgery altered her personality. While this negates Meinhof's own belief in the cause, and her status as one of the RAF's primary ideologues, this was seen as a persuasive argument.

In fact, it was so persuasive that the West German government, without asking her family for permission, removed Meinhof's brain during the autopsy in her body, giving it to a variety of neuroscientists over several decades to study for pathologies. No pathologies were ever found, and when her daughters learned of the theft, they sued the now German state for the release of her brain, which was granted (Third 2010).

In an article on Meinhof, Amanda Third (2010) uses Hélène Cixous' theory on the metaphorical decapitation of women. Women are figuratively 'decapitated' when they are essentialized as unreasonable and irrational. Third (2010: 85) suggests that, as a violent woman, Meinhof represents a threat to the order of the state. Feminist political theorists have determined that Western democratic thought is dependent upon the conflation of a citizen as a rational actor (see Elshtain 1981; Pateman 1980). As noted in section 15.1, women are essentialized in contrast to an ideal citizen because they are constructed as irrational. Meinhof, therefore, as both violent and as an (irrational) woman, posed a threat to the state. Her 'decapitation' then is a way of containing her violence: making it pathological and something outside of Meinhof's control. It fails to account for her political beliefs that she had for the majority of her life, which negates her political agency, and capacity to act and make decisions autonomously.

Meinhof is a strong example of how 'female terrorists' are often constructed as representing a deeper threat to society than 'male terrorists'. They threaten: the masculine ordering of the state system; democratic practices which rely upon masculine actors; and the very way that many societies construct women as peaceful and givers, not takers, of life (for more on this see Gentry and Sjoberg 2015).

QUESTIONS

1. What are some current constructions of women who engage in terrorism that deny them their political agency?
2. How is Shamima Begum an example of how gender and race intersect to undermine her agency, in a potentially similar way to how Meinhof's gender was used to undermine her?

Yet, these are more examples of how subjective 'terrorism' is known in popular cases, not in the academic discipline of Terrorism Studies. There are two academic discussions that help illustrate this: the new terrorism thesis and the focus on radicalization. The new terrorism thesis was introduced in the 1990s and argued that future terrorist attacks would be much larger events with mass casualties, perpetrated by religious groups (Laqueur 1999 and 1996; Hoffman 2002, 2001, 1999). It looked at events like Aum Shinrikyo's sarin nerve gas attack on the Tokyo subway in 1995, as well as white supremacist Timothy McVeigh's attack on the US federal building in Tulsa, Oklahoma (also in 1995). Yet, as al-Qaeda's activities intensified in the late 1990s, culminating in the 9/11 attacks, new terrorism's focus narrowed to almost only looking at radical Islamism (see Gentry and Sjoberg 2016; Gentry 2020). In the post-9/11 moment, the chain of signification of terrorism was racialized to include 'Arab', 'Muslim', 'Islam', to the detriment of recognizing the other forms of terrorism (Ahmed 2004).

At the same time, 'radicalization' became a buzzword in both Terrorism Studies and in counter-terrorism (Heath-Kelly 2013). Radicalization seeks to understand what attracts certain individuals to terrorism (Borum 2012a and 2012b). Yet, it ignores the literature on mobilization and politicization that came before. Additionally, it is important to look at the discursive linkages that radicalization rests upon. Radicalization presumes that a mental shift has happened within an individual, making them more receptive to the use of violence. This new affinity for the possible use of illegitimate violence, as it is violence not associated with the more powerful and more legitimate state, is classified as irrational (see Gentry 2020: 137–138)—something that is also racialized and linked with violence (see section 15.2 on essentialization). When it comes to radicalization counter-terrorism policy, it has been shown that in both word and action, the UK's counter-terrorism policy, CONTEST, and its counter-radicalization pillar, Prevent, focuses extensively on radical Islamism. Muslims from all walks of life have become the ones who are bear the brunt of Prevent's objectives (Heath-Kelly 2012: 70). Prevent and its element of suspicion 'have become a tool of power exercised by the state and non-Muslim communities against, and to control, Muslim communities' (Githens-Mazer and Lambert 2010: 901). Muslims have a 1 in 500 chance of being referred to Prevent, which is 40 times higher than any other UK population (Versi 2017).

The way we perceive a person's use of violence is often shaped by how we understand that person as an individual. What is their gender? What is their ethnic identity? What is their assumed religion or cultural origin? These assumptions uphold various structures and are used to make sense of individuals and their actions, violent or not. Structures foreclose the ability to recognize an individual and their violence as legitimate or not. Equally, structures also force or 'guide' particular people along particular paths. Therefore, the next section 15.3 will look at why someone might use violence because of the way that they perceive gender and race.

15.3 WHEN GENDER AND RACE ARE THE DRIVING FORCES: THE INCEL REVOLUTION

Thus far this chapter has focused on how intersectional factors shape *understandings* of terrorist violence. It is now going to shift to examine how intersectional factors become the driving forces *for* terrorist violence. Intersectionality began as a concept to understand how people felt and experienced multiple lived oppressions, initially gender and race. Those gendered and racialized oppressions stemmed from misogyny and racism. Therefore, this section will look at terrorist violence that is driven by intersecting hatred, specifically the Incel Revolution ('involuntary celibate'), which is a loosely conceived subculture social movement comprised of male supremacists sharing a misogynistic (a hatred of women) ideological mission. 'Incels' and toxic masculinity have only recently started to receive serious attention from the counter-terrorism community, particularly in relationship to their white nationalism and racially motivated violence (Hoffman, Ware, Shapiro 2020). It is terrorism that should be widely conceived as 'misogynistic terrorism' (see CBC 2018; Penny 2014).

It is not easy to talk about misogyny. In fact, the *first book* to focus solely on a philosophy of misogyny was not written until Kate Manne's 2018 book, *Down Girl*. In *Down Girl*, Manne differentiates between sexism and misogyny, although they are both part of patriarchal (a system or government whereby men hold the majority of the power) structural forces. According to Manne (2018: 13), 'sexism [is] the branch of patriarchal ideology that *justifies* and *rationalizes* a patriarchal social order' where as 'misogyny [is] the system that *polices* and *enforces* its governing, norms, and expectations'. In talking about violence and terrorism, misogyny is more apt as 'misogyny . . . uphold[s] patriarchal order . . . by visiting hostile or adverse social consequences on a certain (more or less circumscribed) class of girls or women to enforce and police social norms' (Manne 2018: 13). Misogyny is a policing system, one that classifies and punishes women, girls, transgender, and non-binary people for acting outside of acceptable norms (Manne 2018: 27). Therefore, misogyny maintains order via political violence or the threat thereof: 'It is a form of coercive control—just as terrorism aims to be—and it uses violence or the threat of violence to gain this control' (Gentry 2020: 174).

15.4 VIOLENT ACTORS ASSOCIATED WITH MISOGYNISTIC TERRORISM

- **Anders Breivik:** Conducted a two-part attack on 22 July 2011 in Norway killing and injuring a total of 355 people (see also Case Study 15.1).
- **Marc Lépine:** Canadian mass shooter who entered the École Polytechnique in Montreal on 6 December 1989, murdering 14 women, wounding 10 women and four men.
- **Alek Minassian:** Committed a van attack in Toronto on 23 April 2018, which killed 10 and hospitalized 15 people.
- **Elliot Rodger:** In a gun and vehicle rampage targeting women at the University of California, Santa Barbara, on 23 May 2014, Rodger killed six people and injured 14.
- **Dylann Roof:** Typically seen as a white supremacist, there were also elements of misogyny in his church shooting in Charleston, South Carolina on 17 June 2015, in which he killed nine and injured one person.

Only recently has 'toxic masculinity' entered common vocabulary. Misogyny and toxic masculinity link multiple forms of violence from sexual harassment, domestic abuse, online abuse, and mass shootings. The UN has found that a third of all women globally will experience some form of sexual violence, and the WHO reports that a third of all women globally will experience domestic abuse (both reports available on the UN and WHO websites respectively). In the US, a third of all girls and young women face emotional abuse and bullying daily (see here YWCA.org). In the UK, crimes related to trans-misogyny (prejudice against transgender women) have risen 81 per cent between 2018 and 2019 (BBC 2019). Misogyny and toxic masculinity are also at the centre of the Incel Rebellion. This rebellion is similar to a social movement in that it is composed of individuals and groups whose ideology supports (violent) action (Della Porta 2008; Gentry 2004). The actors are mainly young white men who 'share grievances' against women and ethnic minorities (Collins and Zadronzy 2018). There are multiple groups of men who contribute to toxic masculinity: Whereas 15 per cent of total gun homicide victims in the US between 2008–12 were female, 50 per cent of the victims of mass shootings . . . were female (Everytown Research 2016).

15.5 GROUPS/ONLINE COMMUNITIES WITH MISOGYNISTIC IDEALIZATIONS

- **Men's Right Activists:** Men who believe that Feminism and laws that support women in divorce and childcare settlements adversely affects men.
- **Pick Up Artists:** A movement of men whose goal is to 'seduce' women. It aims to teach all men 'The Game,' or to learn a specific sequence of events to seduce women, seeing them as passive in sex and only there to fulfil men's sexual needs.
- **Incels:** Men who see themselves as 'INvoluntary CELibates' or beta males.
- **Red Pill Forum:** A Reddit forum that believes it reveals the truth about the power between the sexes, believing that women use men for their own purpose, are entitled, and that Feminism and women's rights harm men.
- **4Chan:** An online forum associated with toxic masculinity and white supremacy.
- **incel.me**: online forum targeting those who see themselves as incels.

(Anti-Defamation League 2018; Valenti 2018; Conger 2018; Gentry 2020, chapter 5.)

The men involved are often conceived framed as independent actors, something akin to lone wolf actors, because their violent acts are often conducted alone. Consider Anders Breivik's twin attacks in Norway; Elliot Rodger's van and shooting in Santa Barbara, California US; and Alec Minassian's van attack in Toronto. Yet, the agency of misogynistic terrorists is often minimized because of their whiteness and presumed mental health problems. Furthermore, misogynistic terrorists are not isolated individuals—in misogynistic terrorism the offenders are often inspired by, and immersed in, online and community politicalization processes (Valenti 2018). In online forums like Reddit or 4Chan they find support and encouragement from like-minded individuals, ones that often idealize men like Rodger and Breivik.

Shared online forums are an articulation of the larger movement's ideological misogynistic stance. The Red Pill, an extremist men's rights forum on Reddit, is filled with articles, commentary, and blog posts that demonstrate its misogynistic leanings. Toxic masculinity maintains strict gender roles. The 'alpha male' claim is a central to the Red Pill. 'Alpha' males are conceptualized as the only men who hold women's interest because they are physically fit and domineering in attitude. Alpha males have 'game,' which is a 'sexual strategy' men need to adopt because women, in a biologically essentialist move, select mates 'to locate the best DNA [sic] possible, and to garner the most resources' (Red Pill 2011). In juxtaposition, Beta males are of 'low value to women' because they do not dominate them, something that women inherently (biologically) desire (Red Pill 2015). This leads Beta males into a life of involuntary celibacy, or 'incel,' a 'man who wants to get laid, but can't' (Red Pill 2015).

The ideology of toxic masculinity sets out a vision of the world in which women are compliant, submissive, and sexually attractive. It blames Feminism for most, if not all, social ills. Women are seen to have 'too much freedom to choose their partners, which leaves some men cheated out of their sexual birthright' (Anti-Defamation League 2018, 12). Violence—rape, beatings, or murder—is often an outcome of the entitlement this group of men feel towards women. Neo-Nazi Andrew Anglin stated: 'women crave men who call them stupid and claim they shouldn't have any rights. They also crave being tied up, beaten, and raped' (Anti-Defamation League 2018: 7).

Additional statements and manifestos left by toxic male actors are further examples of their ideological support for violence. These are widely-read and referred to within online forums. Misogyny and racism are evident in the shooters' manifestos, and in the websites that keep their memory alive, effectively presenting these men as martyrs to a cause that serve to inspire others. Marc Lépine, a Canadian mass murderer from Montreal who in 1989 murdered 14 women in the Ecole Polytechnique massacre, was driven by his hatred of Feminism and the harm that women, by entering the workforce, have done to men.

Similar anger and entitlement appear up in most of the writings from these men. Elliot Rodger saw himself as an incel, unable to fit into university to life, and owed by the women who had sexually rejected him. In 2014, he targeted women at the University of California, Santa Barbara in the US and killed six people:

> 'I was ready and capable of fighting back against the cruelty of women. The hatred that festered inside of me...had empowered me in a dark, twisted way. I was now armed with weapons...with the willpower to exact the most catastrophic act of vengeance the world will ever see' (Rodger 2014, 124).

Dylann Roof's two manifestos, the first he wrote before his attack on the Emanuel African Methodist Episcopal Church in 2005, and the second he wrote from jail, mainly focus on race (Roof is a white supremacist and neo-Nazi). However, Roof also discusses women and the value they hold for white men. For instance, women in interracial relationships are

PHOTO 15.2 A memorial on Utøya Island to those killed by Norwegian domestic terrorist Anders Breivik.

'victims' in need of 'saving' (Roof 2014: 5). He told one of the Black men that he shot during his attack that, 'I have to do this, because y'all are raping our women...'. Anders Breivik's loathing of women follows similar lines (see Photo 15.2). Breivik believes that the 'politically correct' project 'intends to deny the intrinsic worth of native Christian European heterosexual males' (Jones 2011). Breivik is haunted by a 'terror of feminization'—or the weakening of masculinity—and that only restoration of patriarchy can save European culture (Goldberg 2011). It is Feminism's attack on the nuclear family that has led a 'demographic collapse' 'opening Europe to Muslim colonization' (Jones 2011).

Race is also threaded throughout all these men's actions. Before Rodger drove to University of California, Santa Barbara's campus, he killed his two Chinese roommates and their Chinese friend. He described them as 'utterly repulsive' (Rodger 2014: 128). Rodger was incensed that his sister's interracial boyfriend had previously dated 'a pretty brunette white girl' and he had not (Rodger 2014: 128–129). Roof's actions are more associated with racism; yet his hatred was not limited to Black people (although they are the ones he focused upon). He used the white supremacist, neo-Nazi code '1488,' in which '14' refers to a micro-creed, fourteen words long—'We must secure the existence of our people and a future for white children,' 'and 88 is code for 'Heil Hitler,' as 'H' is the eighth letter (Ball 2017). Securing white reproduction is a key feature of both white supremacy and misogynistic tendencies. Buying into racialized stereotypes, Roof believed that all Black people are violent and have 'lower IQ's, lower impulse control, and higher testosterone levels' (Roof 2014: 3). He saw himself as the only person able to stop Black crime (Roof 2014: 5).

Just as Marc Lépine's massacre from 1989 is frequently referenced, the actions of the men such as Roof, Breivik, and Roger also inspire other attacks. These men have been written as martyrs to a revolutionary cause. In Alek Minassian's attack in 2018, he praised Rodger directly, and self-identifies as an incel (Crilly et al. 2018). In a Facebook post, Minassian wrote:

> 'Private (Recruit) Minassian Infantry 00010, wishing to speak to Sgt 4chan please. C23249161. The Incel Rebellion has already begun! . . . All hail the Supreme Gentlemen Elliot Rodger!' (Collins and Zadronzy 2018).

Immediately after his attack in Toronto, Canada, which killed 10 and injured 16 people, others posted supportive sentiments on incel.me, including ones that constructed him as the latest martyr to the Incel Revolution.

This growing social movement of misogynistic hate and incel-led violence is held together by virulent and violent supremacism and racism. It is therefore important for counter-terrorism communities to understand the dynamics of gender and racism as motivating forces behind the use of violence. Without understanding the dynamics of how masculinity is understood, essentialized, and idealized within this movement, the violence cannot be appropriately challenged.

15.6 CONCLUSION

This chapter has demonstrated how terrorism as a concept and form of violence is understood in relation to gender and race structures. Using the concept of intersectionality, the chapter demonstrates how the concept of terrorism is tied to gendered and racialized social constructs. As such, violence labelled as terrorist is always seen as illegitimate and non-credible. Terrorism is perceived as significantly worse than state violence, because of how gender and race are used as delegitimizing forces in socio-political life.

Additionally, it has explored how gender and race are used as motivating and legitimating forces *for* violence, particularly in the case of the 'Incel Revolution' and related misogynistic-motived attacks. The rising social movement driven by toxic masculinity and intersecting misogynistic and racist oppressions have led to violent acts committed by seemingly unrelated actors. Yet, when looking at these 'disparate' actors' ideologies, one can see that there are significant similarities in how they think about women and race.

In summary, the chapter argues that violence, terrorism, and the terrorist actor are not objectively defined, but concepts that exist within subjective understandings—dependent upon how one understands particular social hierarchies, including (but not limited to) gender and race. Therefore, the chapter urges students of terrorism to think critically about how gendered and/or racialized bias might be at work when describing an act of terrorism or a terrorist actor.

DISCUSSION QUESTIONS

1. Take the example of the Malhuer Nature Reserve takeover discussed in the Introduction. If the men involved were Muslim or Black and not white, would the law enforcement response have been different and what does this tell us about terrorism *and* counter-terrorism?
2. Reflect upon what you know about the people who have joined ISIS. Why does the press treat men and women differently?
3. What are some other forms of gender or race idealizations/essentializations that take place within terrorism or counter-terrorism not discussed in this chapter?
4. How do other structures, such as heteronormativity or religious bias, play a role in how we understand terrorism?
5. Find some examples of terrorist groups that use race or gender to legitimize violence—how do they make this known?

 Visit the online resources for pointers on how to answer the discussion questions, links to useful web sources, and guidance on accessing databases:
www.oup.com/he/Wilson-Muro1e

GUIDE TO FURTHER READING

Gentry, C. E. (2020), *Disordered Violence: How Gender, Race, and Heteronormativity Structure Terrorism* (Edinburgh: Edinburgh University Press). *In this book, Gentry looks at the subjective nature of terrorism, from its definition, how actors are portrayed, radicalization, to the idea of 'misogynistic terrorism'. She argues that the subjectivity is dependent upon gender, race, and heteronormativity as power structures that shape Terrorism Studies and Critical Terrorism Studies.*

Gentry, C. E. and L. Sjoberg (2015), *Beyond Mothers, Monsters, Whores: Rethinking Women's Violence in Global Politics* (London: Zed Books). *In the second edition of this book, Gentry and Sjoberg look at how women who commit acts of political violence, including genocide, suicide bombings, and torture, are portrayed within three gendered narratives, mother, monster, and whore, that serve to deny or remove women's agency.*

Puar, J. K. (2018) *Terrorist Assemblages: Homonationalism in Queer Times*. Durham: Duke University Press. *In this deeply theoretical text, Puar looks at post-9/11 USA and how the discursive structure of heteronormativity allied with nationalism. As the US government, society, and citizens dealt with the aftermath of the 9/11 attacks and the Global War on Terror, a form of homonationalism emerged that asserted certain masculinized and patriotic ideals that governed particular bodies in prescriptive ways.*

Stampnitzky, L. (2013) *Disciplining Terrorism: How 'Experts' Invented Terrorism*. Cambridge: Cambridge University Press. *Stampnitzky traces the origins of Terrorism Studies, examining how it took shape between academics, policymakers, and the military. She looks at various social forces, including the growth of new-Conservatism in the US in the 1980s, that shaped how the public and the academic community came to know and study the phenomenon of terrorism in very particular ways.*

Third, A. (2014) *Gender and the Political: Deconstructing the Female Terrorist*. New York: Springer. *Third offers a discourse analysis of gender and terrorism focused on the United States in the 1960s. She looks at how political violence and terrorism emerged at the same time as the feminist movement, examining the evolution of a Western discourse of threat and legitimacy.*

REFERENCES

Ahmed, S. (2004) *The Cultural Politics of Emotion*. Edinburgh: Edinburgh University Press.

Alison, M. (2003) 'Cogs in the Wheel? Women in the Liberation Tigers of Tamil Eelam', *Civil Wars*, 6 (4): 37–54.

Almasy, S. (2018) 'Video Shows Austin Bomber Blow Himself Up as Officers Closed In,' CNN, 31 August <https://edition.cnn.com/2018/08/31/us/austin-serial-bomber-video/index.html> (last accessed 9 October 2019).

Anonymous (1976) 'The Female Terrorist and her Impact on Policing', *Top Security Project*, 2 (4): 242–5.

Anti-Defamation League (2018) *When Women Are the Enemy: The Intersection of Misogyny and White Supremacy*, <https://www.adl.org/resources/reports/when-women-are-the-enemy-the-intersection-of-misogyny-and-white-supremacy> (last accessed 9 October 2019).

Aust, S. (2008) *The Baader-Meinhof Complex*. London: Bodley Head.

Aust, S. (1987) *The Baader-Meinhof Group: The Inside Story of a Phenomenon*. London: Bodley Head.

Ball, E. (2017) 'United States v. Dylann Roof', *The New York Review of Books*, 9 March, <https://www.nybooks.com/articles/2017/03/09/united-states-versus-dylann-roof/> (last accessed 25 November 2018).

Barkawi, T. and M. Laffey (2006) 'The Post-colonial Moment in Security Studies', *Review of International Studies*, 32 (2): 329–352.

BBC (2010) 'Profile: Major Nidal Malik Hasan', 12 October, <https://www.bbc.co.uk/news/world-us-canada-11525580> (last accessed 8 October 2019).

BBC (2019) 'Transgender Hate Crimes Recorded by Police Go Up 81%', 27 June, https://www.bbc.co.uk/news/uk-48756370 (last accessed 11 August 2021).

Berntzen, L. E. and Sandberg, S. (2014) 'The Collective Nature of Lone Wolf Terrorism: Anders Behring Breivik and the Anti-Islamic Social Movement', *Terrorism and Political Violence*, 26 (5): 759–779.

Blakeley, R. (2009) *State Terrorism and Neoliberalism: The North in the South*. Abingdon: Routledge.

Borum, R. (2012a) 'Radicalization into Violent Extremism I: A Review of Social Science Theories', *Journal of Strategic Security*, 4 (4): 7–36.

Borum, R. (2012b) 'Radicalization into Violent Extremism II: A Review of Conceptual Models and Empirical Research', *Journal of Strategic Security*, 4 (4): 37–62.

CBC (2018) 'The Current Transcript for April 26, 2018', <https://www.cbc.ca/radio/thecurrent/the-current-for-april-26-2018-1.4636157/thursday-april-26-2018-full-episode-transcript-1.4637420> (last accessed 25 November 2018).

Chakrabarty, D. (1992) 'Provincialising Europe: Post-coloniality and the Critique of History', *Cultural Studies*, 6 (3): 337–357.

Collins, B. and Zadrozny, B. (2018) 'After Toronto Attack, Online Misogynists Praise Suspect as "New Saint"', *ABC News*, 24 April, <https://www.nbcnews.com/news/us-news/after-toronto-attack-online-misogynists-praise-suspect-new-saint-n868821> (last accessed 25 November 2018).

Conger, C. (2018) 'How Pickup Artists Work', *How Stuff Works*, <https://people.howstuffworks.com/pickup-artist.htm> (last accessed 9 October 2019).

Cooper, H. A. A. (1979), 'Women as Terrorist', in F. Adler and R. J. Simon (eds.), *The Criminology of Deviant Women*. Boston: Houghton Mifflin.

Crenshaw, M. (ed.) (1995), *Terrorism in Context*. University Park, PA: Penn State Press.

Crilly, R., Guly, C., and Molloy, M. (2018) 'What Do We Know About Alek Minassian, Arrested after Toronto Van Attack?', *The Telegraph*, 24 April, <https://www.telegraph.co.uk/news/2018/04/24/do-know-alek-minassian-arrested-toronto-van-attack/> (last accessed 25 November 2018).

Cunningham, K. J. (2003) 'Cross-Regional Trends in Female Terrorism', *Studies in Conflict and Terrorism*, 26 (3): 171–195.

Della Porta, D. (2008) 'Research on Social Movements And Political Violence', *Qualitative Sociology*, 31 (3): 221–230.

Devetak, R. (2013) 'Poststructuralism', in S. Burchill and A. Linklater (eds.), *Theories of International Relations*. London: Palgrave.

Elshtain, J. B. (1981) *Public Man, Private Woman: Women in Social and Political Thought*. Princeton, NJ: University of Princeton Press.

Elshtain, J. B. (1987) *Women and War*. Chicago, IL: University of Chicago Press.

Gentry, C. E. (2004) 'The Relationship between New Social Movement Theory and Terrorism Studies: The Role of Leadership, Membership, Ideology and Gender', *Terrorism and Political Violence*, 16 (2): 274–293.

Gentry, C. E. (2014) 'Epistemic Bias: Legitimate Authority and Politically Violent Nonstate

Actors', in Caron E. Gentry and Amy E. Eckert (eds.), *The Future of Just War: New Critical Essays*. Athens, GA: University of Georgia Press, 17–29.

Gentry, C. E. (2018) 'Gender and Terrorism', in Caron E. Gentry, Laura Shepherd, and Laura Sjoberg (eds.), *The Routledge Handbook on Gender and Security*. Abingdon: Routledge, 140–150.

Gentry, C. E. (2019) 'Women and Terrorism', In Erica Chenoweth, Richard English, Andreas Gofas, and Stathis N. Kalyvas (eds), *The Oxford Handbook on Terrorism*. Oxford: Oxford University Press, 414–428.

Gentry, C. E. (2020) *Disordered Violence: How Gender, Race, and Heteronormativity Structure Terrorism*. Edinburgh: Edinburgh University Press.

Gentry, C. E. and Sjoberg, L. (2016) 'Female Terrorism and Militancy', in Richard D. Jackson (ed.), *Routledge Handbook of Critical Terrorism Studies*. Abingdon: Routledge, 145–156.

Gentry, Caron E. and Sjoberg, L. (2015) *Beyond Mothers, Monsters, Whores: Rethinking Women's Violence in Global Politics*. London: Zed Books.

Githens-Mazer, J. and Lambert, R. (2010) 'Why Conventional Wisdom on Radicalization Fails: The Persistence of a Failed Discourse', *International Affairs*, 86 (4): 889–901.

Goldberg, M. (2011) 'Norway Massacre: Anders Breivik's Deadly Attack Fuelled by Hatred of Women', *The Daily Beast*, 24 July, <https://www.thedailybeast.com/norway-massacre-anders-breiviks-deadly-attack-fueled-by-hatred-of-women> (last accessed 26 November 2018).

Hamilton, C. (2013) *Women and ETA: The Gender Politics of Radical Basque Nationalism*. Manchester: Manchester University Press.

Hanna, J., Karimi, K., Morris, J., and Almasy, S. (2018), 'Police: Austin Bomber Left 25-Minute Confession Video on Phone', *CNN*, 31 August, <https://edition.cnn.com/2018/03/21/us/austin-explosions/index.html> (last accessed 21 November 2018).

Heath-Kelly, C. (2012) 'Reinventing Prevention or Exposing the Gap? False Positives in UK Terrorism Governance and the Quest for Pre-Emption', *Critical Studies on Terrorism*, 5 (1): 69–87.

Heath-Kelly, C. (2013) 'Counterterrorism and the Counterfactual: Producing the "Radicalization" Discourse and the UK PREVENT Strategy', *The British Journal of Politics and International Relations*, 15 (3): 394–415.

Hoffman, B. (1999) 'Terrorism Trends and Prospects', in I. Lesser, J. Arguilla, B. Hoffman, D. F. Ronfeldt, and M. Zanini (eds.), *Countering the New Terrorism*. Santa Monica, CA: RAND, 7–38.

Hoffman, B. (2001) 'Rethinking Terrorism in Light of a War on Terrorism,' Testimony Before the Subcommittee on Terrorism and Homeland Security, US House of Representatives, 26 September, <https://www.rand.org/content/dam/rand/pubs/testimonies/2005/CT182.pdf> (last accessed 22 November 2018).

Hoffman, B. (2002) 'Rethinking Terrorism and Counterterrorism Since 9/11', *Studies in Conflict and Terrorism*, 25 (5): 303–316.

Hoffman, B. (2006) *Inside Terrorism*. New York: Columbia University Press.

Hoffman, B., Ware, J., and Shapiro, E. (2020) 'Assessing the Threat of Incel Violence', *Studies in Conflict and Terrorism*, 43 (7): 565–587.

Jenkins, B. M. (1980) *The Study of Terrorism: Definitional Problems*. Santa Monica, CA: RAND.

Jones, J. C. (2011) 'Anders Breivik's Chilling Anti-Feminism', *The Guardian*, 27 July, <https://www.theguardian.com/commentisfree/2011/jul/27/breivik-anti-feminism> (last accessed 25 November 2018).

Kenber, B. (2013) 'Nidal Hasan Sentenced to Death for Fort Hood Shooting Rampage,' *The Washington Post*, 28 August, <https://www.washingtonpost.com/world/national-security/nidal-hasan-sentenced-to-death-for-fort-hood-shooting-rampage/2013/08/28/aad28de2-0ffa-11e3-bdf6-e4fc677d94a1_story.html?utm_term=.b4d0fdb96c96> (last accessed 23 November 2018).

Kirby, A. (2007) 'The London Bombers as "Self-Starters": A Case Study in Indigenous Radicalization and the Emergence of Autonomous Cliques', *Studies in Conflict and Terrorism*, 30 (5): 415–428.

Laqueur, W. (1996) 'Postmodern Terrorism,' *Foreign Affairs*, 75 (5): 24–36.

Laqueur, W. (1999) *The New Terrorism: Fanaticism and the Arms of Mass Destruction*. Oxford: Oxford University Press.

Loken, M. and A. Zelenz (2018) 'Explaining Extremism: Western Women in Daesh', *European Journal of International Security*, 3 (1): 45–68.

MacDonald, E. (1991) *Shoot the Women First*. Washington, D.C.: Fourth Estate.

Manne, K. (2018) *Down Girl: The Logic of Misogyny*. Oxford: Oxford University Press.

Martini, A. (2018) 'Making Women Terrorists into "Jihadi Brides": An Analysis of Media Narratives on Women Joining ISIS', *Critical Studies on Terrorism*, 11 (3): 458–477

McEvoy, S. (2009) 'Loyalist Women Paramilitaries in Northern Ireland: Beginning a Feminist Converzation About Conflict Resolution', *Security Studies*, 18 (2): 262–286.

McClintock, A. (2013) *Imperial Leather: Race, Gender, and Sexuality in the Colonial Contest*. Abingdon: Routledge.

Morgan, R. (1989) *The Demon Lover: The Roots of Terrorism*. New York: Washington Square Press.

Muppidi, H. (2006) 'Shame and Rage: International Relations and the World School of Colonialism', in R. L. Riley and N. Inayatullah (eds.), *Interrogating Imperialism*. Basingstoke: Palgrave Macmillan, 51–61.

Nayak, M. (2006) 'Orientalism and "Saving" US State Identity after 9/11', *International Feminist Journal of Politics*, 8 (1): 42–61.

Parashar, S. (2009) 'Feminist International Relations And Women Militants: Case Studies From Sri Lanka And Kashmir', *Cambridge Review of International Affairs*, 22 (2): 235–256.

Parashar, S. (2011) 'Gender, Jihad, and Jingoism: Women as Perpetrators, Planners, and Patrons of Militancy in Kashmir', *Studies in Conflict and Terrorism*, 34 (4): 295–317.

Pateman, C. (1980) '"The Disorder of Women:" Women, Love, and the Sense of Justice', *Ethics*, 91 (1): 20–34.

Penny, L. (2014) 'Let's Call the Isla Vista Killings What They Were', *New Statesman*, 25 May 2014, https://www.newstatesman.com/lifestyle/2014/05/lets-call-isla-vista-killings-what-they-were-misogynist-extremism (last accessed 8 October 2019).

Red Pill (2011) 'Schedules of Mating', <https://therationalmale.com/2011/08/23/schedules-of-mating/> (last accessed 26 November 2018).

Red Pill (2015) 'Updated Glossary of Terms and Acronyms', <https://www.reddit.com/r/TheRedPill/comments/2zckqu/updated_glossary_of_terms_and_acronyms/> (last accessed 26 November 2018).

Richardson, L. (2006) *What Terrorists Want: Understanding the Enemy, Containing the Threat*. New York: Random House.

Rodger, E. (2014) 'Manifesto', <https://www.documentcloud.org/documents/1173808-elliot-rodger-manifesto.html> (last accessed 25 November 2018).

Roof, D. S. (2014) 'Manifesto', <https://assets.documentcloud.org/documents/3237779/Dylann-Roof-manifesto.pdf> (last accessed 25 November 2018).

Shepherd, L. J. (2006) 'Veiled References: Constructions of Gender in the Bush Administration Discourse on the Attacks on Afghanistan Post-9/11', *International Journal of Feminist Politics*, 8 (1): 19–41.

Sjoberg, L. (2009) 'Feminist Interrogations of Terrorism/Terrorism Studies', *International Relations*, 23 (1): 69–74.

Sjoberg, L. (2013) *Gendering Global Conflict: Toward a Feminist Theory of War*. New York: Columbia University Press.

Sjoberg, L. and Gentry, C. E. (2007) *Mothers, Monsters, Whores: Women's Violence in Global Politics*. London: Zed Books.

Sjoberg, L. and Gentry, C. E. (eds.) (2011), *Women, Gender, and Terrorism*. Athens, GA: University of Georgia Press.

Smith, L. T. (2012) *Decolonising Methodologies: Research and Indigenous Peoples*. London: Zed Books.

Spaaij, R. (2010) 'The Enigma of Lone Wolf Terrorism: An Assessment', *Studies in Conflict and Terrorism*, 33 (9): 854–870.

Stampnitzky, L. (2013) *Disciplining Terrorism: How 'Experts' Invented Terrorism*. Cambridge: Cambridge University Press.

Third, A. (2010) 'Imprisonment and Excessive Femininity: Reading Ulrike Meinhof's Brain', *Parallax*, 16 (4): 83–100.

Tickner, J. A. (1992) *Gender in International Relations: Feminist Perspectives on Achieving Global Security*. New York: Columbia University Press.

Valenti, J. (2018) 'When Misogynists Become Terrorists', *The New York Times*, 26 April, <https://www.nytimes.com/2018/04/26/opinion/when-misogynists-become-terrorists.html> (last accessed 25 November 2018).

Versi, M. (2017) 'The Latest Prevent Figures Show Why the Strategy Needs an Independent Review', *The Guardian*, 10 November, <https://www.theguardian.com/commentisfree/2017/nov/10/prevent-strategy-statistics-independent-review-home-office-muslims> (last accessed 24 November 2018).

Wallace-Wells, B. (2018) 'The Inscrutable Terror of the Austin Bombings', *The New Yorker*, 28 March, <https://www.newyorker.com/news/dispatch/the-inscrutable-terror-of-the-austin-bombings> (last accessed 21 November 2018).

Weinberg, L. and Eubank, W. L. (1987) 'Italian Women Terrorists', *Studies in Conflict and Terrorism*, 9 (3): 241–262.

Wight, Colin (2015) *Rethinking Terrorism: Terrorism, Violence, and the State*. Basingstoke: Palgrave Macmillan.

CHAPTER 16

Terrorism by Insurgents and Rebels

JAKANA THOMAS

16.1 INTRODUCTION

> **KEY CONCEPTS**
>
> **Terrorism** In the context of this chapter, this is defined as: 'premeditated use or threat to use violence by individuals or subnational groups against noncombatants in order to obtain a political or social objective through the intimidation of a large audience beyond that of the immediate victims' (Enders, Sandler, and Gaibullov 2011: 321).

Although *transnational* terror attacks attract substantial attention and engender outsized anxiety, most acts of terrorism around the globe are actually perpetrated by assailants that reside in the same country they target. That is, the majority of terror attacks can be classified as *domestic terrorism*. According to Enders, Sandler and Gaibullov (2011), between 1970 and 2007, there were more than three and a half times more domestic attacks than transnational attacks. Berkebile (2017) puts the proportion of domestic attacks higher, at between 80 and 90 per cent of all attacks. Moreover, nearly half of these domestic attacks were conducted in the context of a rebellion (Findley and Young 2012). Despite the frequency of civil war-related terror, few studies seek to understand the frequency and value of terrorism in this particular context. This chapter explores the use of terrorism by rebel organizations involved in a sustained domestic struggle against a government, and explains why violent political organizations may view terrorism as a viable means to achieve victory over a state opponent. Ultimately, by theorizing about what groups hope to achieve with their use of terrorism, we gain a better understanding of why this particular tool is so attractive in rebellion, and therefore so prevalent.

Acts of terrorism are commonly perpetrated around civil conflicts (Stanton 2013). As many as two-thirds of attributed global attacks occurring between 1970 and 2004 were conducted by recognized rebel organizations while around half took place in declared war zones (Findley and Young 2012). These domestic terror attacks were used to start, restart, prolong and end wars. Given the availability of other strategies and tactics, why do actors rely on terror?

> **KEY CONCEPTS**
>
> **Civil Conflict/War** An organized domestic struggle between a state and a non-state entity over a political, economic or social policy that leads to a significant number of fatalities (i.e. at least 25 deaths). A civil conflict escalates to a civil war when a higher death count is registered (i.e. at least 500 deaths).

The basic answer to the puzzle of domestic conflict-related terror is that terrorism is compelling violence that can generate significant benefits for actors that use it. Rebel organizations primarily utilize violence against civilians to help them achieve their war aims. These aims may include broad political or social goals as well as smaller *process* goals. While broad goals may encompass drastic changes to the political, economic and social structures in a state, process goals focus on smaller day-to-day objectives that allow rebels to eventually achieve their more ambitious aims. Recruitment and fundraising are two process goals that terrorism can help advance. Debates remain on the efficacy of terrorism (see Chapter 19: 'Is Terrorism Effective?'), there are several convincing reasons to believe that visiting violence upon the civilian population would help rebel groups accomplish their objectives.

First, terrorism can be used to bolster groups with limited fighting capacity and reduced military prospects. Terrorism is thought to be a tool of the weak and a last resort for groups that have tried other strategies and failed. Asymmetric insurgencies or guerrilla wars, which feature rebels that are much weaker than their state opponents, often feature terror, as violence against civilians can level the playing field between unequally matched opponents. Put simply, terrorism keeps rebels active for longer. Second, rebel groups use violence against civilians to establish and maintain territorial control. Not only can terror help subdue a population that would otherwise resist rebel rule, terrorism can also demonstrate the state's inability to effectively govern its own territory. Doing so affords rebels the opportunity to show civilians that their leadership is preferable to the state's. Rebel organizations may provide positive benefits at the same time they intimidate civilians with violence. By providing benefits in the form of social services, protection or material goods, rebels can persuade the population to endure violence and reject the state. Finally, terrorism can help dissidents wear down their targets or sow discord into a political process that makes an opponent give up, providing the clearest mechanism by which terrorism helps a group achieve its goals. Each of these arguments highlight the ways in which terrorism during civil war can be intentional and strategic.

16.2 REBEL RELATIVE STRENGTH

Terrorism is both a 'tool of the weak' and a last resort. Martha Crenshaw (1981: 387) suggests that terrorism is the preferred tool of a 'minority that by its own judgement lacks other means.' Thus, when militants have tried other tactics with little success, they are likely to resort to terrorism as a last effort to attain their goals (Crenshaw 1981). Teichman (1989) argues that 'struggles of national liberation are struggles of the poor against the rich, the weak against the strong. As such they cannot succeed unless inexpensive methods are used.' In this regard, terrorism is particularly attractive for relatively weak or less rich organizations because the cost is typically low, while potential returns are high. For instance, while the 9/11 attacks to the US were believed to cost around $500,000 from initial planning to execution, many domestic attacks cost less than the price of a mobile phone, while others are cheaper than the average textbook.

In 2007 Harkat-ul-Jihad-e-Islami Bangladesh (or HuJi, an Islamic fundamentalist organization) detonated two bombs in Hyderabad, India, which killed and injured more than 90 people. The cost? $50 (Acharya 2009). Hoffman (2003) suggests that the makeshift suicide bombs used in Israel likely cost around $150, while estimates put a remote-controlled bomb at around $400. These attacks can be financed relatively cheaply while imposing great damage on targets. Suicide terrorism is especially useful for addressing material power asymmetries between a weak group and a much stronger government adversary (Horowitz 2010; Hafez 2006). Thus, it is practical that groups with few resources but big demands would incorporate terrorism in order to contend with a much more imposing government. Indeed, studies find that when rebels are weak relative to their state foes, they are more likely to adopt terrorist tactics or victimize civilians (Stanton 2013). Battle losses also explain rebels' turn toward terrorizing civilians. As rebels lose more, they terrorize more. States with stronger militaries experience greater rates of terrorism. Since most rebel groups are weaker than the states they fight, terrorism is part of many civil wars.

In civil wars, imbalances in military capabilities force rebel organizations to resort to unconventional tactics. Unconventional or irregular tactics are those where militants avoid direct confrontations with the state and rely instead on 'hit and run' attacks, that are often associated with insurgencies. The use of irregular/guerrilla warfare, according to Kalyvas (2006), is an unambiguous statement of a group's relative weakness. Terrorism is also a form of irregular violence (Lake 2002). Both terrorist and insurgent tactics eschew direct confrontations for clandestine, sporadic attacks, and can be used to achieve similar objectives. Terrorism and guerrilla warfare are both thought to be 'weapons of the weak designed to harass the enemy and gradually erode will' (Moghadam et al. 2014: 5). Both tactics are designed to alleviate or address unevenness in the distribution of military power between a rebel group and the state. However, while guerrillas launch attacks at the state in a battle, terrorists inflict direct harm on civilians or non-combatants, even if the ultimate aim is to compel the state to change its policies. Therefore, insurgency and terrorism are two ways that weaker militant groups attempt to force concessions from a stronger adversary.

> **KEY CONCEPTS**
>
> **Insurgency** A domestic conflict where lightly armed rebel units challenge a much more capable state opponent using indirect, hit-and-run attacks (Price 1977). These conflicts are also referred to as irregular rebellions or guerrilla wars.

If relative weakness causes a group to adopt both terrorism and insurgent tactics, groups that adopt one tactic should be likely to use the other. This appears to be true, despite alleged differences between guerrilla and terrorist organizations in terms of their size, capabilities and goals. In fact, although organizations like al-Qaeda, Hamas, and ISIS have gained notoriety as terrorists, they actually only engage in terrorism 'on the side.' Their primary activities are war-fighting (Moghadam et al. 2014: 3). By all accounts, groups that are generally classified as 'terrorists' often focus as much, if not more direct attention on battling the state. The overwhelming majority of global terror groups operating between 2002 and 2012 were involved in organized domestic conflicts at the same time that they were waging campaigns of terror and did far more damage to state entities than civilian communities; only about one-third of these terror attacks targeted civilians directly (Moghadam et al. 2014). In Western Europe, combatants fighting on behalf of the state made up nearly half of all fatalities from domestic terror incidents between 1965 and 2000 (Sanchez-Cuenca and De La Calle 2009).

Terrorism and insurgency are often used in tandem as is demonstrated by Figure 16.1, which examines the use of terrorism in civil conflicts between 1960 and 2008. The darkest bar reflects the total number of terror attacks in each type of conflict, while the lighter bars display the number and severity of attacks across each type of target.

These data show that terrorism is both most frequent and most severe during insurgencies compared to other types of rebellion; terrorism was used in more than 85 per cent of cases classified as insurgencies. On average, such conflicts experience 83 terror attacks in a given year. Non-insurgencies, which include conventional and symmetrical non-conventional conflicts, however, average only 23 terror attacks per year. Additionally, more deaths from terrorism were recorded in irregular conflicts; insurgencies averaged 244 deaths while other types of conflicts together averaged about 142 fatalities per year.

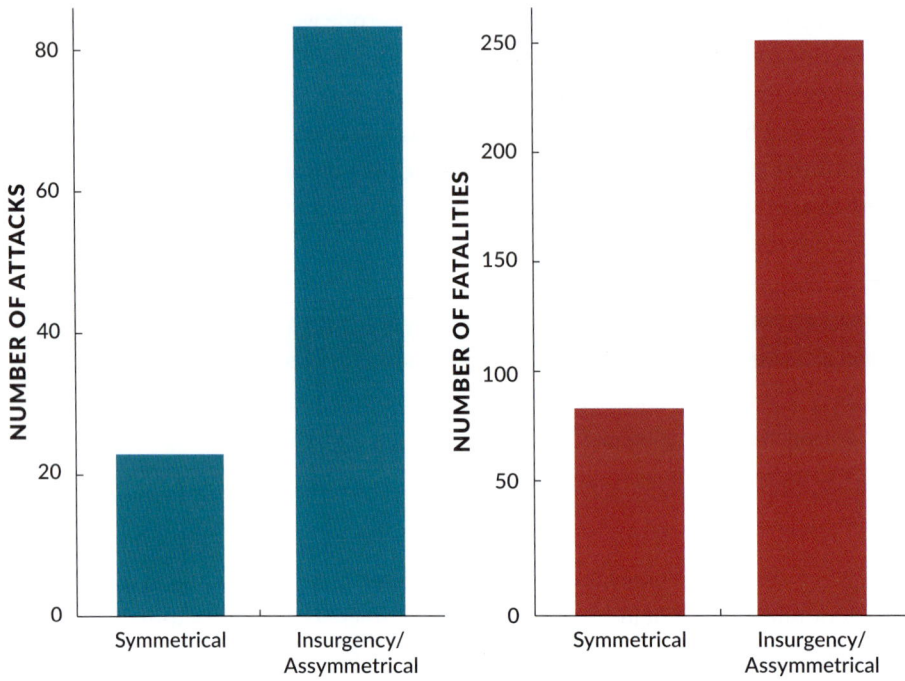

FIGURE 16.1 Frequency and severity of terrorism by insurgents, 1960–2008. Incidents from the Global Terrorism Database (LaFree and Dugan 2007) are matched to Kalyvas and Balcell's (2010) conflict typology using replication files from Krcmaric (2018). The left-hand graph examines the number of terror attacks by insurgents and non-insurgents, while the right-hand graph displays the number of fatalities from terror attacks.

KEY CONCEPTS

Conventional conflict Military engagement where both states and rebels use sophisticated techniques, are heavily armed and fight in traditional battles defined by clear frontlines.

KEY CONCEPTS

Symmetrical non-conventional conflict Balanced conflicts where neither the state nor the rebel group are strong enough to engage in sophisticated set-piece battles with well-defined frontlines. Instead, both states and rebels may use unconventional tactics to strike out at their enemy.

Since a defining feature of an insurgency is the imbalance between state and non-state military forces, the trends support the notion that terrorism is used to address rebels' *relative* weakness. That is to say that the power disparity between belligerents, not a rebel

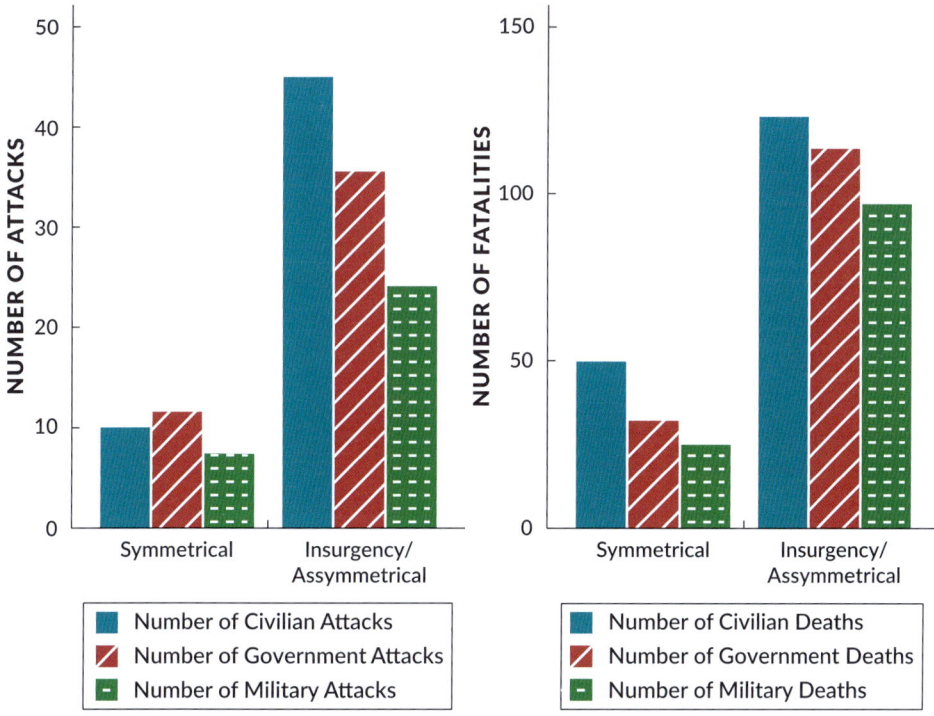

FIGURE 16.2 Targets of terrorism by insurgents, 1960–2008. Incidents from the Global Terrorism Database (LaFree and Dugan 2007) are matched to Kalyvas and Balcells' (2010) conflict typology using replication files from Krcmaric (2018). The left-hand graph displays the number of terror attacks by insurgents and non-insurgents across target types, while the right-hand graph examines the number of fatalities from terror attacks by target.

groups' inherent weakness, leads to the reliance on terrorist tactics. If all weak rebel groups found terrorism attractive, situations where both the rebel and state armies were both weak would also see more terrorism. This is not the case, however. Terrorism is actually *least* common in symmetrical non-conventional (SNC) conflicts, or disputes where the state and rebels *both* have limited military power. This is reflected in Figure 16.1.

What is more, insurgents do not appear to use terrorism only to strike out at the government. Figure 16.2 shows us that although insurgent rebels attack state entities quite often, civilians are actually their main targets. The disparity becomes even more apparent when rates of terrorism against civilian targets are compared with attacks against only state military forces. While there are about 45 insurgent attacks on civilian targets in a given year, the mean number of terror attacks against the military stands at only 24. This suggests that terrorism is used to accomplish something distinct from guerilla attacks on the state. The following sections explore the distinct logic of attacking civilians in a war against the government.

CASE STUDY 16.1

Terrorism by UNITA

The rebel organization, National Union for the Total Independence of Angola (UNITA) is a useful case to demonstrate the effect of military asymmetry on the use of terrorism. UNITA fought a decades-long war against the government of Angola from the mid-1970s until 2002 using both conventional and guerrilla tactics. Over the span of the war, the organization was estimated to have been manned by as many as 60,000 rebels and at its peak reached parity with the Angolan state (Cunningham et al. 2013). At its weakest point, the organization was estimated to comprise only a couple of thousand fighters. Most importantly, UNITA used terrorism quite liberally.

According to the Global Terrorism Database, the organization was implicated in over 400 terror attacks between 1978 and 2002. However, UNITA did not use terrorism consistently across that time. Instead, the group's use of terrorism varied with its military strength, particularly relative to the government's. Figure 16.3 demonstrates that UNITA executed attacks

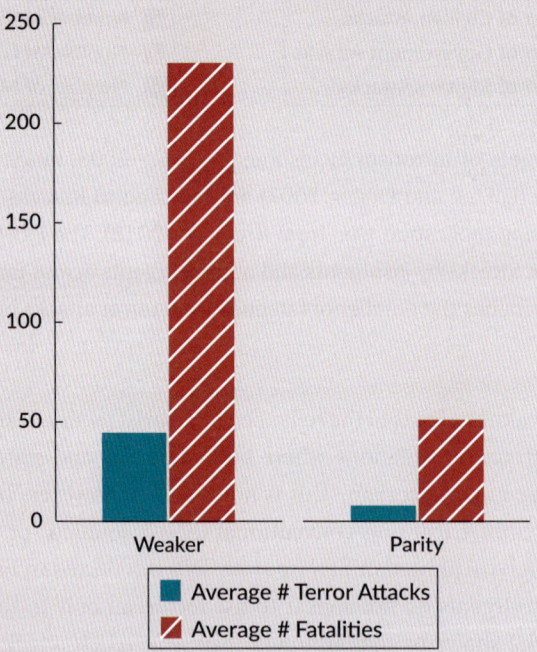

FIGURE 16.3 Frequency of UNITA terrorism, 1989–2002. Incidents from the Global Terrorism Database (LaFree and Dugan 2007) are matched with data on rebel strength from Cunningham et al.'s (2013) Nonstate Actor dataset. The left-hand figure displays the frequency and severity of UNITA attacks when the organization is judged as weaker than the state, while the right-hand figure provides information on UNITA attacks when the organization is equally matched with the state.

more frequently in years it was judged to be weaker than the state. These attacks were also deadlier. When the organization was unable to hurt the state directly, it tended to aim its violence at the undefended and defenceless civilian population. Conversely, UNITA used far less terrorism in years its strength matched the government's, labelled here as parity. When the group was considered to be as strong as the Angolan military, it launched only about 8 attacks in a given year. Nearly 180 more civilians were killed, on average, in years where UNITA's army was weaker than government forces.

The types of targets UNITA attacked also hint at the group's strategy. Although UNITA directed its violence at a range of targets, civilians were hit hardest overall and particularly so when the group was doing poorly on the battlefield. Figure 16.4 shows during periods of UNITA's relative weakness, attacks focused disproportionately on producing civilian casualties. UNITA's terror attacks killed on average 192 civilians a year—more than four times the number of government personnel slain—when the rebel group was weaker than the state army. The group continued to use terrorism when it was strong enough to contest the state on the battlefield, but these attacks were less frequent and tended to harm individuals associated with the government rather than civilians. Figure 16.4 highlights that under more favourable military

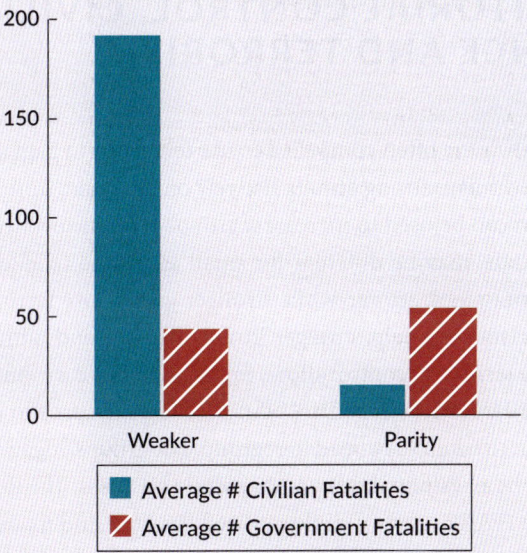

FIGURE 16.4 Severity of UNITA terrorism by target, 1989–2002. Incidents from the Global Terrorism Database are matched with data on rebel strength from Cunningham et al.'s (2013) Nonstate Actor dataset. The left-hand figure displays the severity of UNITA attacks when the organization is judged as weaker than the state, while the right-hand figure provides information on UNITA attacks when the organization is equally matched with the state. The darker bar examines civilian fatalities, while the lighter bar considers all government fatalities.

conditions, UNITA's attacks killed about 15 civilians in a given year, whereas those same conditions led to the deaths of more than three times the number of government personnel.

> UNITA appears to have used terrorism as a substitute for conventional military operations. When its own organizational weakness prevented the group from hurting its primary enemy in battle, the rebels hoped to injure the state through its attacks on civilians. UNITA's behaviour suggests a trade-off between military and civilian deaths and supports the general argument that terrorism during civil war is caused by disparities in military power. Parallels can be drawn between weak rebels and school yard bullies; both prey on those believed to weaker in order to deflect from their own power deficiencies.
>
> **QUESTIONS**
>
> 1. Why would attacks against the civilian population be viewed as acceptable substitutes for attacks against the Angolan army?
> 2. Why would UNITA's attacks on the civilian population harm the state rather than the rebel group itself?

16.3 TERRITORIAL CONTROL, CIVILIAN COMPLIANCE AND TERRORISM

Although weaker rebels are often compelled to use terrorism to gain a military advantage over a stronger government, strong groups also rely on terrorism during war. While across the board, terrorism can be used to increase a group's leverage over the state, the logic of attacks against civilians may be different for small and large rebel organizations. Weak groups use terrorism to look strong, while stronger groups use terror to look legitimate. In particular, terrorism may help stronger groups liberate and administer territory, an important aim since territorial control allows militants to build a robust insurgency (Kalyvas and Balcells 2010). Territorial control affords rebels the space to organize a rebellion and a place to retreat to when they need to regroup. For groups engaged in criminal enterprises, territory can be an essential resource to sustain business. The Revolutionary Armed Forces of Colombia (FARC), for example, utilized the land and its inhabitants to sustain a booming cocaine enterprise. In other conflicts like that in the Democratic Republic of Congo, rebel organizations benefitted from occupying and extorting resource-rich territories. The extraction of gemstones, drugs and even timber has helped prolong rebellions around the world (Ross 2004).

While territorial control is beneficial for rebels, the road to dominance is likely to be difficult and destructive, which is why terrorism is frequently employed in areas that insurgents do not yet fully control (De La Calle and Sanchez-Cuenca 2012). To establish control over a given area, civilians will need to be subdued, as they often resist rebel rule (Arjona 2015). Violence can be an effective means of exerting dominance over an area. As Stuart Elden (2009) suggests, 'to control a territory is to exercise terror; to challenge territorial extent is to exercise terror.' Contested control, in particular, can spur violence against civilians, as competitors attempt to force the population to cooperate and prevent mass defection that could weaken their authority (Kalyvas 2006; Metelits 2009). Yet the decision to use terror can be risky when attempting to govern, as attacks against civilians may alienate supporters and cause the population to instead seek protection from the opposing side (Kalyvas 2006; Polo and Gleditsch 2016). Violence therefore, has its productive limits.

Scholars have found that selective, intentional targeting of individual 'guilty' civilians can increase cooperation, while indiscriminate attacks against innocent civilians can be counterproductive (Kalyvas 2006). In order to discriminate between guiltless and culpable civilians, however, combatants need accurate intelligence on instances of compliance and defection at the individual level. Therefore, high value is placed on information and parties will often go to great lengths to extract it from the civilian population. While some belligerents attempt to terrorize civilians into collaborating, others recognize there are more benign ways to elicit compliance. Many rebel groups make efforts to persuade the civilian population with a mix of coercive and benevolent strategies. Territory-holding rebels have strong incentives to place emphasis on the latter and develop cooperative relationships with civilians to secure vital material benefits, including taxes, information, shelter and recruits, that increase its standing (Stewart and Liou 2016). While terrorism can crush opposition, it does little to generate sustained civilian loyalty. Governance efforts, on the other hand, can help achieve this goal. A clear link has been established between territorial control and the provision of services (Ishiyama and Widmeier 2013; Berman and Matanock 2015). Seizing territory enables a violent group to set up a proto-state, which rivals the authority and legitimacy of the government.

> **KEY CONCEPTS**
>
> **Proto-state** A non-state political institution that performs many similar functions to the state without the sovereignty that comes with statehood. These entities are also referred to as quasi-states or states within states.

Power vacuums left by the absence of the government from a particular territory enables rebels to offer essential services, especially protection, in exchange for compliance. According to Ahmad (2017: 25), 'When a state descends into civil war, no party has a clear monopoly on force, and security must be purchased from competing warlord protection rackets. Each of these rackets not only protects its clients but also threatens them and attacks other rackets.' Therefore, territorial control, service provision and violence come together to form political order in civil war zones (Ahmad 2017).

16.4 REBEL SOCIAL SERVICE PROVISION

Violent groups branded as terrorists are often involved in the *provision of social services* including administering institutions in the education, health and security sectors. Groups including Hamas, Fatah, Hezbollah, Liberation Tigers of Tamil Eelam (LTTE), and al-Qaeda are well known for setting up extensive bureaucracies and public service outfits. Hamas, for example, has run charities, schools, mosques, and media outlets in the West Bank and Gaza since its inception (Berman 2011; Szekely 2015). The LTTE also developed expansive security, judicial, health, and educational institutions in Tamil Eelam (Mampilly 2012; Wagstaff and Jung 2017; see Photo 16.1). Social services benefit the communities to which they are provided, yet social service provision is also associated with more terrorism (Asal et al. 2019; Heger et al. 2017). That is, groups that provide public goods often also produce the worst of public ills—terrorism.

> **KEY CONCEPTS**
>
> **Public Good** A good or service provided to members of a community that is typically free and non-excludable. Public goods generally refer to social services, such as education, healthcare, security and judicial systems.

PHOTO 16.1 Terrorist groups can also provide social services to boost their popularity amongst citizens. The Palestinian organisation Hamas has run charities, schools, and in 2020 built quarantine rooms in response to Covid-19—pictured here in Rafah, April 2020. One thousand quarantine rooms were built by Hamas in Gaza.

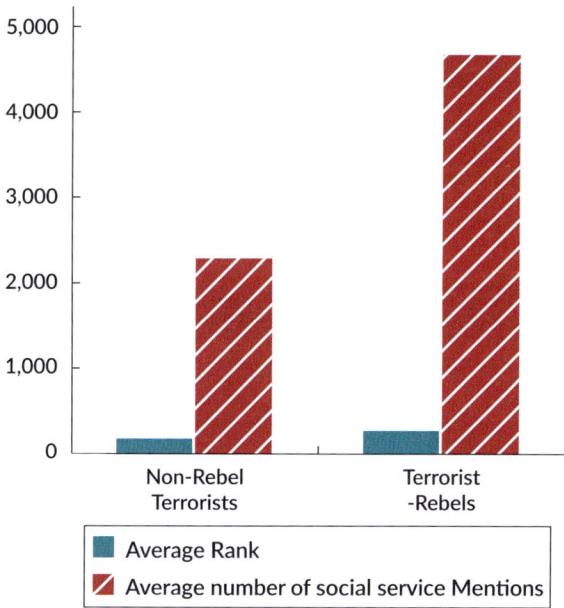

FIGURE 16.5 Average mentions of terrorist social service provision, 1970–2011. Terrorist-Rebels refer to violent organizations that simultaneously execute terror attacks while participating in an organized conflict with the state, while non-rebel terrorists are groups that utilize terror but are not parties to a domestic conflict. These data match Heger and Jung's (2017) 'Terrorist and Insurgent Organization Social Services' dataset (TIOS) with UCDP civil conflict data (Petterson et al. 2020) to identify rebel groups that use both terrorism and provide services.

Heger and Jung (2017) identify nearly 400 groups that have utilized terrorism since 1980 and their levels of social service administration. This data, which records the number of times each terror group was mentioned for its provision of public goods in the news, shows that terrorist groups engaged in rebellion are more often mentioned for their contributions to public services than groups that engage in terrorism outside of conflicts. Figure 16.5 demonstrates that terrorist-rebel groups are twice as likely to be mentioned for their service work than terrorist groups that are not parties to civil conflicts. The activities of rebel groups that utilize terrorism were mentioned about 4669 times, while terrorists that do not operate within a rebellion were mentioned for their service provision only 2287 times. Among the top 20 social service providers, 35 per cent are coded as rebel groups that use terrorism. This is notable given that only 25 per cent of the terrorist organizations in the data qualify as rebels. Among the top three providers of public goods, Hamas and Fatah score the second and third highest. Hamas in particular is a powerful force in the Palestinian territories.

This raises the question: if groups that use terrorism generally do so from a position of weakness, why do we see so many groups that appear to be of higher capacity, such as Hamas and Fatah, also using terrorism? The short answer is that while weaker groups may be forced to adopt terrorism, other groups choose terrorism because it can help them achieve long-term strategic aims as well as smaller goals that may eventually benefit their greater ambitions.

CASE STUDY 16.2

Explaining the Taliban's Social Service Efforts in the Context of Terrorism

As the UNITA case explored in Case Study 16.1 demonstrates, terrorism is not only used by weak groups during war. The Taliban, which have been engaged in a decades-long insurgency against the government of Afghanistan, uses both guerrilla and terrorist tactics, but should not be considered weak. On the contrary, the group has been considered one of 'the most accomplished rebels of modern times' (Berman 2011: 30). This assessment is supported by the Afghan National Security Forces' failure to defeat the organization militarily as well as the Taliban's ability to capture and govern large amounts of Afghan territory. At its peak, the organization controlled as much as 90 per cent of the country (Elden 2009). While the Taliban's share of territory has diminished over the course of the 'Global War on Terror', it has been increasing in recent years. In 2019, the Taliban controlled or contested government control in nearly half of Afghanistan's districts. In August 2021, it overthrew the government.

Despite recent US proclamations that the Taliban is an 'armed insurgency' not a 'terrorist group,' the organization does use terrorism while also offering support to other terrorists. According to the Global Terrorism Database, over 8,700 terror attacks in Afghanistan between 2001 and 2018 have been attributed to the Taliban, with the majority falling outside of what could be considered 'legitimate warfare activities'. Attacks have exploded in recent years, with 2015 standing out as one of the organization's most destructive years. During Afghanistan's presidential elections in 2019, the Taliban carried out more than 200 terror attacks in an attempt to upend the electoral process and deter voting. These incidents were preceded by many attacks aimed at pressuring the government to commit to peace talks with the group.

The inclination toward terrorism is also evident in its relationships with other organizations. Even as the Taliban fought against ISIS' reign of terror, it continued to maintain ties with al-Qaeda, the terror group responsible for the 9/11 terror attacks, and the Pakistan-based Haqqani network. Regardless of its appeals to legitimacy and decency, the Taliban has undoubtedly embraced terrorism.

However, the organization is also known for its effective governance of Afghanistan, and scores among the top 20 service providers in the Terrorist Social Service Provision dataset. Like the FARC, which brutalized the civilian population in Colombia, the Taliban has developed a substantial bureaucracy that includes health, educational, and criminal justice systems (Mampilly 2012). During the Covid-19 pandemic from 2020, for instance, the Taliban's Islamic

PHOTO 16.2 Afghan military forces patrol the streets of Kabul, Afghanistan, as the Taliban carried out attacks to disrupt political campaigns in the lead-up to the elections in September 2019.

Emirate Health Commission staged public awareness campaigns, provided the population with masks, gloves and disinfectants, erected quarantine centres and treated the sick. The organization also welcomed healthcare and aid workers back into its territories in an effort to manage the pandemic, but also continued to abduct healthcare providers and target pharmacies. How can we make sense of a group that actively terrorizes civilians while providing public goods to that same population?

Both terrorism and public goods provision can be used to boost an organization's image domestically and internationally. By coupling these strategies, the Taliban appears to be playing the long game, hoping that both the positive incentives and negative reprimands increase the organization's power and control when the war ends. Not only does violence encourage obedience from civilians, it also undermines the state by demonstrating that the Taliban itself is the only entity capable of stopping the conflict in Afghanistan. Essentially, by demonstrating its own strength, the Taliban's seeks to highlight the Afghan government's weakness. One Taliban commander from Nangahar province underscored this point noting that 'compared to 10 years ago . . . the world sees [the Taliban] as more legitimate, and all of that is through [their] violence' (George 2019). Revealing that the incumbent is incompetent, however, does little to show that the Taliban is the preferred alternative. This is where their demonstration of good governance comes in. By governing their own territories well, the Taliban can prove its ability to provide leadership superior to the current government's. This strategy appears to be working. Not only is their judicial system perceived to be fairer and less corrupt, citizens have noted that the Taliban's Covid-19 response has topped the state's. The 2019 peace deal inked between the US and the Taliban, which is expected to be a precursor to an agreement with the Afghan government, also validates the group's mixed terror-governance strategy. Therefore, it is no surprise that following the historic settlement with the US in 2019 and in the midst of a global pandemic, the Taliban has stepped up its use of terrorism alongside its public works.

QUESTIONS

1. How can violence offer legitimacy to an organization such as the Taliban?
2. How much effort does the Taliban have to expend on providing public goods to offset their use of terrorism in Afghanistan?

Service provision may be used to gain compliance from the population in areas they administer. Governance institutions anchor militants into the community and ensure they are able to engage in effective surveillance and oversight of the civilian population. Public goods provision will be most fruitful when rebels are in competition with the state or other non-state actors for the population's support (Wagstaff and Jung 2017), and when resources are scarce, and the government is either absent or weak. Public projects enable violent groups to offer relief to neglected communities and fill voids left by ineffective governments (Berman 2011). These circumstances allow rebels to trade public benefits for civilian loyalty.

Service institutions can build a group's popularity and increase the public's reliance on the organization's goodwill. As a result, terrorist rebel groups may see substantial legitimacy gains from erecting civilian institutions (Mampilly 2012). This may be necessary since the use of terrorism can damage a rebel group's reputation (Fortna, Lotito and Rubin 2018), which is especially costly for organizations that rely on civilian supporters to function (Polo 2019). Seemingly-random attacks on the population may generate new grievances and alienate existing supporters. Civilians may also oppose acts of terror aimed at enemy supporters if such attacks delegitimize the broader movement (Fortna, Lotito, and Rubin 2018). Terrorism is generally considered to be amoral (Lake 2002; Asal 2012; Moghdam et al.), and the reluctance to negotiate with terrorists is widespread. Therefore, while beneficial in one respect, a group's use of terrorism may also bring about significant downstream consequences.

The provision of resources to the population, however, may offset civilian grievances produced by a group's reign of terror, and increase a rebel organization's legitimacy. By providing more services in an effective manner, organizations are able to rally support among even those who are not attracted to its goals or vision (Berman 2011; Szekely 2015). Maintaining effective institutions may help rebels win civilian hearts and minds. Such a strategy is sensible, given counterinsurgency expert, David Galula's (2006) argument that both insurgents and counterinsurgents are largely waging a political battle for the undecided population. In this regard, Galula urges effective counterinsurgents to develop economic, social, cultural and medical projects geared toward the civilian population during their military campaigns. Terrorists and insurgents wisely adopt similar strategies. It is argued that the LTTE did just this; the organization attempted to augment the effects of its violence and coercion by building legitimacy through the delivery of social services (Terpstra and Frerks 2017). In this way, public works can be helpful in offsetting the pernicious effects of terrorizing the civilian population. They can work to boost a rebel organization's popularity, sometimes ensuring militant's success in electoral politics after wars end (Ishiyama and Widmeier 2013).

16.5 THE STRATEGIES OF TERRORISM

As discussed in section 16.4, terrorism can be helpful for ensuring civilian compliance and for gaining territory from the state. These are sometimes called process goals. But how might terrorism help achieve longer term, broader strategic goals? Though the terror inflicted by some rebel organizations appears to serve no logical end, most terrorism appears to be motivated by a coherent strategy or logic (Lake 2002; Kydd and Walter 2006). Terrorism can be useful for advancing a wide-range of political aims, from negotiations to substantive political concessions and compromise settlements. Broadly, terrorism can be used to advance a number of strategies that attempt to compel the state directly through punishment or indirectly by denying them civilian support, which threatens their legitimacy to rule. By undermining the state and building viable military and political organizations, rebels are able to use terror to make the state offer significant policy concessions.

Kydd and Walter (2006) identify several different strategies that groups may be pursuing when they use terrorism. Attrition, intimidation, provocation are all strategies that hinge on the idea that terrorism can be painful to the government. The *attrition* strategy is used to demonstrate a group's willingness to impose substantial costs on the state if it does not alter its policies (Crenshaw 1981; Kydd and Walter 2006). Terror attacks can be especially devastating when used in a war of attrition as these attacks hit governments where it hurts most. Attacks in areas populated by government supporters can offer violent organizations more 'bang for their buck', as terrorism can engender more shock and awe in places that states are expected to be able to protect (Koren 2017: 249). Terrorists often target capital cities, for instance, to coerce elites (Koren 2017). These attacks in the seat of government can also impose severe economic costs on the regime and its supporters (Ash 2018). Foreign investments are even found to fall with increasing violence against civilians (Koren 2017).

According to Crenshaw (1981: 380), terrorism is the 'systematic inducement of fear and anxiety to control and direct a civilian population', suggesting that terror is used primarily to alter the behaviour of civilians. This is what an *intimidation* strategy aims to do. Here, terrorism compels the population to defect from leaders of the state (Kydd and Walter 2006). Violence against civilians can be used to demonstrate that the state is illegitimate because it is unable to protect its own civilians. From a social contract perspective, states exist primarily to provide organization and security to its citizens and are expected to be the sole violence specialists within a territory. Citizens give up their individual freedoms and sovereignty, as well as tax money, to be protected by the government. Terrorism can reveal that the regime is ill-equipped to or disinterested in fulfilling this important purpose. However, violence often hurts governments more than the organization's perpetrating the attacks, since it is only the state's obligation to protect citizens. Accordingly, research shows that acts of civil disobedience increase after sustained campaigns of civilian victimization (Koren 2017), providing direct evidence that states are in fact held accountable for their inability to adequately protect the population.

Scholars argue that Western democracies (Pape 2006; Crenshaw 1981; Kydd and Walter 2006) and weak states (Crenshaw 1981) are most likely to be targets of attrition and intimidation strategies because of their unwillingness and inability to secure the state at any cost. Liberal states may hesitate to restrict citizens' civil liberties, while other types of states are unable to do so. Authoritarian regimes however, may be less likely to fall prey to attrition or intimidation strategies, but they may be more suitable candidates for a *provocation* strategy. Here, terrorism is used by violent actors that hope to force the state into a repressive response that undermines its own civilian support. Put differently, militant groups use violence to harass the government into heavy-handed counterterrorism measures that mainly harm civilians. Such a reaction to terrorism is not inconceivable, as governments are rarely able to discriminate between insurgents and ordinary civilians (Kalyvas 2006). Carter (2016) provides evidence for provocation, asserting that Western European governments often overreact to terrorism in a way that victimizes the very population it is charged to protect. This strategy has been exploited by Basque separatists like the ETA against the Spanish government, the Zionist Irgun against the British government in Mandate Palestine (Bueno de Mesquita and Dickson 2007), Boko Haram against Nigeria (Thomas 2014), and the Irish Republican Army (IRA) against the UK (Carter 2016).

Although it seems risky to provoke the government's response, doing so actually benefits rebels that can provide safety for affiliates. Government repression enables rebels to recruit new members by offering protection exclusively to the group's collaborators. Strong government responses to terrorism can also radicalize moderates, inclining them toward the terrorists' cause and building support for extremist goals (Lake 2002). Government repression may remove constraints on rebels that would otherwise refrain from attacking civilians (Polo 2020). Together, the intimidation and provocation strategies represent a dilemma for states. Governments face a backlash when their attempts at counterterrorism inflict harm on civilians and also when they fail to formulate an effective response that actually protects civilians from terrorists. Both strong and weak state responses to terror are likely to create sympathy and support for terrorists. How hard is it for states to execute a moderate response? As it turns out, very hard.

The three aforementioned strategies are expected to harm the government and lead to state losses, either by depriving the regime of domestic (and international) support, or targeting the state's assets directly. While attrition strategies impose heavy costs on the state to induce elites to change the state's policies, intimidation and provocation are designed to undercut the states' civilian support, which undermines its legitimacy. When used successfully, these strategies should be associated with a greater willingness of the state to give in to the demands of groups using terrorism. This expectation has garnered empirical support from studies on both terrorism and civilian victimization. More terrorism is associated with a greater probability that the state will come to the negotiating table, as well as a larger number of concessions on rebels' key demands in post-Cold War Africa (Thomas 2014). Similarly, African conflicts that see high levels of civilian abuse by rebels are more likely to end in negotiated settlements (Wood and Kathman 2014). Pape (2006) finds that suicide terror campaigns around the world have been successful at compelling democratic states to concede to rebel's demands; suicide terrorism forced American, French, and Israeli withdrawals from Lebanon in the 1980s and compelled Sri Lanka to support significant Tamil autonomy in the 1990s. Some scholars still doubt, however, that terrorism can be an effective means by which rebels advance their war aims. Fortna (2015), for example, finds that when rebels engage in small-scale bombing campaigns against civilian targets, they are actually less likely to sign negotiated agreements. Abrahms (2012) finds that foreign terrorist organizations do not typically achieve their long-term outcome objectives, even if they do succeed at meeting their process goals. If terrorism does not lead to concessions, what else could it be useful for?

While concessions are important for many violent dissident groups, a subset do not use terrorism in an effort to strike a better bargain with the state. Groups that pursue a *spoiling* strategy, for example, engage in acts of terror to derail a peace process (Stedman 1997; Kydd and Walter 2006). This strategy is likely to emerge when at least two parties have committed to a compromise settlement, but all parties do not view peace or the terms of that peace as beneficial (Stedman 1997).

This strategy can explain Hamas' terrorism in the 1990s. The group used violence in an attempt to undermine the Oslo peace process and its rival, Fatah, which stood to gain control over a future Palestinian state (Berman 2011). Hamas is believed to have planned significant terror attacks to coincide with major events during the Arab-Israeli peace process in order to convince observers that the leaders of the Palestinian Authority were untrustworthy. This dynamic also played out in the peace process in South Africa. Multiple groups engaged in strategic violence at important points during negotiations (Sisk 1993). While the African National Congress (ANC) engaged in terror to thwart its political rivals, the Inkatha Freedom Party (IFP) used attacks to avoid exclusion from the peace deal. Critically, the Pan-Africanist Congress of Azania (PAC) engaging in a campaign of terror strategically to derail peace talks between the ANC and the South African apartheid government.

Evidence confirms that terrorism can destabilize peace by extending the duration of a conflict and increasing the likelihood that it recurs (Findley and Young 2015).

A final strategy, *outbidding*, is the result of competition between two militant groups for civilian support and is, therefore, also most likely to arise in a multiparty conflict. In this scenario, terrorism is used to demonstrate that the most violent group is more committed than its less violent counterparts. Again, Hamas, utilized terrorism against Israel to separate itself from the secular Fatah movement and 'to present themselves as the true nationalists' while casting their opponent as collaborators of the Israeli government (Berman 2011: 130–131). Researchers also point out that internal rifts between factions within the same organization may encourage violence (Biberman and Zahid 2019). In particular, Biberman and Zahid (2019) argue that outbidding between disparate factions within Tehreek-e-Taliban Pakistan and Riyadus-Salikhin was the cause of school massacres in Pakistan and Russia, respectively. Despite some case-specific evidence, broader quantitative support for this theory is mixed. Some studies, such as by Conrad and Greene (2015), and Nemeth (2014) find clear evidence of outbidding, while others find no consistent support for a relationship between terrorism and domestic competition (Findley and Young 2012).

16.6 CONCLUSION

Terrorism is used frequently in civil war, but not by all rebels. Violent actors make strategic decisions about the types of violence they use during conflicts. While some groups target only militaries, others attack civilians; some also adopt mixed-strategies that couple organized armed resistance with campaigns of terror. To understand a group's tactical choice in a civil war, it is often necessary to examine the military constraints that it faces. More capable groups are likely to eschew indiscriminate terror, while weaker groups may rely on it. Groups of all stripes may find selective and moderate civilian victimization worthwhile. This is because terrorism can be used to win a game of 'mercy' against the state. Here, militants apply enough pressure and pain on the regime until it concedes defeat. By targeting civilians, terrorists can undercut the state's base of support, damage the economy, and hurt elites directly, which can all help bolster a group's war effort. Such a strategy is most helpful when rebels are unable to cause enough damage to the state on the battlefield. Terrorism, therefore, can be considered as a complement to other strategies in war.

Terrorism is not only used in conjunction with violence but can be picked up by organizations that use nonviolent resistance as well. The tactic can be used at one point and neglected at another. As Tilly (2004) suggests, there is no clear class of actors called 'terrorists;' there are simply actors that use terrorism and terrorize. Applying the loaded 'terrorist' label to specific actors, makes it difficult to fully grasp the range of actors that use the tactic, including states. It makes it hard to put the actions of organizations like the African National Congress into context. The ANC, South Africa's current governing party, was regarded as a legitimate revolutionary organization that fought against apartheid and oppression. Many herald the nonviolent strategy adopted by the organization to achieve its lofty goals, but less attention is paid to the organization's use of terrorism. Though it was founded on the principle of nonviolent resistance, it also relied on violence, including brutal attacks against political opponents, to achieve its aims. To contextualize the organization's turn to violence, the ANC's leader, Nelson Mandela, proffered that 'there came a point in [the] struggle when brute force of the oppressor could no longer be countered through passive resistance alone' (Mandela 1999). Mandela realized early that success through nonviolence would be difficult, painstakingly slow and arduous. This prompted the organization to consciously adopt military strategies, including guerrilla warfare and terrorism, better suited to contend with the well-endowed, highly repressive state. Ultimately, both violence and nonviolence contributed to the organization's success.

Terrorism is not a panacea; it can come at a cost. Though the ANC generally kept civilian casualties to a minimum, the use of terrorism did hurt the organization's legitimacy. Yet, while nonviolent resistance is generally viewed positively, some groups judge that it is not as effective as violence for achieving large demands. Organizations base their tactical choices, in part, on how much they expect to achieve. However, during a civil war, concerns about one's legitimacy are real and should not be ignored. Thus, it is not uncommon that organizations engage in activities that boost their legitimacy, while also utilizing terrorism. We learned, for instance, that terrorism and civilian governance tend to go hand and hand. Groups may also strategically switch between tactics to achieve a similar purpose.

DISCUSSION QUESTIONS

1. Why is terrorism a distinct form of political violence from insurgency or guerrilla warfare?
2. Which actors use terrorism in civil wars?
3. Which types of strategies can terrorism be used to further?
4. Is terrorism an effective tactic for goal attainment in civil war? Why or why not?
5. What are the major explanations for the use of violence against civilians during rebellions?
6. How do we understand the decision to govern and terrorize the civilian population?

GUIDE TO FURTHER READING

Although we have touched on the strategic nature of terrorism within this chapter, there are a number of other important works that more deeply describe the strategies of terrorism and explain what rebel groups aim to achieve by employing terror during a domestic conflict. Some of the works follow:

Berman, E. (2011) *Radical Religious and Violent: The New Economics of Terrorism*. MIT Press. *Examines the relationships between religious radicalism, terrorism, and social welfare provision.*

Crenshaw, M. (1981) 'The Causes of Terrorism.' *Comparative Politics*, 13: 4, 379–399. **Seminal article examining several leading rationalist explanations of terrorism.**

Kydd, A. and Walter, B. (2006) 'The Strategies of Terrorism,' *International Security* 31: 1, 49–80. **Important article examining potential strategies nonstate actors attempt to further in their use of terrorism.**

Lake, D. (2002) 'Rational Extremism: Understanding Terrorism in the Twenty-First Century', *Dialog-IO*, 1.1, 15–28. **Adopts a bargaining perspective to clarify what extremist political groups hope to gain by using terrorism.**

Pape, R. (2006) *Dying to Win: The Strategic Logic of Suicide Terrorism*. NY: Random House Incorporated. **Book focused specifically on examining the logic of suicide terrorism against liberal democratic states.**

Tilly, C. (2004) 'Terror, Terrorism, Terrorists,' Sociological Theory, 22: 1, 5–13. **Develops the idea that terror tactics can be used by a broad cross-section of political actors to support various goals and strategies. Importantly, it advances the idea that terrorism is not just a tool of nonstate armed groups but is also utilized by states.**

REFERENCES

Abrahms, M. (2012) 'The Political Effectiveness of Terrorism Revisited'. *Comparative Political Studies*, 45 (3): 366–393.

Acharya, A. (2009) 'Small Amounts for Big Bangs? Rethinking Responses to 'Low Cost' Terrorism'. *Journal of Money Laundering Control*, 12 (3): 285–298.

Ahmad, A.(2017) *Jihad & Co.: Black Markets and Islamist Power*. Oxford: Oxford University Press.

Arjona, A. (2015) 'Civilian Resistance to Rebel Governance'. in *Rebel Governance in Civil War*, Ana Arjona, Nelson Kasfir, and Zachariah Mampilly, eds. Cambridge: Cambridge University Press, 180–202.

Asal, V. et al. (2019) 'Carrots, Sticks, and Insurgent Targeting of Civilians'. *Journal of Conflict Resolution*, 63 (7): 1710–1735.

Asal, V. (2012) 'Killing Civilians or Holding Territory? How to Think About Terrorism'. *International Studies Review*, 14 (3): 485–490.

Ash, K. (2018) 'The War Will Come to Your Street: Explaining Geographic Variation in Terrorism by Rebel Groups'. *International Interactions*, 44 (3): 411–436.

Berkebile, R. E. (2017) 'What is Domestic Terrorism? A Method for Classifying Events from the Global Terrorism Database'. *Terrorism and Political Violence*, 29 (1): 1–26.

Berman, E. (2011) *Radical, Religious, and Violent: The New Economics of Terrorism*. MIT Press.

Berman, E., and Matanock, A. M. (2015) 'The Empiricists' Insurgency'. *Annual Review of Political Science*, 18: 443–464.

Biberman, Y. and Zahid, F. (2019) 'Why Terrorists Target Children: Outbidding, Desperation, and Extremism in the Peshawar and Beslan School Massacres'. *Terrorism and Political Violence*, 31 (2): 169–184.

Bueno de Mesquita, E. and Dickson. E. S. (2007) 'The Propaganda of the Deed: Terrorism, Counterterrorism, and Mobilization'. *American Journal of Political Science*, 51 (2): 364–381.

Carter, D. B. (2016) 'Provocation and the Strategy of Terrorist and Guerrilla Attacks'. *International Organization*, 70 (1): 133–173.

Conrad, J. and Greene, K. (2015) 'Competition, Differentiation, and the Severity of Terrorist Attacks'. *The Journal of Politics*, 77 (2): 546–561.

Crenshaw, M. (1981) 'The Causes of Terrorism'. *Comparative Politics*, 13 (4): 379–399.

Cunningham, D. E., Skrede Gleditsch, K., and Salehyan I. (2013) 'Non-state Actors in Civil Wars: A new Dataset'. *Conflict Management and Peace Science*, 30 (5): 516–531.

De la Calle, L. and Sánchez-Cuenca, I. (2012) 'Killing Civilians or Holding Territory? How to Think About Terrorism'. *International Studies Review*, 14 (3): 481–484.

Elden, S. (2009) *Terror and Territory: The Spatial Extent of Sovereignty*. University of Minnesota Press.

Enders, W., Sandler, T., and Gaibulloev, K. (2011) 'Domestic Versus Transnational Terrorism: Data, Decomposition, and Dynamics'. *Journal of Peace Research*, 48 (3): 319–337.

Findley, M. G. and Young, J. K. (2012) 'Terrorism and Civil War: A Spatial and Temporal Approach to a Conceptual Problem'. *Perspectives on Politics*, *10* (2): 285–305.

Findley, M. G. and Young, J. K. (2015) 'Terrorism, Spoiling, and the Resolution of Civil Wars'. *The Journal of Politics*, *77* (4): 1115–1128.

Fortna, V. P. (2015) 'Do Terrorists Win? Rebels' Use of Terrorism and Civil War Outcomes'. *International Organization*, *69* (3): 519–556.

Fortna, V. P., Lotito, N. J., and Rubin, M. A. (2018) 'Don't Bite the Hand that Feeds: Rebel Funding Sources and the Use of Terrorism in Civil Wars'. *International Studies Quarterly*, *62* (4): 782–794.

Galula, D. (2006) *Counterinsurgency Warfare: Theory and Practice*. Greenwood Publishing Group.

George, S. (2019) 'Inside the Taliban's Afghanistan, Violence Remains the Path to Power'. *Washington Post Blogs*, December.

Hafez, M. M. (2006) 'Rationality, Culture, and Structure in the Making of Suicide Bombers: A Preliminary Theoretical Synthesis and Illustrative Case Study'. *Studies in Conflict & Terrorism*, *29* (2): 165–185.

Heger, L. L. and Jung, D. F. (2017) 'Negotiating With Rebels: The Effect of Rebel Service Provision on Conflict Negotiations'. *Journal of Conflict Resolution*, *61* (6): 1203–1229.

Heger, L. L., Jung, D. F., and Wong, W. H. (2017) 'Linking Nonstate Governance and Violence'. *Journal of Global Security Studies*, *2* (3): 220–236.

Hoffman, B. (2003) 'The Logic of Suicide Terrorism', *Atlantic Monthly*, *291* (5).

Horowitz, M. C. (2010) 'Nonstate Actors and the Diffusion of Innovations: The Case of Suicide Terrorism'. *International Organization*, *64* (1): 33–64.

Ishiyama, J. and Widmeier, M. (2013) 'Territorial Control, Levels of Violence, and the Electoral Performance of Former Rebel Political Parties after Civil Wars'. *Civil Wars*, *15* (4): 531–550.

Kalyvas, N. S. (2006) *The Logic of Violence In Civil War*. Cambridge University Press.

Kalyvas, S. N., and Balcells, L. (2010) 'International System and Technologies of Rebellion: How the end of the Cold War Shaped Internal Conflict'. *American Political Science Review*, *104* (3): 415–429.

Krcmaric, D. (2018) 'Varieties of Civil War and Mass Killing: Reassessing the Relationship Between Guerrilla Warfare and Civilian Victimization'. *Journal of Peace Research*, *55* (1): 18–31.

Koren, O. (2017) 'Why Insurgents Kill Civilians in capital cities: A Disaggregated Analysis of Mechanisms and Trends'. *Political Geography*, *61*: 237–252.

Kydd, A. H., and Walter, B. F (2006) 'The Strategies of Terrorism'. *International Security*, *31* (1): 49–80.

LaFree, G. and Dugan, L. (2007) 'Introducing the Global Terrorism Database'. *Terrorism and Political Violence*, *19* (2):181–204.

Lake, D.A. (2002) 'Rational Extremism: Understanding Terrorism in the Twenty-first Century'. *Dialogue IO*, *1* (1): 15–28.

Mampilly, Z. C. (2012) *Rebel Rulers: Insurgent Governance and Civilian Life During War*. Cornell University Press.

Mandela, N. (1999) 'The Sacred Warrior: The Liberator of South Africa Looks at the Seminal Work of the Liberator of India'. *CNN*. December 27.

Metelits, C. (2009) *Inside Insurgency: Violence, Civilians, and Revolutionary Group Behaviour*. NYU Press.

Moghadam, A., Berger, R., and Beliakova, P. (2014) 'Say Terrorist, Think Insurgent: Labelling and Analysing Contemporary Terrorist Actors'. *Perspectives on Terrorism*, *8* (5).

Nemeth, S. (2014) 'The Effect of Competition on Terrorist Group Operations'. *Journal of Conflict Resolution*, *58* (2): 336–362.

Ross, M.L. (2004) 'How do Natural Resources Influence Civil War? Evidence from Thirteen Cases'. *International Organization*, *58* (1): 35–67.

Pape, R. A. (2006) *Dying To Win: The Strategic Logic of Suicide Terrorism*. Random House Incorporated.

Pettersson, T. and Öberg, M. (2020) 'Organized Violence, 1989–2019'. *Journal of Peace Research*, *57* (4): 597–613.

Polo, S. M. T. (2020) 'The Quality of Terrorist Violence: Explaining the Logic of Terrorist Target Choice'. *Journal of Peace Research*, *57* (2): 235–250.

Polo, S. M. T., and Gleditsch, K. S. (2016) 'Twisting Arms and Sending Messages: Terrorist Tactics in Civil War'. *Journal of Peace Research*, *53* (6): 815–829.

Price, H. E. (1977) 'The Strategy and Tactics of Revolutionary Terrorism'. *Comparative Studies in Society and History*, *19* (1): 52–66.

Sánchez-Cuenca, I., and De la Calle, L. (2009) 'Domestic Terrorism: The Hidden Side of Political Violence'. *Annual Review of Political Science*, *12*: 31–49.

Sisk, T.D. (1993) 'The Violence-negotiation Nexus: South Africa in Transition and the Politics of Uncertainty'. *Negotiation Journal*, *9* (1): 77–94.

Stanton, J. A. (2013) 'Terrorism in the Context of Civil War'. *The Journal of Politics*, *75* (4): 1009–1022.

Stedman, S.J. (1997) 'Spoiler Problems in Peace Processes'. *International Security*, *22* (2): 5–53.

Stewart, M.A., and Liou, Y. (2017) 'Do Good Borders Make Good Rebels? Territorial Control and Civilian Casualties'. *The Journal of Politics*, 79 (1): 284–301.

Szekely, O. (2015) 'Doing Well by Doing Good: Understanding Hamas's Social Services as Political Advertising'. *Studies in Conflict & Terrorism*, 38 (4): 275–292.

Teichman, J. (1989) 'How to Define Terrorism'. *Philosophy*, 64 (250): 505–517.

Terpstra, N., and Frerks, G. (2017) 'Rebel Governance and Legitimacy: Understanding the Impact of Rebel Legitimation on Civilian Compliance with the LTTE Rule'. *Civil Wars*, 19 (3): 279–307.

Thomas, J. (2014) 'Rewarding Bad Behaviour: How Governments Respond to Terrorism in Civil War'. *American Journal of Political Science*, 58 (4): 804–818.

Tilly, C. (2004) 'Terror, Terrorism, Terrorists'. *Sociological Theory*, 22 (1): 5–13.

Wagstaff, W. A. and Jung, D. F. (2017) 'Competing for Constituents: Trends in Terrorist Service Provision'. *Terrorism and Political Violence*, 32 (2): 293–324.

Wood, R. M. and Kathman, J. D. (2014) 'Too Much of a Bad Thing? Civilian Victimization and Bargaining in Civil War'. *British Journal of Political Science*, 44 (3): 685–706.

CHAPTER 17

Old and New Terrorism

PETER R. NEUMANN

■ CHAPTER SUMMARY

The discussion about the 'new terrorism' hypothesis was one of the most significant debates to have taken place in terrorism studies in recent decades. Originating in the 1990s, its proponents argued that terrorists were becoming different and more dangerous: an increasing number was motivated by religion; their organizations were transforming from hierarchical, army-like structures into networks; and the attacks they carried out were no longer selective, but aimed to kill as many as possible. The 'new terrorism', they believed, was going to be a more profound—if not, strategic—challenge for the countries that were targeted by it. Yet especially after the September 11th attacks on the US, which seemed to confirm many of the 'new terrorism's' predictions, critics started challenging the concept. They pointed out that none of its alleged elements were unprecedented, and that whatever transformation there might have been had not been as complete or absolute as the term suggested, and that 'old' forms of terrorism continued to pose a threat. No one 'won' the debate, but the back and forth between proponents and critics of the paradigm has provided useful insights into the changing nature of terrorism. It crystallized some of the major issues in the field: the role of religion, the impact of globalization and modern communication technologies on group structures and recruitment, as well as the evolution of terrorist tactics. It provides a useful prism through which to look at the evolution of terrorism. Most importantly, it has brought out a more nuanced—and, arguably, more sophisticated—understanding of all these trends and developments broadening and deepening our understanding of a constantly evolving phenomenon.

17.1 INTRODUCTION

In Bruce Hoffman's *Inside Terrorism,* the chapter on religiously motivated terrorism starts not with a discussion of al-Qaeda or Islamic State (ISIS), but the story of a small group of Jewish terrorists nearly two thousand years ago. The Zealots—from which the contemporary word 'zealot' is derived—sought to end Roman rule in what is today's Israel. Their victims were Roman officials, soldiers, and Jewish collaborators. Instead of firearms or dynamite, which were invented many centuries later, they used a primitive dagger, the *sica*. As Hoffman explains, 'The Zealot would emerge from the anonymous security of a crowded marketplace, draw the *sica* that had been concealed beneath his robes, and in plain view of those present, dramatically slit [the victim's] throat.' The intended effect was identical to that of contemporary terrorism, namely to 'send a powerful message to a wider, watching audience', spread fear and terror, and—ultimately—cause their targets to withdraw or make concessions (Hoffman, 2017: 83).

Hoffman's message seemed clear: there was nothing new about terrorism, nor should anyone be surprised that terrorists were acting in the name of religion (see also Chapter 8 'The History of Terrorism'). The 'connection between terror and religion', he argued, was as old as humanity, long preceding the rise of secular ideologies, such as nationalism and communism. Yet, in what became known as the 'new terrorism' debate, Hoffman appeared to take a different stance. Instead of continuity, he emphasized how terrorism had changed, and that mass casualty attacks by al-Qaeda and other groups constituted a 'new' kind of terrorism. One of its defining features, he pointed out, was the prominence of religion, which had fundamentally changed the way in which terrorists operated.

Could these positions be reconciled? How did the 'new terrorism' differ from the old, and what did the arguments between supporters and opponents teach us about the nature and dynamics of contemporary terrorism? This chapter provides an overview of what emerged as one of the central debates among terrorism researchers in the 1990s and 2000s. It begins with a review of the its origins and a brief summary of conceptual issues. In the following sections, we then examine each of the issues that proponents believed was 'new': the increased role of religion; the 'network'-like character of terrorist groups; and the greater lethality of terrorist attacks.

What the chapter will demonstrate is that neither supporters nor opponents of the 'new terrorism' idea were entirely correct, and that seemingly contradictory statements like Hoffman's could indeed be reconciled. Although no one had 'won', therefore, the debate was nevertheless a useful way of making sense of the changing character of terrorism, not least because it produced more nuanced understandings of key issues like religion, the impact of globalization, the role of the internet, and changes in tactics and targeting. Significantly, it also reinforced the need for a more rigorous framework for conceptualizing—and measuring—the evolution of terrorism.

17.2 ORIGINS

It is hard to pinpoint when exactly the idea of the 'new terrorism' emerged. As early as the mid-1980s, Brian Jenkins noted that terrorism was changing, and that terrorist groups were becoming dangerous: 'Terrorists will escalate their violence, their attacks will become more indiscriminate' (Jenkins, 1985: 30). Even earlier, David Rapoport had written about the rise of religiously motivated terrorism (Rapoport, 1983), which he (later) described as the 'fourth wave' (Rapoport, 2002). Yet it was only in the 1990s that the term became widely used. During this period, many of the most notorious groups of the 1970s and 1980s, such as the Irish Republican Army (IRA), the Palestinian Liberation Organization (PLO), and the Red Army Faction (RAF), were ending their campaigns or engaged in peace processes, while 'new' and seemingly more dangerous forms of terrorism were on the rise. In early 1993, jihadists launched their first attack on the World Trade Center; in 1995, a Buddhist-inspired cult (Aum Shinrikyo, led by Shoko Asahara) released nerve gas on the Tokyo underground; and in the same year, Timothy McVeigh set off a truck bomb in Oklahoma City, USA, which killed 168 people—the single most devastating terrorist attack within the United States prior to September 11th, 2001 (Neumann, 2009: 2–3).

PHOTO 17.1 Aum Shinrikyo founder Shoko Asahara. Aum carried out the 1995 gas attack on the Tokyo subway killing 13 and injuring thousands.

Against this background, Walter Laqueur wrote that changes in technology and virtually all other aspects of terrorism had produced a vastly different phenomenon, and that '[n]ew definitions and new terms may have to developed for new realities' (Laqueur, 1996). In subsequent works, he focused on terrorists' desire and capacity to produce large number of fatalities, especially through the use of weapons of mass destruction, which utilized chemical, biological, radiological or nuclear materials (Laqueur, 1999; see also Gurr and Cole, 2000; Stern, 2000). It was this aspect, which he believed had elevated terrorism from the level of 'nuisance' to that of a strategic threat. The 'new terrorism', he concluded, 'could claim more victims, do more material damage, and unleash far greater panic than anything the world has ever seen' (Laqueur, 1996).

A related aspect was the rise of religion. Building on Rapoport's work, Hoffman not only documented the increasing prominence of religiously motivated groups (Hoffman, 1999), but spelled out what he believed were likely implications and consequences. In a 1993 paper, he argued that 'holy terror' was different in its 'sense of morality', justification, and constituencies, resulting in greater, less predictable violence and more absolutist demands (Hoffman, 1993). Mark Juergensmeyer, a sociologist of religion, arrived at similar conclusions. Based on interviews with terrorists from different religious traditions, including Christianity, Islam, Judaism, and Sikhism, he showed that the 'new' terrorists often thought of themselves as being involved in 'cosmic wars', confronting 'satanic' and 'evil' enemies with whom no compromise was possible (Juergensmeyer, 2000a, 2000b).

The third new element was the more networked nature of terrorist groups. According to an influential study by the American think-tank RAND, which contained a chapter on 'Networks, Netwar, and Information-Age Terrorism' by John Arquilla, David Ronfeldt, and Michele Zanini, globalization and the rise of information technology had allowed terrorist organizations to 'flatten' their hierarchies and operate across greater distances. 'Networked groups', they claimed, had become more frequent, and were capable of carrying out more—and more significant—attacks (Lesser, 1999: 67).

Much of the early debate was among proponents of the new paradigm. Writing in early 2000, for example, Daniel Benjamin and Steve Simon, two officials at the US National Security Council, warned of Osama bin Laden's power and influence, claiming that the leader of al-Qaeda had formed a global network whose determination to acquire weapons of mass destruction and inflict catastrophic damage on the United States was undiminished. In their view, bin Laden was—quite literally—'the new face of terrorism' (Benjamin and Simon, 2000a, 200b). Hoffman did not disagree with their assessment of bin Laden, but believed that the emphasis on weapons of mass destruction had been exaggerated. In Hoffman's words: '[A]s fanatical and irrational as this new breed of terrorists may seem, [they ...] have remained remarkably conservative operationally'. He concluded that 'the gun and the bomb' remained 'the terrorists' weapons of choice' (quoted in Roy, 2000).

Al-Qaeda's attacks against the United States on 11th September 2001 tragically confirmed many of the more pessimistic predictions. Although no chemical, biological or nuclear weapons were used, the death and destruction far exceeded the levels of terrorist violence that had previously been known; they were carried out by a group that claimed to act in the name of religion; and they appeared to operate like a loosely structured global network. If anything, the careful and empirically balanced writings of scholars like Hoffman suddenly seemed inappropriately cautious for what appeared like a new era of 'super-terrorism' (Freedman, 2002), 'mega-terrorism' (Garwin, 2002), or even 'hyper-terrorism' (Heisbourg, 2003).

> **KEY CONCEPTS**
>
> **The New Terrorism** A term which emerged in the 1990s and has been used to describe more networked, religiously motivated terrorists whose attacks are intended to cause mass casualties.

17.3 CONCEPTUAL ISSUES

One of the earliest—and most consistent—criticisms of the 'new terrorism' related to its *use by policymakers*. Because it suggested that terrorism had become more different—and more dangerous—than ever before, politicians started using the concept in order to legitimize new policies and exceptional powers. Rather than adapting the counter-terrorism 'toolbox' with which terrorist groups had been defeated or contained in the past, they argued that new instruments, methods and measures were needed (Copeland, 2001: 10). US President George Bush (President from 2001 to 2009), for example, warned of the 'new realities and dangers posed by modern terrorists', amounting to 'a threat like no other our nation has ever faced', while British Prime Minister Tony Blair (leader from 1997 to 2007) spoke of a 'new global terrorism' that 'was driven not by a set of negotiable political demands, but by religious fanaticism' (quoted in Field, 2009: 195–196). As Martha Crenshaw noted, the idea of a 'new terrorism' allowed policymakers to compare the challenge of terrorism to 'the existential threat of Communism during the Cold War, not past terrorism' (Crenshaw, 2011: 55).

Other scholars focused on challenging the historical *validity of the concept*. Many pointed out that religiously motivated terrorism had existed for millennia, and that there was nothing new about religion as a motivation and justification for acts of violence (see, for example, Copeland, 2001: 9; Spencer, 2004: 16). Others took issue with the idea that the 'new terrorism' was more lethal and likely to use weapons of mass destruction than previous forms of terrorism, arguing that ethno-nationalist and far-right extremists had long histories of mass casualty terrorism, including several attempts at using chemical, biological, radiological, and nuclear weapons (Tucker, 2001). Not least, the critics claimed that network-like structures were not a recent phenomenon, and that terrorist groups had never been as hierarchical as the 'new terrorism's' proponents alleged (see, for example, Duyvesteyn, 2004). For Crenshaw, the historical ignorance of the 'new terrorism' paradigm was so blatant that she believed its only appeal was to politicians and 'newcomers to the field', who found it 'convenient not to have to take the time to study the long and complicated history of the terrorist phenomenon' (Crenshaw, 2011: 64).

Large parts of the debate revolved around conceptual issues, such the *meaning of 'newness'*. Critics defined 'new' as unprecedented ('a phenomenon that has not been witnessed before') (Duyvesteyn, 2004: 439), 'not existing before' or 'discovered recently or now for the first time' (Spencer, 2006: 4), which allowed them to argue that the 'new terrorism' was not—in fact—new, as all of its elements—mass casualties, religion, and networks—had existed in earlier manifestations of terrorism. By contrast, supporters of the 'new terrorism' claimed that 'newness' was based on 'new' combinations of existing phenomena. Neither Hoffman nor any of the paradigm's other proponents denied the 'essential historical continuities' within which the 'new terrorism' had emerged (Kurtulus, 2011), and pointed out that 'new' was often used in the context of 'rapid evolutionary change', which they believed had taken place during the 1980s and 1990s (Neumann, 2009: 12).

Related to this were questions about the appropriate *period of comparison*. Opponents of the 'new terrorism' tended to pick their examples from the entire (known) history of terrorism, arguing that the existence of, say, religiously motivated groups many centuries ago was evidence of how the concept was flawed (Spencer, 2006: 14). Arguably, even proponents of the 'new terrorism', such as Laqueur, were not always consistent in relation to the period(s) of time their claims related to (Laqueur, 1999). A notable exception was Hoffman, who made it clear that he was comparing the terrorism of the 1990s to that of the preceding decades. When he argued that religion was 'new', therefore, he did not imply that it had never previously been a factor, but—simply—that it had become more prominent when compared to the 1960s, 1970s, and 1980s (Hoffman, 1999: 16). From his perspective, it was perfectly possible, therefore, to write that terrorism and religion had a long history—as he pointed out in the case of the Zealots (see section 17.1)—while, at the same time, making the case that religion was a 'new' motivation in the context of 'modern international terrorism' (Hoffman, 2017).

Another source of confusion was *the extent* to which terrorism was meant to have changed. The critics argued that the 'new terrorism' paradigm had created the false impression that most, if not all, terrorism had suddenly turned into something different. Yet, databases showed that ethno-nationalist groups remained the most important perpetrators of terrorism worldwide, and that the greater lethality could be explained with a very small number of attacks that had caused a disproportionate number of fatalities (Tucker, 2001: 12). This was also true for the use of weapons of mass destruction, which remained too rare represent a discernible pattern (Tucker, 2001: 12). Although supporters of the paradigm insisted that they had never claimed a complete transformation, some conceded that other terms, such as Rapoport's idea of a 'wave', might have been more appropriate. According to Ersun Kurtulus, for example, 'when a new wave of terrorist activity... emerges, there is nothing like a radical and complete breach between the new and the old' (Kursulus, 2011: 484). Neumann made a similar observation:

> [T]he transformation from old to new terrorism has neither been uniform nor universal. While most terrorist groups have been affected—in some way or another—by the powerful forces that have triggered the rise of the new terrorism, this does not mean that they have all [suddenly] become religiously driven, mass-casualty producing networks ... In the majority of cases, it seems as if existing groups have adopted aspects of the new terrorism while resisting others ... (Neumann 2009: 47).

Instead of abandoning the concept, however, he suggested modifying it:

> The ideas of old and new terrorism can [still be helpful as a method for disaggregating ...] how terrorism and/or terrorist groups have changed ... Rather than thinking in absolutes, it may be more accurate therefore to speak of new*er* and old*er* terrorism (Neumann, 2009: 48).

17.4 RELIGION

Regarding the first and most frequently mentioned element—the increasing importance of religion—the supporters of the 'new terrorism' had a relatively strong empirical case. Using data from the RAND database of international terrorism, Hoffman demonstrated how the share of terrorist groups with religiously inspired ideologies rose from being virtually non-existent in the late 1960s and throughout the 1970s to over a third in the mid-1990s (Hoffman, 1999: 15–16). Meanwhile, Kurtulus documented a consistent pattern whereby ethno-nationalist terrorist groups in many of the world's most entrenched conflicts were overtaken by groups with a more explicitly religious character, such as the Shiite Hezbollah replacing the more secular Amal militia in Lebanon; the emergence of the Sunni group Hamas as competition for the Palestinian Liberation Organization (PLO); or the transformation of the nationalist independence struggle in Chechnya into the fight for a Salafist Emirate (Kurtulus, 2011: 483).

Significantly, these developments were reflections of a wider trend. Beginning in the 1980s, many scholars had noted a 'religious revival' in numerous countries and across different religious traditions (see, for example, Kepel, 1993). Following a long period of secularization, religious activists from India to the United States started asserting their influence, where possible within the existing political system, but also—and increasingly— through radical action outside established structures. As Neumann pointed out, the rise of religiously motivated terrorism had to be understood within the context of these wider— and indeed, global—political developments (Neumann, 2009: 84–94).

The 'new terrorism' hypothesis was less convincing, however, when it came to implications and consequences. Most of the early literature portrayed members of religiously motivated terrorist groups as fanatics, who could not be understood in rational terms, and whose only purpose was to trigger a global Armageddon. Juergensmeyer's idea of 'cosmic wars' (Juergensmeyer, 2000a), Hoffman's insistence that religiously motivated terrorists were unconstrained (Hoffman, 1993: 2–3), and Benjamin and Simon's suggestion that people like bin Laden 'do not want a place at the table; they want to shatter the table' (Benjamin and Simon, 2000a) created an almost apocalyptical, millenarian idea of what the 'new terrorists' were like. The principal piece of evidence seemed to be the Japanese cult Aum Shinkrikyo, whose 1995 nerve gas attack on the Tokyo underground had—literally—sought to bring about the end of the world. With terrorists like these, the proponents of the 'new terrorism' argued, none of the traditional political strategies for countering terrorism—for example, negotiations, or involvement in political processes—would ever work (see, for example, Laqueur, 1996).

It was only through the debate between supporters and opponents of the 'new terrorism' that a more sophisticated understanding emerged. While millenarian groups, such as Aum Shinrikyo, had 'otherworldly' aims that no political process or engagement could accommodate, the label 'religious' covered a much wider range of aims and political motivations. Even al-Qaeda, for example, could be somewhat ambiguous. While undoubtedly religious in its ideology, motivation, and the ultimate aim of establishing a global Caliphate, it also expressed its objectives in nationalist terms—for example, by calling for a withdrawal of Western troops from Saudi Arabia (see, for example, Scheuer, 2007)—and linked up with groups like the Somali al-Shabaab, which scholars believed had mostly nationalist objectives (see, for example, Jarle Hansen, 2016). Another example was the Palestinian group Hamas, whose core aspiration—the destruction of Israel and the establishment of a Palestinian state—was nationalistic, while the system of government it sought to create was based on Islamic law and therefore religious. Its strategy and tactics reflected this hybridity. Because it justified its 'struggle' in religious terms, it found it more difficult to compromise on territorial claims than its secular rivals of the Palestinian Liberation Organization (PLO). At the same time, the way it waged its conflict with Israel was rational, and at no point had the aim of 'bringing about Armaggedon' (Gunning, 2007). Though undoubtedly religious, there were many respects in which Hamas was fundamentally different from Aum Shinrikyo.

The same was true for individual recruits. Although every religiously inspired group had its fair share of fanatics—which included ideologues and 'spiritual sanctioners' who produced theological justifications for aggressive acts of violence and the killing of civilians (Silber and Bhatt, 2007: 7)—not everyone was necessarily a 'true believer'. On the contrary, the range of motivations and level of religiosity varied widely depending on individuals' background and needs as well as the places in which they were recruited.

As many scholars pointed out, a significant percentage of Western recruits for groups like al-Qaeda and ISIS had little knowledge or understanding of Islam, but embraced extremist interpretation of the religion in order to resolve conflicts of identity and personal crises (Wiktorowicz, 2005; Roy, 2017). Particularly in the case of ISIS, this included large numbers of small-time criminals, for whom the promise of adventure, action, and power was (at least) as important as the religious promise of salvation, and whose commitment to religious doctrine—and the idea of dying for the faith—was consequently very low (Basra and Neumann, 2016). In conflict zones, such as Iraq, Afghanistan, or Somalia, where terrorist groups held territory and transformed into insurgencies, recruits were often motivated by local rivalries, the desire for revenge, payment, and social or tribal dynamics. More so than elsewhere, individual radicalization was driven by the same combination of factors and patterns that also explained the recruitment of (more) secular groups, with large numbers being what David Kilcullen described as 'accidental guerrillas' (Kilcullen, 2011). While religion was not irrelevant, therefore, the way in which it manifested itself, and the degree to which it governed individual members' actions, was more complex than the supporters of the 'new terrorism' seemed to suggest.

One of the ongoing debates has been about the role of Islam. Most of the early proponents of the 'new terrorism' were keen to point out that the 'revival of religion' had taken place in all religions, and that religiously motivated terrorism was becoming more important in Christianity, Judaism, and even—as Aum Shinrikyo's case demonstrated—versions of Buddhism. Juergensmeyer's earlier work, for example, focused on Sikh extremists in India (Juergensmeyer, 1988), whereas Hoffman had written on the role and influence of the so-called Christian Identity movement in the United States (Hoffman, 1993: 6–9). Rapoport, on the other hand, while making it clear that his idea of the 'religious wave' included terrorist from all religious traditions, emphasized that 'Islam is the most important religion in this wave' and should therefore 'get special attention' (Rapoport, 2002). After the September 11th attacks, this quickly became conventional wisdom, with a burgeoning popular literature that 'essentialized' Islam, and attempted to show how it was uniquely prone to facilitating violence (see, for example, Lewis, 2004). Scholars who disagreed with this view pointed out that Christianity, and indeed secular ideologies, had equally long records of legitimizing violence (see, for example, Cavanaugh, 2009), that Islamically inspired terrorism was a response to domestic oppression and Western military interventions (see, for example, Hafez, 2003; Mamdani, 2004), and—perhaps most importantly—that Islam was a very large faith, of which only a small strand—Salafi-Jihadism (a hybrid religious-political ideology based on the Sunni sect of Islamism)—actively promoted the kind of terrorism that groups like al-Qaeda and ISIS engaged in (Maher: 2015). Whatever one's position, there could be no doubt that the ongoing scholarly debate has helped produce a more nuanced understanding of the relationship between violence and religion—and Islam in particular.

KEY CONCEPTS

Millenarianism Belief that fundamental, transformational change is about to happen, and that the (terrorist) group needs to pre-empt it or play a role in bringing it about.

CASE STUDY 17.1

How Religious is ISIS?

At first sight, the idea that ISIS—the most violent jihadist group in recent history—is anything less than committed to its religiously fundamentalist agenda seems outlandish. Yet, since the group split from al-Qaeda in 2013–14, there has been a spirited debate on the role and importance of religion in the group's doctrine and praxis. On the one hand, scholars like William McCants and the journalist Graeme Wood consistently articulated the idea of Islamic State as a thoroughly religious organization. In a widely cited article for *The Atlantic*, Wood wrote:

> The reality is that the Islamic State is Islamic. Very Islamic. Yes, it has attracted psychopaths and adventure seekers, drawn largely from the disaffected populations of the Middle East and Europe. But the religion preached by its most ardent followers derives from coherent and even learned interpretations of Islam (Wood, 2015).

McCants produced an entire book, which documented how the group and its leader, Abu Bakr al-Baghdadi, had been led throughout its history by Salafi-jihadist doctrine and—especially—medieval prophecies, which emphasized the significance of modern-day Syria as the place in which a final confrontation between Islam and its Western enemies will take place (McCants, 2015). This was reflected, for example, in the group's efforts to capture the Syrian village of Dabiq, where that confrontation was meant to take place, and the fact that its online magazine was named after it.

Others, however, were more sceptical. The investigative journalist Christoph Reuter discovered how much of the leadership of ISIS consisted of former officers of Saddam Hussein's secular Iraqi regime, and that its methods resembled those of his army, suggesting that religion may have been used as a tool for mobilizing supporters, but was rarely a genuine motivation (Reuter, 2015). Meanwhile, the analyst Hassan Hassan demonstrated that ISIS was highly skilled at manipulating tribal loyalties, and that much of the fervour with which local supporters were fighting seemed to be driven by political and/or sectarian grievances, rather than medieval prophecies (see Weiss and Hassan, 2015). Not least, Olivier Roy argued that 'adventure-seeking' and other non-religious motivations were more important than Wood believed, and that Western recruits joined Islamic State not because of its particular theology or religious doctrine, but as an outlet for 'youthful rebellion' (Roy, 2017).

As with many debates in the field, there was no clear-cut conclusion. But the different contributions raised valid and important questions, and enabled researchers to develop a more sophisticated approach towards understanding the role of religious justifications in terrorism and political violence. For example, they showed how important it was to distinguish between the views of leaders and followers, account for different motivations and mechanisms in the places from which recruits originated, as well as understand the way in which religion, identity, sectarianism and politics can overlap.

QUESTIONS

1. To what extent has ISIS's violence been driven by prophecies and religious imperatives?
2. How did Islamic State differ from al-Qaeda in ideological terms, if at all?

17.5 NETWORKS

The idea that terrorist groups had become less hierarchically structured was not a purely theoretical speculation. It was inspired by the rise of the so-called Arab Afghans, a group of up to 20,000 jihadists who had met while fighting against the Soviet occupation of Afghanistan in the 1980s (see Hegghammer, 2010). Once the conflict had ended, they turned into a loose network of 'veterans', which never operated as a single group, rarely claimed responsibility for its actions, coalesced around a small number of spiritual leaders, and operated across the entire globe. Long before parts of this network became known as al-Qaeda, some of its members engaged in attacks on Western targets, such as the 1993 bombing of the World Trade Center. According to proponents of the 'new terrorism', its structure and modus operandi appeared 'swarm'-like, and was reliant on modern information technologies as well as global travel and migration (Arquilla, Ronfeldt, and Zanini, 1999; Neumann, 2009: 68–74). For Western governments, whose counter-terrorism doctrines had focused on hierarchical groups operating within a small number of jurisdictions, this was a new and difficult challenge.

Related to this was the rise of 'amateurs', which Hoffman had written during the 1990s. Because organizational structures were looser and more flexible, it became possible for people who had no training and were not full members of a group to claim affiliation and take part in operations. Involvement in terrorism, Hoffman argued, no longer (necessarily) required a lengthy process of selection and initiation, during which a person would become integrated into a quasi-military hierarchy (Hoffman, 1999b: 36–37; 2002: 309). This meant that processes of radicalization would take less time and draw in more people that were unknown to the authorities. The ultimate manifestation of this trend was what journalists started calling 'lone wolves'—'amateur' terrorists who were inspired by a terrorist 'cause', had consumed copious amounts of online propaganda, and decided to act entirely on their own, without any physical association or direct communication with a leadership. Although it was impossible for terrorist groups to know where and when they would strike, this enabled them to operate a form of 'leaderless resistance' (see Weinberg, 2019), which exaggerated their strength and activated more supporters—and in more places—than had previously been possible.

Implicit in many of these claims was the assumption that globalization had enabled networks to become more international. The principal inspiration was—yet again—the Arab Afghan movement, which had dispersed across the world and ended up participating in various conflicts, while maintaining dense networks of contacts and engaging in joint operations whenever individuals such as Osama bin Laden (founder of al-Qaeda) took the initiative and provided funding. According to Kurtulus, the fact that someone like bin Laden was able to direct a 'jihadist *internationale*' from his various bases in Sudan and Afghanistan, with real-time communications and the speedy movement of assets, people and funding across great distances, would have been inconceivable in earlier periods (Kurtulus, 2011: 490–491), because it was dependent on satellite phones, the internet, and the international banking system (Arquilla, Ronfeldt, and Zanini, 1999; Navias 2019: 49–57). Arguably, this was the one element of the 'new terrorism' that was genuinely unprecedented, as it was based on technological innovation and levels of international 'connectedness' that had never previously existed.

According to the sceptics, however, the 'new terrorism' paradigm had exaggerated the extent to which earlier terrorist groups were hierarchically structured (see, for example, Crenshaw, 2011: 62–63). The most frequently cited example was the 19th-century Anarchist movement (see, for example, Spencer, 2004: 16), which authors such as Rapoport and Hoffman have referred to as the 'starting point' of modern terrorism (Rapoport, 2002; Hoffman, 2017: 7–21). With members across Europe and North America, the Anarchists succeeded in creating a (near-)global movement, which—over a 35-year period—was responsible for assassinating the Tsar of Russia, the Empress of Austria, the King of Italy, Presidents of France and the United States, as well as dozens of innocent people who they suspected of being members of the bourgeoisie. Many of their tactics and strategies have remained influential to this day. For example, they were the first modern terrorists to articulate the 'propaganda of the deed', whereby acts of 'individual martyrdom' were designed to inspire supporters and provoke state repression. They also promoted 'lone wolf' terrorism: Johann Most, a German immigrant to the United States, produced a booklet on *Revolutionary War Science* (of which he printed hundreds of copies) that contained bomb-making instructions and encouraged readers to carry out attacks against targets they considered suitable (see Neumann, 2016: 10–17).

Responding to these claims, supporters of the 'new terrorism' conceded that the Anarchists had indeed formed international networks and maintained various channels of communication. Nevertheless, they argued, the extent and speed of communication was vastly slower, so that—despite having a common cause and some interaction with fellow radicals in other countries—the movement was essentially a network of national groups rather than a genuinely transnational enterprise. Furthermore, individuals like Most remained a rare exception—not least because the means for spreading their ideas were far more limited before the rise of the internet (Neumann, 2009: 20–21). The same, they said, was true for leftist revolutionaries in the 1970s and 1980s, who knew each other, had networked at the same Palestinian training camps, and fought for similar causes, but—for the most part—engaged in national campaigns, with little day-to-day coordination or communication (Kurtulus, 2011: 488–489).

Indeed, the most significant challenge to the 'network' hypothesis was not about historical precedents, which supporters of the 'new terrorism' paradigm could easily dismiss as exceptions, but the nature of al-Qaeda and the Arab Afghan 'network' from which it emerged. Because of the much greater interest in al-Qaeda, which followed the September 11th attacks, it became clear that what seemed like a diffuse network had been less chaotic and unstructured than it appeared at the time of the first World Trade Center attack in 1993. In fact, a consensus has emerged among al-Qaeda researchers that the group had functioned in a (more or less) hierarchical way in the years leading up to the 2001 attacks, and that it had been forced into operating like a network only as a result of losing its Afghan sanctuary (Field, 2009: 203). At best, therefore, it could be argued that the Arab Afghans operated different types of structure depending on the circumstances they were in: hierarchies in countries where they were part of national insurgencies or had been granted 'safe haven'; networks in neighbouring territories or places where they had large numbers of activists but could not operate openly; and 'leaderless resistance' in Western countries. It was not so much that networks had 'replaced' hierarchies, as the early proponents of the 'new terrorism' suggested, but—rather—that globalization had given them the flexibility to adapt their structures to whatever the circumstances required.

> **KEY CONCEPTS**
>
> **'Leaderless resistance'** Term first coined by far-right extremists, which refers to the idea of purely 'inspired' attacks, with no need for hierarchies or networks.
>
> **Lone wolf** In the context of this chapter, a popular, but highly ambiguous concept which may be related to an attack's modus operandi ('lone attacker'), the absence of operational links to a terrorist group or network, and/or the attacker's process of radicalization.

17.6 LETHALITY

The 'new terrorism's' third major claim was that terrorists were killing more people. Instead of 'wanting a lot of people watching', as Brian Jenkins' had suggested, they 'wanted a lot of people dead' (Jenkins, 1975). Authors like Laqueur imagined that terrorists would soon adopt the kind of weapons that were described in science fiction novels, including 'earthquake machines' and 'artificial meteors with which to bombard the earth' (Laqueur, 1999: 81, 264). Although Hoffman and most other proponents of the 'new terrorism' never went this far, they too believed that terrorists were increasingly killing people for the sake of killing (Hoffman, 1999: 10). These developments, they argued, were primarily the consequence of another novelty: the rise of religion. In their view, religiously motivated terrorists were less accountable to real-world constituencies, less willing to compromise on their demands, and more prepared to sacrifice themselves as well as large numbers of 'infidels' (Hoffman, 1993: 3; Juergensmeyer, 2000b). The prime example for this was the steady rise of martyrdom operations and suicide bombings, which—in addition to the perpetrators—caused more fatalities on average than 'conventional' operations (see Horowitz, 2015).

Some of the ensuing debate revolved around the use of particular tactics. Following the September 11th attacks, large numbers of scholars attempted to make sense of suicide attacks, demonstrating that their use was not necessarily linked to religion, and that—prior to the civil war in Iraq—the groups responsible for the largest numbers of suicide operations were the (secular) Tamil Tigers and the Kurdish Workers' Party (PKK), while (Sunni) jihadists had adopted the tactic only in the mid-1990s (see Horowitz, 2015). Robert Pape argued that notions like martyrdom and sacrifice were not unique to religion, and that suicide operations—whether religiously motivated or secular—followed a 'strategic logic', which had nothing to do with theological reasoning (Pape, 2003). Even so, neither he nor any of the other critics who published their research after 2001 any longer disputed that there was a 'statistical link', as Duyvesteyn put it, between the rise of jihadist groups, the spread of suicide bombings, and 'a high number of fatalities in their terrorist attacks' (Duyvesteyn, 2004: 448).

More controversial was the alleged rise in weapons of mass destruction use, which even some proponents of the 'new terrorism' believed had been overstated. After September 11th and the discovery that al-Qaeda had experimented with chemical weapons, many analysts returned to Benjamin and Simon's predictions, speculating that such attacks would be the logical next step (see, for example, Blum et al., 2005). Yet, the evidence remained thin. Although jihadists have consistently expressed their intention to acquire weapons of mass destruction, and occasionally experimented with chemical and biological agents, virtually all of these experiments have resulted in failure. Nor was it clear that, had they been successful, they would have produced greater numbers of fatalities than conventional bombings (see Mowatt-Larsen, 2010). Even ISIS—the largest, most powerful terrorist organization in recent history, which had repeatedly expressed its interest in developing weapons of mass destruction, and possessed the time, territory, money, and manpower to do so—did not succeed. As Hoffman predicted, even in the age of 'new terrorism', terrorists remained operationally conservative. In fact, rather than becoming more complex, terrorist attacks seemed to become simpler, utilizing everyday goods, such as knives and cars, and requiring no preparation or 'infrastructure' at all (Neumann, 2016: 129–136).

The most fundamental objection, however, was that the link between ideology and lethality was not as straightforward as the 'new terrorism' hypothesis suggested. As the critics pointed out, it was wrong to argue that religiously motivated terrorists did not care about 'real-world' constituencies: groups like Hamas stood for elections, and had to justify their military operations to voters; Hezbollah was not just a political party and large welfare provider, but participated in Lebanon's government; and even al-Qaeda faced popular pressure when it started targeting (Sunni) Muslim civilians in Iraq and Algeria (see Neumann, 2009: 130–132). Meanwhile, there was plenty of evidence that 'older' terrorist groups, such as the Tamil Tigers or far-right extremists, had engaged in mass-casualty attacks at levels that were like those of the supposedly 'new', religiously motivated terrorists (Crenshaw, 2011: 60).

What united these groups were ideologies based on (ethnic, racial, or religious) identity, which allowed them to declare entire populations as their 'enemies'. In selecting targets, what mattered was not if people were 'civilians', but whether they were 'our' civilians. This was fundamentally different from groups with universalist doctrines—especially Marxists and leftists, as well as ethno-nationalists who had adopted 'anti-imperialist' programmes. Over its entire 27-year history, for example, the Red Army Faction (RAF) (also known as Baader-Meinhof Group) killed just 34 people, and never once targeted large groups of civilians. The 'story', therefore, was not just about the increasing prominence of religion, but—more generally—the decline of 'universalism' and the rise of 'identitarian' doctrines (Neumann 2009: 118–126).

In tactical terms, the consequence was not just an increase in lethality, but less discrimination. ISIS, for example, launched terrorist attacks in European cities that killed hundreds, but it also carried out individual executions—for example, of Western journalists—that did not necessarily result in many people killed. The group was not killing people randomly, or for the sake of killing people. From its perspective, the decisive factor was not people's legal status, age, gender, or (necessarily) the 'body count', but their victims' identity and—most importantly—the sense of terror such killings were able to spawn (see Neumann and Smith, 2008: 9–11).

KEY CONCEPTS

CBRN terrorism Terrorist attacks that utilize chemical, biological, radiological, or nuclear materials.

Mass casualty attacks Typically refers to terrorist attacks that are intentionally aimed at producing large numbers of civilian casualties, often directed at 'soft' targets, for example, shopping centres, public transportation, restaurants, or cafes.

CASE STUDY 17.2

The 2004 Madrid Bombings

The March 2004 bombings of commuter trains in Madrid were the most lethal terrorist attack in Spanish history, killing 191 people and injuring thousands. Immediately after they had taken place, the Spanish government declared that the Basque separatist group ETA (which stands for Basque Homeland and Liberty) was responsible. Yet, three days later, the police found evidence that pointed in a completely different direction. As it turned out, the bombing had been carried out by a jihadist network which was loosely connected with al-Qaeda (see Jordan and Horsburgh, 2004).

In retrospect, ETA had always seemed like an unlikely culprit. Throughout its history, the group conceived of its 'struggle' as a 'dual' fight for both socialism and national self-determination. Although different faction held sway at different times, even during its most nationalist periods, it always aligned with socialist and Marxist political forces. (At one point, it even argued that the precondition for Basque independence was a Marxist revolution across the entire Iberian Peninsula.) Consequently, it never conceived of ordinary

PHOTO 17.2 The monument to the victims of 2004 bombings in front of Atocha Railway Station in Madrid, Spain.

Spanish people—or, rather, what it regarded as the Spanish 'working classes'—as their enemies, and never targeted them purely based on their nationality. Although the group was ruthless and never hesitated to kill its opponents, it carried out only a small number of mass-casualty attacks, of which only two in its more than 50-year history killed more than ten people. As the journalist Paddy Woodworth explained: 'The bombs in Madrid claimed twice as many victims in one bombing as ETA had ever claimed in an entire year and nine times as many as the group had killed in any single atrocity' (Woodworth, 2004).

When the bombings took place and the Spanish Interior Minister immediately blamed ETA, even some of its strongest critics defended the group. In the words of a Basque peace activist, who had often condemned the group's reckless behaviour, 'These attacks just did not fit with the strategy and logic of ETA ... It has never deliberately sought to kill civilians, and it always sends a warning' (quoted in Neumann, 2009). Although it was known that ETA was planning attacks on the transport system, such attacks would have looked very different and resulted in fewer fatalities. ETA itself provided the explanation why. In statements released after the bombings, it made it clear that it would 'never' attack Spanish workers whom it regarded as allies in the struggle against imperialism. One of its political leaders told newspapers that there was 'a big difference' between ETA's strategy and the idea of 'attacking trains carrying people into work from working-class areas' (quoted in Neumann, 2009). From ETA's perspective, the latter was totally inconceivable.

Jihadists, by contrast, had never had any such hesitations, especially when operating in what they called the 'lands of war', in other words, countries that were hostile to their aspirations. Spain had one year earlier joined America's Coalition to invade Iraq, and any operation to 'repel and punish' the invaders was therefore justified—if not, required—from a jihadist perspective. Indeed, less than 24 hours after the attack, a statement claiming responsibility for the attack on behalf of al-Qaeda explained: 'We ... have not felt sad for the so-called civilians. Is it OK for you to kill our children, women old people and youth in Afghanistan, Iraq, Palestine and Kashmir? And it is forbidden to us to kill yours?' (quoted in Neumann, 2009) While it remains unclear whether the statement's authors were in direct contact with the attackers, it clearly summed up their 'us versus them' mentality. In their view, virtually any action was justified as long as it targeted members of the enemy group. The contrast with groups like ETA, which navigated between the nationalist and universalist parts of their ideology, could not have been greater.

QUESTIONS

1. Is a group's ideology the key factor in explaining its lethality?
2. Does greater lethality increase or decrease a terrorist group's chances of political success?

17.7 CONCLUSION

The discussion about the 'new terrorism' hypothesis was one of the most significant debates to have taken place in terrorism studies in recent years. Originating in the 1990s, its proponents tried to make sense of what they believed was a rapidly changing phenomenon. Terrorists, they believed, were becoming different and more dangerous: an increasing number was motivated by religion; their organizations were transforming from hierarchical, army-like structures into networks; and the attacks they carried out were no longer selective, but aimed to kill as many as possible. The 'new terrorism', which was powered by the forces of globalization and the global chaos and confusion which had followed the end of the Cold War, was going to be a more profound, strategic—if not, existential—challenge for the countries that were targeted by it.

Especially after the September 11th attacks, which seemed to confirm many of the 'new terrorism's' predictions, critics started challenging the concept. They pointed out that none of its alleged elements were unprecedented, and should therefore not be described as 'new'. They also argued that whatever transformation there might have been had not been as complete or absolute as the term suggested, and that 'old' forms of terrorism continued to pose a threat. By suggesting that there had been a complete rupture, the risk was that analysts would dismiss the continuities that existed between 'older' and 'newer' forms of terrorism, and fail to draw on the lessons and insights that were learned in previous decades of engagement with the phenomenon. Another danger was that policymakers would use the concept as an excuse for introducing excessive measures in the 'Global War on Terror', comparing the threats posed by jihadist groups to the 'existential threat' of the Cold War rather than the more limited challenge to security and state authority posed by terrorist groups of the past.

Yet, the critics' positions could be challenged too. Some of the historical examples and precedents they cited were centuries old, raising questions as to how representative they were, and to what extent they were relevant to the idea that modern terrorism had undergone a transformation. In their effort to refute the 'new terrorism's' claims, it occasionally seemed like they were denying *any* change, claiming that terrorism had essentially stayed the same. This position was not just untenable, given the rise of the 'Afghan Arabs', jihadist terrorism and attacks like those on 11th September 2001, it was also profoundly ahistorical, because it failed to put forward any theory of change through which the evolving character of terrorism could be explained.

What have we learned from the 'new terrorism' debate? First, it demonstrated how important it was to be empirically and conceptually rigorous. Proponents of the paradigm should have been clearer about what they meant by 'new', or—perhaps—use a different terminology altogether. Except for Hoffman, supporters and opponents frequently operated with examples and anecdotes whose empirical validity and representativeness were impossible to assess. No doubt, part of the problem was—and continues to be—the lack of reliable terrorism data, especially for the decades and centuries that preceded the creation of databases by RAND and the University of Maryland. But this should not have prevented them from developing a more coherent framework, spelling out their assumptions, developing an evidence base, and defining periods of comparison.

Secondly, whatever one thinks of the 'new terrorism' label, the debate has provided useful insights into how terrorism has changed. Terrorism studies scholars often focus on very small phenomena—say, the use of a particular tactic by a specific group—but rarely come together to discuss wider developments and ideas. Next to the (ongoing) debate about the definition of terrorism, and the back and forth about the role of ideology and social networks in processes of radicalization, the 'new terrorism' debate has crystallized some of the major issues in the field: the role of religion, the impact of globalization and modern communication technologies on group structures and recruitment, as well as the evolution of terrorist tactics. It provides a useful prism through which to look at these changes, and connect them to wider trends.

Finally, the 'new terrorism' has brought out a more nuanced—and, arguably, more sophisticated—understanding of all these trends and developments. While most scholars now accept that religion is a more important factor in terrorism today than it used to be, they realize that not all kinds of religiously inspired ideology are the same. While they understand that group structures can be diffuse, they know that hierarchies have not entirely disappeared. And although terrorist attacks have statistically become more lethal, the underlying driver has not necessarily been the desire to 'kill people for the sake of killing people', but—rather—the rise of groups with ideologies based on identity and other 'exclusivist' ideologies. In all these respects, the debate about the 'new terrorism' has made a significant contribution to broadening and deepening our understanding of a constantly evolving phenomenon.

DISCUSSION QUESTIONS

1. To what extent has the rise of the internet and global communications changed terrorism?
2. What technological developments are likely to be embraced by terrorists in the future?
3. Did the rise of al-Qaeda and jihadist terrorism justify the Global War on Terror and other exceptional measures taken to combat terrorism?
4. Should far-right terrorism be classified as 'old' or 'new'?
5. Based on the issues and factors described in this chapter, what forms of terrorism are likely to emerge next?

Visit the online resources for pointers on how to answer the discussion questions, links to useful web sources, and guidance on accessing databases:
www.oup.com/he/Wilson-Muro1e

GUIDE TO FURTHER READING

Benjamin, D. and Simon, S. (2000b) 'America and the New Terrorism', *Survival*, 42:1, 59–75. *Benjamin and Simon, who worked in the US National Security Council at the time, were the first senior practitioners to warn of the 'New Terror' in a clear and concise way.*

Duyvesteyn, I. (2004), 'How New Is the New Terrorism?', *Studies in Conflict and Terrorism*, 27:5, 439–454. *Isabelle Duyvesteyn's article is one of the key refutations of the 'new terrorism' hypothesis, written from the perspective of a historian.*

Hoffman, B. (1999) 'Terrorism Trends and Prospects', in Ian O. Lesser, Bruce Hoffman, John Arquilla, David Ronfeldt, and Michele Zanini (1999), *Countering the New Terrorism*. Santa Monica, CA, and Washington DC: RAND, 7–38. *Bruce Hoffman was one of the first scholars to articulate the different aspects of the 'new terrorism'.*

Kurtulus, E. N. (2011) 'The "New Terrorism" and Its Critics', *Studies in Conflict and Terrorism*, 34:6, 476–500. *Ersun Kurtulus' article tries to provide a synthesis of all the arguments, showing why, despite its limitations, 'new terrorism' may still be a useful way of thinking about change in terrorism.*

Rapoport, D. C. (2002) 'The Four Waves of Rebel Terror and September 11', *Anthropoetics*, 8:1, available at http://anthropoetics.ucla.edu/ap0801/terror/. *David Rapoport's 'four waves' are one of the key concepts in terrorism studies, showing why and how terrorism changes.*

REFERENCES

Arquilla, J., Ronfeldt, D., and Zanini, M. (1999) 'Networks, Netwar, and Information-Age Terrorism', in Ian O. Lesser, Bruce Hoffman, John Arquilla, David Ronfeldt, and Michele Zanini, *Countering the New Terrorism*. Santa Monica, CA, and Washington DC: RAND, 39–83.

Basra, R. and Neumann, P. R. (2016) 'Criminal Pasts, Terrorist Futures: European Jihadists and the new Crime-terror Nexus', *Perspectives on Terrorism*, 10 (6): 25–40.

Benjamin, D. and Simon, S. (2000a) 'The New Face of Terrorism', *New York Times*, 4 January 2000.

Benjamin, D. and Simon, S. (2000b), 'America and the New Terrorism', *Survival*, 42 (1): 59–75.

Blum, A. et al. (2005) 'Nonstate Actors, Terrorism, and Weapons of Mass Destruction', *International Studies Review*, 7 (1): 133–170.

Callimachi, R. (2017) 'Not "Lone Wolves" After All: How ISIS Guides World's Terror Plots', *New York Times*, 4 February.

Cavanaugh, W.T. (2009) *The Myth of Religious Violence*. Oxford: Oxford University Press.

Copeland, T. (2001) 'Is the "New Terrorism" Really New?: An Analysis of the New Paradigm for Terrorism', *The Journal of Conflict Studies*, 21 (2): 1–16.

Crenshaw, M. (2011) *Explaining Terrorism: Causes, Processes, and Consequences*. New York and London: Routledge.

Duyvesteyn, I. (2004) 'How New Is the New Terrorism?', *Studies in Conflict and Terrorism*, 27 (5): 439–454.

Field, A. (2009) 'The "New Terrorism": Revolution or Evolution?', *Political Studies Review*, 7 (3): 195–207.

Freedman, L. (2002) (ed.), *Superterrorism: Policy Responses*, Oxford: Blackwell.

Garwin, R. L., (2002) 'The Technology of Megaterror', *MIT Technology Review*, September.

Gill, P., Horgan, G., and Deckert, P. (2014) 'Bombing Alone: Tracing the Motivations and Antecedent Behaviours of Lone-actor Terrorists', *Journal of Forensic Science*, 59 (2): 425–35.

Gunning, J. (2007) *Hamas in Politics: Democracy, Religion, Violence*, London: Hurst & Co.

Gurr, N. and Cole, B. (2000) *The New Face of Terrorism: Threats from Weapons of Mass Destruction*. London: I.B. Tauris.

Hafez, M. (2003) *Why Muslims Rebel: Repression and Resistance in the Muslim World*. Boulder, CO: Lynne Rienner.

Hegghammer, T. (2010) 'The Rise of Muslim Foreign Fighters: Islam and the Globalization of Jihad', *International Security*, 35 (3): 53–94.

Heisbourg, F. (2003) *Hyperterrorism: The New War*. Paris: Odile Jacob.

Hoffman, B. (1993) '"Holy Terror": The Implications of Terrorism Motivated by a Religious Imperative', *RAND Paper*, P-7834, 1–14; available at https://www.rand.org/pubs/papers/P7834.html.

Hoffman, B. (1999) 'Terrorism Trends and Prospects' in Ian O. Lesser, Bruce Hoffman, John Arquilla, David Ronfeldt, and Michele Zanini (1999), *Countering the New Terrorism*. Santa Monica, CA, and Washington DC: RAND, 7–38.

Hoffman, B. (1999b) 'Terrorism and Weapons of Mass Destruction: An Analysis of Trends and Motivations', *RAND Paper*, P-8039-1; available at https://www.rand.org/pubs/papers/P8039-1.html.

Hoffman, B. (2002) 'Rethinking Terrorism and Counterterrorism since 9/11', *Studies in Conflict and Terrorism*, 25 (5): 303–316.

Hoffman, B. (2017) *Inside Terrorism*, 3rd edition. New York: Columbia University Press.

Horowitz, M. C. (2015) 'The Rise and Spread of Suicide Bombing', *Annual Review of Political Science*, 18: 69–84.

Jarle Hansen, S. (2016), *Al-Shabaab in Somalia: The History and Ideology of a Militant Islamist Group*. London: Hurst & Co.

Jenkins, B. M. (1975) 'Will Terrorists Go Nuclear?', *RAND Paper*, P-5541; available at https://www.rand.org/pubs/papers/P5541.html.

Jenkins, B. M. (1985) 'Future Trends in International Terrorism', *RAND Paper*, P-7176; available at https://www.rand.org/pubs/papers/P7176.html.

Jordan, J. and Horsburgh, N. (2004) 'Mapping Jihadist Terrorism in Spain', *Studies in Conflict and Terrorism*, 28 (3): 169–191.

Juergensmeyer, M. (1988) 'The Logic of Religious Violence: The Case of the Punjab', *Contributions to Indian Sociology*, 22 (1).

Juergensmeyer, M. (2000a) 'Understanding the New Terrorism', *Current History*, April.

Juergensmeyer, M. (2000b) *Terror in the Mind of God: The Global Rise of Religious Violence*, Berkeley. CA: University of California Press.

Kepel, G. (1993) *The Revenge of God: The Resurgence of Islam, Christianity and Judaism in the Modern World*. University Park, PA: Penn State University Press.

Kilcullen, D. (2011) *The Accidental Guerrilla: Fighting Small Wars in the Midst of a Big One*. London: Hurst & Co.

Kurtulus, E. N. (2011) 'The "New Terrorism" and Its Critics', *Studies in Conflict and Terrorism*, 34 (6): 476–500.

Laqueur, W. (1996) 'Postmodern Terrorism', *Foreign Affairs*, 75 (5): 24–36.

Laqueur, W. (1999) *The New Terrorism: Fanaticism and the Arms of Mass Destruction*. Oxford: Oxford University Press.

Lesser, I.O., Hoffman, B., Arquilla, J., Ronfeldt, D., and Zanini, M. (1999) *Countering the New Terrorism*. Santa Monica, CA, and Washington DC: RAND.

Lewis, B, (2004) *The Crisis of Islam: Holy War and Unholy Terror*. New York: Random House.

Maher, S. (2015) *Salafi-Jihadism: The History of an Idea*. London: Hurst & Co.

Mamdani, M. (2004) *Good Muslim, Bad Muslim: America, the Cold War, and the Roots of Terror*. New York: Pantheon.

McAdam, D. (1986) 'Recruitment to high-risk activism: the case of Freedom Summer', *The American Journal of Sociology*, 92 (1): 155–169.

McCants, W. (2015) *The ISIS Apocalypse: The History, Strategy, and Doomsday Vision of the Islamic State*. New York: St Martin's Press.

Mitchell D. S. and Arvin, B. (2007) 'Radicalization in the West: The Homegrown Threat', New York City Police Department.

Morgan, M. (2004) 'The Origins of the New Terrorism', *Parameters*, Spring 2004, 29–43.

Mowatt-Larsen, R. (2010) *Al Qaeda Weapons of Mass Destruction Threat: Hype or Reality*.Cambridge, MA: Belfer Center; available at https://www.belfercenter.org/publication/al-qaeda-weapons-mass-destruction-threat-hype-or-reality.

Navias, M. (2019) *Finance and Security: Global Vulnerabilities, Threats, and Responses*. London: Hurst & Co.

Neumann, P. (2009) *Old and New Terrorism: Late Modernity, Globalization and the Transformation of Political Violence*. Cambridge: Polity Press.

Neumann, P. (2016) *Radicalized: New Jihadists and the Threat to the West*. London: I.B. Tauris.

Neumann, P. and Smith, M. L. R. (2008) *The Strategy of Terrorism: How It Works, and Why It Fails*. New York and London: Routledge.

Pape, R. A. (2003) 'The Strategic Logic of Suicide Terrorism', *American Political Science Review*, 97 (3): 343–361.

Rapoport, D. C. (1983) 'Fear and Trembling: Terrorism in Three Religious Traditions', *American Political Science Review*, 78 (3): 658–677.

Rapoport, D. C. (2002), 'The Four Waves of Rebel Terror and September 11', *Anthropoetics*, 8:1, available at http://anthropoetics.ucla.edu/ap0801/terror/.

Reuter, C. (2015) *Die schwarze Macht: Der 'Islamische Staat' und die Strategen des Terror*. Hamburg: DVA.

Roy, O., Hoffman, B., Paz, R., Simon, S., and Benjamin, D. (2000) 'America and the New Terrorism: an Exchange', *Survival*, 42 (2): 156–172.

Roy, O. (2017) *Jihad and Death: The Global Appeal of Islamic State*. London: Hurst & Co.

Scheuer, M. (2007) *Imperial Hubris: Why the West Is Losing the War on Terror*. Washington DC: Potomac Books.

Schuurmann, B. et al. (2019) 'End of the Lone Wolf: The Typology that Should Not Have Been', *Studies in Conflict and Terrorism*, 42 (8): 771–778.

Spencer, A. (2006) 'Questioning the Concept of "New Terrorism"', *Peace, Conflict and Development*, 8: 1–733.

Stern, J. (2000) *The Ultimate Terrorists*. Cambridge, MA: Harvard University Press.

Tucker, D. (2001) 'What Is New about the New Terrorism and How Dangerous Is It?', *Terrorism and Political Violence*, 13 (3): 1–14.

Weinberg, L. (2019) 'Lone Wolf Attacks Prove Louise Beam Was Right About "Leaderless Resistance"', *Fair Observer*, 7 August 2019; available at https://www.fairobserver.com/global-terrorism-news/lone-wolf-attacks-louis-beam-leaderless-resistance-domestic-terrosrim-us-news-88710/.

Weiss, M. and Hassan H. (2015) *ISIS: Inside the Army of Terror*. New York: Regan Arts.

Wiktorowicz, Q. (2005) *Radical Islam Rising: Muslim Extremism in the West*. London: Rowman and Littlefield.

Wood, G. (2015) 'What ISIS Really Wants', *The Atlantic*, March 2015; available at https://www.theatlantic.com/magazine/archive/2015/03/what-isis-really-wants/384980/.

Woodworth, P. (2004) 'Was it Eta, or a strike by Al Qaeda', *The Times*, 12 March 2004.

CHAPTER 18

Social Media and Terrorism

DONALD HOLBROOK

■ **CHAPTER SUMMARY**

This chapter examines the role social media have played in the evolution of terrorism. It begins by dissecting the key components of social media before highlighting the key ways in which their emergence has impacted modern terrorism. These relate to notions of asymmetry where terrorists seek to maximize their impact against materially stronger adversaries, the networked aspect of terrorism and the importance of communication—broadly defined—for terrorists. The chapter looks at how terrorists have adopted social media techniques in various parts of the world and assesses some of the pitfalls, as well as benefits, this adoption can bring. The final section delves deeper into the important relationship between online habits and behaviours on the one hand and their 'real life' implications in the physical world on the other.

18.1 INTRODUCTION

On Saturday afternoon 21 September 2013, four men with links to the East African terrorist group Al-Shabab launched an attack on the Westgate shopping centre in a wealthy district of Nairobi, the capital of Kenya. The heavily-armed assailants threw grenades and fired from automatic rifles, taking control of the sprawling complex. During the four-day siege that ensued, the attackers murdered 67 people, mostly civilians, and inflicted close to 200 non-fatal injuries. This had been a carefully-planned attack which largely caught the authorities by surprise, prompting criticism of their delayed response (McConnell, 2015).

The terrorists' planning for this attack, however, had not been limited to their immediate tactical objectives. During the siege, Al-Shabab launched an orchestrated and pre-planned media campaign on Twitter, taunting the Kenyan authorities, challenging their version of events as the attack unfolded—including premature announcements that it had ended—and highlighting some of the causes which they purported to be advancing. The terrorist groups' media arm employed the same hashtags that others were using to cover the siege on Twitter, including #WestgateMall and #Kenyan government. The tweets justified the attack as a response to the suffering Somalians were enduring because of Kenya's involvement in counter-insurgency operations in the country, the launch of which in December 2011 coincided with Al-Shabab's first forays on Twitter. More profoundly, Al-Shabab used Tweets to compete directly with alternative sources of information from official government outlets or established media organizations, dismissing some of the accusations levelled against them, and providing an alternative narrative to the events and their context (Anzalone, 2013).

Twitter, and social media more broadly, had thus become an important tool to Al-Shabab, forming part of its operational repertoire. Through exploiting the benefits of immediacy and autonomous communication that such platforms provided, the group managed to elevate its position, maximize the impact of its violence, and increase its visibility.

Social media represent a new way in which terrorists and their sympathizers can operate and, in turn, affects counterterrorism efforts and initiatives seeking to undermine them. Terrorist organizations dedicate substantial energy to exploiting such platforms and individuals susceptible to their messages partake in online networks that promote and facilitate their agendas.

This chapter explores the way in which social media have impacted the evolution of terrorism. It begins by clarifying the key concepts of social media, social networks, and their relevance to terrorism and political violence. It then explores how social media relate to three interconnected dimensions of terrorism: asymmetry in the political landscape, reliance on networks, and communication. The ways in which terrorists have sought to exploit social media in different parts of the globe are traced, as are potential pitfalls of these interactions. Finally, the chapter looks in more detail at the interplay between virtual engagement online and their potential to affect physical behaviours offline.

18.2 CONCEPTS AND DEFINITIONS

The term 'social media' dates back to 2003–2004 when new platforms for virtual interaction through the internet, particularly MySpace and Facebook, were launched. The proliferation and rise in popularity of these online channels and virtual networks has been rapid with equally profound changes to the way in which information is shared, choices are made and implemented, and social networks are formed (Droogan et al., 2018: 171).

> **KEY CONCEPTS**
>
> **Social Media** *Social media* are 'web-based applications and interactive platforms that facilitate the creation, discussion, modification, and exchange of user-generated content'. *Social networks*, online platforms such as Facebook and Instagram where people interact and share content, are one type of social media. Other applications that fall under this category include blogs, business networks such as LinkedIn, social gaming, and virtual worlds, microblogs like Twitter, photo sharing such as Flickr, online product reviews, social bookmarking, YouTube videos, and digital forums (Aichner and Jacob, 2015: 258–260).

The components of social media consist of 'networked database platforms that combine public with personal communication' (Meikle, 2016: 6). Let us look at the parts of this definition in a little more detail. The networked element refers to the technological advancements of 'Web 2.0'—a term that also stretches back to the genesis of social media to emphasize the new participatory qualities of the world wide web—to link individuals together in different locales. As Zuckerman quipped: 'Web 1.0 was invented to allow physicists to share research papers. Web 2.0 was created to allow people to share pictures of cute cats' (in McCaughey, 2014: 1). The opportunities this has provided for grassroots, user-generated output to be created, shared and amplified has revolutionized all spheres of human interaction, from social relations to commerce and political activism.

The 'database platform' aspect of our definition refers to the core business model of social media which combines content, computing and communication to create a pool of data which a user's usage of these platforms creates. Public and personal communication, in turn, highlights how individual users converge in user-generated content platforms in a networked digital environment. As Meikle observes: 'The public space of the media industries and the personal space of the individual response can now occupy the same space—social media' (2016: 7).

This constitutes a fundamental shift from 'old media', when large numbers of consumers concentrated around relatively small numbers of information outlets, such as established news networks and material from their correspondents. Through social media, platforms themselves do not actually create any of their own media, but allow the users to do so instead (Meikle, 2016). Whereas terrorists were traditionally reliant on their ability to use their attacks and other activities to attract the attention of the press or the TV news networks, social media allows them to circumvent, even dominate, these traditional platforms and create their own networks of distribution (Hoffman, 2017b).

Terrorists have proven adept in the past at employing new communication technologies, such as advances in printing that enabled them to distribute manifestos to potential recruits, or 24-hour news coverage which gave access to new audiences across the world. In one sense, therefore, the emergence of social media represents a new chapter in this history of communicational innovation. Yet, this new digital environment also shapes the way in which terrorism—and political activism more generally—evolves (Taylor and Currie, 2012). As Ramsay observes, 'we forget that technology doesn't just help us to get more of what we want. It changes what we want, and how we understand our very existence' (2011: 33).

18.3 SOCIAL MEDIA AND THE NATURE OF TERRORISM

Social media is particularly important to the way we understand terrorism for three related reasons.

Firstly, we can consider the impact of social media with respect to notions of asymmetry. Terrorism, particularly after the 11th September 2011 terrorist attacks in America (9/11), is often seen to exist within the confines of asymmetric warfare (Martin and Weinberg, 2016; Stepanova, 2008), where a materially weaker attacker tries to use different tactics to gain the upper hand against its enemy. While terrorist organizations, such as al-Qaeda and ISIS, can acquire substantial material strength, they nonetheless employ tactics outside the norms and laws of conventional warfare in order to undermine and weaken vastly more powerful adversaries (Thornton, 2007; Ayalon and Jenkins, 2014; Di Lellio and Castano, 2015). Terrorists are agitators who rely on their ability to be nimble, innovative, provocative, clandestine, and unpredictable to dominate and dictate the agendas of their conventionally stronger foes. While technological innovation—including developments in the media communication industry—have always been an essential part of this interplay between terrorists and their targets, the social media revolution has greatly enhanced the ability of terrorists and their supporters to augment their resolve while requiring minimal investment.

Consider, for instance, the importance of encrypted communication. During major conventional confrontations between superpowers, securing—and decrypting— communication between elements of a fighting force or between allies engaged in war attracted huge investment and energy and played a major part, for instance, in the conclusion of World War II. Today, terrorists can install freely available applications, such as Telegram, Signal or Tox, or access 'deep web' (the part of the web that is not indexed by conventional search engines, also known as hidden or dark web). forums that allow them to exchange data and information with minimal risk that their exchanges can be intercepted. As the director of Britain's signals intelligence agency—GCHQ—observed: 'Techniques for encrypting messages or making them anonymous which were once the preserve of the most sophisticated criminals or nation states now come as standard' (Hannigan, 2014). The encrypted messaging application Telegram, for instance (see Photo 18.1), has been used by members of ISIS to communicate internally—including exchanges with individual attackers—as well as to distribute a variety of instructional and ideological content to followers (Mazzoni, 2018), prompting pressure from authorities for a 'back-door' (access provided by the platforms themselves on a case-by-case basis to hidden messages that are otherwise beyond the agencies' reach) (Tan, 2017). Such requests, in turn, have raised concerns about privacy and civil liberties.

Secondly, social media accentuate and elevate the networked dimensions of terrorism. Terrorist actors exist both as organized entities operating as relatively cohesive groups and a looser phenomenon of individuals acting more autonomously in the interests of a perceived social base that celebrates and promotes political violence. Both actor types—and their hybrids—draw support and inspiration from each other and these synergies are greatly strengthened by using social media. There are clear facilitative dimensions

PHOTO 18.1 Social media apps such as Telegram have been used by terror groups including ISIS and al-Qaeda to communicate via encrypted messages.

to digital networking: participants can communicate globally, and often secretly, and—by extension—identify avenues for fund-raising, financial transaction, recruitment and liaison, capacity building, intelligence gathering, and other dimensions of organizational planning.

This networked aspect has more profound 'cultural' implications too. Groups are provided with the opportunity to share their cultural output—recorded songs, visuals, films, memoirs, stories, reflections, lectures—with a global audience and tailor their messages to individual communities, even persons. Social media is uniquely suited for the purposes of such targeted communication. This element is referred to as 'narrowcasting' or 'niche marketing' and consists of structuring media messages that are aimed at specific segments of a population that are defined by characteristics such as values, preferences, demographic attributes or location.

KEY CONCEPTS

Narrowcasting/Niche Marketing Social media relies on *user-generated content*, where individual users of social media applications create media content such as written passages, photographs and videos that are posted online and shared across platforms and networks. The business model of the application designers and hosts rests on the data that these interactions generate. This includes the generation of targeted communication and filtered content based on preference, network, background and choice history that aims digital matter at specific portions of an online community. This targeted communication is sometimes referred to as *narrowcasting or niche marketing*, and is used by businesses and political campaigners as well as other users of social media platforms.

A system of narrowcasting is also inherent in the way in which many content-rich social media platforms operate, which provides the ideal conditions for virtual movements to become embedded. Coding used by YouTube, for example, provides 'suggestions' of videos for further viewing based on existing consumption habits, thus linking output from similar sources. Studies have suggested this feature has contributed to the visibility and networked appearance of extremist outlets that otherwise would have remained more obscure, though YouTube has also sought to counter its exploitation by extremists (Droogan et al., 2018). Through these networked qualities, personalities, ideological currents and concepts are kept alive online—even supplemented by enthusiastic fans and supporters—whereas offline their prominence may have faded more quickly.

Examining the substance of grassroots Islamist extremism, Sageman argued that new channels of communication through the internet had greatly enhanced the leaderless qualities of this movement, suggesting that 'the structure of the Internet has become the structure of global Islamist terrorism' (2008: 121). Subcultures—social groups organized around shared interests and practices with common styles and identity labels—thus acquire important virtual dimensions (Thornton, 1997; Pisoiu, 2014; Ramsay, 2013). While Islamist extremists have been seen as innovators in this regard, a new generation of far-right extremists are increasingly attuned to the mobilizing potential of social media, as we explore further in the next section (Lee, 2017). A strategic document produced by National Action—a neo-Nazi group founded in Britain in 2016—emphasized the need to learn from existing social media activism, including from Islamist militants, in order to broaden the movement appeal: 'Part of raising the social status of nationalism is going to be providing a look—a style that is fashionable, but we own and is associated with us. Ideally this has to be for an urban environment—we need respect' (National Action, 2013: 5).

Thirdly, the dawn of social media has been significant since communication is central to the way in which we understand and conceptualize terrorism. An early study on the topic observed that 'terrorism and mass communication [are] linked to each other. Without communication there can be no terrorism' (Schmid and de Graaf, 1982: 1). The violence draws attention to sentiments and messages designed to influence specific audiences (Schmid and McAllister, 2011: 246). As Wilkinson argued in 1997: 'when one says "terrorism" in a democratic society, one also says 'media' (1997: 54). The rapid development of online platforms since then has made this communicative task much easier to achieve.

Jenkins once described terrorism as an act of theatre (1974: 4): choreographed violence where the victims served as a loudspeaker, attracting much more attention to a cause or agenda than would otherwise have been achieved through a simple manifesto or peaceful activism. The relevance of this analogy has endured. Hours before Anders Breivik, the Norwegian terrorist who murdered 77 of his fellow citizens on 22 July 2011, launched his attack, he posted a video 'trailer' on YouTube to advertise his fifteen-hundred-page manifesto that he wanted to publicize (*Daily Telegraph*, 2011). Social media played a central role in another terrorist attack that was partly inspired by Breivik's actions. Case Study 18.1 traces how Brenton Tarrant used social media platforms in a targeted way in order to broadcast his murder of Muslim worshippers attending prayer in Christchurch, New Zealand.

CASE STUDY 18.1

Christchurch Terror Attacks

In the afternoon of 15 March 2019 Brenton Harrison Tarrant, a 28-year-old Australian, opened fire on worshippers who had gathered for Friday prayers at two mosques in Christchurch, New Zealand. He shot 100 people, killing 50. Tarrant assembled an arsenal of firearms, ammunition, and explosives to carry out his attack, but planned its execution explicitly with the aim of maximizing its propaganda impact via social media. He filmed his entire attack using a helmet-mounted video camera that fed the footage to Facebook Live, a live streaming feature of the social media platform that was launched in 2015.

Prior notice of the attack, and the planned live-stream on the attacker's Facebook account, had been posted on Twitter as well as the anonymous internet forum '8chan', popular with far-right extremists including Tarrant himself (see also Chapter 15). According to Facebook, the original 17-minute video was viewed by 200 users live, and later by an additional 4,000 users. It was first reported 12 minutes after it ended, but had already spread widely. Within 24 hours, Facebook had deleted 300,000 copies of the video from its platform, as well as 1.2 million copies at the point of upload (BBC News, 2019). But by then, the video has spread even further, via 8chan, where extremists promoted it and even produced and distributed their own edited versions, but also via more established platforms such as YouTube, Reddit, and Twitter. Tarrant's 'manifesto'—a 74-page document prepared in advance of the attack setting out apparent motives—was similarly distributed via commercial social media platforms and more ideologically orientated forums, including 8chan. Mainstream news organizations, in turn, reposted material from both the manifesto and the video as they reported the events, prompting criticism of their reliance on terrorists' own output in their efforts to cover the news, thus elevating prominence and visibility of such content (Wakefield, 2019).

In his manifesto, Tarrant—echoing a format used by the Norwegian terrorist Anders Breivik who inspired him—posed a series of questions in a mock interview for which he provided some abstruse answers. Concerning the question 'From where did you receive/ research/ develop your beliefs?', Tarrant replied: 'The internet, of course. You will not find the truth anywhere else' (17).

PHOTO 18.2 New Zealand, 2019: People walk past the flower wall along Rolleston Avenue after the memorial service for the victims of the Christchurch mosque shootings.

Indeed, the Christchurch attack has been described as 'a mass murder of, and for, the internet' (Roose, 2019), from the way in which Tarrant planned and publicized his attack, the pool of extremists on 8chan and elsewhere who celebrated and promoted it, the language he used in his video and manifesto, and the way in which these seemed to spread almost uncontrollably online. Tarrant even made a reference to a popular YouTube star moments before he launched his attack, mimicking the type of ironic trolling (insulting) that often characterizes postings on extremist social media forums.

The Christchurch shootings thus illustrate not only how social media can impact the execution of a terrorist attack and the way in which it is depicted and perceived, but also the presentation, style and outlook that is adopted by the perpetrator in the first place.

QUESTIONS

1. What does the Christchurch attack tell us about terrorism in the age of social media?
2. How may the challenges that the attack represents with respect to social media be mitigated?

Through social media terrorists and their sympathizers gain control over a message that has conventionally been retained by established media organizations. The scope of this communication, as it has always been, is both internal and external. Cordes referred to the latter as the 'propaganda aspect', concerning efforts to persuade others, and the former as the 'auto-propaganda aspect', inward-facing communication intended to 'persuade the terrorist the enemy is real, the cause just, and the terrorist's existence not only justified, but called for due to the "urgency" of the moment' (2001: 151, 156). Public relations therefore have become a central feature of terrorist campaigns, and—by extension—some of the preventative measures intended to counter them. Section 18.4 looks at this interplay between terrorism and social media at a more granular level.

18.4 TERRORIST USE OF SOCIAL MEDIA

Social media are relevant to key dimensions of the way in which we understand terrorism. It has, by extension, impacted all areas where terrorists operate, though to differing degrees. Speaking about the global impact of these developments, Hoffman (2017a) reflected on the way in which the advent of social media usage had altered the picture: 'Ease, interactivity, networking, reach, frequency, usability, stability, immediacy, publicity and permanence are among the benefits to terrorist groups like ISIS who have nimbly adapted these technologies for their nefarious purposes.' Those with shared identities and grievances now have new opportunities to form collectives around them. In countries where social media usage is high, and level of government control is relatively low, social media usage has been identified in a wide range of terrorism-related activities, though these are also the areas that have attracted the majority of existing research on the topic.

A 2018 Europol report on the terrorist threat in Europe found that 'online propaganda and networking via social media are still essential to terrorist attempts to reach out to EU audiences for recruitment, radicalisation and fundraising' (2018: 6). Another Europol report found that by 2017, 150 social media platforms were being exploited by terrorists for propaganda dissemination, though there had been a reduction in the abuse of mainstream platforms such as Facebook and Twitter due to industry and government efforts to counter these activities (2017: 53).

A study by RAND Europe on terrorism trends in the United Kingdom found that the 'internet plays a part in almost every national security investigation conducted by the security and intelligence agencies and police in the UK. Terrorism cases in the UK without a "digital footprint" are increasingly rare' (von Behr et al., 2013: 3). The independent reviewer of terrorism laws in the UK, in turn, found that social media platforms, including PalTalk Messenger, Telegram, Kik Messenger, Twitter, Viber, WhatsApp, and Facebook had featured, and sometimes played significant roles, in major terrorist plots that concluded in court in 2016, aiding activities such as communication, financial transaction, logistics and target identification (Hill, 2017).

Platforms like Facebook have provided a 'virtual bridge' between so-called foreign fighters and other travellers who left their homes to join Islamist extremist organizations partaking in the civil war in Syria, especially between 2013 and 2016, and curious or sympathetic domestic social media users who might be susceptible to overtures, including direct recruitment efforts, from those who journeyed to the battlefield, seeking to reach out and influence others. For instance, after 19-year-old Aqsa Mahmood, who left her family home in Glasgow to join ISIS in November 2013, arrived in Syria, and used her Tumblr blogs to reach out to other young women to urge them to join her (Fantz and Shubert, 2015).

A study by the START consortium into terrorists' use of social media in the United States found that such platforms were 'playing an increasingly important role in the radicalization processes of U.S. extremists', featuring in close to 90 per cent of identified cases examined in 2016 (2018: 1). The most common types of usage were consumption and dissemination of media content, followed by participation in extremist dialogues, especially within the far-right. The START study found that fewer used social media to facilitate extremist activities directly, though we have since seen prominent examples of such facilitation through social media. Far-right-dominated platforms such as Gab and Parler, for instance, were used to coordinate the storming of the US Capitol building on 6 January 2021 (Frenkel, 2021).

The START study also found that use of social media appeared to accelerate the process of radicalization, with the time period between initial documented interest in extremism and attempted participation in extremist action becoming shorter, compared to those cases where social media did not appear to play a role. Conversely, however, those who had been most active on social media platforms were found to have a lower success rate in terms of actual outcomes, whether in the form of formulating terrorist plots or travelling overseas to become combatants. Those who were most successful in their orchestration of terrorist plots, in turn, abstained from social media usage altogether (START, 2018). This is explored next.

Social media usage has penetrated across the Arab nation also, albeit to differing and fluctuating degrees, depending on state-enforced limitations on the use of the internet more generally. A UNESCO report on youth and violent extremism on social media found that 'Arab youth are major consumers of social media networks and especially Facebook, which is one of the top ten most used sites by Arab Internet users', with implications for the way in which political activism had developed (Alava, Frau-Meigs, and Hassan, 2017: 30). Terrorist groups operating in the region, especially ISIS-linked organizations, have developed a sophisticated repertoire of Arabic language media content that is shared and promoted via social media, using such platforms to expand their reach and capacity. One US intelligence officer suggested: 'that the internet is a major reason why ISIS is so successful, and so worrying, as far as global terror movements go' (Frenkel, 2016).

Meanwhile, internet bandwidth availability in Africa increased twenty-fold between 2008 and 2012, and mobile phone data-service subscriptions increased sixty-fold in the first decade of the 21st century, making the continent the world's fastest growing mobile phone market. By the end of 2015 46 per cent of Africa's overall population had subscribed to mobile services, which are relied on for a range of day-to-day services, including online banking (Cox et al., 2018a: 7–8). Some terrorist organizations active in different parts of the continent, in turn, have sought to exploit a rise in smartphone usage to expand their operations. ISIS-linked operatives, again, are seen as something of a leader in this regard, using platforms such as Telegram, Kik, and WhatsApp to engage with potential recruits, including supplementing offline engagement. Al-Shabab, the al-Qaeda affiliate in East Africa discussed in section 18.1, is active on Twitter, but has also sought to reach out to potential supporters via closed chatrooms. Boko Haram, the ISIS affiliate group operating in northeast Nigeria and neighbouring regions has also stepped up its activities on Twitter, as well as using social media to publicize new audio or video statements, though it has also faced a backlash on these channels by users condemning the group's activities (Cox et al., 2018b: 3; Alava, Frau-Meigs, and Hassan, 2017: 31).

In many parts of Asia, Facebook and Facebook Messenger have become embedded, while Twitter, Line and Skype are also popular. Indonesia, for example, has 76 million regular Facebook users, and ranks fourth in the world by total number of users (Alava, Frau-Meigs, and Hassan, 2017: 34). 80 per cent of the Bangladeshi population is reportedly on Facebook, which has increasingly supplanted older technologies as the main source of news (Droogan et al., 2018: 177). Social media are also popular in China, though their domestic platforms, such as WeChat, prevail.

Terrorists have managed to exploit this proliferation of usage, primarily for communication and propaganda distribution, but also for facilitative endeavours such as financing and 'administering digital training environments'. Terrorists in Pakistan have used mobile phones to 'live-stream' their attacks to elevate its impact and propaganda value, while organizations in Philippines have used platforms such as YouTube, Facebook, Twitter, and Telegram to enhance their 'branding' and marketing initiatives, especially in order to accentuate apparent links with global terrorist networks. Indeed, brand management on social media has become a central preoccupation of many terrorist organizations. The Jamaat-e-Islami group in Bangladesh, for instance, dedicates particular effort to scan social media for unwanted commentary in an attempt to 'control' the narrative around it (ibid. 170, 173, 178).

Such efforts to combat negative publicity point to the fact that the advent of social media presents terrorist organizations, operatives and sympathizers with challenges, as well as opportunities. Just as these ubiquitous platforms can be exploited by promoters of political violence, they can also be used by those seeking to counter these operations, whether from informal grassroots initiatives, civil-society organizations, or official strategic communications campaigns. Social media usage can also expose other vulnerabilities and weaknesses that can undermine those seeking to support terrorism through online means. Social media, in short, represent a double-edged sword for terrorists, bringing great benefits but also potential pitfalls. The next section expands on these dynamics in more detail.

18.5 SOCIAL MEDIA AS A DOUBLE-EDGED SWORD

The spread of social media usage can work against terrorists in several key ways. Firstly, the communicative revolution brought by Web 2.0 represents something of a contradiction in terms of the visibility of terrorists and their sympathizers. On the one hand, the proliferation of encrypted platforms has provided opportunities for clandestine communication that can be hard for the authorities to detect. But on the other hand, other more open dimensions of social media have provided new opportunities for surveillance. Indeed, it is telling that those who were most active on social media, among a pool of radicalized individuals in the United States, were also the least likely to have been successful in their extremist involvement, partly because they left more digital crumbs for the authorities to pick up, compared to those who abstained from social media use altogether (START, 2018).

Those who are sympathetic toward a particular extremist cause often feel the urge to display these allegiances on their social networks, just as other social media users are keen to advertise their loyalties and affiliations. Many young recruits to extremist networks and causes will have grown up with widespread use of social media on a day-to-day basis. In fact, senior ISIS commanders in Syria and Iraq were forced to confiscate mobile phones used by volunteers who were posting images and other uploads from the battlefield, from which security and intelligence agencies could then use to locate their positions or track their activities (Droogan et al., 2018: 174). Beyond detection, moreover, active social media usage can also provide law-enforcement and prosecutors with a new set of digital evidence that can be used to secure convictions in court, as new opportunities to establish guilt and intent may have been provided.

Secondly, as noted at in section 18.1, social media and the participatory aspects of Web 2.0 more broadly have shaped political activism in horizontal and leaderless directions. There has been a democratization of political protest in general where established leaderships can be challenged or side-lined more easily than before. This can impact terrorist use of social media also. Web 2.0 promotes supporter-generated content: while leaders of established groups are provided with new opportunities to distribute their messages, individual users can also disseminate their own content that may well gain more prominence than more 'established' voices. This can challenge the message consistency from a given movement if individual members produce material that contradicts the position adopted by movement leaders. Indeed, the boundaries of a movement or a group become hazy if there are multiple voices that on social media seem to carry near equal weight. Leaders may also find it hard to keep other participants at bay who wish to outflank them or produce rival currents in competition for the same resources or followers. The virtual domain, in short, is volatile and hard to preserve (Creswell and Haykel, 2017: 31).

Thirdly, the largest social media and networking platforms are major profit-making enterprises and the misuse of these platforms can threaten their business model, for instance, if users abandon them due to loss of reputation or governments make their operating environment more stringent due to their lack of confidence in the ability of these businesses to self-police and censor. Resulting pressure, especially on mainstream platforms, to develop tools to counter the spread of extremist content glorifying terrorism has thus made it harder for the proponents of such content to survive online. Facebook as an example of this, has developed tools to detect extremist content, and employs staff to review and remove material that is deemed to breach guidelines, including terroristic material (Saltman, 2017). In June 2017, major tech companies—including Google, Facebook, and Microsoft—formed the 'Global Internet Forum to Counter Terrorism', designed to disrupt attempts by terrorists to exploit any platforms that were part of their portfolio, including through dedicated efforts to remove content (Macdonald, 2018). Providers, especially more minor platforms, are aided in these efforts by dedicated government bodies that monitor the misuse of the internet, including social media, for terrorist purposes, such as the European Union Internet Referral Unit (EU IRU).

Fourthly, many have suggested that terrorists' use of social media to spread propaganda and reach out to potential recruits offers opportunities to counter their extremist rhetoric directly. After all, since social media levels the playing field (metaphorically), perhaps extremist outlets can be challenged and exposed in the same virtual arenas where they are seeking to spread their message. The independent reviewer of terrorism laws in the UK argued that the 'the omnipresence of social media provides a great opportunity to meet the evils of terrorism, to take the opportunity to prove them wrong' (Hill, 2017). Many such initiatives have since been launched, often with a social media focus, and the topic has attracted the attention of international bodies such as the United Nations. In May 2017, the Security Council adopted Resolution 2354 which is dedicated to countering terrorist narratives (UN, 2017).

The effectiveness of any of these efforts to reduce the threat of terrorism remains unclear. There are also concerns that state-led initiatives to police the internet and social media may have a detrimental effect on free speech online and will provide governments with tools or precedent to supress legitimate political dissent (Human Rights Watch, 2018). Furthermore, if mainstream platforms appear too hazardous, there is a risk that terrorists and extremists may migrate to other platforms that are more difficult to track and penetrate, due to technologies they employ or a reluctance by their designers to cooperate with governments and provide access to or remove content and users. After being removed from Twitter, for instance, large numbers of far-right activists migrated to a social networking platform called 'Gab', which describes itself as a 'free speech social network' launched in 2016. Critics accuse it of providing a haven for neo-Nazis (Roose, 2018). Some neo-Nazis have also been found to use online gaming servers to create their own bespoke chatrooms and means to share content (Sandford and De Simone, 2018).

The flip-side to this uptick in extremists' use of more obscure social media platforms, however, is that they lose their ability to reach large and geographically dispersed audiences, which, as this chapter has demonstrated, is a fundamental benefit of social media to begin with. If terrorist groups operate on closed or clandestine platforms alone, they risk managing little more than speaking to an existing audience of supporters. Indeed, analysts found that senior members of ISIS became concerned that they were losing their ability to reach out to larger audiences after they moved large swathes of their media enterprise from open platforms to Telegram, prompting them to plan coordinated 'media raids' for rapid dissemination of content through established platforms before it would be removed (Europol, 2018: 31).

The efficacy and utility of terrorists' use of social media can thus be approached from several different perspectives. Fundamentally, however, this dynamic also raises more profound questions about the relationship between the offline space and physical environments more broadly. Do online musings, behaviours, and choices necessarily translate to offline settings, where their impact might be greater? There is no easy way of answering this question, which is also much broader than simply relating to terrorist use of social media. But it is an important consideration that is relevant to this topic and will be explored in more detail in section 18.6.

18.6 LINKING VIRTUAL AND PHYSICAL WORLDS

The link between online and offline experiences is not well understood, and subject to extensive and ongoing debate in a variety of domains and disciplines. More broadly, the effects of media consumption or viewing habits—online or offline—on physical behaviour are another major topic of debate (Salam and Stack, 2018). The question surrounding social media and terrorism centres on the extent to which social media activity in support of terrorism impacts its physical manifestations beyond the benefits of facilitation for those already involved in violent groups.

Many have sought to emphasize the importance of physical interactions and socialization that have not merely been replaced by social media online. Burke (2011) for instance observed that 'Twitter will never be a substitute for grassroots activism, [it] won't help Al-Shabaab retake Mogadishu or the Taliban reach Kabul in any meaningful way', adding that 'terrorism is a social activity like any other. Militant or moderate, you can spend as much time as you like online, but eventually you have to come back to the real world'. Such questions were raised again as countries across the globe grappled with the Covid-19 pandemic. With millions confined to their homes many relied on the internet to make sense of events around them. The World Health Organization spoke of an 'infodemic', as conspiracy theories about the disease spread like wildfire. But what would the impact be in the 'real world'? (Hao and Basu, 2020).

Research has even suggested that some of those who participate in interactive virtual spaces that glorify terrorism satisfy any 'activist' needs and associations online, without any intention of translating these into more direct offline behaviour. Ramsay's (2013: 186) study of jihadi use of internet forums, for instance, found that 'the online violent radical milieu may actually generate its own *positive* reasons for non-engagement [through] a set of meaningful and, so it would seem, pleasurable practices of its own'. If users online could assume virtual roles and engage in debates and exchanges with their like-minded peers, in short, they may have satisfied what they were trying to achieve without necessitating or prompting deeper engagement or physical involvement.

CASE STUDY 18.2

Lee Rigby

On 22 May 2013, Lee Rigby, an off-duty soldier, was targeted by two assailants as he approached his military accommodation in south-east London. The attackers, Michael Adebolajo and Michael Adebowale, had been known to the security services for some time. Michael Adebowale had come to the attention of the authorities for extremist posts he had made on social media.

Adebowale had been active on Facebook for some time before the attack and was open about his desire to harm the UK. These extremist posts brought him to the attention of the authorities as early as autumn 2011. He had held eleven Facebook accounts in the months leading up to the attack, seven accounts were deleted by Facebook, mostly due to their association with known terrorist accounts or Islamist extremist groups (Intelligence and Security Committee of Parliament, 2014: 128–129), but his ability to use the platform was not compromised since he could simply re-open new accounts once others had been closed. Some of Adebowale's exchanges on Facebook, meanwhile, did not lead to accounts being closed, even though they appeared to be of an extremist nature. In one exchange with an associate a few months before the attack, for instance, Adebowale reportedly remarked: 'let's kill a soldier' (Intelligence and Security Committee of Parliament, 2014: 131). He also reportedly made references to his desire to become a 'lone wolf', and die for his cause. These extremist posts did not appear to have triggered Facebook's detection mechanism for problematic material, nor were they communicated to the authorities.

In the parliamentary investigation that followed the attacks, social media providers were criticized for not doing more to flag and remove the content. The intelligence community was also questioned as to their failure to intervene when an individual had been so explicit on social media about the desire to become a militant, even detailing his preferred target.

In their response to the parliamentary committee, security and intelligence agencies pointed to four key and related challenges in detecting concerning posts of this nature and the *risk* they posed, which would affect the way in which resources would be allocated and targets prioritized. First, it was difficult to assess the intent and capability of an individual making extremist references online, or indeed to connect online personas with offline individuals. Secondly, some of these exchanges were hard to access, either due to encryption or because they had not been identified by service providers or platforms. Thirdly, the volume of communication posed challenges both for platforms and monitoring agencies. As a representative from GCHQ noted: 'The internet is vast—there are 204 million email messages sent every minute, 100,000 tweets and a million Facebook posts. GCHQ only has the capability to access a tiny fraction of this information, and resource constraints mean that only a very small fraction of that can ever be stored or processed.' Fourthly, the commonality of extremist views on social media caused added problems of resource prioritization. When asked about Adebowale's references to jihad and becoming a 'lone wolf', the director of Britain's domestic intelligence agency, MI5, remarked: 'those sorts of things said, and worse, on these sorts of [sites] are very common; and the challenge that we have is to try to discern rhetoric from intent in these things [...]. The vast majority of it, [...] translates into no action at all. No action at all' (ISCP, 2014: 148, 78).

QUESTIONS

1. What does this Case Study tell us about risk assessment based on social media evidence?
2. What tools can effectively employed online, and what is the role of platforms such as Facebook in this regard?

This raises the problem of assessing the risk associated with social media postings and activities that glorify or promote terrorism. How likely are such sentiments to translate into physical harm? Many who call for violent attacks or even claim to be participating in violence themselves are simply engaged in 'a type of grandstanding common to the Internet, without ever having had any real commitment and/or intention to engage in violence at all'. Threats of violence online are common (Conway, 2017: 80). Case Study 18.2 explores this dilemma in more detail.

18.7 CONCLUSION

When we consider the multiple social, geopolitical, and technological developments that have shaped terrorism across the world, the dawn of social media and the participatory web represents a recent chapter in a very long history. Yet its emergence, beyond the invention of the internet, has generated a huge amount of interest, attention, and research. This is partly because social media platforms are so open and ubiquitous. There simply is so much more 'data' for us to look at and analyse, and it has never been easier to access. But translating all this information into something tangible, actionable, and interpreting this data in meaningful ways represent significant challenges that we should not underestimate.

The impact of social media on people's lives across the world has been profound, but also complex. Social media has affected human interaction everywhere, and because of the way in which terrorism is constituted, popular usage of social media concerns some of its key components. As we traced in this chapter, terrorists have become more adaptive and agile in an asymmetric playing field. Social networks are virtual and boundless, so loyal communities can form and spread even if they are geographically dispersed. And terrorists can speak and share more widely, quickly, cheaply, and securely than ever before.

But terrorists' use of social media brings potential hazards too. The way in which these hazards constrain terrorists and their sympathizers in the digital space and the way operatives might wish to mitigate them will have consequences that will shape the future evolution of this domain. Access to data and ubiquity of platforms means that some individuals, networks and communication channels may become more detectable than before. The 'flattening' of online political resistance, moreover, may well have more significant consequences for the vitality, salience, and stability of leadership within these realms. Leaders may be more easily challenged or circumvented with potentially profound consequences. If terrorist groups, movements or leaderships seek to counteract these dangers by migrating to more closed or hidden platforms, that too will shape how social media affects terrorism and undermines its key benefit. Finally, if social media platforms remain operable, open and accessible, it is harder to control debate and access to information. This is a complex issue for governments, educators, and any other authority seeking to limit exposure to harmful content online, but could also undermine efforts to rationalize extremism and militancy if, for instance, conspiracy theories that underpin them become more easily debunked.

As this chapter has discussed, there are even more profound questions about the impact of social media on terrorism and its evolution to which we have few answers. Social media stands as its own entity. It do not reflect the 'real' physical world in a precise mirror image. Most of us who use social networks, for instance, likely try to depict a more attractive, consistent, and interesting version of our lives than is reflected by the day-to-day reality of our existence. Terrorists, their supporters and sympathizers are not any different. The way in which the virtual relates to the physical is therefore central to this debate, as it is to questions surrounding the impact of media and the internet more broadly.

So how do we understand terrorist use of social media? These platforms and applications work in unison with other processes, whether online or offline, that provide further context and opportunities. As we have seen, social media may produce completely new opportunities for individuals, especially those without existing social connections that might introduce them to new extremist cohorts. Social media may also supplement and constitute one virtual component of a much more complex interaction taking place offline. And some individuals may abstain from social media use altogether. 'From a risk assessment perspective', according to one study on the internet and terrorism., 'there is no easy offline versus online violent radicalization dichotomy to be drawn. It may be a false dichotomy. Plotters regularly engage in activities in both domains. Often their behaviours are compartmentalized across these two domains' (Gill et al., 2017: 100).

As students and researchers, therefore we need to be careful as we seek to navigate this space. We need to ensure that our assumptions about what we observe online rests on an empirical understanding of the way in which these experiences play out for the individuals we are trying to study. What is clear, though, is that social media now form a central component of many terrorist campaigns, networks and groups, that have invested significant resources, time and money, in their deployment and development. They would hardly have done so unless they were sure about their significance and impact (Conway, 2017: 91).

DISCUSSION QUESTIONS

1. Do social media aid or inhibit terrorism?
2. Who should lead efforts to combat terrorists' use of social media and how can these efforts be encouraged?
3. What are the consequences of targeting terrorists' use of social media?
4. How can a balance be struck between addressing citizens' right to privacy vis-à-vis their right to security?
5. How do we assess if efforts to target terrorist use of social media are being effective?
6. How will this terrain evolve? What challenges are we likely to face in the future?

Visit the online resources for pointers on how to answer the discussion questions, links to useful web sources, and guidance on accessing databases: www.oup.com/he/Wilson-Muro1e

GUIDE TO FURTHER READING

Centre for Analysis of Social Media (2021) https://demos.co.uk/research-area/casm/ (as of August 2021). *This is a resource offering regularly updated material concerning wider issues relating to social media research and its future issues and trajectories.*

Conway, M. (2017) 'Determining the Role of the Internet in Violent Extremism and Terrorism: Six Suggestions for Progressing Research', *Studies in Conflict and Terrorism*, 40:1, 77–98. *Conway provides an overview of key debates relating to the study of the internet and terrorism, offering context to understanding the role of social media in this regard.*

Cronin, A. (2019) *Power to the People: How Open Technological Innovation is Arming Tomorrow's Terrorists*. NY: Oxford University Press. *Giving us the broader picture, Audrey Cronin discusses social media in the wider context of technological developments that have aided and impacted the evolution of modern terrorism.*

Ramsay, G. (2013) *Jihadi Culture on the World Wide Web*. NY: Bloomsbury. *Ramsay offers a comprehensive analysis of how online virtual spaces involving promotion of violent extremism can constitute distinct microcultures. His book is an important theoretical contribution to our understanding of the impact of social media on terrorism.*

VoxPol library (2021) https://www.voxpol.eu/library/ (as of August 2021). *This resource offers a regularly updated library of research papers relating to extremist use of the internet, especially social media.*

REFERENCES

Aichner, T. and Jacob, F. (2015) 'Measuring the Degree of Corporate Social Media Use', *International Journal of Market Research*, 57 (2): 257–275.

Alava, S., Frau-Meigs, D., and Hassan, G. (2017) 'Youth and Violent Extremism on Social Media: Mapping the Research', Paris: United Nations Educational, Scientific and Cultural Organization.

Anzalone, C. (2013) 'The Nairobi Attack and Al-Shabab's Media Strategy', *CTC Sentinel*, 6 (10).

Ayalon, A. and Jenkins, B. M. (2014) 'War by What Means, According to Whose Rules?', Rand Corporation, https://www.rand.org/pubs/conf_proceedings/CF334.html (last accessed January 2019).

BBC News (2019) 'Facebook: New Zealand Attack Video Viewed 4,000 Times' 19 March, https://www.bbc.com/news/business-47620519 (as of March 2019).

Burke, J. (2011) 'Al-Shabab's Tweets Won't Boost its Cause', *The Guardian*, 16 December, https://www.theguardian.com/commentisfree/2011/dec/16/al-shabab-tweets-terrorism-twitter (as of February 2019).

Conway, M. (2017) 'Determining the Role of the Internet in Violent Extremism and Terrorism: Six Suggestions for Progressing Research', *Studies in Conflict and Terrorism*, 40 (1): 77–98.

Cordes, B. (2001) 'When Terrorists do the Talking: Reflections on Terrorist Literature', in D. Rapoport (ed.), *Inside Terrorist Organizations* (2nd edition, 150–172). London: Frank Cass.

Cox, K., Marcellino, W., Bellasio, J., Ward, A., Galai, K., Meranto, S., and Persi Paoli, G. (2018a) 'Social Media in Africa: A Double-edged Sword for Security and Development: Research Report', United Nations Development Programme/ RAND Europe.

Cox, K., Marcellino, W., Bellasio, J., Ward, A., Galai, K., Meranto, S., and Persi Paoli, G. (2018b) 'Social Media in Africa: A Double-Edged Sword for Security and Development: Executive Summary', United Nations Development Programme/ RAND Europe.

Creswell, R. and Haykel, B. (2017) 'Poetry in Jihadi Culture', in Hegghammer, T. (ed.) *Jihadi Culture: The Art and Social Practices of Militant Islamists*. Cambridge: Cambridge University Press.

Daily Telegraph, 'Norway killings: Breivik posted hate-filled video on YouTube hours before attacks', 24 July 2011, https://www.telegraph.co.uk/news/worldnews/europe/norway/8657473/Norway-killings-Breivik-posted-hate-filled-video-on-YouTube-hours-before-attacks.html (last accessed January 2019).

Di Lellio, A. and Castano, E. (2015) 'The Danger of "New Norms" and the Continuing Relevance of IHL in the post-9/11 era', *International Review of the Red Cross*, 97 (900): 1277–1293.

Droogan J., Waldek L., and Blackhall R. (2018) 'Innovation and Terror: An Analysis of the Use of Social Media by Terror-related Groups in the Asia Pacific', *Journal of Policing, Intelligence and Counter Terrorism*, 13 (2): 170–184.

Europol (2017) 'Internet Organized Crime Threat Assessment (IOCTA)', see https://www.europol.europa.eu/activities-services/main-reports/internet-organised-crime-threat-assessment-iocta-2018 (as of January 2019).

Europol (2018) 'European Union Terrorism Situation and Trend Report', available from https://www.europol.europa.eu/activities-services/main-reports/eu-terrorism-situation-and-trend-report (as of January 2019).

Fantz, A. and Atika Shubert, A. (2015) 'From Scottish Teen to ISIS Bride and Recruiter: The Aqsa Mahmood Story', *CNN* (24 February), https://edition.cnn.com/2015/02/23/world/scottish-teen-isis-recruiter/index.html (as of August 2021).

Frenkel, S. (2021) 'The Storming of Capitol Hill was Organized on Social Media', *The New York Times*, https://www.nytimes.com/2021/01/06/us/politics/protesters-storm-capitol-hill-building.html (as of August 2021).

Frenkel, S. (2016) 'This is How ISIS Uses the Internet', *Buzzfeed News* (12 May), https://www.buzzfeednews.com/article/sheerafrenkel/everything-you-ever-wanted-to-know-about-how-isis-uses-the-i (as of August 2021).

Gill, P., Corner, E., Conway, M., Thornton, A., Bloom, M., and Horgan, J. (2017) 'Terrorist Use of the Internet by the Numbers Quantifying Behaviours, Patterns, and Processes', *Criminology & Public Policy*, 16 (1): 99–107.

Hannigan, R. (2014) 'The Web is a Terrorist's Command-and-control Network of Choice', *Financial Times* (3 November), https://www.ft.com/content/c89b6c58-6342-11e4-8a63-00144feabdc0 (last accessed January 2019).

Hao, K. and Basu, T. (2020) 'The Coronavirus is The First True Social-Media "Infodemic"', *MIT Technology Review* (February 12), https://www.technologyreview.com/2020/02/12/844851/the-coronavirus-is-the-first-true-social-media-infodemic/ (as of August 2021).

Hill, M. (2017) 'Terrorism and Social Media Conference'—Keynote Speech, available from http://www.cyberterrorism-project.org/tasm-conference-2017 (as of January 2019).

Hoffman, B. (2017a) 'Terrorism and Social Media Conference'—Keynote Speech, available from http://www.cyberterrorism-project.org/tasm-conference-2017 (as of January 2019).

Hoffman, B. (2017b) Inside Terrorism (3rd edition). New York: Columbia University Press.

Human Rights Watch (2018) 'Germany: Flawed Social Media Law: NetzDG is Wrong Response to Online Abuse', (14 February), https://www.hrw.org/news/2018/02/14/germany-flawed-social-media-law (as of January 2019).

Intelligence and Security Committee of Parliament (2014) 'Report on the Intelligence Relating to the Murder of Fusilier Lee Rigby' (24 November). London: House of Commons.

Jenkins, B. (1974) 'International Terrorism: A New Kind of Warfare', *The Rand Paper Series*, P-5261, Santa Monica: Rand.

Lee, B. (2017) 'Crest Guide: Understanding the Farright Landscape', Centre for Research and Evidence on Security Threats (July).

Macdonald, S. (2018) 'How Tech Companies are Successfully Disrupting Terrorist Social Media Activity', *The Conversation* (26 June), http://theconversation.com/how-tech-companies-are-successfully-disrupting-terrorist-social-media-activity-98594, as of January 2019.

Martin, S. and Weinberg, L. B. (2016) 'Terrorism in an Era of Unconventional Warfare', *Terrorism and Political Violence*, 28 (2): 236–253, DOI: 10.1080/09546553.2014.895330

Mazzoni, V. (2018) 'Exploring the Jihadi Telegram World: A Brief Overview', *European Eye on Radicalization* (21 June), https://eeradicalization.com/exploring-the-jihadi-telegram-world-a-brief-overview/ (last accessed January 2019).

McCaughey, M. (2014) *Cyberactivism on the Participatory Web* (ed.). New York: Routledge.

McConnell, T. (2015) 'Close Your Eyes and Pretend to be Dead', *Foreign Policy* (21 September) https://foreignpolicy.com/2015/09/20/nairobi-kenya-westgate-mall-attack-al-shabab/

Meikle, G. (2016) *Social Media: Communication, Sharing and Visibility*, London: Routledge.

National Action (2013) 'Strategy and Promotion', September.

Pisoiu, D. (2014) 'Subcultural Theory Applied to Jihadi and Right-Wing Radicalization in Germany', *Terrorism and Political Violence*, 27 (1): 9–28.

Ramsay, G. (2011) 'Consuming the Jihad: An Enquiry into the Subculture of Internet Jihadism', thesis submitted for the degree of PhD at the University of St Andrews.

Ramsay, G. (2013) *Jihadi Culture on the World Wide Web*. New York: Bloomsbury.

Roose, K. (2018) 'On Gab, an Extremist-Friendly Site, Pittsburgh Shooting Suspect Aired His Hatred in Full', *New York Times* (28 October), https://www.nytimes.com/2018/10/28/us/gab-robert-bowers-pittsburgh-synagogue-shootings.html (as of January 2019).

Roose, K. (2019) 'A Mass Murder of, and for, the Internet', *The New York Times*, 15 March, https://www.nytimes.com/2019/03/15/technology/facebook-youtube-christchurch-shooting.html#click=https://t.co/ZNo66KmK6m (as of March 2019).

Sageman, M. (2008) *Leaderless Jihad: Terror Networks in the Twenty-first Century*. University of Pennsylvania Press, Philadelphia.

Salam, M. and Stack, L. (2018) 'Do Video Games Lead to Mass Shootings? Researchers Say No', *New York Times* (23 February), https://www.nytimes.com/2018/02/23/us/politics/trump-video-games-shootings.html (as of February 2019).

Saltman, E. M. (2017) 'Terrorism and Social Media Conference'—Keynote Speech, available from http://www.cyberterrorism-project.org/tasm-conference-2017 (as of January 2019).

Sandford, D. and De Simone, D. (2018) 'British Neo-Nazis Suggest Prince Harry should be shot', *BBC News* (5 December), https://www.bbc.com/news/uk-46460442 (as of January 2019).

Schmid A. P. and de Graaf J. (1982) *Violence as Communication: Insurgent Terrorism and the Western News Media*. London: Sage.

Schmid A. P. and McAllister B. (2011) 'Theories of Terrorism', in Schmid AP (ed.) *The Routledge Handbook of Terrorism Research* (201–272). Abingdon: Routledge.

START (2018) 'The Use of Social Media by United States Extremists', *Research Brief*, College Park: The National Consortium for the Study of Terrorism and Responses to Terrorism.

Stepanova, E. (2008) *SIPRI Research Report No 23 Terrorism in Asymmetrical Conflict: Ideological and Structural Aspects*, SIPRI, Stockholm.

Tan, R. (2017) 'Terrorists' Love For Telegram, Explained: It's Become ISIS's app of Choice', *Vox*, https://www.vox.com/world/2017/6/30/15886506/terrorism-isis-telegram-social-media-russia-pavel-durov-twitter (last accessed January 2019).

Taylor, M. and Currie, P. M. (2012) *Terrorism and Affordance*. New York: Continuum.

Thornton, R. (2007) *Asymmetric Warfare: Threat and Response in the Twenty-First Century*. Cambridge: Polity Press.

Thornton, S. (ed.) (1997) *The Subcultures Reader*. London: Routledge.

UN (2017) 'Unanimously Adopting Resolution 2354 (2017), Security Council Urges Member States to Follow New Guidelines on Countering Terrorist Narratives', see https://www.un.org/press/en/2017/sc12839.doc.htm (as of January 2019).

Von Behr, I., Reding, A., Edwards, C., and Gribbon, L. (2013) 'Radicalisation in the Digital Era The Use of the Internet in 15 Cases of Terrorism and Extremism', Cambridge: RAND Europe.

Wakefield, J. (2019) 'Christchurch Shootings: Social Media Races to Stop Attack Footage', BBC News, 16 March, https://www.bbc.com/news/technology-47583393 (as of March 2019).

Wilkinson, P. (1997) 'The media and terrorism: A Reassessment', *Terrorism and Political Violence*, 9 (2): 51–64.

CHAPTER 19

Is Terrorism Effective?

DIEGO MURO

■ **CHAPTER SUMMARY**

Does terrorism work? Is terrorism successful in delivering the expected results for its perpetrators? This chapter on the efficacy of terrorism argues that terrorism can be successful in delivering tactical returns, but it is largely ineffective in realizing strategic goals. The chapter considers the pros and cons of using coercive intimidation to pursue political ends from both a theoretical perspective and a case study approach. It also outlines some of the methodological problems inherent in the academic debate that has taken place thus far on the subject, and suggests ways forward for making future scholarship in this area more inclusive, systematic, and effective than it has been to date.

19.1 INTRODUCTION

Does terrorism work? Is terrorism successful in delivering the expected results for its perpetrators? Finding answers to these two questions is of great importance to scholars, practitioners, and societies, especially those who continue to suffer terrorist attacks. From a scholarly perspective, it is critical to reach some consensus on whether past terrorist campaigns delivered the political goals that terrorists sought. From a policy perspective, it is essential to understand how terrorism can fail in order to identify vulnerabilities, and create a hostile environment for the survival of terrorist groups. In other words, the debate on the efficaciousness of terrorism has academic and practical implications in setting the historical record of terrorism and devising more efficient counter-terrorism policies.

This chapter on the effectiveness of terrorism is divided into five sections. At the first major section, 19.2 'Is Terrorism an Effective Tactic?' provides an overview of the scholarly debate on the political returns of terrorism, and concludes there is no consensus among experts. Section 19.3 explains why the effectiveness debate has not been resolved, and outlines some of the methodological problems inherent in the controversy that has taken place thus far on the subject. Section 19.4 discusses the pros and cons of using coercive intimidation to pursue political ends from both a theoretical perspective and a case study approach. The section also argues that terrorism can be effective in delivering tactical returns, but is largely ineffective in realizing strategic goals. Section 19.5 suggests ways forward for making future scholarship in this area more inclusive, methodical, and productive than it has been to date. Finally, the conclusion (section 19.6) summarizes the key arguments about the efficaciousness of terrorism.

19.2 IS TERRORISM AN EFFECTIVE TACTIC?

Scholars of terrorism are divided between those who think that terrorism works and those who think that it does not. One of the challenges experts face when trying to establish the efficacy or inefficacy of terrorism is identifying clearly when non-state terrorist actors have been fully effective, when they have been moderately effective, and when they have clearly failed. This and other controversies divide the camp between those who maintain that the use of violence against civilians by clandestine groups is an efficacious tool for achieving political objectives, and those who argue that it is not.

Alan Dershowitz figures in academic research that has explored how terrorists have succeeded in furthering their political goals. In his 2002 book, *Why Terrorism Works*, Dershowitz enumerates a series of terrorist actions where perpetrators not only went unpunished, but were rewarded for their crimes. From the 1960s onwards, terrorist acts resulted in increased publicity and freedom for terrorists because states, the media, and ultimately the citizens gave in to terrorism. For Dershowitz, the prime examples were Palestinian terrorist groups like the Popular Front for the Liberation of Palestine (PFLP). Despite launching a campaign of hijacking and blowing up planes in the late 1960s, Palestinian terrorism gained legitimacy and recognition from heads of state throughout the world. In the words of Dershowitz, 'the international community responded to terrorism between 1968 and 2001 by consistently rewarding and legitimizing it, rather than punishing and condemning it' (Dershowitz 2002: 85).

Other authors besides Dershowitz stress the efficacy of violence and the threat of violence for political purposes. David Lake (2002, 20) has maintained that terrorism is a 'rational and strategic' tactic because it enables terrorists to achieve a superior bargaining position. Likewise, Robert Pape has sustained that 'suicide terrorism has been rising largely because terrorists have learnt that it pays' (Pape 2003: 343). Andrew Kydd and Barbara Walter (2006: 49) have further argued that 'extremist organizations such as al-Qaeda, Hamas and the Tamil Tigers engage in terrorism because it frequently delivers the desired response.' According to these scholars, terrorists would view indiscriminate violence, suicide attacks in particular, as successful in producing the desired results. Ehud Sprinzak and Jakana Thomas also concur with Pape's argument that terrorism works, and point to government overreaction and terrorists' imposition of unacceptable costs as reasons for the political effectiveness of the tactic (Sprinzak 2000; Thomas 2014). Relatedly, Gould and Klor have also argued that 'terrorism can be an effective strategy' and, in the case of Israel, they determine that Israelis became 'more willing to grant concessions as a result of terrorism' (Gould and Klor 2010: 1459–1460).

KEY CONCEPTS

Terrorism as a method? Louise Richardson defines terrorism as a 'a method that entails the use of violence or force or the threat of violence or force with the primary purpose of generating a psychological impact beyond the immediate victims or object of attack for political motive' (Richardson 2015: 146). If we choose to define terrorism as a method or tactic (instead of a specific ideology, political movement or form of psychotic behaviour) then it is possible to evaluate whether this particular procedure is suitable for obtaining the political goals that terrorists have set for themselves.

However, the works of Lake, Kydd and Walter, Pape, and Gould and Klor have also been criticized because they give disproportionate attention to a handful of effective terrorist groups (in Palestine, Sri Lanka, Turkey, or Israel) and because their measurement strategies of 'success' are highly subjective. Indeed, determining the 'political returns' of violence is often complicated by the fact that government concessions can range from a launch-pad into politics, to a chance to avoid prison, not to mention the reluctance of governments to acknowledge the existence of peace talks or concessions (Bapat 2005).

Not all experts agree that terrorist violence can be successful in delivering the expected results for its perpetrators. A second set of scholars do not go as far as to say that terrorism simply 'does not work', and are quick to make a series of academic concessions (Thomas 2014). From their perspective, terrorism is tactically effective in harming civilians, instilling fear or capturing the attention of an audience. They also concede that the use of indiscriminate violence by clandestine groups often increases the recognition of a given grievance, terrorizes victims, forces governments to overreact and contributes to organizational survival. However, this second group of authors is much more critical of those who contend that the strategic use of terrorism and the indiscriminate targeting of civilians can force governments to make substantial policy concessions, especially in established democracies. They predominantly take a strategic view of terrorism and focus their attention on what the acts of violence are supposed to deliver in the long run (e.g. strategic goals). Furthermore, they doubt that terrorism is 'rational' given that less costly strategies such as campaigns of nonviolent resistance are twice as effective as their violent counterparts (Chenoweth and Stephan 2011).

> **KEY CONCEPTS**
>
> **The tactics and strategy of terrorism** Terrorist groups are usually weaker than the states they target and, as a result, are vulnerable to government retaliation. By contrast, states typically have considerable advantages in resources, capabilities, and public support. This power disparity explains why violent non-state groups adopt 'weapons of the weak' such as targeting civilians in order to intimidate governments into changing policy or granting concessions.
>
> Bombings and shootings of non-combatants remain the tactics of choice for terrorists. These tactics are adopted in anticipation of how the enemy government will respond and to bring about political change of some type, which is the strategic goal.
>
> The distinction between strategy and tactics is essential to the conduct of warfare. Broadly speaking, strategy is the planning, coordination, and general direction of military operations to meet overall political and military objectives. Tactics implement strategy by short-term decisions on the movement of troops and employment of weapons on the battlefield. The military theorist Carl von Clausewitz put it succinctly: 'tactics is the doctrine of the use of armed forces in battle, strategy the doctrine of the use of individual battles for the purpose of war' (Howard 2002: 36).

Max Abrahms figures prominently among the set of scholars who claim that terrorism does not work. The focus of Abrahms' work is on terrorists' capacity to secure their strategic goals, which they rarely achieve. He is quick to concede that terrorism is effective in obtaining tactical goals such as producing fear and harm. He also maintains that terrorism is ineffective politically, and that such strategic inefficacy is inherent in the tactic of targeting civilians, but admits that strategic incentives alone do not necessarily explain terrorists' actions (Abrahms 2012). He also argues that clandestine groups may use violence to send signals to an audience, to advance the groups' long-term goals and interests, or to produce positive reactions inside the group, but: 'terrorist success rates are actually extremely low' (Abrahms 2006: 43–44).

Other researchers have concluded that coercive violence against civilians rarely results in political success. Thomas Schelling (1991: 20) argues that terrorism 'almost never appears to accomplish anything politically significant' and David Rapoport (2001: 54) confirms that, 'by their own standards, terrorists rarely succeed.' Peter Neumann and Michael Smith also concur in arguing that 'campaigns of terrorism—shocking and brutal as they may seem—rarely succeed in achieving their stated objectives' (Neumann and Smith 2008: 100). All these academics agree that past terrorist campaigns had occasional tactical success in the form of human cost or economic disruption, but they largely resulted in strategic failures, at least in terms of their self-proclaimed goals. Empirical studies have also confirmed that only a handful of terrorist groups in modern history have managed to accomplish their political objectives (Kalyvas 2004; Abrahms 2006, 2013; Jones and Libicki 2008; Cronin 2009; Fortna 2015). Contrary to the view of the first group of scholars who argue that terrorism often works, this second group suggest that terrorism is highly correlated with political failure.

To summarize, the debate on the efficacy of terrorism divides a group of scholars who argue that terrorism is effective (Dershowitz, Pape, Walter, Kydd, Gould, Klor, Sprinzak, and Thomas) from those who argue that terrorism does not work (Abrahms, Kalyvas, Rapoport, Schelling, Neumann, Smith, Jones, Libicki, Cronin, and Fortna). A third group of authors—English, Krause, Muro, Phillips and Richardson—do not see the question in a binary, and suggest more nuanced approaches. Their work aims to identify some of the methodological obstacles to moving the debate forward, and suggests multi-level and longitudinal frameworks for analysing the political effectiveness of terrorism. In short, they suggest that effectiveness needs to be studied recurrently over a period of time at the individual, organizational and country level in order to find a persuasive synthesis.

19.3 WHY CAN'T SCHOLARS AGREE?

There is some agreement in the field that terrorist groups typically fail to achieve their self-proclaimed goals (Crenshaw 1987; Schelling 1991; Abrahms 2006; Fortna 2015). According to Kurth Cronin, of the nearly 500 groups she studied in her book *How Terrorism Ends*, only about 5 per cent came to an end after achieving their stated aims (Cronin 2009: 81). Abrahms also sustains that terrorism is a coercive method with a poor record, and estimates the rate of success at 7 per cent (Abrahms 2006). Jones and Libicki similarly examined the demise of 648 terrorist groups between 1968 and 2006 and concluded that 10 per cent of the groups ended their campaigns after obtaining victory in the form of significant policy concessions (Jones and Libicki 2008). According to Jones (2017), large-scale insurgency (an active revolt or uprising) has a superior track record in comparison to terrorism (35 per cent), whereas Chenoweth and Stephan have argued that nonviolent civil resistance has the most favourable record (52 per cent, according to Chenoweth and Stephan 2011).

Historically, only a handful of well-known terrorist campaigns have skilfully used political violence to create compliant behaviour in their opponents. This is the case of the ethno-nationalist campaigns in British-ruled Palestine, Cyprus and Algeria in the aftermath of World War II. As argued by Bruce Hoffman, the tactical 'successes' and political victories won by groups like the Irgun (the Zionist paramilitary organization that operated in Mandate Palestine between 1931 and 1948), EOKA (the Greek Cypriot nationalist paramilitary organization to end British rule in Cyprus), and the FLN (the National Liberation Front Algeria) demonstrated that—notwithstanding the repeated denials of the governments they confronted—terrorism does 'work' (Hoffman 2006: 61). Paul Wilkinson further established a connection between nationalism and effectiveness when arguing that if 'the success of terrorist movements is to be judged by their ability to realize their long-term political objectives, then those in the nationalist category have the best record' (Wilkinson 2011: 21).

The question 'when does terrorism work?' assumes that terrorism can sometimes be effective. If terrorism was completely ineffective, why would so many groups continue to use this coercive instrument in so many regions? And what would explain the rising number of worldwide terrorist incidents since the 1970s? It is entirely possible that violent extremists are misguided and ignore the poor record of terrorist campaigns of the past. But it is also possible that illegitimate violence is seen by perpetrators as the 'weapon of the weak' for a cause with little chance of success. There may also be short-term considerations, privately held goals or the desire to respond to a pressing grievance that prevail over the realization of long-term strategic goals (e.g. decolonization, revolution, regime change, etc.). Nonetheless, there must be some well-founded expectation that political violence can be useful. Otherwise, why would so many groups use it in the first instance?

Determining whether a group has been successful or not is a challenging task. The examples of EOKA, Irgun or the FLN are historical examples of success because they managed to realize their ultimate goal, which was to break free from colonial power. Their violent campaigns forced the British and French authorities to overreact with counterproductive and self-defeating measures that increased indigenous support for guerrilla warfare. It is also possible to argue that doomsday cults like Aum Shinrikyo (and terrorist organization founded by Shoko Asahara in 1984) and the Branch Davidians (a religious sect which was founded in 1955 by Benjamin Roden) failed to bring about the apocalypse or Christ's second coming. But what about cases which obtained tactical successes but failed to realize their long-term goals? What about the terrorist campaigns of the IRA in Ireland and ETA in Spain (see Case Study 19.1)? Arguably, their ethno-nationalist mobilizations failed in defeating their government opponents and establishing new sovereign states but were successful at capturing attention, instilling fear, polarizing society, imposing a credible story of 'conflict', and institutionalizing organizations that challenged elected governments for decades (Muro 2008; English 2012; Leonisio et al. 2017). The fuzziness of goals and the need to distinguish between publicly stated goals and privately held ones are examined in Case Study 19.1.

CASE STUDY 19.1

The End of ETA

The Basque organization ETA (Euskadi Ta Askatasuna, Basque Homeland and Freedom) laid down its arms on 20 October 2011 after 43 years of violent campaigning. The separatist campaign took 845 lives, plus hundreds of displaced and injured people as well as an estimated economic cost of about 10 per cent of the Basque region's GDP (see Photo 19.1).

ETA had emerged during the dictatorship of General Franco (1939–1975) but its lethality increased in the late 1970s as Spain transitioned to democracy. ETA killed 845 individuals during its campaign, 802 during the democratic period (95 per cent) and 43 under the dictatorship (5 per cent). Most victims were members of the Civil Guards, Spain's national police force, and both local and national politicians who were opposed to ETA's separatist demands.

The goals and history of ETA are linked to the so-called Basque Movement of National Liberation (*Movimiento de Liberación Nacional Vasco*—MLNV), a self-named network of organizations founded in 1974 and made up of a number of interconnected political groups, social agents and NGOs with interests in the field of feminism, environmentalism, internationalism, Basque culture, youth, students, and prisoners' rights. The key actors of this network that legitimized the use of terrorism and provided social and political support for ETA's actions were the political party Herri Batasuna (and successors), and the trade union LAB (Muro 2008).

These satellite organizations nourished ETA with the necessary human, material, moral, and logistical resources to continue fighting Spain and account for the terrorist organization's longevity. Without this radical ideology and activism, ETA would not have been a resilient insurgent group but an underground movement incapable of fighting a 'Long War' against Spanish security forces. The existence of a stable radical social environment (up to 15 per cent of the Basque electorate) allowed ETA to fight a war of attrition against the Spanish state with the goal of forcing the authorities to allow secession.

The use of terrorist violence delivered some tactical results in the forms of policy concessions and peace negotiations as well as provoking some excessive use of force on the part of Spanish security forces (e.g. torture or GAL death squads). Within the Basque context, ETA's campaign of extortion, murder, and kidnappings was widely reported by the media and this publicity allowed ETA to become a powerful and influential actor. ETA intimidated opponents, polarized society, and disseminated its interpretation that violence was an indicator of a wider ethnic struggle opposing Basques and Spaniards (and also French). However, as ETA disarmed

PHOTO 19.1 The flag of the Basque Country on the left, and the Spanish flag on the right.

and dissolved itself, the Spanish government refused to make political concessions or improve the conditions of imprisoned ETA members (etarras).

ETA's violent campaign is an example of how terrorism can deliver tactical gains and strategic loss. Having failed to achieve its goal of creating an independent socialist state for the seven regions in northern Spain and south-west France that separatists claimed as their own, ETA unilaterally decided to end its 'armed activity' after years of operational decline. In the end, terrorism was also detrimental for the Basque secessionist cause, which came to be associated with indiscriminate violence against civilians.

But why did ETA declare a unilateral ceasefire in 2011? What are the causal factors that led the Basque group towards its end? A combination of internal and external variables account for its demise. The main external cause was Spain's counter-terrorist policy (and the close collaboration with France) that eventually brought about the operational decline of the organization and delegitimized its violent activism. The main internal cause was the gradual loss of social support and the realization by ETA leaders that terrorism, defined as the deliberate creation and exploitation of fear through violence or the threat of violence in the pursuit of political change, was ineffective in gaining policy concessions. In short, the efficiency of Spain's counter-terrorist policy and the loss of social support brought about ETA's demise (Leonisio, Molina, and Muro 2017).

QUESTIONS

1. Was ETA's terrorist campaign effective?
2. Was ETA defeated or did it disband voluntarily?

Unpacking the range of tactical and strategic goals is essential if scholars and students aspire to incorporate complex cases in which both instances of success and failure can be detected. Expanding the range of classification possibilities allows researchers to distinguish between the goals of the individual vs. those of the organization, the leaders vs. the rank and file and the goals of the organization vs. those of the support base. For example, there is evidence of 'bias to action' in terrorist groups where radical leaders and 'trigger-happy' recruits favour indiscriminate violence as a way of promoting themselves, getting to the top of the organizational chart and dictating action over reflection. There is also evidence that the priority for any living organization, terrorist groups included, is its own survival (Della Porta 2013; Young and Dugan 2014). Groups act to advance their goals, but also for reasons of 'their own' such as prolonging their own longevity through cooperation or violent rivalry (Phillips 2014, 2015; Acosta 2016). The need to address inner needs (organizational disarray, ideological dissent, competition for leadership, splintering, etc.) may also account for specific actions that cannot be explained by solely referring to long-term strategic objectives (Staniland 2014). In short, the concepts 'effective' and 'ineffective' cannot capture the complexity of a terrorist campaign.

Judging the efficacy of terrorism largely depends on the definition of 'effectiveness,' and the operationalization of both 'success' and 'failure.' Scholars may define effectiveness as a discrete variable that takes on the values of 'victory' or 'defeat,' or as an elastic measurement that can take on different values (e.g. total defeat, tactical advance, partial victory, total victory, etc.). Using a continuous variable with a wider range of values enables the coding of campaigns that ended with clear victory or defeat but also those that obtained mixed results. Success may mean different things to different terrorist groups and the idea of success itself may change over time as circumstances and aims evolve. An additional complication lies in the fact that terrorist groups may have a multiplicity of goals (internal, organizational, ideological, military, propaganda, etc.) and that some will be realized whereas others will not. How do researchers code victory in one area and defeat in another? For example, how should one evaluate a group that gains some policy concessions and popularizes a widely felt grievance, but fails to survive as an effective violent organization? The group's judgement could be that failure in maximizing casualties and producing high costs among the opponents is compensated for the fact that the community of reference has been 'awoken,' either politically or by the start of an insurgent movement. These are some of the challenges researchers face when operationalizing fuzzy concepts into measurable indicators.

Peter Krause has suggested that the crux of the matter is the conceptual definition of political effectiveness (Krause 2017). Coding a variety of political outcomes produced by the terrorist campaign is only possible if a distinction is first made between short-term tactical returns and long-term strategic results. Terrorist groups have a variety of time horizons and they combine strategic demands with the tactical use of violence to create fear. According to Brian Jenkins, 'incidents in which terrorists deliberately aim to kill large numbers of people or cause widespread damage are relatively rare' (Jenkins 1975: 4).

At the same time, it is important to distinguish between clear cases of failure and success. Between these two extremes, one can have an interval where cases of organizational success or partial failure can be accommodated. A combination of these six concepts (tactical-strategic, partial success/failure, and complete success/failure) would create a 2 by 4 table in which the effectiveness of terrorist groups could be coded in at least eight different ways. This table would allow for the debate on effectiveness to move beyond dummy variables and identify success in relation to a wider range of goals. As argued by Richard English (2016), terrorist campaigns are not black-and-white phenomena but a series of events which may not lead to the realization of the stated goals, but to the partial success of secondary aims.

19.4 WHEN AND WHERE DOES TERRORISM WORK?

If terrorism can sometimes work in delivering short-term goals we then need to turn our attention to 'when' and 'where' terrorism will work. Tactical and strategic success may be dependent on many variable and contextual settings, the most important of which will be the groups' longevity (see also Chapter 13). A terrorist group which lasts a few months cannot implement lasting change, and needs to either prioritize organizational survival, or risk extinction.

At the most basic level, however, the duration of the terrorist campaign as well as its efficacy will depend on three crucial elements:

(1) The terrorists' relationship with their communities
(2) The types of goals they fight for
(3) The efficacy of the counter-terrorist effort

First, terrorist efficacy will depend on the military capabilities of the clandestine group, the relationship with its support base, the ability to fundraise and recruit, and the power to persuade two key audiences: enemy governments and the population they represent or wish to control. Some degree of institutionalization and the ability to form an efficient organization will be necessary but not sufficient factors for success.

Existing research argues that there is a relationship between organizational capabilities and the power to hurt. For example, Asal and Rethemeyer (2008) argue that membership size and other organizational resources are significant predictors of terrorist lethality. At the same time, terrorist groups that exclusively focus on their internal workings and neglect the aggrieved populations they claim to represent often find it difficult to survive (Rapoport 2004: 58; Mesquita and Dickson 2007). Using excessive force or indiscriminate violence can provoke effects such as an excessive response from the state or a backlash from the constituency of sympathizers. The social perception of what constitutes a legitimate target is not easily transformed and terrorist groups must operate within the moral boundaries of their constituency, or risk a negative reaction from the supporters they claim to represent. In democracies, this means that groups who target civilians indiscriminately are unlikely to gain the policy concessions they desire (Abrahms 2006, 2012). Ultimately, an organization's popularity and survival depend on a consistent stream of support.

Second, the effectiveness of a terrorist campaign will depend on whether the goals of the group are attainable or not. Those fighting for tangible goals and specific policy concessions find that terrorism has a useful agenda-setting function in influencing the salience of issues. As argued by Martha Crenshaw, terrorism is useful in putting a matter of political change on the public agenda (Crenshaw 1988: 17). Furthermore, organizations with limited goals tend to be more successful than groups with maximalist demands who reject incremental change (Rapoport 2004: 59). Organizations that demand specific policies such as regional autonomy or economic transfers for their constituency have more probabilities of obtaining policy concessions than those with non-negotiable causes like realizing Armageddon or overthrowing global capitalism.

The strategic goals of left-wing terrorist groups such as the Red Brigades or the Red Army Faction were not achieved because the so-called 'armed struggle' failed to replace capitalist imperial powers with dictatorships of the proletariat, which were unrealistic objectives. Likewise, dogmatist groups like ISIS who aim to create a new state in the sovereign territory of Iraq and Syria while challenging the foundations of the Westphalian system faced a more daunting task than groups that pursue tractable goals. This distinction between types of goals echoes Paul Wilkinson's distinction between 'corrigible' and 'incorrigible' terrorism. 'Corrigible terrorists,' he argued, include those fighting for attainable, practical goals which are negotiable in the end. 'Incorrigible terrorists' include those fighting for ideological and 'pure' causes which are neither tangible nor negotiable (Wilkinson 2011: 7).

Thirdly, efficacy will also depend on the counter-terrorism and resilience of targeted societies. According to Cronin, terrorism virtually always fails, 'as long as policymakers are wise enough to avoid ceding power to this treacherous use of force' (Cronin 2009: 206). Walter has also argued that ethnic minorities who fight for self-determination decide whether to challenge based in part on whether the government has made concessions in the past, and whether the government can be expected to do so in the future (Walter 2006). Beyond the strategic environment in which perpetrators and governments operate, the fact is that terrorists continue to take up weapons against failed states and advanced democracies.

This is not to say, however, that all individuals have the same statistical chance of being a target of terrorism. People in stable democracies have a higher probability of dying from heart disease, a car accident or even falling out of bed than from a terrorist attack. The majority of terrorist incidents are concentrated in a handful of states with problems of governance. In 2016, for example, three-quarters of deaths from terrorism affected only five countries: Iraq, Afghanistan, Nigeria, Syria, and Pakistan. If an additional five countries were added to the list—Somalia, Turkey, Yemen, the Democratic Republic of Congo, and South Sudan—the attacks perpetrated against these ten countries accounted for 86.5 per cent of all terrorist attacks in 2016. Furthermore, only 2 per cent of all 186,110 terrorist fatalities in the 2002–16 period occurred in OECD countries (typically democratic countries). Evidence suggests that richer democracies are less affected by terrorism than areas of conflict and that, when they are affected, they have more legitimate resources to combat it (Aksoy et al. 2012; Chenoweth 2013).

CASE STUDY 19.2

Shining Path

Sendero Luminoso (Shining Path, see Photo 19.2) can be used to illustrate the difference between tactical success and strategic failure as well as the difficulty in distinguishing between terrorist groups and insurgencies.

The Communist Party of Peru—Shining Path (PCP-SL) (Spanish: Partido Comunista del Perú—Sendero Luminoso), more commonly known as the Shining Path, was a revolutionary party and terrorist organization that aimed to replace the 'bourgeois' Peruvian state with a communist regime. The PCP-SL fought a 'people's war' against the Peruvian state between 1980 and 2000 and at the peak of its organizational power had about 3,500 active terrorists (senderistas).

Abimael Guzmán was the founder and charismatic leader of Shining Path. He was an admirer of Mao Zedong's Cultural Revolution in China (1966–1976) and a firm believer that the peasantry (not the working class) needed to use brutal methods to obtain revolutionary goals. The hierarchical structure of Shining Path made it possible for 'decapitation' to bring about the downfall of the Maoist group. Guzmán was arrested in 1992 and his last successor, Comrade Artemio, was captured in 2012.

The followers of the group used both guerrilla warfare and urban terrorism. The revolutionary insurgents followed the Maoist (the form of communism developed by Mao Zedong) model of 'people's war' in which guerrilla warfare started in the countryside and ended in cities, just before the masses would gain power. The group maintained its rural stronghold in the Andean highlands, but was also able to routinely target the capital city of Peru, Lima. The senderistas used urban terrorism against civilians (politicians, trade unionists, journalists, elected officials, etc.), police stations, and critical infrastructure (such as roads, bridges, railways, and energy grids).

According to a 2003 report from the Truth and Reconciliation Commission, the internal conflict resulted in 69,000 people killed or 'disappeared', and other thousands of victims of sexual violence, torture, and forced displacement. The Maoist group was responsible for 31,000 deaths (44 per cent), mostly civilians and members of the military. The remaining deaths and disappearances were linked to the actions of the Peruvian security forces, anti-rebel peasant militias trained by the military, terrorist groups such as the Túpac Amaru Revolutionary Movement (MRTA) as well as drug trafficking organizations. A 2019 study disputed the casualty figures from the Commission and argued that the Peruvian state accounted for a larger share of killings than the Shining Path.

IS TERRORISM EFFECTIVE?

PHOTO 19.2 Revolutionary propaganda poster from The Shining Path (Sendero Luminoso). The poster is a complicated montage of images: front and centre under the banner of Maoism, a demonstration of indigenous people burn the American flag, and demand the implementation of Maoist policies. Above in the sky is the triumvirate of Karl Marx, Vladimir Lenin, and Mao Zedong, joined by Abimael Guzmán, the Shining Path leader imprisoned by the Peruvian government in 1992.

Shining Path did not achieve its strategic goal of overthrowing the state by guerrilla warfare and creating the People's Republic of Peru, but it did manage to terrorize Peruvian society for decades, especially the impoverished peasantry of rural areas. The tactical and organizational goals of the groups evolved and changed under increasing pressure of the Peruvian security forces. Shining Path's goals shifted from waging a revolutionary and peasant war from the Andean regions of Ayacucho, Huancavelica, and Apurímac, to both using insurgent tactics and urban terrorism. At the time of writing in 2021, Shining Path have publicly recognized the failure of the 'armed struggle', but the few dozen members left refused to disband.

QUESTIONS

1. Were the goals of Shining Path 'realistic'?
2. Was Shining Path a terrorist or an insurgent group? And was it effective?

The effectiveness debate cannot be resolved until researchers define precisely what is meant by 'effectiveness' and make explicit their coding challenges when deciding whether a violent campaign has succeeded or failed. A way forward could be to unpack the term 'political effectiveness' into short-term tactical and long-term strategic goals, and acknowledge that its operationalization has to assume that victory and defeat are poles of a continuous variable, not a binary one. A rich understanding of the conditions faced by terrorists on the ground (as provided by qualitative researchers) would also allow quantitative scholars to have an in-depth understanding of success and failure. Finally, the efficaciousness of political violence also depends on elements such as the strength of the group (e.g. capabilities and constituency), its ultimate aims and the response of the government and audience that is being targeted, namely the counter-terrorist policy.

19.5 WHAT DO TERRORISTS WANT?

Ultimately, the existing divide over the question of effectiveness is partly explained by the fact that scholars differ in how they define the *real* goals of terrorist groups, and whether their campaigns have ended in success or failure. There is also a history of selection bias where scholars tend to focus on successful terrorist groups for which there is abundant data. These methodological discrepancies account for the scholarly dispute but they cannot explain why terrorists continue to use a violent action that analysts consider to be ineffective. A productive resolution of the debate will only come to those who take seriously the 'working conditions' of terrorists and closely examine how terrorism might work for them.

Why do terrorists continue to adopt a method considered to be ineffective? The answer is that terrorists believe that the benefits outweigh the costs, and estimate this coercive tactic to be superior to other available alternatives (such as conventional politics or non-violent campaigns of protest). From the terrorists' perspective, indiscriminate violence against non-combatants can be beneficial in areas such as getting the attention of the enemy, ensuring organizational survival, and gaining recognition for a cause, to name a few. These are briefly examined next.

Terrorism can help in popularizing a grievance, gaining social support, and provoking a counter-reaction from the opponent. Political violence is useful for spreading fear, provoking a government reaction, and magnifying the voices of terrorists, as well as for obtaining support from the constituencies the group claims to represent. In short, terrorism is not generally supposed to occur in the absence of public support for it. Thus, terrorism is also useful in 'politicizing' an issue and creating a cycle of social mobilization that accompanies the violent dimension.

Political violence can sometimes evolve in parallel to a wave of mobilization that scholars have dubbed a 'cycle of protest,' which is a 'phase of heightened conflict across the social system, with a rapid diffusion of collective action from mobilized to less mobilized' (Tarrow 1998, 142). Ultimately, the decision to take up weapons for propagandistic and psychological impact is a way of acquiring power for those who do not have it, and are too weak to confront the state openly (Crenshaw 1988: 16).

Because of the increased ability to influence others, terrorists are able to project an image of influence that far exceeds their actual strength. Even if the overall violent campaign fails to obtain the end results, it is always possible for militants to justify political violence by the wider impact on a community of reference. For example, the popularity of the Jihadist-Salafist cause that is often associated with al-Qaeda and ISIS owes much of its success to the backlash against the US counter-terrorist strategy, particularly the Global War on Terror, and the full-scale invasions of Iraq and Afghanistan, as well as other combat operations in Yemen, Pakistan, and Syria. The worldwide campaign against terrorism allowed the global jihadist movement to disseminate the message that America was at war with Islam, and that it was necessary to expel the 'crusaders' from Muslim lands. Ultimately, the global insurgent movement that emanated from al-Qaeda corroborated the belief that terrorism can be useful in provoking a response from opponents, disrupting and discrediting the process of government, and widening the support base.

Terrorism can also help organizations survive. The history of terrorism demonstrates that many groups do not outlast their first year of existence and that even disciplined groups who survive more than 12 months are not very lethal (Vittori 2009; Phillips 2019). Movements that manage to build cohesive organizations during an initial phase later endure state repression and 'outbid' possible competitors in the marketplace of political violence in a second phase (Kydd and Walter 2006; Phillips 2014). By the time they have consolidated organizational power, their efforts to survive might have diverted them from the original goals that justified their emergence in favour of prioritizing the provision of both cohesion and discipline. What is clear is that managing the internal life of groups and consolidating organizational power is essential to building an effective combat machine.

In the case of the Colombian FARC (Revolutionary Armed Forces of Colombia—People's Army), the complex relationship between drug trafficking and political violence drove the largest guerrilla group in Colombia to mutate into a narco-guerrilla outfit with significant interests in drug production and trafficking. The metamorphosis of the FARC during the 1990s begged the question of whether the guerrilla force had become an armed group that used drug trafficking to secure revenues for war, or whether it had simply transformed into a paramilitary group of drug dealers with political interests. The point is that cocaine crops increased the military standing of the FARC, but also diverted its attention from its political strategy to seize national power.

Ultimately, groups like the FARC face a dilemma balancing organizational control and political effectiveness, which is in itself contingent on a particular constellation of competitors and opponents, the most important of which is the state. Existing work on organizational structures has recognized this dilemma of internal organizational control and external projection, and argues that violence might be strategically useful in helping insurgent groups maintain cohesion and survive. Paul Staniland, for example, has argued that material resources alone do not determine the success or failure of insurgent groups, and other factors such as ideology and organization bolster or undermine group survival (Staniland 2014: 221). In short, terrorism can be instrumental in prolonging conflicts and lengthening the life spans of groups that engage in it.

Terrorism can be an effective means of communicating with audiences. As indicated by Brian Jenkins, the primary role of 'violent propaganda' is to communicate a message to a specific government and to world opinion, which may explain why terrorists 'want a lot of people watching and a lot of people listening and not a lot of people dead' (Jenkins 1975). Even for groups like ISIS, who used suicide missions to inflict the maximum damage possible on the opponent, the effect of violence on audiences is still an important part of their decision-making calculus. The use of videos distributed through social media—and the level of effort these groups devote both to capturing their acts and delivering them globally with high-production values—demonstrates the importance of audience reactions to their activities (Roy 2017). The main purpose of these propaganda machines is to publicize their cause to the enemy and sympathizers, but also to potential recruits, who are supposed to be inspired by the sacrifice of individual Mujahideen. After all, terrorism allows a few determined individuals to inflict considerable damage on the state, which is a far more powerful enemy.

A good example of how terrorism can expand the support base and instil fear among opponents would be the US military withdrawal from Lebanon after a suicide attack that struck a chord with the American audience. In October 1983, 241 marines were killed with the loss of one assailant. Four months later President Ronald Reagan pulled out all the American combat troops there, rather than face another suicide mission. In this example, a suicide operation created major benefits in terms of visibility, prestige, and popularity for Islamic Jihad (and elements of what would eventually become Hezbollah—a Lebanese Shia Islamist political party and militant group).

Non-state terrorist actors will continue to use or threaten to use violence against civilians because it can help them survive, strengthen their support structures, popularize a cause or grievance, provoke a counter-reaction and discredit the government. This list of tactical gains is not exhaustive but highlights some of the returns that account for why terrorist groups on the ground continue to use violence to the bewilderment of experts, who often adopt a 10,000-foot view which overstates the long-term objectives of political violence.

Contrary to the approaches of analysts and strategists who privilege outcome goals (e.g. Abrahms) organizations on the ground are mainly concerned with their own survival. An organization that collapses and disappears no longer has the ability to fight the 'long war' against its opponents, and it is understandable that pragmatic leaders may privilege short-term organizational needs over utopian goals. The disconnect between the study of terrorism and its practice (as indicated by the real-world conditions terrorists face every day) explains the lack of progress in the effectiveness debate.

Ultimately, the effectiveness debate can only move forward if scholars resolve their methodological disputes but also incorporate the view from the ground. This is an area where historical research and in-depth qualitative studies can challenge the coding strategies of large databases of terrorist incidents. It is also essential to address the multi-dimensional aspect of political efficacy (including organizational, tactical, and strategic), and expand the levels of analysis to incorporate the micro, meso and macro dimensions.

19.5.1 Ways forward for the effectiveness debate?

Scholars are unlikely to resolve the effectiveness any time soon. The positions are too distant from each other to be reconciled, and there are fundamental methodological disagreements that prevent a productive resolution.

First, the definition of 'terrorism' used by scholars varies greatly and that has implications as to what cases are examined and what cases are excluded from the sample (e.g. cases of narco-guerrilla like the Colombian FARC). Second, the definition of 'effectiveness' is rarely made explicit. Whereas some scholars focus on the tactical returns of violence, others focus on the strategic goals of terrorists (e.g. revolution, secession, etc.). Third, there is the issue of 'selection bias', where successful groups with long histories of violence are often used as illustrations whereas lesser-known terrorist groups with brief histories are ignored. The clue to resolving the effectiveness debate is the strength of terrorism as much as its weakness.

19.6 CONCLUSION

Is terrorism effective? There are two opposing views in the debate on whether terrorism works. The first posits that terrorist violence is an effective tactic for inducing government concessions and swaying public opinion. The second view argues that terrorists very rarely achieve their core political ends and that terrorist groups only obtain tactical victories before they become unstable and disintegrate. While most terrorist organizations fail to achieve their political objectives, groups across regions continue to use terrorism at increasing rates. How is this possible, given the dismal achievements of terrorism? Why do terrorists continue to use a tactic that does not work?

Terrorist tactics have been used as an instrument to survive, gain supporters, and communicate the goals and resolve of the terrorist group. As a form of fighting, terrorism has a political logic, and it is chosen by perpetrators to improve their effectiveness relative to alternative tactics (insurgency, guerrilla warfare, nonviolent civil resistance, etc.), which may be perceived as ineffective.

Examples of tactical gains such as organizational survival, acquiring sympathizers, boosting status, or provoking a response from the opponent are common, but it is much harder to find clear instances of strategic success where terrorist groups accomplished the political goals they set for themselves, be it secession, overthrowing capitalism or expelling an occupying force. Eventually, the tactical use of terrorism brings cohesion to the group's organization, ideology, goals and constituencies. On occasions, terrorism is seen as a tactic of 'last resort' and in others, it is a last desperate effort to accomplish political change.

The political logic of terrorism is not merely to ensure survival and growth but to create the conditions where victory can take place. Future research in this area will need to examine the perceptions of terrorists in order to comprehend their cost-benefit calculations. The way forward also involves turning the effectiveness question on its head and revisit the efficaciousness of counter-terrorism.

Ultimately, collective security is a relational act that brings the state and the terrorist group into conflict with each other. Terrorist campaigns are often studied in isolation and it is essential to 'bring the state back in' to provide a full picture of the insecurity spiral involving these two actors. At its most basic level, the effectiveness of counter-terrorism determines the effectiveness of terrorism, and vice versa. Also, the debate on effectiveness has been dominated by quantitative approaches but unpacking the true meaning of effectiveness for perpetrators can only be provided by qualitative research. A more inclusive research agenda will be in a better position to reconcile existing findings that contradict one another such as those referring to longevity, lethality, and effectiveness.

Establishing the instrumental character of terrorism in pursuing political objectives could provide important clues as to when counter-terrorism will work. What should be the overall goal of agencies which aim to combat and prevent terrorism? To disrupt the operational, logistical and financial activities of violent extremists or to apprehend individual terrorists and defeat the groups they belong to?

When striking a balance between short-term and long-term goals, policymakers and security officers could bear in mind that most terrorist groups fail to achieve their strategic goals but often strike some tactical success along the way (such as advertising, provocation, morale building, weakening the government to name a few). This empirical fact can reinforce our democratic principles and belief that balanced legal frameworks and the democratically established rule of law will eventually prevail. However, the numerous instances of partial success seem to suggest that nonstate actors will continue to use violence against civilians to threaten, coerce, and intimidate the societies we live in.

DISCUSSION QUESTIONS

1. Why is there no agreement on the effectiveness debate?
2. Does terrorism work in delivering tactical and strategic goals?
3. Why has terrorism increased since the 1970s if this tactic is ineffective in delivering political goals?
4. Does success depend on whether the terrorist's goals are negotiable or non-negotiable?
5. What does 'efficacy' or 'success' mean for a terrorist organization?
6. How would you describe the transformation of a terrorist group into a political party? As success or failure?

Visit the online resources for pointers on how to answer the discussion questions, links to useful web sources, and guidance on accessing databases:
www.oup.com/he/Wilson-Muro1e

GUIDE TO FURTHER READING

Although we have touched on the political effectiveness of terrorism within this chapter, there are a number of other important works that more deeply describe how terrorism works and explain what success and failure means for non-state terrorist actors.

Abrahms, Max (2012) 'The Political Effectiveness of Terrorism Revisited'. *Comparative Political Studies* 45.3: 366–393. *This paper argues that terrorism does not work and puts forward a theory of why governments resist compliance when their civilians are targeted.*

English, Richard (2016) *Does Terrorism Work?* Oxford: Oxford University Press. *This book provides a historian's answer to the question of effectiveness debate and focuses on four case studies: Al-Qaeda, the Provisional IRA, Hamas, and ETA.*

Fortna, Virginia Page (2015) 'Do Terrorists Win? Rebels' Use of Terrorism and Civil War Outcomes', *International Organization* 69.3: 519–556. *The paper evaluates the advantages and disadvantages of terrorism relative to other tactics used in civil war. The author concludes that terrorist rebel groups are less effective than non-terrorist groups.*

Krause, Peter (2013) 'The Political Effectiveness of Non-State Violence: A Two-Level Framework to Transform a Deceptive Debate', *Security Studies*, June, 22(2): 259–294. *Krause provides a methodological critique of the debate and suggests a fruitful two-level framework that distinguishes between strategic and organizational goals.*

Kydd, Andrew and Walter, Barbara (2006) 'The Strategies of Terrorism', *International Security*, Vol. 31, No. 1, 49–80. *This is a classic piece that portrays terrorism as a form of costly signalling. Terrorists wish to signal that they have the strength and will to impose costs on those who oppose them and employ five primary strategies.*

Thomas, Jakana (2014) 'Rewarding Bad Behaviour: How Governments Respond to Terrorism in Civil War', *American Journal of Political Science*, Vol. 58, No. 4, 804–818. *This paper examines markers of success and demonstrates that rebel groups are both more likely to be granted the opportunity to participate in negotiations and offered more concessions when they execute a greater number of terror attacks during civil wars.*

REFERENCES

Abrahms, M. (2006) 'Why Terrorism Does Not Work', *International Security*, 31: 42–78.

Abrahms, M. (2012) 'The Political Effectiveness of Terrorism Revisited', *Comparative Political Studies*, 45 (3): 366–393.

Acosta, B. (2016) 'Dying for Survival: Why Militant Organizations Continue to Conduct Suicide Attacks', *Journal of Peace Research*, 52 (2): 180–196.

Aksoy, D. (2014) 'Elections and the Timing of Terrorist Attacks', *The Journal of Politics*, 76 (4): 899–913.

Aksoy, D., Carter, D. B., and Wright, J. (2012) 'Terrorism in Dictatorships', *The Journal of Politics*, 74: 810–826.

Asal, V. and Rethermeyer, R. K. (2008) 'The Nature of the Beast: Organizational Structures and the Lethality of Terrorist Attacks', *Journal of Politics*, 70: 437–449.

Bapat, N. A. (2005) 'Insurgency and the Opening of Peace Processes', *Journal of Peace Research*, 42 (6): 699–717.

Chenoweth, E. and Stephan, M. (2011) *Why Civil Resistance Works: The Strategic Logic of Nonviolent Conflict*. New York: Columbia University Press.

Chenoweth, E. (2013) 'Terrorism and Democracy', *Annual Review of Political Science*, 16: 355–378.

Crenshaw, M. (1987) 'Theories of Terrorism: Instrumental and Organizational Approaches', *Journal of Strategic Studies*, 10 (4): 13–31.

Crenshaw, M. (1988) 'The Logic of Terrorism: Terrorist Behaviour as a Product of Strategic Choice', in Walter Reich, (ed.), *Origins of Terrorism: Psychologies, Ideologies, Theologies, States of Mind*. Washington, DC: Woodrow Wilson Center Press.

Cronin, A. K. (2009) *How Terrorism Ends*. Princeton, NJ: Princeton University Press.

Della Porta, D. (2013) *Clandestine Political Violence*. Cambridge: Cambridge University Press.

Dershowitz, A. (2002) *Why Terrorism Works: Understanding the Threat, Responding to the Challenge*. New Haven, Conn.: Yale University Press.

English, R. (2009) *Terrorism: How to Respond*. Oxford: Oxford University Press.

English, R. (2012) *Armed Struggle: The History of the IRA*. London: Pan.

English, R. (2016) *Does Terrorism Work?* Oxford: Oxford University Press.

Fortna, V. P. (2015) 'Do Terrorists Win? Rebels' Use of Terrorism and Civil War Outcomes', *International Organization*, 69 (3): 1–38.

Gould, E. D. and Klor, E. F. (2010) 'Does Terrorism Work?', *Quarterly Journal of Economics*, 125 (4):1459–1510.

Hoffman, B. (2006) *Inside Terrorism*. New York: Columbia University Press.

Howard, M. (2002) *Clausewitz: A Very Short Introduction*. Oxford: Oxford University Press.

Jenkins, B. M.(1975) 'International Terrorism: A New Mode of Conflict', in David Carlton and Carlo Schaerf (eds), *International Terrorism and World Security*. London: Croom Helm.

Jenkins, B. M. (1975) 'Will Terrorists Go Nuclear?', RAND Paper. Accessed from: https://www.rand.org/pubs/papers/P5541.html

Jones, S. D. (2017) *Waging Insurgent Warfare*. Oxford: Oxford University Press.

Jones, S. G. and Libicki, M. C. (2008) *How Terrorist Groups End*. Santa Monica, CA: RAND.

Kalyvas, S. (2004) 'The Paradox of Terrorism in Civil War', *The Journal of Ethics*, 8 (1): 97–138.

Krause, P., 2013 'The Political Effectiveness of Non-State Violence: A Two-Level Framework to Transform a Deceptive Debate', *Security Studies*, 22 (2): 259–294.

Krause, P. (2017) *Rebel Power: Why National Movements Compete, Fight, and Win*. Ithaca, NY: Cornell University Press.

Kydd, A. and Walter, B. (2006) 'The Strategies of Terrorism', *International Security*, 31 (1): 49–80.

Lake, D. A. (2002). 'Rational Extremism: Understanding Terrorism in the Twenty-First Century', *Dialogue-IO*, 1: 15–29.

Leonisio, R., Molina, F., and Muro, D. (eds.) (2017) *ETA's Terrorist Campaign: From Violence to Politics, 1968–2015*. London and New York: Routledge.

Mesquita, E. B. & Dickson, E. S. (2007) 'The Propaganda of the Deed: Terrorism, Counterterrorism, and Mobilization', *American Journal of Political Science*, 51 (2): 364–381.

Muro, D. (2008) *Ethnicity and Violence. The Case of Radical Basque nationalism*. London and Abingdon: Routledge.

Muro, D. (2019) *When Does Terrorism Work?*. London and Abingdon: Routledge.

Neumann, P. R. and Smith, M. L. R. (2008) *The Strategy of Terrorism: How it Works, and Why it Fails*. London: Routledge.

Pape, R. A. (2003) 'The Strategic Logic of Suicide Terrorism', *American Political Science Review*, 97 (3): 343–361.

Phillips, B. J. (2014) 'Terrorist Group Cooperation and Longevity', *International Studies Quarterly*, 58 (2): 336–347.

Phillips, B. J., (2015) 'Enemies with Benefits? Violent Rivalry and Terrorist Group Longevity', *Journal of Peace Research*, 52 (1): 62–75.

Phillips, B. J., (2019) 'Do 90 Percent of Terrorist Groups Last Less than a Year? Updating the conventional wisdom', *Terrorism and Political Violence*, 31 (6): 1255–1265.

Rapoport, D. C. (2001) 'The International World as Some Terrorists Have Seen It: A Look at a Century of Memoirs', in Rapoport, David C. (ed.) *Inside Terrorist Organisations*. London: Frank Cass.

Rapoport, D. (2004) 'The Four Waves of Terrorism', in Cronin, A. K. and Ludes, J. M. (eds.) *Attacking Terrorism*. Washington, DC: Georgetown University Press, 46–73.

Richardson, L. (2015) *Conceptualizing Terrorism*. Oxford: Oxford University Press.

Roy, O. (2017) *Jihad and Death: The Global Appeal of Islamic State*. Oxford: Oxford University Press.

Schelling, T. (1991) 'What Purposes Can International Terrorism Serve?', in *Violence, Terrorism, and Justice*. Raymond Gillespie Frey and Christopher W. Morris (eds.). New York: Cambridge University Press.

Sprinzak, E. (2000) 'Rational Fanatics', *Foreign Policy*, Vol. September–October, 63–73.

Tarrow, S. (1998) *Power in Movement: Social Movements and Contentious Politics*. Cambridge/New York: Cambridge University Press.

Young, J. K. and Dugan, L. (2014) 'Survival of the Fittest: Why Terrorist Groups Endure', *Perspectives on Terrorism*, 8 (2).

Vittori, J. (2009) 'All Struggles Must End: The Longevity of Terrorist Groups', *Contemporary Security Policy*, 30 (3): 444–466.

Walter, B. F. (2006) 'Information, Uncertainty, and the Decision to Secede', *International Organization*, 60 (1): 105–135.

Wilkinson, P. (2011) *Terrorism Versus Democracy: The Liberal State Response*. London: Frank Cass.

Thomas, J. (2014) 'Rewarding Bad Behaviour: How Governments Respond to Terrorism in Civil War', *American Journal of Political Science*, 58 (4): 804–818.

PART THREE

Countering Terrorism

| PART ONE | The State of Terrorism Studies | 15 |

| PART TWO | Issues and Debates in Terrorism Studies | 135 |

| PART THREE | Countering Terrorism | 389 |

20	Counterterrorism Agencies and Their Work	391
21	Responding to Terrorism Nonviolently	413
22	Counterterrorism and Human Rights	434
23	Foreign Policy and Countering Terrorism	454
24	International Organizations and Counter-Terrorism	477
25	Terrorism, Counter-Terrorism, and Technology	497
26	Preventing and Countering Violent Extremism	518
27	Disengagement and Deradicalization Programmes	538
28	Victims of Terrorism and Political Violence	558
29	The End of Terrorist Campaigns	575

CHAPTER 20

Counterterrorism Agencies and Their Work

MARTIN INNES AND HELEN INNES

■ CHAPTER SUMMARY

This chapter focuses upon the work of counterterrorism, both in its moments of high illumination, and when operating more 'in the shadows'. We begin by setting out the defining dilemma of counterterrorism efforts in liberal democracies—the 'demand' posed by the volume of potential risks and threats, inevitably outstrips the available 'supply' of counterterrorism assets. The chapter then attends to policy frameworks that shape and structure counterterrorism interventions by seeking to bring about an end to terrorist activities. The key roles and responsibilities of military, intelligence, and criminal justice agencies are described, highlighting country-level variations in the organization of these arrangements. The chapter shows that in practice, agencies operate in a blended way influenced by several factors, one of which is the spectrum of terrorist threats, and another is the transformations wrought by digital and social media. Mapping the changes in the organization of counterterrorism, one direct effect highlighted is how issues of transparency, oversight, and accountability have become increasingly important.

20.1 INTRODUCTION

Successful terror attacks remain rare (Crenshaw and LaFree, 2017). But when they do occur, the contours of social reaction often follow a pattern (Innes et al., 2018). The period immediately following a terror attack becomes a significant moment where the veil of secrecy that shrouds much counterterrorism work is partially lifted. It moves out of the 'shadows', albeit only partially and temporarily, becoming more publicly visible.

This enhanced visibility is brings to the fore issues of moral ambiguity; the occurrence of terrorist violence both justifies the need for a counterterrorism apparatus, but also illuminates its limits and frailties. The post-attack situation is important for understanding the organization and conduct of counterterrorism, but it provides an incomplete picture. In general terms, much of what is done to counter and manage the risks and threats of politically motivated violence is performed in a relatively low-visibility and clandestine manner. In the post-attack moment, it breaks cover not just as a matter of practicality, but also to try and convey public reassurance that the security apparatus of the state is being deployed to protect from serious harms.

20.2 THE DEMAND AND SUPPLY CHALLENGE

In many terror attacks over the past two decades, the perpetrators had previously come to the attention of the authorities for some reason. In part, this reflects how 'demand', in terms of the numbers of potential terrorist actors, outstrips the 'supply' of counterterrorism resources. Consequently, difficult decisions are taken about what risks and threats to prioritize and actively manage through surveillance and intelligence collection, and which to leave aside.

> **KEY CONCEPTS**
>
> **Demand** In the context of this chapter, this is the quantity of risks and threats that have to be managed by available counterterrorism resources and assets.
>
> **Supply** A short-hand term that captures how key services and interventions are organized, and the amount of investment in them.

The underlying problem of supply and demand equates to a large volume of potential risks and threats that create a demand that inevitably outstrips the available supply of counterterrorism assets. Supply-side factors are never simply just a correlate of the level of demand, but rather differ between countries and contexts. This reflects a range of influences including a country's history of being exposed to terrorism, its legal culture, and traditions.

The contemporary counterterrorism system in liberal democratic countries tends to be built around several key components, that structure and organize responses:

- There is typically (though not in the US, UK, and Canada) a separation between agencies with lead responsibility for managing 'domestic' terrorism and those focusing upon 'international terrorism', albeit their work and agendas intermingle in practice and in relation to specific cases.
- Both police and military perform particular functions and roles. In most jurisdictions, police involvement pivots around specialist units, rather than mainstream generalist officers.
- Police and military usually have primacy for the conduct of different kinds of interventions, supported by intelligence agencies who focus upon the systematic collection, processing and analysis of human and signals intelligence. Especially in Western-liberal democracies, such as the United States, Canada, and the UK, reflecting concerns about the ethics and pragmatics of surveillance, it is usual to have an agency focused upon domestic monitoring, and a different agency leading on foreign collection. For instance, this is the pattern in the UK where MI5 has been focused on domestic monitoring; while MI6 faces outwards to the wider world (Andrew, 2009) Equivalent roles in the USA have been respectively covered by the Federal Bureau of Investigation (FBI) and the Central Intelligence Agency (CIA).
- Reflecting the pace of technological change, many countries have now also developed a more specialist technological capacity and capability to monitor the array of digital communications and digital media that might afford foresight into the intentions and plans of terrorist groups. For example, in the US this is undertaken by the National Security Agency rather than the FBI, CIA, or military intelligence.

Reflecting the involvement of multiple agencies with partially overlapping remits, an increasingly important role in the counterterrorism apparatus is played by units with a specialist co-ordination role. Taking France as an example, counterterrorism investigations, whether they are domestic or foreign in focus, adopt similar logics and practices to other criminal investigations, albeit under the direction of specialist judges from the counterterrorism section of the Public Prosecutor's Office. That said, reflecting its status as a former colonial power, the French military maintains a presence in African countries in the Sahel region for example (in collaboration with Burkina Faso, Chad, Mali, Mauritania, and Niger) to combat jihadist groups.

To scale the demands on counterterrorism agencies, it is worth roughly mapping their volume of activities. For example, by the end of 2019, there had been 45 attacks in 7 countries since 2017, spanning the France, Germany, Belgium, Spain, Finland, and Sweden.

According to Europol's most recent EU Terrorism Situation and Trend report (TE-SAT, 2020) for the European Union, in 2020 there were:

- 57 foiled, failed, and completed terrorist attacks reported by 6 EU Member States.
- 449 individuals were arrested on suspicion of terrorism-related offences in 17 EU Member States, with the highest numbers in France, Belgium, Spain, Germany, and Italy.
- 21 people died because of terrorist attacks in the EU and 54 people were injured.

In the UK at any one time, there are approximately 500 active counterterrorism investigations, involving around 3,000 'subjects of interest' (HM Government, 2018). The British Security Service reports having about 20,000 previous 'subjects' of counterterrorist investigations in its databases. Home Office statistics show that, as of 30 June 2020, there were 243 persons in custody for terrorism-related offences in Great Britain, an increase of 24 on the previous year (Home Office, 2020). There has been a significant shift in the composition of the presenting risks, with a rapidly rising number of cases focused upon far-right terrorism in Western countries (BBC News, 2019), including the 2016 murder of British Labour party MP Jo Cox, and an attack on a London mosque in Finsbury Park in 2017. The British Security Services took over primacy for right-wing terrorism investigations from the police in 2020.

It has been acknowledged that terrorism metrics are increasing over time, albeit there are year-on-year fluctuations. Nesser (2015) describes yearly increases in the number of attacks across Europe between 2000 and 2004, after which time the numbers fell back somewhat, until a sharp increase in 2010. Between 2011 and 2014, there was a sequence of increases and then in 2017 the UK alone encountered five attacks in six months, with an especially large number of casualties associated with the Manchester Arena bombing following a concert by American singer Ariana Grande in 2017. In Australia, between 2014 and 2015, the Australian Security Intelligence Organisation (ASIO) doubled the number of adverse security assessments made in relation to passports and reported 400 ongoing terrorism investigations (Safi, 2015). During this period, three separate Islamist-inspired attacks were committed in Australian within a 13-month period: the September 2014 stabbing of two police officers in Melbourne; the December 2014 siege of a Sydney café; and the October 2015 fatal shooting of a New South Wales police officer (Mullins, 2016).

Accompanying this trajectory has been a diversification in attack methodologies. In the early 2000s when al-Qaeda represented the principal strategic terrorist threat, the key task for counterterrorism agencies was to detect and intercept sophisticated bomb plots. However, with the ascendancy of ISIS around 2014, there was a palpable shift away from these hard-to-design and deliver strategies, requiring high technical expertise and significant planning and preparation on the part of the perpetrators. They were replaced by methods that relied upon brute simplicity, harnessing everyday objects such as cars, vans, and knives to kill. Such methods require very little skill, relying only upon instilling a level of commitment and motivation among those primed to carry them out.

Since 2014, vehicle ramming attacks have occurred in Canada, France, the United States, the United Kingdom, Tajikistan, and Germany. In Norway between 1970 and

2010, terrorism attacks were small in scale and impact, but from 2014 its security service responded to an increased terror threat from extreme Islamists, raising the threat level three times. By 2018, the threat profile was shifting again as support for right-wing extremism was on the rise. Norway suffered two high profile right-wing attacks in 2011 and 2019 from so-called 'lone-wolf' actors. The first by Anders Breivik, who targeted a youth summer camp (see Case Study 15.1), and the second, a shooting by Philip Manshaus at a mosque (Counter Extremist Project, 2020).

Given the scale of demand, prioritizing risks and threats is an important function of the counterterrorism apparatus overall. As revealed by several enquiries launched following terror attacks, for a variety of reasons, and in common with all risk management-based systems, this approach sometimes fails. The following sections 20.3–20.4 consider how approaches to counterterrorism seek to confront this challenge in a coordinated and evidence-based way, through wide-ranging government policy and interventions aimed at accelerating the demise of terrorist activity.

20.3 COUNTERTERRORISM POLICY

Large-scale, multi-faceted government counterterrorism policies seek to manage the risk, stop support for terrorist causes, and protect the lives of citizens and economic interests. This section focuses on the UK CONTEST Strategy on the grounds that it has been highly influential on subsequent strategies developed by a number of European governments, and indeed the European Union's own framework (Coolsaet, 2010; EU, 2020). The core aim and strands of CONTEST are set out in the Key Concepts box.

KEY CONCEPTS

Prepare Processes and systems to anticipate a range of different types of potential attack. Includes both cross-governmental responses and community resilience.

Prevent Activities designed to inhibit and interdict processes of violent radicalization, and those who seek to propagate extremist ideas. This is the most public-facing and politically contentious strand of CONTEST.

Protect Activities often derived from the principles of situational crime prevention to reduce risks and threats to elements of the critical national infrastructure. Minimizes the opportunities for an attack and limits the consequences should one occur.

Pursue The identification and securing of motivated offenders is more in the traditions of police and security service involvement in counterterrorism work.

Its organization around four principal strands is reflected in policy elsewhere. Canada's 2011 strategy of 'Building Resilience against terrorism' is organized and prioritized around the principles of Prevent, Detect, Deny, and Respond (Government of Canada, 2011). Australia's National Counter-Terrorism Strategy and Plan, maintained by the Australia-New Zealand Counter-Terrorism Committee (ANZCTC, 2017), sets out arrangements, governance, and operational responsibilities for its counterterrorism governments and agencies around the principles of Preparedness, Prevention, Response, and Recovery. Norway's Action Plan to prevent radicalization and violent extremism was directly influenced the British Prevent strategy.

The stated aim of the CONTEST strategy is 'to reduce the risk to the UK and its interests overseas from terrorism so that people can go about their lives freely and with confidence' (HMG, 2011). Sir David Omand (2010) set out how the aspiration for it was to enable a 'whole of government' response to the risks and threats posted by international terrorism, in particular the pressing concerns about al-Qaeda at the time.

Analyses of CONTEST have stressed how this cross-government response to terrorism induces a pre-cautionary, preventive, and pre-emptive stance (Walker and McKay, 2015; Mythen, Walklate, and Khan, 2013). This is not dissimilar to what is happening in criminal justice policy more generally, where conduct is 'criminalized' in anticipation of it causing harm (Ashworth and Zedner, 2014; Heath-Kelly, 2013). This suggests a subtle shift has accompanied the implementation of CONTEST; when the focus of counterterrorism is principally overseas, the guiding disposition is far more 'militaristic'. In a domestic context, it 'leans' far more on the logics and practices of criminal justice.

The Prevent strand has proven especially politically contentious, with repeated allegations that it institutionalizes government 'spying' upon communities (Kundani, 2009), and casting Muslims as a de facto 'suspect community' (Pantazis and Pemberton, 2009). Prevent has been subject to three systematic revisions in its lifetime, with a fourth pending. In 2008, the UK government felt it paid insufficient attention to genuinely preventative modes of working and judged it to be overly reliant upon more established 'Pursue' practices. Funding was made available to try and incentivize, with some success, civil society and non-governmental organizations to engage with the challenges of countering extremism in their local communities. Further revisions in 2011 were more explicitly ideologically motivated, reflecting a change to the coalition government the year before. The new administration was of the view that previous versions of Prevent focused upon integrating activities of counter-radicalization, deradicalization and community cohesion building, whereas they now wanted to establish a clearer distinction between counterterrorism, and integration and cohesion work. In 2015, the UK Conservative government explicitly widened Prevent's focus beyond violent extremism, to encompass all forms of extremism (HMG, 2015). When first introduced, Prevent was firmly focused upon Islamist-inspired risks and threats, but it has shifted to include far-right extremism as a core element. This is in part, a correction, but also a reflection of wider trends where the far-right terrorist threat has risen in many countries. UK Government figures for 2017–18 record a total of 394 Prevent referrals to 'Channel', the early intervention multi-agency safeguarding process against violent extremist or terrorist behaviour. Of these, 45 per cent concerned Islamist extremism and 44 per cent right-wing extremism (Home Office, 2018).

20.4 INTERVENTION OUTCOMES

Cronin (2009) identifies seven principal ways that 'terrorism ends', in terms of how and why groups desist from deploying violence in pursuit of their political aims and eventually disintegrate (see also Chapter 29). The challenge for counterterrorism agencies is to engineer situations that accelerate these desistance processes, with the constrained resources that they have. Consistent ongoing pressure upon individuals and their relationships with each other continually risks terrorist groups imploding from mistakes, burnout and collapse. Cronin asserts that interventions conducted by criminal justice agencies and/or the military, especially when they cohere with other trends, do have a role in promoting desistance from terrorism.

Deterrence-based models have long dominated both criminal justice and counterterrorist policies. Such models maintain that an individual's prohibited behaviour can be altered by the threat and imposition of punishment. La Free Dugan and Korte (2009) identified six British counterterrorist interventions aimed at reducing political violence in Northern Ireland between 1969 and 1992, and tested their impact on the risk of new attacks. They first hypothesized a positive 'deterrence model' founded on the belief that assertive policing and the threat of severe consequences would deter individuals and groups from future violence. An alternative proposition was that such interventions would induce a negative 'backlash' effect, increasing violence. The data showed strongest support for backlash models, with only one military surge ('Operation Motorman') deterring violence.

The six interventions tested in the La Free study were all assertive, intrusive, and coercive. As Wilkinson (2001: 102) contends, since 1969, the Northern Ireland conflict exemplified 'the use of military in aid of the civil power', whereby the army were mobilized in support of the police and civil authorities. Whilst distinct from the full militarization of counterterrorism responses seen in some other countries, it nonetheless represents something of a departure from the criminal justice-based approach that many maintain should always be the default option for liberal democratic policies (English, 2014). Strategies aimed at decreasing the benefits of terrorism through non-military means, such as improving the legitimacy of government, solving widespread grievances that produce strain, or attending to situational features that increase the costs of terrorism, might be more effective than strategies based only on increasing punishment (La Free and Dugan, 2009). In the case of Northern Ireland, violence began to recede only when Irish and British Governments began working closer together to find a political settlement, with the Anglo-Irish agreement giving those associated with paramilitary violence a pathway into the political process.

There remains the possibility that antiterrorist interventions might both decrease and *increase* subsequent violence. Certainly, the route to lasting peace in Northern Ireland via the Good Friday Agreement has not been smooth, nor have the fractures disappeared. Avoiding a 'blowback' effect that generates support for the terrorists' cause is a key challenge for all counterterrorism agencies. This is because the aims of their terrorist adversaries can be advanced either by the actions of groups themselves, or by forms of over-reach and over-exertion, that unintentionally degrade the perceived legitimacy of and public permission for particular counterterror interventions.

Sluka's (1989) ethnographic study of the Divis Flats in Belfast, Northern Ireland is one of the most incisive studies of this challenge. Whereas media and public policy rhetoric tends to distinguish between a small group of committed terrorists and everyone else, Sluka constructs a more complex and nuanced picture of the social reality of support and opposition to terrorism. Informed by extensive fieldwork, he argues for a 'spectrum' of positions, rather than just two, that can be adopted by the general public. On the one hand, are people committed to political causes who provide ongoing and active assistance, both material and psychological, to those who directly commit the violent acts. At the other end of the spectrum are those implacably opposed to both the means and ends of the active terrorists. Of most interest to Sluka though, is the range of positions in between these two polarities. The belief and attitudes of people in the middle parts of the spectrum are liable to ebb and flow according to the actions and reactions of the terrorists and counterterror agents. For instance, he evidenced how IRA violence that harmed innocent civilians typically led to a decline in their popular support. But by far the most significant factor shaping community attitudes and opinions were the interventions of the Royal Ulster Constabulary and the British Army; when they were perceived to have over-reacted to an event, this increased public support for the paramilitary groups. Further support for the general tenor of this argument is to be found in the work of Hillyard (1993). Hillyard maintains that the oversimplification of the general public as either being 'for' or 'against' the terrorists results in counterterror agencies constructing a de facto 'suspect community'.

Over-reaction when countering terrorism can then function as a motivator and mobilizing force for terrorist campaigns. Sluka's account suggests the work of counterterrorism is also a 'legitimacy contest'. Unless a terrorist campaign can tap into a reservoir of social support somewhere, then it is unlikely to be sustained over a particularly long period (see Chapter 13 on the 'Longevity of Terrorist Groups'). Commenting upon the situation in Israel for instance, Ganor (2005) stressed that the various groups who engage in terrorist activities in that setting are, in effect, in competition for popular support and activists. The perceived legitimacy of the claims and counterclaims forwarded by the various groups are therefore pivotal to their capacity to continue their opposition to the Israeli government and its policies. In the Northern Ireland context, a need to secure and sustain a degree of popular legitimacy led IRA and other similar organizations to engage in activities specifically intended to try and enhance their standing in the eyes of the public.

Case Study 20.1 is used to show how in less democratic, more authoritarian countries, the lines between terrorist activity, state counterterrorism agencies, and public opinion are blurred. In this example, state-sponsored intervention induced longer term downstream consequences for counterterrorism agencies internationally.

CASE STUDY 20.1

Countering Terrorism in Russia

Following the fall of the Soviet Union (1988–1991), the powerful Russian state intelligence agencies had to be re-made, with several organizations established to take on functions previously centralized under the KGB (translated as the 'Committee for State Security', which was the main security agency for the Soviet Union from 13 March 1954 until 3 December 1991). The lead agency for counterterrorism in Russia today is the Federal Security Service (FSB), with policy support from the Ministry of Interior (MVD). Depending on the specifics of the case or situation, other security and intelligence agencies can also be involved.

A test of this strategy occurred on the 23 October 2002 (see Photo 20.1), when a group of heavily armed Chechen separatist fighters seized around 850 hostages from the audience at a Moscow theatre. Their demands were that the Russian government withdraw their military forces from Chechnya. As the days passed, international media attention grew and the pressure on the Russian government to resolve the siege increased.

The key problem for Russian special forces in attempting a forced entry of the building was that the physical design meant they would have to fight their adversaries down a series of narrow corridors and a heavily defended staircase before getting to where the hostages were being held. So instead, a decision was taken to pump the theatre full of gas prior to an assault, to incapacitate the defenders. Many of the details about what happened next, such as who authorized this plan and what precisely the gas was, remain shrouded in mystery. Special forces entered the building on 26 October. Not all of the hostage-takers were overcome by the gas, and a firefight ensued. After around two hours, all of the Chechens were killed. Unfortunately, as many as 300 hostages also died because of the gas (although this is still unclear, official records stated that 130 hostages died).

The Russian state's reaction to what transpired culminated in new anti-terror laws, Russian military action against Chechen separatists, a growth in public support for President Vladimir Putin, and war with Chechnya. However, an official investigation by the Moscow City Prosecutor's Office over 3.5 years failed to establish key information, such as the number of hostages released by the operation and the number of militants who seized the theatre.

In 2007, the official investigation was suspended and an independent investigation into the Moscow Theatre siege was set up, involving amongst others the former FSB officer Aleksander Litvinenko and the journalist Anna Politkovskaya. Based upon their investigations,

PHOTO 20.1 October 2002. Russian special forces soldiers carry out hostages during the storming of the theatre building captured by Chechen terrorists, after the three-day standoff which left many hostages in addition to the 40 hostage-takers dead, almost all of them gassed by Russian forces in a controversial army assault.

they alleged the FSB were aware of the presence of the Chechen group in Moscow prior to the attack. Moreover, the Chechens had been encouraged to act by an 'agent provocateur' (an agent who is employed to include others to break the law in order to be convicted) working for the FSB, whose name was in the list of hostage-takers and who left the scene alive.

In effect, Russia's lead counterterrorism agency was accused of both manipulating the terrorists into staging the attack, and acting to influence public opinion at a time when domestic and international pressure was mounting for Vladimir Putin to negotiate with Chechen moderates. Both Litvinenko and Politkovskaya were assassinated in 2006, the former in the UK. Political assassinations are modes of violence that can be plausibly defined as forms of state-sponsored terrorism, and in recent years, investigating them has become an increasingly common feature of the work of Western counterterrorism agencies, with Russian state actors implicated in the deaths of exiled Chechens living in Vienna and Berlin.

QUESTIONS

1. Thinking about the country where you live, investigate any major terror attacks which have been used to reform the organization and responsibilities of individual counterterrorism agencies.
2. Find some examples of counterterrorism agencies who have used agent provocateurs, and analyse risks of doing so.

20.5 IMPLEMENTING APPROACHES TO COUNTERTERRORISM

All counterterrorism agencies distribute their assets across a variety of 'offensive' and 'defensive', reactive, and proactive postures (Crelinsten, 2009, 2014; English, 2014). They can be mapped back to the strands of counterterrorism policy outlined in section 20.3. For example, interventions under Prevent/Prepare in policy by and large represent an anticipatory, preventative, and proactive approach, whereas Pursue or Response are aligned with reactive, retrospective action.

Each of these approaches intersect with different elements integral to the conduct of counterterrorism work. Focusing our discussion here are three elements: military; intelligence; and criminal justice. Each bring to the fore key logics and practices that shape counterterrorism work. A proactive approach, for example, is reliant on intelligence-led policing, and/or the use of intelligence technologies and military cooperation across borders.

20.5.1 Military

From a Western liberal democratic standpoint, a militaristic counterterrorism strategy tends to be externally oriented, and pivots around defining specific terrorist incidents, either rhetorically or legally, as 'acts of war'. It is undoubtedly a reactive 'hard power', offensive response, with adversaries typically cast as 'enemy combatants', rather than as having engaged in 'criminal' acts (Shapiro and Byman, 2006). That said, some countries lean on their military assets more than others, engaging them more readily in their counterterrorism response efforts both at home and abroad. For example, Israel operates a 'targeted assassination' programme as a formal component of their national responses to terrorism. But even the UK government has had recourse to deploy troops to key locations to support police officers during periods of heightened threat (Rayner, 2017).

The epitome of the military frame of counterterrorism was the US response to the 9/11 attacks. As the deadliest ever attack on US soil (2,977 people died), the magnitude and horror of the attack triggered rapid legislative change and military engagement abroad. It was a crisis 'reflex' that experts agree was ill-judged, exaggerated, and ultimately counterproductive; arguably a response that the terrorists themselves were seeking (English, 2010; Nacos et al., 2011; Crenshaw and LaFree, 2017).

The 'Global War on Terror' rhetoric adopted by the United States set out terms of military engagement without limit or end. Challenging other states to join the US in its response, President George W. Bush's position identified foreign states as the 'problem' and changing their behaviour as the preferred solution (Dunn, 2005). This ultimately led to America and allies fighting a war in Afghanistan and then Iraq, the latter predicated on faulty British intelligence that Saddam Hussein, President of Iraq, possessed weapons of mass destruction and had ties to al-Qaeda. These long-lasting conflicts hugely divided public opinion at the time, and the backlash against foreign occupation and involvement in the affairs of volatile states continues to be felt (Pape, 2006), playing a part in radicalizing people globally, and directly propagating the inception of ISIS.

20.5.2 Intelligence

Intelligence is information that when collected, processed, and interpreted affords insight and foresight in respect of potential risks and threats. All agencies engaged in counterterrorism work maintain an intelligence capacity and capability to inform their decision-making, but for some it is their main purpose. As Gearty (2007) asserts, agencies whose principal focus is intelligence tend to exhibit a preference for early, proactive interventions, disrupting the activities of those believed to be planning an attack, oftentimes through extra-legal interventions.

Many countries maintain a distinction between domestic intelligence activities directed at their own citizens, and those where the principal interest is the activities of other states and their agents. In today's networked world these are increasingly permeable distinctions at an operational level, and agencies tend to use similar processes and systems to generate their intelligence products.

Key types of intelligence are:

- 'HUMINT' or 'Human Intelligence' that comes from agents, spies and informants, and covert human intelligence sources (CHIS). These intelligence methods rely on actors' maintaining close contact to subjects of interest, without them revealing their intentions as a way of exfiltrating secret information.
- 'SIGINT' or 'Signals Intelligence' is the more technologically dependent conceptual partner of HUMINT. It centres on the covert monitoring of, and listening to, communications 'chatter' across all the electronic means and devices that people use today, with a particular interest in defined targets and subjects of interest
- 'OSINT' or 'Open Source' intelligence utilizes publicly available data and has recently seen a rapid growth (see also Chapter 7 on open source databases). Whereas the preceding two methods focus upon accessing secrets, open source methods scan across and make links between the vast quantities of public data available in the contemporary media ecosystem, especially social media platforms.

Almost all agencies tend to try and use a blend of human and technologically sourced material, indicative of how there are two fundamental intelligence problems that must be resolved. The first is accessing secrets that target individuals, organizations and agencies want to restrict access to. The second is linking multiple pieces of information and data that, in isolation may tell you very little, but blended are far more revealing. Given the vast array of available data and information that can be harnessed in our contemporary digitally networked society, an inevitable discrepancy results between what is collected and what is processed (Silver, 2012). Identifying the right risks and threats to collect information about, represents a significant challenge to all intelligence operatives.

The dynamics and methods of intelligence work have been profoundly 'disrupted' by the transformations associated with the information age (Herman, 2001; Treverton, 2003). The speed and scale of information routinely publicly available has surged, especially due to the proliferation of social media (see Chapter 18). In response, there has been a 'scramble' within intelligence agencies around the world to upgrade their tactics and techniques, with significant investments being made in the 'open source' domain.

This reflects how the rhythms and routines of countering terrorism are being altered by social media (Innes, Dobreva, and Innes, 2019) Just as these platforms are disrupting the institutional and interactional ordering of society more generally, these communication technologies are also directly impacting the construction, communication, and conduct of terrorist acts and their management. They have amplified the volume of misinformation and disinformation that police and other first responders must contend with in their sense-making work, when producing a definition of the situation in terms of 'who did what to whom and why?'

Terrorist groups and so-called 'lone-wolf' actors are adept at utilizing social media platforms to broadcast their motivations and propaganda to a wide audience. The apotheosis of this was the 'made for media' spree shooting undertaken by Brenton Tarrant in Christchurch New Zealand in 2019 (see Case Study 18.1). The often-rapid online radicalization of terrorists and how to effectively police the virtual space is a growing challenge for counterterrorism efforts globally, and will function as a driver of social, legal, and technological reform in the future. However, for all the attention and interest steered toward digital intelligence, we should not neglect the continued value of more 'analogue' methods when developing covert human intelligence sources and agents.

Case Study 20.2 illustrates the centrality of intelligence in the counterterrorism apparatus of different countries and ongoing efforts to remove barriers to intelligence sharing. There is a division of labour between multiple agencies performing particular roles with the shared aim of ensuring effective coordination across the counterterrorism system, but for some the emergence of mechanisms for 'mass surveillance' is a worrying development.

CASE STUDY 20.2

Co-ordinating Approaches across Agencies

The German Joint Counter-Terrorism Centre (GTAZ) was established in 2004 to improve intelligence sharing between individual agencies. A new unit was initiated within GTAZ to harmonize individual risk assessment processes, in an effort to ensure that a standardized method was applied to assess actors engaging with extremist ideas. The unit aimed to minimize frictions and 'rubbing points' within the German counterterrorism system. Although this move was delayed by the Covid-19 pandemic, by 2022 a new anti-terrorism centre in Berlin will house around 1200 staff from the Special Operations Command, Mobile Task Force and Department for Combating Islamic Terrorism. The idea behind this change is that physical co-location and shared infrastructure will remove some of the barriers to effective intelligence sharing and joint action.

A not dissimilar set of motives lay behind the establishment of the Department of Homeland Security in the United States (see Photo 20.2). In this case, intelligence issues were brought into sharp focus by the findings of the 9/11 Commission who identified that, prior to the hijacked airliners being flown into the Twin Towers and Pentagon in 2001, there was probably sufficient intelligence available that the attack could have been prevented. Unfortunately, multiple agencies were in possession of different bits of information, and no single agency was able to see everything available. The result was a failure to 'connect the dots' in a way that would have generated a signal that an attack was imminent.

In part, this problem is an artefact of America's especially complex intelligence and law enforcement landscape, where there are an unusually large number of agencies with some kind of counterterror remit. This resulted in lots of redundancy, mission overlap, and jostling for lead responsibilities for specific cases.

Effective intelligence sharing and inter-agency friction are not challenges unique to the American system. They are found elsewhere and have been a recurrent finding of many

PHOTO 20.2 The US DHS (Department of Homeland Security) was founded because of 9/11.

post-attack reviews and public enquiries. Some commentators are worried about the potential to grow mass-surveillance systems and have suggested that some division between agencies may be desirable to limit the power of state surveillance and protect human rights (Muižnieks, 2016).

QUESTIONS

1. Why have units specializing in joint-tasking and coordination become increasingly important in counterterrorism?
2. What are the potential advantages and disadvantages of having multiple agencies engaged in the delivery of counterterrorism?

20.5.3 Criminal justice

The criminal justice framing of counterterrorism asserts that the violence should be defined primarily a criminal act, and thus subject to criminal justice system responses. Although there is some overlap with the military and intelligence, the police mindset is fundamentally more concerned with collecting evidence and case-building in order to bring offenders to justice through the criminal justice process. In viewing counterterrorism approaches on a spectrum, Gaulke (2010) places enforcement of the law at the mid-point, anchored by 'suppression' and 'accommodation' at either end. Suppression is founded on military action and the suspension of normal legal safeguards for suspects, whilst accommodation involves tackling terrorism by addressing motivations for terrorist violence. All are limited. A suppression approach risks instigating action that is disproportionate. The long-term work associated with an accommodation approach risks perceptions of legitimizing the terrorist's cause for no immediate benefit. Relying on the criminal justice system to enforce law and criminalize terrorism creates a dependency on the reactiveness of the legal system after the event.

Post 9/11, counterterrorism work has been punctuated by repeated examples of what Innes and Levi (2017) label a 'legislative reflex' where, in the wake of terrorist attacks, politicians perceive that they need to be seen 'doing something' and almost instinctively reach for new laws. This is exemplified by the situation in the UK where, since 2001 the list of key statutes introduced includes: the Antiterrorism Bill, Crime and Security Act 2001, which allowed for detention without trial (later overturned by the courts); the Prevention of Terrorism Act 2005 introducing the 'control order' (also overturned); the Terrorism Act 2006, enabling the Treasury to freeze the assets of suspects; the Counterterrorism Act 2008, under which police were permitted to continue questioning suspects after charge; the Terrorist Asset-Freezing Act 2010; and the 2015 Counterterrorism and Security bill.

Grasping for new legislative answers to innovations in terrorist attack methodologies has become part of the domestic societal response to terrorist attacks. Foley's comparative analysis of Britain and France, two liberal democratic countries facing a broadly similar level of Islamic terrorist risk and threat, shows how the French system deals with terror cases via a special judiciary. This reduces the need for more 'piecemeal' legislative change that is required under the British system, where intelligence and judiciary operate more discretely (Foley, 2013). The different structures of these control agencies underpin the more 'muscular' and assertive policies and interventions seen in France, and accounts for why Britain has tended to avoid mass-arrests and large-scale initiatives in favour of targeted arrests and intelligence-led disruption. Foley attributes 'influencing factors' at the level of society, state and agency expressed as deep institutional, organizational and cultural norms, as framing how contemporary terrorism is configured and understood in each country, and consequently what kinds of countermeasures secure public permission.

Within policing, Innes and Thiel (2008) point to a tension about whether specialist counterterrorism officers represent the most effective way to respond to the current threat of Islamist extremism, compared to a broader effort encompassing neighbourhood policing teams. From a proactive perspective, the latter are potentially better placed to deal with the myriad of hate crimes, community tensions and local injustices that may 'prime' certain individuals to become more vulnerable to and interested in radical and extremist ideologies (Innes et al. 2007). This is counterposed with a more 'reactive' policing posture that focuses attention upon individuals representing more of a 'clear and present' danger (rather than a population of individuals who might arrive at this destination at some point in the future). Ongoing indecision and tension about which strategy to prioritize has resulted in operational policing that incorporates elements of both stances (Lambert, 2011).

The case against widening police involvement to formally incorporate community policing assets is set out by Thacher (2005). He suggests that the danger of involving local police in national security issues is that they will become 'contaminated' in the eyes of communities, because of the almost inevitable focus on mitigating serious potential risks and threats. The concept of a 'suspect community' attempts to capture how police and allied agencies collectively treat all members of a community or group as potential terrorists, or at least sympathetic to their campaigns (Abbas, 2018), failing to differentiate between the 'real' terrorists and 'normal' members of the public. The discrimination and harassment consequently experienced by ordinary people induces them to express more support than they might otherwise have done for the terrorists. Bratton and Kelling (2006) were troubled by the potentially negative consequences that might flow from asking local policing to focus explicitly upon countering Islamist-inspired terrorism. A particular concern being that policing resources will be subject to 'mission drift', away from managing crime to managing terrorism risks (Manning, 2010).

Whilst such worries are both pertinent and incisive to the 'prevention' strand of counterterrorism work, the general trend does seem to be to establish a softer role for community policing officers. This reflects a view among senior police that, despite considerable expansion in resourcing intelligence assets, levels of threat do not seem to be receding and if anything, are diversifying. A new approach recognizes the increasing interconnections between neighbourhood and national security (Innes and Thiel, 2008). In the wake of the cluster of terrorist attacks that took place in the UK during the first half of 2017, several senior police leaders went on the record to publicly state the value and importance of Neighbourhood Policing assets to countering terrorism, citing greater community connections developed from local neighbourhood policing teams. These provide a channel for passing community intelligence to the police about possible national security risks and threats. Such official statements reflect a growing awareness and perception that, whilst assertive intelligence-based operations can be effective in neutralizing or mitigating potential threats, if they are not perceived as proportionate and targeted by communities, then they may simply amplify public concern and antipathy towards the police, effectively supporting the terrorists' cause (Pickering et al., 2008).

20.6 INTERACTIONS AND COLLABORATIONS

The preceding sections 20.5–20.5.3 have separated out the work of key agencies to clarify their respective roles and functions. In practice however, there is far more co-ordination, co-operation and sometimes competition between them. This is especially pronounced in the United States, reflecting a more de-centralized institutional landscape with thousands of law enforcement organizations and large numbers of federal agencies with a potential counterterrorism role. As a result, the 'Joint-Terrorism Task Force' concept has become pivotal to the US operating model. Such taskforces involve temporary coalitions of staff from across different relevant agencies, brought together to work on defined risks or threats. As Fosher (2009) describes, such arrangements are riven with frictions and tensions. Different agencies have distinct traditions and decision-making hierarchies that must be navigated and negotiated in order to get the work done, leaning heavily on workers' informal networks and tacit knowledge, rather than the formal procedures detailed in policy documents.

The operational vehicles in Europe are rather different from those in North America but there is a similar accent upon the importance of collaboration and co-ordination, especially with regards to intelligence sharing. One key institutional reform encouraged by the 9/11 attacks has been a significant growth in the number and reach of 'transnational' counterterror institutions (Jacobson, 2006), functioning as multilateral intelligence clearing houses to quickly move data between states that know about a threat to those that might need to know, without comprising the source or its methods (Ganor, 2005; Steven and Gunaratna, 2004). Whilst acknowledging such developments, it is important we do not over-state their consequences or influence. European counterterror institutions have a reputation for inactivity and are struggling to keep pace with the rapid evolution in terrorist threat postures and methodologies that have been observed over the last two decades.

20.7 CONCLUSION

Criminologists sometimes deploy the concept of a 'signal crime' to describe how specific high-profile incidents induce changes to the ways people think, feel or behave (Innes, 2014). This is an appropriate concept for thinking about how and why counterterrorism agendas and methodologies must evolve and adapt. Terrorist violence is enacted to 'terrorize, polarize, and mobilize' a public audience in pursuit of a political motivation. Attending to terrorism as a communicative action is integral to the ways in which the violence is designed to work upon public perceptions and attitudes, but it has also been slightly neglected. For understandable reasons, the design and delivery of counterterrorism interventions has focused upon the violence and how to prevent it, rather than its communicative properties. However, both dimensions are important for effective counterterrorism.

For this reason, this chapter has deliberately attended to the role that new communication technologies are having in shifting the predispositions and practices of counterterrorism agencies. Some aspects of counterterrorist work have become less covert, emerging from the shadows somewhat. This is especially true for preventative anti-radicalization activities and the target-hardening situational countermeasures layered into our environment. That said, there is a difference between what happens in the emotionally charged post-attack moment and the more patient and pain-staking activities that define counterterror work 'in ordinary time' (Innes et al., 2018). It is notable that some of the most important recent innovations in counterterrorism practice have focused upon managing the immediate post-attack situation in an effort to mitigate the overall public harm of terrorism.

Ultimately, there is a certain synchronicity between those performing counterterrorism tasks and their adversaries. Each are trying to innovate in ways that afford them a competitive advantage over their opponents. For those positioned on the counterterrorism side, this chapter has drawn attention to several fundamental ethical and practical dilemmas that have to be navigated and negotiated (Wilkinson, 2001). These include how much to invest in 'upstream' prevention efforts, versus more reactive interventions. Whilst preventing terrorist violence is the ultimate objective, there is an attendant danger that, if insufficiently targeted, such countermeasures can cast groups subject to them as suspect communities.

There remain significant challenges even though the work of counterterrorism agencies has become increasingly sophisticated, nuanced, and informed by a research evidence base. The nature of these challenges gravitate around the ways politically motivated violence is becoming simultaneously more sophisticated (such the use of drones and chemical nerve agents) and elemental (carried out with knives and vehicles). It is also conducted by a greater diversity of threat actors, as evidenced by the involvement of Russian state operatives in the Skripal poisonings in Salisbury in 2018, and those with far-right ideological proclivities in countries such as New Zealand, Norway, and the United States.

DISCUSSION QUESTIONS

1. How have growing concerns about far-right inspired terrorism impacted the roles of police, intelligence, and military?
2. Why do risk and threat assessments sometimes fail to detect and thus prevent terrorist plots?
3. What are the primary challenges for counterterrorist agencies operating in an era of social media?
4. How did the period of public sector austerity following the 2008 global economic crash, impact upon the work of counterterrorism?
5. What are the risks of using Neighbourhood/Community Policing approaches as part of the counterterrorism effort?

 Visit the online resources for pointers on how to answer the discussion questions, links to useful web sources, and guidance on accessing databases: www.oup.com/he/Wilson-Muro1e

GUIDE TO FURTHER READING

As with terrorism studies more generally, material on the work of counterterrorism institutions is distributed across a range of academic disciplines.

Andrew, C. (2009) *The Defence of the Realm: The Authorized History of MI5* (London: Allen Lane). *An example of agency specific historical accounts.*

English, R. (2010) *Terrorism: How to Respond.* Oxford: Oxford University Press. *A wide-ranging account setting out the key issues and challenges of responding to terrorism.*

Foley, F. (2013) *Countering Terrorism in Britain and France: Institutions, Norms and the Shadow of the Past* (Cambridge: Cambridge University Press). *Provides a comparative assessment of agencies and their histories in Britain and France.*

Innes, M., Roberts, C., and Lowe, T. (2017) 'A disruptive influence: Prevent-ing problems and countering violent extremism policy in practice', *Law and Society Review*, 51/2: 252–81. *Is a more focused account of the Prevent strand of the CONTEST strategy.*

Innes, M., Innes, H., Dobreva, D., Chermak, S., Huey, L., and McGovern, A. (2018) *From Minutes to Months: A Rapid Evidence Assessment of the Impact of Media and Social Media during and after Terror Events*. Ottawa, Ontario: Public Safety Canada.

Wilkinson, P. (2001) *Terrorism Versus Democracy: The Liberal State Response*. Abingdon: Frank Cass. A seminal text that places responding to terrorism in a political context.

REFERENCES

Abbas, M. (2018) 'Producing "Internal Suspect Bodies": Divisive Effects of UK Counterterrorism Measures on Muslim Communities in Leeds and Bradford'. *British Journal of Sociology* 70/1 https://onlinelibrary.wiley.com/doi/abs/10.1111/1468-4446.12366

Andrew, C. (2009) *The Defence of the Realm: The Authorized History of MI5*. Allen Lane.

Ashworth, A. and Zedner, L. (2014) *Preventive Justice*. Oxford: Oxford University Press.

Australia-New Zealand Counter-Terrorism Committee (ANZCTC) (2017) *National Counter-Terrorism Plan*. Australia-New Zealand counter-terrorism committee. https://www.nationalsecurity.gov.au/Media-and-publications/Publications/Documents/ANZCTC-National-Counter-Terrorism-Plan.PDF

BBC News (2019) Fastest-growing UK Terror Threat 'From far-right'. 19/09/2019. https://www.bbc.co.uk/news/uk-49753325

Bratton, W. and Kelling, G. (2006) 'Policing Terrorism', *Civic Bulletin* No.43, Manhattan Lust for Policy Research (http://www.manhattan-institute.org/html/cb_43.htm) (last accessed 06 January 2008).

Canada. Public Safety Canada (2011) *Building Resilience against Terrorism: Canada's Counter-terrorism Strategy*. Ottawa, Ont: Public Safety Canada. https://www.publicsafety.gc.ca/cnt/rsrcs/pblctns/rslnc-gnst-trrrsm/index-en.aspx

Coolsaet, R. (2010) EU Counterterrorism Strategy: Value Added or Chimera? International Affairs (Royal Institute of International Affairs 1944), 86 (4): 857–873.

Counter Extremist Project (2020) Violent Right-Wing Extremism and Terrorism—Transnational Connectivity, Definitions, Incidents, Structures and Countermeasures. https://www.counterextremism.com/sites/default/files/CEP%20Study_Violent%20Right-Wing%20Extremism%20and%20Terrorism_Nov%202020.pdf

Crenlinsten, R. (2014) Perspectives on Counterterrorism: From Stovepipes to a Comprehensive Approach. http://www.terrorismanalysts.com/pt/index.php/pot/article/view/321/html

Crelinsten, R. (2009) *Counter-Terrorism*. Cambridge: Polity Press.

Crenshaw, M. and La Free, G. (2017) *Countering Terrorism*. Brookings Institution Press.

Cronin, AK. (2009) *How Terrorism Ends: Understanding the Decline and Demise of Terrorist Campaigns*. Princeton University Press.

Dunn, DH. (2005) 'Bush, 11 September and the Conflicting Strategies of the "War on Terrorism"'. *Irish Studies in International Affairs*, 16: 11–33.

English, R. (2014) 'Introduction: The Enduring Illusions of Terrorism and Counter-Terrorism', in R. English (ed.) *Illusions of Terrorism and Counter-Terrorism*. Oxford: Oxford University Press.

English, R. (2010) *Terrorism: How to Respond*. Oxford: Oxford University Press.

European Union (2020) A Counter terrorism Agenda for the EU: Anticipate, Prevent, Protect, Respond. https://ec.europa.eu/home-affairs/sites/homeaffairs/files/what-we-do/policies/european-agenda-security/20201209_counter-terrorism-agenda-eu_en.pdf

Foley, F. (2013) *Countering Terrorism in Britain and France: Institutions, Norms and the Shadow of the Past*. Cambridge: Cambridge University Press.

Fosher, K. (2009) *Under Construction: Making Security at the Local Level*. Chicago: University of Chicago Press.

Ganor, B. (2005) *The Counter-Terrorism Puzzle: A Guide for Decision-Makers* (Edison, NJ.: Transaction).

Gaulke, A. (2010) Obama nation?: US Foreign Policy One Year on: Redefining the Global War on Terror? IDEAS reports—Special Reports, Kitchen, Nicholas (ed.) SR003. LSE IDEAS, London School of Economics and Political Science, London, UK http://eprints.lse.ac.uk/43580/1/Obama%20nation_redefining%20the%20global%20war%20on%20terror%28lsero%29.pdf

Gearty, C. (2007) 'Dilemmas of Terror', *Prospect* (October) 34–38.

Government of Canada (2018) Building Resilience Against Terrorism: Canada's Counter-terrorism

Strategy, 139. https://www.publicsafety.gc.ca/cnt/rsrcs/pblctns/rslnc-gnst-trrrsm/index-en.aspx

Heath-Kelly, C. (2013) 'Counter Terrorism and the Counter Factual: Producing the "Radicalisation" Discourse and the UK Prevent Strategy'. *The British Journal of Politics and International Relations*, 15 (3): 394–415.

Herman, M. (2001) *Intelligence Services in the Information Age*. London: Frank Cass.

Hillyard, P. (1993) *Suspect Community: Peoples' Experience of the Prevention of Terrorism Acts in Britain*. London: Pluto Press.

HM Government (2011) CONTEST The United Kingdom's Strategy for Countering Terrorism. Cm8123. https://assets.publishing.service.gov.uk/government/uploads/system/uploads/attachment_data/file/97995/strategy-contest.pdf

HM Government (2015) Prevent Duty Guidance. https://www.legislation.gov.uk/ukdsi/2015/9780111133309/pdfs/ukdsiod_9780111133309_en.pdf; https://assets.publishing.service.gov.uk/government/uploads/system/uploads/attachment_data/file/248645/Serious_and_Organised_Crime_Strategy.pdf

HM Government (2018) CONTEST. The United Kingdom's strategy for countering terrorism. Cm 9608. London: Crown Copyright. https://assets.publishing.service.gov.uk/government/uploads/system/uploads/attachment_data/file/716907/140618_CCS207_CCS0218929798-1_CONTEST_3.0_WEB.pdf

Home Office, (2020) Operation of Police Powers Under the Terrorism Act 2000 and Subsequent Legislation: Arrests, Outcomes, and Stop and Search. Great Britain, year ending June 2020. https://assets.publishing.service.gov.uk/government/uploads/system/uploads/attachment_data/file/918494/police-powers-terrorism-jun2020-hosb2620.pdf

Home Office (2018) Factsheet: Prevent and Channel statistics 2017/18. https://homeofficemedia.blog.gov.uk/2018/12/13/factsheet-prevent-and-channel-statistics-2017-2018/

Innes, M., Abbott, L., Lowe, T., and Roberts, C. (2007) *Hearts and Minds and Eyes and Ears: Reducing Radicalisation Risks through Reassurance-Oriented Policing*. London: ACPO.

Innes, M. and Thiel, D. (2008) 'Policing Terror, in Newburn, T. (ed.) *The Handbook of Policing* 2nd edition, Cullompton: Willan, 553–579.

Innes, M. (2014) *Signal Crimes: Reactions to Crime, Disorder and Control*. Oxford: Oxford University Press.

Innes, M. and Levi, M. (2017) 'Making and Managing Terrorism and Counter-terrorism'. Chapter 20 in Liebling, A., Maruna, S., and McAra, L (eds) *The Oxford Handbook of Criminology* (6th edition). Oxford: Oxford University Press.

Innes, M., Dobreva, D., and Innes, H. (2019) 'Disinformation and Digital Influencing after Terrorism: Spoofing, Truthing and Social proofing'. *Contemporary Social Science*, 16 (2). https://doi.org/10.1080/21582041.2019.1569714

Jacobson, M. (2006) *The West at War*. Washington Institute for Near East Policy.

Kundani, A. (2009) *Spooked! How Not to Prevent Violent Extremism*. London: Institute of Race Relations.

Lambert, B. (2011) *Countering Al Qaeda in London: Police and Muslims in Partnership*. Hurst & Company, London.

La Free, G., Dugan, L., and Korte, R (2009) 'The Impact of British Counter-terrorist Strategies on Political Violence in Northern Ireland: Comparing Deterrence and Backlash models'. *Criminology*, 47 (1): 17–45.

Manning, P. (2010) *Democratic Policing in a Changing World*. Boulder: Paradigm.

Muižnieks, N. (2016) 'Human Rights in Europe Should not Buckle Under Mass Surveillance'. *Open Democracy*, 12 February. https://www.opendemocracy.net/en/digitaliberties/human-rights-in-europe-should-not-buckle-under-mass-surveillance/

Mullins, S. (2016) 'Counterterrorism in Australia: Practitioner Perspectives'. *Journal of Policing, Intelligence and Counterterrorism*, 11 (1): 93–111. https://www.tandfonline.com/doi/full/10.1080/18335330.2016.1161228

Mythen, G., Walklate, S., and Khan, F. (2013) 'Why Should we Have to Prove we are Alright? Counter-terrorism, Risk and Partial Securities'. *Sociology*, 5 (3): 1–16.

Nacos, BL., Block-Elkon, Y., and Shapiro, RY. (2011) *Selling Fear: Counter-Terrorism, the Media and Public Opinion*. The University of Chicago Press.

Nesser, P. (2015) *Islamist Terrorism in Europe*. London: Hurst.

Omand, D. (2010) *Securing the State*. London: C. Hurst & Co.

Pantazis, C. and Pemberton, S. (2009) 'From the "old" to the "new" Suspect Community: Examining the Impacts of Recent UK Counter-terrorist Legislation'. *British Journal of Criminology*, 49 (5): 646–666.

Pape, R. (2006) *Dying to Win: The Strategic Logic of Suicide Terrorism*. Random House: New York.

Pickering, S., McCulloch, J., and Wright-Neville, D. P. (2008) *Counter-terrorism Policing*:

Community, Cohesion and Security. Springer: New York.

Rayner, D. (2017) What is Operation Temperer? Theresa May becomes first PM to deploy up to 5,000 soldiers on streets. *Daily Telegraph*, 23/05/2017. https://www.telegraph.co.uk/news/2017/05/23/operation-temperer-theresa-may-becomes-first-pm-deploy-5000/

Safi, M. (2015) ASIO Terrorism Investigations Doubled to 400 in 2014–15, Agency Report Finds. *The Guardian*. http://www.theguardian.com/australia-news/2015/nov/02/asio-terrorism-investigations-doubled-to-400-in-2014-15-says-agency-report

Shapiro, J. and Byman, D. (2006) 'Bridging the Transatlantic Counterterrorism gap'. *Washington Quarterly, 29* (4): 36–7, 40, 43.

Silver, N. (2012) *The Signal and the Noise*. Penguin Group.

Sluka, J. (1989) *Hearts and Minds, Water and Fish: Support for the IRA and INLA in a Northern Ireland Ghetto*. Connecticut: JAI Press.

Steven, G. and Gunaratna, R. (2004) *Counterterrorism: A Reference Handbook*. Santa Barbara: ABC Clio.

TE-SAT (2020) European Union Terrorism Situation and Trend Report (TE-SAT) 2020. https://www.europol.europa.eu/activities-services/main-reports/european-union-terrorism-situation-and-trend-report-te-sat-2020

Thacher, D. (2005) 'The Local Role in Homeland Security'. *Law and Society Review, 39* (5): 635–676.

Treverton, G. (2003) *Reshaping National Intelligence for an Age of Information*. Cambridge: Cambridge University Press.

Walker, C. and McKay, S. (2015) 'Community Surveillance and Terrorism', in Pearse, J. (ed.) *Investigating Terrorism: Current Political, Legal and Psychological Issues*. Chichester: Wiley-Blackwell.

Wilkinson, P. (2001) *Terrorism Versus Democracy: The Liberal State Response*. Abingdon: Frank Cass.

CHAPTER 21

Responding to Terrorism Nonviolently

SONDRE LINDAHL AND RICHARD JACKSON

■ **CHAPTER SUMMARY**

This chapter introduces and explores the theory and practice of responding to terrorism nonviolently. It examines some of the main failures and limitations of violent or force-based counterterrorism, and the reasons for this failure, before examining alternative nonviolent approaches which have historically been used to reduce the incidence of terrorism and transform violent conflict into political conflict. It then explores the literatures on subjects such as nonviolent resistance, unarmed peacekeeping, non-warring communities and social defence which provide important suggestions and guidance for further developing approaches to nonviolent counterterrorism.

21.1 INTRODUCTION

After terrorism became a key international security concern in the 1970s, governments responded to it in a variety of ways, including the use of military force, intelligence-led and police operations, heightened security measures, mass surveillance, the enactment of new laws, economic sanctions, counter-radicalization programmes, negotiations and dialogue, amnesties, political reforms, public diplomacy campaigns and many more (see Crelinsten 2009; Lindahl 2016). However, the terrorist attacks perpetrated by al-Qaeda on 11 September 2001 proved to be a turning point in how counterterrorism was conceptualized and conducted by countries around the world. The globally televised attacks shattered the image of terrorism as a relatively minor but nonetheless serious international security threat, and replaced it with the widely accepted belief that terrorism posed a serious existential threat to states and the entire international system.

The immediate response by the United States and its close allies to the 9/11 attacks was to declare a 'Global War on Terror' (GWOT), which as the term implies, entailed the employment of coercive strategies based on military force and direct violence aimed at eliminating terrorists and destroying their capacity to launch future attacks (Jackson 2005). There was a widespread consensus following the attacks that this 'new' form of terrorism could only be countered and defeated through responding with even greater counter-violence than the terrorists could deploy. As Crelinsten (2009: 19) explains: 'how we conceive of terrorism determines to a great extent how we go about countering it and what resources—money, manpower, institutional framework, time horizon—we devote to the effort'. Once terrorism was conceived of as a new form of warfare, it made perfect sense to respond to it using the weapons and strategies of war and military violence—what we call a force-based approach.

Importantly, this force-based approach treats terrorists as exogenous threats to the societies they operate within, and assumes that they must be eliminated. As such, force-based counterterrorism is a negatively defined approach in which the goal is to reduce future terrorism by employing greater counter-violence in order to neutralize prospective terrorists. This stands in opposition to the nonviolent approach which argues for a positively defined approach in which potential acts of terrorism are prevented by putting in place policies and practices that treat terrorists as endogenous to the societies they operate within. It assumes that counterterrorism should not mirror the use of political violence, but instead focus on how policies and practices can be put in place so that violence is rejected by all actors as a way of resolving the conflict. This approach is also based on assumptions about the political nature of terrorism, and that nonviolent policies and practices are best suited to recognize and address the underlying causes of terrorist attacks.

In the decades since 2001, new counterterrorism approaches such as 'countering violent extremism (CVE)' and 'counter-radicalization'—these approaches focus on contesting the extreme ideologies which are thought to drive acts of terrorist violence—have arguably moved into the centre of the counterterrorism paradigm, at least for many Western countries and their close allies (Martini, Ford, and Jackson 2020). Elsewhere, military occupation and drone killing programmes continue in areas of the Middle East and North Africa, as does extraordinary rendition (the extra-legal kidnap and imprisonment of suspected terrorists), the use of enhanced interrogation or torture, and limited military operations. In short, the use of force retains a central place within global counterterrorism approaches, and few question its legitimacy or efficacy as a response to terrorist attacks.

However, after nearly two decades of major global counterterrorism efforts, assessments by scholars, and military officials clearly show that the GWOT has failed in terms of all its main strategic, political and humanitarian goals. Further, with a civilian death toll of over a million (PSR 2015), trillions of dollars expended, and serious damage to human rights, civil liberties, societal norms and many societies' 'ways of life' (Wolfendale 2007), it can be argued that the counterterrorism 'cure' has so far been more harmful than the terrorism 'disease' itself. A case can even be made that force-based counterterrorism has made terrorism worse, given that levels of terrorism experienced in many parts of the globe have greatly *increased* since the US-led invasion of Afghanistan in October 2001, and even more so after the invasion of Iraq by the US, UK, Australia, and Poland in March 2003 (the first stage of the Iraq War), as documented in global terrorism datasets. Some scholars have suggested that force-based counterterrorism has become a self-fulfilling prophecy: it provokes as much, if not more, terrorism than it prevents (Zulaika 2009).

This aim of this chapter is to examine the theory, practice and potential of nonviolent approaches to counterterrorism. It begins by outlining the limitations and failures of violent, force-based forms of counterterrorism, particularly as seen in the ongoing GWOT, and contemporary approaches. Located in an understanding of the political causes of terrorism and the inherent limitations of violence as a political or security tool, the chapter then examines how negotiations, dialogue, conflict resolution, reforms, peacebuilding, and other forms have been used historically to settle conflicts involving terrorism and increase security in the midst of violent political conflict. The final part of the chapter explores what research from fields like nonviolent resistance, unarmed peacekeeping, non-warring communities, and social defence could contribute to new thinking about nonviolent forms of counterterrorism.

21.2 THE FAILURES OF FORCE-BASED COUNTERTERRORISM

The argument that nonviolent responses to terrorism are more likely to be both effective and ethical ways to reduce violence and resolve conflict is based first and foremost on a realistic assessment of the failures and inherent weaknesses of force-based counterterrorism (Jackson 2017). A force-based approach relies on using coercive physical force to eliminate or neutralize terrorists, and to destroy, deter, and degrade terrorist capabilities to launch attacks. It mirrors terrorism by countering violence with even greater violence, for example, by using tactics like military invasion, torture, drone killings, shoot to kill policies, and other militarized measures. Central to this approach is the assumption that one can reduce and counter the threat of terrorism by either eliminating actual or potential terrorists, or deterring would-be terrorists through demonstrating a willingness to use even greater force and violence than the terrorists themselves. Although the force-based approach may seem intuitive, in practice it has largely failed to effectively counter and prevent future terrorism. These failures can be summarized under sections 21.2.1. The empirical failure of force-based counterterrorism and 21.2.2 The theoretical and ethical failures of force-based counterterrorism.

21.2.1 The empirical failure of force-based counterterrorism

The most conspicuous example of how force-based counterterrorism has failed is the observation that after nearly two decades, at the time of writing in mid-2021, Western military forces are still present in Afghanistan and Iraq. The two countries are marred by violence and political instability, and in terms of preventing terrorism, the invasions have accomplished the opposite. In 2018, the US started negotiations with the Taliban (the military organization currently waging war within Afghanistan), in part due to the realization that the group cannot be militarily defeated and eliminated as a political actor in the country (see Case Study 21.1 below). In 2021, the new Biden administration announced that the US would withdraw its forces from the country by 31 August 2021. The story is even worse in Iraq where the invasion and subsequent occupation policies helped create the conditions that allowed ISIS to emerge and spread across the region, conditions which include the large-scale suffering caused to civilians by the invasion and occupation. A 2016 report concluded that the war in Iraq had resulted in one million civilian casualties, the displacement of approximately three million people, as well as the death of 4,800 coalition soldiers (*Blood and Treasure: The Costs of the Iraq War*, 2016; see also PSR, 2015).

Financially, since 2001, the US has appropriated and is obligated to spend an estimated US $6.4 trillion in budgetary costs related to and caused by the GWOT (Crawford 2019). In December 2019, the *Washington Post* newspaper shed further light on the empirical failures of the global war on terror, releasing the so-called 'Afghanistan Papers' (see *The Afghanistan Papers: Interview with Ambassador Michael Flynn* 2019). These documents included assessments from over 400 officials and insiders of the war in Afghanistan as part of a federal project examining the root failures of the war. They paint a dismal picture of the war. For example, Dougles Lute, a three-star Army general who served in Afghanistan told government interviewers in 2015, 'We didn't have the foggiest notion of what we were undertaking' (*The Afghanistan Papers: Interview with Ambassador Douglas Lute* 2019). Several other US officials acknowledged that their warfighting strategies were fatally flawed, and enormous sums of money were wasted.

Such an assessment of the empirical failures of force-based counterterrorism is not limited to Afghanistan and Iraq, but can also be applied to military intervention against terrorists in other states, such as Pakistan, Syria, Yemen, Somalia, Mali, Chechnya, Palestine, Kashmir, to name but a few. A broader evaluation would suggest that, among a great many other negative effects, the GWOT has increased global insecurity, destabilized regions such as the Middle East and the Horn of Africa, and resulted in a proliferation in the number of terrorist groups. More broadly, it is difficult to find any clear empirical examples of successful force-based counterterrorism.

In addition to this broad assessment, a closer empirical examination of specific methods supports the conclusion that force-based counterterrorism either fails to reduce levels of terrorism or actually makes terrorism worse. A study by Araj (2008: 284) found that rather than reducing the amount of terrorism, 'harsh state repression is a major cause of suicide bombing'. Likewise, Piazza (2017: 102) concluded that while 'forms of repression that close off nonviolent avenues of dissent and boost group grievances increase the amount of domestic terrorism a country faces, types of repression that raise the costs of terrorist activity have no discernible effect on terrorism'. Other empirical research has confirmed that states often experience more terrorism after they engage in military intervention and occupation (Piazza and Choi 2018; Pape 2005). Tamil (LTTE) terrorism against India following military intervention in Sri Lanka in 1987, and Chechen terrorism against Russia following the Russian military invasion of Chechnya in 1994 (see also Case Study 21.1), are all examples of this effect.

More specifically, there have been studies on the effectiveness of targeted killing of terrorists by drone strikes, or so-called leadership decapitation strategies, in recent years (Abrahms and Mierau 2017: 831). This reflects an increased reliance on drone killings by the US and its allies since the Barack Obama administration (2009–2017). These studies, perhaps because they are often based on different metrics, data and methods, have produced contrasting and overall, inconclusive findings. For example, while some scholars such as Byman (2006) argue that drone strikes can be a useful counterterrorism tool, a larger number of studies finds that they are either ineffective, or counterproductive (Bolland and Ludvigsen 2018). Abrahms and Mierau (2017), for example, conclude that leadership decapitation leads to greater indiscriminate violence by militant groups. Studies have found that employing torture as a counterterrorist tool is similarly ineffective (Schiemann 2015; Rejali 2007; Goodman-Delahunty, Martschuk, and Dhami 2014).

In short, the empirical record of employing violent and coercive approaches aimed at eliminating or deterring terrorist groups strongly suggests that it is in fact a very poor method of counterterrorism, as well as being unethical and harmful in its consequences. Not only is it unlikely to achieve even minimal goals such as reducing the number of terrorist attacks, but it also comes with a great many negative consequences in terms of civilian casualties, destabilization, refugees, the undermining of human rights protections, increased Islamophobia (fear and prejudice against Muslims) and xenophobia (prejudice against people from other countries), and much more.

A final consideration here is a practical one, namely, that in order to make good policy, it is important to have good information about what different options exist, what the costs and benefits and potential harms of each option are, and what options work best under different circumstances. As van Dongen (2010: 227) argues, 'Awareness of the full range of options is a vital element in the development of any sound policy . . . The field of counter-terrorism studies seems, unfortunately, to fall short of even the first step—an overview of the options.' The next crucial step is to engage in rigorous empirical evaluation to determine what works, and whether the costs and harms of different actions justify the benefits. There is a growing consensus that governments and researchers have largely failed in this task. As one of the most comprehensive studies of counterterrorism effectiveness explains:

> 'Counter-terrorism policy needs to be rational, effective, and cause as little harm as necessary. There is only one way to determine whether counter-terrorism strategies are effective – by conducting methodologically valid evaluations of those strategies. It is clear that current counter-terrorism policies, strategies and tactics lack this evidence base. In other words, programs are being used without any knowledge, understanding, or even attempts to determine whether they are effective' (Lum, Kennedy, and Sherley, 2008: 41).

In fact, the study concluded that 'some evaluated interventions either didn't work or sometimes *increased* the likelihood of terrorism and terrorism-related harm' (Lum, Kennedy, and Shirley, 2006/09: 3). More worryingly, they did not find 'any evidence that the minuscule proportion of government counterterrorism spending related to research has been directed towards evaluating these [counterterrorism] programs' (ibid. 4). What this means in practice is that governments have continued to enact costly and often harm-inducing counterterrorism policies with little or no evidence about whether they are actually effective, or what kind of consequences they have produced.

21.2.2 The theoretical and ethical failures of force-based counterterrorism

There are theoretical reasons for the failures of force-based counterterrorism outlined in 21.2.1. The first is that there was a widespread belief among officials and scholars following 9/11 that the attacks had 'wiped the slate clean of the conventional wisdom on terrorists and terrorism, and, by doing so, ushered in a new era of conflict' (Hoffman, 2004). In a practical sense, this meant that previous knowledge of how to respond effectively to terrorism, and what the limitations and costs of force-based counterterrorism are, based on previous historical experiences, for example in Northern Ireland, Palestine, Egypt, and Spain, were wilfully ignored (see Jackson 2012, 2015).

Another reason is that from a theoretical perspective (supported by empirical studies) we can argue that there is a widespread misunderstanding of the relationship between violence, force, coercion, and power (Jackson 2018, 2019). In particular, the relationship between brute force and coercion is deeply misunderstood (Holmes 2013: 185) in the sense that the effectiveness of violence to deter or compel opponents depends entirely on how people respond to the violence, not the violence itself. In essence, the capacity to hurt and destroy bears no direct relation to the ability to coerce (see Wallace 2016): violent actions or threats, as demonstrated in the GWOT, can produce submission and deterrence *or* resistance and retaliation, and the outcome is never predictable. In countries such as Afghanistan, Iraq, Pakistan, Israel, Northern Ireland, and Somalia, the attempted use of overwhelming military force has arguably produced greater levels of determined resistance than submission and deterrence.

Further, violence can be understood as a phenomenon with a history, and as a double-act 'between human subjects, subjects whose experience of violence interpolates them in a repetition effect from which they cannot free themselves' (Young 2010: 4–5). Violence, therefore, does not just erupt from nowhere, and it is rarely without any kind of meaning, because it emerges as a response to a situation that has already been given meaning. As Howes (2013: 436) puts it, 'killing people does not have predictable political results. . . which makes it difficult to know what meanings people will assign to it or what actions they will take in response to it.' Arguably, the meaning taken by many actors in the Middle East from the invasion of Iraq in 2003 was that the West hated Muslims, and violent resistance to Western domination was necessary for survival. Importantly, this mirrored the meaning that many Americans assigned to the 9/11 attacks. The point is that neither the United States nor al-Qaeda fully anticipated (or intended) the way in which their opponent would respond to their violence. The unpredictability of violence makes it a poor choice for policy, especially in terms of evaluating its effectiveness.

Related to this, and in keeping with social theory, it is important to recognize that violence is never purely instrumental, but rather is *constitutive* of identities, ethics, practices, and politics (see Frazer and Hutchings 2008). What this means is that the practices of the GWOT molds and structures society through the institutionalization of the counterterrorism system, and the normalization of violence as a legitimate political or security instrument. It constructs at both the national and global levels, a securitized context in which political violence is viewed as normal and expected, thereby perpetuating cycles of violent conflict.

Another aspect of violence—specifically, the necessity of defining enemies and dehumanizing them sufficiently to justify killing—helps to explain, and lies at the heart of, the ethical failures of force-based counterterrorism. After 9/11, once terrorists were assumed to be inherently 'evil' and therefore undeserving of human rights, all kinds of violence and abuse directed against them in the service of counterterrorism, became permissible. Consequently, human rights groups, journalists and lawyers all over the world have documented and publicized the many thousands of cases of grave human rights violations committed by governments in the name of counterterrorism, including the widespread use of torture, prisoner abuse, drone killings, mass surveillance, wrongful imprisonment, and other repressive actions.

> **KEY CONCEPTS**
>
> **Force-based counterterrorism** State responses to acts of terrorism which employ coercive physical force aimed at eliminating or neutralizing terrorists, and intended to destroy, deter and degrade terrorist capabilities to launch attacks. Based primarily on the military or state security organizations, examples include military invasion, torture, drone killings, shoot to kill policies, search and destroy missions, extraordinary rendition, hostage rescue, and more.
>
> **Counterterrorism policy evaluation** The systematic collection and analysis of information to make judgements about the process, content, implementation and impact of counterterrorism policies. The aim is to check the effects of policies and assess their necessity, efficiency, costs, and validity in order to improve future policymaking.

21.3 ALTERNATIVES TO FORCE-BASED COUNTERTERRORISM

Compared to the literature discussing force-based approaches, the literature on nonviolent or peace-based approaches to counterterrorism is fairly small. In part, this is because, as we have explored, since 9/11 terrorism has been constructed and understood as both a form of evil violence and a new type of warfare. In this understanding, terrorism has also been de-politicized and de-coupled from the idea of strategic political action. In such a conceptual and policy framework, it makes little sense to engage in political dialogue with, or make concessions to, terrorist groups, or even to consider them as serious political actors. Here, we are focusing on approaches such as dialogue and direct negotiation with terrorist groups, reconciliation and conflict resolution, concessions and reforms, amnesties and pardons, political settlements, and the like. While there are other measures such as economic sanctions, strengthening homeland security, enacting counterterrorism laws, mass surveillance and intelligence-gathering which are not based on the direct use of force, these are better understood as defensive anti-terrorism measures designed to mitigate vulnerabilities, rather than offensive counterterrorism measures designed to prevent, deter or respond to acts of terrorism.

The broader focus on force-based counterterrorism has given the impression that when faced with the threat of terrorism, states have no other option but to fight back using counter-violence. However, a closer look at historical campaigns of terrorism reveals there are a great many alternatives to the use of force, many of which have been effective at reducing its incidence, increasing security and resolving the political conflicts that motivated actors to adopt terrorist tactics in the first place. In fact, looking empirically at how the majority of terrorist groups have ended, we see that historically very few of them were defeated or transformed through the use of direct military force. As Figure 21.1 illustrates, the vast majority

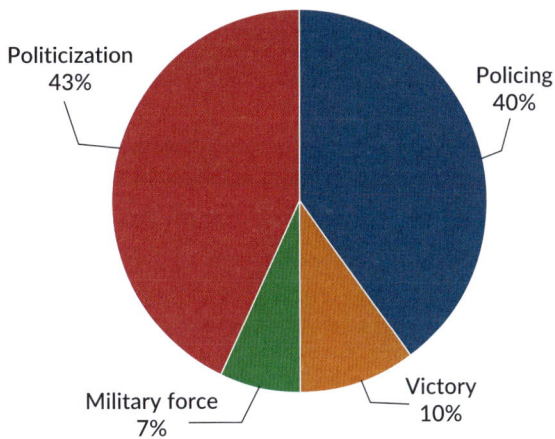

FIGURE 21.1 How terrorist groups end (based on Jones and Libicki 2008: 19).

of them end and stop their violence following police and intelligence work which undermines the group's activities; when internal divisions lead the group to splint or disintegrate; or when the group transforms into a political actor which decides to pursue its goals through normal political channels instead of violent contestation (see, for example, Murua 2017).

The most common alternative approach to force-based counterterrorism is the use of dialogue and negotiations as part of an attempt at conflict resolution and promoting a political settlement (see Goerzig 2010; English 2009). It is typical for states to opt for this approach only after years of employing military force without any conclusive gains. Some of the most prominent examples include the Oslo Accords between Israel and the PLO, the Good Friday Agreement between the UK government and the paramilitary groups in Northern Ireland, and the peace talks between the Taliban and US in Afghanistan (see Case Study 21.1). It has become something of a truism that while every government publicly proclaims that they never negotiate with terrorists, most governments will do so, albeit first in secret and only after they find that the use of force has not worked or involves too many costs.

CASE STUDY 21.1

Afghanistan: Negotiating with the Enemy

In response to the 9/11 attack, the US and a Coalition of four allies, in addition to the NATO-led ISAF military mission, launched a major military campaign to capture or kill Osama bin Laden, disrupt the use of Afghanistan as a base for terrorist operations, and overthrow the Taliban regime. Despite a large-scale military and civilian occupation and ongoing military operations over two decades, the US failed to defeat the Taliban insurgency or build a secure, prosperous democratic state. Despite long-standing public rhetoric referring to the Taliban as a terrorist organization, and a long-standing policy of never negotiating with terrorists, the US government began negotiations to end the conflict with representatives of the Taliban in 2018. In 2019, President Trump announced that a peace treaty had been signed with the Taliban (see Photo 21.1). Although the peace agreement faced obstacles to its enactment in 2020, the tentative agreement is an important recognition that the employment of overwhelming military force failed to defeat a terrorist organization, while direct negotiations provided a pathway towards ending the violence, the withdrawal of foreign troops, and political reconciliation.

The case of Afghanistan underlines the political nature of terrorism, and the importance of addressing its political causes through nonviolent means such as direct dialogue. In 2021, the Biden administration controversially announced the withdrawal of US forces from Afghanistan, despite ongoing violent conflict.

QUESTIONS

1. How do we explain the failure of the world's greatest superpower to defeat the Taliban?
2. Why did the United States start negotiating with the Taliban, despite labelling them as a 'terrorist organization'?

PHOTO 21.1 In 2019 the US government and the Taliban signed a historic agreement.

The point is that while it is difficult to find clear examples where a major terrorist campaign was defeated through military force alone—the defeat of the LTTE in Sri Lanka or the defeat of left-wing opponents to the Argentinian dictatorship are arguable exceptions—there are a number of prominent examples where terrorism and political violence declined during and following genuine political dialogue and conflict resolution attempts, including Northern Ireland, Israel, and South Africa. Contrary to the objection that negotiating with terrorists encourages more groups and individuals to take up terrorism as a way of gaining political concessions, the majority of cases demonstrates the opposite: direct negotiations about the political issues motivating the terrorist groups most often leads to a decline in political violence (Goerzig 2010). This is because terrorism is a strategy—a means to an end—and when terrorist groups can negotiate directly and participate in a political process, the use of terrorism most often becomes counter-productive.

Directly related to this, the transformation of terrorist groups into political parties or movements through processes of dialogue with the broader movements from which they emerge, combined with political reforms, has also proven to be an effective method of getting terrorist groups to lay down their arms or marginalizing them to the point where they disappear. In Northern Ireland (see Case Study 21.2 below), Palestine, Spain and elsewhere, former terrorist groups and militants, and the broader grievances of the populations they represent, have been channelled into political processes rather than violent resistance. Given that many terrorist campaigns occur in situations where political aspirations and opportunities to have a voice in the political system are denied, this makes perfect sense.

CASE STUDY 21.2

The Good Friday Peace Agreement

For decades, Northern Ireland was dominated by the Troubles, a violent conflict centred on latent political and nationalistic issues which erupted in the late 1960s between republican paramilitary groups such as the IRA and Irish National Liberation Army (INLA), loyalist paramilitaries such as the Ulster Volunteer Force (UVF) and Ulster Defence Association (UDA), British state security forces such as the British Army and RUC, and political activists.

The Troubles ended with the Good Friday Agreement in April 1998 (see Photo 21.2). The conflict was dominated by violence and terrorism, and more than 3,500 people were killed during the conflict. In the 1990s, following years of secret dialogue between the UK government and paramilitary representatives, gradual steps were taken towards a peace agreement. The Good Friday Agreement was the culmination of a long and complex process involving the British and Irish governments, unionist and republican parties, some representing paramilitary organizations, and changing international and domestic conditions. The agreement included a devolved, inclusive government, a programme for the release of prisoners, troop reductions, targets for paramilitary decommissioning, provisions for polls on Irish reunification, and civil rights measures for the two communities in Northern Ireland. While some analysts argue

PHOTO 21.2 The Good Friday Agreement was signed in 1998 and ended most of the conflict of the Troubles in Northern Ireland. It was a major development in the peace process in Northern Ireland in the 1990s.

that military pressure was decisive in pushing the parties towards concessions, there is little question that the peace agreement could not have been achieved in the absence of serious dialogue and a commitment to political reform. Importantly, Northern Ireland has not experienced a return to previous levels of violence, and this is in large due to the political agreement which included all the various actors and stakeholders, and thus removed the support for armed struggle as a legitimate tactic.

QUESTIONS

1. What conditions and processes made dialogue possible in Northern Ireland?
2. Could the Northern Ireland conflict have been resolved without political dialogue, and if not, why not?

Another dimension of this is that a great many terrorist campaigns have occurred, and continue to occur, in response to a perceived or real injustice or grievance, such as when a society is militarily occupied or colonized by a foreign power or rival group. For example, there were a number of prominent terrorist campaigns against European colonial powers in Africa, Asia and elsewhere in the decades after the Second World War. During this period, popularly supported liberation movements, sometimes with a terrorist flank, sought to gain political independence. When the colonial powers made concessions, especially when they gave full independence to their colonies, the terrorist campaigns ended because they had achieved their goals. Prominent examples here include terrorist campaigns in Cyprus against the British, Jewish terrorism in Palestine, and the armed struggles in Zimbabwe and South Africa against apartheid regimes.

What this history suggests is that force-based counterterrorism is not the only effective or legitimate response to terrorism, especially when it is part of a broader movement seeking social and political justice, the end of occupation or greater independence. In some circumstances, direct negotiations and dialogue, concessions, the end of military occupation and political independence could be a much more effective policy. Many would argue that such approaches need to be seriously explored in the ongoing conflicts in Palestine, Afghanistan, Iraq, Chechnya, the Philippines, Somalia, and elsewhere.

Importantly, in many cases, local community actors, civil society and broader political movements will pressure violent groups to desist from terrorism if they perceive that the authorities are willing to engage in genuine dialogue and reform. This is arguably the reason why ETA in Spain declared a final ceasefire and decided to pursue its goal of an independent Basque nation politically (Murua 2017). It was also a key factor in the Good Friday Agreement (see Case Study 21.2). Directly related to this, peacebuilding operations and programmes which work to promote reconciliation, the disarmament and demobilization of armed groups, train local leaders in conflict resolution, provide alternative employment for former combatants, generate local capacities for security provision, engage in anti-violence and counter-radicalization programmes and the like, can also offer an alternative approach to violence reduction (Ingiriis 2018; D'Estaing 2017).

Another nonviolent approach we can observe historically involves offering terrorists amnesties or pardons in exchange for giving up armed struggle. This is something we have seen in places like Italy where there was a terrorism campaign by the Red Brigades, in Northern Ireland where the Good Friday Agreement included the release of prisoners convicted of terrorism, and in South Africa where pardon was exchanged for participating in the truth and reconciliation commission. More recently, programmes for returned foreign fighters from the Middle East and/or right-wing nationalist terrorists in countries like Indonesia, Denmark, Germany, Singapore, and elsewhere have worked with returnees or former militants, providing counselling, mentoring, skills training and employment support, as opposed to imprisonment and harsh restrictions, as a way of rehabilitating and reintegrating former fighters or militants into the community. This approach of treating returned fighters as politically motivated human beings, rather than as inhuman 'evildoers', appears to work well in diverting people from further violence.

21.4 EXPLORING THE POTENTIAL OF NONVIOLENT COUNTERTERRORISM

The preoccupation with force-based counterterrorism has meant that relatively little effort has thus far gone into exploring the potential of nonviolent approaches. Taking nonviolent responses to terrorism seriously involves, first, acknowledging the political roots of terrorist violence, and second, exploring alternative ways in which groups and individuals respond to political violence more broadly.

21.4.1 Counterterrorism and the political

To argue that terrorism, and by extension counterterrorism, is a type of political violence is not new. In a review of terrorism books in the 1970s, Arblaster (1977: 421) observed that much writing on terrorism preferred to concentrate on the moral, tactical or psychological dimensions of the subject, and evaded the political dimension, thereby failing to 'reflect collective political situations and political commitments'. Arblaster suggested that nationalism, which can be combined with both left- and right-wing ideologies, was the most widespread common factor, and that it is at the political level that the explanations for terrorism, and the solutions, should be sought. This chapter argues similarly that terrorism is *political* violence, a strategy of political contention and a symptom of political conflict, as can be clearly seen in Palestine, Northern Ireland, Sri Lanka, Colombia, Spain, Turkey, and Iraq. Even al-Qaeda was motivated by well-defined political goals such as expelling US forces from the Arabian Gulf and supporting Palestinian liberation (see Lawrence 2005).

So what does this mean for counterterrorism? In short, it means that terrorism is not a form of violence perpetrated by inherently evil actors hell-bent on destroying the world. It means that the explanations for acts of terrorism are, in large part, to be found at the political level and counterterrorism should start from this premise. It means that counterterrorism must shift away from its current *negatively* defined approach of countering violence with violence, and instead, counterterrorism should be reconceptualized as a *positively* defined condition of working politically to prevent the use of violence. Importantly, it means that terrorism, while sometimes horrific, is a threat that we can deal with within the realm of ordinary politics, instead of through the exceptional paradigm of war.

> **KEY CONCEPTS**
>
> **Nonviolence** Forms of political action aimed at social change which rejects the use of violence against human beings or causing direct harm to humans. Sometimes referred to as nonviolent resistance, it is based the employment of forms of moral and/or disruptive force to compel or convince opponents, and can involve hundreds of different tactics and approaches.

Conflict resolution The theory and practice of resolving conflicts between individuals, groups and states through dialogue-based or largely nonviolent approaches, including legal methods, negotiation, mediation, conciliation, reconciliation, diplomacy, peacekeeping and many more.

Unarmed civilian peacekeeping The use of trained but unarmed civilians to protect other vulnerable civilians in the midst of violent political conflict through strategies of nonviolent resistance.

Social defence A nonviolent alternative to military defence based on widespread political, economic and social non-cooperation in order to resist and oppose military aggression or political repression.

Peacebuilding A holistic approach to conflict resolution aimed at resolving injustice or transforming the structural conditions that generate deadly forms of conflict.

21.4.2 Exploring nonviolent alternatives

It is one of the enduring weaknesses of terrorism studies as a field that it has not fully engaged with all the research and practice from other fields of study which also deal with the causes and resolution of violent conflict (see Jackson 2012). This is in part due to the origins of the field when it attempted to conceptualize terrorism as a unique kind of immoral and nihilistic violence that was purportedly unlike other forms of political violence (Stampnitzky 2013). Nevertheless, following other scholars (English 2009), we suggest that there is both an imperative to begin seriously investigating nonviolent responses to counterterrorism, and a number of existing bodies of research which could facilitate new theory and practice development in this respect.

In addition to the long-standing literature which examines the successes of dialogue, diplomacy, negotiation and mediation in resolving violent conflicts, including conflicts involving acts of terrorism (see Goerzig 2010), a potentially important literature for nonviolent counterterrorism is the large and ever-growing field of nonviolent resistance studies. For over a decade now, scholars have examined the use of nonviolent resistance as a form of political action aimed at overthrowing authoritarian regimes, changing state policies, resisting military occupations, and winning independence for subnational groups (see Chenoweth and Stephan 2011; Bartkowski 2013). Part of the significance of this research is that it demonstrates that repressive state violence, as well as the repressive violence of armed groups who come to control a population such as ISIS, can be effectively responded to with collective nonviolent strategies, and there are a large number of creative, nonviolent options for resistance and protection. We suggest that it could be useful to examine the hundreds of cases of nonviolent resistance to uncover potential nonviolent strategies, tactics and approaches which could inform nonviolent counterterrorism.

Second, there is an emerging literature on what have been called 'nonwarring communities' in places like Colombia, Somalia, Syria, and elsewhere where forms of nonviolent community action have proved to be quite effective in resisting violent incursions by armed groups, including communities under the rule of ISIS (Stephan 2015). Anderson and Wallace (2013) and Kaplan (2017), for example, examined more than a dozen communities from several war-afflicted states who used local institutions, autonomous self-rule, and a variety of creative strategies and tactics to 'nudge' armed actors into concessions, avoid entanglement in the violence, protect the security of their members, and demand accountability from armed groups. Based on the understanding that all armed groups in a conflict nevertheless require the cooperation of civilians, these studies are uncovering the ways in which civilians can exert agency in nonviolent ways to resist, deter or compel armed actors. Such studies clearly provide a potentially rich source for the exploration of bottom-up, locally situated nonviolent counterterrorism.

Third, there is a growing literature detailing and examining the successes of unarmed peacekeeping and nonviolent accompaniment in situations of violent conflict, including in situations like Colombia, Sri Lanka, and South Sudan where acts of terrorism by both state and nonstate actors have been common (see Wallace 2016). This literature examines cases where UN troops chose to be unarmed, as well as cases involving civilian-based nonviolent peace-forces such as Peace Brigades International. Again, the importance of this literature is that it provides solid evidence that military force does not have a monopoly on security provision or deterrence, but that nonviolent actors and strategies can influence and deter armed actors without the use of violent coercion. It speaks to the potential of replacing armed military or police forces with unarmed peacekeepers in situations of violent conflict, including terrorist campaigns, and illustrates the agency of local actors in constructing their own security.

Fourth, there is a long-standing literature on civilian-based forms of national defence, often called social defence (see Bartkowski 2015). Rooted in both the realistic recognition that most small or medium-sized states in the world would be unable to defend themselves from invasion by the most powerful states using military force, and that there are actual cases of successful nonviolent resistance to powerful occupiers (such as Lithuanian popular resistance against Soviet occupation in the early 1990s), such approaches provide strategies for broad civil non-cooperation and raising the costs of invasion and occupation. In fact, Burrowes (1996: 164) suggests that his strategic framework of social defence has the 'ability to formulate a strategy of nonviolent defence against *any* type of military aggression'. This literature should be investigated to see how it could be applied to defence against the violent aggression of terrorist campaigns.

Another important priority in the development of nonviolent counterterrorism is the importance of prevention. Instead of simply reacting to acts of terrorism after they occur, counterterrorism could learn a great deal from the long-standing field of conflict prevention (see Ackermann 2003) which focuses on ensuring that societies maintain high standards of human rights and group rights protection, the promotion of social justice and democratic participation, and developing early warning capabilities so that when political conflict begins to intensify, it can be managed and resolved before it tips over into violence.

It is important to note that none of these literatures imply that nonviolence works every time or in every case; there is no known method that works in every case. But, knowing that nonviolent resistance, non-warring communities and unarmed peacekeeping, among others, has worked in a great many cases and different areas opens up our intellectual horizons to new possibilities, and demands that we seriously explore the potential of nonviolent alternatives to the ineffective and destructive counterterrorism approaches which have dominated policy and practice until now.

21.5 CONCLUSION

In this chapter, we have explained why nonviolent responses to terrorism ought to be taken more seriously, and outlined some areas of research which could provide important theory and practice for nonviolent counterterrorism. Our approach is premised on the noted failures of force-based counterterrorism, including the inherently problematic and unethical way that violence operates as a form of political action. In the context of a broader terrorism discourse which understands terrorism to be a uniquely threatening form of evil (Jackson 2005), it is controversial to suggest that states respond nonviolently to acts of terrorism. Some might consider it to be unrealistic and naïve. Nonetheless, we have outlined the compelling reasons why nonviolent counterterrorism is likely to be more effective, less damaging and more ethical than current approaches. Certainly, given the record of the GWOT to date, it is the policy of responding to terrorism with military force which would appear to be rather naïve and unrealistic.

However, despite the many nonviolent ways in which campaigns of terrorism have been ended historically, and despite the well-known failures of force-based counterterrorism and the need for alternatives, to date studies on responding to terrorism nonviolently have been relatively few and far between. Certainly, it is difficult to find studies which go beyond a critique of the GWOT or current forms of counterterrorism to suggesting an alternative nonviolent approach. An exception to this state of affairs is Lindahl's (2018) 'critical theory of counterterrorism'. His approach, which is summarized in Table 21.1, is based on the principles we have articulated in this chapter, including the need to treat terrorism as a political phenomenon, the importance of maintaining means-ends consistency and aiming for more than simply the elimination of terrorists, the importance of directing action towards prevention, and the crucial importance of the rigorous evaluation of counterterrorism to ensure that it is not causing more harm than good. Based on these principles, and investigating the many ways in which nonviolent political action has been used in political campaigns, unarmed peacekeeping and social defence, we believe that a practical toolkit of nonviolent counterterrorism can be developed, tested, applied, and evaluated in the coming years.

TABLE 21.1 The CTS Model of Counterterrorism

THE CTS MODEL OF COUNTERTERRORISM		
1. Key assumptions		
	A.	Is primarily a label not a scientific fact.
	B.	Needs to be contextualized.
	C.	Derives from, and embedded in, deep politics.
2. Basic Principles		
	A.	Dare to know: Entails a radical rethinking of ontology, epistemology, and the agenda of counterterrorism.
	B.	Emancipation: Provides the normative and ethical foundation for the model. It is a continuous process which holds that security has to be concerned with enhancing the emancipatory space for all people. It is also the higher-order choice that bears on lower-order choices in strategies and tactics.
	C.	Means/ends relationship: There is an inviolable connection between the means we use and the changes we want to bring about.
	D.	Nonviolence: As a way of life. Commensurate with emancipation and means/ends consistency. It is a morally preferable way of countering terrorism, and empirically better suited to deal with political conflicts.
	E.	Holism: Because there is not a single effective method of counterterrorism, it has to contextualize acts of terrorism and address across the political apparatus.
3. Strategies and tactics		
	A.	Adhere to the higher-order choice of emancipation and emphasize means/ends consistency, nonviolence, and holism in both short- and long-term strategies.
	B.	Short-term response: disaster management model, respect orthodox legal framework, and avoid creating a culture of fear followed by draconian measures.
4. Priorities		
	A.	Prevention is the single most important dimension of the model.
	B.	Counterterrorism as positive peace, and more commitment and resources must be devoted to addressing the structural issues that are conducive to terrorism in the first place.
5. Evaluation		
	A.	Proportionality
	B.	Effectiveness
	C.	Legitimacy

Source: Lindahl 2018: 107

DISCUSSION QUESTIONS

1. How has the conception of the terrorism threat influenced the way in which states have responded to it?
2. Why has the global war on terror and forced-based counterterrorism been so unsuccessful in countering and preventing terrorism?
3. Why have nonviolent approaches to counterterrorism been so ignored, particularly when there are historic examples of methods like peace negotiations which have been successful in previous campaigns?
4. Why might dialogue and negotiations provide terrorists with an incentive to lay down their weapons?
5. What can we learn about possible strategies of nonviolent counterterrorism from the experiences of nonviolent resistance, non-warring communities, unarmed peacekeeping, and social defence?

 Visit the online resources for pointers on how to answer the discussion questions, links to useful web sources, and guidance on accessing databases:
www.oup.com/he/Wilson-Muro1e

GUIDE TO FURTHER READING

English, R. (2009) *Terrorism: How to Respond*. Oxford: Oxford University Press. *Based on years of research, a book which provides a powerful set of arguments for treating terrorism as a political problem that cannot be resolved through force alone.*

Goerzig, C. (2010) *Talking to Terrorists: Concessions and the Renunciation of Violence*. Abingdon: Routledge. *A study of how dialogue and negotiations can be a successful response to terrorism, and a confirmation that dialogue and concessions to terrorist groups does not lead to more terrorism, as some critics argue.*

Jones, S. and Libicki, M. (2008) *How Terrorist Groups End: Lessons for Countering Al Qaeda*, Rand Corporation. *An important empirical study which demonstrates the limited role that force plays in ending terrorist campaigns.*

Kaplan, O. (2017) *Resisting War: How Communities Protect Themselves*.Cambridge: Cambridge University Press. *An important study which demonstrates the range of ways that local communities can resist and prevent violence without the use of armed force, even in cases where terrorism is occurring.*

Lindahl, S. (2018) *A Critical Theory of Counterterrorism: Ontology, Epistemology, Normativity*. Abingdon: Routledge. *The first major study to outline a critical terrorism studies approach to countering terrorism, including the application of the CTS model to the case study of Norway after the Breivik attack.*

Wallace, M. (2016) *Security Without Weapons: Rethinking Violence, Violent Action, and Civilian Protection*, Abingdon, UK: Routledge. *A study which uncovers the limits of using violent force, and the real-world potential of protecting civilians from armed actors without the use of weapons.*

REFERENCES

Abrahms, M. and Mierau, J. (2017) 'Leadership Matters: The Effects of Targeted Killings on Militant Group Tactics', *Terrorism and Political Violence*, 29 (5): 830–851.

Ackermann, A. (2003) 'The Idea and Practice of Conflict Prevention', *Journal of Peace Research*, 40 (3): 339–347.

Anderson, M. and Wallace, M. (2013) *Opting Out of War*, Boulder, CO: Lynne Reinner.

Araj, B. (2008) 'Harsh State Repression as a Cause of Suicide Bombing: The Case of the Palestinian-Israeli Conflict', *Studies in Conflict & Terrorism*, 31 (4): 284–303.

Arblaster, A. (1977) 'Terrorism: Myths, Meaning and Morals', *Political Studies*, 25 (3): 413–424.

Bartkowski, M., ed. (2013) *Recovering Nonviolent History: Civil Resistance in Liberation Struggles*. Boulder, CO: Lynne Rienner.

Bartkowski, M. (2015) *Nonviolent Civilian Defence to Counter Russian Hybrid Warfare*, White Paper, The John Hopkins University Center for Advanced Governmental Studies, available online at: http://advanced.jhu.edu/academics/graduate-degree-programs/global-security-studies/program-resources/publications/white-paper-maciej-bartkowski/ (last accessed 04 September 2015).

Bolland, T. and Ludvigsen, J. (2018) '"No Boots on the Ground": The Effectiveness of US Drones Against Al Qaeda in the Arabian Peninsula', *Defence & Security Analysis*, 34 (2): 127–143.

Burrowes, R. (1996) *The Strategy of Nonviolent Defence: A Gandhian Approach*. New York: State University of New York Press.

Byman, D. (2006) 'Do Targeted Killings Work?', *Foreign Affairs*, 85 (2): 95–111.

Chenoweth, E. and Stephan, M. (2011) *Why Civil Resistance Works: The Strategic Logic of Nonviolent Conflict*. New York: Columbia University Press.

Crawford, N. C. (2019) *United States Budgetary Costs and Obligations of Post 9/11 Wars through FY2020: $6.4 Trillion*. Boston. Available at: https://watson.brown.edu/costsofwar/files/cow/imce/papers/2019/US Budgetary Costs of Wars November 2019.pdf?utm_source=Daily on Defence (2019 TEMPLATE)_11/15/2019&utm_medium=email&utm_campaign=WEX_Daily on Defence&rid=84648.

Crelinsten, R. (2009) *Counterterrorism*. Cambridge: Polity.

D'Estaing, S. G. (2017) 'Engaging women in countering violent extremism: avoiding instrumentalisation and furthering agency', *Gender and Development*, 25 (1): 103–118.

English, R. (2009) *Terrorism: How to Respond*. Oxford: Oxford University Press.

Frazer, E. and Hutchings, K., 2008. 'On Politics and Violence: Arendt Contra Fanon', *Contemporary Political Theory*, 7: 90–108.

Goerzig, C. (2010) *Talking to Terrorists: Concessions and the Renunciation of Violence*. Abingdon: Routledge.

Goodman-Delahunty, J., Martschuk, N., and Dhami, M. (2014) 'Interviewing High Value Detainees: Securing Cooperation and Disclosures', *Applied Cognitive Pyschology*, 6: 883–907.

Hoffman, B. (2004) 'Foreword', in Silke, A. (ed.) *Research on Terrorism. Trends, Achievements & Failures*. Abingdon: Frank Cass, xvii.

Holmes, R. (2013) *The Ethics of Nonviolence: Essays by Robert L. Holmes*, edited by P. Cicovacki. New York, NY: Bloomsbury.

Howes, D. (2013) 'The Failure of Pacifism and the Success of Nonviolence'. *Perspectives on Politics* 11 (2): 427–466.

Ingiriis, M. H. (2018) 'Building Peace from the Margins in Somalia: The Case for Political Settlement with Al-Shabaab', *Contemporary Security Policy*, 39 (4): 512–536.

Jackson, R. (2005) *Writing the War on Terrorism: Language, Politics and Counterterrorism*. Manchester: Manchester University Press.

Jackson, R. (2012) 'Unknown Knowns: The Subjugated Knowledge of Terrorism Studies', *Critical Studies on Terrorism*, 5 (1): 11–29.

Jackson, R. (2015) 'The Epistemological Crisis of Counterterrorism', *Critical Studies on Terrorism*, 8 (1): 33–54.

Jackson, R. (2017) 'CTS, Counterterrorism and Nonviolence', *Critical Studies on Terrorism*, 10 (2): 357–369.

Jackson, R. (2018) 'Pacifism: The Anatomy of a Subjugated Knowledge', *Critical Studies on Security*, 6 (2): 160–175.

Jackson, R. (2019) 'Pacifism and the Ethical Imagination', *International Politics*, 56 (2): 212–227.

Jones, S. and Libicki, M. (2008) *How Terrorist Groups End: Lessons for Countering Al Qaeda*. Rand Corporation.

Kaplan, O. (2017) *Resisting War: How Communities Protect Themselves*. Cambridge: Cambridge University Press.

Lawrence, B. (2005) *Messages to the World: The Statements of Osama bin Laden*. London: Verso.

Lindahl, S. (2016) 'Critical Evaluation of Counterterrorism', in Jackson, R., ed., *Routledge*

Handbook of Critical Terrorism Studies. Abingdon: Routledge, 214–224.

Lindahl, S. (2018) *A Critical Theory of Counterterrorism: Ontology, Epistemology, Normativity*. Abingdon: Routledge.

Lum, C., Kennedy, L., and Sherley, A. (2006, 2009) 'The Effectiveness of Counter-Terrorism Strategies', *Campbell Systematic Reviews*, (2): 1–50; available online at: https://campbellcollaboration.org/.../251_147ebbe46e2519dc1da62c-1c1146c121.html.

Lum, C., Kennedy, L. W., and Sherley, A. (2008) 'Is Counter-terrorism Policy Evidence-based? What Works, What Harms, and What is Unknown', *Psicothema*, 20 (1): 35–42.

Martini, A., Ford, K., and Jackson, R., eds. (2020) *Encountering Extremism: Theoretical Issues and Local Challenges*. Manchester, UK: Manchester University Press.

Middle East Eye (2016) *Blood and Treasure: The Costs of the Iraq War* Available at: http://www.middleeasteye.net/news/blood-and-treasure-costs-iraq-war-1660190585 (last accessed 4 July 2016).

Murua, I., (2017) 'No More Bullets for ETA: The Loss of Internal Support as a Key Factor in the End of the Basque Group's Campaign', *Critical Studies on Terrorism*, 10 (1): 93–114.

Pape, R. (2005) *Dying to Win: The Strategic Logic of Suicide Terrorism*. New York, Random House.

Piazza, J. (2017) 'Repression and Terrorism: A Cross-National Empirical Analysis of Types of Repression and Domestic Terrorism', *Terrorism and Political Violence*, 29 (1): 102–118.

Piazza, J. and Choi, S. (2018) 'International Military Interventions and Transnational Terrorist Backlash', *International Studies Quarterly*, 62: 686–695.

PSR (Physicians for Social Responsibility) (2015) *Body Count: Casualty Figures after 10 Years of the 'War on Terror'*, IPPNW Germany, available online at: http://www.psr.org/assets/pdfs/body-count.pdf, (last accessed 22 May 2017).

Rejali, D. (2007) *Torture and Democracy*. Princeton University Press.

Schiemann, J. (2015) *Does Torture Work?* Oxford: Oxford University Press.

Stampnitzky, L. (2013) *Disciplining Terrorism, How Experts Invented 'Terrorism'*. Cambridge: Cambridge University Press.

Stephan, M. (2015) 'Civil Resistance vs. ISIS', *Journal of Resistance Studies*, 1 (2): 127–50.

The Afghanistan Papers: Interview with Ambassador Douglas Lute (2019) *The Washington Post*. Available at: https://www.washingtonpost.com/graphics/2019/investigations/afghanistan-papers/documents-database/ (last accessed 27 January 2020).

The Afghanistan Papers: Interview with Michael Flynn (2019) *The Washington Post*. Available at: https://www.washingtonpost.com/graphics/2019/investigations/afghanistan-papers/documents-database/documents/flynn_michael_ll_11102015.pdf?v=26 (last accessed 27 January 2020).

van Dongen, T. (2010) 'Mapping Counterterrorism: A Categorisation of Policies and the Promise of Empirically Based, Systematic Comparisons', *Critical Studies on Terrorism*, 3 (2): 227–241.

Wallace, M. (2016) *Security Without Weapons: Rethinking Violence, Violent Action, and Civilian Protection*. Abingdon, UK: Routledge.

Wolfendale, J. (2007) 'Terrorism, Security and the Threat of Counterterrorism', *Studies in Conflict & Terrorism*, 30 (1): 75–92.

Young, R. (2010) 'The Violent State', *Naked Punch Supplement*, Issue 2. Available at: https://issuu.com/naked_punch_review/docs/supplementyoung.

Zulaika, J. (2009) *Terrorism: The Self-fulfilling Prophesy*. Chicago, IL: University of Chicago Press.

CHAPTER 22

Counterterrorism and Human Rights

FRANK FOLEY

■ **CHAPTER SUMMARY**

This chapter examines how counterterrorism policies and operations affect human rights in liberal democracies. It analyses how practices such as detention without trial, torture and extra-judicial killings impact negatively on human rights. The chapter also reverses the causal arrow to consider whether and how human rights standards can have an effect on counterterrorism policy and practice. Can norms of individual liberty significantly constrain a state's response to terrorist groups? And does respect for human rights help or hinder the effectiveness of counterterrorism? The chapter presents a framework which enables readers to critically analyse the academic literature on these questions. It illustrates the key factors and mechanisms at play through case studies, ranging from Northern Ireland in the 1970s to the United States 'war' against jihadist terrorism.

22.1 INTRODUCTION

Counterterrorism has been a top priority policy issue in international politics in recent decades as transnational terrorist groups have attacked leading powers ranging from the United States to France to Russia. With countries such as these pushing the issue of terrorism up the global agenda, governments' increased focus on counterterrorism has had significant implications for human rights. State practices including torture, extra-judicial killings, detention without trial and digital surveillance have had a decidedly negative impact on human rights. Nevertheless, some scholars believe that human rights are not as weak as they may seem in a counterterrorism and national security context. As this chapter will outline, there is an active debate among experts on whether human rights standards can significantly constrain liberal democratic state responses to terrorist groups. Another major question is whether derogating from human rights helps or hinders the effectiveness of state counterterrorism.

Human rights are generally understood to be those 'fundamental moral rights of the person that are necessary for a life with human dignity' (Forsythe, 2012: 3). Principles, such as the right to life or the right not to be tortured, have a long history. Yet it took the horrors of World War II and the holocaust for states to fully accept that human rights were not just a domestic matter, but also needed to be recognized in international law. In 1948, states agreed the Universal Declaration of Human Rights, an international agreement adopted by the United Nations, while the 1949 Geneva Conventions which were negotiated in the aftermath of WWII stated that some individual rights should be respected even by countries engaged in armed conflict. Human rights were advanced in the following decades by both 'hard law' (authoritative rules which are legally binding) and 'soft law' (norms or principles which are not legally binding). For example, the European Convention on Human Rights led to the creation of hard law, as national courts and a supranational court provide binding judgements about what is legal and illegal in specific situations. However, soft law is also very important. Despite being non-binding in a legal sense, some major human rights treaties and United Nations resolutions can nevertheless influence policymaking and the behaviour of states (Forsythe, 2012: 14–15). Beyond their litigation work, non-governmental organizations (NGOs) have also engaged in advocacy work and pressure campaigns which have influenced some states towards the greater implementation of human rights norms (Risse and Sikkink, 1999). In many ways, therefore, human rights are more firmly established in world politics today than ever before. Yet these rights are also being challenged by a range of forces including the rise of neo-authoritarianism in China and other states which violate human rights (such as Saudi Arabia, Turkey, Yemen, Syria, and Russia), the advance of nationalist and populist politics, and the greater prominence of terrorist groups and state responses to terrorism.

Counterterrorism, for the purposes of this chapter, refers to policies formulated and actions taken by states (or international organizations) to reduce or prevent terrorism, or mitigate the effects of terrorism. It encompasses many activities ranging from protective security measures, which harden targets against potential attacks, to emergency management which aims to respond speedily once an attack has taken place (Crelinsten, 2019). International diplomacy is important for coordinating state responses to terrorism, while foreign aid, domestic social policy, and counter-radicalization programmes can be used to try to reduce the numbers of people seeking to get involved in terrorism over the long term. Anti-terrorist legislation and legal processes, as well as police, intelligence, and military operations against terrorism have a major impact on human rights, and will be a central focus of this chapter.

> **KEY CONCEPTS**
>
> **Human Rights** Fundamental moral rights, acquired at birth and inherent to all human beings, which are necessary for a life with human dignity. Key human rights include the right to life (or prohibition of the arbitrary deprivation of life), the prohibitions of torture and slavery, and the right to a fair trial.
>
> **Counterterrorism** Policies formulated and actions taken by states to reduce or prevent terrorism, or mitigate the effects of terrorism. Encompasses a wide range of elements including legislation and legal processes, as well as police, intelligence and military operations against terrorism.

This chapter presents a framework which enables students to critically analyse the academic literature on the complex relationship between counterterrorism and human rights. As this relationship works differently across different political regime types, to aid analytical coherence, the chapter focuses primarily on liberal democratic states. It begins by outlining how some counterterrorism practices, such as detention without trial, torture, and extrajudicial killings, have impacted negatively on human rights in liberal democracies. We then reverse the causal arrow to consider whether and how human rights standards can influence counterterrorism policy and practice. Can norms of individual liberty significantly constrain a state's response to terrorist groups? Finally, the chapter assesses the debate on whether derogating from human rights enables the state to better fight terrorism or has counterproductive consequences which reduce the effectiveness of a counterterrorism campaign.

22.2 HOW COUNTERTERRORISM AFFECTS HUMAN RIGHTS

A wide range of empirical cases studies lend support to the belief that states' increased efforts on counterterrorism have had a negative effect on their adherence to human rights (see, for example, Galli, 2015; Donohue, 2008; Adelman, 2007). Table 22.1 gives an overview of how four types of counterterrorism actions (placed across the top) impact on

TABLE 22.1 Counterterrorism actions and human rights

INTELLIGENCE	RESTRICTION	DECISIVE INTERVENTION	CUSTODY & TRIAL
Privacy	Freedom of expression	Prohibition of arbitrary arrest	Prohibition of arbitrary detention
Freedom of expression	Freedom of movement	Prohibition of enforced disappearances	Prohibition of torture, inhumane or degrading treatment
	Right to enter own nation	Life (arbitrary deprivation of life)	Fair trial (by impartial tribunal; within reasonable time)

specific human rights as defined by international conventions and treaties (these rights make up the rest of the table). Though not comprehensive, it indicates the range of different types of counterterrorism actions and their potential to affect many human rights. The following section outlines a range of examples which illustrate how the human rights listed in the table have been undermined by responses to terrorism in democratic states.

Let us now consider in turn how legislative and operational counterterrorism may affect human rights. At the core of any corpus of anti-terrorism legislation is a legal framework for dealing with terrorist suspects. To understand how that legal framework operates in a democratic state, it is useful to break it down into three parts: the pre-trial process, terrorism trials, and terrorist offences (Foley, 2013: 176). In the *pre-trial process* a central question is: when a terrorist suspect is arrested, how many days can they be held without being charged? In the United States, this period cannot exceed 48 hours (Epifanio, 2011). Spain, by contrast, has permitted incommunicado detention for up to 13 days in terrorism cases, and provided for a delay in the arrival of a lawyer to advise the suspect—a system which has the potential to facilitate torture or ill treatment in detention, according to successive UN reports (Scheinin, 2008: 15–16). Beyond this initial period, how long does it take for a case to reach trial? Among liberal democracies, France has one of the more draconian systems in this respect as the length of time between arrest and trial can be up to four years in terrorism cases (Foley: 2013: 187). This has raised questions about whether France has fully respected suspects' right to a trial within reasonable time. Thus, whether it is the prohibition of torture or rights of due process, there is considerable variation in the extent to which anti-terrorism legislation infringes on human rights in the pre-trial phase.

In the next stage of the process—*terrorism trials*—there is also significant variation across countries. At one end of the spectrum, some states try terrorist suspects in ordinary civilian courts, providing considerable protection of the right to a fair trial. For instance, the UK has used ordinary courts to deal with terrorist suspects linked to al-Qaeda and ISIS. These trials do not derogate from the procedures of ordinary English justice, and a

PHOTO 22.1 Terror detention times vary around the world: in Australia this is 48 hours, the same for the US, whereas France and Spain have longer maximum detention periods. In the UK it is 24 hours.

jury composed of member of the public decides on the guilt or innocence of defendants. Other states have used special terrorism trials within the civilian justice system. France abolished jury trial in terrorism cases in 1986, following some cases in which jurors had been threatened. This was a derogation from ordinary procedure in respect of the *Cour d'Assises*, a criminal trial court which considers more serious terrorism offences, and many of the judges who sit in these trials are specialized in adjudicating on terrorism cases (Shapiro and Suzan, 2003: 77).

The most controversial type of terrorism trial has been that located in systems of military justice. Alongside the terrorism trials which take place in American civilian courts, the US government set up a parallel system of justice in 2002 when it created military commissions at the Guantanamo Bay detention camp. Foreign nationals thus face charges of involvement in international terrorism in military-run trials in which the procedures and rules of evidence are looser and more favourable to the authorities than they are in US civilian courts. The commissions have been reformed repeatedly following a Supreme Court ruling in 2006 that they were unconstitutional and following Acts of Congress (Jimenez-Bacardi, 2013). Yet they have proved to be a largely ineffective means of securing justice. Of the some 750 people that have been detained at Guantanamo Bay over the years, only a handful have been prosecuted and convicted of terrorism. The rest have mostly been transferred to other countries, while about 26 remain there under indefinite detention without charge or trial (Human Rights First, 2018), thus violating detainees' right to a fair trial. Other countries, such as Malaysia and Singapore, cited terrorist threats from al-Qaeda, and later ISIS, as justification for passing laws which also permitted indefinite detention without trial (Tan, 2018).

In understanding how states legally deal with terrorist suspects, a third element to consider is *terrorist offences*. Human rights are best served if such offences are clearly and narrowly defined. For instance, many British terrorist suspects have been convicted of conspiracy to cause an explosion. To secure a conviction on this charge, the prosecution needs to show that all suspects had the same intention (to cause explosions) and that they had agreed to carry it out (Foley, 2013: 200). If terrorism offences are more loosely defined, it can raise questions about the authorities' respect for the right to a fair trial. In France for example, it is an offence to participate in an 'association established with a view to the preparation [of] . . . acts of terrorism'. This offence has been interpreted very broadly in numerous cases, including the controversial 'Chalabi' case of 1998 when it was used to bring 138 people before a mass trial (Foley, 2013: 202–205, 298–300).

Beyond the legal framework for dealing with terrorist suspects, anti-terrorism legislation ranges more broadly across the powers of investigation, detention and executive action. Several liberal democracies passed anti-terrorism legislation after 9/11, which increased the authorities' power to detain or deport foreign nationals suspected of links to terrorism. In terms of investigative powers, the US and other states introduced legislation which expanded the ability of their security agencies to carry out special searches, plant bugging devices, and implement phone tapping, computer, and internet surveillance for the purposes of gathering intelligence on terrorism (Epifanio, 2011: 404–406). In 2013, a major leak by an American whistle-blower, Edward Snowden, revealed that the US, UK, Canadian, and other governments had engaged in an 'astonishingly large-scale monitoring' of populations' phone and internet activity, raising questions about whether they had violated their citizens' right to privacy (Lyon, 2014: 2).

In addition to legislation, a second major dimension of counterterrorism is the state's operational response to terrorism. The harder edge of this dimension includes operations to arrest, disrupt, or kill suspected terrorists. Arrest operations can infringe on human rights in cases where there are insufficient grounds for arrest or when raids are indiscriminate. The French security agencies, for instance, have on several occasions arrested large numbers of people from Muslim communities in major raids, most notably during the terrorist crises of 1995 and 2015. French officials have admitted that during certain periods, it was explicit police policy to arrest the maximum number of people possible; in effect, to do 'fishing expeditions' (Foley, 2019: 533). Such operations have had implications for human rights, in particular the prohibition of arbitrary arrest. There are other restrictions, short of arrest and prosecution, which are used to disrupt terrorist suspects. Britain has used 'control orders' to confine suspects to their homes for much of the day, restrict their use of the internet and ban them from meeting certain individuals. Such measures, which infringed on individuals' rights to freedom of movement and expression, were reduced in scope over time by UK court rulings and government reforms (Foley, 2013: 215–219).

The killing of suspected terrorists can be uncontroversial in certain cases, especially when done in self-defence to shut down a live terrorist attack. Major questions are raised, however, when states seek to kill suspects pre-emptively. Israel has assassinated countless leaders and members of Palestinian militant groups in recent decades, provoking international outrage on a number of occasions (Byman, 2011). The US under President Barack Obama (in power from 2009 to 2017) greatly increased its use of drone strikes, conducting thousands of so-called 'targeted killings' of terrorist suspects in countries such as Afghanistan, Pakistan, and Yemen. While the Obama administration argued that it was respecting international law for the use of force in self-defence, American 'targeted killing' operations have been widely condemned as violations of human rights, notably the right to life or prohibition of the arbitrary deprivation of life (McDonald, 2017). The Indonesian government has also been criticized as its special counterterrorism police unit, Densus 88 (or Detachment 88), has been implicated in the extra-judicial killing of many terrorist suspects since its creation following the 2002 Bali bombings (Tan, 2018). All too often, innocent civilians are the victims of such operations. One of the most notorious cases of this came at the height of Colombia's fight against the FARC (or 'Revolutionary Armed Forces of Colombia'). Between 2002 and 2008, Colombian army brigades routinely killed civilians who they falsely claimed were combatants in order to show 'positive' results in the form of rising enemy body counts. Allegations have been made in over 3,600 such cases, and at least 1,600 mid- and low-level soldiers have been convicted for these unlawful killings (Human Rights Watch, 2019).

This section has outlined how legislative and operational responses to terrorism have major implications for human rights. The next section, 22.3, reverses the causal arrow to consider whether human rights standards have a significant impact on counterterrorism.

22.3 DO HUMAN RIGHTS STANDARDS SHAPE COUNTERTERRORISM?

What are the key factors that shape the development of counterterrorism policy and practice? In particular, do human rights standards have an important influence on counterterrorism? Can these standards significantly constrain a state's response to terrorist groups? Scholars offer different answers to these key questions. This section outlines their debate and traces their arguments back to broader worldviews or theories of International Relations (IR).

Scholars writing from a broadly realist perspective in IR theory would not expect human rights to have a major influence on how states respond to terrorist groups. For realists, the key interests of any government are power, security and order. If it is necessary to violate or ignore human rights in order to safeguard these interests, governments will not hesitate to do so (Chong, 2014: 27–30). The assumption from this perspective is that governments are rational actors, which calculate their actions to maintain or increase their political power. As Carey, Gibney and Poe (2010: 129) argue, states use repression and violate human rights 'when they perceive their power to the threatened.' According to this view, one needs to focus on the nature of the terrorist threat—not human rights norms—to understand a government's approach to counterterrorism. Thus, Laura Donohue warns that highly destructive terrorist attacks could prompt liberal democratic states to take radical steps to 'protect themselves from potential harm.' Based on a detailed study of the US and UK, she suggests that, faced with radical terrorist threats, leaders in these states could brush aside concerns about human rights and make authoritarian responses to terrorism that 'fundamentally change the [state] structure of each country' (Donohue, 2008: 359–360).

Several strands of legal scholarship and research in critical security studies give further reasons to be sceptical about the influence of human rights on state responses to political violence. Legal experts have noted how governments often take the opportunity to introduce draconian anti-terrorism legislation in the aftermath of major terrorist attacks. As Fiona de Londras (2011: 8) puts it: 'domestic law-making processes tend not to cope particularly well in times of crisis. Panic, fear and populist impulses can conspire to create an atmosphere where the imperative turns towards combating a risk, and where that risk is presented . . . as being particularly grave or dangerous.' Critical security scholars draw attention to the social and political processes through which our knowledge of security threats is produced. In regard to counterterrorism, they have highlighted how states justify their legislative and operational crackdowns through discourses of 'exceptionalism'. After a terrorist attack, the argument is often made that 'exceptional times require exceptional measures' (Neal, 2010: 1). As time passes, however, the exception becomes the norm. Neal (2012a: 261) shows how the 'norm/exception binary becomes blurred' as laws passed during an emergency continue to exercise a major influence on politics and the law long after 'the symbolic impact of major terrorist attacks has faded'.

Governments have other strategies to justify and sustain a draconian response to terrorism. The literature on 'securitization' examines the processes by which a particular group or issue comes to be seen as a threat or a question of 'national security'. For example, Stuart Croft shows how the discourse of Britain's 'political and cultural elite' called a 'single British Muslim community' into being variously as a 'radical other' (to be feared and demonized) and as an 'orientalized other' (to be engaged and patronized). The invocation of this radical other or enemy within helped to bolster the argument for 'extraordinary measures' and anti-terrorism legislation (Croft, 2012: 198–201, 235–237).

Rebecca Sanders (2018) examines how the US government made convoluted legal arguments and manipulated legal norms in order to enable its prosecution of the Global War on Terror, including the operation of controversial military commissions at Guantanamo Bay. To facilitate its violations of human rights, all the government needed was a veneer of 'plausible legality,' she writes. This raises major doubts about the ability of international law to regulate or constrain state responses to terrorism. Furthermore, the increasing prominence of nationalist and populist politics over the last decade poses a significant new threat to human rights. Claiming to be motivated by counterterrorism concerns, in 2015 the then Presidential candidate Donald Trump advocated torture, and pledged to ban Muslims from entering the United States. While his ability to implement his agenda as US President was mixed, his rhetoric has contributed to a normalization of brutality, extreme right-wing policies, and a political backlash against international human rights norms (Birdsall and Sanders, 2020). Overall, a common theme of these various literatures is that governments have powerful material, legal, and ideational resources at their disposal to facilitate the maintenance of a repressive response to terrorism in which human rights play only a very limited role.

By contrast, several other strands of literature have identified ways in which human rights standards can have a significant influence on counterterrorism. One strand, which can be traced back to a broadly liberal perspective in IR theory, draws attention to the importance of international law, treaties and institutions for the protection of human rights. Rejecting the realist view of national interest as overly narrow, liberals suggest that states have signed up to such treaties and institutions because they have a long-term interest in the protection of human rights. For example, all states are better off if their prisoners of war are not mistreated (Chong, 2014: 31–32). Some, including the US President George W. Bush administration, have argued that since terrorist groups do not sign up to the Geneva Conventions, the standards of international law for humanitarian treatment in war do not apply to such groups. However, most legal experts—including the US Supreme Court—have held that reciprocity is not the only relevant principle in such cases and that international law does apply to suspected terrorists (Sanders, 2011: 615–617).

In practice, also, governments have not enjoyed complete freedom of action—even in cases such as Guantanamo Bay, outlined above, and torture under the 'war on terror.' Ruth Blakeley (2013) has shown how 'collective social action' by NGOs and human rights lawyers, through the structure of domestic and international law, helped to stymie the George W. Bush administration's torture programme (see Case Study 22.1). The US supreme court also ruled against the government's military commissions at Guantanamo Bay and insisted upon a greater protection of rights for detainees. The British government introduced its own version of indefinite detention without trial of foreign terrorist suspects in 2001, but this was effectively thrown out by the UK's highest court in 2004. In explaining such rulings, Fiona de Londras argues that international human rights law has emboldened superior courts in the two countries to 'resist repressive detention laws'. Indeed, these courts 'acted in a less deferential manner than was the case in earlier situations of emergency or war'. Through this mechanism, she concludes, 'human rights have . . . fought back against counter-terrorist detention in the "War on Terror"' (de Londras, 2011: i, 278, 283).

Comparative research has illustrated across multiple cases the importance of the judiciary and parliament in shaping anti-terrorist and emergency legislation. Lynch (2015) shows that when the legislature has strong veto powers and there are sufficient opportunities for judicial challenge through the courts, the result is increased accountability over the government's passing of emergency laws. But scholars have produced different findings on whether anti-terrorist legislation is generally subject to sufficient checks and balances by parliament. In his research on the British case, Neal (2012b: 357) finds that 'counterterrorist law is all too often made in a rushed, reactive, and repetitious way, marginalizing the deliberative, critical, and democratic functions of legislatures and leading to outcomes that later prove to be unconstitutional ….'. While this is the majority position in the literature, there are dissenting views, such as Bright's (2014) finding that parliament does provide a good level of scrutiny. He reaches the opposite conclusion to that of Neal on the British case. Based on a quantitative analysis of UK legislation between 2007 and 2012, Bright finds that the introduction of security legislation actually causes parliamentarians to increase their scrutiny activities, owing to the high importance of such legislation. In theory, at least, this increased scrutiny should bring with it a greater chance that individual rights will be not be disregarded.

Constructivism in IR theory has been drawn on to shed light on some additional reasons why human rights have an influence on counterterrorism. From this perspective, ideas that are viewed as legitimate have a lot of power—and human rights constitutes one set of ideas that has gained increasing legitimacy around the world over the last century (Chong, 2014: 33–34). If such ideas are internalized by domestic political or governmental actors, they can have a significant effect. Even within the George W. Bush administration in the years after 9/11, some officials—notably legal advisors—had internalized, or at least were influenced by, international human rights norms. These officers dissented against the administration's detention and interrogation policies. Indeed, some scholars have found that their dissent played an important role in constraining these policies and bringing them more into alignment with international law over time. The dissenters repeatedly clashed with hardliners who wanted to maintain key elements of the administration's war on terror. Based on his research on this case, Arturo Jimenez-Bacardi (2013: 129) concluded: 'Understanding the normative clashes between members within the executive bureaucracies is key for uncovering the causal mechanism that can lead to state compliance with humanitarian and human rights law.'

Some studies delve further into the varying configurations of ideas and norms found in different national contexts. Foley (2013) asks why Britain and France—two comparable Western European nations—have often differed in their response to jihadist terrorism. This study draws attention to the influence of domestic, historically-grounded, norms; it finds that there is effectively a normative consensus in France that the security of the Republic supersedes other considerations. In Britain, by contrast, there is a greater degree of norm competition as the idea of security-maximization has been contested in public debate by elite actors invoking contradictory norms such as 'traditional British liberties' and respect for communities. This configuration of norms has helped to constrain UK counterterrorism, while the normative consensus in France has enabled its authorities to mount more invasive police operations against terrorism than Britain and create a more draconian anti-terrorist legal regime (Foley, 2013: 1–6, 55–58). Domestic norms thus emerge as a crucial factor for explaining why comparable nations may uphold human rights to different degrees when responding to terrorism. From this perspective, historically-grounded norms can constrain counterterrorism in a way that helps to protect human rights. Case Study 22.1 illustrates the influence of norms and other factors on one of the most controversial aspects of America's contemporary response to terrorism.

CASE STUDY 22.1

Torture in the US 'War on Terror'

In September 2002, Cofer Black, a leading official of the US Central Intelligence Agency (CIA), faced a congressional committee and declared: 'there was a before-9/11 and an after-9/11. After 9/11, the gloves came off' (Black, 2002). Under the orders of President George W. Bush, the CIA had developed a secret 'enhanced interrogation' programme, which gave officials licence to use a range of brutal methods, including waterboarding, 'rectal feeding', and sleep deprivation for up to a week, usually standing or in painful stress positions. These torture techniques were used on terrorist suspects not only at Guantanamo Bay but also at secret CIA prisons—or 'black sites'—in many countries around the world including Romania, Poland, Lithuania, and Thailand. Using 'extraordinary rendition', the US abducted or took custody of individuals outside of any legal process in order to fly them to countries, which were known to use torture, for the explicit purpose of interrogation (SSCI, 2014) (see also Case Study 14.1 from Chapter 14 'Can States Be Terrorists?').

In many ways, the United States use of torture after 9/11 is a classic case of one of the arguments outlined in the main text—that human rights are cast aside when a state faces a heightened terrorist threat. It illustrates how governments have often been able to circumvent the international anti-torture norm and shape public discourse on this issue through powerful rhetorical strategies of denial, exception or 'plausible legality' (Blakeley and Raphael, 2017; Neal, 2010; Sanders, 2011). This case also illustrates other dynamics, however. Some security officials within the US government strongly objected to the torture programme from early on (Ralph, 2013: 117–119). When the programme was exposed to the public, certain types of evidence, and the timing of their release, led mainstream US politics to make a transition from denial to acknowledgement and criticism of the government's perpetration of torture (Del Rosso, 2015). The administration revoked some of its harshest interrogation techniques, Congress passed legislation to regulate the treatment of detainees and President George W. Bush decided to close the black sites. The United States' defection from the international prohibition against torture became increasingly controversial among its allies and ultimately failed to secure the support of international society (Keating, 2014). As time went on, international human rights norms were not so easily cast aside.

When President Obama came to office in 2009, he publicly repudiated the Bush administration's torture programme, stating that it had damaged American values and the country's reputation around the world (Obama, 2009). He signed an executive order explicitly restricting the interrogation techniques that US officials could use—something that Bush had refused to do—and ordered that the CIA could not operate any secret prisons. Obama also set up the High-Value Detainee Interrogation Group, which emphasizes conventional techniques, such as building rapport with the suspect as a means of extracting information (Ralph, 2013: 129–135). It appeared that human rights norms in respect of torture had firmly re-asserted themselves in US counterterrorism.

These norms soon faced a growing challenge, however, from the rise of nationalist and populist politics in the United States. Donald Trump assumed office in 2017, having promised to inflict 'a hell of a lot worse than waterboarding' on terrorist suspects. Yet he faced stiff and uniform opposition from US national security officials who had been stung by the extensive criticism that they had received for carrying out torture under the Bush administration. The US Congress had also asserted itself, notably by passing section 1045 of the 2016 National Defence Appropriation Act, which made specific restrictions on the interrogation techniques that can be lawfully used and explicitly banned waterboarding (Birdsall and Sanders, 2020).

Referring to this law, senior Republican Senator John McCain (2016), himself a victim of torture in Vietnam in the 1960s, made clear his disdain for Trump's promises days after the latter had been elected president. 'If they started waterboarding, I swear to you that [we] would have them in court in New York in a minute,' he said, 'and there is no judge in America that wouldn't say they are in violation of the law because it is specifically in law now prohibited. So, I don't give a damn what the President of the United States wants to do . . . We will not waterboard. We will not torture.' McCain was proved right. In the years that followed his election, as far as we know, Trump did not revive the use of torture in America's response to terrorism.

QUESTIONS

1. What factors best explain the differences between the George W. Bush, Barack Obama, and Donald Trump US administrations' respective approaches to the question of torture?
2. Did human rights standards have a significant effect on the United States' interrogation techniques during the Global War on Terror? If so, why? If not, why not?

22.4 HUMAN RIGHTS AND THE EFFECTIVENESS OF COUNTERTERRORISM

Does respect for human rights help or hinder the effectiveness of counterterrorism? Public discourse often assumes that there is a 'balance' or a trade-off between human rights and security: more of one means less of the other (Donohue, 2008: 1–6).

Academics such as Richard Posner also argue that the 'balance' metaphor is well-founded: 'there is a basic tradeoff between security and liberty . . . [In] advanced liberal democracies . . . an appreciable increase in security will require some decrease in liberty, and vice-versa.' When faced with a terrorist threat, 'a well-functioning government will supply more security and less liberty, because the value gained from the increase in security will exceed the value lost from the decrease in liberty' (Posner and Vermeule, 2006: 1098–1099). From this point of view a state that fully respects human rights, such as fair trial and freedom from arbitrary arrest, is likely to be less effective in countering terrorism. If the government is restricted in its ability to gather intelligence on individuals and make broad police sweeps, that can allow terrorists to slip through the authorities' fingers. The implication is that more arrests—even arbitrary arrests—are likely to catch more terrorists. If suspects are afforded a fair trial and their guilt or innocent is decided by a jury composed of member of the public, this could offer terrorists another opportunity to get away.

When it comes to fighting terrorism abroad, some authors go further in emphasizing that a forceful military response is necessary over and above the protection of human rights. The nature of jihadist terrorism requires this, they contend. Writing in a professional journal of the US Army War College, Ralph Peters (2004: 24–31) argued that the primary task of the war on terror was 'to kill the enemy. You must be willing to kill in the short term to save lives and foster peace in the long term.' Michael Rubin (2010: 220) similarly argues against any notion that governments should respect rights or moderate their counterterrorism operations in order to win the 'battle of ideas' against jihadist groups and maintain the support of Muslim communities. Such ideas are 'naïve' because terrorist groups often control the communities around them. 'Countering terrorism is not a popularity contest,' Rubin concludes.

There is no shortage of arguments, however, against unrestrained counterterrorism operations and the idea that there is a trade-off between human rights and security. Researchers have argued that this 'balance' metaphor is seriously flawed for several reasons. Laura Donohue (2008: 3) questions whether such consequentialist argumentation is appropriate in the first place: 'Some rights are fundamental to liberal democracy and cannot be relinquished' without changing the nature and values of democratic states and societies. Even if one sets aside this concern, she argues, the balance metaphor misses a key empirical point. While counterterrorist legislation has the potential to increase security, Donohue's research on the US and UK indicates that its most important effect is actually how it increases executive power. Evan Shor elaborates further on this line of analysis in his quantitative study of 130 countries, which examines whether counterterrorist legislation is effective in achieving its main goal: reducing terrorist acts and their severity. This analysis finds that laws which focused mainly on protecting infrastructure, limiting the distribution of weapons and tracking telecommunications were associated with a subsequent reduction of terrorist attacks (Shor, 2016: 544). Overall, however, Shor found that the effects of most types of counterterrorist legislation are 'counterproductive and harmful'.

In particular, draconian legislation which gave special powers to courts and security forces was associated with a subsequent increase in terrorist attacks. Furthermore, 'the accumulation of wide-ranging legislation has a deleterious long-term effect, increasing terrorist levels after a decade or more of laws. Countries that use counterterrorist legislation often and repeatedly are more likely to suffer from terrorist attacks in years to come' (Shor, 2016: 525, 543–544).

Why may draconian counterterrorism measures, which violate human rights, lead to a growth in the terrorist threat? Classic studies in the literature, such as Wilkinson (2006), suggest that state repression generates grievances and contributes to radicalization within target communities, leading greater numbers of people to join terrorist groups. For example, studies of the Basque terrorist group, ETA, show how police abuse and intimidation during the 1970s and 1980s helped to legitimize violence for many Basques and solidified 'a new generation of ETA recruits', firm in the conviction that they were fighting 'an oppressive Spanish state whose methods were no different from [the dictator] Franco' (Argomaniz and Vidal-Diez, 2015). Apart from fuelling recruitment, repression may give terrorist groups greater motivation to use violence as a means to try to coerce the state into changing its policies (Pape, 2003, 2005). Rights violations and perceived injustice and can also elicit a 'backlash' or acts of retaliation from the terrorist group (see Case Study 22.2).

This is not just a question concerning the interaction between the state and terrorist groups, however. More broadly, the violation of human rights reduces the effectiveness of counterterrorism because it also undermines key relationships, which a government needs in order to be successful over the longer term. This may be especially true when governments violate key physical integrity rights through actions such as torture, arbitrary detention, disappearances, and extrajudicial killings. Norms which protect individuals' bodily integrity are widely shared across cultures and their violation causes particular offence (Risse and Sikkink, 1999: 2–3). Walsh and Piazza (2010) argue that violating these physical integrity rights alienates the government from key constituencies in the population, reducing the chances that individuals will provide intelligence to state agencies about terrorist operatives hiding in the community. It is also controversial within broader domestic politics, increasing the opposition of other political forces in the country, thereby damaging the efficacy of the government's counterterrorism policy. The authors also suggest that such rights violations can damage vital international cooperation against terrorism by compromising the ability or willingness of other states to work closely with the offending government. Conversely, countries that respect these key human rights avoid damaging important relationships and they achieve better counterterrorism outcomes. For Walsh and Piazza (2010: 551) this explains why—in their quantitative analysis of 195 countries—they found that those which respected physical integrity rights consistently experienced fewer terrorist attacks. Case Study 22.2 is a classic example of the relationship between human rights violations and the effectiveness of counterterrorism.

CASE STUDY 22.2

British Operations in Northern Ireland in the 1970s

On 30 January 1972, soldiers from the British Army were among the security forces sent to police a civil rights demonstration in Derry, Northern Ireland. Some of the marchers broke off from the main demonstration and began to throw stones and other missiles at the soldiers. As the Irish Republican Army (IRA) paramilitary group had previously killed several members of the British Army, the soldiers were tense and aggressive when they launched an arrest operation into the nationalist Bogside area of Derry. Mayhem, confusion, and shock ensued as the Army proceeded to kill thirteen civilians and fatally wound a fourteenth. The nationalist community was outraged by the killings, the day came to be known as 'Bloody Sunday,' and support for militant republicanism grew dramatically (English, 2003: 149–151). As the republican leader Gerry Adams (1996: 181) wrote in his autobiography, 'money, guns and recruits flooded into the IRA'. A leading historian of the IRA, Richard English (2003: 151–152), confirms that hundreds joined the IRA after Bloody Sunday, but that for many this was just the culmination of a pattern of repressive British operations, which had included curfews, indiscriminate house searches, and internment without trial.

Apart from boosting recruitment, these repressive operations illustrated a second pattern – outlined in the main text—which is that they generally failed to deter the IRA and often caused instead something of a 'backlash' effect. LaFree et al. (2009) examined six key British counterterrorist interventions and found that only one of them—Operation Motorman—was associated with a subsequent reduction in IRA violence. Two of the operations had no significant effects, while three of them—including internment without trial—led to a substantial increase in levels of terrorist violence. It appears that violating human rights, such as the right to life and to a fair trial, did not help the state to combat terrorism effectively and increase security. Rather than there being a trade-off between human rights and security, the Northern Ireland example has prompted authors such as Dickson (2012: 291) to conclude that the 'protection of human rights is not just consistent with [counterterrorism] operations but actually essential to its effectiveness.'

Other scholars warn, however, against what John Bew (2014: 158–159) has called the tendency of some commentators to 'relegate any display or use of "hard power" to the category of abuse or strategic error'. These scholars have focused, for example, on how the large-scale deployment of Operation Motorman enabled the British Army to take back the 'no go' areas of Belfast and Derry in July 1972. Smith and Neumann (2005: 413) note how Motorman led to a reduction in IRA violence, arguing that this 'shattered the IRA's military bargaining strategy'. It is not argued, however, that violating human rights will help the state to combat terrorism more effectively. Bew (2014: 160) acknowledges the UK's 'big strategic

PHOTO 22.2 Derry, Northern Ireland on 30 January 1994—a Bloody Sunday Memorial March.

errors' in Northern Ireland and recognizes that Bloody Sunday is 'the example *par excellence* of the dangers of kinetic operations in urban areas'. Indeed, the most repressive methods used in Northern Ireland are widely acknowledged in the UK today as having been counterproductive, and Prime Ministers, such as David Cameron (UK PM from 2010 to 2016), have apologized for the worst excesses. Narratives laying out these counterproductive effects have, in part, influenced the British government to take a more 'proportionate' approach in its campaign against jihadist terrorism than it did in the past in Northern Ireland (Foley, 2021; Foley, 2013: 59–60).

QUESTIONS

1. Does the case of Northern Ireland indicate that there is a 'balance' or a trade-off between upholding human rights and maintaining security?
2. Did repressive counterterrorist operations make a significant contribution to reducing IRA violence?

22.5 CONCLUSION

Many actors beyond the state, from terrorist groups and militias to organized crime groups, commit major violations of human rights. Yet governments are particularly powerful actors. Their control over populations and the tools at their disposal can enable them to imprison, torture, and kill on a wide scale (Carey, Gibney, and Poe, 2010: 128). At the same time, governments have the capability to advance human rights and ensure the implementation of due process through the criminal justice system. As Donnelly (2003: 35–37) puts it, 'the modern state has emerged as both the principal threat to the enjoyment of human rights and the essential institution for their effective implementation'. This chapter has outlined how liberal democratic states' increased focus on counterterrorism in recent decades has led them to perpetrate major human rights violations including detention without trial, extra-judicial killings, and perpetrating or colluding in torture. They have also infringed on citizens' rights to privacy, freedom of expression and freedom of movement. Governments have been enabled to do this by a range of legal, rhetorical and other strategies, which they have used to justify and sustain these draconian counterterrorism policies.

Yet, as Donnelly indicated, the state is also an important force for the maintenance of human rights. The chapter reviewed how state institutions—most notably, the judiciary—have been influenced by international human rights law in a way which has helped to moderate governments' responses to terrorism. Human rights standards also influenced some officials within government and their dissent played an important role in rolling back some of the worse abuses of state counterterrorism. Domestic norms have been invoked by civil society in some countries in a way that helped to constrain security practice and protect human rights. Not only governments, but also opponents of state abuses have been able to deploy effective rhetorical strategies in some cases (Foley, 2021). Even in the fraught terrain of counterterrorism and national security, human rights have been able to 'fight back' (de Londras, 2011).

It is also far from certain that derogating from human rights helps governments to better fight terrorism in the first place. Some argue that 'taking the gloves off' will enable the state to better wear down the enemy through more arrests, killings and imprisonments. We have seen, however, that state repression can generate grievances, which leads to more people joining terrorist groups, thus boosting their overall strength and ability to perpetrate further attacks. It can also alienate key constituencies. While only a small proportion will join terrorist groups, more may become alienated from a draconian state and unwilling to provide it with vital, on-the-ground intelligence on suspected terrorist operatives. Drawing leaders' attention to these counterproductive effects may help disabuse some of the notion that infringing on people's rights is necessary for effective counterterrorism. Yet, whether influenced by cognitive biases or their own populist political calculations, some will continue to believe that human rights are an obstacle to their country's fight against terrorism.

DISCUSSION QUESTIONS

1. How does legislative and operational counterterrorism impact on human rights?
2. What strategies have governments used to justify and sustain draconian counterterrorism policies?
3. Have human rights standards significantly constrained state responses to terrorism?
4. Is there a 'balance' between upholding human rights and maintaining security?
5. Does respect for human rights help or hinder the effectiveness of counterterrorism?

 Visit the online resources for pointers on how to answer the discussion questions, links to useful web sources, and guidance on accessing databases:
www.oup.com/he/Wilson-Muro1e

GUIDE TO FURTHER READING

Blakeley, R. (2013) 'Human Rights, State Wrongs, and Social Change: The Theory and Practice of Emancipation'. *Review of International Studies* 39/3: 599–619. *A study of how 'collective social action' through human rights architecture forced a reversal of some of the Bush administration's repressive policies under the 'War on Terror.' Blakeley counters the Marxian critique of human rights, arguing that it fails to acknowledge the 'emancipatory potential of human rights'.*

Carey, S., Gibney, M., and Poe, S. (2010) *The Politics of Human Rights: The Quest for Dignity*. Cambridge: Cambridge University Press. *Introductory text, which draws on empirical research to elucidate key issues in human rights from a broadly rational choice perspective.*

De Londras, F. (2011) *Detention in the 'War on Terror': Can Human Rights Fight Back?* Cambridge: Cambridge University Press. *Argues that international human rights law has emboldened domestic courts to resist draconian counterterrorism detention policies in the US and the UK.*

Foley, F. (2013) *Countering Terrorism in Britain and France: Institutions, Norms and the Shadow of the Past*. Cambridge: Cambridge University Press. *Outlining key differences between British and French counterterrorism, this study shows how domestic, historically-grounded, norms and institutions are crucial factors for explaining why comparable nations may uphold human rights to different degrees when responding to terrorism.*

Parker, T. (2019) *Avoiding the Terrorist Trap: Why Respect for Human Rights is the Key to Defeating Terrorism*. London: World Scientific. *Extensive analysis by a counterterrorism practitioner on the underlying causes of terrorist violence and why a strategy which fully respects human rights and the rule of law is the most effective approach to combating terrorism.*

Walsh, J. and Piazza, J. (2010) 'Why Respecting Physical Integrity Rights Reduces Terrorism', *Comparative Political Studies* 43/4: 551–577. *Quantitative analysis of 195 countries, which finds that those which respected physical integrity rights consistently experienced fewer terrorist attacks.*

REFERENCES

Adams, G. (1996) *Before the Dawn. An Autobiography*. Dingle: Brandon.

Adelman, H. (2007) 'Canada's balancing act: protecting human rights and countering terrorist threats', in A. Brysk and Shafir, G. (eds.), *National Insecurity and Human Rights: Democracies Debate Counterterrorism* (Berkeley: University of California Press), 137–156.

Argomaniz, J. and Vidal-Diez, A. (2015) 'Examining Deterrence and Backlash Effects in Counter-Terrorism: The Case of ETA', *Terrorism and Political Violence*, 27 (1): 160–181.

Bew, J. (2014) 'Mass, Methods, and Means: The Northern Ireland 'Model' of Counter-insurgency', in M. L. R. Smith, Jones, D., and Gventer, C. (eds.) *The New Counter-insurgency Era in Critical Perspective* (Basingstoke, Palgrave Macmillan), 156–172.

Birdsall, A. and Sanders, R. (2020) 'Trumping International Law?', *International Studies Perspectives*, 21 (3): 275–297.

Black, C. (2002) 'Unclassified: Testimony of Cofer Black', Joint Investigation into September 11th: Fifth Public Hearing—26 September 2002—Joint House/Senate Intelligence Committee Hearing: https://fas.org/irp/congress/2002_hr/092602black.html

Blakeley, R. and Raphael, S. (2017) 'British Torture in the "War on Terror"'. *European Journal of International Relations*, 23 (2): 1–24.

Blakeley, R. (2013) 'Human Rights, State Wrongs, and Social Change: The Theory and Practice of Emancipation', *Review of International Studies*, 39 (3): 599–619.

Bright, J. (2014) 'In Search of the Politics of Security', *British Journal of Politics and International Relations*, 17 (4): 585–603.

Byman, D. (2011) *A High Price: The Triumphs and Failures of Israeli Counterterrorism*. New York: Oxford University Press.

Carey, S., Gibney, M., and Poe, S. (2010) *The Politics of Human Rights: The Quest for Dignity*. Cambridge: Cambridge University Press.

Chong, D. (2014) *Debating Human Rights*. Boulder, Colorado: Lynne Rienner Publishers.

Crelinsten, R. (2019) 'Conceptualising Counterterrorism', in A. Silke (ed.) *The Routledge Handbook of Terrorism and Counterterrorism* (Abingdon: Routledge).

Croft, S. (2012) *Securitizing Islam: Identity and the Search for Security*. Cambridge: Cambridge University Press.

De Londras, F. (2011) *Detention in the 'War on Terror': Can Human Rights Fight Back?* Cambridge: Cambridge University Press.

Del Rosso, J. (2015) *Talking About Torture: How Political Discourse Shapes the Debate*. New York, Columbia University Press.

Dickson, B. (2012) 'Counterinsurgency and Human Rights in Northern Ireland', in P. Dixon (ed.), *The British Approach to Counterinsurgency: From Malaya and Northern Ireland to Iraq and Afghanistan* (Basingstoke: Palgrave Macmillan), 291–313.

Donnelly, J. (2003) *Universal Human Rights in Theory and Practice*. Ithaca: Cornell University Press.

Donohue, L. (2008) *The Cost of Counterterrorism: Power, Politics, and Liberty*. Cambridge: Cambridge University Press.

English, R. (2003) *Armed Struggle: The History of the IRA*. London: Macmillan.

Epifanio, M. (2011) 'Legislative Response to International Terrorism', *Journal of Peace Research*, 48 (3): 399–411.

Foley, F. (2013) *Countering Terrorism in Britain and France: Institutions, Norms and the Shadow of the Past*. Cambridge: Cambridge University Press.

Foley, F. (2019) 'France', in A. Silke (ed.) *The Routledge Handbook of Terrorism and Counterterrorism*. Abingdon: Routledge.

Foley, F. (2021) 'The (De)legitimation of Torture: Rhetoric, Shaming and Narrative Contestation in two British cases', *European Journal of International Relations*, 27 (1): 102–126, DOI: 10.1177/1354066120950011.

Forsythe, D. P. (2012) *Human Rights in International Relations*. Cambridge: Cambridge University Press.

Galli, F (2015) *The Law on Terrorism: The UK, France and Italy Compared*. Brussels: Bruylant.

Human Rights First (2018) 'Guantanamo by the numbers', 10 October: https://www.humanrightsfirst.org/resource/guantanamo-numbers

Human Rights Watch (2019) 'Colombia', in *Human Rights Watch World Report 2019*: https://www.hrw.org/world-report/2019/country-chapters/colombia

Jimenez-Bacardi, A. (2013) 'The Power and Limits of International Law: Challenging the Bush Administration's Extra-Legal Detention System', in A. Brysk (ed.), *The Politics of the Globalization of Law: Getting from Rights to Justice*. Abingdon: Routledge, 127–143.

Keating V. C. (2014) 'Contesting the International Illegitimacy of Torture: The Bush Administration's Failure to Legitimate its Preferences within International Society', *British Journal of Politics and International Relations*, 16 (1): 1–27.

LaFree, G., Dugan, L., and Korte, R. (2009) 'The Impact of British Counterterrorist Strategies on Political Violence in Northern Ireland: Comparing Deterrence and Backlash Models', *Criminology*, 47 (1): 17–45.

Lyon, D. (2014 'Surveillance, Snowden, and Big Data: Capacities, Consequences, Critique', *Big Data & Society*, 1 (2): 1–13.

Lynch, M. (2015) 'A Theory of Human Rights Accountability and Emergency Law: Bringing in Historical Institutionalism', *Journal of Human Rights*, 14 (4): 504–524.

McCain, J. (2016) Comments at the Halifax International Security Forum, 20 November: https://www.youtube.com/watch?v=oMlpZ9zd0dA (starts at: 3.45)

McDonald, J. (2017) *Enemies Known and Unknown: Targeted Killings in America's Transnational War*. London: Hurst & Co.

Neal, A. (2010) *Exceptionalism and the Politics of Counter-terrorism: Liberty, Security and the War on Terror*. Abingdon and New York: Routledge.

Neal, A. (2012a) 'Normalization and Legislative Exceptionalism: Counterterrorist Lawmaking and the Changing Times of Security Emergencies', *International Political Sociology*, 6 (3): 260–276.

Neal, A. (2012b) 'Terrorism, Lawmaking, and Democratic Politics: Legislators as Security Actors', *Terrorism and Political Violence*, 24 (3): 357–374.

Obama, B. (2009) 'Protecting Our Security and Our Values', Speech at the National Archives Museum, Washington, D.C., 21 May: http://www.realclearpolitics.com/articles/2009/05/21/obama_guantanamo_speech_transcript_96610.html

Pape, R. (2003) 'The Strategic Logic of Suicide Terrorism', *American Political Science Review*, 97 (3): 342–361.

Pape, R. (2005) *Dying to Win: The Strategic Logic of Suicide Terrorism*. New York: Random House.

Peters, R. (2004) 'In Praise of Attrition', *Parameters* XXXIV: 24–32.

Posner, E. and Vermeule, A. (2006) 'Emergencies and Democratic Failure', *Virginia Law Review*, 92 (6): 1091–1146.

Ralph, J. (2013) *America's War on Terror: The State of the 9/11 Exception from Bush to Obama*. Oxford: Oxford University Press.

Risse, T. and Sikkink, K. (1999) 'The Socialization of International Human Rights Norms into Domestic Practices: Introduction', in T. Risse, Ropp, S. C., and Sikkink, K. (eds.), *The Power of Human Rights: International Norms and Domestic Change*. Cambridge: Cambridge University Press, 1–38.

Rubin, M. (2010) 'Counterterrorism Strategies: Do We Need Bombs over Bridges? Yes: More Creative Military Strategies are Needed', in S. Gottlieb (ed.) *Debating Terrorism and Counterterrorism: Conflicting Perspectives on Causes, Contexts, and Responses* (Washington, CQ Press).

Sanders, R. (2011) '(Im)plausible Legality: The Rationalisation of Human Rights Abuses in The American "Global War on Terror"', *The International Journal of Human Rights*, 15 (4): 605–626.

Sanders, R. (2018) *Plausible Legality: Legal Culture and Political Imperative in the Global War on Terror*. New York: Oxford University Press.

Scheinin, M. (2008) *Report of the Special Rapporteur on the promotion and protection of human rights and fundamental freedoms while countering terrorism: Mission to Spain*. United Nations Human Rights Council/10/3, 16 December.

Shapiro, J. and Byman, D. (2006) 'Bridging the Transatlantic Counterterrorism Gap', *Washington Quarterly*, 29 (4): 33–50.

Shapiro, J. and Suzan, B. (2003) 'The French Experience of Counterterrorism', *Survival*, 45 (1): 67–98.

Shor, E. (2016) 'Counterterrorist Legislation and Subsequent Terrorism: Does it Work?', *Social Forces*, 95 (2): 525–557.

Smith, M. L. R. and Neumann, P. (2005) 'Motorman's Long Journey: Changing the Strategic Setting in Northern Ireland', *Contemporary British History*, 19 (4): 413–435.

SSCI [Senate Select Committee on Intelligence] (2014) *Committee Study of the Central Intelligence Agency's Detention and Interrogation Program*, 3 December 2014.

Tan, A. (2018) 'Evaluating Counter-terrorism Strategies in Asia', *Journal of Policing, Intelligence and Counter Terrorism*, 13 (2): 155–169.

Walsh, J. and Piazza, J. (2010) 'Why Respecting Physical Integrity Rights Reduces Terrorism', *Comparative Political Studies*, 43 (4): 551–577.

Wilkinson, P. (2006) *Terrorism versus Democracy*. Abingdon, Oxon: Routledge.

CHAPTER 23

Foreign Policy and Countering Terrorism

RASHMI SINGH

■ CHAPTER SUMMARY

Foreign policy intersects and interacts with terrorism and countering terrorism in many ways. To fully understand the formulation of foreign policy and policies countering terrorism we need to view the foreign and domestic as two ends of a continuum, rather than as sharply delineated. This chapter explores the dialectic between foreign policy and countering terrorism by mapping how the core instruments of foreign policy, i.e. diplomacy and culture, economic statecraft, and the military are also the core instruments of policies countering terrorism. In exploring this overlap, this chapter demonstrates that countering terrorism and foreign policy are interdependent and mutually constitutive. The chapter concludes by exploring how the interdependent, co-constituted, and co-produced nature of foreign policy and countering terrorism—when combined with a state's overemphasis on countering the terrorist threat—may serve to hinder its fight against terrorism.

23.1 INTRODUCTION

In 2011, Eliza Manningham-Buller, the former director-general of MI5, explicitly linked the British intervention in Iraq in 2003 to the 7/7 attacks in London in 2005. She argued that as a state's foreign and domestic policy are intertwined, actions taken abroad should be expected to have an impact on the homeland (Manningham-Buller 2011). Certainly, foreign policy intersects and interacts with both domestic and international terrorism, as well as domestic and international policies countering terrorism. In fact, to fully understand the formulation of foreign policy and policies countering terrorism, one needs to view the foreign and domestic as two ends of a continuum rather than as separate. This chapter begins by defining the contours of foreign policy and countering terrorism, before arguing that they not only dynamically interact with each other but also impact upon each other in the process. In other words, foreign policy and countering terrorism are best described as interdependent, mutually constitutive as well as bidirectional. This chapter also illustrates this interdependence by discussing how foreign policy and countering terrorism are executed in the international arena via the exact same policy instruments, i.e. diplomacy and culture, military force, and economic statecraft. It concludes that the interdependent, co-constituted, and bidirectional nature of foreign policy and policies countering terrorism inherently pose distinct challenges for students and researchers.

23.2 CONCEPTS AND DEFINITIONS

23.2.1 Foreign policy

Foreign policy has a long history. Indeed, reflections on foreign policy as well as foreign policy activity can be traced back to ancient times. China, for instance, has over two millennia of foreign policy, representing perhaps the longest record of any organized state (Fairbank 1969). Within the Indian context, Kautilya's *Arthashastra* (circa 300 BC) represents the fullest text cogently addressing the subject of an empire's foreign affairs (Modelski 1964; Zaman 2007). Similarly, we can also trace reflections on foreign policy for over 2,000 years in the West, from the ancient works of Herodotus and Thucydides to those produced by Niccolò Machiavelli and Hugo Grotius in the 16th and 17th centuries AD.

There exists, perhaps because of this long history, much discussion and debate regarding the exact contours of foreign policy and how best to study it. The common sense understanding of foreign policy sees it as the set of strategies and tactics employed by states to pursue their national objectives in relation to, or with, other states. The study of these strategies and tactics is called foreign policy analysis (FPA). However, there is disagreement amongst specialists about what constitutes foreign policy and what might be the best ways to undertake FPA. Despite these differences there is a consensus that foreign policy lies 'at the hinge of domestic politics and international relations' (Hill 2003: 23). See the Key Concepts box for a fuller definition.

> **KEY CONCEPTS**
>
> **Foreign Policy** Foreign policy is the 'sum of official external relations conducted by an independent actor (usually but not exclusively a state) in international relations' (Hill 2016: 4). It is worth engaging with the individual components of this definition for the sake of clarity. First, the idea of an 'independent actor' allows us to take into consideration the activities of not only state actors in the international system, but also non-state entities such as the European Union, multi-national corporations, or even terrorist groups like ISIS or ETA. In the same vein, the assertion that 'external relations' are 'official' underscores that foreign policy includes 'outputs from all parts of the governing mechanisms of the state or enterprise not just the foreign ministry' (Hill 2016: 4). Third, the definition also highlights that policy (as opposed to decisions) is the result of the 'sum' total of these official relations 'because actors usually seek some degree of coherence towards the outside world', which in turn expects them to engage in a reasonably rational and predictable manner (Hill 2016: 5). Lastly, the policy is 'foreign' because the world is more clearly divided into distinctive communities than it is homogenized and, as such, communities needs strategies for dealing with those they deem to be 'foreign'/ 'other'/ 'from the outside'.

At the core of foreign policy analysis lies 'an investigation into decision-making, individual decision-makers, processes and conditions that affect foreign policy and the outcomes of these decisions' (Alden and Aran 2017: 3). Consequently, FPA focuses upon the actors directly involved with the formal decision-making apparatus of a state or non-state entity as well as the full constellation of informal sources that influence and impact foreign policy. The study of foreign policy focuses upon the state and individual decision-makers to understand their impact on world politics. However, a proliferation in the varieties of actors over the last few decades has created an increasingly complex, multi-level international environment that has pushed FPA scholars to expand their outlook and include a fresh range of non-state and transnational actors into their analysis, most notably terrorist groups and multinational enterprises (see Key Concepts box).

> **KEY CONCEPTS**
>
> **The Structure-Agency Debate** There is a long-standing debate in the social sciences around the whether structure or agency is more important in shaping human behaviour. This debate extends to International Relations (IR) where different schools of IR theory approach the issue from widely varying positions.

> 'Structure' is best described as the patterned social or material arrangements (Olanike, 2011) that form society/the system as a whole. These patterned social and material arrangements are not only recurrent but also function as factors of influence that determine and constrain, to varying degrees, the actions, decisions, and behaviours of individuals/actors 'socialized into that structure' (Olanike 2011: 71). Agency, on the other hand, references the existence of 'free choice' and thus the capacity of actors (i.e. agents) to act autonomously by exercising free will.
>
> There are different positions as to how much the structure constrains or determines the behaviour of the actors. For some, the structure is determinant, i.e. the actors act the way they do due to structural constraints. For others, structural constraints exercise minimal influence and action is mostly or fully determined by the actor's own choices and free will. While for still others, the agent and structure are intricately interdependent and one determines the characteristics and behaviours of the other, i.e. they are mutually constitutive.

Some key points to bear in mind throughout the chapter include that foreign policy:

- Has a long and rich *history*.
- Is a *process* made up of three stages: *initiation, formulation, and implementation*.
- Takes into account both external and internal variables which are known as the *determinants of foreign policy*.
- Is *multi-factorial* and *multi-level*.
- Places a strong emphasis on the role of human *agency*.
- Analyses a country's *relations* with the state, non-state, and transnational actors.

23.2.2 Countering terrorism

Commonly, the term counter-terrorism is used rather loosely to refer to two different but related measures employed to combat terrorism, namely counter-terrorism and anti-terrorism. As a sub-category of combating terrorism, **counter-terrorism** refers to the 'offensive measures usually involving lethal force taken directly against terrorist operatives' (Smith 2002: 12). **Anti-terrorism**, references the hugely diverse set of passive or defensive measures adopted to thwart a terrorist attack from occurring. To these two measures countering terrorism we can also add a third sub-category, i.e. of '*consequence management*', a term which emerged in the United States in the 1990s to refer 'to all measures used to mitigate the effects of terrorist attacks' (Smith 2002: 12). It should be noted that the term 'counter-terrorism' in the context of this chapter references the sub-category of combating terrorism, while '*countering terrorism*' is used as the umbrella term for all three sub-categories.

Another way to understand these three elements is to understand them as the counter-measures adopted by governments to address each phase of terrorist activity that occurs before, during, and after the 'boom', i.e. the terrorist attack (see Figure 23.1).

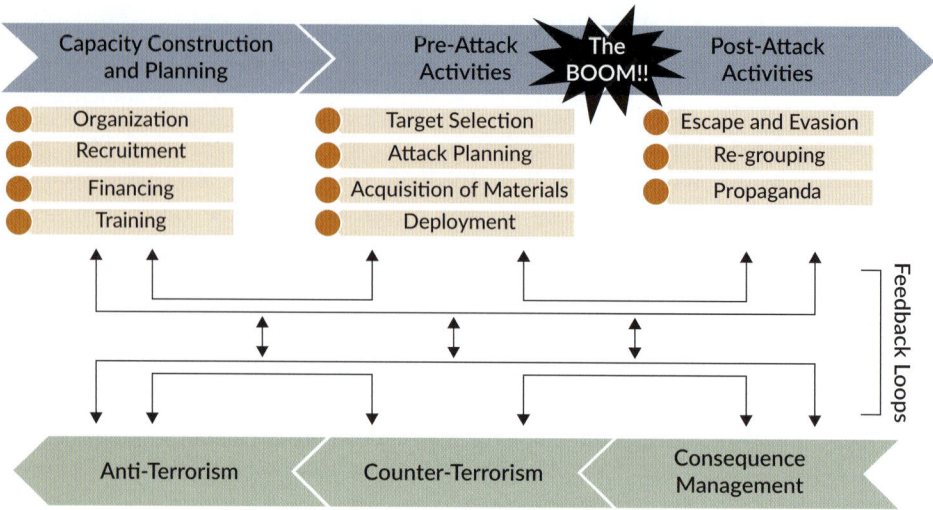

FIGURE 23.1 The key phases of terrorism and corresponding countering terrorism responses.

In the preparatory phase before any attack, terrorist groups are usually involved in activities like capability development, recruitment, training, financing activities, intelligence, surveillance and reconnaissance activities, the acquisition of material resources, planning and risk assessment and so on. Terrorist behaviour during an attack is organized around the activities of entry, execution, and exit/extraction. Similarly, post-attack activities by terrorist organizations usually include reconstitution, assessment, exfiltration and evasion, propaganda and persuasion activities, and so on. Hence, defensive **anti-terrorism** countermeasures, such as threat identification, intelligence gathering and surveillance, coalition building, etc. usually target the preparatory phase of terrorist behaviour and tend to be in place well before a terrorist group formulates its intent to attack (Smith 2002; Pelfrey 2005). An offensive **counter-terrorism** response that includes armed action by the military and law enforcement, well formulated crisis management capabilities, negotiations and other highly specialized response activities (e.g. chemical, biological, and radiological agent detection and identification) addresses the crisis phase of the terrorist attack. Lastly, **consequence management**, also includes a wide range of activities from vulnerability and response assessment to public health, law enforcement and judicial responses and is directed towards post-attack activities of terrorist organizations. More critically, lessons from each phase feed into the development of more effective countermeasures in the future, thereby bringing the response cycle full circle.

Each of these three countermeasures deal with very different stages of the terrorist attack cycle and thus with a considerably different manifestation of the terrorist threat.

As such, it is important to recognize that each countermeasure uses different institutional arms and capabilities of the state, ranging from the military to the judiciary. Even when the same institutional instruments are employed across these categories, which of their capabilities are harnessed, and how, can be potentially very different. This variety enables us to understand the broad typologies of state responses to terrorism which can be roughly categorized as ***military-led approaches***, that apply a mix of pre-emption, deterrence, and retribution; ***regulatory or legal-judicial responses*** that focus on enhancing criminal penalties for terrorist activities; and ***appeasing options*** that can range from accommodation to concession (Rees and Aldrich 2005: 907; Crelinsten 2009, 2014; Livingstone 1990; Wardlaw 1982). These approaches along with their accompanying institutional arms and capabilities are usually applied in tandem and used to combat not only domestic terrorist activity but also international and transnational terrorism (see Key Concepts box). Thus, the many institutions, decision-makers, and influencers involved with countering terrorism are also involved in the formulation of foreign policy. In other words, a state's countering terrorism concerns impact its foreign policy choices just as foreign policy affects the policies and practices of countering terrorism at home and abroad.

> **KEY CONCEPTS**
>
> **Domestic Terrorism** Also sometimes known as homegrown terrorism, is when the site, targets, perpetrators and cause of a terrorist attack and related activity are all from and within the borders of a given state.
>
> **International Terrorism** involves actions in which the location of terrorist attacks and activity is different from the geographic space(s) of prime concern to the terrorist or terrorist group and their cause.
>
> **Transnational Terrorism** Involves actions in which victims, perpetrators, and sites of violence represent different states and nationalities and transcends any given state boundaries. The same can be said for their cause and ideology. Therefore, individuals from different states and nationalities come together in another country to organize terrorist attacks and other support activities in yet another country.

Remember that countering terrorism:

- Is a term loosely used to refer to three distinct sub-categories of countering terrorism: *anti-terrorism*, *counter-terrorism*, and *consequence management*
    - The sub-category of anti-terrorism references the many passive or defensive measures adopted to thwart a terrorist attack from occurring
    - The sub-category of counter-terrorism refers to the 'offensive measures usually involving lethal force taken directly against terrorist operatives' (Smith 2002: 12)

- The sub-category consequence management refers 'to all measures used to mitigate the effects of terrorist attacks' (Smith 2002: 12)
- Each of the sub-categories of countering terrorism address different stages of the terrorist attack cycle
  - Anti-terrorism countermeasures address the preparatory phase of terrorist activities
  - Counter-terrorism countermeasures address the crisis phase of terrorist activity
  - Consequence management countermeasures address the post-attack phase of terrorist activity

The primary obligations of a government are to safeguard its national independence, integrity and security. A state's national security policy focuses upon identifying and preventing risks and threats to the integrity, safety, and security of its territory, property, and citizenry. Policies and practices countering terrorism, as a subset of national security, thus form a country's first line of defence against terrorism. Terrorism poses one of the most critical threats to both domestic and international peace and security in the world today. Transnational terrorism demonstrates how the strategies, ambitions and actions of specific non-state actors can influence both domestic and international politics. This is a challenge that no single country can address on its own, underscoring the importance of international cooperation and partnerships in the field of countering terrorism. Today, a state's countering terrorism concerns exert a significant influence upon its foreign policy choices and behaviour. Its domestic and international countering terrorism policies and practices are, in turn, impacted by its foreign policy interests, ambitions, and actions.

This interdependency is demonstrated in the terrorist targeting of Spain on 11 March 2004, when ten bombs exploded on three commuter trains in Madrid, killing 191 and injuring over 1,500. The attack was conducted by an ad hoc coalition of individuals who were unaffiliated or members of different Islamist organizations. The group, dubbed the 11-M network, used terrorism to compel Spain to withdrawal its troops from Iraq where, as a coalition partner in the 'Global War on Terror', it militarily supported the US-led operations in Afghanistan and Iraq (Rose et al. 2007). The Spanish government capitulated to this blowback against its foreign policy/countering terrorism policy stance when it announced that it was pulling its troops out of Iraq shortly thereafter.

This illustrates how policies countering terrorism and foreign policy are dynamically (co)related, (co)constituted and bidirectional. They are clearly related to each other, and any change in one tends to influence how the other evolves (and vice versa). Thus, any shift in foreign policy generates an impact upon countering terrorism, which in turn influences foreign policy in an ever-changing, ever-evolving pattern of interaction between the two. Moreover, as foreign policy and countering terrorism are bidirectional, they both possesses an equal capacity to influence and bring about change in the other.

23.3 THE OVERLAPPING INSTRUMENTS OF FOREIGN POLICY AND COUNTERING TERRORISM

If we understand foreign policy as a process, comprising the three stages of initiation, formulation, and implementation, we must also identify how these decisions and capabilities are translated into actions. There are three mechanisms by which foreign policy is executed. Often referred to as the instruments of foreign policy these are: diplomacy and culture, economic statecraft, and the military. It is important to understand that a state's resources are first operationalized into capabilities with its many institutions and bureaucracies continually taking decisions that shape their character and evolution (Hill 2016). These capabilities are, in turn, translated into actions at an international level through the instruments of foreign policy.

A state's objective conditions (its resources), derived from history and geography, are elements such as size, population, levels of industrialization, mineral deposits to name but a few that constitute 'the basic forces of foreign policy' (Hill 2016: 146). As resources determine the limits of a state's impact on the world, they are an important measure of its overall influence in the international system. However, objective conditions alone are not sufficient to understand state behaviour in the international arena or predict the course of its relations with other actors (Phillips 2000). First, while resources are immensely important, they are not 'in themselves operational instruments of foreign policy' and to 'reach the level of instruments . . . [they] must first be operationalized into *capabilities*' (Hill 2016: 146). Capabilities are essentially a government's operationalized resources, such as technological capability, armed services, or educational levels. Thus, capabilities trace their foundations to a state's objective conditions, but they are also shaped by the continuous decisions taken by various governmental departments and bureaucracies. Instruments, in turn, give states 'externally projectable power' (Puchala, cited in Hill 2016), and fall into the four broad categories mentioned above. Second, national interest (of which security, and hence countering terrorism, are an intrinsic part) and foreign policy instruments are important correlates to objective conditions and guide state behaviour, both internally and externally. This is because national interest and foreign policy instruments serve to link *capabilities* with a country's *normative preferences* (i.e. its actual interests), which together determine how a country behaves on the world stage (Phillips 2000).

While the same levels of conceptualization are lacking in the field of combating terrorism, one can argue that, like in foreign policy, how countering terrorism policies are conceived, created, and executed tends to be premised on an intricate combination of factors such as national interest, existent or perceived threats, preferences, choices, options, and capabilities. Similarly, the generation of policies countering terrorism can also be understood as processes organized around the three stages of initiation, formulation, and implementation (see Figure 23.2).

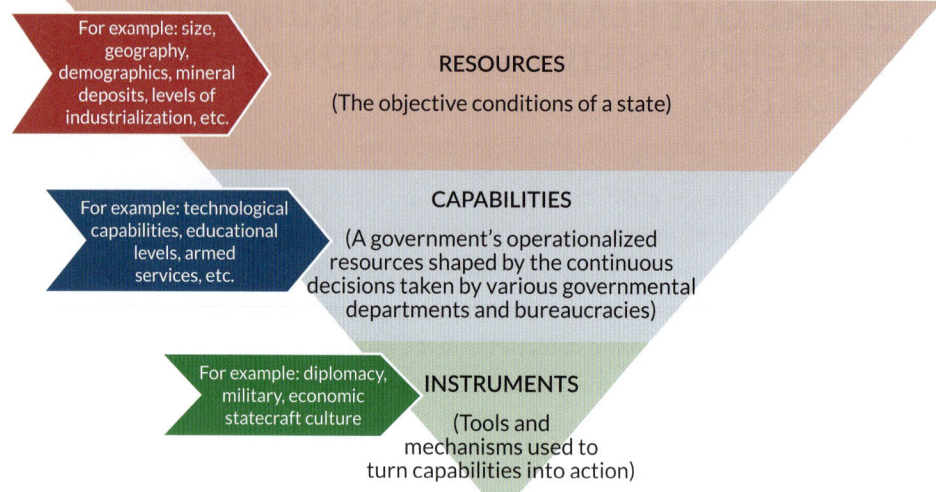

FIGURE 23.3 The pyramidal relationship between the key constituent elements of foreign policy and countering terrorism policy.

This suggests that, just like in the case of foreign policy, we must also seek to understand how countering terrorism decisions and capabilities are translated into actions in the international arena. Countering terrorism too consists of many different policy instruments and a country can engage with state or non-state terrorist threats in a wide variety of ways. We have seen that, like foreign policy, the policies and practices of countering terrorism involve the participation of multiple departments and agencies, from the judiciary to the military. Thus, the countering terrorism strategy of a country also leverages three key instruments, i.e. diplomacy and culture, economy, and the military, to combat the threat of international and transnational terrorism (Pillar 2001).

In this regard, it is important to emphasize that the broad categories of policy instruments used by both foreign policy and countering terrorism are the one and the same. Moreover, in both foreign policy and countering terrorism, these instruments are used in combination or with some potential held in reserve. Arguably then, the pyramidal relationship between resources, capabilities and instruments, as seen in Figure 23.3, can also be applied to understand how policies countering terrorism are founded in a country's objective conditions, how these resources are operationalized into capabilities which are, in turn, translated into instruments of countering terrorism that are actioned when a state faces an international or transnational terrorist threat.

Once again, policies countering terrorism and foreign policy overlap in a variety of ways. Now that we've established this overlap, this section 23.4 will explore how the three instruments of foreign policy are the very same instruments leveraged by states to project and implement their policies countering terrorism, both domestically and internationally.

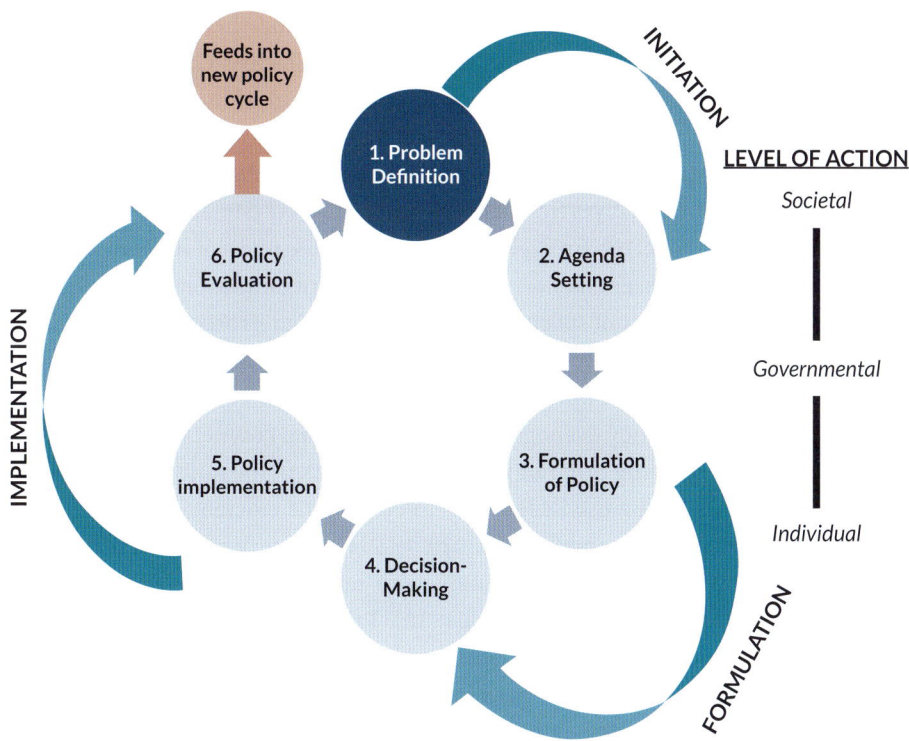

FIGURE 23.2 The foreign policy and countering terrorism policy cycle.

23.4 DIPLOMACY AND CULTURE: MORE THAN DIALOGUE

Diplomacy is 'a communication—the use of language by representatives of one state, aimed at influencing the actions of one or more others' (Sartori 2005: 3–4). While diplomacy is often confused with foreign policy, they are not the same. The foreign policy of a state establishes its goals, determines its strategies and tactics. Diplomacy is one of the tools by which foreign policy is executed. In other words, it is an instrument of foreign policy. Diplomacy can also function as an instrument of countering terrorism and represents a powerful tool in the fight against modern terrorism. International countering terrorism diplomacy 'is the sum of the policies, strategies, programmes and efforts taken by national authorities to mobilize international networks of senior political leaders and counter-terrorism professionals in the fight against terrorism' (Gohel and Forster 2020: 102).

The reach of modern terrorist groups, like al-Qaeda, ISIS, and Hezbollah stretch beyond the boundaries of a single state. Combating such terrorist networks that operate in multiple countries across the world requires an unprecedented cooperative effort.

Countering terrorism diplomacy essentially seeks to weave together multiple countering terrorism efforts into one cohesive whole, and thus more effective. Contemporary diplomacy is often described as 'multi-track diplomacy' because, in addition to the traditional formal contacts between the representatives of different states, it also includes the participation of many new actors—from large international organizations to non-governmental organizations and representatives from citizens' associations (Pesto 2010).

Similarly, countering terrorism diplomacy is not the sole remit of professional diplomats in foreign ministries, embassies, and international organizations. Instead, officers responsible for a whole host of specialized tasks combating terrorism at multiple levels in different departments need to cooperate with not only the foreign ministry in their own county but also their counterparts in other countries. 'Typically, ministries of foreign affairs exercise policy oversight for all international counter-terrorism engagements and capacity-building programmes. Senior officers in the military often serve as quasi-diplomats and can be used effectively to coordinate efficient counter-terrorism diplomatic strategies' (Gohel and Forster 2020: 102). Regulatory agencies, such as those responsible for the security of civil aviation, also need to coordinate and cooperate with their foreign counterparts (Pillar 2001: 10). Pillar (2001) argues that the role of multilateral diplomacy is especially important in the post-9/11 world of transnational terrorism as it provides 'broad sanctions for measures that would have less legitimacy if taken by an individual state [and]. . . strengthens an international norm against terrorism' (2001: 10–11).

Underlying this discussion are two related issues that impact our understanding of how diplomacy is leveraged to counter the terrorist threat. The first is an inherent disagreement regarding the peaceful character of diplomacy. For many, diplomacy is the antithesis to war and the use of force while others are more reluctant to draw such a sharp distinction. This leads us to the second issue that underpins not just diplomacy but all three instruments of foreign policy and countering terrorism under discussion here: power. Power, and more precisely the distinction between hard and soft power (Nye 1990a, b) are critical to understanding the significant overlaps between these three policy instruments as well as between foreign policy and countering terrorism (see key concepts).

KEY CONCEPTS

Hard Power Hard power is seen as coercive and founded on the use of coercive tactics, such as the threat or the use of military force, the use of economic sanctions and pressures etc. Hard power is closely associated with the capabilities of a particular state and its ability to change the behaviour of other states through the directed and aggressive use of its material resources. As such, hard power is the capability to mould the international system in one's favour through the use of such coercive tactics that force others to follow one's will.

> **Soft Power** Soft power as a concept is closely associated with the work of Joseph Nye who argues that soft power is founded on the idea of shaping the preferences and behaviours of others in the international system through appealing, attracting, persuading and co-opting as opposed to through the use of coercion and force. In other words, soft power leverages influence and non-coercive instruments, such as culture, political values, diplomacy and foreign policy, in order to change the behaviours of others by making them desire the same outcomes one does.

Two points are worth emphasizing here. First, power is best understood as a spectrum and consequently there is no clear point where hard power ends and soft power begins. Second and related to this idea of a 'continuum of power' (Hill 2003, 2016), while diplomacy is mostly associated with communication/dialogue, cooperation, and negotiation (softer power), it can also be coercive (George and Simons 1994) when there is either a veiled or open threat of force behind what is ostensibly an appeal for cooperation. In other words, diplomacy carries the potential of the use of coercive, physical hard power.

Culture plays a prominent role in foreign policy, both as a foundation of foreign policy and especially linked to soft power. Culture also plays a role in countering terrorism, albeit one that is perhaps less explored than in foreign policy. One way in which culture is operationalized in both foreign policy and countering terrorism strategy is through public diplomacy.

Public diplomacy is the effort to *create* soft power via a government-sponsored use of diplomacy and information to reach out to, and make a good impression upon, the public of another country (Pesto 2010; Seib 2011). This goes beyond just selling a positive image to a target public; it involves 'building long-term relationships that create an enabling environment for government policies' (Nye 2019: 12). Unlike cultural diplomacy, which entails a reciprocity of cultural exchange, public diplomacy is much more unilateral. Effective public diplomacy is a valuable part of a strategy countering terrorism where it can help create an environment where violent extremism cannot gain a foothold. Public diplomacy can therefore function as a powerful *preventative* tool in countering terrorism (Seib 2019). This is explored in more detail in Case Study 23.1.

CASE STUDY 23.1

US Public Diplomacy in the Post-9/11 Era: Success or Failure?

The United States has used public diplomacy since the two World Wars. Public diplomacy was also used during the Cold War and printed publications, cultural exchanges, movie, radio, television, etc. are some of its most common means. After the Cold War, the importance of public diplomacy waned, and it was largely forgotten until 9/11 when there was a sudden and renewed interest in its use (Lasmar 2011: 226). In July 2002, the US Congress passed a bill approving significant funding for various public diplomacy undertakings. Since then, a number of public diplomacy programmes are directed towards winning the 'hearts and minds' of foreign publics with regards to combating terrorism and anti-Americanism. During the Global War on Terror, all major public diplomacy programmes were specifically designed to respond to Muslim and Arab perceptions of the United States. The Shared Values Initiative, for example, was a series of short videos portraying Muslim Americans in the United States but never really gained traction (Lasmar 2011). TV stations in some Muslim countries found the videos so dull they refused to air them (Seib 2019: 163–164). Other unsuccessful campaigns included the publication of 'Hi' magazine targeting Muslim teenagers and an international educational exchange campaign for young Muslims called Partnerships for Learning. There is some consensus that the public diplomacy programmes adopted immediately after 9/11 were a complete disaster. What is worse, much of the Muslim world viewed these efforts as propaganda directed towards furthering America's imperialist designs in the region. Many of these early programmes were fully or partially terminated by 2005 (Lasmar 2011: 230).

Some, like Philip Seib, argue that this changed with the creation of the US Global Engagement Centre (GEC) in 2016. The GEC, responsible for countering terrorist propaganda, initiated a programme that used Facebook profile data to 'identify young people who appeared

PHOTO 23.1 A small unit inside the US State Department, the GEC, used guerrilla marketing tactics, including on the video-streaming site YouTube, to target young Muslims and bombard them with anti-terrorism messages.

interested in extremist causes. The content was forcefully anti-jihadist' (Seib 2019: 164). Advertisements were also placed on YouTube with anyone searching for ISIS videos on the site. These advertisements were viewed more than 14 million times in six months.

The GEC (see Photo 23.1) also outsourced the task of message development to actors better placed to know the target audience. Thus, Arab media corporations, such as the Saudi-owned Middle East Broadcasting Centre, were recruited to develop entertainment content that would advance US national interests in the region. One result of this endeavour was 'Black Crows', 'a television series aired during Ramadan in 2017 [that] depicted Islamic State with unrestrained harshness, particularly how the group treated women' (Seib 2019: 165). Unfortunately, viewership figures cannot be used to gauge the impact and/or success of this campaign.

QUESTIONS

1. What does this Case Study tell us about some of the challenges involved in the deployment of public diplomacy as a tool of counter-terrorism strategy?

2. What are some important means of public diplomacy and what role does new media play in this regard?

23.5 THE MILITARY ARM—DEFENCE AND DETERRENCE

The military is another instrument used in both foreign policy and countering terrorism. In both cases, the role of the military is to provide the state with the capacity to threaten an opponent with the use of force (coercive diplomacy) and to enable the fully-fledged use of force (war) when deemed necessary. Both the threat and actual use of force are options for the already powerful in the international system (Hill 2003). The use of armed force in the conduct of foreign relations is often seen as a failure, even if the military action taken is successful. This is because military actions tend to have long-term consequences and complications which are both harmful and unforeseeable. As Seib (2019) argues, the use of conventional military force as the principal counter-terrorism strategy indicates that efforts to limit terrorist recruitment and activity have already failed. For most states victory in both foreign policy and countering terrorism lies in *avoiding*, as much as possible, the use of the military arm.

There is some evidence to suggest that the use of military pressure, i.e. the *threat* of the use of force, can be quite effective in achieving specific policy objectives. President John F. Kennedy's threat of the use of force during the 1962 Cuban Missile Crisis is perhaps the most iconic example of the successful use coercive diplomacy (George and Simons 1994). However, with any threat of the use of force comes the real risk of escalation and fully-fledged war, which could mire a nation in a protracted, resource draining conflict, compromising its other policy objectives and even resulting in its defeat. An excellent example of the failure of coercive diplomacy is the US attempt to pressure Saddam Hussein into withdrawing his troops from Kuwait between August 1990 and January 1991. Hussein's belief that the US and its allies would not risk a full-scale war eventually resulted in the US launching Operation Desert Storm, which marked the beginning of the First Gulf War (Hill 2003). Certainly, history has many examples of military pressures that degenerated into full-scale wars with varying results. Thus, war continues to carry too high a potential cost for a state for which reason it remains undesirable. Nevertheless, the military certainly has a role to play in the foreign and countering terrorism policies and practices of a country and the short-term and decisive use of overwhelming force can be successful. In countering terrorism, the military can prevent and respond to terrorist attacks as well help mitigate their consequences. Thus, the role of the military can be viewed through the twin lenses of defence and deterrence.

Defence involves mobilizing a country's military forces to either *proactively* or *reactively* protect it from terrorist activity while deterrence is the credible use of the military in a *preventative* role to confront the threat of terrorism or an actual terrorist attack (Taillon 2001: 136). These varying roles provide an effective framework for understanding the different ways the military can be leveraged as an instrument of countering terrorism policy. However, while this can guide our understanding these roles by no means represent strict categories. For instance, proactive or reactive military action can also have a preventative effect.

Deterrence includes defending and protecting high-profile targets of terrorist attacks such as critical infrastructure, important buildings, installations, and individuals that represent typical targets of terrorist groups. Certainly, the fortification of embassies and efforts to protect diplomats has effectively reduced terrorist attacks on these potential targets (Duyvesteyn 2008; Hughes 2011; Lum, Kennedy, and Sherley 2006). Another preventative role fulfilled by the military, which is also part of countering terrorism diplomacy, is the training of allied forces as part of a policy of cooperatively combating terrorism. An example of defence is the mobilization and deployment of Indian military forces in the region of Jammu and Kashmir in 1990 to address what began as an indigenous armed insurgency against the Indian state. This local insurgency was rapidly hijacked by cross-border terrorism, conducted by groups such as Lashkar-e-Taiba (LeT) and Jaish-e-Mohammad (JeM) amongst others, that were based in Pakistan and trained and funded by the Pakistani state. The Indian army has been permanently stationed in the region since then and has undertaken numerous military operations to defend against terrorist activity.

Proactive defence includes the use of the military in pre-emptive interventions, targeted assassinations and interdiction. Pre-emption involves 'striking in advance of hostile action to prevent its occurrence and to avoid suffering injury' (Livingston 1990: 222). Pre-emption is therefore the 'quintessential proactive policy' (Arce and Sandler 2005: 184) where terrorist groups, their assets, and infrastructure are targeted to limit possibilities of

PHOTO 23.2 Indian army soldiers in Northern Kashmir's Baramulla district. The Indian army in 2021 are still present in the regions of Jammu and Kashmir in order to defend against terrorist activity from groups such as LeT and JeM.

future terrorist campaigns. In late February 2019, India conducted pre-emptive airstrikes on a training camp run by JeM near Balakot in Pakistan in response to a suicide attack by the group in its Pulwama district (see Photo 23.2). India justified the airstrikes by arguing that it had 'credible intelligence' JeM was planning to conduct another suicide terror attack in the country (Financial Times 2019).

Targeted killings involve 'naming individuals and ordering their assassination' (Cronin 2009: 24) and are grounded in the rationale that eliminating the key leadership of a terrorist group is critical to its weakening, and the suppression of future terrorist activity. However, there are legal and moral problems involved with this course of action. Post-9/11 the George W. Bush, Barack Obama, and Donald Trump administrations have all conducted targeted strikes against their adversaries. This deeply controversial US countering terrorism policy makes use of UAV (unmanned aerial vehicles) to target al-Qaeda and other terrorist groups in spaces as varied as Pakistan, Yemen, Somalia, and Syria. Israel too has a long history of using this policy against groups like Hezbollah and Hamas. Apart from the moral dilemma there are other problems with targeted killings, including the fact that there is empirical evidence to suggest that their use is usually followed by an escalation of terrorist activity, and that they tend to bolster the culture of martyrdom (Byman 2006; Gross 2003; Luft 2003; Heymann 2001).

The proactive use of military force can also include the interdiction of terrorist personnel and resources. For instance, the January 2002 case of the Israeli security forces which intercepted a maritime smuggling vessel, the *Karine A,* that was on its way to the Gaza Strip and carrying around 50 tons of weapons and explosives (Singh 2017).

Reactive defence policies use military force to respond to a terrorist attack and include retaliatory strikes and hostage rescue. Retaliation is an important reactive tool in countering terrorism and retaliatory strikes can be conducted against both state sponsors of terrorism and non-state actors. Retaliatory operations are coercive in nature because they seek to compel 'terrorist groups to desist from perpetuating further attacks and [force] their state sponsors to cease assisting them' (Hughes 2011: 54). One of the most emblematic examples of retaliatory counter-terrorism are the US airstrikes against Libya in 1986, conducted after the bombing of a disco in Berlin that was frequented by US servicemen. There is some debate if retaliatory policies of countering terrorism work or not, with some arguing that they cause an escalation in terrorist activity (Enders, Sandler, and Cauley 1990; Silke 2005; Lum, Kennedy and Sherley 2006) versus others who argue for a decrease in terrorism (Pruncun and Mohr 1997; Hanle 2007; Duyvesteyn 2008: 337).

Hostage rescue operations are potentially the most well-known and legitimate examples of the military's use in reactive policies of countering terrorism. Especially when responding to international terrorism, the use of the military in hostage rescue missions is not only 'morally defensible' it is 'clearly defined' and 'can be conducted within a legal constitutional framework' (Charters cited in Duyvesteyn 2008: 334). Hostage rescue involves the storming of a hardened site with the intent of neutralizing the terrorists within and saving the prisoners. These operations are extremely high-risk and become even more complex if the hostages to be rescued are held offshore or in a foreign country (Hughes 2011). An example of this in practice is the Israeli Defence Force's 1976 raid on the Ugandan airport of Entebbe, which successfully rescued over one hundred hostages held there by Palestinian and West German terrorists.

23.6 ECONOMIC STATECRAFT: FOREIGN AID, SANCTIONS, AND THE FINANCING OF TERRORISM

Economic statecraft is a versatile instrument of foreign policy and countering terrorism. The use of economic instruments for foreign policy and countering terrorism goals is conceptually distinct from economic diplomacy, which focuses upon the promotion of national prosperity. Economic statecraft, on the other hand, makes uses of economic instruments that are at the disposal of the state to achieve given foreign policy and/or countering terrorism goals. Economic statecraft normally makes use of the existing tools of economics such as trade, investments, and aid. In fact, only sanctions are a 'purpose-built foreign policy instrument' and apart from this, economic statecraft essentially makes use of what already exists and is occurring (Hill 2003: 148).

Unlike military force, economic statecraft works extremely slowly. In an era of global capital flows and trade liberalism, the use of economic instruments, especially the unilateral use of these instruments, is both difficult and complex. Although due to a combination of pressures ranging from an increasing number of states trying to avoid risks associated with the use of military force to a growing perception that economic tools are more ethical, there is a paradoxical increase in the use of economic statecraft as a policy instrument in foreign policy (Hill 2016: 155) and countering terrorism. Foreign aid and sanctions are some of the key tools of economic statecraft used to attain foreign policy and counter-terrorism objectives.

Foreign aid is the voluntary and intentional transfer of capital, goods and/or services from a donor country or international organization to a recipient country. There are many types of foreign aid, such as development aid: one of the most common forms of assistance which seeks to alleviate poverty and assist economic and social development. When it comes to aid, rich countries in the Global North have a significant advantage over poorer countries in the Global South. However, aid can be used coercively. For instance, over time many Western countries have made developmental assistance contingent upon recipients undertaking specific social and political reforms (Smith 1998).

Sanctions, on the other hand, are an openly coercive mechanism of economic statecraft. Punitive in nature and hotly debated, sanctions are the 'withdrawal of customary trade and financial relations for foreign- and security-policy purposes. They can be *comprehensive*, prohibiting commercial activity regarding an entire country, like the long-standing US embargo of Cuba, or *targeted*, blocking transactions by and with particular businesses, groups, or individuals' (Masters 2019). Sanctions can function bilaterally or multilaterally, and include a range of actions and threats.

Policies countering terrorism utilize all these available tools of economic statecraft—including foreign aid and sanctions. In the post-9/11 era, any effective countering terrorism policy needs to prevent and combat the financing of terrorism at a global level. The first step in the Global War on Terror was taken on 23 September when President George W. Bush signed executive order (EO) 13224 to freeze the assets and financial transactions of all persons and entities suspected of conducting and/or supporting terrorist activity. This was done *two weeks before* the start of military operations in Afghanistan (Lasmar 2020; Heng and McDonagh 2009). Shortly thereafter, there was a flurry of international activity to combat the financing of terrorism. At the United Nations, the Security Council led the efforts to adopt a series of resolutions countering terrorist activity, including countermeasures directed at the financing of terrorism (Einsiedel 2016). Similarly, the Financial Action Task Force on Money Laundering (FATF) expanded its mission to include the 'development of standards . . . and strengthening the agreed international standards for combating money laundering and terrorist financing' (FATF 2019).

Since then, the practices involved in the prevention and combating of terrorism financing have evolved tremendously. A complex network of sanctions has been created to inhibit the range of activities linked to financing terrorism. Secondly, this system of sanctions is supported by a related proliferation in national and international legislation. Together, experts argue that these measures are fundamentally reshaping the financial regulatory environment (Lasmar 2020; Master 2019) and pose a huge challenge for financial institutions by raising the risks of being, even unwittingly, involved in terrorist activity. Indeed, the 'penalties for sanctions violations can be huge in terms of fines, loss of business and reputational damage' (Masters 2019). These issues are further illustrated by Case Study 23.2.

CASE STUDY 23.2

The Use of Sanctions to Combat the Financing of Terrorism

Although sanctions against non-state actors are generally linked to post 9/11 actions against al-Qaeda and other terrorist groups, their use dates to 1995 when the US Treasury Department's Office of Foreign Assets Control (OFAC), the US financial intelligence and enforcement agency, issued two executive orders: against terrorists in the Middle East, and drug cartels in Colombia (McBrien 2016). Since then, the use of economic sanctions to disrupt the transnational financing of terrorism has grown considerably. Take the example of the now-defunct Lebanese Canadian Bank (LCB), whose assets at one time were worth a total of US $5.5 billion.

In October 2011, the US Treasury Department identified the active role of LCB and its subsidiaries in laundering the proceeds of a Lebanon-based drug trafficking network linked to Hezbollah, a designated terrorist organization in the United States. The network, led by drug kingpin Ayman Joumaa, used the LCB to launder as much as $200 million of narcotic proceeds per month (US Department of Treasury 2011). The proceeds were laundered through various methods including bulk cash smuggling operations, and trade-based money laundering schemes using cars purchased in the United States and consumer goods overseas. Joumaa's operations extended through 25 countries in 5 continents and involved more than 18 independent networks (McBrien 2016).

Investigations revealed that Joumaa's network of operations was directly linked to the financing of Hezbollah. Several LCB managers were linked to Hezbollah officials and some of the bank's subsidiaries were owned by known supporters of the group. Invoking the Patriot Act, OFAC designated Ayman Joumaa under the Kingpin Act and applied a series of sanctions. These included the designation of individuals and entities in over 20 countries (McBrien 2016), banning the LCB from dealing in US dollars, and bringing various lawsuits against the bank for its alleged connections with Hezbollah. The LCB eventually agreed to settle by paying a fine of $102 million to the US government. The sanctions applied were effective in disrupting the network's activities, denying it access to the US financial system and barring it from trading with individuals and entities within US jurisdiction (Committee on Foreign Affairs 2017).

The complexity and sophistication of this scheme as well as the sheer geographic scope of its transactions demonstrate how important foreign policy is for the success of targeted sanctions. Policies of intelligence sharing are critical for gathering the information on who is involved in, and how to disrupt, such networks. Likewise, international cooperation is paramount for the effective implementation of sanctions. The financing of terrorism has an increasingly transnational component in which the adoption of financial sanctions by individual countries alone is not effective as terrorists just shift to other countries or already operate globally. Therefore, the successful fight against the financing of terrorism requires active foreign policies promoting cooperation amongst the criminal justice systems of different countries.

QUESTIONS

1. What kinds of individuals and entities might be relevant candidates for sanctions' listings?
2. How can international co-operation enhance the fight against the financing of terrorism?

23.7 CONCLUSION

This chapter began by defining the core concepts of foreign policy and countering terrorism before discussing the key policy instruments by which both are executed in the international system. In all cases it was shown that foreign policy and countering terrorism are closely and intricately related. To conclude, a few points are worth re-emphasizing.

First, the instruments of policy discussed here—diplomacy and culture, economic statecraft, and the military—are not sharply delineated. Policy instruments neither exist, nor are they used, in isolation. Not only are there natural synergies between these different instruments and their means, they are also almost always used in tandem to fulfil key foreign policy objectives, and confront the challenge of terrorism. However, providing such training is not simply a case of leveraging the military arm. Instead, it is an exercise in diplomacy, negotiating the terms of cooperation in the global fight against transnational terrorism, that can also potentially include other instruments, such as public diplomacy (culture) or even military aid (economic statecraft), as seen in the case of US military aid extended to countries like Uzbekistan and Kyrgyzstan (Kucera 2012).

Second, there is a certain bidirectionality that exists between foreign policy and policies countering terrorism. It is not only countering terrorism that can drive foreign policy but also foreign policy that can give direction to countering terrorism. Finally, and somewhat related to the bidirectional nature of foreign policy and countering terrorism, we saw that both foreign policy and countering terrorism are clearly mutually constituted and co-produced. This interdependence presents a very particular challenge to our study.

When states work directly with other governments for countering terrorism, they must perforce compromise elements of their foreign policy. Take, for example, the United States' willingness to criticize or pressure countries like, Pakistan, Saudi Arabia, or Egypt, which is encumbered by the fact that it relies upon them to either fight against terrorist groups, or permit it to use their territory to fight terrorism. Students and researchers must be cognizant of the fact that because of the interdependent, co-constituted, and co-produced nature of foreign policy and countering terrorism, a state's overemphasis on countering the terrorist threat may hinder its fight against terrorism.

Note: The author would like to thank the Brazilian National Council for the Development of Science and Technology (CnPQ) for the grant that made this research possible.

DISCUSSION QUESTIONS

1. How can you characterize the relationship between foreign policy and counterterrorism?
2. Which policy instrument is best suited to counter the threat of transnational terrorism and why?
3. Can soft power be an effective component of counter-terrorism strategy? Discuss.
4. What types of roles can the military play in the fight against terrorism? Discuss with examples.
5. What is coercive diplomacy and how can this be used in counter-terrorism strategy?

 Visit the online resources for pointers on how to answer the discussion questions, links to useful web sources, and guidance on accessing databases:
www.oup.com/he/Wilson-Muro1e

GUIDE TO FURTHER READING

Cronin, A. K. (2009) *How Terrorism Ends: Understanding the Decline and Demise of Terrorist Campaigns*. Princeton, NJ: Princeton University Press. *To understand, with examples, a range of countermeasures that can be applied to end terrorist campaigns.*

Hill, C. (2016) *Foreign Policy in the Twenty-First Century*. London: Palgrave. *For an in-depth, nuanced understanding of foreign policy and FPA.*

Pillar, P. R. (2001) *Terrorism and U.S. Foreign Policy*. Washington, D.C.: Brookings Institution Press. *To see how terrorism, countering terrorism, and foreign policy are interdependent and mutually constituted.*

Wilkinson, P. (2011) *Terrorism vs. Democracy: The Liberal State Response*. London: Routledge, 3rd edition. *For understanding how the instruments of countering terrorism are leveraged.*

REFERENCES

Alden, C. and Aran, A. (2017) *Foreign Policy Analysis: New Approaches*. Oxon: Routledge, 2nd edition.

Arce, D. G and Sandler, T. (2005) 'Counterterrorism: A Game-Theoretic Analysis', *Journal of Conflict Resolution*, 49 (2): 183–200.

BBC News (2019) 'Balakot: Indian Air Strikes Target Militants in Pakistan, https://www.bbc.com/news/world-asia-47366718 (as of 14 October 2021)

Byman, D. (2006) 'Do Targeted Killings Work?', *Foreign Affairs*, 85 (2): 95–111.

Committee on Foreign Affairs House of Representatives (2017) *Attacking Hezbollah's Financial Network: Policy Options* (Washington, D.C.: U.S. Government Publishing Office).

Crelinsten, R. (2009) *Counterterrorism*. Cambridge: Polity Press.

Crelinsten, R. (2014) 'Perspectives on Counterterrorism: From Stovepipes to a Comprehensive Approach', *Perspectives on Terrorism*, 8 (1): 2–15.

Cronin, A. K. (2009) *How Terrorism Ends: Understanding the Decline and Demise of Terrorist Campaigns*. Princeton, NJ: Princeton University Press.

Duyvesteyn, I. (2008) 'Great Expectations: The Use of Armed Force to Combat Terrorism', *Small Wars and Insurgencies*, 19 (3): 328–351.

Einsiedel, von S. (2016) 'Assessing the UN's Efforts to Counter Terrorism', *United Nations University Centre for Policy Research*, Occasional Paper, 8: 1–5.

Enders, W., Snadler, T., and Cauley, J. (1990) 'UN Conventions, Technology and Retaliation in the Fight Against Terrorism: An Econometric Evaluation', *Terrorism and Political Violence*, 2 (1): 83–105.

Fairbank, John K. (1969, April) 'China's Foreign Policy in Historical Perspective', in *Foreign Affairs*, https://www.foreignaffairs.com/articles/asia/1969-04-01/chinas-foreign-policy-historical-perspective (as of January 2020).

FATF (2019) *History of the FATF*, https://www.fatf-gafi.org/about/historyofthefatf/ (as of June 2020).

George, A. L. and Simons, W. E. (1994) *The Limits of Coercive Diplomacy*. Boulder, Colorado: Westview Press.

Gohel, S. M. and Forster P. K. (2020) *NATO Counter-Terrorism Reference Curriculum*, https://www.nato.int/nato_static_fl2014/assets/pdf/2020/6/pdf/200612-DEEP-CTRC.pdf (as of June 2020).

Gross, M. (2003) 'Fighting by Other Means in the Mideast: A Critical Analysis of Israel's Assassination Policy', *Political Studies*, 51 (2): 350–68.

Hanle, D. J. (2007) *Terrorism: The Newest Face of Warfare*. Nebraska: Potomac Books.

Heng, Y. K and McDonagh, K. (2009) *Risk, Global Governance and Security: The Other War on Terror*. London: Routledge.

Heymann, P. B. (2001) 'Dealing with Terrorism: An Overview', *International Security*, 26 (3) 24–38.

Hill, C. (2003) 'What Is to Be Done? Foreign Policy as a Site for Political Action', in *International Affairs*, 79 (2): 233–255.

Hill, C. (2003) *The Changing Politics of Foreign Policy*. Houndsmill: Palgrave Macmillian.

Hill, C. (2016) *Foreign Policy in the Twenty-First Century*. London: Palgrave.

Hughes, G. (2011) 'The Military's Role in Counterterrorism: Examples and Implications for Liberal Democracies', in *The Letrot Papers Series* (Carlisle, PA: Strategic Studies Institute, U.S. Army War College).

Kucera, J. (2012) 'US Military Aid to Central Asia: Who Benefits?', *Open Society Foundations Occasional Paper Series No. 7*, https://www.opensocietyfoundations.org/uploads/811a2e90-cbe9-490e-9aa6-dea12976eff3/OPS-No-7-20121015.pdf (as of June 2020).

Lasmar, J. (2011) *The Impact of the Global War on Terror on the Primary Institutions of International Society*, The London School of Economics and Political Science, Ph.D. thesis.

Lasmar, J. (2020) 'O Regime das Sanções Financeiras Internacionais', *IPLD* (06 June), https://www.ipld.com.br/editorial/o-regime-das-sancoes-financeiras-internacionais (as of June 2020).

Livingstone, N. C. (1990) 'Proactive Responses to Terrorism: Reprisals, Pre-emption and Retribution', in C. Kegley (ed.), *International Terrorism: Characteristics, Causes, Controls* (New York: St Martin's Press), 219–227.

Luft, G. (2003) 'The Logic of Israel's Targeted Killing', *Middle East Quarterly*, 10 (1): 3–7.

Lum, C., Kennedy, L. W. and Sherley, A. (2006) 'Are Counter-Terrorism Strategies Effective? The Results of the Campbell Systematic Review on Counter-Terrorism Evaluation Research', *Journal of Experimental Criminology*, 2: 489–516.

Manningham-Buller, E. (2011) 'Terror', *BBC Reith Lecture Series: Securing Freedom*, https://downloads.bbc.co.uk/rmhttp/radio4/transcripts/2011_reith3.pdf (as of August 2021).

Masters, J. (2019) 'What are Economic Sanctions', *The Council on Foreign Relations*, https://www.

cfr.org/backgrounder/what-are-economic-sanctions (as of June 2020).

McBrien, R. J. R. (2016) 'Financial Tools and Sanctions: Following the Money and the Joumaa Web', in Hughes, M. and Miklaucic, M., *Impunity: Countering Illicit Power in War and Transition* (Washington, D.C.: Center for Complex Operations, US Army NDU).

Modelski, G. (1964) 'Kautilya: Foreign Policy and International System in the Ancient Hindu World', *The American Political Science Review*, 58 (3): 549–560.

Nye, J. (1990a) *Bound to Lead: The Changing Nature of American Power*. New York: Basic Books.

Nye, J. (1990b) 'Soft Power', *Foreign Policy*, (80): 153–171.

Nye, J. (2019) 'Soft Power and Public Diplomacy Revisited', *The Hague Journal of Diplomacy*, 14 (1–2): 7–20.

Olanike, F. D. (2011) *Gender and Rural Development*. Munster: LIT Verlag.

Pelfrey, W. V. (2005) 'The Cycle of Preparedness: Establishing a Framework to Prepare for Terrorist Threats', *Journal of Homeland Security and Emergency Management*, 2 (1).

Pesto, H. (2010) 'The Role of Diplomacy in the Fight Against Terrorism', *Connections: The Quarterly Journal*, 10 (1): 64–81.

Phillips, A. L. (2000) *Power and Influence after the Cold War: Germany in East-Central Europe*. Oxford: Roman and Littlefield Publishers Inc.

Pillar, P. R. (2001) 'The Instruments of Counterterrorism', *U.S. Foreign Policy Agenda*, 6 (3): 10–13.

Prunckun Jr, H. W. and Mohr, P. B. (1997) 'Military Deterrence of International Terrorism: An Evaluation of Operation El Dorado Canyon', *Studies in Conflict and Terrorism*, 20 (3): 267–280.

Rees, W. and Aldrich, R. J. (2005) 'Contending Cultures of Counterterrorism: Transatlantic Divergence or Convergence?', *International Affairs*, 81 (5): 905–923.

Rose, W., Murphy, R., and Abrahms, M. (2007) 'Does Terrorism Ever Work? The 2004 Madrid Train Bombings', *International Security*, 32 (1): 185–192.

Sartori, A. E. (2005) *Deterrence by Diplomacy*. Princeton, NJ: Princeton University Press.

Seib, P. (2011) *Public Diplomacy, New Media, and Counterterrorism*. Los Angeles, CA: Figueroa Press).

Seib, P. (2019) 'US Public Diplomacy and the Terrorism Challenge', *The Hague Journal of Diplomacy*, 14 (1–2): 154–168.

Silke, A. (2005), 'Fire of Iolus: The Role of State Countermeasures in Causing Terrorism and What Needs to Be Done', in Bjørgo, T. (ed.), *Root Causes of Terrorism: Myths, Relaity an Ways Forward*. London: Routledge.

Singh, R. (2017) 'A Preliminary Typology Mapping Pathways of Learning and Innovation by Modern Jihadist Groups', *Studies in Conflict and Terrorism*, 40 (7): 624–644.

Smith, A. J. (2002) 'Combating Terrorism', *Military Review*, Leavenworth, 82 (1): 11–18.

Smith, K. E. (1998) 'The Use of Political Conditionality in the EU's Relations with the Third World'. *European Foreign Affairs Review*, 3 (2): 253–274.

Taillon, J. Paul de B. (2001) *The Evolution of Special Forces in Counter-Terrorism*. Westport, CT: Praeger.

US Department of Treasury Press Center (2011) 'Treasury Identifies Lebanese Canadian Bank Sale as a "Primary Money Laundering Concern"', *US Department of Treasury* (October 2011), https://www.treasury.gov/press-center/press-releases/Pages/tg1057.aspx (as of June 2020).

Wardlaw, G. (1982) *Political Terrorism: Theory, Tactics and Countermeasures*. New York: Cambridge University Press.

Zaman, Rashed U. (2006) 'Kautilya: The Indian Strategic Thinker and Indian Strategic Culture', *Comparative Strategy*, 25 (3): 231–247.

CHAPTER 24

International Organizations and Counter-Terrorism

CHRISTIAN KAUNERT AND ORI WERTMAN

■ CHAPTER SUMMARY

In recent years, the role of international organizations in combating terrorism has become increasingly important. This has been in no small measure due to the increasingly transnational and global character of the terrorist threat, which has rendered cross-border cooperation particularly crucial. However, for all its advantages, counter-terrorism within international organizations also presents specific challenges. This chapter will examine counter-terrorism cooperation within the United Nations (UN), as well as within regional organizations, including the Association of Southeast Nations (ASEAN), European Union (EU), and the North-Atlantic Treaty Organization (NATO). It will examine the counter-terrorism activities of each of these international organizations, their success and the challenges that they have faced. The chapter will also consider the extent and the modalities of the counter-terrorism cooperation amongst these international organizations.

24.1 INTRODUCTION

In the aftermath of 9/11, the role of international organizations in combating terrorism has become progressively more important. This has been partly because of the increasingly transnational and global character of terrorism threats, which have rendered cross-border cooperation crucial. However, for all its advantages, Counter-Terrorism (CT) cooperation within international organizations also presents specific challenges. This chapter will examine CT cooperation within the United Nations (UN), as well as within regional organizations, including the Association of Southeast Nations (ASEAN), the European Union (EU), and the North-Atlantic Treaty Organization (NATO). It will examine the CT activities of each of these international organizations, their successes, and the challenges that they have faced. The chapter will also consider the extent and the modalities of CT cooperation amongst these international organizations. For these purposes, the chapter will be structured as follows: in the first part, we will review the individual CT policies of the UN, followed by the ASEAN and the EU. Finally we investigate the NATO-EU CT cooperation, illustrating how two international organizations cooperate in order to combat global terrorism.

24.2 UN COUNTER-TERRORISM COOPERATION

Since 1963, the UN has developed fourteen conventions and four protocols related to terrorism and CT (Hamilton, Colonnese, and Dunaiski, 2016: 13). Yet, while multilateral cooperation is essential to countering the terrorist threat, the primary responsibility for the implementation of the United Nations Global CT Strategy rests with member states. In that sense, the UN has a prominent role in both promoting coordination and coherence at the national, regional, and global levels, and providing assistance to member states. Therefore, the UN implements its CT aims by using the tool of Security Council resolutions, which practically impose CT obligations on member states; conducting capacity building activities that assist the latter to meet their obligations in the field of CT; and mandating sanctions via the Security Council against states, entities, and individuals that sponsor and are affiliated with terrorism (Einsiedel, 2016: 1).

KEY CONCEPTS

International Organization Composed primarily of member states and established by a treaty or other instrument governed by international law and possessing its own legal personality.

United Nations An international organization founded in 1945, which currently comprises 193 member states.

> **Association of Southeast Asian Nations** An international organization founded in 1967, which currently comprises 10 member states in Southeast Asia.
>
> **European Union** An international organization founded in 1993, which acts as a political and economic union of 27 European countries.
>
> **North Atlantic Treaty Organization** An international organization founded in 1949, which acts as an intergovernmental military alliance between 30 European and North American countries.

In retrospect, like other organizations such as the EU and ASEAN, the UN has undergone its own internal process regarding to the perception of the terror threat and concerning how to confront against terrorism. The UN Security Council started to get involved in CT activities in the early 1990s as the new phenomenon of state-sponsored terrorism started to rise (see also Chapter 14 'Can States Be Terrorists?') (Einsiedel, 2016: 1). Thereafter, the UN Security Council began to impose sanctions on various countries involved in terrorist activities, such as Libya (UNSCR 748, 1992), Sudan (UNSCR 1070, 1996), and Afghanistan (UNSCR 1267, 1999), although, the Security Council refrained from taking action against other countries that sponsored terrorism, such as Iran (Einsiedel, 2016: 1).

24.2.1 UN Counter-Terrorism Cooperation after 9/11

The first turning point for the UN in the field of terrorism was 9/11 (see also Chapter 2 'What Are Terrorism Studies?'). Following al-Qaeda's terror attacks, the UN Security Council was at the forefront of the fight. On the 12 September 2001, the Security Council adopted Resolution 1368, calling all States to cooperate against 9/11 terrorist attacks (UNSCR 1368, 2001). In practice, resolution 1368 set a legal precedent in giving member states the right to self-defence against terrorist organizations under Article 51 of the UN Charter for the first time. This decision effectively provided legal legitimacy to the American invasion of Afghanistan following the 9/11 terror attacks. (Einsiedel, 2016: 2). The next step for the UN was adopting Security Council Resolution 1373 on September 28, 2001, which legally forced all member states to implement concrete steps to fight terrorism, including border controls and international cooperation on CT measures (Einsiedel, 2016: 2; UNSCR 1373, 2001; Karlsrud, 2017: 1216).

In April 2004, the UN made another important move in the field of counter-terrorism in adopting Resolution 1540. This resolution, which stems from the discovery of the Pakistani nuclear scientist A. Q. Khan's clandestine nuclear proliferation network, required member states to take steps to prevent non-state entities from acquiring and distributing weapons of mass destruction (Einsiedel, 2016: 2; UNSCR 1540, 2004). In September 2006, the UN adopted a Global Counter-Terrorism Strategy, which has been updated and reviewed a number of times to account for changes in international CT practice (Karlsrud, 2017: 1217–1219; Hamilton, Colonnese, and Dunaiski, 2016: 14).

PHOTO 24.1 New York, NY, USA, inside the UN General Assembly meeting room.

24.2.2 UN Counter-Terrorism Cooperation after the rise of ISIS

One of the most substantial turning points for the UN's CT agenda occurred in 2014, following the rise of ISIS, and concerns over foreign fighters. In practice, these phenomena have led to a wider perception that conducting only CT steps were not enough to curb the danger of violent extremists (Einsiedel, 2016: 3). Therefore, to better address these concerns, the UN has taken a number of steps to increase accountability for terrorist crimes and has emphasized the importance of strengthening judicial cooperation.

In September 2014, the Security Council adopted resolution 2178, which required all member states to take legal action against citizens who travel and join terrorist organizations (Einsiedel, 2016: 3; UNSCR 2178, 2014). This has been the centrepiece of UN CT initiatives after the rise of ISIS, which was followed by another concrete step by the UN Secretary-General in December 2015, establishing a 'Plan of Action to Prevent Violent Extremism'. This plan aimed to encourage member states to conduct preventive measures that prevent individuals from radicalizing and joining extremist groups (Einsiedel, 2016: 4).

Another related CT measure by the UN was Security Council resolution 2322, in which the Security Council recognized the importance of strengthening international legal cooperation aimed at preventing, investigating and prosecuting terrorist acts (UNSCR 2322, 2016; UNODC, 2018: 1). In June 2017, the General Assembly conducted a further measure in the field of CT by adopting resolution 71/291, in which the UN enhanced its capability to assist member states in implementing the UN Global CT Strategy (UNGAR 71/291, 2017).

24.2.3 Criticism about the UN Counter-Terrorism Policy

Despite the wide progress the UN has made regarding CT, there is still considerable criticism of the organization's response to the phenomenon of global terrorism. Since member states have been unable to agree on a definition of terrorism, efforts to adopt an all-encompassing comprehensive counter-terrorism convention have eluded the UN. This disagreement was particularly on the questions of whether the definition of terrorism should include so-called 'state terrorism', which are measures executed by the military forces of a state against civilians, and whether people under foreign occupation should retain the right of violent resistance. The fact that there is no agreed definition of terrorism raises serious human rights concerns, as this allows governments to justify their prosecution of legitimate political dissent as combating terrorism (Karlsrud, 2017: 1216; Einsiedel, 2016: 1).

CASE STUDY 24.1

UN and EU Financial Sanctions Regime after 9/11

Following the 9/11 terrorist attacks in the US, the UN Security Council began to adopt measures against terrorism (Bantekas, 2003: 315). One of the steps conducted was the freezing of the assets of terrorist individuals and entities in general, such as Taliban and al-Qaeda. These freezing measures were also followed and implemented by the EU in December 2001. Thus, in order to confront terrorism, Council Common Position on combating terrorism 2001/930/CFSP outlined a series of measures to be implemented by the EU. These concrete steps included freezing funds and other financial assets of individuals and groups that involved in terrorist acts on the territory of the EU (CCPCT, 2001a). In addition, Council Common Position 2001/931/CFSP requires EU member states to enhance judicial and police cooperation between them on CT, and an annex list of persons, groups and entities that involved in terrorism was also issued by this Council Common Position (CCPCT, 2001b).

QUESTIONS

1. Do you think the United Nations is well equipped to act as a global legislator in counter-terrorism?
2. Should the EU always follow the UN when drawing up its counter-terrorism legislation?

24.3 ASEAN COUNTER-TERRORISM COOPERATION

Formed at a time when Southeast Asian countries were split by ideological conflict and war, ASEAN was established mainly as a forum for diplomatic engagement in order to facilitate regional rapprochement and guarantee domestic regime security (Khong and Nesadurai, 2007: 40–41).

The 1990s witnessed the emergence of a regional stand towards terrorism in ASEAN (Emmers, 2003; Gunaratna, 2007). This was, however, mostly evident in the organization's discussions on transnational crime, the rubric under which terrorism was placed. Following 9/11, ASEAN was forced to take a more assertive stand on international terrorism, particularly in response counter-terrorism moves in the US and the subsequent normative pressure emanating from this. In November 2001, the heads of ASEAN member states signed the ASEAN Declaration on Joint Action on Counter Terrorism which articulated terrorism as 'a direct challenge to the attainment of peace, progress and prosperity of ASEAN and the realisation of ASEAN Vision 2020' and declared the commitment of ASEAN countries 'to counter, prevent and suppress' terrorism in all its forms as per relevant UN resolutions and international law (ASEAN, 2001). The declaration emphasized the need to strengthen and deepen counter-terrorism cooperation at all levels through the discussion and exploration of 'practical ideas and initiatives to increase ASEAN's role in and involvement with the international community . . . to make the fight against terrorism a truly regional and global endeavour' (ASEAN, 2001). It did not however specify exactly how ASEAN's commitment to counter the threat of terrorism would be fulfilled, reflecting the lack of political consensus on not only an ASEAN definition of terrorism, but also measures with which it should be tackled at the regional level. Nonetheless, it represented a key step in framing terrorism as a security threat in the region (Emmers, 2003).

The Bali bombings in October 2002, together with terrorist attacks in the Philippines, served to powerfully drive home the realities of international terrorism in ASEAN (Caballero-Anthony, 2004: 176). Historically, domestic terrorist threats such as those propagated by the Abu Sayyaf Group (ASG) and the Moro Islamic Liberation Front (MILF) in southern Philippines, and the National Revolutionary Front (BRN, Barisan Revolusi Nasional) and Pattani United Liberation Organisation (PULO) in southern Thailand, were seen to be essentially home-grown, with weak linkages across countries. Consequently, threat perceptions with respect to international terrorism varied within the region, and responses to challenges raised by such groups were mainly located at the national level, with little by way of a regional dimension to them. The Bali bombings revealed dramatically the extent to which al-Qaeda had 'co-opted Islamist militant groups such as the Abu Sayyaf Group (ASG) and the Moro Islamic Liberation Front (MILF) in the Philippines . . .[and] infiltrated Jemaah Islamiyah (JI), an Indonesian Islamist group, and developed it as a regional network spanning East and Southeast Asia and Australia' (Acharya, 2006: 1). At the Eighth ASEAN Summit on 4 November 2002 in Phnom Penh, ASEAN Leaders issued a further Declaration on Terrorism, condemning the terrorist attacks and expressing solidarity with Indonesia and the Philippines (ASEAN, 2002). In January 2004, the first ASEAN Plus Three (APT) Meeting on Transnational Crime took place in Bangkok, which included China, South Korea, and Japan. Meetings of ASEAN Chiefs of National Police (ASEANOPOL) have also focused on how to deal with and prevent transnational crime, including terrorism. In 2007, ASEAN leaders adopted the ASEAN Convention on Counter Terrorism (ACCT), which provides for the framework for regional cooperation to counter, prevent and suppress terrorism in all its forms and manifestations and to deepen cooperation among law (ASEAN, 2007). A binding treaty requiring ratification by national parliaments of member states, the ACCT came into force in May 2011 following its ratification by six of the ten member states.

The main sources of terrorist activity in the region are al-Qaeda and ISIS. Given the regional character of the terrorist threat within ASEAN, which is mainly embodied by al-Qaeda and ISIS, it is widely considered that it cannot be eradicated by any single state and that a regional CT strategy is therefore necessary. In order to eradicate the terrorist threat posed by al-Qaeda and ISIS, ASEAN leaders realized the need to work together within the region and enhance CT cooperation between the region and the rest of the world. Thus, ASEAN members gradually invested in developing CT policies, strategies, and plans as well as extra-regional, regional, sub-regional, bilateral, and national measures (Gunaratna, 2018: 113; Borelli, 2017: 14).

According to Gerstl (2010), ASEAN's treatment of terrorism is in line with the organization's wider political strategies of 'depoliticization' and 'ASEANization' of terrorism. The former refers to the notion that ASEAN has consciously 'depoliticized' terrorism, i.e. it has taken an issue which has been securitized (at least rhetorically) and removed it from the realm of political discourse (i.e. depoliticized it) thereby making it possibly to deal with it 'as a matter for expert resolution by executive order, often through means that are perceived as purely technical in nature. ASEANization, on the other hand, refers to 'the contextualization of a security threat or political issue under the principles of sovereignty, non-interference and regime legitimacy' (Gerstl 2010: 62). Using this approach, it becomes possible to argue that the evolution of counter-terrorism policies within ASEAN at the regional and sub-regional levels is the consequence of deliberate political strategies—mainly state leaders—with the clear political objective of preserving and upholding the domestic political interests of ASEAN member states (who are also the primary audiences in such instances, as well as the ASEAN consensus model and core values).

In the meantime, terrorism continued to attack Southeast Asia, mostly executed by JI: In August 2003, 12 people were murdered at the Marriot Hotel in Jakarta, Indonesia; in September 2004, 8 people were murdered at the Australian Embassy in Jakarta; in October 2005, 20 people were murdered in Bali (Gunaratna, 2018: 117). Therefore, in order to eradicate the terrorism threat, ASEAN leaders realized the need to work together within the region and enhance CT cooperation with rest of the world (Gunaratna, 2018: 113). In practice, the suggestion that a regional CT treaty should be developed was first put forward by Indonesia at the ASEAN Government Legal Officers' Programme meeting in August 2003 (Gunaratna, 2018: 117).

In February 2004, a Regional Ministerial Meeting on CT was held in Bali, attended by ASEAN foreign ministers as well as those from Australia, Canada, China, Fiji, France, Germany, India, Japan, New Zealand, Papua New Guinea, South Korea, Russia, Timor-Leste, United Kingdom, United States, and the European Union. The meeting led to the establishment of two work teams: First, enforcement officers came together to share operational experiences, formulate best-practice models, develop an information base and facilitate a more effective flow of criminal intelligence. Second, senior legal officials met to report on the adequacy of regional legal frameworks for CT cooperation and to identify areas for improvement of cooperation and assistance (Gunaratna, 2018: 120).

In November 2004, the Mutual Legal Assistance Treaty (MLAT) was signed. The MLAT's goal was to enhance the effectiveness of the law enforcement agencies of ASEAN member states in the investigation and prosecution of offences through cooperation and mutual legal assistance in criminal matters (Tan and Nasu, 2016: 1225–1226). Nevertheless, the most important achievement of ASEAN's CT regional effort was the signing of the ASEAN Convention on CT (ACCT) in 2007. Yet it came into force in May 2011 after Brunei's ratification as the sixth country, and in January 2013, Malaysia became the tenth and last country to ratify the ACCT (Gunaratna, 2018: 118). In practice, the ACCT is the cornerstone in enhancing the region's strategic role in the global strategy on CT and its capacity to confront terrorism in all its forms and manifestations, as it covers crucial grounds from definition issues to the concept of deradicalization, including Chemical, Biological, Radiological, and Nuclear (CBRN) defence (Gunaratna, 2018: 119; ASEAN, 2007). Moreover, the legal significance of the ACCT is twofold. First, it introduces an element of intent as commonly found in the definition of terrorism adopted in many countries, though whether states are required to include it in domestic CT legislation is subject to interpretation. Second, it establishes a shared commitment to exclude the nature of the motive behind the act, such as a political, religious, or ideological motivation on the part of terrorists from criminalization of terrorism within the region. This aspect is particularly important due to the political, religious, racial, ethnic, and ideological diversity that exists in Southeast Asia, where criminal investigations and trials can easily be politicized on those grounds (Tan and Nasu, 2016: 1226). As a result, the intensified collaboration of the Indonesian police and law enforcement agencies with their regional and Western counterparts and a new transnational focus of national CT policies in Southeast Asia in general have yielded concrete results. For instance, the arrest, trial, and execution of the Bali bombers in 2008, and the killing of Noordin Mohamad Top, a key JI member, in September 2009 (Gerstl, 2010: 58).

Despite all endeavours, ISIS' siege of Marawi, the Philippines, in May 2017 made ASEAN countries realize that they needed to strengthen their CT cooperation. The endeavour of ISIS to capture the city and declare it as an Islamic Territory, resulted in an urban battle between the militants and the Philippine government security forces. Although ISIS was eventually defeated after five months, ASEAN member states understood that the level of cooperation between them was insufficient. Thus, as ISIS planned to replicate Mosul or Raqqa in Asia, the siege of Marawi was a wake-up call to all ASEAN countries and a warning sign that the devastation in Iraq and Syria could be replicated in Southeast Asia (Gunaratna, 2018: 122–123; Tan, 2018: 139). In order to contain this threat, Indonesia, Malaysia and the Philippines launched joint trilateral maritime and air patrols off the Sulu archipelago in Mindanao and Sabah in June 2017, which eventually disrupted the operation of ISIS and dramatically reduced the number of maritime attacks, including kidnappings at sea (Gunaratna, 2018: 123–124; Tan, 2018: 142). Eventually, in September 2017, during the Eleventh ASEAN Ministerial Meeting on Transnational Crime hosted by the Philippines, ASEAN adopted the ASEAN Plan of Action in Combating Transnational Crime 2016-2025. The aim of the Plan of Action is to continue ASEAN member states' close cooperation to prevent and combat transnational crimes as well as to enhance ASEAN's capacity to address transnational crimes in an effective and timely manner (Gunaratna, 2018: 119; ASEAN, 2017). Another important step to combat terrorism was the establishment of 'Our Eyes' in February 2018, in which each participating country agreed to share strategic intelligence on terrorism. In practice, 'Our Eyes' centres will be established in each country member (currently Brunei, Indonesia, Malaysia, the Philippines, Singapore, and Thailand), which will maintain communications, share CT intelligence and discuss operational cooperation among and across national defence establishments (Tan, 2018: 142-143; Gunaratna, 2018: 124–125).

Finally, the '3R' (resilience, response, and recovery) framework has been announced at the ASEAN Defence Ministers' Meeting Retreat held in Singapore in February 2018. The 3R framework not only provides a coherent and comprehensive regional approach against terrorism, but it also strengthens ASEAN's centrality, coordination and partnership among the various CT initiatives of the ASEAN member countries. Moreover, the framework recognizes the historical differences and varying force capabilities among the ASEAN member states and thus seeks to enhance CT cooperation among the ASEAN militaries by leveraging their niche capabilities to better complement the efforts of home front or internal security agencies (Tan, 2018: 144).

Despite some progress, various legal and political challenges have hampered the willingness of governments to exchange personnel, build common databases, conduct joint training and operations, and share expertise, experience, and resources. According to Gunaratna (2018: 113), one of the biggest obstacles to a coordinated strategy is the 'ASEAN Way' of policymaking, which based on consensus, respect of national sovereignty and non-interference in domestic matters. Furthermore, multilateral intelligence-sharing is exceptionally rare in the region as governments prefer to exchange threat information bilaterally. As a result, the production of legislation, ratification process, and implementation are not fast enough to keep pace with the dynamic threat (Gunaratna, 2018: 127). Another aspect is the CT strategies of militarization by the Southeast Asian governments, providing their armed forces key roles in the global war on terror. Yet, although they work to protect their citizens from terrorism, this prospect raises questions over how national governments are to avoid stepping on civil liberties domestically (Tan, 2018: 140–144). Hence, in order to contain, isolate and eliminate the threat of terrorism, the challenge for Southeast Asia is to work together (e.g. exchange personnel, create common databases, conduct joint training and operations, and share expertise, resources, and experience) beyond what is already in place, as the current and emerging threat cannot be eradicated by any single state (Gunaratna, 2018: 128; Tan, 2018: 143).

24.4 EU COUNTER-TERRORISM COOPERATION

Terrorism is a long-standing problem in Europe and a source of concern in all EU's member states (Kaunert, Leonard, and Wertman, 2019). Consequently, governments and policy-makers in most EU member states are urged by their public to deliver adequate responses to these threats (Wensink et al. 2017: 14). This section outlines the role of the EU institutions in counter-terrorism: the European Commission, the Council Secretariat, the EU Counter-Terrorism Coordinator, the European External Action Service and the High Representative/VP, and the European Parliament. EU institutional actors have played a crucial role in shaping the development of the EU counter-terrorism. Member states have often pushed towards dealing with these new items on the political agenda as security threats, which have traditionally called for national solutions. However, 9/11 led to the member states to recognize that greater co-operation was needed on counter-terrorism. They chose the EU as the best vehicle for this. The European institutions seized on 9/11 and managed to channel this process towards developing 'European' rather than 'national' solutions.

24.4.1 EU Counter-Terrorism Institutions

The EU has five prominent institutions/figures that outline its counter-terrorism role:

(1) European Commission: an executive branch of the European Union that is responsible for proposing legislation, implementing decisions, upholding the EU treaties, and managing the day-to-day business of the EU.

(2) Council Secretariat: General Secretariat of the Council of the European Union that assists the Council of the European Union, the Presidency of the Council of the European Union, the European Council, and the President of the European Council.

(3) EU Counter-Terrorism Coordinator: works **closely with the EU institutions** to advance EU efforts to tackle terrorism and coordinates the work of the Council in combating terrorism.

(4) European External Action Service and the High Representative/VP: steers the foreign and security policies on behalf of the EU.

(5) European Parliament: composing 705 members, it is one of three legislative branches of the European Union and one of its seven institutions. Together with the Council of the European Union, it adopts European legislation, commonly on the proposal of the European Commission.

Retrospectively, European cooperation in the field of CT is a relatively recent development. Operational cooperation on internal security issues, such as terrorism, started in the 1970s under the auspices of the TREVI Group (Kaunert, Leonard, and MacKenzie, 2012). Thus,

PHOTO 24.2   The European Commission building in Brussels, Belgium.

although the 1970s and 1980s were the most violent decades for Europe in term of terror attacks, with more than four hundred victims per year in peak years (Gaub and Pauwels, 2017: 4), terrorism was hardly a priority on the common EU agenda, as the cooperation in the field of CT was informal and was not officially a part of the institutional structure of the European Community (Wensink et al. 2017: 16; Torelli, 2017: 13). Only in 1993, when the Treaty of Maastricht entered into force, the CT cooperation was included in the EU's legal framework. Yet even then, the EU's achievements in this area remained rather low-key and modest for a time (Kaunert, Leonard, and MacKenzie, 2012; Kaunert, 2010b).

In essence, the EU's CT agenda has been to a large extent 'crisis-driven', and was heavily influenced by four major shock waves:

(1) 9/11;
(2) the Madrid and London terror attacks (2004 and 2005 respectively)
(3) the Syrian Civil War (from 2011) and rise of ISIS, the foreign terrorist fighters phenomenon, and the attacks on *Charlie Hebdo* (2005, see also Case Study 5.2), the Bataclan Theatre attacks in Paris, 2015, and the 2016 Brussels bombings at Brussels Airport in Zaventem and the Maalbeek metro station;
(4) the 2016 Nice and Berlin truck attacks, and a series of small-scale attacks, featuring the rise of the lone actors and the weaponization of ordinary life (Kaunert, Leonard, and MacKenzie, 2020).

The first turning point for the EU was 9/11 terror attacks, when the EU began to truly develop its CT policy (Kaunert and Leonard, 2019: 6; Argomaniz 2011; Bossong, 2013; Kaunert, 2010b, 2007, 2005). Shortly after al-Qaeda's terror attacks, the European Council stated that combating terrorism is an EU priority objective. Thus, the EU adopted an Action Plan on Combating Terrorism, which identifies the need for the EU to perform a greater role in the efforts of the international community to prevent and stabilize regional conflicts (Torelli, 2017: 13; Wensink et al., 2017: 32).

The second turning point came following the terror attacks in Madrid (March 2004) and London (July 2005). Thus, despite the EU's gradually converging perception regarding the threat of terrorism, the EU developed a more coherent CT policy only after these two terror attacks (Wensink et al., 2017: 32). Following the Madrid terror attack, in which 192 were killed, some measures were taken including the improvement of border controls, judicial cooperation, and information exchange, together with the appointment of an EU counter-terrorism coordinator in 2004 (Torelli, 2017: 14; Wensink et al., 2017: 33; Council of the European Union, 2004: 14). Nevertheless, the London attacks in 2005, in which 52 were murdered, brought about an EU CT Strategy and a parallel Strategy for Combating Radicalization and Recruitment to Terrorism in 2005 (Council of the European Union, 2005: 6; Torelli, 2017: 14; Wensink et al., 2017: 33). Practically, the Madrid and London attacks enhanced the counter-terrorism cooperation between the EU and the Global South, as the EU's policymakers realized the strong transnational dimension of the terrorist threat (Kaunert, 2010a). In addition, by illustrating the importance of combating terrorism globally in its 2005 Counter-terrorism Strategy (Council of the European Union, 2005: 6), the EU focused on forging closer ties with third countries in the fight against terrorism, such as collaboration with Middle East and North Africa (MENA) countries (Kaunert, Leonard, and Wertman, 2019).

The third turning point for the EU's CT efforts was the Syrian Civil War, the rise of ISIS, and the Paris attacks in 2015. These attacks motivated the EU to reconsider its counter-terrorism policies (Wensink et al., 2017: 34). The civil war in Syria and rise of ISIS attracted five thousand foreign fighters from the EU, most of them joined extremist groups. Eventually, 30 per cent of those fighters returned to Europe. While not all of these returnees became terrorists, many of them have been exposed to sustained radicalization and violence, and therefore may pose a significant menace to their homelands. Practically, the threat from foreign fighters was demonstrated by two terrorist attacks in France in January and November 2015, in which 147 were murdered. In both attacks, some of the terrorists received training in Yemen and Syria (Wensink et al., 2017: 34–35). Thus, the appearance of new Jihadist cells among other European countries emphasized further watersheds in the perception of the terrorist threat across the EU. ISIS proved itself even more resolute to directly target Europe by primarily resorting to EU citizens travelling back and forth from MENA. As a result, the EU changed its CT approach and deradicalization policies in December 2015 (Torelli, 2017: 15–16).

Together with an enhancing of EU framework decisions, this new approach added new criminal offences that address the foreign terrorist fighters' phenomenon, including the receiving of terrorist training, travelling and attempting to travel abroad for terrorism, and funding or facilitating such journeys (Wensink et al., 2017: 35). Furthermore, it illustrated the necessity of 'security dialogues' with a range of partners, including neighbouring countries (European Commission, 2015: 4). In that context, the March 2016 Brussels terror attack in which 32 were murdered, appeared to be related to the above mentioned international support networks. As a result, a sense of urgency to ameliorate the mechanisms of data exchange and mutual legal assistance grew within EU member states. Therefore, the EU took additional steps in proposing and adopting measures and policies related to the prevention of radicalization, the detection of travel for suspicious purposes, the criminal justice sector, and cooperation with third countries. Finally, due to the rise of the 'lone actor' phenomenon, the attacks in Nice in July 2016, in which 86 were killed, and the attack in Berlin in December 2016, in which twelve were murdered, also seemed to exemplify a shift in the threat perceptions by EU citizens (Wensink et al., 2017: 36).

The fourth and final turning point for the EU's CT efforts were after the three European terrorist attacks of 2017, in Manchester, London, and Barcelona, in which 46 were murdered. In essence, these attacks intensified the sense of a looming terrorism threat within the EU member states. Thus, becoming aware of the interconnectedness of its own security and the security of its neighbours and other states around the globe, the EU started in 2017 negotiations for 'agreements on the transfer of personal data between Europol and Algeria, Egypt, Israel, Jordan, Lebanon, Morocco, Tunisia and Turkey' in hopes of strengthening the Europol's international position (European Union External Action, 2017; European Commission, 2018).

CASE STUDY 24.2

The European Court of Justice and the Kadi Case

The European Court of Justice (ECJ) adopted a more critical stance in his fighting against terrorism. One of the most prominent ECJ rulings are the decisions in Kadi (Case C-402/05) and Al-Barakaat (Case C-415/05) in 2008. Mr Kadi, a Saudi resident who owned assets in Sweden, and Barakaat, a charity for Somali refugees, were included on the EU 1267 Committee list of terrorist suspects whose assets should be frozen by the EU member states. However, both claimed that their assets' freezing was illegal as it was conducted without any legal procedure such as a court hearing.

The verdict of the ECJ was the following: European Courts were accorded jurisdiction to review all measures adopted by the EU that were necessary in order to implement the UNSCRs, like the financial sanctions against suspected terrorists. Any EU legal act needs to respect fundamental rights, and, thus, can be reviewed. The human rights standards of the EU apply completely. Once European Courts rule that some fundamental rights of a person included on the EU lists have been breached, there would be a legal need to remove that person from the lists.

QUESTIONS

1. Do you agree that human rights concern should trump UNSC resolutions?
2. Do you accept that the ECJ can overturn UNSC resolutions for the territory of the EU?

24.5 MULTILATERAL COUNTER-TERRORISM COOPERATION: NATO AND THE EU

As we have seen in the examples detailed in section 24.4.1, international organizations operate against the threat of global terrorism. Along with the individual CT efforts of each organization, international organizations cooperate with each other on a number of different levels against the phenomenon of terrorism. The case of NATO-EU CT cooperation presented in this section is a classic example of how this cooperation is actually conducted (Kaunert and Wertman, 2019).

In essence, the transatlantic relationship is a key pillar in the NATO-EU CT collaboration, particularly the relationship between the EU and the US. In fact, EU-US cooperation has reached a consistent level of intensity, ranging from dialogue to various agreements requiring the transfer of the personal data of EU air passengers to the US authorities (Kaunert and Wertman, 2019: 70). In this context, aiming to strengthen their collaboration in various fields such as CT, a joint declaration was signed by NATO and the EU in Warsaw on 8 July 2016. The declaration was the starting point of this cooperation, with a view to giving new impetus and substance to the NATO-EU strategic partnership (Argano, 2018; NATO Multimedia Library). A new EU-NATO joint declaration was signed two years later, illustrating a shared vision of how the two organizations would cooperate against common security threats including CT (NATO, 10.7.2018; Helwig, 2018).

While NATO is a significant player in military CT, as the organization conducts its endeavours across a wide spectrum of effective CT operations and policies, European CT cooperation is a relatively recent development. Thus, NATO is involved in the Global Coalition against ISIS, conducts Operation Sea Guardian in the Mediterranean to guarantee freedom of navigation and the protection of critical infrastructures (Mesterhazy, 2017: 11). In essence, NATO's CT Policy Guidelines focus on three main areas: Awareness, Capabilities, and Engagement. With regard to the Awareness level, NATO supports national authorities and thus ensures shared awareness of the terrorist menace via consultations, strengthened intelligence-sharing and continuous strategic analysis and assessment. On the Capabilities domain, the goal of NATO is to ensure that the organization has suitable capabilities to confront terrorism. In the Engagement aspect, given the global CT effort requires a holistic approach, NATO's aim is to enhance cooperation with partner states and other key international players (NATO, 2018).

In essence, NATO and the EU hold different approach on the question of how to fighting terrorism. Nevertheless, each organization has its own reason for cooperation in the field of CT. First, given the EU cannot deal with the issue of the territorial defence of each European member state nor wishes to acquire these capabilities, the former needs NATO for reaching a collective security. Second, in order to stabilize Europe's tumultuous neighbourhoods, from North Africa, the Balkans and the former Soviet countries in Eastern Europe, NATO-EU collaboration is an essential element to accomplish this goal. Thus, combining the EU's 'soft power' skills with NATO's 'hard power' capabilities has a tremendous contribution in this matter. Finally, NATO-EU coordination and cooperation assist to avoid competition and overlap between the two organizations' security echelons (Raik and Järvenpää, 2017: 1–3).

The 2016 Joint Declaration in Warsaw enhanced the NATO-EU CT cooperation, as the two organizations agreed to accelerate their cooperation against terrorism by adopting steps to enhance the mechanism of data exchanging and coordinate their CT support for partner states (NATO, 2018; European External Action Service, 2017). In practice, there are four field of CT cooperation between NATO and the EU:

First, in the Defence and Security Capacity-Building domain, the EU and NATO have conducted CT joint operations and partnership initiatives in the MENA region, Afghanistan, and Kosovo (Mesterhazy, 2017: 14–15). Second, in the Chemical Biological Radiological Nuclear (CBRN) weapons proliferation field, NATO-EU cooperation focused on the menace of ISIS inspiration to conduct any form of lethal weapon against its enemies, an activity that illustrated through the NATO Joint CBRN Defence Centre of Excellence and the EU CBRN Centre of Excellence (Mesterhazy, 2017: 13). Third, in the maritime security sphere, NATO and the EU conduct their CT partnership in the Mediterranean and Aegean Sea, concentrating on both the tactical and operational domains. One of the prominent examples of how this cooperation works is Operation Sophia, in which NATO's Sea Guardian operation supports the EU's endeavours to confront networks of people smuggling networks throughout the Mediterranean. (Mesterhazy, 2017: 15; NATO, 2018).

Finally, another domain ripe for NATO-EU CT cooperation is cybersecurity. Given ISIS and other terror organizations, and sometimes even individuals, use encryption to hide their relationships from intelligence agencies, the field of cybersecurity has even a greater importance in CT measures. In addition, the internet and social media are also extensively assisted by the internet in general and social media in particular, especially for propaganda distribution. However, the internet and social media are also powerful recruitment fundraising tools for the terror organizations. In order to strengthen their CT collaboration, EU cyber defence teams were invited to participate in NATO's Cyber Coalition exercise. Moreover, NATO confirmed the involvement of the EU Agency for Network and Information Security (ENISA) as an observer (Mesterhazy, 2017: 14).

While NATO and the EU aim to strengthen their CT cooperation, several impediments hinder this partnership. First, there is not a shared common understanding and perception of European defence, as each EU member state holds its own perception. In addition, there is a substantial difference between NATO and EU in regarding how to confront the phenomenon of terrorism. One the hand, USA, UK, and France tend to perceive terrorism mainly through the prism of military measures. On the other hand, most EU member states perceive it as an issue requiring judicial cooperation, crime prevention, and law enforcement (Kasapoglu, 2018: 12; Argano, 2018). The latter's view stems from the fact that Europe has yet to experience the kind of transformation process that occurred in the US following 9/11, which caused Washington to substantially rethink its CT measures (Monaco, 2017).

Although NATO and EU wish to join hands in their fight against terrorism, the two organizations have not established new formal cooperation mechanisms. Hence, since both organizations conduct their CT operations and initiatives without a common strategy and shared understanding of the potential limitations of their respective capabilities, NATO and EU's capacity-building endeavours lack sufficient coordination mechanisms (Mesterhazy, 2017: 15). In this respect, the EU and NATO could do more to ameliorate communications to identify shortfalls and devise complementary strategies for confronting the terrorist menace (Aversano-Stabile et al., 2018: 5; Mesterhazy, 2017: 1).

Since the 2016 Joint Declaration, NATO-EU Counter-Terrorism cooperation has mainly evolved across four domain areas:

(1) Defence and Security Capacity-Building
(2) CBRN Weapons Proliferation
(3) Maritime Security
(4) Cybersecurity

24.6 CONCLUSION

This chapter outlined and examined the role of the international organizations in counter-terrorism. Certainly, the role of international organizations in combating terrorism has become significantly more important, whether that be the United Nations, the European Union, NATO, or ASEAN. Clearly, the transnational and global character of the terrorist threat has rendered cross-border cooperation particularly crucial. At the same time, it is also shown to have presented several challenges. The legal orders of the United Nations (UN), the European Union (EU), the North-Atlantic Treaty Organization (NATO), and the Association of Southeast Nations (ASEAN) can easily clash with one another. The European Court of Justice has shown its willingness to prioritize European interests over global interests. National constitutional courts, such as in the United States or in Germany have done similar things. This chapter has demonstrated the importance but also the controversies of the counter-terrorism cooperation amongst these international organizations, notably in relation to human rights. What are the broader points emanating from counter-terrorism cooperation within international organizations? Firstly, international organizations are needed because of the increasing transnational character of terrorism. Secondly, while they are needed, the range of legal powers between different international organizations is very substantial. One end of the spectrum, the European Union has very strong powers and can even enter the legislative process against terrorism. On the other end of the spectrum, ASEAN is merely intergovernmental in nature, and, thus, according to the ASEAN way, non-binding or intervening in domestic affairs. The United Nations, while primarily similar to ASEAN in the non-binding nature of many resolutions, also displays features of legislating of a sort—most notably the various UN Security Council Resolutions mentioned before. Finally, this range of competences can be healthy, as it provides the analyst with ample scope to evaluate the effectiveness of each of those organizations.

DISCUSSION QUESTIONS

1. Do international organizations help or hinder counter-terrorism?
2. Who should lead counter-terrorism efforts at the global level? Can the United Nations be a world legislator in counter-terrorism?
3. How can international organizations cooperate with one another more efficiently in counter-terrorism?
4. Does the EU provide an effective framework for counter-terrorism cooperation at the European level?
5. How effective is the EU in counter-terrorism compared to other regional organizations, such as ASEAN or NATO?

GUIDE TO FURTHER READING

Kaunert, C. and Leonard, S. (2019) 'The Collective Securitization of Terrorism in the European Union', *West European Politics*. *Christian Kaunert and Sarah Leonard's article is the most recent and most comprehensive source written about this topic and highly recommended. It gives an explanation of the development of the entire area of EU counter-terrorism and explains why the field has developed in the way that it has since 9/11.*

The next three books are standard recent sources on Post-9/11 Counter-Terrorism in the EU (Argomaniz, Bures, and Bossong) and on ASEAN (Emmers).

Argomaniz, J. (2011) *The EU and Counter-Terrorism: Politics, Polity and Policies after 9/11*. London: Routledge. Javier Argomaniz's book examines the institutionalization of EU counter-terrorism in particular. *His book offers a comprehensive empirical account of the polity, policy, and politics of EU counter-terrorism, based on an analysis of academic literature, official documents, and about 50 interviews with policymakers, experts, and practitioners.*

Bossong, R. (2013) *The Evolution of EU Counter-Terrorism: European Security Policy after 9/11*. London: Routledge. *Raphael Bossong's book traces the evolution of the EU's fight against terrorism from the late 1970s until the end of the first decade after 9/11. He provides a historical analysis on both EU-internal and international counter-terrorism policies and features.*

Bures, O. (2011) *EU Counterterrorism Policy—A Paper Tiger?* London: Routledge. Oldrich Bures' book is an exemplary work which analyses the development of EU counter-terrorism in great depth. *The book offers a critical analysis of the measures the European Union has taken to combat terrorism and how, in a number of key areas, EU counter-terrorism policy is more of a paper tiger than an effective counter-terrorism device.*

Emmers, Ralf (2009) 'Comprehensive security and resilience in Southeast Asia: ASEAN's approach to terrorism', *The Pacific Review*, 22(2): 159–177. *Ralf Emmers article is the analytical counterpart to Kaunert and Leonard's article for ASEAN. He analyses how the Association of Southeast Asian Nations (ASEAN) tackled the threat of terrorism since 9/11 and the Bali bombings. Overall, however, his article is not optimistic about ASEAN's role in promoting regional resilience against the threat of terrorism in Southeast Asia.*

Note:

This chapter draws on previous research by the authors, most notably:

Kaunert, C. and Wertman, O. (2019) 'Counter-Terrorism Cooperation between NATO and the EU', in Lindstrom, G. and Tardy, T. (eds.) *The EU and NATO: The Essential Partners*. European Union Institute for Security Studies-EUISS, 63–71.

REFERENCES

Acharya, A. (2006) 'Securitization in Asia: Functional and Normative Implications', in Caballero- Anthony, Melly, Ralf Emmers and Acharya (eds.) *Non-traditional Security in Asia: Dilemmas in Securitisation*. London: Ashgate.

Argano, M. E. (2018) *NATO's Impact on the European International Security and Counterterrorism Policy*. EULOGOS Athena.

Argomaniz, J. (2011) *Post-9/11 European Union Counter-Terrorism: Politics, Polity and Policies*. London: Routledge.

ASEAN Declaration on Joint Action to Counter Terrorism (November 5, 2001). Available at: https://asean.org/?static_post=2001-asean-declaration-on-joint-action-to-counter-terrorism

ASEAN Work Programme to Implement the ASEAN Plan of Action to Combat Transnational Crime (May 17, 2002). Available at: https://asean.org/?static_post=work-programme-to-implement-the-asean-plan-of-action-to-combat-transnational-crime-kuala-lumpur-17-may-2002

ASEAN Convention on Counter Terrorism (2007). Available at: https://asean.org/?static_post=asean-convention-on-counter-terrorism

ASEAN Plan of Action in Combating Transnational Crime (September 20, 2017). Available at: https://asean.org/wp-content/uploads/2012/05/ASEAN-Plan-of-Action-in-Combating-TC_Adopted-by-11th-AMMTC-on-20Sept17.pdf

Aversano-Stabile, A. Lasconjarias, G. and Sartori, P. (2018) *NATO-EU Cooperation to Project Stability* (Istituto Affari Internazionali- IAI). Available at: https://www.iai.it/en/pubblicazioni/nato-eu-cooperation-project-stability

Bantekas, I. (2003) 'The International Law of Terrorist Financing', *American Journal of International Law*, 97 (2): 315–333.

Borelli, M. (2017) ASEAN Counter-Terrorism Weakness. *Counter Terrorist Trends and Analyses*, 9 (9): 14–20.

Bossong, R. (2013) *The Evolution of EU Counter-Terrorism: European Security Policy After 9/11*. London: Routledge.

Caballero-Anthony, Melly. (2004) 'Re-visioning Human Security in Southeast Asia', *Asian Perspective*, 28 (3): 155–189.

Council Common Position on Combating Terrorism (2001a), 2001/930/CFSP. Available at: https://eurlex.europa.eu/LexUriServ/LexUriServ.do?uri=OJ:L:2001:344:0090:0092:EN:PDF

Council Common Position on Combating Terrorism (2001b), 2001/931/CFSP. Available at: https://eur-lex.europa.eu/LexUriServ/LexUriServ.do?uri=OJ:L:2001:344:0093:0096:EN:PDF

Council of the European Union (2004) *Declaration on Combating Terrorism*, 7906/04, Brussels.

Council of the European Union (2005) *The European Union Counter-Terrorism Strategy*, 14469/4/05, Brussels.

Einsiedel, S. (2016) *Assessing the UN's Efforts to Counter-terrorism*. United Nations University.

Emmers, Ralf (2003) 'ASEAN and the Securitization of Transnational Crime in Southeast Asia', *The Pacific Review*, 16 (3): 419–438.

European Commission (2015) *The European Agenda on Security*, COM (2015) 185, Brussels.

European Commission (2018) *Security Union: Strengthening Europol's cooperation with third countries to fight terrorism and serious organized crime*, Available at: https://ec.europa.eu/home-affairs/news/security-union-strengthening-europols-cooperation-third-countries-fight-terrorism-and-serious_en

European External Action Service (2017), 'EU and NATO Cooperation to Expand to New Areas, including Counter-terror; Military Mobility; Women, Peace and Security', 6 December. Available at: https://eeas.europa.eu/headquarters/headquarters-homepage/36854/eu-and-nato-cooperationexpand-new-areas-including-counter-terror-military-mobility-women_en.

European Union External Action (2017) *EU Sets Out New Measures to Counter Terrorism*, Available at: https://eeas.europa.eu/headquarters/headquarters-homepage/34141/eu-sets-out-new-measures-counter-terrorism_en

Gaub, F. and Pauwels, A. (2017) 'Counter-terrorism Cooperation with the Southern Neighborhood', *European Union Institute for Security Studies*. Available at: https://www.iss.europa.eu/content/counter-terrorism-cooperation-southern-neighbourhood

Gerstl, A. (2010) The Depoliticisation and 'ASEAN-isation' of Counter-Terrorism Policies in Southeast Asia: A Weak Trigger for a Fragmented Version of Human Security. *ASEAS—Austrian Journal of South-East Asian Studies, 3* (1): 48–75.

Gunaratna, R. (2007) 'Combating Al Jama'ah Al Islamiyyah in Southeast Asia', in Anne Aldis and Graeme P. Herd, eds., *The Ideological War on Terror: Worldwide Strategies for Counter-terrorism*, 113–127, London: Routledge.

Gunaratna, R. (2018) 'ASEAN's Greatest Counter-Terrorism Challenge: The Shift from "Need to Know" to Smart to Share', in Echle, C., Gunaratna, R., Rueppel, P., and Sarmah, M. (eds.). *Combatting Violent Extremism and Terrorism in Asia and Europe: From Cooperation to Collaboration* (Konrad-Adenauer-Stiftung and S. Rajaratnam School of International Studies), 111–128.

Hamilton, K., Colonnese, F., and Dunaiski, M. (2016) *Children and Counter Terrorism*. United Nations Interregional Crime and Justice Research Institute-UNICRI.

Helwig, N. (2018) *New Tasks for EU-NATO Cooperation: An Inclusive EU Defence Policy Requires Close Collaboration with NATO* (SWP-Berlin).

Karlsrud, J. (2017) Towards UN Counter-Terrorism Operations? *Third World Quarterly*, 38 (6): 1215–1231.

Kasapoglu, C. (2018) *A Guide for EU-NATO Security Cooperation on Foreign Terrorist Fighters in the Euro-Mediterranean Region* (Konrad Adenauer Stiftung). Available at: https://www.kas.de/single-title/-/content/foreign-terrorist-fighters-in-the-euro-mediterranean-area1

Kaunert, C. (2005) 'The Area of Freedom, Security and Justice: The Construction of a European Public Order', *European Security*, 14 (4): 459–483.

Kaunert, C. (2007) 'Without the Power of Purse or Sword: the European Arrest Warrant and the Role of the Commission', *Journal of European integration*, 29 (4): 387–404.

Kaunert, C. (2010a) 'The External Dimension of EU Counter-Terrorism Relations: Competences, Interests, and Institutions', *Terrorism and Political Violence* 22 (1): 41–61.

Kaunert, C. (2010b) *European Internal Security: Towards Supranational Governance in the Area of Freedom, Security and Justice?* Manchester University Press.

Kaunert, C. and Leonard, S. (2019) 'The Collective Securitization of Terrorism in the European Union', *West European Politics, 42* (2): 261–277.

Kaunert, C., Leonard, S., and MacKenzie, A. (2012) 'The Social Construction of an EU Interest in Counter-terrorism: US Influence and Internal Struggles in the Cases of PNR and SWIFT', *European Security, 21* (4): 474–496.

Kaunert, C., Leonard, S., and MacKenzie, A. (2020) *The EU as a Global Counter-Terrorism Actor*. London: Edward Elgar.

Kaunert, C., Leonard, S., and Wertman, O. (2019) 'EU Counter-terrorism Cooperation with the Middle East and North Africa', in Cusumano, E. and Hofmaier, S. (eds.). *Projecting Resilience across the Mediterranean* Palgrave, 87–102.

Kaunert, C. and Wertman, O. (2019) 'Counter-Terrorism Cooperation between NATO and the EU', in Lindstrom, G. and Tardy, T. (eds.). *The EU and NATO: The Essential Partners* (European Union Institute for Security Studies-EUISS), 63–71.

Khong, Y. and Nesadurai, H. (2007) 'Hanging together, institutional design, and cooperation in Southeast Asia: AFTA and the ARF', in Acharya, A. and Johnson, A. (eds.) *Crafting Cooperation: Regional Institutions in Comparative Perspective*, 32–82, Cambridge: Cambridge University Press.

Mesterhazy, A. (2017) *NATO-EU Cooperation after Warsaw* (NATO Parliamentary Assembly, Defence and Security Committee). Available at: https://www.nato-pa.int/document/2017-eu-and-nato-cooperation-mesterhazy-report-163-dsctc-17-e-rev1-fin

Monaco, L. (2017) 'A Strategy for the War on Terrorism', *Foreign Affairs*.

NATO (2018) 'Countering Terrorism'. Available at: https://www.nato.int/cps/en/natohq/topics_77646.htm

NATO Multimedia Library, 'Intelligence/Information Sharing in Combating Terrorism'. Available at: http://www.natolibguides.info/intelligence

Raik, K. and Järvenpää, P. (2017) *A New Era of EU-NATO Cooperation: How to Make the Best of a Marriage of Necessity*. International Centre for Defence and Security.

Tan, S. S. (2018) 'Sending in the Cavalry: The Growing Militarization of Counterterrorism in Southeast Asia', *PRISM*, 7 (4): 138–147.

Tan, S. S. and Nasu, H. (2016) 'ASEAN and the Development of Counter-Terrorism Law and Policy in South Asia', *UNSW Law Journal*, 39 (3): 1219–1238.

Torelli, S. M. (2017) *European Union and the External Dimension of Security: Supporting Tunisia as a Model in Counter-Terrorism Cooperation*. Barcelona: European Institute of the Mediterranean.

United Nations General Assembly Resolution 71/291 (2017). Available at: https://undocs.org/pdf?symbol=en/a/res/71/291

United Nations Security Council Resolution 748 (1992). Available at: https://www.webcitation.org/6IazEBgO0?url=http://www.treasury.gov/resource-center/sanctions/Documents/748.pdf

United Nations Security Council Resolution 1070 (1996). Available at: https://www.refworld.org/docid/3b00f20b8.html

United Nations Security Council Resolution 1267 (1999). Available at: https://www.undocs.org/S/RES/1267(1999)

United Nations Security Council Resolution 1368 (2001). Available at: https://undocs.org/S/RES/1368(2001)

United Nations Security Council Resolution 1373 (2001). Available at: https://www.unodc.org/pdf/crime/terrorism/res_1373_english.pdf

United Nations Security Council Resolution 1540 (2004). Available at: http://archive.ipu.org/splz-e/civ1540/1540.pdf

United Nations Security Council Resolution 2178 (2014). Available at: http://www.securitycouncilreport.org/atf/cf/%7B65BFCF9B-6D27-4E9C-8CD3-CF6E4FF96FF9%7D/s_res_2178.pdf

United Nations Security Council Resolution 2322 (2016). Available at: https://undocs.org/S/RES/2322(2016)

United Nations Office on Drugs and Crime-UNODC (2018) *Supporting Legal Responses and Criminal Justice Capacity to Prevent and Counter Terrorism*. United Nations.

Wensink, W., Warmenhoven, B., Haasnoot, R., Wesselink, R., Van Ginkel, B., Wittendorp, S., Paulussen, C., Douma, W., Boutin, B., Gueven, O., and Rijken, T. (2017) *The European Union's Policies on Counter-Terrorism Relevance, Coherence and Effectiveness*. European Parliament, Policy Department for Citizens' Rights and Constitutional Affairs.

CHAPTER 25

Terrorism, Counter-Terrorism, and Technology

PETER LEHR

■ CHAPTER SUMMARY

Against the backdrop of terrorist attacks against Western cities, this chapter offers a critical appraisal of the role of technology in the fight against terrorism at the so-called 'home front'. The question usually asked is 'what can technology do for us?' However, since technologies have the power to change our behaviour according to the anthropological 'agency of things' approach, a related question needs to be asked as well: 'What can technology do *to* us?' To answer these related questions, we explore a three-pronged 'thesis, antithesis, and synthesis' approach.

25.1 INTRODUCTION

As threats of terror persist against Western liberal democracies, the question is often raised in how far advanced counter-terrorism technologies can contribute to protecting or 'hardening' our cities, our public spaces, and our open societies. While some experts like Mark Mills and Peter Huber (2002) believe that technology, in particular high tech such as identification, scanning, and screening systems, might be the proverbial 'silver bullet' or a 'magical response' in our fight against terrorism, others such as David Lyon (2004) say that technology will not save us. There is a need for a detached appraisal of counter-terrorism technologies—an appraisal that critically assesses advantages and disadvantages of such technologies without getting side-tracked into a mere cataloguing of them. This chapter offers such an appraisal, asking not only the question 'what can technology do <u>for</u> us' but also the complementary but usually overlooked one 'what can technology do <u>to</u> us?' As regards the methodology, this chapter outlines three-pronged 'thesis, antithesis and synthesis' approach, which means that the argument that 'our technology will win' ('thesis') will be examined first, followed by an examination of the counter-argument that 'technology won't protect us' ('antithesis'), and a critical discussion of both perspectives to find a way forward ('synthesis').

25.2 THESIS: OUR TECHNOLOGY WILL WIN

The events of 11th September 2001 (usually rendered as 9/11) are widely seen as a watershed moment in history. Even now, there is the still lingering-on conviction that terrorism has morphed from a sub-category of organized crime to a sub-category of warfare (Crelinsten 2009, 9). While this is debatable, it can certainly be said that 9/11 acted as a formidable pacemaker for counter-terrorism: on the domestic level for example, many countries hurriedly passed anti-terrorism legislation. On the regional level, bodies such as the European Union (EU), and the Arab League or the Association of Southeast Asian Nations (ASEAN) coordinated their member states' responses in order to combat this transnational threat more effectively and efficiently. On the international level, a 'Global War on Terrorism' (GWoT) was launched, with the USA in the lead.

The events of 9/11 also resulted in a search for 'silver bullets' that would help to win the war on terrorism. Technology was quickly identified as such a potential 'silver bullet'. Mills and Huber for example argued that '[i]n the post-September 11 world, we know we have to see the plastic explosives in the truck before they detonate, the anthrax before it's dispersed, the sarin nerve gas before it gets into the air-conditioning duct—and not just see it but recognize it. Our imaging systems will have to distinguish between the scaffolding on a Wonder Bra and the wiring on a bomb' (Mills and Huber 2002: 1–2).

It would be even better if we could identify known or suspected terrorists in order to intervene before the attack can be carried out. It is these 'pro-active' counter-terrorism aspects—identifying, detecting, recognizing—that are the focus of this chapter. However, as this chapter will use a broader definition of 'technology' that goes beyond Mills and Huber's, we will also briefly discuss low-tech-based reactive or passive measures that mainly aim at mitigating the consequences of a successful terrorist attack (for a more detailed debate, see Lehr 2019).

> **KEY CONCEPTS**
>
> **Technology** The *Cambridge English Dictionary* (undated) defines technology as the '(study and knowledge of) the practical, especially industrial, use of scientific discoveries'. The term itself is a composite derived from the Greek words *tekhne* (meaning 'art' or 'craft') and *logia* (meaning 'branch of learning'). Hence, *tekhnologia* can be rendered very simply as 'systematic treatment'.

In the aftermath of the Brighton Hotel Bombing in England on 12 October 1984, the IRA stated that terrorists need 'to be lucky only once while [counter-terrorists] will have to be lucky always' (as quoted in Taylor 2001: 265). This statement hints at an inconvenient truth: preventing terrorist attacks from happening is not always possible. Hence, when counter-terrorist specialists talk about harnessing sophisticated technologies, they usually think in terms of layered defences: firstly, detecting and apprehending terrorists in the planning stage of a terrorist attack; secondly, detecting and apprehending terrorists on their way to carry out an attack before they reach their chosen target; and thirdly, minimizing the number of casualties and the physical damage if and when terrorists succeed to reach their target and carry out their attack.

The first layer of defences consists of detecting and thwarting terrorists in the planning phase of an attack. The most important step here is to correctly identify known or suspected terrorists. In the case of 'expeditionary terrorism' (Kilcullen 2016: 119) for example, perpetrators have to enter the country they target from abroad—which means they have to cross borders. In the 1960s and 1970s, an immigration officer would have made a visual inspection of the individuals and their passports before waving them through (or not). In present day, this visual inspection is backed up by a much more thorough computerized 'inspection' of the passport holders: modern biometric passports contain small microchips with computer-readable information about at least two types of their holders' biometrics, their 'face prints' and their fingerprints (on face prints, see Malčik and Drahansky 2012). There are other biometrics as well, such one's iris, one's voice, or even one's walk which are also fairly unique and can be used for the identification of individuals.

However, since many terrorists actually are citizens of the country in which they plan to strike, border controls alone are insufficient to prevent terrorist incidents. Furthermore, biometrics such as fingerprints, iris recognition or voice recognition require the cooperation of individuals to be taken. Hence, from a counter-terrorism perspective, it would be preferable if technologies were in place that could identify terrorists remotely while they walk through our cities without them even knowing that they are monitored.

> **KEY CONCEPTS**
>
> **Biometrics** Biometrics, a term coined from the Greek words 'bios' (life) and 'metron' (measurement), can be defined as 'the statistical use and analysis of (unalterable) biological data' or 'the use of data extracted from the body' (Lyon 2004: 299) under the assumption that everybody possesses unalterable features that are unique to a person, depending on the biometrical modality in question (see for example Al-Abed, Charrier, and Rosenberger 2012).

Fortunately, from a counter-terrorism perspective, such solutions exist in the shape of 'smart' CCTV systems. As opposed to older CCTV systems that consist only of one or several cameras (for example, there are six million such systems deployed in the UK, 420,000 of them in London, see Hare 2019). The most advanced 'smart' CCTV systems are now equipped with video software that analyses patterns of behaviour to discern 'normal' and expected behaviour from 'abnormal' and unexpected behaviour, such as individuals loitering in the same spot in a public space or a street for a long time, people running where everyone else is walking, people carrying backpacks or suitcases in areas where such items are unusual, or sudden commotions within a crowd of people. If unexpected behaviour is detected, an alarm is triggered to let a human operator decide whether to take further action or not (Strittmatter 2018).

An example of such a system is the *Mannheimer Weg 2.0* ('Mannheim Method 2.0') of the south German city of Mannheim. This system consists of 70 CCTV systems deployed at 28 locations and sending live feeds to a control centre. About 20 of these systems are equipped with behaviour-analytical software that automatically scans the feed for unexpected behaviour, to then alert a human operator who decides whether police intervention is required or not. Interestingly, and mainly due to privacy issues (discussed in more detail in this section), the system does not include facial recognition or audio recording, and is also programmed to delete image feeds within 72 hours (Spiegel Online 2018; RNZ 2019).

In the future, such smart CCTV systems are likely to be complemented by 'smart glasses' equipped with Augmented Reality (AR) software and worn by police officers. Early versions of such glasses already exist, with the *Google Glass* rolled out in April 2013 being the first of its kind (Clark 2013). As regards counter-terrorism, or policing in general, AR glasses have been rolled out to a number of Chinese police forces from mid-2018 onward: 'The smart specs [connect] to a feed which taps into China's state database to root out potential criminals via facial recognition. Officers can identify suspects in a crowd by snapping their photo and matching it to the database' (Russell 2018) (see Photo 25.1 below).

PHOTO 25.1 2018. A police officer wears a pair of smart glasses with facial recognition at Zhengzhou East Railway Station in China's central Henan province.

Since this technology is a powerful tool for crime prevention in general and counter-terrorism in particular, it is certain that it will be further improved and used by security services across the world.

> **KEY CONCEPTS**
>
> **Virtual Reality (VR)** Virtual Reality simulates a more or less realistic alternative environment, usually via headsets featuring a small screen mimicking a somewhat restricted 'normal' view. Depending on the system used, and the power of the computer creating this virtual reality, the user either is restricted to simply look around, or can, to a certain extent, interact with objects (or simulated persons or creatures) via game controllers.
>
> **Augmented Reality (AR)** Compared to VR, Augmented Reality only 'augments', that is 'adds to', our view of the 'real' world by overlaying it with additional information that might be useful, depending on where we are and what we are looking for. This has been popularized in gaming, including *Pokémon Go*—an AR game based on catching virtual creatures overlaid into the player's reality.

All these identification efforts revolve around one very essential 'back office' in the shape of computer systems: without computerized databases set up for collecting, collating, managing, and disseminating data derived from various identification, monitoring, and surveillance systems, all efforts to thwart terrorist attacks would be unsuccessful. Current computer systems run by various intelligence services such as the USA's National Security Agency (NSA) or the UK's Government Communications Headquarters (GCHQ) proactively search social media or listen in on phone calls to detect suspicious behaviour, to profile individual terrorists or suspects, and to carry out a network analysis: who is talking with whom, where, and about what?

This automated process is known as *data mining and acquisition*—facilitated by our habit, as 'digital persons' (Solove 2004: 1), to leave 'digital footprints' when we move through the internet, when we pay contactless, or when we use the 'Internet of Things', defined as all the high-tech, computer chip-equipped devises: smart phones, smart watches and other wearables, smart meters, smart homes, devices such as Amazon's Alexa, Apple's Siri, or Google Home (McEwen and Cassimally 2014).

> **KEY CONCEPTS**
>
> **Data Mining** Data mining (or data analytics) refers to a process also known as 'Knowledge Discovery from Databases' or KDD which turns raw data into meaningful information (Gandy 2002: 3). In other words, 'knowledge discovery refers to non-trivial extraction of implicit, previously unknown, and potentially useful knowledge from data' (Chen 2006: 17).

In the context of countering terrorism, the underlying assumption is that 'prospective datamining could be used to find the "signature" of terrorist cells embedded in larger networks' (Fienberg 2008: 197). Currently, the (still largely elusive) aim of data mining is knowledge discovery in real time, while 'it' happens, in the hope to predict terrorist incidents to prevent them before being carried out. There are some serious side effects to large-scale data mining, such as a loss of privacy, and possibly civil liberties (discussed later in this section). But as ex-US National Security Agency 'spy technology chief' Eric Heseltine points out in the case of the United Kingdom and its signals intelligence service GCHQ: 'If GCHQ wants to protect the UK, it is a requirement for them to understand what kind of [data] traffic is going on inside the UK – because in the end stages of an attack, there will be communications inside the UK between people co-ordinating this stuff' (as quoted in Hastings 2019).

How important all these identification, surveillance, and observation technologies including data mining can be gleaned by the fact that several planned terrorist attacks, such as the Transatlantic airliner bombing plot of 2006 on board airlines from the UK, US and Canada, could be prevented: the perpetrators left traceable digital footprints such as phone calls, emails, use of social media, and internet search histories that helped counter-terrorism forces to piece together enough information about the impending attack to intervene before it was too late. In this regard, it should be noted that nobody is born a terrorist. Citizens that commit terrorism have all generated evidence trails for the state to follow, such as pictures taken for passports, ID cards, driver licences etc., or police photographs in the case of minor crimes, long before becoming terrorists.

Despite all these identification and behavioural analytics technologies, some terrorists might be able to evade identification efforts for a variety of reasons, including failures in intelligence sharing. Hence, a second layer of defence is required, consisting of technologies that can detect and identify suspicious objects or substances carried by terrorists while on their way to a chosen target—thus enabling police forces to swiftly intervene in order to neutralize the threat. This is what Mills and Huber mean when they point out that we need to detect and identify dangerous substances before it's too late (Mills and Huber 2002: 1–2). What they have in mind are scanning technologies such as metal detectors, full-body scanners, and explosive detection systems. Frequent travellers are already familiar with most of them from the security checks at airports.

Metal detectors come in the shape of baggage scanners, portal scanners (also known as Walk-Through Metal Detectors/WTMD) or as hand-held devices colloquially known as 'wands'. The user-friendliness of WTMD systems, both for operators as well as for those having to step through them, resulted in a swift adoption for access control of sensitive public and private sector facilities. Many shopping centres have adopted WTMD systems as well, also checking bags if and when required. Nevertheless, smuggling weapons or improvised explosive devices (IEDs) onto the premises is rendered more challenging, which means potential attackers might look elsewhere for easier targets. Although such detectors would not have deterred the perpetrators of the attacks in Paris, 13/14 November 2015, the deployment of these systems to increase security of locations which are either sensitive or attract crowds is a step in the right direction.

> **KEY CONCEPTS**
>
> **Metal Detectors** Metal detectors systems work by creating a magnetic field which is interrupted by anything metallic, thus triggering an alarm. In the case of baggage scanners, secondary checks will be conducted, overseen by a human operator. In the case of alarms triggered by a Walk-Through Metal Detectors (WTMD) system, this usually leads to a thorough pat-down by security personnel.

In a time of a changed threat environment, that is in the aftermath of the Transatlantic aircraft plot of 2006 where the perpetrators planned to detonate liquid explosives, or the failed al-Qaeda bombing attempt of Christmas Day 2009 on a flight from the Netherlands to the US where a terrorist planned to set off explosives sewn into his underwear; metal detectors are no longer enough. They would not be able to spot such hidden explosives. Ceramic or nylon knives would also remain invisible for such systems. Hence, full-body scanners were introduced to fill this gap. Currently however, even state-of-the-art full-body scanners are neither able to penetrate the skin deep enough to detect items hidden in someone's body, nor can they detect items hidden in shoes. The next generation of technology however will be able to do just that. Also, future baggage scanners will be able to detect more than metal: '3D' luggage scanners will also be able to detect and correctly analyse electronics and liquids—which may result in the end of the 100ml liquids carry-on rule on flights (currently in force as a result of the Transatlantic aircraft liquid bomb attempt) (Duffy 2019).

> **KEY CONCEPTS**
>
> **Full-Body Scanners** Depending on the type, a full-body scanner either 'projects low-level X-ray beams over the body to create a reflection of the body displayed on the monitor [or] bounces harmless electromagnetic waves off the body' (Price and Forrest 2016: 312).
>
> The first generation of full-body scanners created rather detailed greyscale pictures of passengers' bodies. Hence, the process of going through a backscatter body scanner was likened to a 'virtual strip search' by civil rights groups such as the American Civil Liberty Union (ACLU) (Klitou 2008), while in the UK, child protection groups feared that these systems could be abused to take nude pictures of children. Current systems however simply use a generic, 'standardized stick-figure on a screen, to indicate to the security officer areas of the individual's body which should receive a targeted hand-search' (Department for Transport 2016: 2). Furthermore, all information generated via the scan is immediately deleted once the process is completed (ibid.).

Last but not least, explosive detection systems (EDS) and explosives trace detectors (ETD) should also be mentioned. Unfortunately, current systems produce a high rate of 'false positives' (that is, they misidentify harmless substances as dangerous ones)—after all, potassium as an ingredient for gunpowder is also found in bananas, while glycerine as an ingredient of nitro-glycerine also is one of the main ingredients of cosmetics. Hence, they are of limited utility only.

> **KEY CONCEPTS**
>
> **Explosive Detection Systems (EDS)** Explosive detection systems (EDS) search for explosives either by way of an image shape analysis that looks for detonators, wires and batteries; or via the known density of explosives which lies between the low density of organic material and the high density of metals (Singh and Singh 2003: 34).
>
> **Explosive Trace Detectors (ETD)** Explosive trace detectors (ETD), colloquially known as 'sniffers', look for chemical fingerprints of explosives—these are the detectors air passengers encounter when they must hand over laptops or mobile phones to a security official who then rubs the device's surface with a reagent-impregnated swab, which is then taken to an analyser unit to test for traces of explosives. At the moment, most commercially available ETD systems are based on ion mobility spectrometry (IMS) or on gas chromatography (Caygill, Davis, and Higson 2012).

All of these different scanner and sniffer technologies have their limitations, and do not really work as stand-alone security solutions. On the other hand, requiring individuals to pass through all of these systems for enhanced security is a time-consuming process. From a counter-terrorism perspective, it would be preferable if firstly, all this scanning and sniffing could be done in one go; and secondly, even more importantly, completed remotely and not necessarily with the consent or even knowledge of people being security-checked. We are looking here at a future generation of security technology in the shape of 'smart corridors' (see Key Concepts box) and even smarter CCTV systems than those we have at present.

> **KEY CONCEPTS**
>
> **'Smart Corridors'** 'Smart corridors' is the most common name for future walk-through passages lined with various scanners and sniffers, plus facial recognition systems. They are envisaged as 'one stop' multimodal security solutions that are also 'able to screen a person for weapons, drugs or explosives in real time without impeding the traffic flow' (Singh and Singh 2003: 33).

Research in this direction is already making some progress, and several such systems have been announced in the last years. However, going public on such advanced solutions after some closely controlled laboratory-condition tests is one thing—rolling them out for the general public to be used at busy airports or main railway stations is completely different. The same can be said for smart CCTV systems or 'smart lampposts' (Livni 2019) which not only include advanced facial recognition and gait recognition cameras, but also remote scanner and sniffer technologies that can detect suspicious items or traces of explosives at a distance on the bodies of individuals in the midst of a crowd. At the moment however, such systems do not yet exist.

As it stands, it is evident that the scanning and sniffing technologies currently used in this second layer are by no means fool-proof. For the foreseeable future, it is thus likely that a certain percentage of terrorists will manage to slip through this net as well, be it because of careful planning, or sheer luck. The third layer of defence therefore is geared to deal with those who are about to strike. This final layer is no longer about threat neutralization but about consequence mitigation: while it is now very likely that the attack can no longer be prevented, its costs in the form of lives lost, and assets damaged or destroyed, can be minimized by carefully deployed defences.

Unlike the defences of the first and second layer, technologies employed here do not need to be high-tech any longer. Rather, low-tech solutions are sufficient in most cases. Examples would be so-called 'street furniture' in the shape of bollards, lamp posts, flower pots, and benches: if made of cement or stainless steel, they can be used as barricades to deny vehicle access to certain areas. Most airports and many rail stations now feature such unobtrusive security measures. Such barricades also come as readily deployable mobile solutions, for example to enhance security of public events by funnelling people through access gates—which come with portal scanners. A case in point would be the Notting Hill Carnival of 25/26 August 2019 in London, or Edinburgh Fringe events in Scotland in the same month. On a much larger scale, the 'Rings of Steel and Glass' of Belfast and the City of London (Coaffee 2004) used such barricades as modern equivalent of ancient city walls, also with the purpose of controlling access by only offering a few gates. This process of securing whole buildings or areas via barricades and access gates is known as 'citadelization'.

> **KEY CONCEPTS**
>
> **'Citadelization' of Buildings** Securing or 'citadelizing' buildings is a straightforward exercise if it is done in the blueprint stage of new buildings: at that stage, adding, or 'designing in', a number of security features is easy. One well-known example is *One World Center* New York which, under the impression of 9/11, was built with a reinforced concrete base as well as extra-wide pressurized stairwells. It also features biological and chemical air filters, while the interior is constantly monitored by about 400 smart CCTV systems (Tarantola 2011).
>
> On the other hand, retrofitting existing buildings with security features is, usually due to confined space, far more difficult. Still, smart CCTV systems and air filters can be added. The original glass fronts also can be replaced by shatterproof glass which, in case of a terrorist attack (or an earthquake for that matter) would not turn into lethal, dagger-like splinters, thus helping to minimize casualties. The entries to the building can be secured with various kinds of detectors, while bollards, concrete or steel flower pots, and other types of street furniture could form barriers protecting it from car or truck bombs. Even sturdy trees can serve that purpose.

Occasionally however, the confined spaces of inner cities render the addition of security measures well-nigh impossible. Trying to *increase* the security of a particular space might even *decrease* its safety. A case in point is London Bridge, which was the location of a terrorist attack in June 2017, and then again in May 2019. In the inquest after the 2017 incident, it emerged that the bridge actually had been fitted with security barriers in the shape of steel guardrails—but since a number of cyclists complained about these 'trip hazards', they had been removed again 'as part of a wider programme to improve safety and "reduce street clutter"' (Dearden 2019, also see BBC 2019b). Furthermore, one should not forget the so-called 'displacement' effect: if one potential target is hardened by protective measures, terrorists simply move on to the next target on their list—of which there are plenty in cities.

This comment brings us to the opposing views i.e. the assertion that our technology will not protect us. This pessimist view flies in the face of optimist technophiles who see technology as a 'silver bullet'. Mills and Huber for example conclude that a) 'it is *only* our technology that will let us survive the enduring war against terrorism', and b) that in the fight of 'their sons against our silicon, [our] silicon will win' (Mills and Huber 2002: 13). That this isn't necessarily true will be discussed next in section 25.3.

25.3 ANTITHESIS: OUR TECHNOLOGY WILL NOT SAVE US

Undeniably, technology is a valuable tool in the fight against terrorism. Whether it will help us win this fight is another question: not all scholars are as sanguine as Mills and Huber. David Lyon for example cautions that this optimism may well be misplaced since '[any] technology can be outwitted, given time and ingenuity' (Lyon 2004: 310). Furthermore, an uncritical application of technology may come with a hefty price-tag in regards to civil liberties and human rights.

First of all, and as already touched on in this chapter, all the technologies deployed at the moment are not as reliable as one would hope. Facial recognition software for example comes with a high rate of 'false positives' (that is, mis-identifications), and also has in-built bias against ethnic minority groups, which is due to the way this software works: it either generates image-based algorithms, which 'use a template-based method to calculate the correlation between a face and one or more templates to estimate the face identity'; or geometry feature-based algorithms, which 'capture the local facial features and their geometric relationship' (Introna and Wood 2004: 185). The algorithm itself consists of just a couple of kilobytes—after all, the microchips of biometric passports are very small when it comes to memory space. This data reduction negatively affects the performance of the algorithms with the result that biases are present. With regard to template-based algorithms for example, Introna and Wood (2004: 186, 192) argue that '[i]t obviously depends on the gallery used to create the standard template as well as the range of potential variations within a population. For example, because minorities tend to deviate the most from the standard template they [...] are easier to identify by the algorithms [and] will have a greater probability of triggering the alarm, [thus being] subjected to a higher probability of scrutiny as false positives, i.e. mistaken identity.'

Technophiles will point out that the year 2004 was a long time ago when it comes to software development, and that current facial recognition systems routinely achieve a much higher rate of accuracy of between 97 and 99 per cent (Chakya 2014; Shiostu 2019). Under controlled laboratory conditions, that may well be the case, but it is doubtful whether the more messy 'real life' use of such systems leads to more reliable outcomes at present. One illustrative example to the contrary in this regard is the attempt by the London Metropolitan Police to use facial detection during the Notting Hill Carnival by 2017 with the modest aim to protect participants from acts of low-level everyday crime such as pickpocketing.

CASE STUDY 25.1

Notting Hill Carnival August 2017

With the intent to protect people from criminals, the London Metropolitan Police decided to deploy facial recognition systems. As was explained well before the event, the 'technology involves the use of overt cameras which scan the faces of those passing by and flag up potential matches against a database of custody images. The database will be populated with images of individuals who are forbidden from attending carnival, as well as individuals wanted by police' (as quoted in Dodd 2017). Not surprisingly given this intrusion into people's privacy, the announcement resulted in strong protests from civil rights groups such as Liberty, Privacy International, StopWatch, and Black Lives Matter (BBC 2017). But worse was in store for the police: even though the database used was small and only contained 500 images, the facial recognition software used during the event returned about 35 false positives (that is, mistaken identities), 'leading to one incorrect arrest and five interventions' (Lamb 2017). In a press release after the event, the Biometrics Commissioner of the British Government admitted that Facial Recognition Technology 'has the potential to be a really useful crime fighting tool, but we are not there yet. It needs to be properly tested and evaluated if it is going to be effective and it will need to be handled carefully by the police and the government if it is going to be trusted by the public' (Wiles 2017).

Although the deployment of facial recognition systems during the Notting Hill Carnival of August 2017 is not a real-world example of counter-terrorism per se, this example illustrates that facial recognition systems still have to overcome a number of rather formidable technological hurdles before they can be added to the array of useful counter-terrorism tools.

QUESTIONS

1. Do you agree that Facial Recognition Technology could be a useful tool in fighting terrorism and serious crime, despite its current problems?
2. Is the intrusion into people's privacy a price that needs to be paid for an increase in safety and security?

It should be noted that most, if not all, of the technologies discussed as potential 'silver bullets' in this chapter to combat terrorism, actually could be called 'dual use' technologies—in the sense that these technologies could be employed by counter-terrorists as well as by terrorists. One example to illustrate this—the case of now widely available drones. While for counter-terrorism purposes, various types of drones could be, or already are, used for airborne surveillance operations, in the hands of terrorists they could easily be weaponized. The larger of these commercially available drones can be jury-rigged to carry explosives which could be flown into a high-value targets by remote control. That terrorists are perfectly aware of this becomes apparent in the cases of ISIS drone strikes on Iraqi army units, or the (failed) drone strike by some Islamic Jihad members on Israeli tanks deployed on the border to Gaza (Doffman 2019). Another example is the failed drone attack on Venezuelan president Nicolás Maduro on 4 August 2018, (Jenkins 2018; also see Grossman 2018) (see Photo 25.2 below). In regard to outwitting defensive technologies, the use of drones by terrorists highlights how physical barricades could be outwitted: simply by flying over them.

PHOTO 25.2 Caracas, Venezuela, 2018. The exact moment in which bodyguards cover the president of Venezuela, Nicolás Maduro, after the explosion of a drone near the stage.

This can be prevented, or at least rendered more difficult, by 'geofencing', that is setting up a virtual three-dimensional perimeter fence that when approached, triggers an alarm and countermeasures (see for example Ijeh et al. 2009). These jam drones, and could be followed by efforts to capture terrorists. However, terrorists are devising 'countermeasures'. As high-tech goes, drones belong to the lower end. In the case of aviation terrorism, there are concerted efforts to harness sophisticated technology in order to outwit protective technology and to get past defences, ever-more sophisticated protective measures notwithstanding. By depending ever more on technology to defeat terrorists, this encourages attackers to do likewise.

CASE STUDY 25.2

Aviation Terrorism—Terrorist Action versus Counter-Terrorist Reaction

After the loss of Air India Flight 182 on 23 June 1985 and of Pan Am Flight 103 on 21 December 1988, both destroyed in flight by time-fused bombs hidden in suitcases, X-ray-based baggage scanners were made mandatory for airports. Furthermore, a computer-assisted passenger pre-screening system (CAPPS) was introduced which allowed for a pre-selection of suspicious travellers, and a practice known as 'passenger-baggage reconciliation': if passengers did not board the plane, their baggage was (and still is) off-loaded. Since these security measures assumed that terrorists would not be willing to sacrifice their own lives, they were not sufficient to prevent 9/11—even though CAPPS pre-selected several of the perpetrators.

In the aftermath of 9/11, further security measures were introduced: carry-on baggage had to be scanned by metal detectors as well, while all passengers had to walk through portal metal scanners. Depending on the threat level, some passengers also had their laptops or other devices checked by so-called explosives trace detectors (ETDs). Additional security measures included the hardening of cockpit doors and the deployment of air marshals to prevent potential hijackers to commandeer a plane.

Terrorists quickly found countermeasures again. The first notable incident happened on 22 December 2001. Al-Qaeda-linked terrorist Richard Reid boarded American Airlines Flight 63 from Paris to Miami, USA carrying a small explosive device hidden in his trainers. Now known as 'shoe bomber', Reid was subdued by passengers and crew before he could ignite the explosives. Fortunately, the countermeasures to shoe bombs were quite straightforward: on demand, passengers now have to take their shoes off and place them on the belt as well.

This time, it took terrorists a bit longer to respond. In August 2006, it emerged that a London-based al-Qaeda cell had assembled liquid bombs in the shape of TATP explosives hidden in soft-drink bottles. The perpetrator took their cue from similar liquid bombs, planned and tested in the Philippines by al-Qaeda terrorist Ramzi Yousef in December 1994. Timely intelligence and police action prevented that plot also—it is highly questionable whether existing security measures would have detected the liquid bombs that were meant to destroy seven transatlantic planes. Governments reacted with inaugurating further security measures—this time introducing limits on liquids that passengers are allowed to take on board, while also mandating that these liquids have to be carried in a transparent, resealable bag to allow visual inspection.

It took al-Qaeda three years to find yet another way to get past security measures—this time in the shape of an 'underwear bomb', worn by AQ operative Umar Farouk Abdulmuttalab. The target was Northwest Airlines Flight 253, departing on Christmas Day 2009 from Amsterdam to Detroit. Abdulmuttalab could board the flight unchallenged since the explosives sewn into his briefs could not be detected by the scanners in use at Schipol Airport. Fortunately, and just like Reid, he had problems igniting the charge, and could be subdued by passengers and crew. In order to counter this novel threat, authorities introduced full-body scanners.

At the time of writing, the underwear bombing plan is nearly a decade in the past, and it is more than questionable whether the much-discussed 'cavity bombs', based on explosive devices hidden in the body (hence the name), will be operational (see for example Corera 2012; Argomaniz and Lehr 2016).

QUESTIONS

1. Why is commercial aviation (airports and airliners) such a tempting target for terrorists?
2. Is this (terrorist) action–(counter-terrorist) reaction pattern unavoidable, given terrorists' ongoing attempts to find new ways to attack commercial aviation?

The danger of a high-tech arms race between terrorists and counter-terrorists is not the most serious issue here. Rather, many technologies, in particular observation and surveillance technologies such as facial identification and data mining technologies, pose a serious danger to civil liberties in general and privacy. To begin with, this chapter outlined that in London alone, roughly 420,000 CCTV systems, old and new, gaze down on pedestrians crossing their fields of vision. Those deployed at King's Cross and at Canary Wharf are smart, i.e. they are equipped with facial recognition software. All the CCTV systems in question are owned and operated by a multitude of public and private actors. The pedestrians being scanned and perhaps identified without their knowledge do not know what happens with all this information garnered. As Stephanie Hare from the *Observer* newspaper warns,

> 'We are just as ignorant about what has been happening to our faces when they're scanned by the property developers, shopping centres, museums, conference centres and casinos that have also been secretly using facial recognition technology on us, according to the civil liberties group Big Brother Watch. But we can take a good guess. They may be matching us against police watchlists, maintaining their own watchlists or sharing their watchlists with the police, other companies and other governments' (Hare 2019).

We do not know what happens with all the data collected when we use the internet and social media, thus leaving the 'digital footprints'. One might well argue that in the time of Facebook, Instagram or Google, leaving 'digital footprints' is not really an issue for all the millions of users regularly posting pictures and stories on these platforms, and indeed, this is a valid argument. But revealing too much about oneself online, or getting one's search histories recorded, is only the tip of the iceberg.

The onslaught on our privacy, and on our civil liberties, in the name of security is far more severe precisely because our ever-increasing digital footprints render it easy for interested intelligence services to tap into the flow of data and to establish immense data bases. Consider for example the US National Security Agencies *Prism* program which was launched in 2007 and allegedly taps 'directly into the central servers of nine leading U.S. Internet companies, extracting audio and video chats, photographs, e-mails, documents, and connection logs that enable analysts to track foreign targets' (Gellman and Poitras 2013). Or the British GCHQ's *Tempora* programme which 'tap[s] into and store huge volumes of data drawn from fibre-optic cables for up to 30 days so that they can be sifted and analysed [and is allegedly] handling 600m "telephone events" each day, had tapped more than 200 fibre-optic cables, and was able to process data from at least 46 of them at a time' (MacAskill et al. 2013). From a counter-terrorism perspective, we must acknowledge that such prospective data mining could be useful 'to find the "signature" of terrorist cells embedded in larger networks' (Fienberg 2008: 197), thus preventing an imminent terrorist attack. But as people in society, are we at ease with such large-scale data mining operations that, by their very nature, tend to compromise privacy rights?

The 2021 *Pegasus* spyware scandal shows that the accumulation of huge volumes of data may just be the start when it comes to the infringement of civil liberties and human rights.

Pegasus, developed by the Israeli technology company NSO Group, 'can stealthily enter a smartphone and gain access to everything on it, including its camera and microphone' (Gurijala 2021). Unnoticed by the owner of the smartphone and without leaving any trace (Amnesty International 2021), it then harvests data such as photos, videos, social media posts, web search histories, call logs, or passwords—while also being able to activate the smartphone's camera and microphone 'for real-time surveillance without the permission or knowledge of the user' (ibid.). The NSO Group claims that Pegasus, designed to infiltrate any operating system and any smartphone on the market, is sold to governments only for the purpose of combating serious crime and terrorism. However, an international investigative journalism initiative known as *Pegasus Project* found that some governments quickly used this spyware for very different purposes—for example to infiltrate the phones of targeted opposition politicians, human rights activists, dissidents, journalists, or leading politicians of foreign governments, including heads of state (Kirchgaessner et al. 2021).

Unleashing sophisticated technical advancements against terrorists in the assumption that technology will win obviously comes with a hefty price tag, not only in terms of the literal financial costs. Rather, as the case of first generation of full body scanners indicates, costs may well involve a certain trade-off between security and civil liberties: do air travellers have to undergo a 'virtual strip search' to board a plane? Or, what about the current requirement for travellers to the United States to surrender smart phones to immigration officials on request, to let them examine social media profiles? And what about the massive amounts of our data collected by various intelligence services. Real time data mining is arguably a very promising tool for preventing terrorist attacks—but one which has courted controversy. The Pegasus spyware scandal for example shows how easily data mining can be abused by governments more interested in eavesdropping on individuals or groups opposed to them than in combating terrorists.

Since many of these examples of technological advancements are very useful tools in the fight against terrorism, counter-terrorist experts will probably likely claim that hard choices need to be made. Margaret Thatcher, former Prime Minister of the UK, for example quipped that '[i]n order to protect democracy, you sometimes have no choice but to use undemocratic means' (as quoted in Ganor 2005: 166). At first glance, this 'hard choices' argument is a compelling one—but it raises several difficult-to-answer questions, among them 'how far can we go' and 'where will we end?'

25.4 SYNTHESIS: THE NATURE OF THE TERRORIST THREAT

To reach a conclusion regarding the advantages and disadvantages of technology, it is useful to step back for a moment to take a look at the bigger picture of the 'action-reaction' cycle between terrorists and counter-terrorists, or the state at large. Usually, it is the terrorists who act, forcing the affected state to react. This reaction often occurs in the shape of an immediate response: something bad happens; the population, represented by the media, clamours for 'something to be done'; and the government springs into action—this is 'the politics of the latest outrage', as Anderson (2000: 228) calls it. New legislation is passed in a hurry, and new powers for police and intelligence services are introduced. This is also the time when silver bullets are sought in the shape of solutions that promise to at least mitigate the impact of terrorism on us, if not completely defeating it. In the context of this chapter, these silver bullets are high-tech solutions. But these silver bullets are both imperfect and harmful, as this chapter has explored. On the one hand, they are not good enough to offer 100 per cent security, on the other, they impinge on our civil liberties and our right to privacy.

The technical aspect is easier to deal with. Even if we are 'not there yet' when it comes to multimodal security solutions—in particular sensor-equipped smart CCTV systems that can detect and identify suspicious substances from a distance—it seems to be a question of time only until such solutions will be available. These still-to-be-developed technologies will not end terrorist attacks once and for all since in our open societies, terrorists simply can move on to an unprotected target. But deploying such technologies will help to at least mitigate the consequences of an attack. Fewer people will be killed or injured, and less damage will be inflicted.

The impact of such technologies on our civil liberties and our privacy is more difficult to gauge. Those who are critical regarding the deployment of surveillance and of data mining and acquisition technologies, may well argue with former US President Benjamin Franklin (1755) that: '[t]hose who would give up essential liberty, to purchase a little temporary safety, deserve neither liberty nor safety.' The fears of these critics might not necessarily be assuaged by time-limits on counter-terrorism measures—after all, time limits can be extended (the US Patriot Act, originally published on 26 October 2001 to deter and punish terrorist acts is a case in point), and surveillance technology, once deployed, is here to stay in any case. Furthermore, it is undeniable that the public's calls for action are welcome at least by some interested parties from the public and private sectors, since it gives opportunities to widen the powers of the state as well, as the influence of private security enterprises. However, since the pressure on the state to react can be quite substantial, it would be misleading to resort to conspiracy theories of a state power grab—especially so since the government typically reacts to protests if the measures seemed to have gone too far—the case of the full-body scanners would be one recent example of that.

A further indication that conspiracy theories revolving around a power-grab by the state are too simplistic is the fact that quite often, the authorities that would gain most from such measures are not always keen to expand their power. An example is the UK Home Office's attempted roll-out of facial recognition technology across the country in the autumn of 2019. Interestingly, and contrary to fears that British police forces would be 'eager to embrace a technology for infringing privacy and increasing state surveillance' (Townsend 2019), the two forces earmarked for a trial of this technology, Kent Police and West Midlands Police, were 'in fact fiercely resistant to piloting facial recognition and den[ied] they agreed to help the Home Office trial this technology' (ibid.). After all, it is no secret that a) there is substantial unease with the public regarding this technology, and b) that this technology still is prone to misidentify a disturbingly high percentage of individuals, even under the best circumstances.

As regards the Internet of Things (things embedded with sensors, software, and other technology to connect with the internet), it should also be mentioned that it was Germany's federal telecoms regulator which recommended in October 2017 that devices capable of parents eavesdropping on the conversations of children (devices the regulator deemed to be 'unauthorized transmitting systems') to be destroyed (Kaufman 2017). One of the arguments leading to the ban was that if parents can eavesdrop on their children and monitor their movements, so can other individuals with ill intent: most devices communicate via unsecured Wi-Fi or Bluetooth connections. The main lesson here however is that it was a state authority that raised the alarm and pushed back against yet another technology that endangers people's privacy—other state authorities, in particular intelligence services, might have had a very different view on that matter.

25.5 CONCLUSION

We are faced with a dilemma—a dilemma that has been neatly summarized by Eric Haseltine, former NSA 'spy technology chief': the decision whether we should try to unleash our sophisticated technologies on terrorists, all possible side effects just discussed notwithstanding, pretty much depends on 'whether [we] think the world is safe or not' (as interviewed in Hastings 2019). In other words, it boils down to the question of how we see the terrorist threat: is it overblown, as for example Mueller (2006) argued? Or is it a threat to the very fabric of our society?

DISCUSSION QUESTIONS

1. Is technology the long-sought silver bullet that will help defeat the terrorist threat?
2. Mills and Huber argue that 'our silicon will win'. Do you agree?
3. What impact could sophisticated surveillance, observation, and identification technology have on the concept of 'citizen'?
4. How far can (or should) liberal democracies go when it comes to protecting their citizens from terrorism?

Visit the online resources for pointers on how to answer the discussion questions, links to useful web sources, and guidance on accessing databases:
www.oup.com/he/Wilson-Muro1e

GUIDE TO FURTHER READING

Coaffee, Jon (2004) 'Recasting the "Ring of Steel": Designing Out Terrorism in the City of London?', in Graham, Stephen (ed.): *Cities, War, and Terrorism. Towards an Urban Geopolitics*. Malden, MA and Oxford: Blackwell, 276–296. *Provides an overview on how City of London police and other actors redesigned the public spaces within the City of London to harden them against terrorist threats.*

Fienberg, Stephen E. (2008) 'Homeland Insecurity: Data Mining, Privacy, Disclosure Limitation, and the Hunt for Terrorists', in Hsinchun Chen et al. (eds.): *Terrorism Informatics. Knowledge Management and Data Mining for Homeland Security*. New York: Springer, 197–218. *Offers a useful and easy to understand introduction on data mining with a focus on counter-terrorism.*

Lehr, Peter (2019) *Counter-Terrorism Technologies: A Critical Assessment*. Cham: Springer. *This monograph discusses the role of technology in terrorism and counter-terrorism, while taking a critical approach that stays clear from technophilia on the one hand and technophobia on the other.*

Lyon, David (2004) 'Technology vs. "terrorism": Circuits of City Surveillance since September 11, 2001', in Graham, S. (ed.): *Cities, War, and Terrorism. Towards an Urban Geopolitics*. Blackwell, Malden/Oxford, 297–311. *Lyon's chapter critically investigates the role of surveillance systems deployed in great numbers after 9/11, also touching on the convergence between public (state) and private (enterprises) surveillance.*

Mills, Mark P. and Huber, Peter W. (2002) 'How Technology Will Defeat Terrorism: At Home and Abroad, Digital Wizardry Will Keep Us Safe.' *City Journal*, Winter. *Mills and Huber's trail-blazing short article is a must-read in the context of counter-terrorism technology since it raises a series of fundamental questions regarding human rights and civil liberties.*

REFERENCES

Al-Abed, Mohamad, Christophe Charrier and Christophe Rosenberger (2012) 'Evaluation of Biometric Systems', in Yang, Yucheng (ed.): *New Trends and Developments in Biometrics*, 149–169. London: Intech Open Limited. https://www.intechopen.com/books/new-trends-and-developments-in-biometrics/evaluation-of-biometric-systems

Amnesty International (2021) 'Forensic Methodology Report: How to Catch NSO Group's Pegasus', *Amnesty International Blog*, 18 July. Index Number: DOC 10/4487/2021. https://www.amnesty.org/en/latest/research/2021/07/forensic-methodology-report-how-to-catch-nso-groups-pegasus/

Anderson, Malcolm (2000) 'Counterterrorism as an Objective of European Police Cooperation', in Reinares, Fernando (ed.): *European Democracies Against Terrorism. Governmental Policies and Intergovernmental Cooperation* (Aldershot: Ashgate, 2000).

Argomaniz, Javier and Lehr, Peter (2016) 'Political Resilience and EU Responses to Aviation Terrorism', *Studies in Conflict and Terrorism*, 39 (4): 363–379.

BBC (2017) 'Groups Call for Notting Hill Carnival face scans to be dropped by Met', *BBC News England*, 17 August. https://www.bbc.co.uk/news/uk-england-london-40963126

Cambridge English Dictionary [online] (undated): 'technology'. https://dictionary.cambridge.org/dictionary/english/technology

Caygill, Sarah J., Davis, Frank, and Higson, Seamus P. J. (2012) 'Current Trends in Explosive Detection Techniques', *Talanta*, Vol. 88, 15 January, 14–29. https://dspace.lib.cranfield.ac.uk/bitstream/1826/6887/1/Current_trends_in_explosives_detection_techniques-2012.pdf

Chakya, Kyle (2014) 'Face-Recognition Software: Is this the End of Anonymity for all of us?', *The Independent*, 23 April. http://www.independent.co.uk/life-style/gadgets-and-tech/features/face-recognition-software-is-this-the-end-of-anonymity-for-all-of-us-9278697.html

Chen, Hsinchun (2006) *Intelligence and Security Informatics for International Security. Information Sharing and Data Mining*. New York: Springer.

Clark, Matt (2013) 'Google Glass Violates Nevada Law, Says Caesars Palace', *IGN*, 8 May. http://uk.ign.com/articles/2013/05/08/

google-glass-violates-nevada-law-says-caesars-palace

Coaffee, Jon (2004) 'Recasting the "Ring of Steel": Designing Out Terrorism in the City of London?', in Graham, Stephen (ed.): *Cities, War, and Terrorism. Towards an Urban Geopolitics*. Malden, MA and Oxford: Blackwell, 276–296.

Corera, Gordon (2012) 'Human Bombs: Are They a Realistic Threat?', *BBC News Magazine*, 23 May. https://www.bbc.co.uk/news/magazine-18161870

Crelinsten, Ronald (2009) *Counterterrorism*. Cambridge and Malden, MA: Polity Press.

Dearden, Lizzie (2019) 'Police Defend Decision not to Install London Bridge Barriers Despite Warning that it was "Viable and Attractive" Terror Target', *The Independent*, 19 June. https://www.independent.co.uk/news/uk/home-news/london-bridge-attack-barriers-terror-target-police-warning-latest-a8965991.html

Department for Transport (UK) (2016) 'Security Scanners Code of Practice'. London: Department for Transport. *Gov.UK Guidance: Security Scanners Implementation Information*. Published: 22 March 2010. Last updated: 20 December 2016. https://www.gov.uk/government/uploads/system/uploads/attachment_data/file/573478/security-scanner-code-of-practice-2016.pdf

Dodd, Vikram (2017) 'Met Police to use Facial Recognition Software at Notting Hill carnival', *The Guardian*, 5 August. https://www.theguardian.com/uk-news/2017/aug/05/met-police-facial-recognition-software-notting-hill-carnival

Doffman, Zak (2019) 'Warning Over Terrorist Attacks Using Drones Given by EU Security Chief', *Forbes*, 4 August. https://www.forbes.com/sites/zakdoffman/2019/08/04/europes-security-chief-issues-dire-warning-on-terrorist-threat-from-drones/#eded2dd7ae41

Duffy, Nick (2019) '3D Scanners Could end Liquid Limits at Airports', *The i Paper*, 26 August.

Fienberg, Stephen E. (2008) 'Homeland Insecurity: Data Mining, Privacy, Disclosure Limitation, and the Hunt for Terrorists', in Hsinchun Chen et al. (eds.): *Terrorism Informatics. Knowledge Management and Data Mining for Homeland Security*. New York: Springer, pp. 197–218.

Franklin, Benjamin (1755) *Pennsylvania Assembly: Reply to the Governor*. November 11. http://franklinpapers.org/franklin/framedVolumes.jsp?vol=6&page=238a

Gandy, Oscar H. (2002) 'Data Mining and Surveillance in the Post-9.11 Environment', *Presentation to the Political Economy Section, IAMCR*. Barcelona, July. http://web.asc.upenn.edu/usr/ogandy/iamcrdatamining.pdf

Ganor, Boaz (2005) *The Counter-Terrorism Puzzle: a Guide for Decision Makers*. New Brunswick/London: Transaction.

Gellman, Barton and Poitras, Laura (2013) 'U.S., British Intelligence Mining Data from Nine U.S. Internet Companies in Broad Secret Program', *Washington Post*, 7 June. https://www.washingtonpost.com/investigations/us-intelligence-mining-data-from-nine-us-internet-companies-in-broad-secret-program/2013/06/06/3a0c0da8-cebf-11e2-8845-d970ccb04497_story.html?utm_term=.7ac02725b7a2

Grossman, Nicholas (2018) *Drones and Terrorism: Asymmetric Warfare and the Threat to Global Security*. London et al.: I.B. Tauris.

Gurijala, Bhanukiran (2021) 'What is Pegasus? A Cybersecurity Expert Explains how the Spyware Invades Phones and What it Does When it gets in', *The Conversation*, 9 August. https://theconversation.com/what-is-pegasus-a-cybersecurity-expert-explains-how-the-spyware-invades-phones-and-what-it-does-when-it-gets-in-165382

Hare, Stephanie (2019) 'Facial Recognition is now Rampant. The Implications for our Freedom are Chilling', *The Observer*, 18 August.

Hastings, Rob (2019) 'Tinker Tailor Soldier Bug', *The i Paper*, 25 June.

Ijeh, Anthony C., Brimicombe, Allan J., Preston, David S., and Imafidon, Chris O. (2009) 'Geofencing in a Security Strategy Model', in Hamid Jahankhani, Ali G. Hessami, and Feng Hsiu (eds.): *Global Safety and Sustainability: 5th International Conference Proceedings*. Berlin and Heidelberg: Springer, 104–111.

Introna, Lucas and Wood, David (2004) 'Picturing Algorithmic Surveillance: The Politics of Facial Recognition Systems', *Surveillance & Society*, 2 (2–3): 177–198. http://www.ssoar.info/ssoar/bitstream/handle/document/20067/ssoar-surveillance-2004-23-introna_et_al-picturing_algorithmic_surveillance_the_politics.pdf?sequence=1

Jenkins, Barry (2018) 'We Should Fear the use of Killer Drones like in Venezuela – all you need is £5,000 and Some Tinfoil', *The Independent*, 11 August. https://www.independent.co.uk/voices/killer-drones-venezuela-president-attack-uk-aircraft-warfare-isis-syria-a8487536.html

Kaufman, Mark (2017) 'German Government Tells Parents to Destroy Children's Smart Watches', *Mashable*, 17 November. http://mashable.com/2017/11/17/german-regulator-tells-people-to-destroy-childrens-smartwatches/?utm_cid=mash-com-fb-main-link#4RPI4gVYbOq5

Kilcullen, David (2016) *Blood Year: Islamic State and the Failures of the War on Terror*. London: Hurst.

Kirchgaessner, Stephanie, Lewis, Paul, Pegg, David, Cutler, Sam, Lakhani, Nina, and Safi, Michael (2021) 'Revealed: Leak Uncovers Global Abuse of Cyber-surveillance Weapon', *The Guardian*, 18 July. https://www.theguardian.com/world/2021/jul/18/revealed-leak-uncovers-global-abuse-of-cyber-surveillance-weapon-nso-group-pegasus

Klitou, Demetrius (2008) 'Backscatter Body Scanners – A Strip Search by Other Means', *Computer Law & Security Report*, 24, 316–325. http://www.sciencedirect.com/science/article/pii/S0267364908000708

Lamb, Hilary (2017) 'Facial Recognition Technology "Fails" at Notting Hill Carnival', *E&T Engineering and Technology*, 1 September. https://eandt.theiet.org/content/articles/2017/08/facial-recognition-technology-fails-at-notting-hill-carnival/

Lehr, Peter (2019) *Counter-Terrorism Technologies: A Critical Assessment*. Cham: Springer.

Livni, Ephrat (2019) 'Hong Kong Protestors are Attacking Smart Lampposts', *Quartz*, 24 August. https://qz.com/1694684/hong-kong-protestors-are-attacking-smart-lampposts/

Lyon, David (2004) 'Technology vs. "Terrorism": Circuits of City Surveillance since September 11, 2001', in Graham, S. (ed.): *Cities, War, and Terrorism. Towards an Urban Geopolitics*. Blackwell, Malden/Oxford, pp 297–311.

MacAskill, Ewen et al. (2013) 'GCHQ Taps Fibre-optic Cables for Secret Access to World's Communications', *The Guardian*, 21 June. https://www.theguardian.com/uk/2013/jun/21/gchq-cables-secret-world-communications-nsa

Malčik, Dominik and Drahansky, Martin (2012) 'Anatomy of Biometric Passports', *Journal of Biomedicine and Biotechnology, 2012*. Article ID 490362. https://www.hindawi.com/journals/bmri/2012/490362/

McEwen, Adrian and Cassimally, Hakim (2014) *Designing the Internet of Things*. London: John Wiley & Sons.

McGoogan, Cara (2017) 'The end of Passport Gates? Dubai to Test "Invisible" Airport Checks Using Facial Recognition', *The Telegraph*, 13 June. http://www.telegraph.co.uk/technology/2017/06/13/end-passport-gates-dubai-test-invisible-airport-checks-using/

Mills, Mark P. and Huber, Peter W. (2002) 'How Technology will Defeat Terrorism: At Home and Abroad, Digital Wizardry will Keep us Safe', *City Journal*, Winter.

Mueller, John E. (2006) *Overblown: How Politicians and the Terrorist Industry Inflate National Security Threats, and Why We Believe Them*. New York: Free Press

Price, Jeffrey C. and Jeffrey S. Forrest (2016) *Practical Aviation Security. Predicting and Preventing Future Threats*. Amsterdam et al.: Butterworth-Heinemann/Elsevier (3rd edition).

RNZ (2019) 'Videoüberwachung immer lückenloser'. *Rhein-Neckar-Zeitung*, 26 August. https://www.rnz.de/nachrichten/mannheim_artikel,-mannheim-videoueberwachung-immer-lueckenloser-_arid,462413.html?fbclid=IwAR3-YCwaTqJ4kE0MqUC91pNKt0nMoSzU5s-_2lKFDI48qQ9Qn_3LJqXM02c

Russell, Jon (2018) 'Chinese Police are Using Smart Glasses to Identify Potential Suspects', *TechCrunch*, 8 February. https://techcrunch.com/2018/02/08/chinese-police-are-getting-smart-glasses/

Shiostu, Christopher (2019) 'Facial Recognition Tech Sucks, but it's Inevitable', *The Next Web*, 9 February. https://thenextweb.com/contributors/2019/02/09/facial-recognition-tech-sucks-but-its-inevitable/

Singh, Sameer and Singh, Maneesha (2003) 'Explosives Detection Systems (EDS) for Aviation Security', *Signal Processing*, 83: 31–55.

Solove, Daniel J. (2004) *The Digital Person: Technology and Privacy in the Information Age*. New York and London: New York University Press.

Spiegel Online (2018) 'Rennen und Fallen sind in Mannheim bald verdächtig: Projekt mit intelligenten Kameras', *Spiegel Online Netzwelt*. 15 February. http://www.spiegel.de/netzwelt/netzpolitik/mannheimer-weg-2-0-pilotprojekt-mit-intelligenten-kameras-startet-bald-a-1193622.html

Strittmatter, Kai (2018) 'Absolute Kontrolle', *Sueddeutsche Zeitung*, 1 February. http://www.sueddeutsche.de/digital/digitale-ueberwachung-in-china-absolute-kontrolle-1.3849464

Tarantola, Andrew (2011) 'How to Terror-Proof the New World Trade Center', *Gizmodo.com*, 9 September. https://gizmodo.com/5838327/terror-proofing-the-new-world-trade-center

Taylor, Peter (2001) *Brits: The War Against the IRA*. London: Bloomsbury Publishing.

Townsend, Mark (2019) 'Police Halts Trial of Face Recognition Systems', *The Observer*, 18 August.

Wiles, Paul (2017) 'Metropolitan Police's Use of Facial Recognition Software at the Notting Hill Carnival, 2017', *Gov. UK Press Release*, 23 August. https://www.gov.uk/government/news/metropolitan-polices-use-of-facirecognition-technology-at-the-notting-hill-carnival-2017

CHAPTER 26

Preventing and Countering Violent Extremism

DANIEL KOEHLER

■ CHAPTER SUMMARY

This chapter provides a practical and current overview of preventing and countering violent extremism work, and the underlying research. Key terms and concepts are introduced and critically discussed, before outlining main gaps, and important routes ahead. Of particular importance are the issues of evaluation and quality standards, as well as staff training, gender specific P/CVE, evidence-based methods, and solid theories of change. It is argued that fundamental differences between 'Western' and 'Eastern' style P/CVE have begun to erode in recent history, with a renewed discourse on the role of ideology on the Western side, and a recognition of civil society partners, as well as non-ideological components (such as psychological, creative arts, and family counselling) within the Eastern framing of P/CVE.

26.1 INTRODUCTION

On 29 November 2019, 28-year-old Usman Khan attended an academic conference on prisoner rehabilitation in London. Later that day, Khan conducted a terrorist attack near London Bridge in the centre of London, using a knife to stab five people, of whom two later died. Khan was wearing a fake suicide vest, and was shot to death by a police officer. He was also wearing an electronic tag, as he was recently released from prison on licence conditions. Khan had been arrested in 2010, and convicted in 2012 of terrorism offences including a bomb plot. It was reported that Khan completed a prison-based rehabilitation programme called the 'Healthy Identity Intervention', and took part in another initiative designed to facilitate a long-term disengagement from terrorism (BBC, 2019). Khan's case sparked an intense public debate in the United Kingdom about the effectiveness, quality, and success rates of terrorist rehabilitation, disengagement, or deradicalization programmes.

Whether or not a successful rehabilitation of highly radicalized individuals is possible, and how this can be done effectively is the main focus of the chapter. However, this is only one side of the story. Usman Khan was not born as a terrorist and changed—i.e. radicalized—to a point of no return. To prevent such processes of change as early as possible is the purpose of preventing and countering violent extremism programmes (P/CVE). In this chapter we will explore key questions regarding the history, design, and main issues with P/CVE, as they have become a cornerstone of many countries' counterterrorism strategies in the last decade.

The chapter begins by clarifying the key concepts of P/CVE and their relevance to terrorism and political violence. We then explore the current practical and academic state of the art within the P/CVE domain, especially in regard to the decrease of discernible P/CVE styles across the globe (sometimes called 'Western' and 'Eastern' P/CVE styles) towards a more standard practice. We then move on to assessing certain evidence-based P/CVE tools and practices, before discussing the two special sub-topics of gender sensitive P/CVE, and evaluation of P/CVE programmes.

> **KEY CONCEPTS**
>
> **P/CVE** Preventing an Countering Violent Extremism (P/CVE) is typically 'an approach intended to preclude individuals from engaging in, or materially supporting, ideologically motivated violence' (Williams, 2017: 153) or simply as 'non-coercive attempts to reduce involvement in terrorism' (Harris-Hogan et al., 2015: 6).
>
> **CVE** Countering Violent Extremism is an umbrella category that includes prevention activities (i.e. before a person becomes involved in extremism) and intervention activities (i.e. deradicalization and disengagement of persons who have become violent offenders and committed extremists).

> **Deradicalization** Deradicalization, in the context of this chapter, is 'the social and psychological process whereby an individual's commitment to, and involvement in, violent radicalization is reduced to the extent that they are no longer at risk of involvement and engagement in violent activity' (Horgan and Braddock, 2010: 153). This means that a person changes their extremist ideology and worldview. The corresponding term 'disengagement' focuses on behaviour: 'the process whereby an individual experiences a change in role or function that is usually associated with a reduction of violent participation' (ibid.). Some people leave extremist groups but remain committed to the cause, while others stay engaged without believing in the ideology.

26.2 A SHORT HISTORY OF P/CVE

The development of concepts for preventing and countering violent extremism date back to 2005 in Europe, when terrorist threats evolved out of so-called 'homegrown extremism' (persons borne or raised in the country they attacked). In the United States, however, the concept arrived much later, and was promoted from 2009/10 by the Office of the Coordinator for Counterterrorism under the Barack Obama administration (2009–2017).

After the September 11th, 2001 attacks the George W. Bush administration (2001–2009) released a National Implementation Plan that featured a 'counter violent Islamic extremism' (CVIE) part, tasked with combating radical and extremist ideology. This approach proved to be highly unpopular until the Obama administration relaunched the concept (Bennett et al., 2020). It is likely that the US strategic thinking in this regard was influenced by the British concept of 'preventing violent extremism' (PVE) (Bennett et al., 2020), which was introduced as part of the Counter Terrorism Strategy (CONTEST) and its pillar 'PREVENT' (see also Chapter 20). The British strategy took shape in 2003, and gained widespread governmental support after the July 7th 2005 London terror attack happened. In the attack, four terrorists seperately detonated four bombs targeting the London public transport, killing 52 victims and injuring over 700 more. Only one of the attackers was not born in Britain, but had moved there at an early age. Effectively, all of the perpetrators were raised in Britain, causing a heated public debate about the reasons for the radicalization and ways to prevent such processes in the future. PREVENT, the government's response to what was dubbed 'homegrown extremism' underwent several updates and changes since its creation in 2006, 2009, and 2015. However, the aims of PREVENT remained more or less the same: to counter violent extremist ideology and strengthen moderate opinions that might pose as an effective counterweight. To achieve such far reaching goals, many different activities and methods became associated with P/CVE in the following years and decades. This in turn has also led some scholars to critique the concept for being too broad and essentially void of any specific meaning or conceptual clarity (e.g. Bjørgo and Horgan, 2009: 3; Horgan, 2009: 17).

The idea to support violent actors, or those on the path to violence, to reintegrate into society and leave behind groups which might have recruited and radicalized them is not new. Disarmament, Demobilization, Reintegration (DDR) programmes have been used in post-civil war contexts since 1989 (Muggah, 2005: 244). Many tools used in DDR programmes, such as education, vocational training, trauma therapy, or reconciliation with communities and victims are also widely used by P/CVE initiatives, in particular programmes designed to work with violent extremist offenders. Such 'deradicalization' programmes were developed in Europe during the late 1980s and mid-1990s (in Norway, Sweden, and Germany) targeting left-wing and right-wing extremists (e.g. Bjørgo, 1997; Koehler, 2021). Internationally, however, such programmes gained wider attention in the course of the US-led Global War on Terror after the September 11th attacks. With financial support from the US, some Middle Eastern countries tried to use theological debates with terrorist prison inmates led by high ranking Islamic scholars in an effort to disprove their religious reasoning and cause them to abandon violence. Programmes existed, for example, in Yemen (Johnsen, 2006) and Saudi Arabia (El-Said and Barrett, 2012), bringing international attention to the idea of 'reversing radicalism' (Ripley, 2008).

This also led to increased academic interest in this approach (Bjørgo and Horgan, 2009; Horgan, 2009). It quickly became clear, that a 'lack of conceptual clarity in the emerging discourse on deradicalization' (Bjørgo and Horgan, 2009: 3) was a barrier for studying such programmes' effectiveness. Scholars criticized the term for being used across many different policies and tools with 'virtually no conceptual development in the area' (Horgan, 2009: 17). This did not stop policymakers adopting the concept for their counterterrorism strategies as a solution to extremism and terrorism other than arresting and killing violent actors (see Figure 26.1).

UNITED NATIONS	EUROPEAN UNION	UNITED STATES
• 2014: Resolution 2178 (rehabilitation of returning foreign fighters) • 2016: General Assembly Resolution A/70/674 (Plan of Action to Prevent Violent Extremism) • 2017: Resolution 2396 (CVE measures as counter-terrorism)	• 2005: Revised European Union Counter-Terrorism Strategy (includes disengagement and exit strategies) • 2016: European Commission (COM(2016) 230 final) deems implementation of de-radicalization programmes an 'absolute priority'	• 2011: US Government National Strategy: Empowering Local Partners to Prevent Violent Extremism in the United States • 2014: Department of Homeland Security: 'Three Cities' Counter Violent Extremism (CVE) Pilot Initiatives. • 2017: Department of Homeland Security: Countering Violent Extremism (CVE) Grant Program

FIGURE 26.1 Examples of counterterrorism policies including a P/CVE component.

To name a few examples: in 2014, the United Nations Security Council (UNSC) adopted Resolution 2178 that called upon all members states to develop and establish effective rehabilitation programmes for so-called 'foreign fighters' returning from Syria and Iraq (UNSC, 2014). Two years later, in January 2016, the UNSC presented a 'Plan of Action to Prevent Violent Extremism' to the General Assembly and listed more than 70 specific recommendations, including a call to introduce 'disengagement, rehabilitation and counselling programmes for persons engaged in violent extremism' (UNSG, 2016: 4). This was then followed up with Resolution 2396, adopted by the UNSC in December 2017. This resolution continued to emphas specific measures to counter terrorism, including CVE (UNSC, 2017).

Not only did the United Nations increasingly lean on P/CVE to combat violent extremism and terrorism, but also the European Union. The revised 'European Union Counter-Terrorism Strategy' of 2005, for example, includes 'disengagement and exit strategies' (EU, 2005: 11) as important tools. In 2016 the European Commission (EC) even stated that the implementation of 'deradicalization' programmes was an 'absolute priority' (EC, 2016: 6) to prevent and fight radicalization.

The United States formulated its first real CVE strategy under the Obama administration in August 2011. As in many other countries (such as Britain and the 7/7 bombings), the P/CVE concept remained more or less dormant until a major terrorist attack happened, in this case the Boston marathon bombing of April 15, 2013 (see Photo 26.1).

PHOTO 26.1 A week after the Boston 2013 marathon bombing on Boylston Street, Boston, MA, USA. Following the attack, P/CVE projects increased.

Following this attack that killed three victims and injured 264, funding for P/CVE projects was significantly increased. In September 2014, another major milestone was set with the 'Three City Pilot' programme promoted by the US government. In this pilot programme initiative, the cities of Boston, Minneapolis, and Los Angeles received grant money to lead the field testing of P/CVE in the US.

In addition to this, the US Department of Homeland Security (DHS) initiated a CVE Task Force which included the Federal Bureau of Investigation (FBI), Department of Justice (DoJ) and the National Counterterrorism Center (NCTC). Under the protection of this CVE Task Force, the first CVE grant programme for civil society organizations was rolled out in January 2017. During the Donald Trump administration (2017–2021), CVE became much more controversial as it was seen first and foremost as a tool to target 'Islamist terrorism' by the Federal Government. As a consequence, some non-governmental organizations even refused to accept awards of grant money (Wang, 2017). Under the Trump administration, the term 'terrorism prevention' replaced P/CVE, only to be changed again to 'preventing and combatting targeted violence' by the Joe Biden Presidential administration (inaugurated in 2021). Again, it was a major violent incident that influenced the development of P/CVE. After the January 6th 2021 far-right-motivated riot and violent storming of the US Capitol building in Washington DC, the need to include domestic extremism in any strategy to combat radicalization to violence became widely accepted. The latest modification to this concept in the US at the time of writing was the May 2021 establishment of the 'Center for Prevention Programs and Partnerships (CP3)', led by the DHS and tasked with combating all forms of 'targeted violence'.

Still, most terms used in this field remain unclear, and sometimes even hinder practical advancements. Altier et al. (2014: 647) found 'that existing research remains devoid of conceptual clarity' with too much overlapping between key concepts and inconsistent use (for an overview see also: Koehler, 2020a). In addition to this conceptual confusion, some regions and cultures have interpreted and used the P/CVE terms differently. Crucially, a contradiction between 'Western' and 'Eastern' style P/CVE became clear.

26.3 'WESTERN' AND 'EASTERN' P/CVE APPROACHES

P/CVE programmes and strategies have become an essential part of global counterterrorism and have had recommendations in key international organizations (such as the United Nations, European Union, or Organization for Security and Co-operation in Europe). Since the early 2000s, about 50 countries have introduced such programmes and strategies (Marsden, 2019). Funding for such programmes has been made available through bilateral development aid (e.g. through the US State Department Global Engagement Center or the United Nations Development Programme), and increased substantially in recent years. Nevertheless, different understandings and 'styles' of P/CVE have only very recently begun to blur, especially between what can be called 'Western' and 'Eastern' P/CVE approaches (Koehler, 2016).

While Western countries have traditionally focused on social work, mental health, and educational tools to prevent and counter a violent radicalization process, Southeast Asian, Middle Eastern, and North-African countries that established programmes in this field have based their approaches on theological debates (including the dismantling of religious reasoning for violence by using equally religious arguments, for example, based on the Quran or Islamic teachings) and a direct ideological confrontation. The main reasons for this were the rule of law, freedom of speech, and religion, as well as democratic principles in Western countries, which essentially formed a barrier against state sanctioned attempts to change a person's ideological (religious or political) worldview. Holding even extremist worldviews when not violating any laws is usually protected by constitutions and other legal frameworks. Muslim majority countries on the other hand in many cases have based their political systems on some form of official interpretation of Islam. This aspect in combination with a general lack of protective rights for the freedom of speech or religion and weak rule of law has resulted in the attempt to challenge what was perceived to be a 'misguided' reading of Islam, for example, through state affiliated religious authorities. This theological confrontation was most prominently featured in the P/CVE programmes of Saudi Arabia, Malaysia, Indonesia, and Singapore (Koehler, 2016).

The differences in approaching P/CVE between Western and Eastern countries has begun to erode in recent years, however. The direct ideological confrontation was found to be ineffective against highly radicalized individuals, even when delivered through leading religious scholars with high degrees of credibility. Therefore, even those programmes originally based purely on theological debates (like in Saudi Arabia) have added various other components, such as mental health counselling, and creative arts or sports (al-Hadlaq, 2015). On the other side, P/CVE programmes in Western contexts have also begun to include more ideological components also, since it has been recognized that ignoring theological or political aspects of extremist recruitment could render other methods ineffective.

However, violent radicalization processes are highly individual and depend on individual context (see Case Study 26.1 for an example). Even though some schools of thought still exist that either reject the role of ideological debates or place a main focus on it, most P/CVE practitioners and scholars today accept the need for an individual and hand-tailored approach to each client. While at the same time safeguarding cultural and legal differences between countries, international organizations have strongly promoted much more diversified toolboxes in P/CVE that would allow for a more flexible handling of individual needs. Still, it must be recognized that the way a country challenges immensely complex violent extremist radicalization processes is determined by many factors, including the available resources, political power structures, government stability, existing civil society actors, strength and structure of the violent extremist milieu, culture, legal framework, and many others.

All of this highlights the immense complexity involved in effective P/CVE and the need for evidence-based tools and methods. After all, how can one be sure to use a tool that is not making matters worse?

26.4 EVIDENCE-BASED METHODS AND TOOLS

This chapter has outlined how P/CVE programmes have spread around the world and become a cornerstone of many counterterrorism strategies. We also have learned that those programmes are very complex, and need to adapt their methods to the individual needs and risk factors of every person they work with. How is it possible then to design and run a programme that aims to address a very individual process like radicalization?

A 'one size fits all' solution does not exist. P/CVE programmes need to be flexible and adaptable to individual needs and vulnerability factors, which results in comparatively high demands regarding the training of P/CVE personnel (Koehler and Fiebig, 2019). Also, since the programmes need to adapt to each person individually, this means that there is a massive challenge of scale, since in many countries the extremist environments include many thousand members and continuously recruit new followers. This means that P/CVE programmes can only be an additional part of the solution to violent extremism and terrorism. However, based on the available evidence-based literature, it is possible to draw some lessons learned about generally accepted practices and methods in the P/CVE field.

Johan Gøtzsche-Astrup (2018: 97) has conducted a meta-analysis which aimed to identify explanations for radicalization with a high degree of empirical validity shown through previous studies. This led him to recommend a variety of prevention and intervention tools, such as: approaches designed to increase the personal motivation for change (e.g. motivational interviewing), mentoring methods to help the person trying to leave extremism behind, and support to find closure after negative life experiences. Other methods could help to cope with fundamental uncertainty, provide personal skills to respond to challenging situations (e.g. education, employment) to avoid losing status. Finally, he also showed that any methods and tools need to be tailored to individual needs and personalities. In short, such methods to help persons leave violent extremism are tailored to each person, and because they are so highly individual can take years to result in lasting results.

Furthermore, anyone working in the P/CVE field must be aware of the various subcultural dynamics, codes, and symbols that provide a collective identity to extremist social environments. It is essential to recognize visual signs (such as codes and symbols, clothing brands, specific language, activities) in order to help others, including family members, teachers, and community leaders to detect and understand radicalization, as well as the reasons for the attraction of young people to such groups and environments. This knowledge about the subcultural dynamics is also the foundation of understanding each person's specific relationship with the group and the social milieu (Miller-Idriss, 2018). Together with the specific ideology of the extremist environment in question, subcultural products and activities (e.g. rallies, concerts) form a 'contrast society': a social space parallel to the mainstream culture with its own norms, rules, and values (Koehler, 2015a), which needs to be studied and understood by P/CVE programme personnel to hand-tailor, plan, and execute a sustainable intervention (Koehler and Fiebig, 2019; Koehler, 2020b). For example, the different gender roles, the acceptability of violence, or social values with more or less importance (like honour, pride, and purity for example) greatly impact the way in which an intervention or prevention measure is perceived and accepted or rejected.

A few additional evidence-based recommendations for specific P/CVE tools exist. Dalgaard-Nielsen (2013: 101), for example, identified 16 academic articles and books published between 1990 and 2012 that include a total of 216 interviews with former members of various extremist or terrorist groups. In these studies, Daalgard-Nielsen found three key themes behind exit processes: 'ideological doubt, doubt related to group and leadership issues, and doubt related to personal and practical issues.' Accordingly, she recommends to P/CVE practitioners to focus on personal doubts of the clients, and use subtle approaches to reduce resistance against the intervention, as well as to employ methods that affirm the person's identity. This is generally seen as more effective than challenging beliefs (ideology) directly.

More specifically, this should be done through 'humanization of the enemy, de-idealizing violence, leveraging internal strain in the extremist groups, leveraging bad leadership and/or personal and practical issues such as guilt feelings, longing for a normal life, and burnout', as well as increase contact with the world outside (Dalgaard-Nielsen, 2013: 106). In sum, Dalgaard-Nielsen mainly recommends communicational approaches focused on the client's experiences in the extremist environment, as well as methods to address practical aspects of leaving, such as helping to find a normal life. Even though these recommendations mainly focus on one extreme end of P/CVE (i.e. deradicalization), they are also valid for earlier stages of potential radicalization processes, or to create resilience against recruitment attempts in the first place. Building and maintaining resilience has emerged as a key theme in P/CVE research (Stephens, Sieckelinck, and Boutellier, 2019).

Regarding the role of communication tools, especially de-escalation strategies, rhetoric, as well as recognizing and handling psychological reactance, and direct confrontational communicative strategies in P/CVE have been found to be questionable, and carrying a high risk of backfiring. This means that some people become even more radical out of a stubborn protection of their worldviews against outside pressure to change (Braddock, 2014). It should therefore be the cornerstone of P/CVE communication to adapt the contents to the person's preferences and needs in order to be more likely to create a cognitive opening for thinking about alternative ideas and values, without this being perceived as a form of 'brainwashing'.

Next to academic literature that looks at entry and exit processes of individuals, a comparatively small number of studies has also explored practical activities of P/CVE programmes. However, which methods can be seen as effective in comparison to others, as well as why, when, and how certain methods are used is mostly unknown so far (for a literature review regarding CVE programme evaluations see for example: Feddes and Gallucci, 2015). A first collection of methods typically used in CVE and deradicalization programmes around the world was provided by Koehler (2016). According to his survey, methods usually belong to either:

a) Ideological/theological deconstruction of extremist worldviews;

b) Social work;

c) Psychological or psychiatric counselling or treatment;

d) Educational tools (such as vocational training or fostering critical thinking skills and background knowledge);

e) Creative arts and sports.

Which effect for what purpose in the CVE or deradicalization work each of the tools under these five categories is supposed to have, remains speculative in most cases. Nevertheless, an established principle in the P/CVE field is that the methods and tools must be based on an individual client assessment of needs and risks in order to achieve a good fit between the person and the intervention approach.

Beyond theological and ideological debating, many associate P/CVE programmes with psychological and mental health counselling (Koehler, 2016). It must be pointed out, that the role of mental health disorders and psychopathologies in violent radicalization processes is very much disputed. It seems that a significant difference exists between group-based extremists (Ruby, 2002) and lone actors (Corner and Gill, 2018). Still, some studies have suggested certain personality traits among violent extremists and terrorists (Misiak et al., 2019). In addition to these potential mental health and personality factors, as well as their role within radicalization processes, it has been found that membership in terrorist or violent extremist groups can also increase the likelihood to develop mental health issues (Weatherston and Moran, 2003; Koehler, 2020b).

In sum, methods and approaches used in the P/CVE field are still mostly not evidence-based but rather the result of established practices from various adjacent fields, such as social work, psychotherapy, or education. How far these tools and methods are equally valuable when creating resilience against a potential future radicalization or countering an ongoing one remains speculative in many cases so far. Only very few methods have been tested in rigorous research, for example, the positive effect of imagining oneself into the position of another person has previously been disregarded: including 'perspective taking' (Noor and Halabi, 2018), or approaches bringing people to think about their legacy and how they will be remembered ('immortality priming') (Williams, 2017).

Even with the growing number of evidence-based methods in the P/CVE field, the key question remains: how can we be certain that these programmes actually work and are successful? What does 'success' even mean in this context? This is the main area of exploration for evaluation experts and researchers who are struggling with many difficulties surrounding this field.

CASE STUDY 26.1

White Supremacist Online Recruiting in the United States

As part of a story on white supremacist online recruiting ('Right-Wing Hate Groups Are Recruiting Video Gamers', 5 November 2018), National Public Radio presented the following case (Kamenetz, 2018):

> 'John, a father of two in Colorado, had no idea what his 15-year-old son had gotten into, until one night. John saw a pile of papers . . . turned them over and found a copy of a notorious neo-Nazi propaganda book . . .
>
> John confronted his son angrily. "I was through the roof." And then, "I went back into my room. I was crying. I felt like a failure that a child that I had raised would be remotely interested in that sort of stuff." Almost every teen plays video games — 97 percent of boys, according to the Pew Research Center, and 83 percent of girls. Increasingly, these games are played online, with strangers. And experts say that while it's by no means common, online games — and the associated chat rooms, livestreams and other channels — have become one avenue for recruitment by right-wing extremist groups.
>
> John's son liked playing first-person shooter games, like Counterstrike: Global Offensive. Games like these are multiplayer — you must form teams with friends or strangers. You can chat in the game, over voice or text, or in separate chat rooms. Some of these are hosted by sites like Discord that make it easy for anyone to create a private chat. John knew his son was spending time playing video games and chatting either out loud or over text, but there were no obvious red flags. "There wasn't anything obvious to me at first because it's common. This is the norm for kids. Instead of hanging out at the drive-in they're all online," he said. Yet it's exactly this way, John says, that his son started hanging out with avowed white supremacists.
>
> These people became his son's friends. They talked to him about problems he was having at school, and suggested some of his African-American classmates as scapegoats. They also keyed into his interest in history, especially military history, and in Nordic mythology. Above all, they offered him membership in a hierarchy: white people against others. "He started to feel like he was in on something. He was now in the in crowd with these guys. It provided some structure and identity that he was searching for at the time." John learned his son had been drawn into conversation with at least one group that the Southern Poverty Law Center calls a Nazi terrorist organization.'

Recruitment and indoctrination into extremist environments is often achieved by the actors behind it through social interactions in the context of casual activities, such as sports, music concerts, or video gaming. By enjoying such casual activities together, extremist actors can gain trust, respect and interest by those they target. Once a first notion of community or collective identity has formed, for example as being in the same gaming clan or enjoying the same style of music, ideological topics are introduced based on the interests and mental openings on the side of the potential recruit. At the same time, positive reinforcement of identity is used to provide a positive feeling and generally enjoyable atmosphere. It is this climate in which radicalization process can flourish and lead to further engagmenet with the extremist environment and its goals.

QUESTIONS

1. How could you have helped John and his son's school to build resilience against such recruitment efforts before it happened?
2. How important do you think online spaces are for radicalization and how could they be harnessed for P/CVE?

26.5 GENDER SENSITIVE P/CVE

For the purposes of this chapter we will examine 'male' and 'female' clients in a binary as these genders have been the basis of research and studies. Research into non-binary and transgender people, for example, is so far limited.

Since terrorist activities and groups are in many if not most cases dominated by cigender-men, counterterrorism has traditionally also focused on male suspects. Even though the relatively young P/CVE field has not explicitly put male clients first but rather established a general notion of individual and hand-tailored approaches to meet the needs of each personal context, this almost automatically meant that male clients formed the majority of cases, and thereby directly influenced the experiences and methods of most programmes. This potential gender blindness has been pointed out repeatedly in recent years by many international organizations, such as the United Nations, the Organization for Security and Co-operation in Europe (OSCE), think tanks like Institute for Strategic Dialogue (ISD), and P/CVE programmes (e.g. Moonshot CVE and OSCE, 2014).

When considering the role of gender in P/CVE work, one has to differentiate roughly into gender specific counselling or intervention targeting female extremists on the one hand, and the role of women and gender in prevention work. Regarding the first aspect, research has begun to shed light on the potentially different entry and exit pathways of women into, and out of, violent extremism and terrorism (e.g. Bloom, 2011). Women might have different roles, aspirations, push and pull factors, different experiences during involvement, as well as reasons for leaving a violent extremist social environment than men. This can be connected either to the specific role ascribed to women by the extremist group and ideology in question, the context factors (such as the country and conflict), or the individual trajectories and background of the female recruit.

Furthermore, it should be recognized that female members of violent extremist groups might face significant problems during reintegration not typically encountered with male clients. This can be the result of different role expectations in the community of which an individual is reintegrating. Membership in violent extremist groups is oftentimes perceived to be a highly impactful experience that has the potential to fundamentally alter a person's sense of self and identity. For example, a community might expect the female former extremist to return to her previous role before radicalization, while she might have developed a new identity at odds with that previous role. Additional practical and psychological issues during rehabilitation typically faced by women are, for example, legal struggles regarding children, especially when the biological father is still a member of the violent extremist milieu. Victimization and abuse are also much more prevalent among female a members of extremist groups, resulting in a higher demand for psycho-therapeutic components of P/CVE programmes targeting women.

Regarding the second aspect of gender and P/CVE, women are by now seen as vital to detect and prevent violent extremism. For example, mothers are usually best placed to identify, predict, and respond to potential violent radicalization processes, which is the reason for the widespread establishment of family counselling programmes in the P/CVE field with a special focus on mothers (Koehler, 2015b). Women can also offer effective counter narratives and help to humanize the victims of violence, as well as to make terrorist activities appear less glamourous. In that role, women can be key to form networks of resilience against violent extremism.

However, the importance of women in the P/CVE field, and gender questions in general, are still very much underrepresented in research and practice (Coomaraswamy, 2015).

26.6 EVALUATION OF P/CVE PROGRAMMES

With the increasing number of P/CVE programmes and their growing importance within counter-terrorism strategies, more resources are allocated to such initiatives. Also, the clientele of P/CVE programmes are, by definition, also at risk of being or becoming dangerous to the society as potential terrorists and violent extremists. As a result, P/CVE programmes are facing extraordinary scrutiny and the public demand for proving their effects and impacts.

Evaluating the impact or quality of P/CVE programmes is challenging (Horgan and Braddock, 2010; Koehler, 2017, see Photo 26.2). A key problem faced by policymakers and evaluators is how it is possible to be sure about real impact of an intervention on a person's mindset, especially when the outcome measure is a so-called 'non-event', meaning something is *not* happening, like a person *not* conducting a terrorist attack. Scientifically, the possibility of other reasons and mechanisms involved in the behavioural change, including even a faked change, make it nearly impossible to determine which intervention had the desired effect, when ruling out experimental research designs for ethical reasons. Conducting trial interventions would require a comparison group not receiving

PHOTO 26.2 Evaluating the effectiveness of P/CVE programmes is difficult.

the intervention, and consciously being exposed to a higher risk of violent radicalization, which could then lead to acts of violence and terrorism. As a result of this, most accounts of P/CVE programmes are rather descriptive, and use proxy indicators to measure 'success', such as participant numbers, recidivism rates: the percentage of persons who completed the programme and still went back to crime or violent extremism, or non-completion rates (Mastroe and Szmania, 2016). However, in addition to the lack of an overall consensus regarding the term P/CVE, unclear and differing use of concepts like 'recidivism' (sometimes understood to mean return to the original extremist group or crime in general, as well as with differeng views on the time period to be observed after the disengagement) or 'participant numbers' further complicate the translation of such impact measures into a solid assessment of the programmes' effect.

Even if these questions seem trivial, they are essential to the wider counterterrorism field because ill-designed and ineffective deradicalization programmes (however 'effective' is framed and measured). These are not only a waste of important resources, but also, more importantly, might increase the threat and risk of terrorism and violent extremism by applying incorrect methods based on inadequate needs assessments, failing to detect high risk cases, giving away critical counter-argumentation techniques, or helping committed extremists and terrorists to re-enter a society without raising the authorities' suspicion. P/CVE is a complex and delicate task that requires high operational standards and procedures, expert training, typological adaption (the ability to identify and apply the appropriate type of programme for the chosen goals and target groups), and detailed programme design according to the specific context and goals.

In response to these evaluation challenges, academics have suggested a variety of approaches in recent years. One evaluation of a Sri Lankan rehabilitation programme for detained Tamil Tiger fighters, for example, used random or delayed interventions as a quasi-experiment (Kruglanski et al., 2014). Another approach suggests using established measurement frameworks from healthcare to measure individual attributes such as anger, frustration, alienation, dissatisfaction, grievances, and so on (Baruch et al., 2018). The selection of these attributes is informed by presumed theories of radicalization drivers, which are debated as well. Another example is based on the evaluation of an Australian rehabilitation programme for terrorist inmates in prison (Cherney and Belton, 2021). The approach chosen here focuses on case managers' notes regarding potentially positive, negative or neutral changes in their clients' situation after counselling sessions.

In addition to this, P/CVE programmes do not simply 'work' or not. Their impact on participants and clients varies with the individual context and person-specific goals or background (see Case Study 26.2 for an example of such a programme). It is also very important to point out the different target groups and eligibility criteria as 'there may be a tendency for initiatives to permit only those prospective participants deemed at relatively low risk of committing post-detainment terrorism to participate. Therefore, a given programme could demonstrate low post-detainment terrorism engagement rates, (perhaps) not because the programme's interventions are especially effective, but that the participants already were at a low risk of reoffending' (Williams and Kleinman, 2013: 112). Therefore, Williams and Kleinman also point out the stakeholders' own responsibility to decide which success measures and metrics are most relevant to them.

Despite the fact that these evaluation approaches are detailed and sophisticated models, the have mostly not been implemented or widely tested in the practical P/CVE field. To date, most evaluation studies that focus on P/CVE programmes are based on anecdotal evidence (i.e. programme description), without 'explicit reference to theory and no empirical quantitative or qualitative data' (Feddes and Gallucci, 2015: 17). This might be due to a perception among P/CVE practitioners that those evaluation approaches are too time intensive, too theoretical, and require too much financial or personal resources. Among practitioners, it is also often pointed out that P/CVE is highly context-specific and needs to adapt to each individual client. Hence, a comparative evaluation between programmes and even within a single initiative meet exceptional methodological challenges (Nehlsen et al., 2020) Whatever the challenges of evaluating P/CVE programmes and arguments against it might be, the fact that significant resources are diverted to this field and that the target clientele of such programmes might pose a high threat if left alone or if confronted with the wrong intervention directly establishes the need for evidence based approaches and strict evaluations to avoid backlash and counter-effects (Koehler, 2017).

CASE STUDY 26.2

The Prevention Project 'Attention?!' (Achtung?!) in Germany

In 2015 the police precinct in the southern German city of Ludwigsburg started a P/CVE programme called 'Attention?!' (Achtung?!) with financial support from the European Union. Aiming to reach teenagers and adolescents between 13 and 16 years of age, the project is composed of several modules a school can choose from. The 'core package' consists of an interactive theatre play designed to show teenagers the risks and emotions involved in different forms of violent radicalization (such as extreme right-wing and jihadist), a discussion forum with trained experts to talk about the play and an exhibition about shared values and norms across cultures and religions. There are also many optional modules, for example a workshop for parents, an online game, educational material, and coursework or training sessions for teachers around the issues of P/CVE. The project was made available state-wide in 2018 with financial support from the state government after European funding had ended. The project is being evaluated, and a clearly visible impact on the knowledge and vulnerability of teenagers regarding radicalization is not yet available.

This project is a good example of a programme in the so-called 'primary prevention' category, meaning it aims to build resilience against extremist recruitment before it happens. The theatre play and the connected education modules are supposed to teach students about the appearance of extremist subcultures, their recruitment strategies and to create awareness about the individual motives that could make someone become involved in violent extremist groups.

For more information on how creative arts are used in the P/CVE, see:

Hussain, L., Gubash, C., and Bruton, B. F. (5 February 2015): 'Saudi De-Radicalization Center Uses Art Therapy to Tackle Extremists'. NBC News.

Terhaag, S. (2020): 'De-radicalization Through the Performative Arts'. *JD Journal for Deradicalization*, Spring (22), 218–248.

QUESTIONS

1. Next to theatre plays, what other forms of creative arts do you think could be used for PVE purposes?
2. Based on what you know about radicalization and P/CVE, how might drama have a positive impact in a student environment?

26.7 CONCLUSION

When we consider the benefits of diverting individuals away from processes that could lead to terrorism, it might seem surprising that P/CVE programmes and strategies have not been used more widely around the world. Compared to the budgets, personnel, and number of conventional counterterrorism tools like imprisonment, intelligence, police, and military-based approaches, P/CVE methods are still highly limited. Furthermore, we cannot 'arrest or kill our way out of terrorism'. Prisons can turn into hotbeds of violent radicalization, and targeted assassinations of terrorists can turn them into martyrs. Furthermore, collateral damage might fuel grievances and produce even more support for the terrorist group. P/CVE offers the promise to be cheaper and more effective in the long run to counter terrorist activities by cutting off the supply chain of new recruits, and by creating various additional benefits such as building community resilience and awareness against violent extremism and terrorism.

However, it is more complicated than that. As this chapter has demonstrated, the P/CVE field is still very much in its infancy and the evidence base for tools and approaches used is slim. Scientific evaluations of effects or programme quality are rare and that means we cannot be sure in most cases of P/CVE programming if the resources put to work are indeed having the desired results. It might even be worse, since ill-designed or faulty P/CVE programmes without a solid monitoring and evaluation structure in place could actually increase risks of violent radicalization. In addition, key issues such as gender sensitive P/CVE programming have not yet been explored enough to ensure that blind spots are minimized.

What we have witnessed in the last 10 years is the significant growth of a global P/CVE industry with government funded projects and programmes being established on a wide scale, as the positive effects of these are generally assumed. It must be pointed out though that this development has outpaced the available evidence produced by high quality research, and some programmes have even been funded and started without the necessary time frame to train expert personnel. There are still many more questions to be answered when it comes to P/CVE, which is a very complex set of methods attempting to influence another complex process (violent radicalization). We are still at the beginning of understanding both sides of the equation and most tools used within P/CVE are merely based on a hypothesis that they might have a positive effect.

This should not, however, prevent further research about P/CVE or funding more projects in this field. On the contrary, these open questions and unclear mechanisms should lead us as students and researchers forward to improve P/CVE, find a solid evidence base, create programmes with better theories of change, and be rigorous in monitoring and evaluating existing programmes. It is the main underlying premise of P/CVE that human beings can change for the better, as well as that they do not turn to terrorism out of an inevitable necessity. Such processes are the result of individual push and pull factors that can be prevented and countered to avoid violence and conflict. Despite all the shortcomings of the P/CVE field, it is still a noble and valid motivation to continue building a professional landscape of programmes that provide help and support to those in need. Such a well-grounded and monitored field of activities holds a strong potential to become an essential complementary set of tools and approaches for other counterterrorism strategies.

DISCUSSION QUESTIONS

1. How would you describe the difference between preventing and countering violent extremism?
2. What are 'Western' and 'Eastern' styles of P/CVE?
3. Why is it so difficult to evaluate the impact of P/CVE programmes?
4. How would you design a gender-specific P/CVE programme?
5. Can you think of some key challenges for P/CVE in the future?

Visit the online resources for pointers on how to answer the discussion questions, links to useful web sources, and guidance on accessing databases:
www.oup.com/he/Wilson-Muro1e

GUIDE TO FURTHER READING

Koehler, D. (2016) *Understanding Deradicalization. Methods, Tools and Programs for Countering Violent Extremism*. New York: Routledge. *This work provides a comprehensive review of the state of the art and different P/CVE programme types and methods from around the world.*

Radicalization Awareness Network (RAN), *Preventing Radicalization to Terrorism and Violent Extremism. Approaches and Practices*, Available on the ec.Europa.eu website. *This collection of good practices from Europe is based on practitioner experiences from programmes spread across the European Union and gives very helpful information on the practical tools used in the P/CVE field.*

United Nations Development Programme (2018) *Improving the Impact of Preventing Violent Extremism Programming. A Toolkit for Design, Monitoring and Evaluation*. Available on the undp.org website. *This toolkit was designed to help practitioners and policymakers to quickly design and launch P/CVE programmes in post-conflict settings.*

United States Institute of Peace (2018) *Taking Stock. Analytic Tools for Understanding and Designing P/CVE Programs*. Available on the usip.org website. *This USIP toolkit takes a broader perspective on P/CVE programme design and includes exercises and methods that help to select the appropriate programme types and contents.*

REFERENCES

al-Hadlaq, A. (2015) 'Saudi Efforts in Counter-Radicalization and Extremist Rehabilitation', in Gunaratna, R. and Bin Ali, M. (eds.) *Terrorist Rehabilitation: A new Frontier in Counter-terrorism Insurgency and Terrorism Series*. New Jersey: Imperial College Press, 21–39.

Altier, M. B., Thoroughgood, C. N., and Horgan, J. G. (2014) 'Turning Away From Terrorism: Lessons From Psychology, Sociology, and Criminology', *Journal of Peace Research*, 51 (5): 647–661.

Baruch, B., Ling, T., Warnes, R., and Hofman, J. (2018) 'Evaluation in an Emerging Field: Developing a Measurement Framework for the Field of Counter-violent-extremism', *Evaluation*, 24 (4): 475–495.

BBC (2019) 'London Bridge: Usman Khan Completed Untested Rehabilitation Scheme', *British Broadcasting Corporation*, 4 December 2019. Available at: https://www.bbc.com/news/uk-50653191.

Bennett, C., Hughes, S., and Meleagrou-Hitchens, A. (2020) 'An Abridged History of America's Terrorism Prevention Programs: Fits and Starts', *Lawfare Blog*, 29 December 2020. Available at https://www.lawfareblog.com/abridged-history-americas-terrorism-prevention-programs-fits-and-starts.

Bjørgo, T. (1997) *Racist and Right-Wing Violence in Scandinavia: Patterns, Perpetrators, and Responses*. Oslo: Aschehoug.

Bjørgo, T. and Horgan, J. (2009) *Leaving Terrorism Behind: Individual and Collective Disengagement*. London/New York: Routledge.

Bloom, M. (2011) *Bombshell: Women and Terrorism*. Philadelphia: University of Pennsylvania Press.

Braddock, K. (2014) 'The Talking Cure? Communication and Psychological Impact in Prison De-Radicalization Programmes', in Silke, A. (ed.) *Prisons, Terrorism and Extremism: Critical Issues in Management, Radicalization and Reform*. London: Routledge, 60–74.

Cherney, A. and Belton, E. (2021) 'Evaluating Case-Managed Approaches to Counter Radicalization and Violent Extremism: An Example of the Proactive Integrated Support Model (PRISM) Intervention', *Studies in Conflict & Terrorism, 44* (8): 625–645.

Coomaraswamy, R. (2015) *Preventing Conflict, Transforming Justice, Securing the Peace. A Global Study on the Implementation of United Nations Security Council resolution 1325*: United Nations. Available at: http://wps.unwomen.org/pdf/en/GlobalStudy_EN_Web.pdf.

Corner, E. and Gill, P. (2018) 'The Nascent Empirical Literature on Psychopathology and Terrorism', *World Psychiatry, 17* (2): 147–148.

Dalgaard-Nielsen, A. (2013) 'Promoting Exit from Violent Extremism: Themes and Approaches', *Studies in Conflict & Terrorism, 36* (2): 99–115.

EC (2016) *Communication from the Commission to the European Parliament, the European Council and the Council delivering on the European Agenda on Security to fight against terrorism and pave the way towards an effective and genuine Security Union*: European Commission (COM(2016) 230 final).

El-Said, H. and Barrett, R. (2012) 'Saudi Arabia: The master of deradicalization', in El-Said, H. and Harrigan, J. (eds.) *Deradicalising Violent Extremists: Counter-Radicalization and Deradicalization Programmes and their Impact in Muslim Majority States*. London: Routledge, 194–226.

EU, The Council of the European Union (2005) *The European Union Counter-Terrorism Strategy*. Brussels.

Feddes, A. and Gallucci, M. (2015) 'A Literature Review on Methodology used in Evaluating Effects of Preventive and De-radicalization Interventions', *JD Journal for Deradicalization*, (5): 1–27.

Gøtzsche-Astrup, O. (2018) 'The Time for Causal Designs: Review and Evaluation of Empirical Support for Mechanisms of Political Radicalization', *Aggression and Violent Behaviour, 39*: 90–99.

Harris-Hogan, S., Barrelle, K., and Zammit, A. (2015) 'What is Countering Violent Extremism? Exploring CVE Policy and Practice in Australia', *Behavioural Sciences of Terrorism and Political Aggression, 8* (1): 6–24.

Horgan, J. (2009) *Walking Away from Terrorism: Accounts of Disengagement from Radical and Extremist Movements*. London/New York: Routledge.

Horgan, J. and Braddock, K. (2010) 'Rehabilitating the Terrorists? Challenges in Assessing the Effectiveness of De-radicalization Programs', *Terrorism and Political Violence, 22* (2): 267–291.

Johnsen, G. (2006) 'Yemen's Passive Role in the War on Terrorism', *Terrorism Monitor, 4* (4): 7–9.

Kamenetz, A. (2018) 'Right-Wing Hate Groups Are Recruiting Video Gamers', *National Public Radio*, 5 November. Available at: https://www.npr.org/2018/11/05/660642531/right-wing-hate-groups-are-recruiting-video-gamers.

Koehler, D. (2015a) 'Contrast Societies. Radical Social Movements and Their Relationships with their Target Societies. A Theoretical Model', *Behavioural Sciences of Terrorism and Political Aggression, 7* (1): 18–34.

Koehler, D. (2015b) 'Family Counselling, Deradicalization and Counter-Terrorism: The Danish and German Programs in Context', in Zeiger, S. and Aly, A. (eds.) *Countering Violent Extremism: Developing an Evidence-base for Policy and Practice*. Perth: Curtin University, 129–136.

Koehler, D. (2016) *Understanding Deradicalization. Methods, Tools and Programs for Countering Violent Extremism* Oxon/New York: Routledge.

Koehler, D. (2017) 'How and why we Should Take Deradicalization Seriously', *Nature Human Behaviour, 1*: 0095.

Koehler, D. (2020a) 'Terminology and Definitions', in Hansen, S. J. and Lid, S. (eds.) *Routledge Handbook of Deradicalization and Disengagement*. London and New York: Routledge, 11–25.

Koehler, D. (2020b) 'Violent Extremism, Mental Health and Substance Abuse Among Adolescents: Towards a Trauma Psychological Perspective on Violent Radicalization and Deradicalization', *The Journal of Forensic Psychiatry and Psychology, 31* (3): 455–472.

Koehler, D. (2021) 'Disengaging from Left-Wing Terrorism and Extremism: Field Experiences from Germany and Research Gaps', *Studies in Conflict & Terrorism*, 1–21. Online first, doi: 10.1080/1057610X.2021.1917639

Koehler, D. and Fiebig, V. (2019) 'Knowing What to Do: Academic and Practitioner Understanding of How to Counter Violent Radicalization', *Perspectives on Terrorism, 13* (3): 44–62.

Kruglanski, A. W., Gelfand, M. J., Bélanger, J. J., Gunaratna, R., and Hettiarachchi, M. (2014) 'De-radicalising the Liberation Tigers of Tamil Eelam (LTTE)', in Silke, A. (ed.) *Prisons, Terrorism and Extremism: Critical Issues in Management, Radicalization and Reform.* London: Routledge, 183–196.

Marsden, S. V. (2019) 'Countering Violent Extremism: A Guide to Good Practice', *Crest Security Review*, Spring 2019(9).

Mastroe, C. and Szmania, S. (2016) *Surveying CVE Metrics in Prevention, Disengagement and De-Radicalization Programs*, College Park, MD: START. Available at: https://www.start.umd.edu/pubs/START_SurveyingCVEMetrics_March2016.pdf.

Miller-Idriss, C. (2018) *The Extreme Gone Mainstream: Commercialization and Far Right Youth Cuture in Germany.* Princeton, NJ: Princeton University Press.

Misiak, B., Samochowiec, J., Bhui, K., Schouler-Ocak, M., Demunter, H., Kuey, L., Raballo, A., Gorwood, P., Frydecka, D., and Dom, G. (2019) 'A Systematic Review on the Relationship Between Mental Health, Radicalization and Mass Violence', *European Psychiatry, 56*: 51–59.

Muggah, R. (2005) 'No Magic Bullet: A Critical Perspective on Disarmament, Demobilization and Reintegration (DDR) and Weapons Reduction in Post-conflict Contexts', *The Round Table, 94* (379): 239–252.

Nehlsen, I., Biene, J., Coester, M., Greuel, F., Milbradt, B., and Armborst, A. (2020) 'Evident and Effective? The Challenges, Potentials and Limitations of Evaluation Research on Preventing Violent Extremism', *International Journal of Conflict and Violence (IJCV), 14* (2): 1–20.

Noor, M. and Halabi, S. (2018) 'Can we Forgive a Militant Outgroup Member? The role of Perspective-taking', *Asian Journal of Social Psychology, 21* (4): 246–255.

OSCE (2014) *GCTF-OSCE International Workshop on 'Advancing Women's Roles in Countering Violent Extremism and Radicalization that Lead to Terrorism'. Report.*, Vienna: Organization for Security and Cooperation in Europe/Gobal Counterterrorism Forum. Available at: https://www.thegctf.org/documents/10295/163336/Final+report_OSCE+GCTF+Vienna+Workskop+on+Women+and+CVE.pdf.

Ripley, A. (2008) 'Future Revolutions. 4. Reverse Radicalism', *Time Magazine*.

Ruby, C. L. (2002) 'Are Terrorists Mentally Deranged?', *Analyses of Social Issues and Public Policy, 2* (1): 15–26.

Stephens, W., Sieckelinck, S., and Boutellier, H. (2021) 'Preventing Violent Extremism: A Review of the Literature', *Studies in Conflict & Terrorism, 44* (4): 346–361.

UNSC (2014) *Resolution 2178 (2014)*: United Nations Security Council (S/RES/2178 (2014)).

UNSC, Council, U.N.S. (2017) *Resolution 2396*.

UNSG (2016) *United Nations Plan of Action to Prevent Violent Extremism.* New York: United Nations Secretary General.

Wang, A. B. (2017) 'Muslim Nonprofit Groups are Rejecting Federal Funds Because of Trump', *Washington Post*, 11 February 2017. Available at: https://www.washingtonpost.com/news/post-nation/wp/2017/02/11/it-all-came-down-to-principle-muslim-nonprofit-groups-are-rejecting-federal-funds-because-of-trump/?utm_term=.1fb379850a62.

Weatherston, D. and Moran, J. (2003) 'Terrorism and Mental Illness: Is There a relationship?', *International Journal of Offender Therapy and Comparative Criminology, 47* (6): 698–713.

Williams, M. J. (2017) 'Prosocial Behaviour Following Immortality Priming: Experimental Tests of Factors with Implications for CVE Interventions', *Behavioural Sciences of Terrorism and Political Aggression, 9* (3): 153–190.

Williams, M. J. and Kleinman, S. M. (2013) 'A Utilization-Focused Guide for Conducting Terrorism risk Reduction Program Evaluations', *Behavioural Sciences of Terrorism and Political Aggression, 6* (2): 102–146.

CHAPTER 27

Disengagement and Deradicalization Programmes

SARAH MARSDEN

■ **CHAPTER SUMMARY**

Disengagement and deradicalization programmes have become an increasingly important part of counter-terrorism efforts. However, they are not new, efforts to move people away from terrorism have been around since the 1980s. This chapter traces the evolution of initiatives which aim to support the transition away from militancy. It considers how different countries have sought to reduce the risk of people reengaging in terrorism, and describes the main features of intervention programmes. Assessing the shifting logic behind disengagement and deradicalization initiatives, the chapter asks why there has been an increasing emphasis on changing attitudes and ideas in contrast with historical efforts which typically focused on behavioural change. Finally, the chapter reflects on the challenges such programmes face in achieving and interpreting their goals.

27.1 INTRODUCTION

By the time Jamal al-Harith died in a suicide car bomb attack on an Iraqi army base in 2017, much of his adult life had been shaped by global jihadism. First arrested in 2002 by the Taliban on the Afghan-Pakistan border, and accused of being a British spy, al-Harith was later taken to Guantanamo Bay detention camp and held for two years on suspicion of being an enemy combatant. Following his release in 2004, the British government is believed to have paid al-Harith compensation of £1 million pounds for complicity in his mistreatment whilst detained. A decade later he crossed the border into Syria and joined ISIS to die with two others attacking an Iraqi-led coalition base near Mosul.

Al-Harith's family claim he was radicalized in 2013, many years after his release from Guantanamo, when he began associating with Abu Qaqa al-Britani, an ISIS recruiter who grew up close to al-Harith's family home in Manchester, UK. However, US intelligence files suggest he may have been involved in jihadism as early as 1992, and that he was affiliated with al-Qaeda. As with most accounts of engagement in terrorism, it is difficult to piece together the full story. What does seem clear is that, given the extended period he was incarcerated, and the extent of his engagement with different security and criminal justice agencies, there were multiple opportunities to intervene to try and prevent al-Harith re-engaging in militancy.

In the aftermath of al-Harith's death, questions were raised about counter-terrorism policy and practice: Why wasn't he monitored more effectively? What role does imprisonment play in extremism? Should greater efforts have been made to deradicalize him? At the heart of these questions is whether it is possible to assess the risk from those who have been involved in extremism, and whether those risks can be reduced through active intervention. In short, is it possible to deradicalize extremists?

This chapter explores the history of efforts to move people away from terrorism. After defining key terms including deradicalization, disengagement, and reintegration, the chapter charts the history of initiatives which attempt to support disengagement from extremism and terrorism. Discussion goes on to consider the contemporary landscape of deradicalization policy and practice, before examining the limited evidence about what reduces the risk of returning to terrorism. The chapter concludes by identifying emerging challenges for policymakers and practitioners tasked with managing and reducing the risk posed by extremists, including interpreting whether deradicalization works.

27.2 CONCEPTUALIZING AND DEFINING DERADICALIZATION

Deradicalization is a relatively new term that came to prominence in the mid-2000s in the aftermath of a series of attacks in Europe, including the Madrid train attack in 2004 and the London transport bombings in 2005. The term 'radicalization' emerged to conceptualize the process by which people became committed to extremist ideas which justified violence. Following on from the idea of radicalization came the concept of deradicalization, a term denoting the rejection of ideas which support violence (Horgan 2009) (see also Key Concepts box).

There are ongoing debates about the concepts associated with deradicalization. A wide range of terms are used to describe efforts to move people away from terrorism, from re-education to rehabilitation, disaffiliation to disengagement, and desistance to deradicalization (Horgan and Taylor 2011). Although they have different emphases, these terms are broadly used to describe a change in someone's commitment to the ideas and behaviours associated with terrorism. What is important is that they relate to a causal process, a means by which those once committed to violence change their ways, whether as a result of an external intervention, or personal choice.

> **KEY CONCEPTS**
>
> **Deradicalization** Typically describes the psychological and sociological process associated with ideological or attitudinal change that means an individual no longer feels they are personally responsible for progressing a political agenda through violence (Horgan 2009: 153).
>
> **Disengagement** Refers to the behavioural process which sees an individual cease involvement in political violence. In contrast to deradicalization, disengagement does not imply that the individual has changed their commitment to the ideas or attitudes which support violence (Horgan 2009: 152).
>
> **Reintegration** Is a broader framework which has been used to draw attention to the wider context the individual is moving into, for example, once they have been released from prison. Reintegration operates across different domains and include political, social and economic forms (Marsden 2017: 3).

Deradicalization remains a controversial idea. One area of debate relates to the emphasis on ideological or attitudinal change, that is, whether deradicalization should be the ultimate goal, or if disengagement, or behavioural change, is sufficient. Two questions sit at the heart of this issue: is deradicalization necessary to reduce the risk of reengaging in terrorism? And, is the emphasis on ideas and attitudes appropriate?

The relationship between attitudes and behaviour is complex. Many people who hold radical views do not go on to use violence, and some of those who use violence are not committed to radical ideas (Horgan and Taylor 2011). A range of factors influence people's move to terrorism, from economic incentives to peer pressure, or a desire for adventure or revenge (Borum 2011) (see also Chapter 9 'What Are the Root Causes of Terrorism?'). These motivations are not always informed by a commitment to radical ideology, which raises the question of whether efforts to deradicalize those involved in terrorism are always appropriate.

A further challenge facing the concept of deradicalization is the heavy emphasis on the individual. Most interventions concentrate on addressing individual-level factors, for example trying to reduce a person's commitment to radical ideas. Positioning the problem in the mind of the individual in this way can overlook contextual factors which influence disengagement trajectories. The more recent emphasis on reintegration has sought to address this by understanding how wider social, political, and economic factors interact with the ideas and attitudes which support violence to influence an individual's route through extremism.

As we will see later in the chapter, the evidence base on deradicalization is not strong. It is therefore not possible to definitively say whether a change in ideas and attitudes will significantly reduce the risk of reengaging in terrorism. As well as a practical challenge, the issue of whether people should be required to change the beliefs they hold about particular political or religious ideas, and their attitudes about how these should be progressed, raises the question of whether the state should dictate what individuals can or cannot believe. The assumption behind deradicalization initiatives is that if a person holds attitudes which support extremist offending, these are an appropriate target for intervention, and for those who have broken the law, it is reasonable to try and change their mind, in some cases against their will.

The question is whether the state is going beyond trying to secure the safety of its citizens and is instead demanding that people adopt a particular set of sanctioned ideas in order to discipline their conduct (ElShimi 2017). This process is made more contentious because there is a widespread perception that Muslim communities in countries such as France, Germany and the UK have been targeted by counter-terrorism policy over the last two decades (Mucha 2017; Choudhury and Fenwick 2011). Hence the move to require people to accept particular attitudes acceptable to the government disproportionately affects certain identity groups in ways which can be harmful and divisive (Githens-Mazer and Lambert 2010). Critics of state-led deradicalization efforts also argue that by focusing attention on changing individual attitudes, the social, economic and political grievances which act as reference points for those involved in radical politics are neglected (Muhanna-Matar 2017).

The counterargument is that, given the potential harm caused by terrorism, it is necessary to intervene to address all those factors that might reduce the risk of engaging in violence. By implication, terrorism offenders subject to deradicalization interventions are held to a different standard to non-politically motivated offenders. For example, countries such as Saudi Arabia require detainees on their deradicalization programmes to have rejected extremism before they are allowed to be released. This kind of change in attitudes is not required for those convicted of non-politically motivated offending and can have significant consequences, increasing the potential people might falsely renounce their beliefs, or leading to long periods of incarceration. Underpinning some of these issues is the challenge that research does not have either, a strong enough evidence base to explain the relationship between extremist ideas and behaviour, or a solid theoretical foundation through which to develop one.

27.2.1 Theorizing deradicalization

One of the characteristics of research on deradicalization is the limited robust engagement with theory. Although research has identified some factors relevant to understanding how and when people move away from terrorism, they are less able to explain, through the application or development of theory, why desistance and deradicalization occur. Nevertheless, models are being developed that are beginning to offer a more nuanced account of some of the core features of disengagement, for example, by analysing the relationship between ideas, attitudes and behaviours in greater depth (Khalil et al. 2019). The empirical evidence base is also evolving as researchers gain better access to those who have disengaged from terrorism.

One of the first empirically informed models to be developed in the field is Kate Barrelle's (2015) Pro-Integration Model (PIM). Based on interviews with those who had left a range of kinds of radical groups, the model is built around five domains (social relations, coping, identity, ideology, and action orientation) made up of 15 disengagement themes reflected in interviewees' experiences. Uniting these five domains is the concept of integration, which assumes that 'disengagement is an identity transition from being an outsider to belonging' (Barrelle 2015: 134).

Beyond specific models seeking to explain desistance from terrorism, there is a meta-model of risk which underpins much research and practice in this field. The dominance of the risk concept is seen in efforts to interpret the risk of re-engaging in terrorism; the level of risk an individual is believed to pose to the public; or someone's changing risk profile, typically assessed through specific indicators used to interpret an individual's progress or regress.

A risk-oriented approach informs work with terrorism offenders as it is the dominant model in the wider criminal justice system (Andrews and Bonta 2010). Rehabilitation initiatives with non-politically motivated offenders are typically informed by the risk-needs-responsivity (RNR) approach. This is oriented around three principles. The risk principle is based on the use of validated risk assessment tools able to accurately predict criminal behaviour and which in turn help practitioners to match the level of intervention with the risk an individual is believed to pose. The need principle proposes that interventions should target criminogenic needs empirically linked to the likelihood of reoffending and which it is possible to change. The responsivity principle takes account of the learning style, capacity, and social and psychological characteristics of the offender when developing and delivering interventions (Andrews and Bonta 2010).

The challenge applying an RNR-based approach to terrorism offenders is that there are believed to be important differences between non-politically motivated offenders and those convicted of terrorism offences. This means that the risk assessment tools developed for 'normal' offenders may not be effective in assessing and managing the risk of terrorism offenders (Logan and Lloyd 2019). There are ongoing efforts to validate risk assessment protocols (Lloyd 2019), however at this stage, the evidence base is not sufficiently robust to determine which factors, if addressed, reliably reduce the risk of reoffending.

As well as an empirical challenge, there are a number of other issues associated with the dominance of risk-based approaches. The first is that it largely overlooks protective factors, or those positive influences which increase someone's resilience to extremism and improve their chances of pursuing a positive future. In the limited research which has looked at the role of protective factors, having good levels of self-control, or family and friends who are not involved in extremism are associated with positive outcomes (Lösel et al. 2018). The same study looked specifically at religious and ethnic extremism and found a number of protective factors that were important for this group including positive parenting; a basic attachment to society; and accepting the legitimacy of the police. However, most protective factors seem to have a relatively small effect on outcomes which suggests the need for support across multiple factors if they are to enable successful reintegration. Much more research is needed to understand the role of protective factors and how best to increase resilience to re-engaging in extremism and terrorism.

A second, broader issue with risk-oriented approaches is their conceptualization of the offender as someone who embodies a series of risks and needs. The underlying assumption is that there is something wrong with them which interventions seek to put right. Rather than a political agent pursuing an ideologically informed agenda, this sees those involved in terrorism as being heavily influenced by external forces or things that are wrong with them, such as limited critical thinking skills. As well as neglecting individual agency and political motivations, this approach can impact the way deradicalization interventions are developed and offenders' willingness to engage with them. If a programme is framed as seeking to address a series of needs or problems with the individual, this can undermine their motivation to engage with the intervention, something which is important for successful outcomes (Ward and Maruna 2007).

An alternative, the strengths or desistance-based approach, is increasingly being incorporated into terrorism offender intervention programmes and is often related to the Good Lives Model (GLM) (Dean 2014). Rather than assuming that offending is informed by individual needs and deficits, the GLM argues that people break the law because of a common desire to achieve a 'good life' in different areas of their lives such as relatedness, work, or spirituality (Ward and Stewart 2003). When the route to achieving these goods is blocked, the GLM proposes that people pursue them through antisocial or illegal means. The implication for intervention programmes is that they should focus on increasing the individual's potential to achieve goods through pro-social, legal means. Research has found that practitioners consider a strengths-based approach an effective and ethical way of working with those involved in extremism (Marsden 2017).

As well as understanding why people move away from terrorism, research is beginning to examine why people re-engage in militancy. One of the few studies to look at this systematically has found that people with links to extremist networks and who remain committed to radical ideas are at greater risk of re-engaging in terrorism, whilst those from wealthier backgrounds are at lower risk (Altier et al. 2019). The age-crime curve, which refers to the common finding that people are less likely to engage in criminality as they age, also holds true for extremists.

Research on the factors which lead people to leave militant groups has developed a good understanding of the push and pull factors implicated in deradicalization and disengagement. So far, the benefits of theorizing this process have not been fully exploited. The dominant underlying model is one of individual-level risk assessment and management which has the potential to neglect important political motivations, and pathologize individuals, by suggesting there is something wrong them. These efforts to interpret and manage risk are a relatively new development in relation to terrorism. This is despite the fact that deradicalization interventions have been in operation for several decades.

27.3 HISTORY AND EVOLUTION OF DERADICALIZATION INTERVENTIONS

Historically, the favoured approach for dealing with terrorism has been to capture, imprison or kill its perpetrators. Alongside this, states came to recognize the benefits of creating incentives for militants to move away from terrorism. Italy set up the *dissociati* programme to deal with members of the *Brigate Rosse* (Red Brigades) (Jamieson 1990). The scheme granted those prisoners willing to renounce violence, make a full confession and denounce the Red Brigades, favourable conditions whilst serving their sentence, enabling them to spend time outside of the prison working and reintegrating into the community. In the early 1980s, Spain instigated a similar 'social reinsertion' scheme for members of Euskadi Ta Askatasuna (ETA). This offered a range of inducements to ETA members affiliated with a nonviolent faction of the movement, and who had not been involved in serious violence, to disengage from terrorism. Incentives included early release from prison and in some cases meant they were effectively granted a pardon. In return they had to renounce ETA, promise to abide by the law, and acknowledge the pain their campaign had caused (Alonso 2011).

Both the social reinsertion measures in Spain and the *dissociati* scheme in Italy required individual prisoners to voluntarily reject terrorism and were more focused on supporting disengagement than deradicalization. They were not designed for those who remained committed to the cause and refused to renounce violence. Some of the first attempts to try and encourage people to change their minds, rather than just work with pre-existing motivation were developed in relation to far-right extremism in Europe (see Case Study 27.1).

CASE STUDY 27.1

Exit Project

In the 1980s and 1990s Norway, Sweden, and Denmark saw increasing levels of xenophobia and racist violence perpetrated by racist gangs, but more often by neo-Nazi groups and those motivated by extreme ethnonationalism (Bjørgo 1997). In the Norwegian town of Brumunddal, the situation became particularly bad. In response, a cross-community group devised an action plan to tackle the problem, one outcome of which was the 'Exit Project - Leaving Violent Youth Groups'.

Officially launched in 1997, Exit had three aims: engage with those who wanted to move away from far-right groups; provide support for their parents; and increase the capacity of professionals by developing and sharing knowledge (Bjørgo 2002). Exit involved teachers, police officers and youth workers who collaborated with parents to work with several hundred of the town's young people. Exit was considered a success. By 2000, only ten per cent of the 100 young people involved in racist violence in 1995 were still part of extremist groups (Bjørgo 2002), and the number of far-right group members the police were in contact with reduced by 78 per cent (Daugherty 2019).

Similar programmes were established in Sweden, Germany, Finland, and Switzerland. Exit Sweden was set up in 1998 and confronted a significant challenge. Whilst in Norway the number of people involved in far-right politics was in the low hundreds, in Sweden it was around 3,000 (Bjørgo 2002). In contrast to Norway's project, Exit Sweden worked directly with individuals, rather than through professional or parental networks, and relied heavily on former members of far-right groups to deliver the interventions (Daugherty 2019).

Exit Sweden developed a five-phase exit process with stages focused on motivation, disengagement, settling, reflection and stabilization (Demant et al. 2008). Interestingly, there is relatively little focus on ideology or deradicalization. This is partly because those they work with are well-schooled in counterarguments, but also because those who contact Exit Sweden typically want support with the social problems associated with being part of a far-right group rather than to explore ideological questions (Lodenius 2014).

Inevitably, such programmes face challenges. There have been issues with organizational and management capacity, including a high turnover of staff and uncertainty over funding. Some of the parents of those enrolled on the programmes themselves hold far-right views, making family reintegration harder to achieve. Evaluations of the programme's effectiveness remain limited. Nevertheless, a 2001 report on the Swedish programme was largely favourable. Of 133 people involved in the programme, 125 were believed to have left the White Power movement (National Council for Crime Prevention 2001).

Exit programmes still operate today including in Germany which has developed a wide range of programmes over the last two decades (Daugherty 2019) including in the Hayat (Turkish and Arabic for 'life') programme which has been adapted to work with those involved in militant Islamism (Koehler 2013).

PHOTO 27.1 Neo-Nazi demonstration in Koblenz, Germany, 2011. Exit Projects were created in response to the rise of neo-Nazi groups in European countries such as Sweden, Denmark, and Norway, and as can be seen in this photo, still operate today in Germany and elsewhere.

QUESTIONS

1. How important do you think it is to tackle ideological issues?
2. What are the pros and cons of former extremists running deradicalization programmes?

Countries facing rising levels of Islamist extremism began developing rehabilitation and deradicalization programmes in the early 2000s. Two of the first were initiated by Saudi Arabia and Yemen in the context of growing levels of violence from al-Qaeda. These initiatives were shaped by the criminal justice context in which they were embedded and are different in character to the European programmes focused on the far-right. In most cases, these initiatives have been developed by the state and are delivered in the context of the criminal justice system.

Perhaps the longest running of the rehabilitation centres focused on militant Islamism is in Saudi Arabia. It has developed a strategy known as PRAC: prevention, rehabilitation, and aftercare (Al-Hadlaq 2015). Delivered in prisons to those convicted of terrorism offences, the first phase of the programme involves religious and psychological counselling. If detainees respond positively, and providing they have not been convicted of an extremely serious offence, they are transferred to a rehabilitation centre to prepare them for release into the community. Provided with a range of activities including arts, recreation, vocational training, and intensive religious counselling, participants and their families are also offered generous financial support to cover housing and cars, with some given support finding a wife (El-Said and Barrett 2012).

The UK was one of the first European countries to develop intervention programmes for those convicted of Islamist-related terrorism. In the mid-2000s a wave of people convicted in the wake of the September 11th attacks began to be released from prison. The prison and probation services needed additional mechanisms to work with these individuals because they were perceived to have different needs. Terrorism offenders were believed to pose a higher risk and the risk factors associated with non-politically motivated offending such as substance abuse, or poor educational attainment, were less relevant for terrorism offenders. Consequently, a new approach was considered necessary and deradicalization interventions began to be trialled in England and Wales. They are now embedded in the criminal justice system and are an important part of the Prevent and Pursue aspects of the UK's counter-terrorism policy, CONTEST.

Most deradicalization initiatives are typically targeted at those convicted of a terrorism offence. However, there has been an increase in programmes for people considered at risk of involvement in extremism. Preventative initiatives often take a similar approach to those used with convicted terrorism offenders and aim to deradicalize individuals by persuading them the views they hold are harmful. From the Exit projects in Europe to the rehabilitation programmes in the Middle East, this overlap between post-conviction and preventative efforts has become increasingly embedded in counter-terrorism policy and practice and is one of the trends in the field of deradicalization over the last few decades.

Reviewing the history of deradicalization initiatives there has been a clear shift in the way this issue is addressed. From an emphasis on enforcing or encouraging disengagement through interdiction, arrest and by providing incentives, over time this has shifted to focus on changing the ideas believed to inform terrorism through deradicalization programmes. More recently still, there has been an effort to prevent terrorism through interventions targeted at those considered at risk of involvement in extremism. The result has been a burgeoning number of programmes across the world and a growing number of actors undertaking deradicalization work.

27.4 CONTEMPORARY DERADICALIZATION POLICY AND PRACTICE

From a small number of countries including Norway, Sweden, and Germany setting up often local level initiatives, deradicalization programmes have become an important part of many states' counter-terrorism efforts. They differ depending on the local context, the structure of the criminal justice system and the scope of the need. It is most common for deradicalization interventions to be delivered whilst the individual is in the criminal justice system, either in prison, or when they have been released into the community on parole. Programmes prioritize different forms of intervention but typically take a multi-modal approach using a range of activities to try and support the move away from terrorism. What follows describes some of the main actors involved in delivering deradicalization programmes and the methods they use. Reviewing the people and practices involved in deradicalization efforts reveals a rapidly developing field that would benefit from a stronger empirical foundation to inform intervention work.

Although statutory bodies are central to deradicalization work, a number of other types of actor are typically involved in delivering interventions. These include community organizations, religious leaders, family members, and increasingly, commercial organizations which deliver deradicalization work. Although it is not uncommon for non-statutory actors to work with non-terrorism offenders, one of the reasons they are often involved with terrorism interventions is due to the ideological foundation of the offence. Because terrorism is very often an attack against a government, policy or country, statutory agencies such as the prison or probation authorities are considered illegitimate by many terrorism offenders. Consequently, it can be difficult for statutory agents to develop the level of trust needed to work on a one-to-one basis with an individual. Recognizing this, countries including the Netherlands, Germany, Denmark, and the UK work alongside non-state actors in the context of multi-agency partnerships to deliver deradicalization work.

CASE STUDY 27.2

The Aarhus Model

A prominent example of a multi-partner approach has been developed in the Danish town of Aarhus pictured in Photo 27.2. The police, schools, social services, and the local community, including the Grimhojvej Mosque, work with those who have been, or are at risk of becoming involved in extremism, including returnees from the conflict in Syria. Begun as a pilot in 2007 in response to growing jihadist violence in Europe, the Aarhus project was put on a more sustainable footing in 2011. It involves general awareness raising and capacity building activities for community members and professionals and schools. A parents' network provides support and advice whilst more targeted work focuses on those considered at risk of becoming involved in extremism, and involves understanding the risk the individual might pose, working with the family, and providing a hotline so people can report their concerns. For those already involved in extremism, or considered at imminent risk of travelling overseas, there is an exit programme, providing support tailored to the individual's needs.

Mentors are central to the Aarhus programme. The mentor works with the individual to explore the difficulties that accompany a life committed to extremism. Mentors provide practical support, helping them find work, education or recreational activities and provides more general support to explore issues they might be facing (Bertelsen 2015). Underpinned by the 'Life Psychology' approach, the Aarhus programme tries to address triggering and moderating

PHOTO 27.2 The Danish city of Aarhus has pioneered a programme that aims to build trust with potential terrorists and returning ISIS fighters.

risk factors and support the move away from terrorism and enable the individual to pursue a more fulfilling life (Bertelsen 2015).

Enabled by a long history of interdisciplinary working between the police, education sector and social services, Aarhus' work is also informed by ongoing engagement with researchers at Aarhus University. These elements of best practice have led to Aarhus being designated a model municipality. Despite this, it is difficult to determine the effectiveness of the programme. Evaluations are not publicly available, and although there is anecdotal evidence of success, it is not clear whether this can be attributed to the project (Agerschou 2014).

Learn more about the Aarhus programme here:

- Aarhus.dk: https://www.aarhus.dk/english/collaborate-with-the-city/inclusive-citizenship/anti-radicalization/
- Arhus Prevention Radicalization: https://efus.eu/files/2016/09/PS_Aarhus_Prevention Radicalization_ENG.pdf

QUESTIONS

1. What do interventions like the one at Aarhus suggest about who should take responsibility for helping extremists reintegrate?
2. How might you gauge the success of deradicalization initiatives?

27.4.1 Partnership working in deradicalization initiatives

Multi-agency cooperation of the kind seen in Aarhus can be difficult to establish because the organizations involved can have differing priorities. For example, the police may be more concerned with investigating the individual to understand the risk they pose to the public, whereas the probation services and community-based organizations may be more focused on rehabilitation (Marsden 2017). Despite the tensions between these aims statutory bodies regularly work with non-statutory organizations. Community-based groups are often better placed to understand the needs of those involved in extremism and have greater credibility and legitimacy in the eyes of the offender. They are able to support the individual's reintegration into positive social networks in the community and sometimes have the capacity to provide ongoing support once the individual is no longer under statutory supervision (Marsden 2017).

Working with community-based organizations carries risks, both for the organization and the statutory bodies who oversee this work. In some countries, including France and the UK, the debate over the targeting of Muslim communities by counter-terrorism policy means that Muslim-led organizations risk undermining the relationship of trust they have with the local community because they are seen to be supporting a controversial set of policies. Statutory organizations such as the police and probation services face issues working with community partners because of differing understandings of risk and practical challenges, for example, associated with how much information it is possible to share securely. Hence, although partnership working is widely recognized as an important part of deradicalization work, there are a number of practical challenges which can impact its effectiveness including differing priorities with respect to rehabilitation and risk management, community distrust, and contrasting working practices.

27.4.2 Deradicalization intervention methods

Interventions are typically tailored to the individual and generally involve a range of activities to try and reduce the risk of people re-engaging in terrorism. These include addressing individual-level factors such as the search for status or the influence of extremist ideology; group level issues like the need for belonging; or enabling factors such as recruiters or the role of extremist networks. Interventions can include support finding work or education, help reintegrating back into the family, recreational activities, psychological support, and ideological or theological guidance.

Mentoring is a common mechanism used to support extremist interventions. It can take a number of forms depending on the nature of the offence and the offender but typically involves one-to-one support delivered in the context of regular meetings. Mentoring in relation to extremism differs from other forms of mentoring. The ideological nature of the offence means that mentors need to have an understanding of the arguments that seek to justify political violence, and the confidence to challenge the views of the person they're working with (Spalek and Davies 2012).

Although a widely used form of intervention, there is much to learn about how mentoring works to support desistance from extremism. A particular area of debate relates to the characteristics needed to be an effective mentor. Some argue that former extremists are well-placed to deter others from becoming involved in extremism. Because they have first-hand experience of life inside militant organizations, they are able to reveal the contradictions and difficulties facing those who join them. However, because 'formers' have left militancy behind, they may have less legitimacy in the eyes of those who are still committed to the cause (Tapley and Clubb 2019). Collaborating with formers therefore seems to have the potential to support positive change, but the evidence about the circumstances under which this is likely to be effective remains weak.

The growing number of children implicated in violent extremism, most prominently in relation to ISIS, means that interventions focused on young people are a growing area of work. One of the first programmes to engage with adolescents involved in militant Islamism is Sabaoon in Pakistan (Peracha, Khan, and Savage 2016). The programme supports the reintegration of adolescent males, and between 2010 and 2015, 175 boys who engaged with the programme were returned to their communities. A monitoring centre followed their progress which found that all of the participants had reintegrated successfully, although seven required longer-term support.

Across the range of interventions that seek to support deradicalization and disengagement there is little clarity over how they are supposed to work. When designing social interventions, it is good practice to develop a 'theory of change' which specifies how the activities are supposed to produce the desired outcomes (Feddes and Gallucci 2015). This remains implicit in many deradicalization programmes, with very few setting out the means by which mentoring, or support into education or training is supposed to help move someone away from extremism. Part of the reason for this is that the evidence base underpinning deradicalization is still developing which means it is not always possible to explain why particular interventions might reduce the risk of someone re-engaging in extremism.

27.5 EMPIRICAL EVIDENCE ABOUT DERADICALIZATION

There are a number of reasons why the evidence base on deradicalization is not strong. As with many areas of terrorism research it is difficult to collect data, either from those directly involved in extremism, or the agencies that work with them. Terrorism is uncommon compared with a crime such as robbery, which means there is limited data. Much existing information is drawn from individuals who have voluntarily withdrawn from extremism, rather than those who have moved away as a result of external intervention, and it is not yet clear if the same processes are at work across these two trajectories. Research therefore commonly relies on incomplete open source data which typically combines multiple cases from different time periods, ideological streams, and offence types. The risk with this approach is that it can overlook the differences between types of offender and the factors that shape their trajectories through terrorism (Gill 2015). Nevertheless, the knowledge base about why people move away from terrorism is developing. This section reviews the evidence about what informs deradicalization and considers some of the conceptual models that have been used to interpret this process.

27.5.1 Push and pull factors

It is common to talk about deradicalization and disengagement in relation to individualized, dynamic push and pull factors (Bjørgo 2009). Push factors are those things which propel the individual away from the extremist group, and pull factors are those which motivate them to re-engage with wider society. Push factors include experiences such as disillusion with the group, its strategy or leadership; a feeling that violence has gone too far; losing faith in the ideology; the psychological or physiological effects of violence; or burnout from the stress of being part of a clandestine group (Altier Thoroughgood and Horgan 2014). Pull factors are often concerned with a desire to lead a 'normal' life. They can include positive interactions with political moderates; the attraction of a partner outside the group, or desire to marry; demands from family members; and financial incentives and amnesties (Altier Thoroughgood and Horgan 2014).

Research is beginning to explore the dynamics of push and pull factors in more detail. In an analysis of 87 autobiographical accounts of militants, Mary Beth Altier and her colleagues (2017) found that push factors were more common than pull factors in accounts of disengagement. This study also suggested that a number of push factors including burnout and disillusionment with the group's strategy, leadership or day-to-day life are more typically found in accounts of disengagement rather than deradicalization. Interestingly, this research also found that when people are strongly committed to an ideology, they are less susceptible to pull factors.

It is important to unpack more general findings such as these to look at how push and pull factors operate in the context of specific types of group. Research comparing left-wing groups commited to anarchist or anti-globalization causes, and right-wing groups such as the Ku Klux Klan or white power skinheads, suggests that disillusion is a factor in exit from both types of movement. Dissatisfaction is fuelled by a perceived lack of organizational capacity; when values do not align with members' behaviour; and where there is a lack of benevolence or compassion (Windisch, Scott Ligon, and Simi 2019). However, distrust appears to be caused by different things across the two ideologies. Infighting and violence lead to distrust within right-wing groups, whilst for left-wing groups trust is lost due to a sense that the group will not protect members from external threats.

Much research and practice is rooted in the assumption that by reducing someone's commitment to radical ideas, there is a lower risk that they will re-engage in militancy.

Studies such as Altier et al.'s (2021) supports this argument. However, some research has challenged this perspective. In work looking at the long-term processes associated with disengagement from violence in Northern Ireland, researchers found that many of those once involved in terrorism remained politically active and, although they rejected violence, they retained strong political beliefs (Ferguson, Burgess, and Hollywood 2015). In other words, they were disengaged but not deradicalized. The researchers also cautioned that efforts to try and change former combatant's ideas and beliefs could be counterproductive, potentially hardening rather than changing their mind.

As well as looking at the role of ideology, research is beginning to explore the importance of the social, political and organizational environment in disengagement processes (La Palm 2017). Although there is much we do not know about the impact of the social context on reintegration (Clubb and Tapley 2018), it does seem clear that context interacts with individual experiences and characteristics to shape the potential for successful reintegration. Research examining an intervention programme in France identified a number of contextual risk factors linked to ongoing involvement in terrorism including having contact with extremist peers and being part of geographical clusters of extremists (Campelo et al. 2018). In Singapore, the Religious Rehabilitation Group run a programme for those in detention that recognizes the importance of social support. Families are provided with help whilst the individual is in prison, and there is a structured means of working with the detainee when they're released, enabled by the Inter-Agency Aftercare Group (Jayakumar 2020). Together this seeks to increase the likelihood that families' needs are met and that they will be a positive influence on the individual, and hence reduce the risk they might re-engage in terrorism.

It is important to recognize that former militants often face significant barriers to reintegration (Dwyer 2013). They may be estranged from their family and lack access to positive social networks. Accessing education or training, or securing employment can be challenging due to the stigma of the offence, particularly when this needs to be disclosed when applying for a job or course. When on parole, offenders often face significant restrictions on what they can do, making social and economic integration difficult. For example, they may not be able to travel easily, use digital devices, or access the internet, all of which makes getting a job harder. Ongoing work on these issues will help shape more robust policy and practice and help practitioners understand what is likely to be effective when designing and delivering interventions.

27.6 CONCLUSION

Deradicalization is a rapidly evolving area of policy, practice, and research. Charting the evolution of this work reveals a number of dynamics. Historically, the emphasis was on enforcing or encouraging disengagement through the use of incentives or arrest. Over time, this has shifted to concentrate on requiring ideological and attitudinal change. This change has raised a number of questions about the nature of the relationship between attitudes and behaviour, and the requirement to conform with state-sanctioned ideas. These issues are particularly important given the increased interest in prevention which targets those who have not yet been involved in extremism but are considered at risk.

The evidence base about whether deradicalization interventions work is growing but there is much we do not know about when and why they are effective. Relatively few interventions build in robust evaluation processes, and those which do monitor their work typically do so in-house and rarely make their assessments public. Only a small number, such as the PRISM programme in Australia (Cherney 2020, 2021; Cherney and Belton 2020), have published research seeking to evaluate their effectiveness. Not least because evaluation in this field is difficult. Few programmes are built on a theory of change (see section 27.4) which specifies how its activities are designed to promote positive change, and there are difficulties identifying appropriate metrics by which to interpret success.

Nevertheless, many states have made deradicalization an important part of their counter-terrorism frameworks. This typically involves multi-agency partnerships delivering interventions on a one-to-one basis. The dominant model underpinning these programmes is the risk paradigm which aims to assess, manage and reduce the risk of people re-engaging in militancy. This remains a valuable framework, however it can overlook protective factors and can be usefully complemented by a strengths-based approach which concentrates on improving people's ability to achieve a 'good life' in positive, legal ways.

There has been significant learning about the concept and practice of deradicalization over recent years, however a number of challenges remain. Moving forward it will be important to contextualize risk factors and pay more attention to the social and political context within which reintegration takes place. This includes taking into account the communities former extremists are moving into and nurturing societal acceptance of reintegrative efforts in order to lower the barriers to reintegration. Finally, greater attention should be paid to developing a theoretically informed account of motivation that does not focus so heavily on individual-level risk factors, but also recognizes the social factors that influence trajectories through extremism, and acknowledges the full range of issues, from status and belonging to political change, that people seek to address through involvement in terrorism. Above all, research has to keep pace with a fast-moving policy space in order that deradicalization initiatives are informed by a robust, critically engaged evidence base.

DISCUSSION QUESTIONS

1. Should interventions focus on deradicalization (attitudinal change) or disengagement (behavioural change)? Why?
2. What are the challenges facing multi-agency deradicalization initiatives? How might they be addressed?
3. Is reintegration a more appropriate framework than deradicalization? Why?
4. What are the strengths and weaknesses of the risk paradigm?
5. What are the risks associated with preventative counter-terrorism policies?

 Visit the online resources for pointers on how to answer the discussion questions, links to useful web sources, and guidance on accessing databases: www.oup.com/he/Wilson-Muro1e

GUIDE TO FURTHER READING

Elshimi, M. S. (2017) *De-radicalization in the UK Prevent Strategy: Security, Identity and Religion*. Taylor & Francis. *Provides a theoretically-informed, critical perspective on the UK's approach to deradicalization.*

Hansen, S. J. and Lid, S. (2020) *Routledge Handbook of Deradicalization and Disengagement*. Routledge. *Brings together a wide range of experts, with chapters on definitional and theoretical issues; different actors involved in deradicalization; and a selection of international case studies.*

Horgan, J. G. (2009) *Walking Away from Terrorism: Accounts of Disengagement from Radical and Extremist Movements*. Routledge. *Drawing on in-depth interviews with former members of extremist groups, this book is one of the seminal works on deradicalization, offering important conceptual and practical insights into how and why people move away from terrorism.*

Koehler, D. (2016) *Understanding Deradicalization: Methods, Tools and Programs for Countering Violent Extremism*. Taylor & Francis. *Reviews the research on deradicalization, providing a valuable overview of how the field has developed, and the theoretical and practical debates about how to interpret and deliver interventions.*

Silke, A. ed. (2014) *Prisons, Terrorism and Extremism: Critical Issues in Management, Radicalization and Reform*. Routledge. *Includes chapters covering a range of contemporary issues related to the management and support of terrorist and extremist offenders.*

REFERENCES

Agerschou, T. (2014) 'Preventing Radicalization and Discrimination in Aarhus', *Journal for Deradicalization*, (1): 5–22.

al-Hadlaq, A. (2015) 'Saudi Efforts in Counter-radicalization and Extremist Rehabilitation', in R. Gunaratna and M. Bin Ali (eds.). *Terrorist Rehabilitation: A New Frontier in Counter-Terrorism*, 7: 21–39. London: Imperial College Press.

Alonso, R. (2011) 'Why do Terrorists Stop? Analysing why ETA Members Abandon or Continue with Terrorism', *Studies in Conflict & Terrorism*, 34 (9): 696–716.

Altier, M. B., Leonard Boyle, E., and Horgan, J. G. (2021) 'Returning to the Fight: An Empirical Analysis of Terrorist Reengagement and Recidivism', *Terrorism and Political Violence*, 33 (4): 836–860.

Altier, M. B., Thoroughgood, C. N., and Horgan, J. G. (2014) 'Turning Away From Terrorism: Lessons From Psychology, Sociology, and Criminology', *Journal of Peace Research*, 51 (5): 647–661.

Altier, M. B., Leonard Boyle, E., Shortland, N. D., and Horgan, J. G. (2017) 'Why They Leave: An Analysis of Terrorist Disengagement Events from Eighty-seven Autobiographical Accounts', *Security Studies*, 26 (2): 305–332.

Andrews, D. A. and Bonta, J. (2010) 'Rehabilitating Criminal Justice Policy and Practice', *Psychology, Public Policy, and Law*, 16 (1): 39.

Barrelle, K. (2015) 'Pro-integration: Disengagement From and Life After Extremism', *Behavioural Sciences of Terrorism and Political Aggression*, 7 (2): 129–142.

Bertelsen, P. (2015) 'Danish Preventive Measures and De-radicalization Strategies: The Aarhus Model', *Panorama: Insights into Asian and European Affairs*, 1 (241): 53.

Bjørgo, T. (2002) 'Exit neo-Nazism: Reducing Recruitment and Promoting Disengagement from Racist Groups'. Norsk Utenrikspolitisk Institutt Paper 627.

Bjørgo, T. (2009) 'Processes of Disengagement From Violent Groups of the Extreme Right', in T. Bjørgo and J. Horgan (eds.), *Leaving Terrorism Behind: Individual and Collective Disengagement*, 30–48. New York: Routledge.

Bjørgo, T. (1997) *Racist and Right-Wing Violence in Scandinavia: Patterns, Perpetrators and Responses*. Oslo: Tano Aschehoug.

Borum, R. (2011) 'Radicalization Into Violent Extremism I: A Review of Social Science Theories', *Journal of Strategic Security*, 4 (4): 7–36.

Campelo, N., Bouzar, L., Oppetit, A., Pellerin, H., Hefez, S., Bronsard, G., Cohen, D., and Bouzar, D. (2018) 'Joining the Islamic State from France Between 2014 and 2016: An Observational Follow-up Study', *Palgrave Communications*, 4 (1): 1–10.

Cherney, A. (2020) 'Evaluating Interventions to Disengage Extremist Offenders: A Study of the Proactive Integrated Support Model (PRISM)', *Behavioural Sciences of Terrorism and Political Aggression*, 12 (1): 17–36.

Cherney, A. (2021) 'The Release and Community Supervision of Radicalized Offenders: Issues and Challenges that can Influence Reintegration', *Terrorism and Political Violence*, 33 (1): 119–137.

Cherney, A. and Belton, E. (2020) 'Assessing Intervention Outcomes Targeting Radicalized Offenders: Testing the pro Integration Model of Extremist Disengagement as an Evaluation Tool', *Dynamics of Asymmetric Conflict*, 13 (3): 193–211.

Choudhury, T. and Fenwick, H. (2011) 'The Impact of Counter-terrorism Measures on Muslim Communities', *International Review of Law, Computers & Technology*, 25 (3): 151–181.

Clubb, G. and Tapley, M. (2018) 'Conceptualising De-radicalization and Former Combatant Reintegration in Nigeria', *Third World Quarterly*, 39 (11): 2053–2068.

Dean, C. (2014) 'The Healthy Identity Intervention: The UK's Development of a Psychologically Informed Intervention to Address Extremist Offending', in *Prisons, Terrorism and Extremism: Critical Issues in Management, Radicalization and Reform*: 89–107. Routledge.

Dwyer, C. D. (2013) '"They Might as well be Walking Around the Inside of a Biscuit tin": Barriers to Employment and Reintegration for "Politically Motivated" Former Prisoners in Northern Ireland', *European Journal of Probation*, 5 (1): 3–24.

El-Said, H. and Barrett, R. (2012) 'Saudi Arabia: The Master of Deradicalization', in *Deradicalising Violent Extremists*, 194–226. Routledge.

National Council for Crime Prevention (2001) English Summary, Exit: A Follow-up and Evaluation of the Organization for People Wishing to Leave Racist and Nazi groups. Available at: https://www.bra.se/download/18.cba82f7130f475a2f1800028108/1371914734840/2001_exit_a_follow-up_and_evaluation.pdf. (last accessed 19 February 2020).

Daugherty, C. E. (2019) 'Deradicalization and Disengagement: Exit Programs in Norway and Sweden and Addressing Neo-Nazi Extremism', in *Journal for Deradicalization*, (21): 219–260.

Demant, F., Slootman, M., Buijs, F., and Tillie, J. (2008) 'Decline and Disengagement', *An Analysis of Processes of Deradicalization*, Amsterdam. IMES Report Series.

Elshimi, M. S. (2017) *De-radicalization in the UK Prevent Strategy: Security, Identity and Religion*. Routledge.

Feddes, A. R. and Gallucci, M. (2015) 'A Literature Review on Methodology Used in Evaluating Effects of Preventive and De-radicalization Interventions', *Journal for Deradicalization*, (5): 1–27.

Ferguson, N., Burgess, M., and Hollywood, I. (2015) 'Leaving Violence Behind: Disengaging From Politically Motivated Violence in Northern Ireland', *Political Psychology*, 36 (2): 199–214.

Gill, P. (2015) 'Toward a Scientific Approach to Identifying and Understanding Indicators of Radicalization and Terrorist Intent: Eight Key Problems', *Journal of Threat Assessment and Management*, 2 (3–4): 187–191.

Githens-Mazer, J. and Lambert, R. (2010) 'Why Conventional Wisdom on Radicalization Fails: The Persistence of a Failed Discourse', *International Affairs*, 86 (4): 889–901.

Horgan, J. G. (2009) *Walking Away from Terrorism: Accounts of Disengagement from Radical and Extremist Movements*. Routledge.

Horgan, J. and Taylor, M. (2011) 'Disengagement, De-radicalization, and the arc of Terrorism: Future Directions for Research', in R. Coolseat (Ed.). *Jihadi Terrorism and the Radicalization Challenge: European and American Experiences*, 2nd edition (173–186). London: Ashgate.

Jamieson, A. (1990) 'Entry, Discipline and Exit in the Italian Red Brigades', *Terrorism and Political Violence*, 2 (1): 1–20.

Jayakumar, S. (2020) Deradicalization in Singapore: Past, Present and Future. ICSR, London. Available at: https://icsr.info/wp-content/uploads/2020/08/ICSR-Report-Deradicalization-in-Singapore-Past-Present-and-Future.pdf (last accessed 22 October 2020).

Khalil, J., Horgan, J., and Zeuthen, M. (2019) 'The Attitudes-Behaviours Corrective (ABC) Model of Violent Extremism', *Terrorism and Political Violence*. Advance online publication. https://doi.org/10.1080/09546553.2019.1699793

Koehler, D. (2013) 'Family Counselling as Prevention and Intervention Tool Against "Foreign Fighters". The German "Hayat" Program', *Journal Exit-Deutschland. Zeitschrift für Deradikalisierung und demokratische Kultur*, 3: 182–204.

La Palm, M. (2017) 'Re-Purposing the Push-Pull Model to Describe Signature Patterns of Terrorist Disengagement by Group: A Validation Study', *Journal for Deradicalization*, (12): 85–118.

Lloyd, M. (2019) *Extremism Risk Assessment: A Directory*. Available at: https://crestresearch.ac.uk/resources/extremism-risk-assessment-directory/ (last accessed 19 February 2020).

Logan, C. and Lloyd, M. (2019) 'Violent Extremism: A Comparison of Approaches to Assessing and Managing Risk', *Legal and Criminological Psychology*, 24 (1): 141–161.

Lodenius, A. L. (2014) 'To Leave a Destructive Life Full of Hate: The Story of Exit in Sweden.' trans. Tanya Silverman, Institute for Strategic Dialogue. Available at: https://annalenalod.files.wordpress.com/2014/10/exit-evaluation-2010-lodenius.pdf (last accessed 19 February 2020).

Lösel, F., King, S., Bender, D., and Jugl, I. (2018) 'Protective Factors Against Extremism and Violent Radicalization: A Systematic Review of Research', *International Journal of Developmental Science*, 12 (1–2): 89–102.

Marsden, S. V. (2017) *Reintegrating Extremists: Deradicalization and Desistance*. Springer.

Mucha, W. (2017) 'Polarization, Stigmatization, Radicalization. Counterterrorism and Homeland Security in France And Germany', *Journal for Deradicalization*, (10): 230–254.

Muhanna-Matar, A. (2017) 'The Limit-experience and Self-deradicalization: The Example of Radical Salafi Youth in Tunisia', *Critical Studies on Terrorism*, 10 (3): 453–475.

Peracha, F., Khan, R. R., and Savage S. (2016) 'Sabaoon: Educational Methods Successfully PCVE', in S. Zeiger (ed.), *Expanding Research on Countering Violent Extremism*: 85–104. Hedayah and Edith Cowan University. Available at: https://s3-eu-central-1.amazonaws.com/hedayah-wp-offload/hedayah/wp-content/uploads/2019/11/17115746/File-410201685227.pdf (last accessed 19 February 2020).

Spalek, B. and Davies, L. (2012) 'Mentoring in Relation to Violent Extremism: A Study of Role, Purpose, and Outcomes', *Studies in Conflict & Terrorism*, 35 (5): 354–368.

Tapley, M. and Clubb, G. (2019) *The Role of Formers in Countering Violent Extremism*. International Centre for Counter-Terrorism.

Ward, T. and Maruna, S. (2007) *Rehabilitation: Beyond the Risk Paradigm*. Routledge.

Ward, T. and Stewart, C. A. (2003) 'Good Lives and the Rehabilitation of Sexual Offenders', in T. Ward, D. R. Laws and S. M. Hudson (eds.), *Sexual Deviance: Issues and Controversies* (21–44). Thousand Oaks, CA: Sage.

Windisch, S., Scott Ligon, G., and Simi, P. (2019) 'Organizational [Dis] trust: Comparing Disengagement Among Former Left-Wing and Right-Wing Violent Extremists', *Studies in Conflict & Terrorism*, 42 (6): 559–580.

CHAPTER 28

Victims of Terrorism and Political Violence

ORLA LYNCH AND CARMEL JOYCE

■ CHAPTER SUMMARY

Victims of terrorism are often thought of as random, unlucky targets of indiscriminate violence. However, psychological and criminological research on victimhood, challenges this simplistic portrayal. As with 'non-political' interpersonal violence, the experience of terrorist victimization is often at odds with any neat, black and white divisions. This complexity is often overlooked in studies on terrorism in favour of a narrower simpler analysis. Furthermore, not all victims are treated equally, and it is not uncommon for competitive victimhood and hierarchies of victimhood to emerge in the aftermath of political violence. This chapter is concerned with understanding how victims and survivors of terrorism are constructed, managed and utilized, by whom and for whom. It will focus on three key issues: firstly, the experience of becoming and being a victim of terrorism, and how this public trauma has a ripple effect that impacts on the individual, their family and society more generally. Secondly, the relevance of key victimological concepts for the case of terrorism and political violence. Thirdly, how victims of terrorism become public victims and are often politicized in the process.

28.1 INTRODUCTION

This chapter will examine how we think about victims of terrorism, how victims of terrorism experience the trauma and the aftermath of the violence, what it means to be a victim of a political and very public attack, and what we can learn from other disciplines that address issues of victimhood in other domains. Specifically, we draw on frameworks from criminology, victimology, and social psychology in order to understand the issues of relevance for understanding victimhood in the case of terrorism and political violence.

> **KEY CONCEPTS**
>
> **Direct victim (primary)** Victim means a person who, individually or collectively, has suffered harm (physical, mental, emotional, economic, or impairment of their fundamental rights), through acts or omissions that are in violation of criminal laws (Newburn, 2017: 366).
>
> **Indirect Victim (Secondary)** The immediate family or dependants of the direct victim and persons who have suffered harm in intervening to assist victims in distress or to prevent victimization (Newburn, 2017: 379).
>
> **Tertiary Victim** Those who are impacted but were not directly involved (e.g. watched the event on television).
>
> **Survivor** The label survivor is often used in multiple ways: it can be used in an objective manner to refer to a victim who was not killed in an attack, but it can also be used to refer to the cognitive and emotional state of individuals who experienced a victimizing experience. In this case the individual tends to see their reaction to the event as a form of growth and uses the term survivor as a descriptor of the active process they're engaged in to move away from a victim status that they see as having more passive implications (Dillenburger, 2008).
>
> **Vicarious Victimization** Vicarious victimization is when individuals experience trauma due to identifying with the victimization of another person (Peterson, 2010).

> **CASE STUDY 28.1**
>
> *Paris Terror Attacks, 2015*
>
> On 13 November 2015 three gunmen stormed the Bataclan Theatre in Paris. They shot and killed 89 concertgoers and wounded hundreds. One survivor committed suicide two years later and was recognized as the 90th victim. ISIS claimed responsibility for the attack as retaliation for French airstrikes in Syria and Iraq (Callimachi, 2015). The Bataclan Theatre attack was one of six locations targeted that night by gunmen and suicide bombers: the other five sites included the Stade De France stadium, and a number of cafes and restaurants.

PHOTO 28.1 November 2015, Paris. Mourners pray outside the Bataclan Theatre in tribute to the victims of the terror attack on 15 November.

The victims came from all walks of life and from 15 countries, and there was global media coverage of the attack. While citizens from all across the world were offering solidarity to the victims and survivors using Facebook flag filters (Ajaka, 2015), graphic video footage and photographs of those killed and injured were broadcast on social and broadcast media. In one instance, a photographer was charged with violating the *Guigou Law*, a legal instrument that prevents the publication without consent of the circumstances of a crime where the dignity of the victim is violated. In this instance, a photographer published an image of a man injured in the Bataclan attacks being resuscitated on the pavement outside the venue. The man later died.

Sometime after the attack there was a police investigation into the attacks and this brought more anguish for the victims and their families. The testimony of a military commander who pointed out that she did not give permission for soldiers who were stationed outside the theatre to enter the Bataclan because she did not want to sacrifice soldiers' lives, was traumatic for the families and survivors. In response to this revelation, the survivors and victims' families filed a legal complaint. In the 2016 parliamentary probe that followed it was acknowledged that a lack of coordination amongst security forces slowed the response to the attack (Faget, 2018).

This legal complaint was in addition to a lawsuit initiated by survivors and victims' families that questioned if state agencies had adequately monitored the attackers in their planning phase, and if police had provided sufficient security for the Bataclan event. However, a Paris court ruled the French state was *not* responsible for failing to avert the terrorist attack as the planning had occurred outside the state (Faget, 2018, see Photo 28.1).

The personal tragedy experienced by the victims and their families was accompanied by a very public reaction to the trauma. It caused a realization amongst the people of Paris and France that the violence witnessed on that day was not just a direct attack on the victims, it was an attack on all individuals going about their day-to-day lives in a busy city. In the aftermath of the attack, Parisians spoke of losing their taste for life (Gregory et al., 2019). In an effort to reconcile the loss and come to terms with the trauma, there have been a number of public and private efforts at remembrance and memorialization. Documentaries, such as 'November 13: Attack on Paris' on Netflix, have been produced recalling the testimonials of survivors. Public memorials have been placed at the six attack locations where annual commemorations are held. In addition to this, a number of survivors have turned to art as a means of sharing their story. For example, Fred Dewilde produced a graphic novel entitled 'Mon Bataclan', as did Catherine Bertrand, entitled 'Chronicles of a Survivor'. A number of survivors penned memoirs, and the street artist Banksy painted a mural of a *sad faced girl* on one of the emergency doors of the Bataclan Theatre. In the case of the Paris attacks, coming to terms with the violence involved both a personal journey for the victims, survivors, and their families but also the public process of recognizing, processing, and memorializing the trauma.

QUESTIONS

1. In this example, revictimization occurs for the victims and their families. How might this have been avoided?
2. Private trauma and public tragedy, while linked to the same event, are very different experiences. How might public events serve to help the private trauma of victims?

The details of the Bataclan attack in Case Study 28.1 highlight the complexity of victimization brought about by terrorist attacks, both for the direct victims and indirect victims. While the survivors and the victims' families continue to live with the impact of the violence, the repercussions are also felt beyond the direct and indirect victims. French society is described as experiencing an awakening—the realization that a threat overshadows their day-to-day lives. While exploring the victim label beyond its traditional conception, we can also consider that on a societal level, those who were impacted through their consumption of the graphic images published on social or print/TV media and as a result now live in fear of terrorism, are also victims. And while these individuals were not intended to be victims directly, they were intended as the audience for the violence. The media coverage of the attacks allowed the perpetrators to better communicate their message by spreading terror to populations far greater than those directly touched by the violence (Schmid, 2012).

While those direct and indirect victims are limited in number, and their suffering is a very personal trauma, the spread of fear to wider audiences effectively destabilizes the sense of security of large segments of the population. And while memories of the violence will fade for the majority of citizens, the legacy of the attack lives beyond the individual memories of those directly impacted in the form of the response: increased security, changes to civil liberties (such the introduction of emergency legislation or martial law), and policymaking, thus further stretching the boundaries of victimhood (Rubin and Peltier, 2017). Now that the concept of victims and victimhood has been explored, we will next examine the impact of terrorism.

28.2 THE IMPACT OF TERRORISM

Research on victims of terrorism is often concerned with the psychological impact of the violence, and particularly a focus on the clinical implications of the attack (Schuster, Stein, Jaycox, et al., 2001). For example, looking at the likelihood that tertiary victims will experience symptoms of Post-Traumatic Stress Disorder (PTSD), as well as therapy, and support measures that are best placed to mitigate the impact of violence (Hersh, 2013). Butler, Panzer, and Goldfrank (2003) examine how terrorist violence may be similar or dissimilar to other victimizing experiences (such as road traffic accidents or natural disasters). While there are similarities in trauma *reactions* that individuals experience regardless of the event, it must be remembered that all victims are unique in that their personal history (pre-attack). Individual culture, religious beliefs, socio-economic status, and ethnicity, are all relevant for how people experience and respond to violence (Green and Pemberton, 2018). However, there are considerations that should be taken into account when thinking specifically about the impact of terrorism on the victims; one is the public and communicative nature of terrorism, and the other is the intent to create harm and fear (Shapland and Hall, 2007).

28.2.1 Terrorism as communication

Terrorism is by its very nature a communicative act. Acts of violence or the threat of violence convey a message. The recipients of the message are many and varied. The victims or recipients of the violence are not the only audience; sometimes the violence against them is the message, and sometimes they serve as a conduit for other intended audiences (Schmid, 2012). Regardless, understanding terrorism is about understanding this communicative aspect of the phenomena. It is also important to understand the experience of *all* parties to the violence. Research on terrorism has focused on the perpetrators, those who carry out or support the violence. It is less common for victims of terrorism to be the primary focus of academic investigation. Since the 9/11 terrorist attacks, there has been a significant shift in focus towards researching victims issues, and victims of terrorism more generally although it is still relatively rare in the field of terrorism studies (Lynch and Argomaniz, 2014).

The lack of research in the field is partly due to the nature of attacks that have featured prominently in research on terrorism over the past two decades. Attention to what might be termed one-off attacks such as 9/11, the 2008 Mumbai shootings, the 2019 London Bridge attack in the UK, and the 2016 truck attack in Nice, France, have supported the narrative of victims being randomly chosen. One-off attacks are overwhelmingly sub-state, and occur in non-conflict environments. In discourse, the focus on these events has led to the dominance of the assumption that victims are 'randomly' chosen and it 'could have been anyone', feeding into the concept known as the ideal victim which we will return to in section 28.3. However, while these one-off attacks have led to a significant number of deaths over the past two decades, there are significantly more victims of terrorism created where the violence is a part of an ongoing conflict, such as during a civil war (United Nations Office on Drugs and Crime, 2018).

The importance of the communicative element of terrorist violence is visible in how the social identity of victims of attacks is made relevant. In most cases of terrorism (except arguably in political assassination) victims are chosen because they represent a particular identity—be it French citizens, Lebanese citizens, or a particular religious minority for example. The identity of victims of terrorism targeted as part of an ongoing conflict is relevant in a similar way. However in the case of terrorism and political violence (TPV) that occurs as part of an ongoing conflict, victimhood is a highly politicized, even weaponized construct. In such cases it is not always clear who is a victim and who is a perpetrator, and the label *victim* is contested and challenged depending on who claims it. 'Victim' when used in these situations is used to discriminate and delineate the boundaries of identity categories—mostly for the ingroup and denied to the outgroup. As a result victimhood has been portrayed as a barrier to an emerging peace, due to a failure of victims to move on, forgive, or reconcile. As a result victims themselves become politicized, even vilified, stigmatized, and denied and presented as the spoilers of the peace (Ferguson, Burgess, and Hollywood, 2010).

28.2.2 Terrorism as intent to create harm and fear

In addition to how the communicative aspect of terrorism impacts on the victims, there is the issue of how the terrorist actor seeks to manipulate perceptions of threat, and an overall fear of terrorism. Creating fear of terrorism is the point of many attacks. While becoming a victim of terrorism is unlikely for most citizens, the belief that one *could* be a victim lies at the heart of the issue. Research on fear of crime suggests that people fear victimization disproportionately to their objective risk (Curiel and Bishop, 2018). So for example, young men are statistically most likely to be the victims of crime, but least likely to report a fear of crime. On the other hand, older people are least likely to be the victim of crime, but most likely to report a greater fear (Reilly, Muldoon, and Byrne, 2004). The level of fear is not related to fact, but to socio-economic status, the physical environment, age, gender, and race, media consumption, and previous experience of victimhood. In the case of terrorism, international events also impact on fear. In the USA, the likelihood of becoming a victim of terrorism is negligible; however, both before and after the events of 9/11 the American public maintains a similar level of fear. Apart from spikes related to various events (such as large-scale attacks or foreign wars) between 40 and 50 per cent of the population are consistently somewhat concerned or very concerned about being a victim of terrorism (Nellis and Savage, 2012; Gallop, 2020).

Despite significant evidence that citizens of the USA are unlikely to experience terrorism, a substantial fear of terrorism remains (Zenko, 2012). There are many contributing factors to the omnipresent fear of terrorism, but one that is relevant here is how terrorist actors seek to manipulate a population's perception of risk. For example, it has been long recognized that both violence and the threat of violence is a part of the phenomenon of terrorism (Silke, 2003), and in many cases maintaining the threat of terrorism over a population is successful as a means of inducing fear. For example, when Osama bin Laden and al-Qaeda declared war on the West in 1996, their overall spreading of fear was successful. Similarly, community control through punishment beatings and disappearances by terrorist groups serve to successfully maintain an environment of threat and compliance amongst a population (Peake and Lynch, 2016).

A widespread fear of terrorism has an impact in both the public and private spheres, and importantly, the mere threat of terrorism suffices for the impact to occur. For the individual, the psychological impact of fear increases the likelihood of mental health problems, and for society, fear of terrorism has an impact on how people vote, and what type of foreign policy and counter-terrorism measures they support. For example, a study in the USA examined public concern about terrorism and found that increased fear of terrorism led to increased support for anti-Muslim counter-terrorism policies (Haner, Sloan, Cullen, Kulig, and Jonson, 2019).

28.2.3 The Just World Hypothesis (JWH)

Why are individuals so concerned becoming a victim of terrorism, when the likelihood of dying or being injured in an attack is negligible? A fear of terrorism is related to beliefs regarding to a sense of fairness, and the control an individual has (or does not have) over their own fate. In a general sense, people like order and seek for order in their social world—we like to believe we can control our own destiny by controlling our behaviour and our environment. Related to this is the belief that *good things happen to good people* and vice versa. We all vary in the *degree* to which we believe this, but it is a cognitive tool we commonly rely on to explain daily day events in our lives (Kaiser, Vick, and Major, 2004).

This way of thinking about the world is called the Just World Hypothesis (JWH), and the more an individual subscribes to this, the less vulnerable they feel to threats in their environment. It gives people a sense of control, and allows people to believe they can influence their environment. However, while many threats can be dismissed as the responsibility of the victim (i.e. victim blaming), other threats cannot be so easily dismissed by reference to the behaviour of the victim. In the case of terrorism, particularly one-off attacks, a person's belief in a fair world is challenged because the victims are often random, innocent, and the violence is seen as unjust. In other-words, there is no way that the victim can be blamed, or have precipitated the violence. The cognitive challenge represented by such attacks can lead to an increase in one's sense of uncertainty about the world, an increase in anxiety, and feeling less safe and secure.

One way that society responds to challenges to one's sense of a just world is to engage in victim blaming, or focus on how a victim may have *facilitated* the violence. This often happens in cases where there are clear delineated identity differences and contextual dissimilarities. For example in the case of terrorist bombings in Beirut, Lebanon in 2015, there is less opportunity to identify with the victims for many people living in the West if ethnic, racial, and social identity differences exist. Given the ongoing civil war in the region, individuals from other places will not see it as comparable to their own environment, and may overestimate the existence of violence in the region. However in contrast to this, in the case of the Bataclan attacks in Paris, for individuals from France or familiar with the city, those killed and injured in the violence were individuals dining out, attending a concert, watching a football game—activities that Europeans could identify with in an environment that they understand as familiar. This encourages individuals to consider that they too are vulnerable to terrorist violence (see also Case Study 28.2).

An alternative response to challenges to one's belief in a 'just world' is to seek revenge, in effect to correct the moral pendulum by punishing transgressors for their actions.

PHOTO 28.2 One of the survivors from the 2005 London bombings was pictured on the front cover of *The Sun* newspaper, but mis-quoted to imply support for Tony Blair's anti-terrorism laws.

This may come in the form of support for military action against a particular target, or support for other government measures such as counter-terrorism legislation. Often, victims of terrorism are co-opted into supporting such measures, occasionally against their will. This happened in the aftermath of the 7/7 London attacks where John Tullock, a survivor of one of the bombings, had his photograph used in a campaign to support the enactment of more draconian anti-terrorist legislation. He did not support the new legislation; however on the front page of *The Sun* newspaper in the UK, under a banner headline declaring 'Terror laws', there was a picture of Tullock, and a misattributed quote stating 'Tell Tony [Blair] He's Right', implying that he supported the new anti-terrorism laws being proposed to parliament.

CASE STUDY 28.2

Terrorism at Home and Abroad

On 12 November 2015, just hours before the multi-site attacks on Paris by ISIS, twin suicide bombings occurred in Beirut, Lebanon. The bombs devastated a shopping district, killed 43 people, and injured hundreds of others. ISIS claimed responsibility for the bombings. The global media coverage that emerged in the following days was heavily skewed towards coverage of the Paris attack. Shortly after the Bataclan and other attacks the victims were being named and memorialized, but there was little coverage of those killed in Lebanon.

Social media companies attended to the Paris attacks by allowing French flag overlays as a display of solidarity, and by activating their safe check-in option, but didn't do the same for Lebanon (Barnard, 2015). Some international landmarks were even lit up in the colours of the French flag, such as the Skytree in Tokyo, Tower Bridge in London, and the Brandenberg gate in Berlin—while the violence in Lebanon was sidelined. This issue is not just related to terrorism, and it is the case that Western coverage of non-Western issues and events is lower than for regional news (El Sayed, 2013). But the underlying assumptions that were displayed in the coverage of the Paris and Beirut attacks point to the ways in which victims of terrorism are treated depending on the context to the violence they experience. The bombings in Beirut were the worst in decades, and like Paris, the violence was unexpected and targeted against civilians. However media coverage conflated the ISIS attacks with the local politics of Lebanon. Consider the headlines that addressed the violence in both locations:

'Deadly explosions rock Hezbollah stronghold in Beirut' (*France 24*) (Ajaka, 2015)

'Terror Strikes in Paris' (*The New Yorker*) (Ajaka, 2015)

The assumption in the language used is that in the case of Beirut, that the target of the attack was linked to Hezbollah, thus connecting the violence to ongoing local political issues, but also dehumanizing the city and its inhabitants. In the case of the Paris attacks headline, the statement is devoid of assumptions about causality.

There are other reasons that the Beirut attacks received less attention. Fewer people died, Beirut is in a region that is widely associated with conflict (the Middle East), and so there is (at least externally) an expectation that violence is inevitable. It is also geographically further away from Europe and the USA. Fewer people in Western countries identify as closely with Beirut as they do with Paris, even if that is due to a familiarity gained through popular culture. However, this is not an isolated case, and the way in which we recognize, support, and memorialize victims is very much dependent on the context of the violence, and the characteristics of the victims.

QUESTIONS

1. What are the assumptions being made about the victims in the Beirut attacks from the media coverage of the attacks?
2. What are the implications of activating the flag overlays on Facebook profile pictures or on national landmarks in the case of the Paris attacks?

28.3 THE IDEAL VICTIM

Closely linked to the relevance of the Just World Hypothesis for understanding terrorism and political violence is the notion of the ideal victim. This is also relevant for how we treat victims, the recognition we give to victims, and the existence of a hierarchy of victimhood where some people are more readily ascribed the victim label than others. The ideal victim is a theoretical victim who is worthy of sympathy based on certain characteristics they exhibit. The notion of the ideal victim emerged from the writings of Nils Christie (1986) whereby he (with little empirical evidence) announced that the ideal victim possesses certain characteristics namely: they are weak, blameless, carrying out a noble task, harmed by malign forces or actors, (unidentifiable forces), and can legitimately claim victim status (Lewis, Hamilton, and Elmore, 2019). Since Christie's work was published, empirical evidence has subsequently supported the notion that people exhibit increased compassion for individuals who meet these and other similar characteristics (ibid.). The recent work of Lewis et al. (2019), points out that in their study of 830 participants that concepts such as innocence, vulnerability, and helplessness were positively correlated with participant's perceptions of who was a legitimate victim, and these perceptions aligned with Christie's (1986) ideal victim characteristics. In addition to this, in this study, victims described as illegitimate were less likely to display the characteristics that aligned with Christie's ideal victim (1986).

It would be reasonable to assume that victims of terrorist attacks would easily meet the criteria of the ideal victim. However this is not always the case. The issue here is not the nature of the attack, but the nature of the victim. While victims may be blameless and/ or innocent, this may be the only characteristic they share with the hypothetical ideal victim. In certain one-off terrorist attacks, given that the general public tend to assume that anyone could have been a victim, it is less likely that victim blaming will take place, and very likely that there will be an outpouring of public sympathy. However, in the case of terrorism that occurs as part of an ongoing conflict (such as a civil war), or for victims of state terrorism (see Chapter 14), very often there is no assumption of blamelessness and innocence for the victims, nor can the victims legitimately claim victim status, and they may well be denied this right by the state (Aguilar and Kovras, 2019; Grossman, 1992; Peake and Lynch, 2016; Shichor, 2007).

28.3.1 Hierarchies of victims

Inequality in the treatment of victims based on the type of attack, the characteristics of the victim, and the social and political context to the violence is commonplace (Jankowick, 2018). The empathy gap is evidenced above in the case of Lebanon (see Case Study 28.2), but is also often evident in the UK, where violence in Northern Ireland associated with the Troubles was often (and is still) overlooked by media outlets in the rest of the UK. Compare, for example, violence in Northern Ireland to Islamist inspired attacks—the former often goes unreported at a national level, whereas the latter attracts 24 hour news coverage (Greenslade, 2013). There are a number of reasons for this, but amongst them is the assumption that people in what individual's perceive to be conflict zones are accustomed to violence, a lack of understanding from observers regarding what is the context to the conflict, and an ability to dis-identify with the victims for a range of reasons. This inequality can also be described as a hierarchy of victimhood, whereby not all victims are seen, nor treated equally.

A hierarchy of victimhood is linked to (McEvoy and McConnachie, 2012):

- A belief in the Just World Hypothesis
- Prioritizing the characteristics of an *ideal victim*
- The notion that there is a clear dichotomy between both victim and perpetrator
- The belief that one can differentiate between *good victims and bad victims*

At the apex of a hierarchy of victimhood are individuals perceived to be innocent victims, and those who most closely aligned with the characteristics matching Christie's (1986) ideal victim. Descending from this apex are other victims whose personal characteristics, or the circumstances of their victimizing experiences, diminishes their similarity to the profile of the ideal victim. In addition to the importance of the notion of an ideal victim is the social identity relationship between them and society. A sense of shared identity is important in how we consider, treat, and respond to victims of violence. Furthermore, the issue of victim precipitation is relevant here—a hierarchy of victimhood prioritizes innocence, so any element of involvement in one's own victimization pushes victims down the hierarchy.

In the case of terrorism and political violence, there is often a substantial public outpouring of grief and sympathy for certain victims, for example children or those killed in service (such as firefighters or police). However, this statement has to be qualified to account for the importance of shared social identity characteristics (ethnicity, nationality, background, religion, culture) between the victims and the observers. Some victims have in the immediate aftermath of the attacks significant social capital or value, and become public symbols of important national characteristics, such as resilience, strength, determination, bravery in the face of terrorist violence.

Linked to the emergence of a hierarchy of victimhood is the notion of competitive victimhood. This refers to a process whereby individuals compete for recognition and resources by virtue of their comparatively more significant experience of victimization. This competitive victimhood is also related to perceptions of innocence, with a direct relationship between the degree of victimhood and total innocence, as well as perceived responsibility for the conflict. For example in the case of the Basque country in Northern Spain, both ETA supporters (Euskadi Ta Askatasuna—a paramilitary group seeking independence for the Basque region) and supporters of the National government and related groups said to have been defending their community in their use of violence, with each group claiming the other side was responsible for initiating the conflict and carrying out atrocities (Argomaniz, 2016). Equally, each group claimed to be the most victimized community and this is part of a claim of moral superiority. In addition, this claim to be more victimized is linked to a group's entitlement to reparations and recognition. However, competitive victimhood is also linked to the maintenance of intergroup conflict due to a group's unwillingness to forgive, a lack of trust, and intergroup empathy (ibid.).

28.4 MEDIA AND TERRORISM VICTIMS

While in the aftermath of violence, victims and their families often engage with the media to seek recognition of their victimizing experience, drawing public attention can have negative consequences. Individuals caught up in terrorist violence are often the focus of intense media scrutiny at the time of a terrorist attack, and this has a significant impact upon their experience of victimization and recovery. Given the very public nature of terrorist attacks, there are expectations of how individuals might behave in the aftermath of the violence, usually related to displays of resilience, stoicism, and some form of post-traumatic growth (PTG). Not showing defeat, and getting on with business as usual are often the expected responses to terrorist attacks, in addition to achieving post-traumatic growth, whereby victims overcome a hugely traumatic event through a journey of personal development (Tedeschi and Calhoun, 1996). An example of how this public reaction to terrorist violence is at often at odds with the individual victim's actual reaction to an attack was demonstrated in the words of Emma Craig, one of the youngest victims of the 7/7 2005 London bombings. She announced on the 10th anniversary of the attacks that 7/7 'may not have broken London, but it did break some of us' (Lambert, 2015). Another example of this dichotomy is documented by Kay Wilson, who survived a mass stabbing attack in a forest near Jerusalem in 2010. She spoke of her personal growth demonstrated by her engagement in public advocacy activities where she aimed to challenge hatred that leads to community division, but also refers to the struggles she faces with flashbacks and survivor's guilt (Collier, 2016). Wilson reflected on how her public and private personas were often conflicting in the aftermath of the violence. Another example from a 7/7 victim John Tullock, whose injured face was prominently featured in print and television media without his permission in the aftermath of the bombing (see Photo 28.2). In addition to this experience with the media at the time of the attack, Tullock's phone was hacked by News of the World journalists in 2006 who sought to intercept messages by listening to his voicemail.

In the time since the 7/7 UK attacks, social media has taken on a hugely significant role in the media portrayal of terrorist attacks and the treatment of victims. Social media has been used by trolls (people who intentionally disrupt online communities) to harass victims and survivors of the Manchester bombings in 2018. Video footage of assassinations have been posted online by ISIS, for example in the case of US journalist James Foley. Facebook profiles have been hacked in the aftermath of attacks, as happened again after the Manchester arena bombing. Furthermore, violence has been live streamed as with the 2019 shootings in Christchurch, New Zealand (see also Chapter 18 'Social Media and Terrorism', and Case Study 18.1). On the other hand, social media has had a range of positive influences. We routinely see the utility of social media groups as a means of support for victims and survivors whether through campaigns (like flag overlays on Facebook profile pictures and check-in functions, see Case Study 28.2) or through the provision of fundraising opportunities. Social media also plays a role in providing a more private form of support, for example, enabling survivors to communicate via encripted chat, and staying in touch using private groups (such as survivors of the Leopold Café attacks in Mumbai, 2008; Ramsay and Anton, 2014).

However, in a report commissioned by Andy Burnham, Mayor of Greater Manchester, in the aftermath of the bombing of the Manchester Arena in 2018 (Kerslake, 2018), the media are criticized for their treatment of the victims and their families. The report points out that families of those killed and the injured were retraumatized by the traditional media's use of social media material from the night of the attack, but also content taken from the social media accounts of the children who were caught up in the violence. In addition, families complained of being harassed by journalists in the immediate aftermath of the attack, and some families describe covert attempts by journalists to capture photographs when they were receiving bad news about their loved ones. A similar situation arose in the aftermath of the Paris attacks of 2015, where graphic video footage taken inside the Bataclan Theatre recorded by hostages was widely shared initially via social media, but ultimately picked up and broadcast by media outlets.

Whether by traditional print and broadcast media, or via social media, one issue that repeatedly appears in the aftermath of terrorist violence is the co-option of a victim's identity for a cause they may not necessarily have supported. One example is that of Lee Rigby. Lee was an off-duty British soldier who was killed in South East London in 2013 by two Islamic extremists (see Case Study 18.2). Since his death, Lee Rigby's name and image has been used repeatedly against the wishes of his family to further the agenda of far-right politics in the UK and abroad. Because Lee was killed by Islamic extremists in the UK, Britain First, a fringe far-right political party, use Lee Rigby's name and image to promote their anti-immigrant Islamophobic messages. Lee Rigby's family have repeatedly pointed out that Lee did not share their racist views, and asked them not to use his name or face on their campaigns. Regardless they have continued to do so, to the point at which Lee Rigby's image is widely associated with the far right (Mortimer, 2016).

While media attention is a double-edged sword for victims, survivors and their families, the need and willingness to engage with the media shifts over time for those impacted by terrorist violence, and also varies across individuals. While media attention may be shunned by victims and their families in the aftermath of a violent attack, in the longer term, victims and survivors often seek out media attention to assist with fundraising for victims' needs, support for memorials, remembrance of those lost and injured or lobbying/political campaigns. However, once the initial attention has decreased in the immediate aftermath of an attack, save around anniversary periods, there tends to be little media attention devoted to the victims and survivors. This is reflected in a publication by the Radicalization Awareness Network, a European Commission organization that brings together practitioners and academics on issues of radicalization. The RAN produced a report that focuses on how victims' organizations can best work with the media to meet their communication needs and how the testimonies of victims can be used to capture the attention of media outlets. RAN also offers media training for victims and victims' groups as they navigate the process of engaging with the media.

28.5 CONCLUSION

Whether in Bagdad, Brussels, Belfast, or Islamabad, terrorism irrevocably alters the lives of its victims, the survivors, their families, and society at large. The victims and survivors of terrorism primarily experience a devastating personal tragedy, but their trauma is often a public and politicized suffering, and as a result their individual experience can only be understood by reference to the context in which it occurred. This chapter has highlighted the key issues of relevance when thinking about victims of terrorism and political violence and the relevance of victimological research for this field. Through examining how victims are perceived and represented and how cognitive strategies, such as the Just World

Hypothesis, and the notion of ideal victims influence these constructions, the complexity of the phenomenon becomes apparent.

Related to the cognitive strategies adopted in reaction to terrorist attacks, the notion of a hierarchy of victimhood was examined, and how the context to the violence was relevant, along with the characteristics of individual and social identity considerations. Importantly, we examined how differences between victims of one-off attacks, and victims of terrorism as part of an ongoing conflict, might be understood in terms of public perceptions of their suffering, notions of innocence, the legitimacy of any claims to victimhood, and the relevance of social identity as both a vehicle to support and deny public sympathy.

Finally we explored the issue of media coverage of terrorist attacks, specifically the experience of victims of terrorism within both traditional and social media. Understanding how victims are treated in the aftermath of attacks, as well as the implications the viral proliferation of images/video on social media have for victims and their families, is essential in order to protect those killed and injured in terrorist violence.

DISCUSSION QUESTIONS

1. What is the impact on society of intense ongoing media coverage in the aftermath of terrorist attacks?
2. How might a widespread fear of terrorism be addressed?
3. In the aftermath of a terrorist attack, when we as individuals reflect on our proximity to the event, our knowledge of the location, our last visit to that place, or the likelihood that we could have been there—what are the implications for how we think about terrorism?
4. If a human rights (as opposed to criminal justice) framework is used to inform victimology, are we all victims now?
5. Explore how media coverage of terrorism has impacted on your sense of safety. Have you changed your behaviour?

Visit the online resources for pointers on how to answer the discussion questions, links to useful web sources, and guidance on accessing databases:
www.oup.com/he/Wilson-Muro1e

GUIDE TO FURTHER READING

For a review of victimological theory, particularly critical approaches, see Walklate, S. (2017) (ed) *Handbook Victims and Victimology*. London: Routledge.

For an overview of the broader impact of terrorism on audiences separate to victims and survivors see Rubin, G. J., Brewin, C. R., Greenberg, N., Simpson, J., and Wessely, S. (2005) *Psychological and*

Behavioural Reactions to the Bombings in London on 7 July 2005: Cross Sectional Survey of a Representative Sample of Londoners, British Medical Journal, vol. 331(7517), 606.

For a case study in unacknowledged and complex victimhood in the case of an ongoing conflict see Peake, S. and Lynch, O. (2016) 'Victims of Irish Republican Paramilitary Violence—The Case of "The Disappeared"', *Terrorism and Political Violence,* vol. 28(3), 452–472.

For an account of the complexities of post-conflict issues related to terrorist campaigns see Moffett, L (2015) 'Reparations for "Guilty Victims": Navigating Complex Identities of Victim–Perpetrators in Reparation Mechanisms', *International Journal of Transitional Justice,* Volume 10(1), 146–167.

For an overview of the international field of victims of terrorism research see Argomaniz, J. and Lynch, O. (2017) *International Perspectives on Terrorist Victimisation.* London: Palgrave.

REFERENCES

Ajaka, N. (2015) 'Paris Beirut and the Language Used to Describe Terrorism', *The Atlantic* https://www.theatlantic.com/international/archive/2015/11/paris-beirut-media-coverage/416457/ (last accessed 6 August 2019).

Aguilar, P. and Koyras, I. (2019) 'Explaining Disappearances as a Tool of Political Terror', *International Political Science Review, 3* (3). https://doi.org/10.1177/0192512118764410

Barnard, A. (2015) 'Beirut, Also the Site of Deadly Attacks, Feels Forgotten', *The New York Times,* 15 November https://www.nytimes.com/2015/11/16/world/middleeast/beirut-lebanon-attacks-paris.html 15 November 2015

Butler, A., Panzer, A. M., and Goldfrank, L. R. (2003) *Preparing for the Psychological Consequences of Terrorism: A Public Health Strategy.* Washington, DC: National Academies Press.

Callimachi, R. (2015) 'ISIS Claim Responsibility Calling Paris attacks "First of the Storm"', *The New York Times* 14 Nov. https://www.nytimes.com/2015/11/15/world/europe/isis-claims-responsibility-for-paris-attacks-calling-them-miracles.html (last accessed 6 August 2019).

Christie N. (1986) 'The Ideal Victim', in Fattah, E. A. (eds.) *From Crime Policy to Victim Policy.* London: Palgrave Macmillan.

Collier, L. (2016) 'Growth After Trauma', *Monitor on Psychology, 47* (10): 48.

Curiel, P. R., Bishop, S. R. (2018) 'Fear of Crime: The Impact of Different Distributions of Victimisation', *Palgrave Commun, 4* (46). https://doi.org/10.1057/s41599-018-0094-8

Darby, J. (1997) 'Finding out More About Northern Ireland', in Darby, J. (1997) *Scorpions in a Bottle.* London: Minority Rights Publications.

Dillenburger, K. (2008) 'A Behaviour Analytic Perspective on Victimology', *The Journal of Behaviour Analysis of Offender and Victim Treatment and Prevention, 1* (1): 5–19.

El Sayed, El A. (2013) 'Images of Muslims in Western Scholarship and Media after 9/11', *Domes. Digest of Middle Eastern Studies, 22* (1): 39–56.

Faget, D. (2018) 'French Court Rejects Lawsuit by Victims of 2015 Paris Attacks', *France 24* 18 Aug. Available online at https://www.france24.com/en/20180718-french-court-rejects-lawsuit-victims-2015-paris-attacks-bataclan (last accessed 6 August 2019).

Ferguson, N., Burgess, M., and Hollywood, I. (2010) 'Who are the Victims? Victimhood Experiences in Post-agreement Northern Ireland', *Political Psychology, 31* (6): 857–886.

Gallop (2020) *Terrorism Trends A-Z.* Available online at https://news.gallup.com/poll/4909/terrorism-united-states.aspx (last accessed 3 March 2020).

Green, S. and Pemberton, A. (2018) 'The Impact of Crime: Victimisation, Harm and Resilience', in Walklate, S. *Handbook of Victims and Victimology.* London; Taylor and Francis: 77–102.

Gregory, J., de Lepinau, J., de Buyer, A., Delony, D., Mir, O., and Gaillard, R. (2019) 'The impact of the Paris terrorist attack on resident physicians', *BMC Psychiatry, 19* (79): 24– 31.

Greenslade, R. (2013) 'Northern Ireland stories are not covered by British National Newspapers', *The Guardian* 18 Oct. Available online at https://www.theguardian.com/media/greenslade/2013/oct/18/northernireland-derry (last accessed 19 March 2020).

Grossman, C. (1992) 'Disappearances in Honduras: The Need for Direct Victim Representation in Human Rights Litigation', *Hastings International & Comparative Law Review, 15* (2): 363.

Haner, M., Sloan, M. M., Cullen, F. T., Kulig, T. C. and Jonson, C. J. (2019) 'Public Concern about Terrorism: Fear, Worry, and Support for Anti-Muslim Policies', *Socius: Sociological Research for a Dynamic World*, 67 (12): 1–16.

Hersh, E. D. (2013) 'Long Term Effect of September 11 on the Political Behaviour of Victims' Families and Neighbors', 110 (52): 20959–20963.

Jankowitz, S. (2018) 'The "Hierarchy of Victims" in Northern Ireland: A Framework for Critical Analysis', *International Journal of Transitional Justice*, 12 (2): 216–236.

Kaiser, C. R., Vick, S. B., and Major, B. (2004) 'A Prospective Investigation of the Relationship Between Just World Beliefs and the Desire for Revenge after September 11, 2001', *Psychological Science*, 15 (7): 503–506.

Kerslake, B. (2018) *The Kerslake Report: An independent review into the Preparedness for and Emergency Response to the Manchester Arena Attack on the 22nd May 2017*. Published Report available online at www.kerslakereview.co.uk, (last accessed 6 August 2019).

Lambert, V. (2015) '7/7 survivor's guilt: It felt Taboo to Admit that the Attack Broke me', *The Telegraph Online Edition*. 11 July. Available online at https://www.telegraph.co.uk/news/uknews/terrorism-in-the-uk/11731785/77-survivors-guilt-It-felt-taboo-to-admit-that-the-attack-broke-me.html (last accessed 5 August 2019).

Lewis, J. A., Hamilton, J. C., and Elmore, J. D. (2019) 'Describing the Ideal Victim: A Linguistic Analysis of Victim Descriptions', *Current Psychology*, online edition. Available online at https://doi-org.ucc.idm.oclc.org/10.1007/s12144-019-00347-1

McEvoy, K and McConnachie, K. (2012) 'Victimology in Transitional Justice: Victimhood, Innocence and Hierarchy', *European Journal of Criminology*, 5: 527–538.

Mortimer, C. (2016) 'Lee Rigby's Family Condemn Britain First for Using his Murder in Party Political Broadcast', *The Independent*, 21 Apr. Available online at https://www.independent.co.uk/news/uk/politics/lee-rigby-britain-first-election-broadcast-bbc-itv-a6993911.html (last accessed 6 August 2019).

Newburn, T. (2017) *Criminology*. London; Routledge.

Peake, S. and Lynch, O. (2016) 'Victims of Irish Republican Paramilitary Violence—The Case of "The Disappeared"', *Terrorism and Political Violence*, 28 (3): 452–472.

Peterson, E. S. L. 'Vicarious Victimization', in Fisher, B. S. and Lab, S. P. (2010) *Encyclopaedia of Victimology and Crime Prevention*. **DOI:** http://dx.doi.org/10.4135/9781412979993.n327

Ramsay, G. and Anton, E. (2014) 'The use of Online Tools by Victims of Terrorism and Victims' Networks in the United Kingdom and Spain', in Lynch, O. and Argomaniz, J. *Victims of Terrorism. A Comparative and Interdisciplinary Study*. London: Routledge.

Reilly, J., Muldoon, O., and Byrne, C. (2004) 'Young Men as Victims and Perpetrators of Violence in Northern Ireland: A Qualitative Analysis', *Journal of Social Issues*, 60 (3): 469–484.

Rubin, A. and Peltier, E. (2018) 'After Grief and Defiance, Arts Help Process 2015 Paris Attacks', *The New York Times* 13 Nov. Available online at https://www.nytimes.com/2018/11/13/world/europe/paris-2015-attacks-bataclan-anniversary.html?auth=login-email&login=email (last accessed 6 August 2019).

Rubin, A. and Peltier, E. (2017) 'The Paris Attacks, 2 years later: Quiet Remembrance and lasting impact', *The New York Times* 13 Nov. https://www.nytimes.com/2017/11/13/world/europe/paris-november-2015.html / (last accessed 6 August 2019).

Schmid, A. P. (2012) 'Strengthening the Role of Victims and Incorporating Victims in Efforts to Counter Extremism and Terrorism'. Available online at https://www.icct.nl/download/file/ICCT-Schmid-Strengthening-the-Role-of-Victims-August-2012.pdf (last accessed 2 November 2020).

Schuster, M. A., Stein, B. D., Jaycox, L. H., Collins, R. L., Marshall, G. N., Elliott, M. N., Zhou, M. S., Kanouse, D. E., Morrison, J. L. and Berry, S. H. (2001) 'A National Survey of Stress Reactions After the September 11, 2001, Terrorist Attacks', *New England Journal of Medicine*, 345: 1507–1512.

Shapland, J. and Hall, M. (2007) 'What do we Know about the Effect of Crime on Victims?', *International Review of Victimology*, 14 (2): 175–217.

Shichor, D (2007) 'Thinking about terrorism and its victims', *Victims & Offenders An International Journal of Evidence-based Research, Policy, and Practice*, 2 (3): 269–287.

Silke, A. (2003) *Victims Terrorists and Society*. London: Wiley.

Zenko, M. (2012) 'America is a Safe Place'. Council on Foreign Relations. Available online at https://www.cfr.org/blog/america-safe-place. (last accessed 13 March 2020).

CHAPTER 29

The End of Terrorist Campaigns

AUDREY KURTH CRONIN

■ CHAPTER SUMMARY

Terrorist campaigns always end, even if those fighting against them have difficulty envisioning how. Over the past two centuries, terrorist campaigns have met their demise following six classic patterns that reappear across hundreds of cases, including: capturing or killing the leader, negotiations, achievement of the objective, failure, state repression, and reorientation to another type of violence. The most effective way to fight a terrorist group is to determine which of these patterns best fit a group, then build a strategy to nudge it in that direction. Without that kind of long-term thinking, counterterrorism gets caught in the action-reaction dynamic of terrorist campaigns, which is intentionally designed to anger policymakers, manipulate state behaviour, shock or inspire audiences, and draw strength to a group. Reactive, tactical counterterrorism prolongs the struggle and extends terrorist campaigns, sweeping outraged policymakers and their publics along with it. Understanding how terrorism ends is the best way, at any stage in a terrorist campaign, to craft effective counterterrorism policy, and to win.

29.1 INTRODUCTION

'Our war on terror begins with al-Qaeda, but it does not end there.

It will not end until every terrorist group of global reach has been found, stopped, and defeated.'

US President George W. Bush, 20 September 2001

Terrorism is a tactic of the weak designed to draw power from the strong. In the aftermath of a terrorist attack, public outrage drives powerful pressure on governments to act against the perpetrators. This is especially true in democracies, whose leaders are expected to protect the lives, livelihoods, and fundamental rights of their citizens. Outraged presidents and prime ministers respond to constituents who have lost loved ones or, more generally, who have forfeited their sense of security, economic stability, and national confidence. Popular anger builds formidable momentum during a terrorist campaign, compelling leaders into short-term responses to stay ahead of it. As a result, policymakers rarely take a strategic perspective to fighting this kind of shocking, publicized violence. More often they are drawn into the action/reaction cycle that actually perpetuates a terrorist campaign and undermines their citizens' best interests over time. The best way to avoid this trap is to understand how terrorist campaigns end, and then act in accordance with that goal. Effective counterterrorism strategies are built on an understanding of what happens during the final phase of campaigns, and why. Looking at how terrorist groups decline and end, comparatively across hundreds of cases, gives us insight into patterns of endings that recur throughout modern history, and it is a more promising way to build effective counterterrorism policies that nudge a group toward its demise.

Thinking about how terrorism ends is the best way to use a group's weaknesses against it, rather than let it exploit a target's weaknesses for their own ends. Counterterrorism is not like a team sport where more or less equal opponents meet on a court or playing field. Rather, it's closer to martial arts, where a weaker actor tries to defeat a stronger one by using tactics of leverage, such as striking at a key point of weakness or throwing an opponent off balance. Fortunately, it's extremely difficult for terrorist groups to act with that kind of concentrated precision, accuracy, and timing, consistently and effectively, every time.

In the aftermath of the 1984 bombing of the Grand Hotel in Brighton, United Kingdom, for example, the IRA released a familiar and oft-quoted statement, 'You have to be lucky all the time. We only have to be lucky once.' Yet over time that's not strictly true. To survive, terrorist groups must continue to attack in ways that are seen to be 'successful'. This means consistently carrying off operations that achieve a group's desired political effects, using publicity to sway a target audience, even as operatives must outrun the vastly superior resources states can muster to fight them (Shapiro, 2013). Most groups struggle to do that effectively, time after time, without tripping up.

Terrorists treacherously kill or harm innocent people and they must be stopped; but that does not mean they are achieving their aims. Terrorism usually fails (see also Chapter 19, 'Is Terrorism Effective?'). How difficult it is to keep a terrorist campaign going becomes apparent in the fact that most groups have short lifespans. According to Cronin, most groups only last an average of about eight years (Cronin, 2009: 75) (see also the more in-depth discussion on lifespan in Chapter 12). Yet on the other side, we'll explore in this chapter, very few governments succumb to terrorism. The days of terrorist campaigns are numbered, and the best way to stop them is to understand how terrorist campaigns end, then do everything in our power to bring that about—or at least to avoid making mistakes that prolong them.

This chapter first explains how we study the endings of terrorist campaigns in a rigorous way, then lays out six historical pathways that emerge from that analysis. The conclusion asserts that knowing how terrorism ends is essential to any effective counterterrorism strategy.

KEY CONCEPTS

Ending a Terrorist Campaign Terrorism is not a new phenomenon. As you know from reading Chapter 8, modern terrorism began in the late 19th century, and some forms of terrorism go back earlier—at least to the 1st century of the common era (e.g. the Sicarii of Ancient Rome). In short, symbolic acts of terrorist violence are nearly as old as recorded human history. Thus, when we speak of 'ending terrorism' or 'how terrorism ends' we do not mean that terrorism as a phenomenon will end—only specific campaigns.

What does it mean for a terrorist campaign to end? In the research from Cronin on hundreds of terrorist groups (2009), it means that a group has entered a ceasefire, renounced violence, entered government, or otherwise indicated a halt to terrorist activities, and has not carried out violence under its own name for at least three years. Terrorist groups are clandestine. With rare exceptions, they must make their presence known by acting if they are to retain members, have a degree of popular support, and be politically viable. This is one reason why the speech made by President Bush in the aftermath of the 11 September 2001 attacks (and quoted at the outset of this chapter) was problematic in its objective to defeat 'every terrorist group of global reach'. Such a generalized aim, eventually shortened to the phrase 'Global War on Terrorism,' set forth an end state that was impossible to achieve.

Having just watched 2,977 people killed in 9/11 on television, Americans and their allies were in a state of shock and anger: the President's sweeping rhetoric makes sense in light of this. But the historical record demonstrates that effective counterterrorism policy must be individually tailored to the challenges of each campaign. Especially in the 21st century, when virtually every terrorist group has some form of 'global reach', trying to end them all is not possible. It is more strategic to look carefully at individual groups, analyse what their strategies and weaknesses are, determine which pattern of ending that group is likely to follow, and devise specific policies that help bring it about. That is an achievable counterterrorism objective—one that has repeatedly paid off throughout the long history of terrorism.

29.2 SCOPE AND METHODS

To determine how most terrorist campaigns end, Cronin undertook an examination of 457 terrorist groups active in the modern era, and yielded lessons for counterterrorism that gradually came into focus across a range of different groups (2019). Before launching into the outcome of that work, however, we should clarify what exactly it covered (and did not cover), and why. Terrorism was defined as an act of violence against innocents that is always illegitimate—separate from the *motivation* for that act, which may or may not seem reasonable. Terrorists often feel they are acting in self-defence, or reciprocating an injustice, or taking the only avenue open to them; indeed, that is what leaders of terrorist groups regularly assert. But the people who die in terrorist attacks also have rights, most notably the right to stay alive. For the purpose of understanding how that violence ends, the important thing is that terrorists violate widely agreed legal and ethical norms by deliberately targeting noncombatants for symbolic purposes.

In addition, only nonstate actors are included in my study of how terrorism ends. State violence against civilians (a far more serious problem) has many powerful mechanisms under international law designed to control or censor it (such as the law of armed conflict, genocide conventions, international humanitarian law, and so forth). The same cannot be said for terrorism by actors who do not control a state government or its armed security forces. The distinction between states and nonstate actors is never black-and-white, because states can use terrorist proxies to engage in 'state-sponsored terrorism,' for example. Nothing in the study of international security, from 'war' to 'sovereignty' to 'terrorism,' is perfectly definable. But for the purposes of studying how this violence ends, nonstate actors are the focus here.

The aim was to understand what happened at the *group* level as a campaign wound down, not at the level of individual operatives. There is also a vast, rich literature about why individuals leave groups, but Cronin's question was slightly different (see Chapter 27 on disengagement). Cases in this large study of how terrorism ends were drawn mainly from an organization-based statistical database called the MIPT Terrorism Knowledge Base, which was later transferred to the National Consortium for the Study of Terrorism and Responses to Terrorism (START), a grant-supported research centre headquartered at the University of Maryland in College Park, Maryland, USA (see also Chapter 7). The online datasets, bibliographies, and other resources of START are excellent resources available to anyone doing research on terrorism (go to start.umd.edu).

Not being satisfied at the time with the relatively short time period covered by existing databases (1968+), Cronin also added earlier cases dating to the late 19th century, such as the Russian group Narodnaya Volya (People's Will), extreme Irish Nationalist groups (e.g. Clan na Gael, the Skirmishers), and a range of anarchist-inspired groups that wreaked havoc between about 1881 and 1934. Groups were driven by all types of political motivations and ideologies, including left-wing, right-wing, ethnonationalist-separatist and religious or 'spiritualist' terrorism—again, because the focus was not the specific motivation, but the symbolic act of violence. To summarize, in examining decades of modern experience with how terrorist campaigns end, the hundreds of groups in Cronin's study shared the following characteristics: each was a nonstate actor, had a political motivation, used symbolic violence aimed at an audience, and purposefully targeted noncombatants (Cronin, 2002/3).

29.3 HOW TERRORISM ENDS

What emerged from Cronin's comparative studying of all these groups were six general pathways out of terrorism that reappeared over and over across international cases: Decapitation, Negotiations, Success, Failure, Repression, and Reorientation (see Key Concepts box). The pathways were not mutually exclusive. A group could display more than one dynamic for ending—for example, engaging in negotiations at the same time members of the group were in-fighting. But as it declined and ended, each terrorist group demonstrated at least one (sometimes more) of these six patterns of decline and ending.

> **KEY CONCEPTS**
>
> The six patterns of decline and ending of terrorist groups:
>
> **Decapitation** Catching or killing the leader.
>
> **Negotiations** Transitioning toward a legitimate political process.
>
> **Success** Achieving the objective.
>
> **Failure** Imploding, provoking a backlash, or becoming marginalized.
>
> **Repression** Crushing a terrorist group with overwhelming force.
>
> **Reorientation** Transitioning to another form, such as a criminal syndicate, insurgency, or conventional army.

The first pathway was *decapitation*, meaning capturing or killing the leader—essentially dealing a blow to the terrorist group by eliminating its head. Particularly when a group has a charismatic leader, someone who has captured media attention by 'claiming' terrorist attacks for example, governments find it difficult to resist targeting them. Capturing and putting such a figure on trial can publicly delegitimize them, strengthening the state by fortifying the rule of law. Leaders of many groups have met that fate, including France's Action Directe, El Salvador's Fuerzas Populares de Liberación, Japan's Aum Shinrikyo, and

Peru's Sendero Luminoso (Shining Path). Delegitimizing a leader by capturing them helps to undermine their ability to gather followers or collect resources.

For example, in 1992 Shining Path's charismatic leader, Abimael Guzmán, was caught by Peruvian security forces dressed in striped pajamas and photographed in police custody behind a cage with iron bars, which was widely publicized in global media. According to the Peruvian Truth and Reconciliation Commission, some 69,000 people had died during Shining Path's campaign of violence (Comisión de la Verdad y Reconciliación Peru, 2003). The striking image of Guzmán, combined with his public statements asking followers to put down their arms, was crucial to the demise of the violent group.

Capturing a leader has other benefits, too. With careful military and police work, an effective apprehension can yield a storehouse of intelligence (as with Peru's Guzmán), force a leader to call off attacks (such as with the Real IRA's Mickey McKevitt), or deromanticize a cause, as with Indonesia's Nazir Abbas, who began criticizing jihadist violence after 2002 civilians died in the 2002 Bali bombing. Capturing a leader can also avoid creating a martyr, as happened with Che Guevara, who was shot by Bolivian forces and then immortalized. There are major risks, however: because it's easier to attack a leader from afar, counterterrorism personnel are often in much greater danger when trying to capture someone. In addition to this, a captured leader can direct followers from prison or even manipulate the media through the platform of a public trial. A leader's ability to attract an audience may not end with their capture.

CASE STUDY 29.1

Aum Shinrikyo

Shoko Asahara was the brutal, charismatic leader of Aum Shinrikyo ('Supreme Truth'), an apocalyptic group founded in Japan in 1984 (see Chapter 17, Photo 17.1). Asahara, who was blind, had tried to gain entrance to Tokyo University in the late 1970s but failed his university entrance examinations. Instead, he became a yoga instructor, opening a Tokyo school called Aum, Inc. There he espoused enlightenment and New Age spiritualist ideas to a growing following. Ultimately the group's ideology was a combination of Tibetan Buddhist, Hindu, Taoist, and Christian apocalyptic beliefs, all centred on Asahara.

Shoko Asahara founded his first monastic community in 1986, forcing new nuns and monks to sever familial ties and relinquish everything they owned. By 1987, he had renamed the movement Aum Shinrikyo. Asahara convincing followers he was both the Messiah and the first enlightened one since Buddha. He also preached that the apocalypse was imminent; therefore, Aum should precipitate its onset and ensure a Japanese-led, post-apocalyptic world order. Gradually, the driving purpose of the community evolved from saving the world, to saving only the enlightened members of Aum Shinrikyo (Danzig et al., 2012).

PHOTO 29.1 The attack on the Tokyo subway in March 1995 was an act of domestic terrorism by members of the cult movement Aum Shinrikyo.

At its peak, the movement had 40,000 members, drawn not just from Japan but also Australia, Germany, Russia, Sri Lanka, Taiwan, and the United States. Particularly notable was the presence of former Soviet scientists who had fled after the demise of the Soviet Union. The group specialized in using high-technology weapons, especially chemical and biological agents, to kill large numbers of civilians and cause popular chaos. They also allegedly wanted to build a nuclear weapon, buying property in Western Australia in order to mine for uranium (Kaplan and Marshall, 1996: 127; Danzig et al., 2012: 50–51, n99). But they are best known for the March 1995 attack on the Tokyo subway with the chemical nerve agent sarin, in which 12 people died and some 5,500 were injured (see Photo 29.1). The sarin attack was the outcome of years of effort in well-funded, advanced laboratories, testing, developing, or using anthrax (B. anthracis), VX nerve gas, chlorine gas, and hydrogen cyanide.

During Aum Shinrikyo's experimentation, the Japanese police were slow to respond to the threat. This was partly because the post-World War II Japanese constitution placed restrictions on police powers, including surveillance, but also because the security services, lacking expertise in the manufacturing of chemical and biological weapons, failed to recognize clues (Jones and Libicki, 2008: 49–52). Aum Shinrikyo was testing out biological weapons for years, including the 1990 spraying of botulism (clostridium botulinum) at two US Naval bases, Narita airport, the National Diet building in Japan, the Tokyo Imperial Palace, and the headquarters of a rival religious group.

Asahara was arrested in May 1995 and put on trial beginning in April 1996. An eight-year spectacle followed, with state-appointed defence lawyers arguing that he was not responsible for what his followers had done, and the defendant refusing to talk. Victims and their relatives became frustrated by the drawn-out process, but it ultimately resulted in death sentences for Asahara and other senior Aum leaders in 2004. In 2018, after exhausting all appeals, seven members of Aum Shinrikyo, including Shoko Asahara, were executed by hanging. As of 2019, the organization had renamed itself Aleph, apologized to victims, and was under court order to pay 1 billion Japanese yen (about $90 million) in reparations to sarin attack victims (Osumi, Japan Times, 2019).

QUESTIONS

1. Do you think the arrest, trial, and execution of Shoko Asahara was the right way to deal with the menace of Aum Shinrikyo?
2. What challenges do democratic governments face in balancing police powers against public safety in domestic counterterrorism?

Governments often prefer to target and kill terrorist leaders instead of capturing them. Killing leaders can be easier than trying to imprison them and gain a conviction through the legal system. If a terrorist attack is imminent, killing the leader may be the only responsible action for a government to take, as their top priority is to protect citizens from harm. Under these circumstances, the attack can be framed as legitimate self-defence under international law (though, the question then shifts to defining what 'imminent' means). Domestic public opinion often supports lethal action. In the aftermath of devastating terrorist attacks, constituents seek vengeance, and for some, a quick execution without trial is justice being served. All these factors drive governments toward assassination of terrorist leaders, a controversial counterterrorism tactic that has dramatically increased among democracies in the past ten years.

Historically, cases of assassination have included the Philippines' counterterrorism efforts against Abu Sayyaf, Russia's campaign against Chechen separatist leaders, and Israel's long-standing practice of targeted killings against Palestinian leaders. But there have been more recent cases too. On 2 May 2011, operating out of Afghanistan, US Special Operations forces (in this case, Navy Sea Air and Land forces, or 'SEALs') carried out a joint CIA-led raid against Osama bin Laden's compound in Abbottabad, Pakistan, killing him and burying his body at sea. Eight years later, during a capture attempt in Idlib province, Syria, on 27 October 2019, Abu Bakr al-Baghdadi, leader ISIS, died by self-detonating a suicide vest after American special forces trapped him in a tunnel.

The US drone campaigns involving attacking members of violent jihadist groups in places like Pakistan and Yemen, using remote-controlled aerial vehicles (UAVs or drones), along with on-the-ground Special Operations Forces, are among the largest ongoing experiments in decapitation of terrorist groups ever attempted (Byman, 2013; Cronin, 2013). The US Barack Obama administration (2009–2017) relied on drone strikes as a key element of their counterterrorism policy against al-Qaeda, executing some 353 strikes in Pakistan and 184 in Yemen, the drone campaign peaking in 2010. Following this, the Donald Trump administration (from 2017 to 2021) similarly increased drone attacks in Yemen and Somalia (New America, 2019).

But our question is when does decapitation *end* terrorist campaigns? Looking comparatively across hundreds of terrorist groups, Cronin found that publicly delegitimizing a leader in the eyes of their followers or potential supporters—by parading them before the media or forcing them to publicly denounce the cause, for example—was strategically more effective in ending a group than killing them, because it undermined support for a cause and had enduring political effects that helped end campaigns (2009). Groups that successfully ended through assassination, on the other hand, were hierarchically structured, characterized by a cult of personality, younger than most other groups (e.g. only two or three years old rather than eight years or more), and lacking a clear leadership succession plan. Al-Qaeda does not fit these conditions, which is one reason it did not end after US Special Forces killed bin Laden in his Abbottabad compound in May 2011. And it is also unlikely that ISIS will end this way, as al-Baghdadi was the third leader of the group (following Ayman al-Zarqawi and Abu Umar al-Baghdadi) and, although events continue to evolve at the time of writing, it appears that a successor leader for ISIS (Abu Ibrahim al-Hashimi al-Qurayshi) is already in place.

A second pathway out of terrorism is **negotiations**. Many governments—in Britain, Israel, Russia, Turkey, the United States, and elsewhere—claim that they don't negotiate with terrorist groups at all, but that is usually untrue and, indeed, it would be irresponsible if it were the case. Negotiations happen on many different levels, from the most public meetings between group leaders and senior government officials (extremely rare) to more informal contacts between clandestine intelligence operatives, or even non-government proxies, on the one hand, and terrorist group members on the other (fairly common). Politicians and policymakers often worry that negotiating with terrorists legitimizes the tactic; but negotiations can also be very effective at de-legitimizing terrorism by demonstrating that a group does not, as it claims, lack better avenues for addressing their grievances (Roberts, 2005). From a government's perspective, they are also both an excellent means of intelligence-gathering, and a way to shift the energy of a group into another channel.

Yet, talks rarely lead to the demise of groups strictly on their own, plus negotiating can be risky from the perspective of both the status quo side and the group. That helps explain why, in Cronin's research on how terrorism ends, only about 18 per cent of the hundreds of groups studied negotiated (Cronin, 2009: 214). Remember that this study included a wide range of terrorist groups, such as very small cells like the German Baader-Meinhof group, or the American Symbionese Liberation Army, which each had a short, violent run and ended differently (Powell, 2015). Those terrorist organizations who entered talks tended to be older and more established, with a longer lifespan (20–25 years) compared to the average group (whose age was about eight years). A 'mutually hurting stalemate,' in which both sides are locked in an ongoing painful conflict that neither can escalate toward victory, is an incubator of negotiations between adversaries. They make a cost-benefit decision that talking is better than continuing the current track (Zartman, 1985). Once talks have started, they tend to persist: only about 10 per cent of those who negotiated gave up on the talks altogether and walked away. The predominant pattern is for talks to drag on, neither succeeding nor failing completely, sometimes joined by another failure dynamic like group internal in-fighting or state repression, and gradually combining to end a group.

Talks are never an immediate cure-all. The best scenarios for ending campaigns are where governments are firm, patient, and persistent in their negotiating. A wide range of organizations such as Basque Separatists (Euskadi Ta Askatasuna or ETA) in Spain, the IRA in Northern Ireland, the Moro Islamic Liberation Front (MILF) in the Philippines, the 19th of April Movement (M-19) and Revolutionary Armed Forces (Fuerzas Armadas Revolucionarias de Colombia, or FARC) in Colombia, and the National Revolutionary Unity (URNG) in Guatemala, have either reduced their violence or ended it altogether in the wake of negotiations. But sometimes the violence actually increases as the talks are underway. Splinter groups may broadcast their dissent by increasing attacks, as was the case in 1998 with the Real IRA's bombing in Omagh during the Good Friday talks. Or governments may lose patience and default to military force, as happened with the lethal Liberation Tigers of Tamil Eelam (LTTE or 'Tamil Tigers'), who were in a Norwegian-brokered peace process for four years (2002–2006) with the Sri Lankan government, then attacked by the Sri Lankan Army (2008–2009). The military offensive tragically killed tens of thousands of Tamil civilians.

Sometimes terrorist campaigns end because they **succeed**. Achieving a political objective, then folding is a third historical pathway toward the end. This is always a sensitive topic, since this type of illegitimate violence against civilians offends common decency and surely deserves to fail. However, success is extremely rare: of the 457 groups studied in depth in *How Terrorism Ends*, across the globe and throughout the decades, only about 5 per cent had by their own standards achieved their objectives. RAND scholars Seth Jones and Martin Libicki found a similar result (4 per cent) (Jones and Libicki, 2008). Political scientist Max Abrahms, examining a much smaller sample of longer-lived groups (28 groups on the US State Department's Foreign Terrorist Organizations list), found terrorism's effectiveness to be less than 10 per cent (Abrahms, 2006). The key point is that numerous scholars have found the success rate of terrorist campaigns to be very low. Terrorism is not a promising enterprise.

Here it's important to distinguish between short-term tactical objectives, such as showing strength or ruthlessness, giving attention to leaders, publicizing the cause, exacting revenge, signaling resolve, or just surviving and threatening people on the one hand, and long-term strategic objectives, which are altruistic-sounding goals that terrorist leaders themselves declare to be the driving purpose for their violence. Strategic goals are extremely difficult to achieve. They may be political, relating to the state—its regime, organization, boundaries, population, economic (redistributing resources or wealth), social (racial or ethnic identity, modernization) or religious (relating to spiritualist identity, values, strictures, virtues), or some combination of these. And reaching ambitious strategic goals cannot be accomplished by a group alone. It requires major counterterrorism policy blunders by the state, such as failing to offer a viable political alternative or taking heavy-handed government actions that drive public support to the group, for example.

Groups that succeed in their strategic political objectives by using terrorism are the exception, not the rule; but a few do so. Two well-known cases are Umkhonto, the military wing of the African National Congress, which reached its political objective when apartheid ended in South Africa; and Irgun Zvai Le'umi (IZL or 'Irgun' for short), which succeeded with the British withdrawal and the establishment of the state of Israel in 1948 (Guelke et al., 2006; Zadka, 1995). When violent groups succeed, individuals who transition into governing roles always distance themselves from acts of terrorism, either by keeping the most violent operatives out of power or by rewriting the history of what they themselves did (Begin, 1997). Even successful former terrorist leaders realize that terrorist tactics are illegitimate and must be disavowed.

The fourth pattern of ending is *failure*. Many groups fail either through implosion, meaning they burn out or collapse in upon themselves; or marginalization through loss of popular support, meaning groups forfeit necessary resources or community protection they need to operate clandestinely. Failure through one of these two big sub-categories—implosion or marginalization—is the most common way that terrorism ends.

Implosion can take many forms. A group may fail to survive across generations, when the first wave of operatives becomes too old to continue the struggle, and no one can replace them. This happened with left-wing groups during the late 1960s and 1970s, such as the Weather Underground and the Symbionese Liberation Army, for example, and with right-wing groups in the 1990s, such as the British neo-Nazi group Combat-18. In-fighting undermines many groups, especially disagreements about ideology or membership—for example, the Japanese group Aum Shinrikyo, the West German Second of June Movement and, again, the British Combat-18 killed their own members who were suspected of disloyalty. Groups may break down into factions, weakening the overall movement, as with the many Palestinian offshoots of the Palestinian Liberation Organization (PFLP, PFLP-GC, DFLP, etc.). Or they can argue over operations, as did the Baader-Meinhof group in Germany. Or they can lose operational control over actions in their name, as happened with the Weather Underground in the United States, and the Ulster Volunteer Force in Northern Ireland. Such errors may indirectly result from counterterrorism pressure; but they all rot a group from within.

Marginalization begins outside the group, losing popular support in the community it is trying either to attract, intimidate, or at least keep minimally tolerant so there is somewhere to hide. There are lots of reasons why popular support may be lost. The group may have lost contact with 'the people,' meaning its goals do not align with what its purported community desires, usually because group members are on the run, and become increasingly extreme in their views. The Italian Red Brigades, German Red Army Faction, and the Japanese Red Army fit this pattern. Sometimes a group becomes so violent it loses contact with reality. In the 1990s, the horrifically vicious GIA in Algeria killed thousands of civilians who might otherwise have been its natural constituency. A government may offer alternatives to what the terrorist group is peddling, such as increased spending, more jobs, land reforms, or specific political concessions that undermine a group's claim to deliver a better future—an important factor in for the IRA during the Troubles in Northern Ireland during the late 1990s. Or a group may lose its sense of ideological relevance, as happened with Marxist groups such as the Spanish First of October Anti-Fascist Resistance Groups (Grupos de Resistencia Antifascista Primero de Octubre, or GRAPO) and the Greek Revolutionary Organization 17 November (17N) following the reunification of Germany and the end of the Soviet Union.

But the most typical, rapid route to a terrorist group's failure is targeting errors that cause backlash among the group's actual or potential public constituency. When a group attacks a target that a wide range of its actual or potential supporters consider illegitimate, that deadly mistake undercuts the group, and transfers public support to the government's response. The history of modern terrorism is replete with examples of groups that set themselves back, or even committed organizational suicide, by making such high-profile mistakes. The 1978 killing of Aldo Moro, who had been a popular Italian politician, repulsed even his political enemies and reversed the upward trajectory of the Red Brigades. The Islamist group al-Gama'a al-Islamiyya (or GAI) in November 1997 killed 62 tourists in Luxor Egypt (see Photo 6.2. Also the site of the Egyptian pyramids), harmed the Egyptian economy, outraged public opinion, and turned the tide of Islamist terrorism in Egypt (Wright, 2006). The Real IRA, which split from the Provisional IRA over the Good Friday talks, in 1998 bombed the small market town of Omagh, killing 29 people (including nine children, most of whom were on a school field trip). The funeral drew both Northern Irish Catholics and Protestants together in outrage, and shortly thereafter RIRA went into sharp decline. Other examples of targeting errors and backlash include the Quebec Liberation Front (Front de Libération du Québec, FLQ, 1963–1971), whose support faded after kidnappings and murders of government ministers in Canada (1970); and Sikh separatists (1981–1995), whose own community turned against them after they killed tens of thousands of people in India (Cronin, 2009: 111).

Al-Qaeda leaders were keenly aware of this problem. Zawahiri more than once argued that the primary battlefield for the movement was in the media, where al-Qaeda had to fight for the support of the Muslim community (or *umma*), which was al-Qaeda's primary objective. Yet between February 1993 and June 2007, at least 40 per cent of the victims of terrorist attacks by al-Qaeda were Muslims, the very people Osama bin Laden and Ayman Zawahiri claimed to serve (Cronin, 2008: 85). By 2013, public support for al-Qaeda was only 13 per cent among Muslims in eleven countries surveyed, while 57 per cent had an unfavourable opinion of the group. In face-to-face interviews with almost 9,000 Muslims conducted by the Pew Research Center, the lowest public support appeared in countries where al-Qaeda or its affiliates were very active: between 2010 and 2013, support in

Nigeria fell by 40 per cent following increased terrorist activity by Boko Haram, for example. Those who lived in countries that had experienced suicide attacks were most likely to condemn them: by 2013, a tiny fraction of Muslims in Pakistan (3 per cent), Indonesia (6 per cent), Nigeria (8 per cent), and Jordan (12 per cent) believed that suicide bombings were often or sometimes justified to defend Islam from its enemies (Poushter, Pew Research Center, 2014).

Long before bin Laden was killed, al-Qaeda had been seriously damaged by its own mistakes, especially killing fellow Muslims, and it was failing to meet its publicly declared aim of mobilizing the community (*umma*) behind its leadership.

However, states cannot merely sit back and wait for groups to end through their own mistakes, because they can kill a lot of innocent people along the way. Instead, effective counterterrorism policy should be designed to take advantage of the operational errors groups nearly always make, drawing attention in the aftermath of tragedy to the human toll terrorist violence takes in the very communities that groups claim they are trying to protect.

A fifth pathway of ending terrorist campaigns is **repression**, meaning state governments using overwhelming armed force to crush a group. This is an instinctive reaction in the aftermath of a major terrorist attack and often the first thing policymakers think to do. Terrorism is a threat to the sinews of the modern nation-state, which bases its legitimacy on the protection of its citizens. Overwhelming force can be deployed internally, as in greatly expanded police powers, or externally, as with military intervention across borders. Notable cases of successful repression include Egypt and the Muslim Brotherhood (1928–1966), and Uruguay's response to the Tupamaros terrorist campaign (Movimiento de Liberación Nacional-Tupamaros, 1968–73). A most dramatic recent case of repression was Russia's 1999 response to Chechen terrorism, in which military forces bombed the city of Grozny to rubble (1999–2000), and killed or displaced virtually the entire Chechen population. Indiscriminate use of state military force is a violation of international law. But if all you want to do is end terrorist attacks within a defined territory, at whatever cost, history and examples such as this demonstrate that it is certainly possible to do so.

The problem is that repression often exports the cause to another place (as with Chechnya and Ingushetia, for example) or mutates it into a new form (as with Egypt and the origins of al-Qaeda). Domestic repression is especially difficult for democracies because it requires 'profiling' of targets, tramples on civil liberties and human rights, tears at the domestic fabric of the state and, by alienating citizens, weakens a government's ability to anticipate future terrorist campaigns. Especially in an age of globalized communications, such overwhelming state action can worsen the terrorist threat over time, by polarizing populations at home, and inspiring additional attacks directed at exploiting domestic divisions. If a state's use of force undermines its own legitimacy, it can open new avenues of surprise attack by those who have lost relatives or otherwise suffered injustice.

CASE STUDY 29.2

Russia's Repression of Chechnya

When the Soviet Union broke up at the end of the Cold War, it was not at all clear what the boundaries of post-Soviet Russia should be. A rapid remaking of the map occurred, with former Soviet subjects such as Lithuania (1990), Estonia (1991), Latvia (1991), Ukraine (1991), Belorussia (1991), Moldova (1991), Uzbekistan (1991), and Kazakhstan (1991) all gaining their independence. The world welcomed the self determination of these new states; but Russia had lost much of its land mass and was reluctant to lose more.

In November 1991, when the Chechens decided to elect their first leader, Dzokhar Dudayev (a former Soviet Air Force general), his first act was to declare Chechnya an independent state too. The Russian government would not stand for it. In 1994, Russian President Boris Yeltsin sent poorly-trained and equipped Russian forces into Chechnya, where they were met by widespread resistance from both Chechen guerrilla fighters and civilians. Casualty figures are disputed, but somewhere from 5,500 to 14,000 Russian troops died. The toll on Chechen civilians was worse, however, with upwards of 50,000 killed, and about a third of the population displaced. The first war in Chechnya was a disaster for both sides.

Just as Russia seemed to be prevailing on the battlefield, the Chechens shifted their tactics to hostage-taking and terrorism. In 1995, Chechen rebel leader Shamil Basayev took 1,200 civilians hostage in a hospital in the Russian city of Budennovsk, one hundred miles north of Chechnya. When the Russians refused to negotiate for the hostages' release, Basayev ordered executions. More than 100 people ultimately died, both in the hostage crisis and in the crossfire when the Russians stormed the town.

Ultimately the Russian government relented and gave Basayev and his fighters safe passage back to Chechnya. But the Chechens had crossed a line at Buddenovsk, showing they were willing to engage in terrorism against Russian civilians. A series of Chechen bombings against trains, train stations, subways, and trolleys continued in places like Moscow, Volgograd, and Trubnya followed. Under pressure, and damaged from a humiliating unpopular military intervention, Yeltsin signed the 1996 Kasavyurt Accords, withdrew Russian troops, and agreed to a 2001 referendum on the future of Chechnya.

The second war in Chechnya started after 1999 incursions by Chechen fighters led by Basayev into neighbouring Dagestan, ostensibly to establish an Islamic republic there. Then a series of bombings of apartment houses in Moscow and Vologodonsk were blamed on Chechen terrorists (although there is ambiguity about whether Russian security forces were involved). The bombs killed nearly 300 people and galvanized Russian public opinion: President Vladimir Putin was elected in part on a campaign promise to 'wipe out' Chechens 'in the outhouse'.

President Putin framed the second intervention as a war against terrorism. Russian military tactics differed markedly from the first war, with better tactics, planning, and intelligence, as well as strict control over media reports. By early 2000, the Russians were occupying most of Chechnya, and Chechen forces were pushed into the mountainous highlands and over the border with Georgia. Again, the Chechens switched to terrorist tactics away from the battlefield (see Photo 29.2).

PHOTO 29.2 January 2000. Russian army troops try to keep warm between fighting Chechen rebels in Gudermes, Chechnya.

On 23 October 2002, they seized the Dubrovka Theatre in Moscow, taking 800 civilians as hostages for three days. The storming of the theatre by Russian special forces killed all 49 Chechens but also 129 civilians, who died of asphyxiation when an anesthetic gas was used to incapacitate everyone. The Dubrovka incident was followed by a quickening pace of terrorist attacks on Russian territory, culminating in the killing of more than 330 people, most of them schoolchildren, in Beslan, North Ossetia, on 3 September 2004.

Chechen terrorist attacks removed all restraints on Russian repression. In the second war, the Russians bombed the Chechen capital, Grozny, and engaged in indiscriminate attacks, forcing virtually all Chechen civilians to flee to neighbouring territories such as Dagestan and Ingushetia, where unrest continues. This demonstrates how if all states want to do is end terrorism within a particular territory, at any cost, you can achieve this with overwhelming military force.

QUESTIONS

1. Was Russia's use of indiscriminate military force in Chechnya justified?
2. How can states maintain the legitimacy of their use of force if they indiscriminately kill civilians in the same way that terrorist groups do?

The last pattern of ending terrorist campaigns is **reorientation**, meaning a group changes its methods, and transitions out of terrorism to something else. This can happen in two directions. Groups can transition away from primarily pursuing political goals and strictly focus on enriching themselves. Criminality and terrorism are not (and have never been) distinct—many groups use criminal activities to fund their terrorist agenda in what some people call the 'crime-terror nexus'. A great many jihadist groups in the Sahel region sustain themselves through lucrative criminal activity, for example. And often former criminals join terrorist groups, or are radicalized in prison, as is common in ISIS. Distinguishing between 'terrorism' and 'criminality' is not as simple as deciding whether someone follows either 'ideology' or 'profit' (Basra, Neumann, and Bruner, 2016).

The best way is to consider the phenomenon to be along a spectrum, with purely political objectives on one end and purely financial motivations on the other. This kind of reorientation happens when a group's central driving purpose moves along the spectrum, from political to financial, and its behaviour shifts accordingly. Examples of groups that have undergone this kind of transition include Abu Sayyaf in the Philippines, the Kosovo Liberation Army, and splinter groups of the IRA such as the New IRA in Northern Ireland. Most criminal groups do not aim to change or destroy governments, since having minimally operating state institutions (led by corrupt officials who might even be on a group's payroll) enables their operations. Plus, they have no interest in governing. Fighting criminal groups requires global cooperation, shared intelligence, and strong legal frameworks, and it is a long-term undertaking that must be led by law enforcement.

The other direction of reorientation is toward more traditional types of military organizations, when a terrorist group gains enough strength to escalate to a full insurgency or even conventional war. Organizations that have successfully transitioned into insurgencies in the past include the Cambodian Khmer Rouge, the Naxalites in India, the LTTE, and the Communist Party of Nepal-Maoists. At their height (~2000–2006), violent factions in Colombia also fit this description, including the Revolutionary Armed Forces of Colombia (Fuerzas Armadas Revolucionarias de Colombia, or FARC), the National Liberation Army (ELN), and the United Self-Defence Forces of Colombia (AUC). Insurgencies threaten state control and may evolve into civil wars.

Most terrorist groups *aspire* to be insurgencies. Insurgencies are more powerful than terrorist groups because an insurgency can hold territory, operating as a military organization, and engaging military forces. They are typically larger than terrorist groups, as well, with membership numbering in the tens of thousands rather than the dozens or hundreds. When a group gains enough strength to operate as a military unit and directly target the forces of a government, it no longer operates within a counterterrorism framework and must be met with a more traditional military response.

This kind of reorientation is always negative for the existing state, as insurgency is a more legitimate form of warfare and a much more serious threat than terrorism, which is always an illegitimate act of violence that often backfires. It is also notable that the rate at which insurgencies have been winning against state opponents has increased in recent decades: for example, one rigorous study that used data from the Correlates of War project (first created in 1963 by political scientist J. David Singer and historian Melvin Small), found that guerrilla factions, insurgencies, and civil war forces won 34.9 per cent of the time against states before 1949, and 55 per cent of the time after 1950 (Arreguin-Toft, 2001).

The most recent, prominent example of this kind of reorientation is ISIS, an entity that successfully transitioned from terrorist group (al-Qaeda in Iraq or AQI) to insurgency (ISIS), to conventional armed force controlled by the so-called Islamic State at the height of its Caliphate (2014–19). At its height in 2014, ISIS had some 30,000 fighters, held territory in both Iraq and Syria, boasted extensive conventional military capability, controlled lines of communication, had extensive infrastructure, governed a local population, and engaged in sophisticated operations targeting traditional military forces.

ISIS emerged from Sunni extremist groups fighting the 2003 US invasion of Iraq, grew with the alienation of Iraqi Sunnis by the Shi'a-dominated Maliki government after US withdrawal, and grabbed the opportunity of the outbreak of the Syrian civil war. Combining with disaffected members Iraqi Sunni tribal leaders, former anti-US insurgents, and former Iraqi military officers, they engaged in a dramatic conquest of much of Iraq in the summer of 2014. By this point, ISIS was clearly no longer just a terrorist group. The government of Iraq and its allies, especially the United States, had no alternative but to fight the so-called Islamic State with conventional military force, to drive it back first toward being an insurgency, and then a transnational terrorist group—which is what it is again now (Cronin, 2015).

Since 2014, ISIS has been seriously degraded, having lost its territory and much of its propaganda capability, although it continues to carry out terrorist attacks within the region, especially in Iraq. Going forward, ISIS-inspired attacks in the United States and, much more seriously, in Europe may continue as trained foreign fighters return. We can only hope that these types of assaults peaked with the November 2015 attacks in Paris (130 killed), the March 2016 bombing of the Brussels airport and metro (32 killed), and the May 2017 bombing of the Ariana Grande concert in Manchester (22 killed), which were all executed as the group was being pummelled in Iraq and Syria.

With ISIS driven out of its Caliphate and militarily defeated, there is no question they have been in serious decline, not least because there is a contrast between the group's raucous claims, and the reality on the ground. Going forward, however, the key question will be whether or not some 130,000 former Islamic State fighters and family members who are held in camps across northern Syria will create the next generation of ISIS, especially since there seems to be no viable plan for either reintegrating them into their native countries, or building humane living standards where they are. This is the kind of counterterrorism mistake that *prevents* groups from failing and ending.

29.4 CONCLUSION

The long history of terrorism demonstrates that this form of violence is not a promising way to achieve an objective. Terrorist groups meet their demise in consistent ways. During a terrorist campaign, policymakers should move beyond asking 'When will the next attack be?' and arrive at the question 'How will it end?' The crucial challenge before them is to determine which of the patterns of endings best fit a given group, then work with that process as it unfolds, steadily pushing the group further in that direction by crafting intelligent counterterrorism policy.

Policymakers who become caught up in the short-term goals, emotions, and spectacle of terrorist attacks relinquish the broader historical perspective that is crucial to the reassertion of state power and legitimacy, a mistake that terrorism's symbolic violence is consciously designed to exploit. It requires foresight and steady leadership to stay the course through to the end of a terrorist campaign, but it can be done.

DISCUSSION QUESTIONS

1. Consider a terrorist group that you know about or are interested in. Which of these six pathways is most likely to lead to its demise?
2. Do you think current counterterrorism policy is effectively driving that terrorist group toward its end?
3. What kinds of counterterrorism mistakes extend the lives of terrorist groups?
4. How are new forms of communications technology such as live-streaming or social media affecting the lifespans of terrorist groups?
5. When an individual engages in terrorism because they are 'inspired' by a group but has no logistical connection to it, does this make it more difficult to end a campaign?

 Visit the online resources for pointers on how to answer the discussion questions, links to useful web sources, and guidance on accessing databases: www.oup.com/he/Wilson-Muro1e

GUIDE TO FURTHER READING

Crenshaw, M. (1991) 'How Terrorism Declines', *Terrorism and Political Violence* 3/1: 69–87. *Crenshaw wrote the first article exploring this topic. It is a classic.*

Cronin, A. K. (2009) *How Terrorism Ends: Understanding the Decline and Demise of Terrorism Campaigns.* Princeton, NJ: Princeton University Press. *The first full study published on how terrorism ends,* expanding on an article published in 2006. Scholars then adapted this approach to explore other types of nonstate violence (e.g. how insurgencies end, how civil wars end) or to focus on individual pathways (decapitation, repression, negotiations, etc.).

Hoffman, B. (2017) *Inside Terrorism*, 3rd edition. New York: Columbia University Press. *This is an accessible overview of the concept of terrorism.*

National Consortium for the Study of Terrorism and Responses to Terrorism (START), at start.umd.edu. *The website is a rich repository of articles, reports, Bibliographies and databases, including the Global Terrorism Database (GTD).*

Pew Research Center, Project on Global Attitudes and Trends; at pewresearch.org. *This project includes data drawn from Muslim-majority countries, offering insight into changing views of terrorism, suicide attacks, Osama bin Laden, al-Qaeda, and other Islamist terrorism-related questions.*

REFERENCES

Abrahms, M. (2006) 'Why Terrorism Does Not Work', *International Security*, 31 (2): 42–78.

Arreguin-Toft, I. (2001) 'How the Weak Win Wars: A Theory of Asymmetric Conflict', *International Security*, 26 (1): 93–128.

Begin, M. (1997) *The Revolt*. New York: Nash.

Byman, D. (2013) 'Why Drones Work', *Foreign Affairs*, July/August: 32–43.

Comisión de la Verdad y Reconciliación Peru (2003) *Informe Final*, Vol. 1, Part 1: *El Proceso, los hechos, las víctimas*. Lima: Navarrete.

Cronin, A. K. (2002/3), 'Behind the Curve: Globalization and International Terrorism', *International Security*, 27 (3): 30–58.

Cronin, A. K. (2008) *Ending Terrorism: Lessons for Defeating Al Qaeda*. International Institute for Strategic Studies Adelphi Paper #394. London: Routledge.

Cronin, A. K. (2009) *How Terrorism Ends: Understanding the Decline and Demise of Terrorist Campaigns*. Princeton, New Jersey: Princeton University Press.

Cronin, A. K. (2015) 'ISIS Is Not a Terrorist Group: Why Counterterrorism Won't Stop the Latest Jihadist Threat', *Foreign Affairs*, March/April: 87–98.

Cronin, A. K. (2013) 'Why Drones Fail', *Foreign Affairs*, July/August: 44–54.

Danzig, R., Sageman, M., Leighton, T., Hough, L., Yuki, H., Kotani, R., and Hosford, Z. (2012) *Aum Shinrikyo: Insights Into How Terrorists Develop Chemical and Biological Weapons*, 2nd edition. Washington, DC: The Center for a New American Security.

Guelke, A., Cox, M., and Stephen, F. (2006) *A Farewell to Arms? Beyond the Good Friday Agreement*. Manchester, UK: Manchester University Press.

Jones, S. G. and Libicki, M. C. (2008) *How Terrorist Groups End: Lessons for Countering Al Qaida*. Santa Monica, CA: RAND Corp.

Kaplan, D. E. and Marshall, A. (1996) *The Cult at the End of the World: The Terrifying Story of the Aum Doomsday Cult, from the Subways of Tokyo to the Nuclear Arsenals of Russia*. New York: Crown.

Osumi, M. (2019) 'Tokyo Court Orders Aum Shinrikyo cult successor Aleph to pay ¥1 billion to victims of sarin attack', *Japan Times*, 10 April 2019; at https://www.japantimes.co.jp/news/2019/04/10/national/crime-legal/tokyo-court-orders-aum-shinrikyo-cult-successor-aleph-pay-%C2%A51-billion-victims-sarin-attack/#.XfaPrNZKiis.

Poushter, J. (2014) 'Support for Al Qaeda was low Before (and after) Osama bin Laden's death', *Pew Research Center*; at https://www.pewresearch.org/fact-tank/2014/05/02/support-for-Al-Qaeda-was-low-before-and-after-osama-bin-ladens-death/.

Powell, J. (2015) *Terrorists at the Table: Why Negotiating Is the Only Way to Peace*. London: St. Martin's Press.

Roberts, A. (2005), 'The "War on Terror" in Historical Perspective', *Survival*, 47 (2): 101–130.

Shapiro, J. (2013) *The Terrorists' Dilemma: Managing Violent Covert Organizations*. Princeton: Princeton University Press.

Wright, L. (2006) *The Looming Tower: Al Qaeda and the Road to 9/11*. New York: Knopf.

Zadka, S. (1995) *Blood in Zion: How the Jewish Guerrillas Drove the British Out of Palestine*. London: Brassey's.

Zartman, I. W. (1985) *Ripe for Resolution*. New York and Oxford: Oxford University Press.

INDEX

Tables, figures, boxes, and photos are indicated by an italic *t*, *f*, *b*, and *p* after the page number

Aarhus model 13, 548*b*
Aberystwyth School of Critical Security
 Studies 39
abortion *see* anti-abortionists
'actor-based approach' 20
Afghanistan
 al-Qaeda/Osama bin Laden 336, 582
 Arab Afghans 335, 336, 337
 civil war 222
 force-based counterterrorism,
  and 416–17, 419, 491
 Global War on Terror, and 270*b*
 insurgencies, motivations of recruits
  for 333
 Northern Alliance 66
 sanctions against 479
 Soviet invasion of 153, 335
 subject to long-running foreign
  military interventions 84
 Taliban 10
  negotiation with 416, 421, 421*b*
  Northern Alliance against 66
  Taliban's social service efforts in
   context of terrorism 314*b*
  targeted killings 440
  terrorism 187, 222, 333
   extent of deaths from 378
 US invasion of 401, 415, 460, 471, 479
  backlash against 382
aircraft hijackings 21–2, 25, 95, 261
 air piracy, hijackings as 76
 aviation terrorism 509*b*
 hijackings in 1960s 76
 marking onset of 'age of terrorism' 76
 PFLP 370
 use of commercial airliners as aerial
  bombs 77
 see also September 11, 2001 al-Qaeda
  attack on US
Alexander I of Yugoslavia, King
 assassination of 21, 78
al-Jamaa al-Islamiyya 7, 106*b*, 107*p*
al-Qaeda 1, 8, 25, 87, 291
 al-Qaeda terrorism failing
  politically 203*b*
 Arab Afghans, and 335, 336, 337
 backlash against the US
  counterterrorist strategy 382

drone strikes against 469
'enhanced interrogation' of al-Qaeda
 suspects 138–9
longevity 239, 244
Madrid 2004 attack *see under* Spain
mass casualty attacks 326
networks and hierarchies 337
objectives 332
operating in multiple countries 463
primary activity as war-fighting 305
social service provision 312
strategy 87
targeting errors causing
 backlash 586–7
 death of Muslim civilians 339, 586
US, attack on *see* September 11, 2001
 al-Qaeda attack on US (9/11)
US rendition, detention, and
 interrogation programme 42*b*
violent ideology, as 6, 164–5
WMD, and 328, 338
worldwide recruitment ring, as 187
see also Bin-Laden, Osama
Al-Qaeda in the Islamic Maghreb
 (AQIM) 8, 173*b*, 174*p*
Al-Shabaab 6, 45
 Nairobi 2013 attack 348
 social media, use of 348
 Somalia, in 45*b*
alternatives to force-based
 counterterrorism *see*
  responding to terrorism
  nonviolently
anarchists/anarchist terrorism
 anarchism, meaning of 166*b*
 anarchist movement
  lone wolf terrorism 180, 336
  near global membership 336
  'propaganda of the deed' 146–7,
   147*b*, 336
  starting point of modern terrorism,
   as 336
 anarchists as insane or weak-
  minded 180
 early view of perpetrators as
  anarchists 179–80
 fading as societal threat after WW1 167
 historically 146–7, 166–7, 179–81, 336

no single profile of anarchist
 terrorist 180–1
poverty, and 180 *see also* far left
 terrorism/left wing groups
animal rights
 Animal Liberation Front 167
 single issue terrorism, as 167
anti-abortionists 62, 149
 religious extremism, and 165, 167
 single issue terrorism, as 167
 targeting abortion clinics 167, 212
 US, in 165, 167
anti-terrorism 48
 addressing preparatory phase of
  terrorist activity 460
 anti-terrorism legislation 441, 498
  expansion of executive powers
   under 439
  infringing on human rights in pre-
   trial stage 437
  legal framework for dealing with
   terrorist suspects 437, 439
  victims co-opted into
   supporting more draconian
   legislation 565*p*, 566
 databases 129
 defensive anti-terrorism
  countermeasures 420, 458
 draconian anti-terrorism legislation
  after attacks 441
 guerrilla marketing tactics 466
 IRA Omagh Bombing leading to
  strengthening of anti-terrorism
  practices 232*b*
 meaning of 457, 458, 459, 460
 UK anti-terrorism legislation 405–6,
  439 *see also* counter-terrorism
Argentina
 'Dirty War' 152, 154
ASEAN counterterrorism
 cooperation 12, 481–5
 '3R' (resilience, response, and
  recovery) framework 485
 al-Qaeda and ISIS as main threat 483
 ASEAN Convention on Counter
  Terrorism 482–3
 ASEAN Declaration on Joint Action
  on Counter Terrorism 482

ASEAN counterterrorism (*Continued*)
  ASEAN Plan of Action in Combating Transnational Crime 485
  Bali 2002 bombings 482, 580
  formation of ASEAN 481
  Mutual Legal Assistance Treaty (MLAT) 484
  need for still further sharing and cooperation 485
  'Our Eyes' centres 485
  Philippines attack 482
  regional strategy, need for 483–5
  strategies of 'depoliticization' and 'ASEANization' of terrorism 483
assassination 79
  assassination of high-level figures 141*b*
    previously typical of terrorism 78–9
    tactic of revolutionary groups, as 84
  historically 141–4
    assassination campaigns 142–3
    firearms in assassinations, use of 144
    gunpowder in assassinations, use of 144
    militant anarchists 146–7, 147*b*
    'tyrannicide' 141
  motivations 141
  political assassinations by Russia 400
  terrorism, and 78, 141*b*
    targeted killings/drone strikes *see* targeted killings
    video footage on social media 570
    urban guerrilla tactics 167
Association of Southeast Nations *see* ASEAN counterterrorism cooperation
Aum Shinrikyo *see under* Japan
aviation terrorism 509*b*
see also aircraft hijackings

Baader-Meinhof Gang *see* Red Army Faction (RAF) *under* Germany
BBC World Service
  avoiding use of term terrorism in reporting foreign conflicts 84–5
Beirut attack by ISIS *see under* Lebanon
Bin-Laden, Osama 25, 164, 169
  attack on US *see* September 11, 2001 attack on USA by al-Qaeda ('9/11')
  CIA raid killing 582, 583, 587
  declaring war on the West 564

directing operations and funding operations 336
fighting for support of Muslim community 586
power and influence 328
stated grievances 203*b*
WMD, and 328–9 *see also* Al Qaeda
biometrics *see under* technology, terrorism, and counterterrorism
Black September
  attack on Israeli Olympic team at 1972 Munich Olympics 22, 22*p*, 26, 64, 261

Cambodia
  Khmer Rouge 266, 590
capacity building 352, 478
  Aarhus model 548*b*
case studies
  Aarhus model 548*b*
  Afghanistan
    negotiations with the enemy 421*b*
    Taliban's social service efforts in context of terrorism 314*b*
  al-Qaeda terrorism failing politically 203*b*
  Al-Shabaab in Somalia 45*b*
  Aum Shinrikyo 580*b*
  aviation terrorism 509*b*
  Charlie Hebdo 2015 attack 85*b*
  Christchurch terror attacks 353*b*
  co-ordinating approaches across agencies 403*b*
  defining terrorism 119*b*
  ETA
    end of ETA 374*b*
    ETA's mixed targeting strategies 226*b*
  EU
    EU at cradle of 'radicalization' 190*b*
    European Court of Justice and *Kadi* case 489*b*
  Exit Project 545*b*, 546*b*
  'Four Waves of Rebel Terror' (Rapaport) 148*b*
  IRA *see under* UK *infra*
  ISIS
    Islamic state terrorism failing politically 206*b*
    role and importance of religion in 334*b*
  Islamic Group (al-Jamaa al-Islamiyya) in Egypt 106*b*, 107*p*
  Israeli-Palestine conflict 63*b*
  Khotso House, destruction of 77*b*

long 1970s decade of terrorism 154*b*
LTTE in Sri Lanka 248*b*
Madrid 2004 bombings 340*b*, 340*p*
Nelson Mandela on terrorism 182*b*
Paris terror attacks, 2015 559*b*
Prevention Project 'Attention?!' (Achtung?!) in Germany 533*b*
racializations of 'lone wolf terrorism' 287*b*
Red Army Faction (RAF) 168*b*
  Ulrike Meinhof and assumptions about women's political violence 289*b*
Revolutionary Organization 17 November in Greece 255*b*
Russia
  countering terror in Russia 399*b*
  Russia's Repression of Chechnya 588*b*
sanctions
  UN and EU financial sanctions regime after 9/11 481*b*
  use of sanctions to combat the financing of terrorism 472*b*
Shining Path 379*b*
Sterling Thesis 24*b*
subjective interpretations of terrorism 65*b*
terrorism at home and abroad 566*b*
terrorism studies and Western-Centrism 27*b*
UK
  British extrajudicial killings in Northern Ireland 272*b*
  British operations in Northern Ireland in the 1970s 448*b*
  IRA Omagh bombing 232*b*, 233*p*
  Lee Rigby murder 361*b*, 571
  Notting Hill Carnival August 2017 (facial recognition technology) 507*b*
UNITA, terrorism by 308*b*
US
  Antifa attack in Charlottesville, Virginia 120*b*, 121*p*
  torture in the US 'War on Terror' 270*b*, 444*b*
  US public diplomacy in post-9/11 era 465*b*
  US rendition, detention, and interrogation programme 42*b*
  white supremacist online recruiting in US 528*b*
causes of terrorism *see* root causes of terrorism
Charlie Hebdo 2015 attack *see under* France

chemical, biological, radiological, and
    nuclear (CBRN) weapons *see*
    weapons of mass
    destruction (WMD)
Chile 267
    enforced disappearances 267
    international isolation 154
    torture, use of 267
China
    foreign policy historically 455
    free press, lack of 119
    Mao Zedong's Cultural
        Revolution 151, 153, 153p
    Uighur separatists 65b
citadelization 506, 506b
civil wars 28, 82, 303
    civil conflict/war, meaning of 303b
    high density of terrorist attacks 222,
        228
    imbalances in military capabilities
        leading to unconventional
        tactics 304–5
    terrorist attacks during 563
    victims
        no assumption of
            blamelessness 568
        victimhood highly politicized 563
civilians/citizenship
    civil wars, killing of civilians in 82
    civilian-based forms of national
        defence 427b, 428
    civilian-based nonviolent peace-
        forces 428
    counterterrorism, effects on 47–8, 52
    cycles of 'tit for tat' violence in
        ethnically divided societies 88
    domestic terrorism 82
    ethnic minorities 47–8
    genocide 82
    hate crimes 88
    IRA attacks 84
    'lone wolf' attacks on civilians *see*
        lone actor/lone wolf terrorism
    non-combatants, meaning of 70
    nonviolent community action,
        effectiveness of 428
    PREVENT duty 48
    states' operations against terrorists,
        civilian deaths in 87
    targeting civilians/non-
        combatants 59, 69–70, 76
        attacks most commonly carried out
            against civilians 225f, 226
        attacks on the public typifying
            terrorism 76
        civilian targeting treated as
            maximalist in nature 228

converting fear into demand for
    policy changes, aim of 230–1
dissuading governments from
    granting concessions 202
fear destabilizing sense of security
    among population 561–2
fear, generating 224, 226
intent to create harm and fear 563
intentional attacks on non-
    combatants to achieve political
    goals 78
jihadist attacks 80
media attention, reduction in 231
not helping terrorist organizations
    achieve their goals 209, 212, 369,
    371, 372
public becoming more able to
    cope 231
public sentiments and perceptions
    as primary targets 230
putting public in fear as primary
    method of terrorism 78–9
rebels/insurgents, by *see under*
    insurgents and rebels, terrorism
    by
tactical gains from violence against
    civilians 383
target selection, fear, and public
    attention 230–4, 232b
targeting choices seldom entirely
    arbitrary 212
targeting particular communities in
    internal conflict 82
targeting public infrastructure 226
terrorists punishing civilian
    attacks 214
vengeance, and 212–13
victims and survivors of non-state
    terrorism 51
victims as innocent bystanders
    78–9
violence promoting backlash
    231–2
terrorists' attitude towards deaths
    of 83–4
unarmed civilian peacekeeping 427b
victims, as *see* victims of terrorism
    and political violence
warnings 82
weaponry, choice of 82
closed source information 31b
Cold War 23, 25, 26
Colombia
    nonviolent community action,
        effectiveness of 428
    Revolutionary Armed Forces of
        Colombia (FARC), and 43

Colombian army killing
    civilians 440
drug trafficking and political
    violence 382
negotiations 584
reorientation 590
territorial control 310
unarmed peacekeeping, success
    of 428
colonialism 65, 286, 373
    anti-colonial terrorism 148
    anti-colonial wave 148b, 150, 151,
        163
    response to injustice of
        colonialism 182
    violent rebellions/violence 286,
        289
colonial imperialism 286
colonial powers 267–8
    concessions, effect of 424–5
    extrajudicial killings in wars of
        decolonization 268
    terrorist campaigns against 424
    torture, use of 268
haphazard erection of national
    borders by colonial
    authorities 163
racialization of anti-colonial
    violence 288
right for colonized people to resort to
    political violence 182, 274
conceptualizations of terrorism 6–7,
    56–73
    components in conceptualization of
        terrorism 67–70
    civilian targeting 69–70
    political motive 69
    psychological impact beyond
        immediate victims 57, 61, 62,
        67, 70, 71
    violence and threat of violence 68
conceptualization of terrorism 57, 61
    conceptualizing, meaning of 60,
        60b
    self-determination, terrorism
        and 62–5
    subjective interpretations of
        terrorism 65b
    terrorism as a method 61–6
defining terrorism 57–9, 60
general 57–9
    association of terrorism with
        particular causes 59
    components in conceptualization
        of terrorism 59, 59b
    importance of determining what
        terrorism is 58

conceptualizations of terrorism
    (*Continued*)
  lack of agreement on defining
      terrorism 57–9
  social construction, terrorism
      as 58*b*, 60
  subjective application of
      terrorism 59, 59*b*
  'terrorism' as distinctive
      phenomenon worthy of
      study 60, 61
  pejorative label, terrorism as 60–1
  terrorism as a method 61–6
    Israeli/Palestine conflict 63*b*
    subjective interpretations of
        terrorism 65*b*
    terrorism as method of
        violence 61–2
conflict prevention 428–9
conflict resolution 415, 420
  CTS focus on 44
  dialogue and negotiations 421, 423
  meaning of 427*b*
  training local leaders in 425
  see also end of terrorist campaigns;
      responding to terrorism
      nonviolently
consequence management *see under*
    foreign policy and countering
    terrorism
constructivism 39, 39*b*, 443
Countering Violent Extremism
    (CVE) *see* preventing and
    countering violent extremism
counterterrorism
  agencies *see* counterterrorism
      agencies
  citizenship, effect on 47–8
  countering political as well as security
      effects of terrorism 44*b*
  CTS Model of 430*t*
  delegitimizing opposition
      movements 44*b*
  disengagement *see* disengagement
      and deradicalization
      programmes
  end of terrorist campaigns *see* end of
      terrorist campaigns
  foreign policy *see* foreign policy and
      countering terrorism
  human rights, and *see* human rights
      and counterterrorism
  international organizations *see*
      international organizations and
      counterterrorism
  meaning of 435–6, 436*b*, 457, 459
    force-based counterterrorism 420*b*

nonviolence *see* responding to
    terrorism nonviolently
preventing violent extremism *see*
    preventing and countering
    violent extremism
state violence, as *see under* states
technology, and *see* technology,
    terrorism, and counterterrorism
victims *see* victims of terrorism and
    political violence
see also anti-terrorism; states
counterterrorism agencies 11, 391–412
  CONTEST counterterrorism
      policy 292, 395–7, 520
    aim of strategy 396
    deradicalization 547
    key concepts 395*b*
    pre-cautionary, preventive, and
        pre-emptive stance 396
    Prevent strand 396–7, 520
  demand and supply challenge
      392–5
    counterterrorism system in liberal
        democracies 393
    demand, meaning of 392*b*
    diversification in attack
        methodologies 394–5
    involvement of multiple agencies
        with partially overlapping
        remits 393
    prioritizing risks and threats,
        importance of 395
    supply, meaning of 392*b*
    terrorism metrics increasing over
        time 394
    volume of activity 393–4
  implementing approaches to
      counterterrorism 401–7
    criminal justice 405–7
    intelligence *see* intelligence
    military 401–2
    interactions and collaborations
        407–8
  intervention outcomes 397–400
    antiterrorist interventions
        increasing violence 398
    criminal justice-based
        approach 397
    decreasing benefits of terrorism
        through non-military
        means 397–8
    deterrence-based models 397
    over-reaction when countering
        terrorism, effect of 398–9
    role of interventions in promoting
        desistance from terrorism 397
    Russia, countering terror in 399*b*

    social reality of support and
        opposition to terrorism 398
    use of military 397
criminal gangs and drug cartels 81–2
criminal justice approach to
    terrorism 397, 405–7
Critical Terrorism Studies (CTS) 6,
    36–55, 262
  counterterrorism 43–8, 430*t*
    citizenship, effect of
        counterterrorism on 47–8
    CTS challenging 43–4, 44*b*
    dialogue and negotiations to end
        terrorist violence, use of 44–5
  critical of 'mainstream' or 'orthodox'
      terrorism studies 38
  critical of focus on non-state
      actors 20
  CTS Model of Counterterrorism 430*t*
  domestic violence as everyday
      terrorism 40
  emancipation 48, 49, 50
    as fundamental concept, as 44
  future challenges 51–2
  general 35, 37–8
  labelling
    political repercussions of 40*b*
    'terrorism' used to label enemies of
        the state 6
  nature and focus of 19, 37
  politics of CTS 48–51
    broadening CTS' interlocutors
        50–1
    CTS vs the state 49–50
    engagement with the state 50
    impact 50*b*
    investigating covert and illegal state
        practices 49
    nonviolent activism 49–50
    reducing state violence 49
    victims and survivors of non-state
        violence, focus on 51
  state action, focus on 6
  state violence 40–8
    legitimization of state violence 45
    see also states
  origins 6, 19, 20, 25
  'terrorism', meaning of 39–40
    discourses of terrorism 39
    terrorism as political rather than
        security issue 40*b*
    whether terrorism as objective
        category exists 39
    theoretical foundations of critical
        approaches 39*b*
culture
  cultural diplomacy 465

prominent role in foreign policy, playing 465
public diplomacy *see under* diplomacy
role in countering terrorism 465
CVE *see* preventing and countering violent extremism
cybersecurity 491, 492

Daesh/Da'ish *see* ISIS/IS/ISIL (Islamic State of Iraq and Syria)
data mining 502, 511–12
  civil liberties, abuse of 511–12
  data mining, meaning of 502*b*
  privacy, and 511–12
databases
  America Terrorism Study 124–5
  Big, Allied, and Dangerous Dataset (BAAD) 122–3
    most extensive open source database on group-level terrorism, as 123
    weaknesses 123
  Extremist Crime Database (ECDB) 124, 126
  Global Terrorism Database (GTD) 22, 29, 116–17, 116*t*, 117*p*, 119*b*
    categories of direct target (victim) types 225–6, 225*f*
    data collection 116–17, 119–20, 128–9, 221
    impact 117
    longevity of terrorist groups 239, 242
    statistics on terrorist attacks 28
  International Terrorism: Attributes of Terrorist Events (ITERATE) 22, 116*t*, 119*b*
    data collection 117
  Lone Actor Terrorist Database 124, 127–8
  Profiles of Individual Radicalization in the US (PIRUS) 124, 125–6
  RAND 22, 45*b*, 116*t*, 119*b*, 208
    data collection 117–18, 120, 331
  Western Jihadism Project 124, 126–7
  Worldwide Incidents Tracking System data (WITS) 116*b*, 119*b*
    data collection 118, 120
  see also open source databases on terrorism
decapitation of leaders *see under* end of terrorist campaigns
definition and meaning of terrorism 1–4, 18–20, 60, 261

civilians as targets of 2
  intentional attacks on non-combatants for political/ideological goals 79
'common sense' approach 19
common use of 'terrorism' affecting conceptual precision 18
conceptualizations of terrorism *see* conceptualizations of terrorism
consistent pattern of symbolic or representative selection of victims 2*b*
CTS approach 39–40
current usage of word terrorism 79–81
discussion and disagreement over 3, 18–20, 57–9
  lack of generally accepted definition of terrorism 118–19, 119*b*
  multiple definitions 114
  terrorism as an essentially contested concept 19–20
elements in definitions of terrorism 119*b*
non-state actors, terrorism applying to 138*b*
political change, related to 2, 3, 18
  politics involving clash of rival powers 2, 3
psychological effect on specific groups to change political behaviour/attitudes 3
state terrorism, defining *see under* states
terror, state oppression as 138*b*
violence, and
  absolutely illegitimate violence, terrorism as 75–6, 80
  act of violence against innocents that is always illegitimate 578
  deliberate creation of state of fear through violence 2, 3
  deliberate use or threat of violence by non-state actors to achieve power 138*b*
  fear caused by excessive violence 2, 3
  heterogeneous violence with political aim, terrorism involving 2, 3
  insurgents' method to seize political power, terrorism as 2*b*
  morality of violence 3
  non-state attacks on civilian targets, terrorism as 208

political violence with transnational dimension 82
premeditated use or threat to use violence against non-combatants 302
psychological effects in broader target audience, terrorism creating 138*b*
socially and politically unacceptable violence, terrorism manifested in 2*b*
systematic inducement of fear and anxiety to control civilian population 317–18
terrorism applying to violence of all kinds of very different agents 20
terrorism signifying 'atrocities targeting the West' 261
threat or use of violence by non-state actors against public interests to effect policy change 221
threatened or actual use of illegal force/violence by non-state actors to attain goals 114
use or threat of violence to generate psychological impact for political motive 370*b*
violence with political motivation 2*b*, 3, 18
democracies
  dependent on public legitimacy 245, 246
  domestic repression, and 587
  frequent targets of terrorism, as *see under* target selection
Denmark
  cartoons of Prophet Muhammad in *Jyllands-Posten* 85*b*
  deradicalization 425, 548
    Aarhus model 13, 548*b*
    Exit Project 545*b*, 546*p*
deradicalization *see* disengagement and deradicalization programmes
diplomacy and culture 12, 455
  coercive diplomacy 467–8
  diplomacy carrying potential use of hard power 465
  contemporary diplomacy as 'multi-track diplomacy' 464
  countering terrorism strategy, as 462, 463–7
    international countering terrorism diplomacy, meaning of 463
    training of allied troops 468
  economic diplomacy 479

diplomacy and culture (*Continued*)
    hard and soft power 464–5, 464*b*, 465*b*
    instrument of foreign policy, diplomacy, and culture, as 461
    international diplomacy 436
    meaning of diplomacy 463
    nonviolent approach, as 427
    public diplomacy
        effort to create soft power 465
        powerful preventative tool in countering terrorism, as 465
        public diplomacy campaigns 414
        US public diplomacy in post-9/11 era 465*b*
    tool by which foreign policy is executed, as 463
disappearances *see* enforced disappearances
discrimination
    against communities of North African origins 43
    counterterrorism, in 43–4
    discriminating between guilty and innocent civilians 311
    state terrorism/violence, discrimination in 43–4
disengagement and deradicalization programmes 13, 58, 538–57
    conceptualizing and defining deradicalization 539–44
        certain identity groups disproportionately affected 541
        complex relationship between attitudes and behaviour 540
        deradicalization remaining controversial idea 540
        heavy emphasis on the individual 541
        insufficient evidence base 541
        terrorism offenders held to different standards 541
        theorizing deradicalization 542–4
    contemporary deradicalization policy and practice 547–51
        Aarhus model 13, 548*b*
        deradicalization intervention methods 550–1
        deradicalization interventions in criminal justice system 547
        partnership working in deradicalization initiatives 550
        programmes adopting multi-modal approach 458
        state and non-state actors delivering programmes 548
    deradicalization, meaning of 194*b*, 520*b*, 540*b*

disengagement, meaning of 103*b*, 194*b*, 540, 540*b*
empirical evidence about deradicalization 551–3
    push and pull factors 552–3
    social context in disengagement processes 553
history and evolution of deradicalization interventions 544–7
    Exit Project 545*b*, 546*b*, 547
    preventative initiatives, increase in 547
    programmes offered by states 544, 546–7
political violence, from 102
reintegration
    emphasis on 541
    meaning of 540*b*
theorizing deradicalization 542–4
    dominant model of individual-level risk assessment 542–3, 544
    Good Lives Model (GLM) 543
    Pro-Integration Model (PIM) 542
    protective factors, role of 543
    re-engagement in militancy, research into 543–4
    risk-needs-responsivity (RNR) approach 542–3
    strengths or desistance-based approach 543
    see also radicalization
domestic terrorism 91, 219
    American Terrorism Study 124–5
    civilians, and 82
    databases 113
    domestic vs international attacks 118*b*
    insurgency and/or civil war, in *see* insurgents and rebels, terrorism by
    meaning 27*b*, 118*b*, 459*b*
    most terrorism as domestic 9, 29, 302–3
    PIRUS, and 126
    repression increasing domestic terrorism 417
    risk of violence 224
    target locations 224
domestic violence
    lacking transnational dimension of terrorism 81
    terrorism, as 40, 81
    Walmart 2019 attack 219–21
drone strikes *see* targeted killings
drug cartels, terrorism as 81–2

education 171
efficacy of terrorism 10, 368–88
    effectiveness of terrorism as a tactic 369–72
        debate over efficacy of terrorism 369–70, 372–7
        difficulties of determining whether a group is successful 373–4, 376
        effectiveness, definition of 376, 381, 384
        efficacy of violence for political purposes 370
        ETA, end of 374*b*
        expectation that political violence can be useful 373
        political effectiveness, definition of 376–7, 384
        strategic view of terrorism questioning whether terrorism works 371–2
        tactics and strategy of terrorism 372*b*
        terrorist groups typically failing to achieve goals 372–3
        terrorist successes 369–70, 373
        use of violence against civilians 369, 371, 372
    effectiveness of terrorist goals, debates around 381–4
        benefits outweighing costs, belief in 381
        civilians, violence against 383
        cycles of protest 381–2
        disconnect between study of terrorism and its practice 383–4
        ideology and organization affecting group survival 383
        means of acquiring power 382
        popularizing grievances by terrorism 381
        projecting image of influence 382
        terrorism as effective means of communicating with audiences 383
        terrorism expanding support base and instilling fear 383
        terrorism helping organizations survive 382–3
        ways forward for effectiveness debate 384
    when and where terrorism works 377–81
        efficacy of the counterterrorist effort 378–9
        elements determining duration of terrorist campaign 377
        Shining Path 379*b*

statistical chance of being victim of terrorism 378–9
terrorists' relationship with their communities 377–8
whether goals of group are attainable 378
see also rationality and terrorism
Egypt
Islamic Group (al-Jamaa al-Islamiyya) in Egypt 106*b*, 107*p*
force-based counterterrorism 418
repression 587
terrorism 80
Luxor massacre 107*p*, 586
US, and 474
end of terrorist campaigns 13–14, 575–93
decapitation by capturing/killing leader 579–83
assassinating terrorist leaders 582–3
Aum Shinrikyo 580*b*
groups successfully ended through assassination 583
publicly delegitimizing leader more effective than killing them 583
ending terrorist campaigns, key concepts in 577*b*
failure 585–7
implosion 585
marginalization 585–6
targeting errors causing backlash 586–7
how terrorism ends 579–91
decapitation by capturing/killing leader 579–83
failure 585–7
negotiations 583–4
pathways out of terrorism 579*b*
reorientation 590
repression 587–8
succeeding in objective 584–5
negotiations 583–4
once started tending to persist 584
rarely leading to demise of groups strictly on own 583
talks never immediate cure-all 584
scope and methods 578–9
enforced disappearances 9, 267, 447, 564
'Dirty War' in Argentina 154
UN Working Group on Enforced or Involuntary Disappearances 267
environmental protection/ecoterrorism 212
single issue terrorism, as 167
ETA *see under* Spain
Ethics Committees 32

ethnic cleansing 119, 265, 267, 276
European Union (EU) 12
EU counterterrorism cooperation 486–9
Action Plan on Combating Terrorism after 9/11 487–8
'deradicalization' programmes as 'absolute priority' 522
'disengagement and exit strategies' 522
enhanced cooperation between EU and Global South 488
EU counterterrorism Institutions 486
European Court of Justice and *Kadi* case 489*b*
foreign terrorist fighters' phenomenon after rise of ISIS 488–9
further international cooperation after 2017 attacks 489
more coherent counterterrorism policy after Madrid and London attacks 488
multilateral counterterrorism cooperation with NATO 490–2
operational cooperation on internal security issues, origins of 486–7
radicalization
EU paper introducing concept of radicalization 190*b*
Radicalization Awareness Network 571
soft power skills 491
UN and EU financial sanctions regime after 9/11 481*b*
extrajudicial killings 40
British extrajudicial killings Ireland, in 268
Northern Ireland, in 272*b*
decolonization, and 268 *see also* targeted killings
extremism
meaning 189*b*
religious extremism *see* religion and religious extremism
violent extremism *see* violent extremism

facial recognition software 507*b*, 511
police concerns about 513–14
'smart CCTV' and 'smart lampposts' 505, 511
'smart corridors' 505*b*
'smart glasses' 500–1, 501*p*
unreliability of 507

far left terrorism/left-wing groups 167
international terrorism evolving from left-wing militants to Islamist radicals 26–7
nationalism, and 426
networks 336–7
new left terrorism 8, 167
target selection 224–5
see also anarchists/anarchist terrorism
far right terrorism/right-wing groups 166
Exit Project 545*b*, 546*b*, 547
Lee Rigby's identity, use of 571
nationalism, and 426
Prevent strategy, and 396–7
rising threat in many countries 396–7
social media, use of 353
storming of US Capitol building in 2021 523
target selection 225
FARC *see under* Colombia
Fatah 63*b*, 319
Hamas, and 319, 320
social service provision 312
fear
destabilizing sense of security among population 561–2
Just World Hypothesis, and 564–6
putting public in fear as primary method of terrorism 78–9
sense of terror from ISIS killings as key 339
target selection, and 224, 230–4
public infrastructure attacks 226
role of fear in target selection 232*b*
violence against public interests to elicit and spread fear 230
violence promoting backlash 231–2
terrorism
deliberate creation of state of fear through violence, as 2, 3
intent to create harm and fear, as 563–4
Financial Action Task Force on Money Laundering (FATF) 471
financing of terrorism
asset freezes 472
Financial Action Task Force on Money Laundering 471
need to prevent financing of terrorism at global level 471
UN Security Council resolutions 472
use of sanctions to combat the financing of terrorism 472, 472*b*

foreign aid
  coercive use of aid 471
  development aid 471
  key tool of economic statecraft, as 471
  meaning of 471
  use in reducing numbers of potential terrorists 436
foreign policy and countering terrorism 12, 454–76
  British intervention in Iraq linked to 7/7/2005 London attacks 455
  consequence management 459
    consequence management countermeasures 460
    meaning 457, 458, 460
  counterterrorism/countering terrorism 457–60
    anti-terrorism, meaning of 457, 458, 459, 460
    consequence management 457, 458, 460
    countering terrorism influencing foreign policy choices 460
    countering terrorism, meaning of 457, 459
    counterterrorism, meaning of 457
    defensive anti-terrorism countermeasures 458, 460
    importance of international cooperation 460
    national security policy focusing on preventing risks 460
    offensive counterterrorism response 458, 459, 460
    phases of terrorism and countering terrorism responses 457–9, 458f
    state responses to terrorism 459
  foreign aid, sanctions, and the financing of terrorism 470–3
    combating financing of terrorism 471–2, 472b
    economic statecraft, effectiveness of 470–1
    difficulties of using economic instruments 471
    foreign aid 471
    sanctions 471, 472, 472b
  foreign policy 455–7
    contours of 455–6
    core of foreign policy analysis 456
    countering terrorism influencing foreign policy choices 460
    determinants of foreign policy 457
    history 455, 457
    human agency, emphasis on 457
    meaning of 456b, 457
    multi-factorial and multi-level 456, 457
    role of 463
    structure-agency debate 456b
    three-stage process of initiation, formulation, and implementation 457, 461
  military arm—defence and deterrence 467–70
    coercive diplomacy, use of 467–8
    defence, meaning of 468
    deterrence, meaning of 468
    harmful consequences of military action, 467
    hostage rescue operations 470
    interdiction of terrorist personnel and resources 470
    pre-emption 468–9
    proactive defence 468–9, 470
    reactive defence 470
    retaliation 470
    targeted killings 469
    threat and actual use of force 467
    training of allied forces 468
    use of armed force seen as failure 467
  overlapping instruments of foreign policy and countering terrorism 461–3
    capabilities of the state 461, 462b
    countering terrorism strategy leveraging key instruments 462
    diplomacy and culture see diplomacy and culture
    foreign aid, sanctions, and the financing of terrorism 470–3
    foreign policy and countering terrorism policy cycle 463f
    instruments 461, 462b
    key constituent elements of foreign and countering terrorism policy 462b
    military arm—defence and deterrence 467–70
    national interest 461
    objective conditions/resources of the state 461, 462b
France
  Action Directe 152b, 167, 579
    decapitation of leader 579
  Algeria, systematic use of torture in 41, 268
  Charlie Hebdo 2015 attack 85b
  counterterrorism 393, 405–6, 550
  detention periods 437
  discrimination against communities of North African origins 43, 560p
  ISIS 2015 attack on Paris 27b, 28, 69, 559b, 565, 566b
  French Revolution 151, 152
    first use of concept of terrorism 21, 145
    'The Terror' 2, 75, 138b, 152b, 261, 285
  terrorism, and
    operational response to terrorism 439
    security of Republic superseding other considerations 443–4
    terrorism trials 438
    terrorist offences, definition of 439
Frankfurt School Critical Theory 39, 39b

gendered and racialized terrorism 9, 281–301
  essentialization 285–8
    gendered ideas about male and female characteristics 285–6
    intersectional oppressions 286
    perceptions of women in terrorism 285–6
    racializations of lone wolf terrorism 287b
    racialized essentializations, perceptions of person's use of violence and 286
    women's engagement in terrorism from beginning 285
  gender and race as driving forces 292–7
    groups/online communities with misogynistic idealizations 295–7
    Incel revolution 292–3, 295–7
    misogynistic terrorism 292–3, 293–4
    misogyny 293, 295–7
    racism 295–7
    toxic masculinity 292–3, 295
    violent actors associated with misogynistic terrorism 293–4
  gender, meaning of 282b
  idealizations 288–92
    actor's violence evaluated through idealizations of gender and race 289
    creating assumptions about how things operate 288
    new terrorism thesis 291

poststructuralism helping in
   analysis of language 289
radicalization 291, 292
Ulrike Meinhof and assumptions
   about women's political
   violence 289b
intersectionality 292
   meaning of 283b
logocentric binaries, meaning
   of 284b
post-culturalism 284b
race, meaning of 283b
subjectivity of who is seen as terrorist
   actor 282–4
   Citizens for Constitutional
      Freedom 282
   Shamima Begum case 282
genocide
   meaning 82
   Nazi genocide 151
geofencing 509
Germany 83
   deradicalization 425, 548
   far right terrorism 166
   Munich Olympics 1972 attack *see*
      Black September
   Nazis
      genocide 151
      use of terrorism to maintain
         power 266
   Prevention Project 'Attention?!'
      (Achtung?!) in Germany 533b
   Red Army Faction (RAF) 7, 9, 99b,
      152b, 168b, 327, 583
      failure of 207, 378, 585
      kidnapping of Hans Martin
         Schleyer 95, 225
      longevity 240
      root causes 168b
      sanctuary in East Germany 24b
      securing survival of organization as
         aim 254
      targets 225
      Ulrike Meinhof 9, 289b *see also* far
         left terrorism/left wing groups
Global War on Terror 11, 83b
   backlash against 382
   failure of 415
   following 9/11 75
   language, use of 45
   mistreatment of prisoners 154
      torture, use of 270b, 271p, 444b
   nature of 414
   Neo-Orientalist bias 288
   US rendition, detention, and
      interrogation programme 42b

globalization 146b
   enabling networks to be more
      international 336
Greece
   Revolutionary Organization 17
      November in Greece 9, 255b
GSPC *see* al-Qaeda in the Islamic
   Maghreb (AQIM)
Guantanamo Bay *see under* United
   States
guerrilla warfare 58, 67, 76, 118–19,
      167, 183, 304–5, 321, 373, 385
   asymmetry of power, and 303, 304–5
   Geneva Convention protocol on 84
   Shining Path 10, 167, 379b
   use of torture against guerrillas 268–9
   weapons of the weak, as 304–5

Hamas 210, 269
   core aspirations 332
   drone strikes against 469
   Fatah, and 319, 320
   justifying military operations to
      voters 339
   longevity 244
   outbidding strategy, adopting 320
   primary activity as war-fighting 305
   social service provision 312, 312p
   strategy
      hybrid nature of 332
      spoiling strategy, adopting 319
hard power 401, 464–5
   meaning of 464b
   NATO 491
hate crimes 88, 89, 92, 119, 121, 219,
      406
Hezbollah 170
   drone strikes against 469
   longevity 244
   operating in multiple countries 463
   participating in Lebanon's
      government 339
   social service provision 312, 339
hijacking of aircraft *see* aircraft
      hijackings
history of terrorism 7–8, 137–56, 261
   ancient world, terror in 140–3
      assassination campaigns 142–3
      assassination, terrorism and 141b
      Assyrian Empire 140
      Nizaris 142–3
      Roman Empire 140, 142
      Sicarii 142
      'tyrannicide' 141, 147
      Zealots 325

continued importance of past
   terrorism 138–43
complexity of past terrorism,
   understanding 138–9
future shape of terrorism,
   understanding 139–40
supporting sense of proportion
   about the present 139
terror in the ancient world 140–3
gunpowder revolution in
   Europe 144
modern terrorism 145–54
   anarchist theory of 'propaganda by
      the deed' 146–7, 147b, 336
   anti-state terrorism in 19th
      century 145–7
   dynamite, use of 147
   Four Waves of Rebel Terror
      (Rapoport) 8, 148–51, 148b, 163,
      167, 327
   globalization 146b
   information circulation 146–7
   long 1970s decade of
      terrorism 151b, 152b
   modern state terror 151–4
   political failure, history of terrorism
      as story of *see* rationality and
      terrorism
   terrorism, new concept of 145
   see also old and new terrorism
homegrown terrorism *see* domestic
   terrorism
hostage rescue operations 470
   Chechen separatists 399b
   Red Army Faction 95
human rights and counterterrorism
      11–12, 154, 434–53
   civil liberties
      data mining, abuse of 512
      impact of surveillance technology
         on 511–12
   counterterrorism, meaning of 435–6,
      436b
   crimes against humanity 82
   effect of counterterrorism on human
      rights 436–40
      anti-terrorism legislation,
         expansion of powers under 439
      killing of suspected terrorists 440
      military justice 438
      negative effect on states' adherence
         to human rights 436–7, 437t
      operational response to
         terrorism 439–40
      pre-trial process 437
      terror detention times 437, 438b

human rights and counterterrorism
    (*Continued*)
  terrorism trials 437–9
  terrorist offences, definition of 439
  European Convention on Human
      Rights 435
  human rights and effectiveness of
      counterterrorism 445–9
    British operations in Northern
        Ireland in the 1970s 448*b*
    draconian legislation associated
        with increase in terrorist
        attacks 447
    executive power increased by
        counterterrorist legislation 446
    physical integrity rights, damage
        caused by violation of 447
    rights fundamental to liberal
        democracy 446
    tradeoff between security and
        liberty 445–6
    violation of human rights
        undermining key
        relationships 447
  human rights, meaning of 435, 436*b*
  human rights standards shaping
      counterterrorism 440–5
    'collective social action' by NGOs,
        impact of 442
    domestic norms as crucial
        factor 443–4
    draconian anti-terrorism
        legislation after attacks 441
    human rights influence on states'
        response to terrorism 440–3
    international human rights norms,
        influence of 443
    international law's ability
        to regulate terrorism
        responses 441–2
    manipulation of legal norms 441
    national security, threats to 441
    nationalist and populist politics,
        threat posed by 442
    role of judiciary and parliament
        in shaping anti-terrorist
        legislation 442–3
    torture in US War on Terror 444*b*
  life, right to 440
  NGOs, role of 435, 442
  prevention of terrorism, human rights
      and 428–9
  privacy, right to 439
    data mining 511–12
    surveillance technology 511

Universal Declaration of Human
    Rights 435
violations of human rights 82
war crimes 82, 265

ideology
  ideological encapsulation 103, 105–6
  ideologically-motivated terrorism
    anarchist terrorism 166–7
    far right terrorism 166
    new left/far left terrorism 167
    radicalization, and role of
        ideology 185–6, 195, 197
    single issue—anti-abortion, animal
        rights, and environmental
        groups 167–8
  longevity of terrorist groups 246–7, 383
  meaning of 165*b*
  role of 553
  violent ideologies 6, 62, 164–5
India 150
  deradicalization 551
  foreign policy historically 455
  Kashmir 59, 65*b*, 223, 468
  Naxalites 590
  pre-emptive airstrikes 469
  religious activists 331
    Sikh extremists 333
  terrorist attacks 304, 468
    LTTE 417
    Mumbai 2008 shootings 563, 570
Indonesia
  al-Qaeda, support for 587
  counterterrorism 484–5, 580
    ASEAN 'Our Eyes' centres 485
  deradicalization 425
  extra-judicial killings 440
  P/CVE programme 524
  social media 357
  terrorist attacks 482, 483
    suicide attacks 587
Institutional Review Boards (IRBs) 32
insurgents and rebels, terrorism by
    9–10, 119, 302–24
  benefits of terrorism 303–4
    asymmetric insurgencies, levelling
        playing field and 303
    helping dissidents wear down
        opponents 303–4
    providing benefits to civilians 303
    recruitment and fundraising 303
    territorial control, gaining 303
    using violence against civilians to
        help achieve goals 303, 304

civil conflict/war, meaning of 303*b*
civilians, and 307
  attacks on civilians alienating
      supporters 311
  civilian compliance and territorial
      control 310–11
  discriminating between guilty and
      innocent civilians 311
  providing benefits to civilians 303,
      312–17
  showing civilians their leadership is
      preferable 303
  terrorism by UNITA 308*b*
  using violence against civilians to
      help achieve goals 303, 304
defining feature of insurgency,
    imbalance between state and
    non-state as 306
insurgency, meaning of 305*b*
insurgent or rebel as neutral
    description 76
majority of terror attacks as domestic
    terrorism 302–3
rebel relative strength 304–10
  civilians, attacks on 307, 308*b*
  irregular/guerrilla warfare
      addressing unevenness of
      power 304–5
  low cost and high returns 304
  targets of terrorism by
      insurgents 307*f*
  terrorism addressing relative
      weakness 306–7
  terrorism and insurgency used in
      tandem 305, 306*f*
  terrorism as last resort 304
  terrorism least common in
      symmetrical non-conventional
      conflicts 306*f*, 307
  terrorists also battling the
      state 305
rebel social service provision 303,
    312–17, 313*f*
  service institutions building
      group's popularity 316–17
  service provision used to
      gain compliance from
      population 317
  social services provided by terrorist
      groups 312–13, 313*f*
  Taliban's social service efforts in
      context of terrorism 314*b*
rebel terrorism arising in 40-year
    waves 30
see also Rapoport, David

INDEX 605

strategies of terrorism 317–20
   attrition strategy 317, 318, 319
   intimidation strategy 317–18, 319
   outbidding strategy 321
   provocation strategy 318, 319
   spoiling strategy 319–20
success of insurgencies against state opponents, increase in 591
territorial control, civilian compliance, terrorism and 310–11
terrorist groups aspiring to be insurgencies 590–1
insurrection/insurgency *see* insurgents and rebels, terrorism by
intelligence 402–5
   blending human and technologically sourced material 402–3
   co-ordinating approaches across agencies 403, 403*b*
   key types of
      HUMINT 401
      OSINT 115*b*, 401
      SIGINT 401
   social media, effect of 403
   transformations from information age 403
International Criminal Court
   genocide 82
   terrorism not among high crimes 82
   war crimes 82
international organizations and counterterrorism 12, 477–96
   ASEAN counterterrorism cooperation 481–5
   EU counterterrorism cooperation 486–9
   multilateral counterterrorism cooperation: NATO and EU 490–2
   cybersecurity 491
   defence and security capacity-building 491, 492
   different approaches on fighting terrorism 490, 491–2
   need for cooperation 490–1
   role of international organizations progressively more important 478
   UN counterterrorism cooperation 478–81
international terrorism 9
   advent of 21–2
   al-Qaeda 396
   anarchists 146

ASEAN 482
defeating poverty as key strand of response to 170
domestic vs international attacks 118*b*
evolving from left-wing militants to Islamist radicals 26–7
first wave of 21
foreign policy, and *see* foreign policy and countering terrorism
hostage rescue operations 470
meaning of 27*b*, 83*b*, 118*b*, 459*b*
military-run trials for international terrorism 438
Orthodox Terrorism Studies focus on 6
prominence given to 26–9
religion as 'new' motivation 330, 331
Soviet Union, and 23, 24*b*
specific agencies focusing on 393
support of foreign states for non-state terrorist groups 83*b*
systematic study of, commencement of 22
target locations 224
IRA/PIRA *see under* Northern Ireland Troubles
Iran 265
   free press, lack of 119
   revolution 153
   state-sponsored terrorism 41, 52
Iraq
   British intervention linked to 7/7/2005 London attacks 455
   civil war 28, 222
   insurgencies, motivations of recruits for 333
   invasion of Iraq, backlash against 382
   ISIS 28
   subject to long-running foreign military interventions 84
   terrorism, extent of deaths from 378
   torture and abuse of detainees held in Abu Ghraib 271
   use of terrorism to maintain power 266
ISIS/IS/ISIL (Islamic State of Iraq and Syria) 8, 87–8
   assassination of leaders 583
   backlash against the US counterterrorist strategy 382
   Barcelona 2017 attack 80
   Beirut attack in 2015 27*b*
   Caliphate 154, 591
   current position of 591

defeat of 591
emergence of 28, 591
Islamic state terrorism failing politically 206*b*
lone actor attacks 88
motivations to join ISIS 332–3
operating in multiple countries 463
Paris attack in 2015 *see under* France
primary activity as war-fighting 305
religious extremism, and 164, 165
   role and importance of religion 334*b*
reorientation from terrorist group to insurgency 591
Shamima Begum case 282
state failure allowing rise of 171
strategy 87
UN counterterrorism cooperation after rise of ISIS 480
victims' identity and sense of terror from killings as key 339
violent ideology, as 62
WMD, and 338
Islamic Courts Union movement 6, 45
Islamic Group, The *see* al-Jamaa al-Islamiyya
Islamic State *see* ISIS
Israel
   attack on Israeli Olympic team at 1972 Munich Olympics 22, 22*p*, 26, 64, 261
   establishment of 585
   hostage rescue operations 470
   Israeli-Palestine conflict 59, 63*b*, 152*b*, 268–9
   killing of suspected terrorists 440, 469
   state terrorism, use of 268–9, 269*p*
Italy 83, 152*b*
   Red Brigades 7, 24*b*, 152*b*
   amnesties or pardons in exchange for giving up armed struggle 425
   dissociati programme 544
   failure of 378, 585
   fate of imprisoned or dead comrades as motivation 255
   see also far left terrorism/left wing groups

Japan 83
   Aum Shinrikyo 165, 327*p*, 373, 580*b*
   decapitation of leader 579
   failure of 207, 585
   'otherworldly' aims 332

Japan (*Continued*)
   religion, and 333
   sarin nerve gas attack 291, 327, 332
   Red Army 152*b*, 154
      failure of 585
jihadist terrorism
   attacks by single individuals as cases of jihadist terrorism 79
   civilians, targeting 80
   dominant role of 79
   lone wolf jihadi plots 194
   novel methods of violence, using 83
   Salafi-Jihadism 333
   Syria civil war leading to jihadi mobilization 191
   terrorists joining jihad through pre-existing social bonds 188–9
   Western Jihadism Project 124, 126–7
judiciary
   criminal justice approach to terrorism 397, 405–7
   International Criminal Court *see* International Criminal Court
   legal-judicial responses to terrorism 459
   role of judiciary and parliament in shaping anti-terrorist legislation 442–3
Just World Hypothesis 564–6

Kashmir, India/Pakistan dispute over 59, 65*b*, 223, 468

League of Nations 21, 60, 78
Lebanon 383
   civilian deaths during invasion by Israel 268–9
   Hezbollah 331, 339
   terrorism
      Beirut 2015 attack 27*b*, 565, 566*b*
      poverty, and 170
      suicide attacks driving US out of Lebanon 91, 222, 228, 319, 383
left-wing groups *see* far left terrorism/left-wing groups
lethality
   terrorism, and 89–90
      radicalization 90
      scale, gravity, and lethality of attacks 89, 90
      new terrorism, and *see under* old and new terrorism
Libya 266
   sanctions 479
      subject to long-running foreign military interventions 84
   supporting terrorists 153, 266
lone actor/lone wolf terrorism 88*b*
   anarchists 180, 336
   Christchurch New Zealand 2019 attacks 88, 353*b*, 403
   far right terrorism 166
   ISIS attacks 88
   jihadi plots 194
   Las Vegas, Nevada 2017 attack 90
   'leaderless resistance' 335
   Lone Actor Terrorist Database 124, 127–8
   mental illness/disorders 194–5
   Nice 2016 attacks 489, 563
   Pulse Nightclub, Orlando 2016 attack 89–90, 89*p*
   Oregon community college 2015 attack 92
   racializations of 'lone wolf terrorism' 287*b*
   San Bernardino, California 2015 attack 92
   social media, use of 403
   socialization process not always gradual 194
longevity of terrorist groups 9, 238–59
   defining longevity of terrorist groups 239–41
      definition of terrorist group 239–40
      longevity, meaning of 240*b*
      relationship between group and terrorist campaign not clear-cut 240
   factors affecting longevity 244–51
      group characteristics 246–50
      intergroup relations 250–1
      state characteristics 244–6
   group characteristics 246–50
      group capabilities 247
      group (peak) size 247
      ideology 246–7
      involvement in crime 247–8, 249–50
   intergroup relations 250–1
      alliances 251
      LTTE in Sri Lanka 248*b*, 250
      rivalries 150–1
   longevity of terrorist groups 241–4
      difficulty of starting terrorism in sustained fashion 243
      groups carrying out attacks for more than a year 243
      most long-lived terrorist groups 243–4
      terrorist groups facing liability of newness 241–2, 242*f*
      use of terrorism not lasting long on average, research claiming 241
   motivations to sustaining terrorism 252–6
      fate of imprisoned or dead comrades 255
      incentives from being member of the group 254
      instrumental/strategic model explaining terrorist decision-making 252–3, 254*b*
      leadership competition leading to escalation of attacks 254
      organizational model explaining terrorist decision-making 254, 254*b*
      revenge/cycle of revenge as motivation 253
      Revolutionary Organization 17 November in Greece 255*b*
      shifting objectives 253
      terrorism helping organizations survive 382–3
   state characteristics 244–6
      geographic location 246
      population 246
      regime type 244–5
      repression 245–6
      state capabilities 245
LTTE *see under* Sri Lanka

Malaysia 268
   counterterrorism 484–5
      ASEAN 'Our Eyes' centres 485
      detention without trial 439
      P/CVE programme 524
media
   depriving terrorists of media attention 214
   freedom of the press, effect of 229
   media attention key to terrorist groups 122
   reduction in media attention, effect of 231
   social media *see* social media
   suicide attackers 211
   symbiotic relationship with groups employing violence 229
   victims of terrorism, and *see under* victims of terrorism and political violence

INDEX 607

mental illness /disorders
　mental health not generally a factor in terrorism 202
　radicalization, and 194–5
　suicide attackers, depression in 211
militant Islamic movements *see* jihadist terrorism
military
　counterterrorism, use in 397, 401–2
　defence and deterrence *see under* foreign policy and countering terrorism
　few terrorist groups defeated through military force 420
　military-led approaches as response to terrorism 459
　hostage rescue operations 470
　military justice 438–9
　pre-emption 468–9
　proactive defence 468–9, 470
　retaliation 470
　senior military officers serving as quasi-diplomats 464
　targeting 222, 226, 227–8
　training of allied forces 468
motivation
　ideology *see* ideology
　nationalism and territorial motivations 163–4
　radicalization *see* radicalization
　religious extremism 164–5, 225
　selective benefits *see under* rationality and terrorism
　sustaining terrorism *see under* longevity of terrorist groups
　target selection *see under* target selection
Munich Olympics massacre *see* Black September

nationalism
　national liberation
　　use of rubric to justify violence 83
　nationalist movements 83
　political phenomenon, as 163
　territorial motivations, and 163–4
　terrorism, and 426
NATO 12
　multilateral counterterrorism cooperation with EU 490–2
negotiations *see* end of terrorist campaigns; responding to terrorism nonviolently
Neo-Orientalist bias 288
new left terrorism *see* far left terrorism/ left-wing groups

new terrorism *see* old and new terrorism
New Zealand
　Brenton Tarrant's Christchurch 2019 attacks 88, 166, 353*b*
　　lone actor attack, as 88, 353*b*, 403
　　social media, streaming of 353*b*, 570
Nigeria 378
　al-Qaeda, support for 587
non-combatant *see under* citizenship
non-state actors
　'actor-based approach' 20
　Al-Shabaab in Somalia 45*b*
　carrying out terrorist violence in response to state repression 43
　claiming responsibility for terrorist attack 41–2
　definition of terrorism, and 21, 138*b*
　responding to state repression 43
　support of foreign states for non-state terrorist groups, international terrorism as 83*b*
　terrorism studies focusing on 20
nonviolent counterterrorism *see* responding to terrorism nonviolently
North-Atlantic Treaty Organization *see* NATO
Northern Ireland Troubles 70
　Bloody Sunday 448*b*, 449*p*
　British extrajudicial killings in Northern Ireland 272*b*
　British operations in Northern Ireland in the 1970s 448*b*
　disengagement from violence in Northern Ireland 553
　far left ideologies, and 167
　Good Friday Agreement 423*b*, 425, 584
　　amnesties and release of prisoners 425
　　political settlement by 397–8, 423*b*
　interventions of RUC and British Army, impact of 398
　IRA/PIRA 31, 101, 327
　　Brighton bombing 576
　　civilians, deaths of 84
　　claimed use of violence against legitimate targets 84
　　emergence of armed campaign 101
　　longevity 239, 243
　　negotiations 584
　　Omagh bombing 232*b*, 233*p*, 580, 584, 586

　　reprisals for IRA attacks on British military in 1920s 268
　　use of violence in combination with other, nonviolent strategies 101
　media overlooking violence in Northern Ireland 568
　New IRA 590
　Real IRA 232*b*, 580, 584, 586
　root causes 160, 161*b*
　responsive/oppositional terrorist campaigns by Loyalist groups 164
　Ulster Volunteer Force 585
Norway
　Anders Breivik 20011 attacks 88, 166, 294, 296*p*, 395
　Philip Manshaus 2019 mosque shooting 395

old and new terrorism 10, 325–46
　conceptual issues 329–31
　　appropriate period of comparison, questions around 330
　　confusion as to extent to which terrorism had changed 330–1
　　historical validity of concept, challenges to 329–30
　　meaning of 'newness', debate around 330
　　new terrorism legitimizing new policies and exceptional powers 329
　　use by policymakers of new terrorism 329
　lethality 337–41
　　alleged rise in use of WMD 338
　　claim that terrorists killing more people 337–8
　　'identitarian' doctrines, rise of 339
　　link between ideology and lethality not as straightforward as claimed 339
　　Madrid 2004 bombings 340*b*, 340*p*, 460
　　mass casualty attacks, meaning of 339*b*
　　suicide operations following strategic logic 338
　networks 335–7
　　amateurs, rise of 335
　　anarchists' network essentially of national groups 336
　　claim that terrorist groups less hierarchically structured 335

old and new terrorism (*Continued*)
  globalization enabling networks to be more international 336
  globalization giving flexibility to adapt their structures 337
  origins of 'new terrorism' 327–9
    more networked nature of terrorist groups 328
    rise of religion 328, 329
    terrorism elevated from 'nuisance' to strategic threat 328
  religion 328, 329, 331–5
    early literature portraying religiously motivated groups as fanatics 331–2
    increasing importance of 331
    individual motivations and level of religiosity varying widely 332
    ISIS, religion and 334*b*
    Islam, role of 333–4
    label 'religious' covering range of aims and political motivations 332–3
    religious 'revival' in numerous countries 331
    Salafi-Jihadism 333
    terrorists killing more people, claim that 337–8
  see also history of terrorism
open source databases on terrorism 7, 113–34
  defining terrorism 119*b*
  future improvements 113, 128–9
    increasing provision of geographic information system 129
    increasingly automated data collection 128–9
    routine inclusion of domestic and international data 128
  materials for creation of open source databases 113, 115*b*
  OSINT 115*b*
  terrorism event databases 113, 114, 115–22
    aims 116
    Antifa attack in Charlottesville, Virginia 120*b*, 121*p*
    biases and inaccuracy in open source data 119–21
    domestic vs international attacks 118*b*
    future of 128–9
    key strengths of event databases 122
    lack of consistency over time 120
    lack of generally accepted definition of terrorism 118–19, 119*b*
    main databases 116–18
    terrorist attacks as unit of analysis 113, 116
    unclassified digital and print media as sources 116
    weaknesses 118–22
    world wide open source event databases on terrorist attacks 116*t*
  terrorism group databases 113, 114–15, 122–3
    BAAD database 122–3
    weaknesses 123
  terrorism open source databases 114–15
    difficulties of conceptualizing and counting terrorism 114
    difficulties of defining and counting terrorist incidents 114
    most data collection methods impossible for terrorism cases 114
  terrorism perpetrator databases 13, 115, 124
    America Terrorism Study 124–5
    Extremist Crime Database (ECDB) 124, 126
    Lone Actor Terrorist Database 124, 127–8
    Profiles of Individual Radicalization in the US (PIRUS) 124, 125–6
    Western Jihadism Project 124, 126–7
    weaknesses of 113, 115
    websites 130*t*
open source information 31, 31*b*
Organization of the Islamic Conference 65
organized crime 69, 119, 249, 450, 498
  drug cartels 81–2
Orthodox Terrorism Studies (OTS)
  evolution of 6, 21–6, 26
    academic study of terrorism since 2001 25–6
    advent of modern, international terrorism 21–2
    pioneers of study of terrorism 22–3
    sub-fields, emergence of 26
  nature of 19, 26–30
    anti-state terrorism, focus on 6, 26–9
    CBRN studies after 9/11 30
    dangers and risks of researching terrorism 32
    difficulty of researching terrorism 31
    future terrorism, consideration of 30
    interdisciplinary subjects influencing development of terrorism studies 25, 29
    international terrorism, focus on 6, 26–9
    'latest outrage' effects 30
    past examples, study of 29
    'thick description' of terrorist behaviour 32*b*, 32
    Western-centrism, terrorism studies and 27*b*
    whether stagnating 30–2
  origins 19

Pakistan
  al-Qaeda, and 203*b*
    Osama bin Laden 582
    support for 587
  conspiracy theories 51
  Haqqani network 314
  Kashmir 59, 65*b*, 223, 468
  pre-emptive air strikes against 469
  terrorism 165, 358, 382, 417, 419, 468
    deaths from terrorism 378–9
    school massacres 320
    suicide attacks 587
    targeted killings in Pakistan 440, 469, 582–3
  US, and 474
Palestinian Liberation Organization (PLO) 63*b*, 327, 332, 585
  sanctuary in East Germany 24*b*
  targets 225
P/CVE *see* preventing and countering violent extremism
peacebuilding 415, 425
  Good Friday agreement *see under* Northern Ireland Troubles
  meaning of 427*b*
  unarmed peacekeeping 428
Peace Brigades International 428
Peru 10
  Shining Path 10, 167, 223, 379*b*
    deaths during campaign 580
    decapitation of leader 580
    failure of 207
  Truth and Reconciliation Commission 580
Philippines
  counterterrorism 482–3, 484–5
    ASEAN 'Our Eyes' centres 485
  assassination 582
  terrorism 80, 482, 484
    negotiations 425, 584
    reorientation 590
    social media, use of 358

police
　avenging 'comrades' killed by police as driver of violent campaigns 101, 104
　combatants and non-combatants, as 70
　counterterrorism role 406-7
　　community policing officers, role of 406-7
　　Neighbourhood Policing assets, importance of 407
　escalating policing 103-4
　　indiscriminate repression leading to solidarization 104
　police brutality, protests against 98
　radicalization, confrontations with police and 109
political agency, lack of 169-70
political violence
　local/national nature of 29
　meaning 18, 97b
　revolutionary terrorism as political violence in own right 23
　rioting as form of 18
　social science of see political violence, social science of
　terrorism as 39, 40b, 426
political violence, social science of 7, 94-112
　clandestine political violence 103-6
　　competitive escalation 103, 104-5
　　escalating policing 103-4
　　ideological encapsulation 103, 105-6
　　organizational compartmentalization 103, 105
　explanatory logic of processual analysis 100-2
　　contingency in sequences of events turning violent 102
　　continuities with other forms of political violence and nonviolent action 101
　　emergence, notion of 100-1
　　interactive escalation 101-2
　　political violence as part of process of escalation 102
　　process and context, relationship between 101-2
　　processes having autonomous causal efficacy 100
　individual radicalization and participation in militant groups 107-9
　　effects of repression and confrontation with police 109
　　'high-risk' activism following 'low-risk' activism 108

　　individual motivations 108-9
　　interpersonal networks strengthened through action 108
　　mobilization via pre-existing social ties 107, 108, 109
　　see also radicalization
　Islamic Group (al-Jamaa al-Islamiyya) in Egypt 106b, 107p
　mechanisms of violent escalation 102-7
　　causal mechanisms, examples of 103
　　clandestine political violence 103-6
　　contentious politics, meaning of 103b
　　social movement families 104-5
　　social movement organizations 104-5
　political violence emerging over time 95-6
　processual approaches 95-6
　　meaning of 96b
　'processual turn' in political violence research 96-100
　　frame alignment 97-8
　　Political Opportunity Structure approach 97, 99
　　Red Army Faction 99b
　　Resource Mobilization Theory 97, 99
　　social movement organizations 97-8
　　social movement theory 97-9
　　social movement organizations 97-8, 104-5
　　unconscious psychological forces, previous focus on 96-7
Popular Front for the Liberation of Palestine (PFLP)
　hijack of airliner in 1968 21-2
　longevity 243, 585
　success of 370
post-structuralism 39, 39b, 284b
　logocentrism, and 284b
poverty and economic deprivation 141, 170
　anarchism, and 180
　foreign aid 471
　terrorism, and 170, 174, 197
preventing and countering violent extremism 13, 518-37
　Countering Violent Extremism (CVE) 414-15
　　meaning of 192b, 518b
　counterterrorism policies including P/CVE component, examples of 521f

　deradicalization, meaning of 520b
　evidence-based methods and tools 525-9
　　building and maintaining resilience 526
　　communication tools 526
　　knowledge of the subcultural dynamics 525-6
　　methods typically used in CVE and deradicalization programmes 526-7
　　no 'one size fits all' solution 525
　　tailored approach 525-6, 527
　　white supremacist online recruiting in US 528b
　evaluation of P/CVE programmes 530-3
　　difficulties of evaluation 530-2
　　most evaluation studies based on anecdotal evidence 532
　　Prevention Project 'Attention?!' (Achtung?!) in Germany 533b
　gender sensitive P/CVE 529-30
　　male clients forming majority of cases 529
　　potentially different entry and exit pathways of women 529-30
　　women having significant problems during reintegration 529-30
　　women key to form networks of resilience against violent extremism 530
　Preventing and Countering Violent Extremism (P/CVE)
　　history of 520-3
　　meaning of 192b, 518b
　Western and Eastern P/CVE approaches 523-5
　　differences in approach eroding 524
　　need for an individual, hand-tailored approach 524
　　see also disengagement and deradicalization programmes
'propaganda by the deed' 146-7, 147b, 336
psychological impact of terrorism
　psychological effect on specific groups to change political behaviour/attitudes 3
　psychological impact beyond immediate victims 57, 61, 62, 67, 70, 71, 138b
　terror as individual psychological state of mind 2
　triggering psychological response as calculated effect of terrorism 263

public, the *see* civilians/
   non-combatants
'puzzle of terrorism' *see* rationality and
   terrorism

racialized terrorism *see* gendered and
   racialized terrorism
radicalization 8, 26, 178–200, 292
   advent of terrorism studies 181–6
      membership of group as a
         dominant motive 185
      psychological motives 184, 185
      role of ideology 185–6
      societal context, psychological
         considerations, and group
         dynamics 184
      structural drivers of political
         violence 182–4
      terrorism as result of a complex
         interplay of factors 185
   assessment of concept 193–5
      gradual socialization in most but
         not all cases 194
      group processes and social bonds as
         crucial ingredient 194
      interaction of personal trajectories,
         group dynamics, and contextual
         factors 193
      no single profile or uniform
         trajectory into terrorism 194
   cognitive and behavioural
      radicalization, weak relationship
      between 192, 195
   competitive escalation, and 104
   conveyor belt theory 192, 195
   Countering Violent Extremism
      (CVE) 192*b*, 414
   disengagement/deradicalization *see*
      disengagement and
      deradicalization programmes
   dynamics shaping processes
      of 103
   early answers to why individuals
      become terrorists 179–81
      anarchists, early view of
         perpetrators as 179–80
      no single profile of anarchist
         terrorist 180–1
   EU policy for preventing
      radicalization 489
   explanation for lethal attacks on
      civilians, as 90
   extremism, and 189*b*, 195
   foreign fighting compared to
      domestic fighting 195
   ideology, role of 185–6, 195, 197
   see also ideology

individual radicalization and
   participation in militant
   groups 107–9
   effects of repression and
      confrontation with police 109
   female activists 109
   'high-risk' activism following 'low-
      risk' activism 108
   individual motivations 108–9, 193,
      332–3
   interpersonal networks
      strengthened through
      action 108
   membership of group as a
      dominant motive 185, 186, 193,
      194, 254
   mobilization via pre-existing social
      ties 107, 108, 109, 192
key variables in making
   terrorists 195–8, 196*f*
   conducive environment 197
   focus on 'vulnerable' young
      people producing inconclusive
      result 196
   ideology 197
   local mobilization hubs 197–8
   opportunity 197
   socialization and mobilization
      process, radicalization as 196
meaning of 103*b*, 179, 189*b*, 292,
   540
mental illness/disorders 194–5
Nelson Mandela on terrorism
   182*b*
PREVENT duty 48, 292, 520
Preventing Violent Extremism *see*
   preventing and countering
   violent extremism
psychological or social
   'pathologies' 107–8, 184, 185,
   292
relative deprivation, frustration,
   and aggression, and 184 *see also*
   relative deprivation
road to radicalization 187–93
   anger and frustration 189–90
   Borum's four-stage model of terrorist
      mind-set 187, 187*f*
   bottom-up mobilization through
      kinship and friendship 107, 108,
      109, 188–9, 192
   EU paper introducing concept of
      radicalization 190*b*
   factors coming together to produce
      violent radicalization 192
   'home-grown' radicals 188
   Moghaddam's staircase to
      terrorism 188, 188*f*

radicalization as dominant paradigm
   for why individuals become
   terrorists 191
radicalization of opinion and
   radicalization of action
   192, 195
Syria civil war leading to jihadi
   mobilization 191
terrorists joining jihad through pre-
   existing social bonds 188–9
root causes, and 162*b*, 182–6
self-radicalization 90, 90*b*, 92
social media, importance of role
   of 356–7
Rapaport, David
'Four Waves of Rebel Terror' 8,
   148–51, 148*b*, 163, 167, 327
rationality and terrorism 8, 201–17
counterterrorism implications
   213–14
   eroding trust in social
      solidarity 214
   hardening targets 214
   improving financial prospects of
      prospective terrorists 214
   knowing priorities of terrorists to
      combat them 214
   teaching terrorists political costs of
      terrorism 214
free riders 210, 210*b*, 211*b*,
   213–14
   'collective action' problem,
      and 210, 211*b*, 214
puzzle of terrorism 202–8
   al-Qaeda terrorism failing
      politically 203*b*
   empirical research showing
      terrorism as losing political
      tactic 202
   history of terrorism as story of
      political failure 207
   Islamic state terrorism failing
      politically 206*b*
   mental health issues not generally a
      factor 202
   practitioners presumed rational
      political actors 202
   terrorism objectively a failure/
      substantively irrational 202–3,
      207–8, 212–13, 213*b*, 214, 227,
      303
rational behaviour, meaning of 208–
   9, 209*b*
rationality, meaning of 209*b*
resolving puzzle of terrorism
   208–13
   'collective action' problem 210,
      211*b*

decision to use terrorism as 'last
    resort' 209–10
  free riders enjoying same political
    benefits/public good without
    risk 210, 210b
  odds of political success not
    zero 209
  risks of terrorism for
    participants 210
  selective benefits 210–11, 211b
  terrorists as social utility
    maximizers 211
  violent acts procedurally
    rational 213, 213b
 selective benefits 210–13, 211b, 214
  attacks helping perpetrators gain
    respect and boost standing 212–
    13, 214
  expected utility 211b, 212, 214
  financial compensation 211, 214,
    254
  social solidarity 211, 214, 254
  suicide attackers 211
  vengeance 212–13, 214
 tactical or process goals, terrorism
    achieving 227–8
 see also efficacy of terrorism
Red Army Faction (RAF) *see under*
    Germany
Red Brigades *see under* Italy
relative deprivation 97
 frustration and aggression,
    and 184
 terrorist violence, and 158, 170, 184,
    188, 193
religion and religious extremism 164–5,
    225
 anti-abortionists 165, 167
 involving all major religions 165
 ISIS, religious extremism and 164,
    165
  role and importance of
    religion 334b
 new terrorism, and *see under* old and
    new terrorism
 religious extremism as
    motivation 164–5, 225
 religious extremism as rationale for
    9/11 64, 329
 root cause of terrorism, religious
    extremism as 164–5
 suicide terrorism not necessarily
    linked to religion 338
 targets for religiously motivated
    groups 225
rendition 41, 49
 extraordinary rendition 420, 444
 meaning of 275, 425

Somalia 46
US rendition, detention, and
    interrogation programme 41,
    42b, 43, 444
reorientation *see under* end of terrorist
    campaigns
repression *see under* end of terrorist
    campaigns
responding to terrorism
    nonviolently 11, 413–33
 alternatives to force-based
    counterterrorism 420–5
 addressing perceived or real
    injustices 424–5
 Afghanistan negotiations with
    Taliban 421b
 amnesties or pardons in
    exchange for giving up armed
    struggle 425
 dialogue and negotiations as part of
    conflict resolution 44–5, 421–5
 few terrorist groups defeated
    through military force 420
 genuine dialogue and reform,
    effectiveness of 425
 Good Friday Agreement,
    negotiations for 423b
 rehabilitating and reintegrating
    former fighters/militants 425
 ways in which terrorist groups
    end 420–1, 421f
 conflict resolution, meaning of 427b
 CTS Model of Counterterrorism 430t
 failures of force-based
    counterterrorism 414–15,
    415–20
 counterterrorism policy evaluation,
    meaning of 420b
 force-based counterterrorism,
    meaning of 420b
 empirical failure of force-based
    counterterrorism 416–18
 theoretical and ethical
    failures of force-based
    counterterrorism 418–20
 nonviolence, meaning of 426b
 peacebuilding, meaning of 427b
 potential of nonviolent
    counterterrorism 426–9
 counterterrorism and the
    political 426–7
 counterterrorism as positively
    defined condition of working
    politically 426
 exploring nonviolent
    alternatives 427–9
 nonviolent community action,
    effectiveness of 428

prevention, importance of 428–9
 social defence 427b, 428
 unarmed civilian peacekeeping,
    meaning of 427b
revenge
 motivation for terrorist attacks,
    as 253
 seeking revenge for terrorism 565–6
revolution
 French Revolution *see under* France
 revolutionary terrorism as political
    violence in own right 23
 terrorism as part of revolutionary
    strategy 2
right-wing groups *see* far right
    terrorism/right-wing groups
rioting 20
 form of political violence, as 18
root causes of terrorism 8, 157–77
 ideologically-motivated
    terrorism 165–6
  anarchist terrorism 166–7
  far right terrorism 166
  new left/far left terrorism 167
  single issue—anti-abortion, animal
    rights, and environmental
    groups 167–8
 political and ideological roots 163–9
  ideologically-motivated
    terrorism 165–6
  nationalism and territorial
    motivations 163–4
  religious extremism 164–5
 relative deprivation *see* relative
    deprivation
 root causes 158–62
  concept focused on structural, or
    societal level, reasons 162, 162b,
    182–4
  defining root causes 160
  effective response to terrorism
    requires understanding of
    causes 158–9
  meaning of 158b, 162b
  radicalization, and 162b
  responsive or oppositional terrorist
    campaigns 164
  types of root causes 161–2
 state reaction 171–4
  GSPC 173b
 structural causes of political
    violence 169–72
  absence of viable political
    opportunity 169–70
  education 171
  poverty and economic
    deprivation 170
  state failure 171–2

Russia/Soviet Union
  Chechen 1999 attack 232, 234
  Chechen 2002 theatre attack 399*b*, 400*p*
  Chechnya, Russia's repression of 588*b*, 589*p*
  human rights violations 435
  invasion of Afghanistan 153
  new left ideologies, collapse of Soviet Union and 167
  repression 587
  Stalin's Great Terror 151, 152*b*
  Sterling Thesis 24*b*

sanctions
  comprehensive or targeted 471
  economic sanctions 414, 420
    hard power, as 464*b*
  inhibiting activities linked to financing terrorism 472
  key tool of economic statecraft 471
  nature of 471
  openly coercive mechanism of economic statecraft, as 471
  penalties for sanctions violations 472
  purpose-built foreign policy instrument, as 471
  UN sanctions 478, 479
    UN and EU financial sanctions regime after 9/11 481*b*
  use of sanctions to combat the financing of terrorism 472*b*
Saudi Arabia
  al-Qaeda, and 165, 203*b*
  deradicalization 521, 524, 541
    PRAC strategy 546–7
    rehabilitation centres focused on militant Islamism 546
  human rights violations 435
  terrorism, definition of 65*b*
  US presence in 165, 203*b*, 474
scanners *see under* technology, terrorism, and counterterrorism
September 11, 2001 attack on USA by al-Qaeda ('9/11') 1, 11, 24, 69, 77, 204*p*
  al-Qaeda terrorism failing politically 203*b*
  boosting research into WMD 25, 30
  effect on terrorism research 25–6, 29–30, 187
  Global War on Terror following 75
  mass death and destruction 329
  no further terrorist attacks on scale of 9/11 83–4
  'one-off' attack, as 563

rationale for attack 87
  religious extremism 164, 329
  seeking reasons for attacks heard as justifications 159
  UN and EU financial sanctions regime after 9/11 481*b*
  UN counterterrorism cooperation after 9/11 479
Shining Path *see under* Peru
Singapore
  ASEAN 'Our Eyes' centres 485
  deradicalization 425
    P/CVE programme 524
    Religious Rehabilitation Group 553
  detention without trial 439
'smart' technology *see under* technology, terrorism and counterterrorism
social defence 428
  meaning of 427*b*
social justice 49, 50, 51, 428–9
social media and terrorism 10, 21, 347–67
  Al-Shabaab use of social media in Nairobi 2013 attack 348
  concepts and definitions 349–50
    components of social media 349
    database platform 349
    social media allowing terrorists to create own networks of distribution 350
    social media, meaning of 349
  cybersecurity, and 491
  digital footprints, use of 511
  intelligence, and 403
    security services monitoring social media 502
  linking virtual and physical worlds 361–3
    importance of physical interactions and socialization 361
    Lee Rigby murder 361*b*
    participation in virtual spaces satisfying 'activist need' 361
  repressive governments using 154
  research, and 31
  significance of role of social media 570
  social media affecting counterterrorism efforts and initiatives 348
  social media and nature of terrorism 350–5
    Christchurch terror attacks 353*b*
    communication central to way terrorism understood 353

encrypted communication, importance of 350–1, 358
impact of social media on notions of asymmetry 350–1
internal and external communication 355
narrowcasting/niche marketing, meaning and effect of 352, 352*b*
social media elevating networked dimensions of terrorism 351–2
social media enhancing leaderless qualities of extremism 352–3, 359
social media as double-edged sword 358–60
  leadership more able to be challenged or side-lined 359
  new opportunities for surveillance using social media 358–9
  policing internet may have detrimental effect on free speech online 360
  pressure on mainstream platforms to counter extremist content 359
  risk extremists may migrate to other platforms 360
  social media providing opportunity to counter extremist rhetoric 359–60
  terrorists' use of more obscure platforms, disadvantages of 360
terrorist use of social media 355–8
  Africa's growing smart phone market, terrorists exploiting 357
  Arab nations, social media usage has penetrated across 357
  Asia, growth of social media in 357
  Christchurch attack, live streaming of 570
  internet/social media playing significant role in terrorist plots 356
  online propaganda and networking essential for recruitment and fundraising 356, 491
  Paris terror attacks, 2015 559*b*
  radicalization, social media's increasingly important role in 356–7
  social media as 'virtual bridge' for foreign fighters/domestic users 356
  social media impacting all areas where terrorists operate 355–6
  terrorists exploiting proliferation of social media usage 358

victims
　　harassment by social media 570
　　social media groups as means of support 570
social movement organizations/families *see under* political violence, social science of
soft power 464–5
　　culture, and 465
　　EU's soft power skills 491
　　meaning of 465*b*
　　public diplomacy creating 465
Somalia
　　Al-Shabaab in 45*b*
　　drone warfare 47*p*
　　insurgencies, motivations of recruits for 333
　　nonviolent community action, effectiveness of 428
　　rendition 46
　　terrorism, extent of deaths from 378–9
South Africa
　　African National Congress (ANC)
　　　　spoiling strategy, adoption of 319
　　　　succeeding in objectives 585
　　　　use of violence by 84, 152*b*
　　apartheid 43
　　Khotso House, destruction of 77*b*
　　Nelson Mandela
　　　　terrorism, on 182*b*
　　　　terrorist or freedom fighter, as 62, 283
　　Truth and Reconciliation Commission 84
　　　　pardons in exchange for participating 425
South Sudan
　　deaths from terrorism 378–9
　　unarmed peacekeeping, success of 428
Soviet Union *see* Russia/Soviet Union
Spain
　　Barcelona 2017 attack 80
　　detention periods 437
　　ETA 163, 167, 226
　　　　competitive victimhood 569
　　　　end of ETA 374*b*, 425, 584
　　　　longevity 239, 240, 243
　　　　mixed targeting strategies 226*b*
　　　　negotiations 584
　　　　'social reinsertion' scheme for ETA members
　　Madrid 2004 attack 69, 189, 340*b*, 340*p*, 460
　　　　withdrawal from Iraq, following 209, 460

state terrorism, use of 269–70
Sri Lanka
　　Tamil Tigers (LTTE) 163, 169
　　　　defeated through use of force 423
　　　　government's aerial bombing of 43–4
　　　　longevity 244, 248*b*, 250
　　　　mass-casualty attacks 339
　　　　reorientation 590
　　　　social service provision 312, 317
　　　　suicide attacks 338
　　unarmed peacekeeping, success of 428
states 20
　　counterterrorism *see* counterterrorism
　　defining state terrorism 262–4
　　　　actual or threatened violence 262–3
　　　　excluding legitimate state action 264
　　　　intent to affect a wider audience than just direct targets 263
　　　　state terrorism versus state-sponsored terrorism 263*b*
　　　　terrorism perpetrated by state or on behalf of state with its approval 263
　　　　triggering psychological response as calculated effect 263, 265
　　　　violence in pursuit of political objective 263
　　domestic repression 587
　　governments defining what is/ is not terrorism 222
　　longevity of terrorist groups, and *see under* longevity of terrorist groups
　　modern state terror 151–4
　　　　Argentina's 'Dirty War' 152, 154
　　　　French Revolution 151, 152, 152*b*
　　　　Islamic State's Caliphate 154
　　　　Mao Zedong's Cultural Revolution 151, 153, 153*p*
　　　　Nazi genocide 151
　　　　Stalin's Great Terror 151, 152*b*
　　national security policy 460
　　primary obligations of government to safeguard national independence and security 460
　　resources of states to terrorize 20
　　state failure 171–2
　　state oppression as terror 138*b*
　　state responses to terrorism
　　　　appeasing options 459
　　　　military-led approaches 459
　　　　regulatory or legal-judicial responses 459

state system as masculine structure 286
state terrorism/violence 9, 40–8, 260–80
　　campaign of deliberate and orchestrated violence by authority's agents 138*b*
　　civilian deaths 87
　　concealing responsibility for violence 42, 87, 263
　　counterterrorism, extreme violence, discrimination, and illegality in 43–4
　　counterterrorism, state violence as 43–8
　　see also counterterrorism
　　CTS, and *see* Critical Terrorism Studies (CTS)
　　defining state terrorism 262–4
　　direct violence 40
　　effects of state terrorism 273–4
　　extrajudicial killings 40, 268, 272*b*, 436, 447
　　generalized terrorism 42
　　indirect violence 40–1
　　legitimization of state violence 45
　　limitations of state terrorism as a concept 274–5
　　limited state terrorism 42
　　nature of 262–4
　　objections to concept of state terrorism 264–5
　　operations directed against terrorists, claiming 87
　　'pro-state' or 'conservative' terrorism 263
　　rendition *see* rendition
　　state terrorism as common form of state violence 41–2
　　state terrorism versus state-sponsored terrorism 263*b*
　　states as primary source of violence in terrorism 40, 48
　　states' monopoly over legitimate violence 265
　　torture *see* torture
　　US rendition, detention, and interrogation programme 42*b*
　　use of terrorism by states 266–73
　　victims, no assumption of blamelessness of 568
　　whether states can be terrorists 265–6
states and non-state actors using different violence 21
terrorism as reaction to state behaviour 172–4

614   INDEX

states (*Continued*)
  use of terrorism by states 266–73
    authoritarian regimes 266–7
    British extrajudicial killings in Northern Ireland 272*b*
    colonial powers 267–8
    liberal democracies 268–9
    totalitarian regimes 266–7
    US Torture in the Global War on Terror 270*b*, 270*p*
structure-agency debate 456*b*
suicide terrorism 26, 91
  addressing material power asymmetries 304
  efficacy of 370
  increase in 338
  ISIS Paris attack 27*b*, 28
  LTTE 339
  media, and 211
  mental health 211
  PKK 338
  rationality, and 211, 212
    striking occupying countries 212
    strategic logic, suicide operations following 338
    US withdrawal from Lebanon after suicide attack 91, 222, 228, 319, 383
    use not necessarily linked to religion 338
  surveillance and detection technology *see* technology, terrorism, and counterterrorism
Syria
  civil war 28, 222
    combat operations in, backlash against 382
    leading to jihadi mobilization 191
  human rights violations 435
  ISIS 28
  nonviolent community action, effectiveness of 428
  state-sponsored terrorism 41, 52
  subject to long-running foreign military interventions 84
  terrorism, extent of deaths from 378

Taliban *see under* Afghanistan
Tamil Tigers/LTTE *see under* Sri Lanka
target selection 8–9, 217–37
  democracies as frequent targets of terrorism 228–30
    civil wars, terrorism as tactic in 228
    democracies especially vulnerable in early years 229–30
    foreign policies, impact of 229
    freedom of the press, effect of 229
    proactive response dilemma 228, 229*b*
    protection of civil liberties by democratic states facilitates attacks 228
    summary of reasons democracies targeted 229*b*
  hard vs soft targets 219*b*
  target locations for terrorism 221–4
    countries as targets for terrorism by non-state actors 222–3, 223*f*
    domestic terrorism 224
    regional trends changing over time 223
    targeting military assets by non-state actors, increase in 222
    terrorist organizations rarely targeting country as a whole 223
    transnational terrorism 224
  target selection, meaning of 221*b*
  target selection, fear, and public attention 230–4
    Chechen 1999 attack in Russia 232, 234
    converting fear into demand for policy changes 230–1
    IRA Omagh bombing 232*b*, 233*p*
    PKK, loss of support for 231, 234
    public becoming more able to cope 231
    public sentiments and perceptions as primary targets 230
    reduced media attention 231
    role of fear in target selection 232*b*
    terrorism helping perpetrators overcome asymmetry of power 230, 303
    violence against public interests to elicit and spread fear 230
    violence promoting backlash 231–2
  target selection, victims, and audiences 224–8
    business targets 226
    categories of direct target (victim) types 225–6, 225*f*
    civilians, attacks mostly against 226
    ETA's mixed targeting strategies 226*b*
    fear, generating 224, 226
    government targets as part of campaigns of attrition 226
    left-wing groups 224–5
    location and timing of attacks often highly symbolic 226
    military targets, focus on 226, 227–8
    public infrastructure attacks 226
    randomness, perception of 224
    religiously-motivated groups 225
    right-wing groups 225
    tactical or process goals, terrorism achieving 227–8
    target audience pivotal to achievement of goals 224–5
    target selection as purposive, intentional, and strategic 224
    Walmart 2019 attack 219–21, 220*p*
    ideological motivation 220–1
    purposive and intentional act 219–20
    soft target, choice of 219
targeted killings
  counterterrorism practice, as 11, 436, 440, 468
  drone strikes, killing of terrorists by 6, 213, 417, 469
  counterproductive nature of 274, 417
  effectiveness of 417, 469
  geofencing 509
  increase in 440, 582–3
  Israel 440, 469
  terrorists' use of 508, 509*b*
  US 274, 417, 440, 469, 582–3
  human rights, violation of 435, 440, 447, 450
  legal and moral problems 469
technology, terrorism, and counterterrorism 12, 497–517
  nature of terrorist threat 512–14
    'action-reaction' cycle 512–13
    deploying technologies to mitigate consequences of attack 513
    Internet of Things 514
    public's calls for action 513
  technology, problems with 507–12
    aviation terrorism 509*b*
    'dual use' technologies/use of drones by terrorists 508, 509*b*
    facial recognition software, unreliability of 507, 507*b*
    geofencing 509
    Pegasus spyware scandal 511–12
    surveillance technologies posing danger to civil liberties 511–12
  technology, success of 498–506
    augmented reality (AR), meaning of 501*b*
    back office computer systems 501–2
    barricades 505–6

INDEX 615

biometrics, meaning of 500*b*
biometrics, use of 499–500
citadelization 506, 506*b*
consequence mitigation 505–6
data mining and acquisition 502, 511–12
data mining, meaning of 502*b*
detecting and identifying dangerous objects or substances 503–5
detecting and thwarting terrorists in planning phase 499
explosive detection systems (EDS) 504, 504*b*
explosives trace detectors (ETD) 504, 504*b*
facial recognition software 500–1, 501*p*, 505, 505*b*, 507, 511
full body scanners 503, 504*b*, 512, 513
future 3D body scanners 504
future 'smart corridors' 505, 505*b*
identifying known or suspected terrorists 499–500
metal detectors 503, 503*b*
preventing terrorist attacks 502–3
'smart' CCTV systems and behaviour-analytical software 500, 505
'smart glasses' with facial recognition software 500–1, 501*p*
'smart lampposts' 505
'street furniture' as barricades 505–6
technology, meaning of 499
virtual reality (VR), meaning of 501*b*
Walk-Through Metal Detectors 503, 503*b*
terror
ancient world, in *see* history of terrorism
meaning of 1–2
campaign of deliberate and orchestrated violence by authority's agents 138*b*
current usage of word terror 79–81
historical use of 2
increasing use of 'terror' 91
state oppression, as 138*b*
individual psychological state of mind, terror as 2 *see also* definition and meaning of terrorism
terrorism
assassination, and *see* assassination

context, terrorism in *see* terrorism in context
countering terrorism *see* counterterrorism
effectiveness of *see* efficacy of terrorism
end of terrorist campaigns *see* end of terrorist campaigns
gendered and racialized *see* gendered and racialized terrorism
history *see* history of terrorism
insurgents and rebels *see* insurgents and rebels, terrorism by
international terrorism *see* international terrorism
last resort, as 170, 209, 304, 385
longevity of terrorist groups *see* longevity of terrorist groups
mass casualty terrorism, advent of 79
meaning *see* conceptualizations of terrorism; definition and meaning of terrorism
old and new *see* old and new terrorism
political violence, and *see* political violence
'puzzle of terrorism' *see* rationality and terrorism
radicalization *see* radicalization
root causes *see* root causes of terrorism
social media, and *see* social media and terrorism
studies *see* terrorism studies
subjective interpretations of 65*b*
suicide terrorism *see* suicide terrorism
target selection *see* target selection
tool of the weak, as 230, 303, 304
terrorism in context 7, 74–93
civil wars 82, 222
current usage of words terror, terrorist, and terrorism 79–81
characterization of anti-government protestors as terrorists 80–1
terrorism as externally generated threat 79
expanding scope of language of terrorism to situations other than political violence 81–2
criminal gangs, especially drug cartels 81–2
domestic violence 81
international dimension 83–7
al-Qaeda and ISIS 87–8

assassination of leading figures 84–5
Charlie Hebdo 2015 attack 85*b*
cycles of 'tit for tat' violence in ethnically divided societies 88
deaths of civilians, terrorists' attitude to 83–4
nationalist movements 83
state's security forces, killing members of 84
states' operations against terrorists 87
lethality and terrorism 89–90
radicalization 90
scale, gravity, and lethality of attacks 89, 90
normative shift in use of term terrorism 75–8
destruction of Khotso House 77*b*
strategy and terrorism 91–2
active campaigns as cause of intense public concern 92
political exploitation of terrorism 91
terrorism applying to active, ongoing transnational campaigns 91–2
victims as innocent bystanders 78–9
deliberate killing of civilians/ non-combatants distinguishing terrorism 79
terrorism studies
CBRN studies after 9/11 30
Critical Terrorism Studies *see* Critical Terrorism Studies (CTS)
dangers and risks of researching terrorism 32
difficulty of researching terrorism 31
effect of 9/11 on 25–6, 29–30, 262
boosting research into WMD 25, 30
future of terrorism research after 9/11 25
future terrorism, consideration of 30
interdisciplinary subjects influencing development of terrorism studies 25, 29
'mainstream' terrorism studies *see* Orthodox Terrorism Studies
radicalization *see under* radicalization
Western-centrism, and 27*b*
'white supremacist' system, operating as 286
terrorists 20*b*
'actor-based approach' 20

terrorists (*Continued*)
  attacks by single individuals as cases of jihadist terrorism 79
  characterization of anti-government protestors as terrorists 80–1
  debates about which actors seen as terrorists 20–1
  evolving from left-wing militants to Islamist radicals 26–7
  longevity of terrorist groups *see* longevity of terrorist groups
  meaning and use of term 20–1
    current usage of word terrorist 79–81
  self-identification
    disappearance of term terrorist as self-identification 75
    self-identification as terrorists in previous centuries 76
  thought-processes of *see* rationality and terrorism
terrorist incidents databases *see* databases
Thailand
  ASEAN 'Our Eyes' centres 485
  terrorism 80, 482
torture, states' use of 40, 41, 49
  colonial powers during wars of national liberation, use of 268
  communism, extirpating 267
  counterterrorism practices post 9/11 11, 274, 374, 415, 416, 417, 419, 420*b*, 435–7, 442, 447, 450
  'enhanced interrogation' 270*b*
  torture and abuse of detainees held in Abu Ghraib 271
  torture in Guantanamo Bay 270*b*
  torture in US Global War on Terror 270*b*, 271*p*, 444*b*
  US rendition, detention, and interrogation programme 42*b*
  human rights, and 435–7, 442, 447, 450
transnational terrorism 197, 459, 462
  influencing domestic and international politics 460
  meaning of 83*b*, 459*b*
  targets 224
Turkey 80, 146, 211
  human rights violations 435
  PKK 163
    loss of support for 231, 234
    suicide attacks 338
    terrorism, extent of deaths from 378–9

United Kingdom (UK)
  anti-terrorism legislation 405–6, 439
  attack in 2017 69
  CONTEST *see under* counterterrorism agencies
  counterterrorism 394, 550
  databases *see* databases
  deradicalization 547, 548
  effects of terrorism legislation on research 32
  Ethics Committees 32
  Government Communications Headquarters (GCHQ) 502, 51
  Harrods, 1983 attack on 76, 84
  human rights 437–8, 439, 443–4
  Lee Rigby murder 361*b*
  London 2005 bombings 69, 189
    British intervention in Iraq linked to 455
  Manchester 2018 bombing 394, 489, 570, 591
  Northern Ireland *see* Northern Ireland Troubles
  Notting Hill Carnival August 2017 (facial recognition technology) 507*b*
  operational response to terrorism 439–40
  police role in counterterrorism 406–7
  PREVENT duty 48, 292
  see also counterterrorism agencies
  Reading 2020 attack 79
  Shamima Begum case 282
  terror trials 437–8
  terrorist offences, definition of 439
  Usman Khan 2019 attack near London Bridge 519, 563
United Nations (UN) 12, 19, 21
  combatants and non-combatants, meaning of 70
  counterterrorism cooperation
    counterterrorism obligations imposed on member states 478
    criticism of UN counterterrorism policy 481
    Security Council resolutions 478
    Security Council sanctions 479
    UN and EU financial sanctions regime after 9/11 481*b*
    UN counterterrorism cooperation after 9/11 479
    UN counterterrorism cooperation after rise of ISIS 480
    UN promoting coordination 478

Enforced or Involuntary Disappearances, Working Group on 267
financing of terrorism, combating 471
  UN Security Council resolutions 471
Global Counter-Terrorism Strategy 171
see also international organizations and counterterrorism
human rights 435 *see also* human rights and counterterrorism
Munich Olympics 1972 attack 64
National Counterterrorism Centre World Incidents Tracking System 70
no universally agreed definition of terrorism 57
  subjective interpretations of terrorism 65*b*
preventing violent extremism 192*b*
Plan of Action to Prevent Violent Extremism 522
rehabilitation programmes for 'foreign fighters' 522
sanctions 478, 479
  UN and EU financial sanctions regime after 9/11 481*b*
unarmed peacekeeping 428
United States (US)
  al-Qaeda's 9/11 attack *see* September 11, 2001 al-Qaeda attack on US
  Al-Shabaab, and 6
  anti-abortionists 165, 167
  Antifa attack in Charlottesville, Virginia 120*b*, 121*p*
  anti-terrorism legislation, expansion of powers under 439
  Boston marathon 2013 bombing 522–3, 522*p*
  CBRN attacks, concerns about 30
  CIA disinformation campaigns 24*b*
  Citizens for Constitutional Freedom 282
  Constitution First Amendment providing permissive research environment 32
  databases *see* databases
  detention periods 437
  experiencing less violence since 1980s 223
  fear of terrorism 563–4
  Guantanamo Bay 438–9, 539
    manipulation of legal norms 441

military commissions 438–9, 441, 442
torture in 270b, 274, 442, 444b
Institutional Review Boards 32
killing of suspected terrorists/drone strikes 274, 417, 440, 469, 582–3
see also targeted killings
Ku Klux Klan 243, 243p
Las Vegas, Nevada 2017 attack 90
military justice 438–9
National Security Agency (NSA) 502, 511
Oregon community college 2015 attack 92
OSINT 115b
P/CVE
CVE strategy, introduction of 522
CVE Task Force 523
domestic extremism 523
funding increased 523
white supremacist online recruiting 528b
preferred target for terrorists, as 27
public diplomacy in post-9/11 era 465b
Pulse Nightclub, Orlando 2016 attack 89–90, 89p
rendition, detention, and interrogation programme 41, 42b, 43, 444
San Bernardino, California 2015 attack 92
sanctions to combat the financing of terrorism, use of 472, 472b
storming of US Capitol building in 2021 523
terrorism trials 438–9
torture in Global War on Terror 270b, 444b
'enhanced interrogation' of al-Qaeda suspects 138–9
US federal building, Tulsa, Oklahoma 1995 attack 291, 327
Walmart 2019 attack 219–21, 220p
Weather Underground 152b, 167, 210, 585
World Trade Center see World Trade Center, attacks on

victims of terrorism and political violence 13, 558–74
direct victim 561
meaning of 559b
fear destabilizing sense of security among population 561–2
ideal victim 567–9
competitive victimhood 569
hierarchies of victims 568–9
impact of terrorism 562–7
form of response as legacy 562
Just World Hypothesis (JWH) 564–6
Paris terror attacks, 2015 559b, 565, 566b, 570
revenge, seeking 565–6
social identity of victims of attacks 563
terrorism as communication 562–3
terrorism as intent to create harm and fear 563–4
terrorism at home and abroad 566b
victimhood portrayed as barrier to emerging peace 563
indirect victim 561
meaning of 559b
media and victims of terrorism, and 569–71
co-option of victim's identity 571
expectations of how individuals might behave 571
need and willingness to engage with media shifting over time 571
public reaction often at odds with victim's reaction 569–70
Radicalization Awareness Network 571
social media, significant role of 570
survivor, meaning of 559b
tertiary victim 561
meaning of 559b
PTSD 562
vicarious victimization, meaning of 559b
violence
definition of 18
conceptualizations of terrorism see under conceptualizations of terrorism
definitions of terrorism, and see under definition and meaning of terrorism
domestic violence as everyday terrorism 40

political violence see political violence
states, and see states
violent extremism see violent extremism
violent extremism 13, 31
PIRUS, and 125
preventing and countering see preventing and countering violent extremism

war crimes 82, 265
war on terror see Global War on Terror
weapons of mass destruction (WMD) 328, 330, 479
al-Qaeda, and 328, 338
boosting research into WMD after 9/11 25, 30
CBRN
Aum Shinrikyo sarin attack 580b
CBRN studies after 9/11 30
CBRN terrorism, meaning of 339b
ISIS, and 338
Western Jihadism Project 124, 126–7
women
female activists, radicalization of 109
gender sensitive P/CVE 529–30
potentially different entry and exit pathways of women 529–30
women having significant problems during reintegration 529–30
women key to form networks of resilience against violent extremism 530
gendered terrorism see gendered and racialized terrorism
Ulrike Meinhof and assumptions about women's political violence 289b
World Trade Center, attacks on
bombing in 1993 by Afghan Arabs 23–4, 327, 337
9/11 see September 11, 2001 al-Qaeda attack on US

Yemen
deradicalization 521, 546
human rights violations 435
targeted killings 274, 440, 469, 582–3
terrorism 222, 382, 417, 488
deaths from 378–9